A History of Classical Malay Literature

The **Institute of Southeast Asian Studies (ISEAS)** was established as an autonomous organization in 1968. It is a regional centre dedicated to the study of socio-political, security and economic trends and developments in Southeast Asia and its wider geostrategic and economic environment. The Institute's research programmes are the Regional Economic Studies (RES, including ASEAN and APEC), Regional Strategic and Political Studies (RSPS), and Regional Social and Cultural Studies (RSCS).

    ISEAS Publishing, an established academic press, has issued more than 2,000 books and journals. It is the largest scholarly publisher of research about Southeast Asia from within the region. ISEAS Publishing works with many other academic and trade publishers and distributors to disseminate important research and analyses from and about Southeast Asia to the rest of the world.

A History of Classical Malay Literature

Liaw Yock Fang

Translated by Razif Bahari and Harry Aveling

Institute of Southeast Asian Studies
Singapore

Yayasan Pustaka Obor Indonesia
Jalan Plaju No. 10,
Jakarta, Indonesia
Ph. 62-21-31926978, 3920114
Fax. 62-21-31924488
Email: yayasan_obor@cbn.net.id
Website: www.obor.or.id
for distribution in Indonesia

ISEAS Publishing
Institute of Southeast Asian Studies
30 Heng Mui Keng Terrace
Pasir Panjang, Singapore 119614
E-mail: publish@iseas.edu.sg
Website: http://bookshop.iseas.edu.sg
for distribution in all countries except Indonesia

With the support of

NATIONAL ARTS COUNCIL
SINGAPORE

All rights reserved. No part of this publication may be reproduced, stored in a retrieval system, or transmitted in any form or by any means, electronic, mechanical, photocopying, recording, or otherwise, without written permission of the publishers.

Copyright © 2013 Liaw Yock Fang
The responsibility for facts and opinions in this publication rests exclusively with the author and his interpretations do not necessarily reflect the views or the policy of the publishers or their supporters.

Title: Liaw Yock Fang, *Sejarah Kesusasteraan Melayu Klasik*
(in Malay) in 1975
Second edition: 1978
Third edition (revised): 1982

First and second editions in Indonesian were published by Erlangga
(1991 and 1993)
Yayasan Pustaka Obor Indonesia published its first edition (in Indonesian) in August 2011
First edition (English language): June 2013
YOI: 702.30.8.2012

A History of Classical Malay Literature/Liaw Yock Fang; translators: Razif Bahari and Harry Aveling.
Ed. 1 – Jakarta: Yayasan Pustaka Obor Indonesia, 2013
x + 506 pp.: 17,5 x 25 cm
ISBN: 978-979-461-810-3 (Indonesia)

ISEAS Library Cataloguing-in-Publication Data

Liaw, Yock Fang, 1936-
    A history of classical Malay literature.
1. Malay literature—History and criticism.
2. Classical literature.
3. Authors, Malay.
I. Title
II. Title: Sejarah kesusastraan Melayu klasik. English
PL5130 L681   2013

ISBN 978-981-4459-88-4 (soft cover)
ISBN 978-981-4459-89-1 (e-book, PDF)

Cover designer: Iksaka Banu
Printed in Indonesia by PT Praninta Jaya Mandiri

Table of Contents

Preface	viii
List of Abbreviations	ix
Chapter I Folk Literature	1
1.1 Tales of Origin	2
1.2 Animal Tales	4
1.3 Javanese Literature	9
1.4 Comic Tales	11
1.5 Folk Epics	27
Chapter II The Indian Epics and The Wayang in Malay Literature	49
2.1 Ramayana	50
2.2 Mahabharata	74
Chapter III Javanese Panji Stories	113
3.1 The Panji Stories	113
3.2 Hikayat Galuh Digantung	116
3.3 Hikayat Cekel Waneng Pati	119
3.4 Hikayat Panji Kuda Semirang	124
3.5 Hikayat Panji Semirang	127
3.6 Hikayat Misa Taman Jayeng Kusuma	131
3.7 Hikayat Dewa Asmara Jaya	133
3.8 Hikayat Undakan Penurat	135
3.9 Javanese Panji Stories	136
3.10 Cambodia and Thailand	138
Chapter IV Literature Belonging to the Period of Transition from Hinduism to Islam	142
4.1 Hikayat Puspa Wiraja	144
4.2 Hikayat Parang Punting	150
4.3 Hikayat Langlang Buana	152
4.4 Hikayat Si Miskin or Hikayat Marakarma	155
4.5 Hikayat Berma Syahdan	156
4.6 Hikayat Indraputra	158

4.7	Hikayat Syah Kobat	160
4.8	Hikayat Koraisy Mengindra	161
4.9	Hikayat Indra Bangsawan	162
4.10	Hikayat Jaya Langkara	166
4.11	Hikayat Nakhoda Muda	168
4.12	Hikayat Ahmad Muhammad	171
4.13	Hikayat Syah Mardan	175
4.14.	Hikayat Isma Yatim	178

Chapter V Literature of the Islamic Age — 184

5.1	Stories from the Quran	187
5.2	Stories of the Prophet Muhammad	214
5.3	Tales of the Prophet Muhammad's Companions	223
5.4	Tales of Islamic Warriors	237

Chapter VI Framed Narratives — 264

6.1	Pancatantra	265
6.2	Hikayat Seribu Satu Malam	275
6.3	Sukasaptati and Hikayat Bayan Budiman	278
6.4	Hikayat Bakhtiar	291
6.5	Hikayat Golam	295
6.6	Hikayat Maharaja Ali	297

Chapter VII The Literature of Islamic Theology — 300

7.1	Hamzah Fansuri	302
7.2	Syamsuddin Al-Sumatrani	305
7.3	Nuruddin Ar-Raniri	309
7.4	Abdur Rauf Singkel	321
7.5	Hikayat Seribu Masalah	326
7.6	Tajus Salatin	328
7.7	Hikayat Wasiat Lukman Hakim	333
7.8	Abd Al-Samad Al-Palimbini	334
7.9	Shihabuddin b. Abdallah Muhammad	336
7.10	Kemas Fakhruddin	337
7.11	Kemas Muhammad b. Ahmad	337
7.12	Daud ibn Abdullah ibn Idris Al-Fatani	337
7.13	Syaikh Ahmad b. Muhammad Zain Patani	339
7.14	Muhammad b. Ismail Daud al-Fatani	339
7.15	Zain al-Abidin b. Muhammad Al-Fatani	339
7.16	Other Indonesian Theologians	339
7.17	Conclusion	339

Chapter VIII Historical Literature ... 345
    8.1   Hikayat Raja-Raja Pasai ... 347
    8.2   Sejarah Melayu ... 350
    8.3   Hikayat Merong Mahawangsa ... 367
    8.4   Hikayat Aceh ... 371
    8.5   Misa Melayu ... 374
    8.6   Hikayat Negeri Johor ... 377
    8.7   Sejarah Raja-raja Riau ... 381
    8.8   Silsilah Melayu dan Bugis ... 383
    8.9   Tuhfat al-Nafis ... 387
    8.10   Hikayat Banjar dan Kota Waringin ... 392
    8.11   Salasilah Kutai ... 396
    8.12   Hikayat Patani ... 399
    8.13   Cerita Asal Bangsa Jin dan Segala Dewa-dewa ... 402
    8.14   Hikayat Hang Tuah ... 404

Chapter IX Classical Malay Law Codes ... 414
    9.1   Undang-Undang Malaka ... 415
    9.2   Undang-Undang Laut ... 419
    9.3   Undang-Undang Minangkabau ... 425
    9.4   Undang-Undang Sungai Ujung ... 433
    9.5   Undang-Undang Dua Belas ... 433
    9.6   Undang-Undang Pahang ... 434
    9.7   Undang-Undang Kedah ... 435
    9.8   Undang-Undang Sembilan Puluh Sembilan ... 437
    9.9   Adat Raja-Raja Melayu ... 438

Chapter X Poetic Forms (Pantun and Syair) ... 442
    10.1   Pantun ... 442
    10.2   Syair ... 447
    10.3   Syair Based on Panji Narratives ... 449
    10.4   Romantic Syair ... 454
    10.5   Figurative Syair ... 465
    10.6   Historical Syair ... 469
    10.7   Religious Syair ... 478

Bibliography ... 491
Index ... 497
Biographical Details ... 505

Preface

This English edition of the *A History of Classical Malay Literature* is based on *Sejarah Kesusasteraan Melayu Klasik,* published by Yayasan Pustaka Obor Indonesia in August 2011. That work follows an earlier two volume edition, published in Jakarta in 1991 and 1993 by the Erlangga Publishing Company. In the ensuing period since then, many new studies on the history of classical Malay literature have appeared. I have included some of these new materials in this book, particularly in Chapter 1. I have also revised various sections in the other chapters, although not extensively. Of course it is not possible to incorporate all the new materials. Therefore, in the bibliography attached at the end of the book, I have provided a record of the books I consider important, including a new catalogue of sources for the history of traditional Malay literature. Readers who are interested can refer to the list of books in the bibliography for more information.

I would like to thank Prof. Dr. Riris K. Toha-Sarumpaet for editing the 2011 edition, and Dr Razif Bahari and Prof. Dr. Harry Aveling for their dedicated attention to the English translation over a two year period. I also wish to thank the late Bapak H. B. Jassin, who is sadly not with us anymore. Pak Jassin was closely involved in the writing of this book. He edited the original Singapore edition of 1975 and wrote the introduction to the third Singapore edition. He also edited the first Indonesian edition. I am forever indebted to him for his kind contributions.

Hopefully this book will be useful for both teachers and students who are interested in Malay literature.

Liaw Yock Fang
Singapore.

May 31, 2013.

List of Abbreviations

BKI   *Bijdragen van het Koninklijk Instituut voor Taal-, Land-en Volkenkunde*, 's Gravenhage.
BSOAS   *Bulletin of the School of Oriental* and (from 1939) *African Studies*, London.
DB   *Dewan Bahasa*, (Magazine), Kuala Lumpur.
EI   *Encyclopaedia of Islam*
JRAS   *Journal of the Royal Asiatic Society*, London.
JMBRAS   *Journal of the Malayan Branch of the Royal Asiatic Society*, Singapore/Kuala Lumpur.
JSBRAS   *Journal of the Straits Branch of the Royal Asiatic Society*, Singapore.
JSS   *Journal of the Siam Society*, Bangkok.
MIS   *Malayan and Indonesian Studies.* Essays Presented to Sir Richard Winstedt on His 85th Birthday. Oxford: Clarendon Press, 1964.
TBG   *Tijdschrift voor Indische Taal-, Land- en Volkenkunde van het (Koninklijk) Bataviaasch Genootschap van Kunsten en Wetenschappen,* Batavia (now Jakarta).
VBG   *Verhandelingen van het Bataviaasch Genootschap van Kunsten en Wetenschappen,* Batavia (now Jakarta).
VKI   *Verhandelingen van het Koninklijk Instituut voor Taal-, Land- en Volkenkunde*
JSEAH   *Journal of South East Asian History*

1 Folk Literature

Folk literature (*sastera rakyat*) is a literature that lives in the midst of the people. A mother may tell a story to her child in the cradle. A storyteller may impart a tale by word of mouth to other villagers who cannot read. (The storyteller him- or herself may not be able to read either). Such stories are passed down orally from one generation to the next. This is a different situation from the written literature that exists in the royal courts of the king (although it should be mentioned here that the boundary between folk literature and written literature is not always clear in Malay literature). Stories of the Mousedeer, for example, were widespread among the common people. As time went by, these stories were gathered and turned into a book at the behest of a ruling nobleman or king. The *Hikayat Hang Tuah*, according to a Russian scholar, also had its genesis in folk literature which was subsequently rearranged and adapted according to the dictates of the palace. Conversely, there were also works of written literature which later became oral literature; for example, the story of a magic bird became the basis for *Hikayat Ahmad dan Muhammad*. Another famous example is the story of a king who understood the language of animals, as found in the *Hikayat Bayan Budiman* (Winstedt, 1958: 62). This story gave birth to a story among the Gayos and Bataks which goes like this:

> There was once a husband who went in search of deer liver for his pregnant wife. In his quest, he killed a black snake which he found fornicating with a white snake. The black snake's mate was very thankful to the man and granted him the gift of animal language. One day, the man heard a conversation between cockroaches which made him laugh. His wife asked him to teach her the language of animals. She said, "Alas, if you don't teach me the language of the animals, I will die." The husband was in a quandary. He cannot teach the language of the animals to his wife. If he teaches her, he himself will die. In the end, he learnt, from a conversation he overheard between a billy goat and a nanny goat, and between a chicken and a hunting dog, how to deal with his wife. He threatened to throw a spear at his wife, and having frightened her off, later married a younger wife.

The birth of oral literature precedes that of written literature. This does not mean, however, that oral literature immediately died with the birth of written literature. Indeed oral literature continues to exist contemporaneoulsy with written literature, especially in the remote areas. The publication of oral stories like *Selampit, Cerita Si Gembang, Cerita Raja Donan* and *Cerita Raja Dera* by Dewan Bahasa dan Pustaka (the Institute of Language and Literature) in Kuala Lumpur bears testimony to this. The Balai Pustaka (Bureau of Literature) in Jakarta has also published four volumes of *Cerita Rakyat* (Folklore).

What constitutes folk literature? Folk literature, also known as oral tradition, covers a wide area; it includes stories, sayings, proverbs, songs, dances, customs, laws, games, beliefs and festivals. The study of folk literature is important, because from it we learn about the worldview, the societal values, as well as the society in, and for, which they are engendered. It was for this reason that UNESCO launched a study of oral traditions in Malaysia and Indonesia. The fruits of this research on the oral traditions of Malaysia can be found in a book edited by Mohd. Taib Osman (Mohd. Taib Osman, 1975).

In this chapter, we will only discuss folk tales. Folk tales can be divided into four categories, as follow:

(1) *Cerita Asal-usul* (Tales of Origin)

(2) *Cerita Binatang* (Tales about Animals)

(3) *Cerita Jenaka* (Comic Tales)

(4) *Cerita Pelipur Lara* (Folk Epics)

1.1 Tales of Origin

The *Cerita Asal-usul* or the aetiological tale is the oldest form of folklore. These stories can in fact be included in the realm of myth, stories that are considered true by their narrators. The Batak origin story tells of the creation of the earth, the sun, the moon, and the first man to inhabit the land of the Batak, as well as the origins of various plants and vegetation; whereas the Malay tale of origin only depicts the origins of various plants and animals. To explain why many tall trees can be found in the jungle that grew along the banks of the river, for example, the Malay tale of origin recounts a story that goes like this:

> Once upon a time, there lived in the jungles of Malaya a race of ogres called the Kelembai whose sorcery can turn a man to stone or wood. They existed in such large numbers in the jungle that the Malays, who felt threatened by them, hatched a plan to drive them out. Fortunately for the Malays, the Kelembais were not known to be very bright. In order to deceive them into thinking that there lived in the jungle a race bigger and more horrible than them, the Malays cut the top off a clump of bamboo and let them grow upright again to assume its full height. The Kelembais thought that only a giant as big enough as them could cut the top of the bamboo. The Malays then laid an elderly grandfather in a cradle they placed in the middle of the forest. When the Kelembais saw the toothless old man, they thought he was a newborn baby. This struck fear in the hearts of the Kelembais [who were frightened by the sheer size of this 'new' adversary]. Eventually, they mistook a rake they found lying along the riverbank for a human comb; and turtles they found there to be gigantic head lice. They didn't dare live in the jungle after that and fled into the horizon. As they fled, they urged anyone they happened to meet along the way to flee with them. Those who refused were turned into trees. That is why there exist many tall and large trees along the river's edge in the jungles of Malaya to this day.

Why are there pockmarks on the corncob? The following story explains why:

> One day, the corn proudly declared that even if there were no more rice in the world, it could

still provide food for humans. Not to be outdone, both the *Dagun*[1] and *Gadung*[2] claimed they too could do the same. So the three of them went to put their case before *Nabi Sulaiman* (King Solomon) who subsequently ruled in favour of the corn. Dagun and Gadung were angered by this and went in search of a thorn. Corn came to know about this and poisoned *Dagun*. This is why the *dagun* is poisonous to this day. Meanwhile, *Gadung* in a fit of jealousy had pricked the corn with a thorn. And that is why corncobs are pockmarked to this day. The case was then brought before theProphet Ilias who told the three to go back to King Solomon to resolve it. Solomon told them that, in order to determine who is right in the matter, they had to fight one another. And so for two weeks they fought. The *mata-lembu* (*Firmiana Malayana*) tree witnessed the fight from upclose and its bark was damaged from being in such close proximity; its heavily scarred trunk is a testimony of this battle to this day. Seeing this, the *peracak* tree was so scared that it ran away on tiptoes. That is why the *peracak* looks so tall and slender in appearance to this very day.

Once upon a time, humans could become animals. Animals, in turn, could perhaps become human beings. Below is a story explaining the origin of a white crocodile:

Once upon a time, there was a skipper named Nakhoda Ragam who sailed from Jering with his beautiful wife, Cik Siti. During their voyage, Nakhoda Ragam often felt the urge to hug his wife, so much so that she had to warn him to be careful as she was sewing. Nakhoda Ragam ignored his wife's warning; he was subsequently pricked by his wife's needle and died. His body was hidden and later buried in Banggor, but his spirit entered into the body of an old crocodile. Whenever a crocodile appears in the waters in that area, seafarers immediately say, "Nakhoda Ragam, your descendants seek your permission to pass." The crocodile will then disappear from the surface of the water.

Similarly, there are stories that explain why the python is not poisonous, why there are stripes on a tiger, and why various species of birds exist. On the origins of an island, there is a story that goes like this (Soetan H. Ibrahim, *Cerita Si Kantan*, Balai Pustaka, Batavia, 1931):

Once upon a time, a poor man lived in the state of Panai in East Sumatra, with his wife and son. His son, who was called Si Kantan, was 16 years old. One day, the Si Kantan's father went to the forest in search of firewood and found a very valuable Semambu cane. He told his son, Si Kantan, to sell the cane in Penang.

Word has it that Si Kantan obtained a lot of money from the sale of the Semambu cane, and with his newfound fortune, led the life of a rich man in Penang. Thereupon, he married a young lady, the daughter of a wealthy merchant. Not long thereafter, he set sail for home to Panai with his wife.

The news of Si Kantan's arrival with his boat laden with riches soon became the talk of the town in the whole of Panai. Si Kantan's mother went to meet her son. But he did not want to acknowledge her as his mother. He thought to himself, "I'd better not admit that this woman is my mother, for I will be ashamed in front of my wife, who's lovely like the full moon. Is it appropriate for someone as rich and noble as I am to have a mother as dirty and deformed as that?"

---

[1] *Dagun* (*Gnetum tenuifolium*), a type of edible root.
[2] *Gadung* (*Dioscorea hispida*), a type of Asiatic bitter yam with a twining stem and poisonous tuber.

> Si Kantan's mother tried repeatedly to meet her son but to no vail. Eventually she prayed: "Oh Allah, My God, if truly he is my son and has turned against me, exact thine own punishment on him for his sins against me."
>
> And by the will of God, there came a heavy rain and a great storm; the river swelled, its waves were huge. Si Kantan's boat was borne aloft and smashed by the raging waves and sank. After that the rain and wind stopped. As soon as the storm and tide receded, Si Kantan's capsized boat suddenly emerged and turned into an island, which was later named Pulau Kantan. It is said that a reticent white monkey can be found on the island which many believe to be the incarnation of Si Kantan's wife. Till today, the island can be seen clearly from the state of Panai.

The origin story may take the form of an explanation for place names: *padang gelang-gelang* (ring worm field), for example, was the place where Merah Silu was infected with ring worms; the kingdom of *Samudra* (meaning 'ocean' in Sanskrit) was named after the large ant (*semut besar*) which Merah Silu ate (*Sejarah Melayu*, chapter 7); and *Singapura* (Singapore, city of the lion) received its name after Sang Nila Utama saw a lion on the island (*Sejarah Melayu*, story 3). Indeed, many similar stories can be found in the *Sejarah Melayu* and other historical texts. A number of these stories and some other tales have been published together by the British scholar W. Skeat (1957). G. E. Maxwell has also translated two of these stories, namely *Puteri Buih* (The Foam Princess) and *Puteri Buluh Betung* (The Bamboo Princess) into English (Winstedt, 1907: 40-42).

1.2 Animal Tales

Animal tales are a popular form of folk literature. Every nation in the world has animal stories, and the same can be said of the Malays. Strangely enough, these stories have a lot in common. The story about the race between the mousedeer and the snail is one example. This story is not only found in Malaya, but also in Java, India, and Europe, the only difference in the story being the animals involved. In India the race involves the tortoise and the *Garuda*, the large, mythical bird-like creature that the Hindu god Vishnu rides. In Europe the race is between the tortoise and the hare or rabbit. Another example concerns stories of animals that do not know how to return an act of kindness. A Malay story, from the state of Perak, tells of a thankless crocodile that wanted to eat a water buffalo that had saved it from being trapped. Stories of animals that do not repay the kindness shown to them can also be found in Kedah. The same stories can also be found in China. The only difference is the animals. In Kedah and China, the animal saved from being trapped is not a crocodile but a tiger, and the rescuer not a water buffalo but a man.

What reason accounts for the fact that the same story can be found everywhere? Is it just a coincidence or has the one story spread to different peoples? Various theories have been put forward by scholars. According to C. Hooykaas, some of these animal stories came from India, and then later spread to Asia and Europe. This may well be true. In India, there are many well-known collections of animal stories, for example, the stories from the *Jataka*, *Pancatantra* and *Sukasaptati*. According to the Indians, regardless of what the beings are, whether deity, *jin* (genie), human or animal, they are just the same. It is possible for humans to become animals and for animals to transform into humans. As such, the animals in these stories are able to speak and think like humans.

Others argue that animal tales existed in all primitive societies and not just in India. In such primitive societies, people still lived in caves, and interacted with animals every day. They also depended on animals for their survival. Therefore, they knew full well the habits of animals. As a result, animals were given human characteristics. The creatures could feel and think like humans. Physical differences were irrelevant. In other words, there is no difference between deities, animals, and humans in primitive societies. In animal tales, there is usually one particular animal that plays the main role. Often, this is a small and weak animal. But by using its intelligence, it can trick other animals and effectively bring the entire jungle under its control. In Malay and Javanese literature, this animal is the *Pelanduk* or *Kancil* (Mousedeer). In Sundanese literature, this animal is the *Kera* (Monkey). Among the Toraja people of Sulawesi, the animal who plays this role is the *Nggasi* or *Kerahantu* (Tarsier). In Champa, Cambodia and Annam, this animal is the Rabbit. Sometimes these animals are defeated by even smaller and weaker animals than themselves. For example, even the intelligent and clever Mousedeer can lose out to the slow Snail in a race.

Malay Versions

Animal tales in Malay with the Mousedeer as their central character usually exhibit three levels of development. At the first level, the Mousedeer is portrayed as a small animal whose life is fraught with constant danger. He manages to survive only by using his sheer intelligence. In order to get to fruits across the river, it asks the Crocodiles to form him a bridge. When trapped, he pretends to be dead. Sometimes he also uses his wits to make fun of other animals. Even so, he is powerless against other animals smaller than himself. The *Hikayat Sang Kancil* (Tales of the Mousedeer), which is very popular in the Malay Peninsula, bears the characteristics of this first level of development.

At the second level, the Mousedeer has become Chief Magistrate of the Jungle. He is one of King Solomon's ministers, whose job is to settle all disputes among men and between animals and other animals. When a merchant complains that an orphan boy has become fat from breathing in the aroma of the merchant's food, the Mousedeer asks the boy to hide behind a curtain and begin counting, saying that the clinking of coins has the same value as the smell of food that he breathed in. The tale of *Pelanduk dengan Anak Memerang* (The Mousedeer and the Baby Otters) is a story that is characteristic of this level of development.

At the third level, the Mousedeer has become King of the Jungle and punishes those who disobey him. The *Hikayat Pelanduk Jenaka* (Humorous Tale of the Mousedeer) is typical of this level of development.

These three types of stories will be respectively discussed below. I will start with the *Hikayat Sang Kancil* (Tale of the Mousedeer) written by Daeng Abdulhamid for Mr. Winstedt. Its contents are as follows. It begins with a story about an animal that repays good with evil. A crocodile has its tail trapped under a fallen tree. A buffalo helps him free himself. But not only does the Crocodile not reciprocate the Buffalo's kindness, he tries to eat him. The matter is referred to a tattered mat and food cover. Both opine that it is simply the way of the world to reward good with evil. When the Mousedeer is consulted, he pretends that he needs to establish the facts of the case and asks the Crocodile to crawl back under the fallen tree. The Mousedeer quickly asks the Buffalo to drop the log, trapping the Crocodile once again. This enrages the Crocodile who vows that he will one day eat the Mousedeer. Next is the story of how the Mousedeer deceives the Tiger. The Mousedeer wants to eat some deer meat and asks the Tiger to catch a deer for him. When the deer is caught, the Mousedeer eats part of the Tiger's share of the meat. The Tiger, feeling that he has been used by the crafty Mousedeer, wants to take his revenge. Because of a subterfuge by the Mousedeer, however, the Tiger ends up eating Buffalo dung; and his tongue is almost severed when it got caught in bamboo. The same thing happens when a python tries to squeeze him around the waist. The next story tells of how the Mousedeer asks some crocodiles to line up to form a bridge so he can cross the river to eat some ripe fruit on the other side. When the Crocodile traps his leg, Mousedeer calmly points out that what Crocodile has caught is not his leg, but a piece of wood.

The Tiger and Crocodile conspire to capture the Mousedeer: the Tiger will hunt him on land while the Crocodile pursues him in the water. But when the Tiger wants to catch the Mousedeer on the riverbank, it is not the Mousedeer who falls into the river but the Tiger. And so, the Crocodile eats the Tiger. The next story depicts the Mousedeer's mischievousness. He pretends to be a teacher instructing pupils in Qur'an recital and canes the Tiger's cub. He then tricks a deer into entering a village, resulting in the deer's capture and slaughter. The dead deer's fawn seeks to avenge its parent's death and hunts the Mousedeer down. In trying to escape, the Mousedeer falls into a deep well. Screaming that the sky is about to come crashing down on them, he tricks the other animals into jumping into the well too, then makes his escape by jumping on their backs while mocking their gullibility.

The Mousedeer was trapped on two occasions. The first time, he pretended to be dead and his body was thrown into the bushes. The second time, he tricked a dog into taking his place in a cage and escaped.

The next story tells the tale of the Mousedeer's arrogance as he seeks out other animals to pit his wit against. First, he challenges the Snail to a race in which he is beaten by the Snail. Then he engages in a quarrel with a Gnat and loses that as well. In the end, he realises the greatness of God and repents. As penance, he helps King Solomon resolve the legal conundrums he faces time and again, and is conferred the title Chief Magistrate of the jungle by King Solomon as a reward. One of the cases he helps resolve is a suit brought in court by a merchant who accuses two orphans of having grown fat by breathing in the aroma of cooking from his kitchen. The Mousedeer asks both children to go behind a curtain and count aloud the silver coins he has given them so that the merchant can hear the clinking of the coins as they count. He then declares that the clinking of the coins signifies payment for the smell of the bread and food enjoyed by the orphans. The moral of the story left by the author at the end of the *hikayat* reads, "Reason is a better paragon of virtue than a thousand stupid and foolish friends."

1.2.1 The Mousedeer and the Baby Otters

According to R. O. Winstedt, the tale of *Pelanduk dengan Anak Memerang* (The Mousedeer and the Baby Otters) is the best example of a cause-and-effect story (what he terms a "clock-story"—an elaboration of a riddle into a narrative) in the Malay language. The story tells of how the Mousedeer kills all of the Otter's babies because the Otter kills fishes in the river. One day the Mousedeer sees the Otter's seven babies playing in its den while both of their parents are out hunting for fish. The

Mousedeer mutters to itself as it thinks of the Otter killing all the fishes. Suddenly the cuckoo birds start a din with their loud cooing. The noise, which reminds the Mousedeer of old battles of days gone, shocks him and he reacts by breaking out into a twelve-step *silat* (Malay martial art) move, his legs stomping here and there. Before he knows it, all the Baby Otters are dead, trampled to death by the Mousedeer's stomping hooves. When they discover this, the Otter and his wife go before King Solomon to seek justice.

In his own defence, the Mousedeer explains that he went on the warpath because he thought the noise made by the cuckoo birds was the sound of battle drums warning of an impending enemy invasion of the city. Actually, the cuckoos created a din because they saw a monitor lizard scurrying with its sharp claws that looked like drawn swords. The Lizard in turn was scurrying with drawn swords because it saw the Turtle carrying a shield. And the Turtle was carrying a shield because it saw the Shrimp bearing crossed spears. Why was the Shrimp bearing spears? Because he saw the Jungle Perch swimming upstream looking sorrowful. The reason why the Perch was so afflicted with sorrow was because many of its kin have been eaten by the Otter. Hearing this, King Solomon summarily decrees the Mousedeer to be innocent. Instead the Otters themselves are held culpable for their own children's death. This story, as well as the *Hikayat Sang Kancil* discussed above, were written by Raja Haji Yahya for Winstedt and published by O. T. Dussek.

Another well-known example of a clock or cause-and-effect story is the tale of the *Bangau* (Stork), sung by children since the old days. My dear readers would surely have sung this song when they were little. The song goes like this.

> Oh Stork, oh Stork, why are you so thin?
> How could I not be thin, when the fish don't rise?
>
> Oh Fish, oh Fish, why don't you rise?
> How could I rise, when the grass is so tall?
>
> Oh Grass, oh Grass, why are you so tall?
> How could I not be tall, the buffalo doesn't eat me.
>
> Oh buffalo, oh buffalo, why aren't you eating grass?
> How could I eat grass, my tummy hurts.
>
> Oh tummy, oh tummy, why do you hurt?
> How could I not hurt, I ate uncooked rice.
>
> Oh rice, oh rice, why weren't you cooked?
> How could I be cooked, the fire wouldn't light.
>
> Oh fire, oh fire, why wouldn't you light?
> How could I light, the wood was all wet.
>
> Oh wood, oh wood, why were you wet?
> How could I not be wet, the rain fell on me.

Oh rain, oh rain, why did you fall on wood?
How could I not fall, frog called me.

Oh frog, oh frog, why do you call the rain?
How could I not call, the snake wanted to eat me.

Oh snake, oh snake, why do you want to eat the frog?
How could I not eat it, it is my food.

1.2.2 Comic Tales of the Mousedeer *(Hikayat Pelanduk Jenaka)*

This book is relatively older than the others as it was mentioned by Werndly as far back as 1736. Different interpretations of the term*"Jenaka"*or *"Jinaka"* have been proposed. Van der Tuuk holds the opinion that *Jinaka* originated from the Sanskrit word *jainaka*, referring to a Jain holy man who was often ridiculed by others. H. Kern argues that *jinaka* is derived from the Javanese word *jaka*, or young man. The infix *in,* which means "living", has been inserted into *jaka*. *Jainana* means acting as a young man. C. A. Mees, who translated these tales into Dutch disagrees with these interpretations. According to him, *jinaka* probably means a sacred or pure Place. He postulates that in the *Hikayat Pelanduk Jenaka*, published by H. C. Klinkert in 1885, a hillock or mound where the Mousedeer withdraws to meditate is often termed *pungsu jantaka* (place of meditation) or, elsewhere, *indra-kila*. *Pungsu jantaka* is the *pusujinaka* referred to in the 1893 version. *Indrakila* is none other than Arjuna's place of meditation and Arjuna is also called Arjuna Janaka or Jenaka.[3]

This *hikayat* has been published twice, in 1885 and 1893. The publisher was the Dutch scholar, H. C. Klinkert. The two editions are quite different: the 1885 edition contains ten stories, while the 1893 edition contains only seven stories. But the plot is the same. Both describe how a small but intelligent mousedeer was able to beat all the other animals and become the King of the Jungle. It is first recounted how Mousedeer obtains his strength: in the 1885 edition, he does this by rubbing his body with the sap from a ficus tree, while in the 1893 edition, by rolling in the grains of the *lalang,* a long, weedy grass. It also contains a story of how the Mousedeer successfully mediates between two archenemies, the Tiger and the Goat, and how this gained the Mousedeer its ever increasing fame. The animals in the jungle beg him to protect them from the menace of a monster. Using his guile, the mousedeer is able to kill the monster. All the animals make their obeisance to the Mousedeer, each bringing him an offering. The Monkey, however, refuses to submit to him and when he is chased out of the jungle, enlists the help of the Elephant, the Lion and the Crocodile. The Elephant, the Lion and the Crocodileare all defeated by the Mousedeer (there are differing accounts of how these animals are vanquished in the two editions). Finally, to punish the Monkey, the Mousedeer tricks him into kicking a beehive. The Monkey is stung so badly that his body swells up all over. The Mousedeer then announces that anyone who refuses to bow to him will receive a similar punishment. And so Mousedeer

---

3   There are also scholars who argue that *"Jantaka"* derives from a nasalised version of the word *"Jataka"*, birth (as in the "birth stories of the previous incarnations of the Buddha"). C. A. Mees also rejects this interpretation (pp. xxii-xxv).

remains on his throne. This story is only found in the 1893 edition. On the other hand, the 1885 edition contains three stories not found in the 1893 issue, namely stories about how:

1. The Mousedeer competes in a river water-drinking contest with the other animals.
2. The Mousedeer catches the monster who has been stealing fish caught by the other animals.
3. The Mousedeer burns the Ant who has killed the Elephant.
   And finally all the animals submit to the authority of the Mousedeer.

From the above discussion, it is clear that the plot in the 1893 edition or the shorter version is more condensed than that of the 1885 edition or the longer version. According to J. Brandes, the shorter version is more original, older and more important. The three stories found only in the longer version are apparently later additions. For example, the ninth story is a variation of the second story. Winstedt agrees that the shorter version is more original and he indicates that it also bears Javanese influences.

It should be mentioned here that the *Hikayat Pelanduk* has also been published in the form of a *syair* (a form of traditional Malay poetry made up of four-line quatrains) in Singapore in 1301 AH, or 1883/84 AD. This *syair* is similar to the long version, but contains only eight stories. The last two stories are not included.

Besides these texts, there are two other collections of mousedeer stories which have been translated from the Javanese language. The first, translated by Winter, is called: *Riwayat dengan Segala Perihal Kancil* (The Life of, and Everything about, the Mousedeer), with 12 color pictures, copied from the Javanese language. The second is *Cerita Kancil yang Cerdik* (The Story of the Clever Mousedeer) by Ng. Wirapustaka, published by Balai Pustaka.

Last but not least, is the *Hikayat Sang Kancil* (Tales of the Mousedeer) which is very popular in the Malay Peninsula.[4] This *hikayat* comprising 20 stories was composed by Daeng Abdulhamid of Perak for Winstedt. Most of these stories are also well-known in Java and other parts of the archipelago. In these tales the Mousedeer is wicked and devious.[5] It dupes other animals and kills innocent baby crocodiles. Finally he himself is defeated by a smaller animal. It is only then that he realises how great God is. He repents and becomes a wise and shrewd judge, who wins praise from King Solomon. It should be mentioned here that the *Hikayat Sang Kancil*, was rewritten in modern Malay by Daud Baharum and published by OUP, Kuala Lumpur.

1.3 Javanese literature

There are three collections of well-known mousedeer stories in Javanese. The oldest is the *Serat Kancil* (Book of Mousedeer) written by Kyai Rangga Amongsastra. This work is written in the traditional Javanese verse form known as the *macapat* and was published by Dr. W. Palmer van den Broekin 1878. In 1889, it was revised by D. F. van der Pant.

---

4 These tales, together with the *Hikayat Pelanduk Jenaka dengan Anak Memerang* was published under the title *Hikayat Pelanduk* in the *Malay Literature Series 13* (MPH 1923).
5 In Achehnese, "*kancil*" means "crafty" or "wicked"; see Snouck Hugronje *The Achehnese* (translated by O'Sullivan), vol.1, p. 158.

Amongsastra's *Serat Kancil* consists of two parts. In the first section, the Mousedeer plays an important role. Eight of the nine stories in the first section, are found in the *Hikayat Sang Kancil* discussed earlier. What is not found is the story of the Mousedeer capturing a monster (which can be found in the *Hikayat Pelanduk*). The second part consists of seven stories; almost all are already well-known mousedeer stories. The only difference is that here, the role of the mousedeer is played by another animal, namely the *Kijang* (barking deer). The first story which depicts a bevy of Baby Otters being trampled to death by the Barking Deer, has a similar motif to the tale of the "Pelanduk dengan Anak Memerang" found in the *Hikayat Pelanduk* (MLS 13). The only difference is that the chaos that sets off the train of events leading to the death of the Baby Otters is begun by the Crab, who is subsequently eaten by the Otter. In "Pelanduk dengan Anak Memerang", the pandemonium was created by none other than the Otter itself. The next story is the story of the clever Barking Deer who can always elude danger.

The second collection of these tales was published by G. C. T. van Dorp in Semarang in 1871. This collection of stories is entitled: *Serat Kancil, awit kalahiraken ngantos dumugi pejahipun wonten ing nagari Mesir mawi kaseharaken* (*The Book of the Mousedeer, from its birth to its death in Egypt, written in verse*). This collection consists of 18 stories. Most of these are well-known tales found in other collections. But there is something special about this collection. In the beginning, it is recounted that the Mousedeer is born of Man. His mother is the Goddess Sungkawa, the daughter of a priest. Unfortunately his mother died giving birth to him (there is no mention of his father). In the tenth and eleventh stories, the Mousedeer becomes a magistrate. In the tenth story, the Mousedeer releases a goat which was about to be eaten by a Tiger. In the eleventh story, the Mousedeer settles a dispute between the Barred Eagle-Owl (*Burung Beluk*) and the Barn Owl (*Burung Daris*) over whether or not the Eagle-Owl's young is a good match for the Barn Owl's young. The fifteenth and seventeenth stories tell how the Mousedeer covers himself with the long quills of the porcupine in order to scare off all the animals she meets with. Finally, in the seventeenth story, the Mousedeer, upon learning that the King of Egypt is looking for a prospective son-in-law, takes it upon himself to be the one to marry the Egyptian princess. Unfortunately, the Mousedeer is captured in Egypt by one of the Egyptian princess's suitors and is killed. This text was translated into Malay by Winter.

The third collection is called the *Serat Saloka Darma* (Book of Poems on Morality) and was written in 1891 by Pangeran Arya Sasraningrat, son of the head of the Paku Alam, Yogyakarta. This collection is made up of only nine stories. Firstly, it tells the story of how the Mousedeer's father helps the Buffalo. This is followed by the story of the Mousedeer's birth, and the race against the Snail. After escaping from danger, the Mousedeer turns over a new leaf and becomes a king. During his reign, the Tiger and the Civet Cat both declare themselves to be teachers of the mystical art (*ilmu kebatinan*). The Civet Cat is captured and exiled. The Tiger, on the other hand, refuses to come before the Mousedeer despite being ordered to do so many times. In the end, the Mousedeer becomes the Tiger's pupil. And the Tiger becomes a palace official in Mousedeer's palace.

This book is written in such a way as to reflect Javanese society. Therefore, in order to fully understand this collection of Mousedeer stories, it is essential to have some knowledge of the Javanese language and way of thinking.

1.3.1 Mousedeer Tales in other Regions of the Archipelago

Tales of the Mousedeer can be found in other regions of the archipelago as well. In Sunda, there is a collection of mousedeer stories that resembles the Javanese ones. But the creature that plays a central role in these stories is not the mousedeer, but the tortoise. In Acheh, there is a collection of 26 stories. The main character is still the Mousedeer. Except for a few, most of the stories are not known in other areas. The story of the Mousedeer is also found on the islands of Roti, Timur and Kangean. The animal that plays the role of protagonist is the Monkey and the stories are largely unknown elsewhere. It should be mentioned here that a collection of the major papers on the Mousedeer tales has been published by Asdi S. Dipodjojo (1966).

Mousedeer tales from outside the Archipelago that have much in common with Malay and Javanese mousedeer stories come from Champa and Annam on mainland Southeast Asia. The animal at the forefront of these tales is the Rabbit, but a large part of these stories reminds one of the Malay-Javanese mousedeer tales. Cambodian Mousedeer tales are somewhat different.

Malay mousedeer tales are often compared to the fox stories of Europe. H. C. Klinkert called the collection of mousedeer stories that he published in 1885, *Hikayat Pelandoek Djinaka of Reinaert de Vos der Maleiers*, meaning *Mousedeer Tales or the Fox of the Malays*.

Actually, there is a huge difference between the Mousedeer tales and the fox stories. The Mousedeer is among the animal kingdom's smallest and weakest creatures. It is his sheer quick wittedness that enables him to survive in the wild. Sometimes he is a little mischievous. But most of the time his intentions are good; he settles disagreements between animals or saves the smaller ones from the threat of larger predators. Perhaps this is why in some collections of stories the Mousedeer is said to have become a fair and wise judge. In contrast, the Fox is a vicious animal, cruel and always menacing small animals with its sharp teeth.

1.4 *Cerita Jenaka* (Comic Tales)

Cerita Jenaka are stories that are full of humour. "*Jenaka*" (Humour), is defined in the major Indonesian dictionary, *Kamus Besar Bahasa Indonesia* (Department of National Education, 2008: 577), as "[something that] evokes laughter, mirth, hilarity, funny." But R. J. Wilkinson in his dictionary, *A Malay-English Dictionary*, explains that "*jenaka*" also means "wily, full of stratagems". In short, a *cerita jenaka* is a story about a comic character, who is either ludicrous, amusing, or sly and quick-witted.

The comic tale is born out of a human proclivity for exaggeration; for example, a ludicrous character like Pak Pandir is created to tell the story of human folly; to depict the role fortuitousness plays in human affairs, an extremely lucky character emerges in the figure of Pak Belalang. So too we find very wily characters such as Si Luncai, extremely down-on-their-luck characters such as Lebai Malang, and farcically funny ones like Abu Nawas and so on.

The comic tale is found all over the world. There is a well-known character in German and Dutch literature called *Uilenspiegel*, that is *uil* (owl) and *spiegel* or mirror. In Arab-Turkish literature, this character is called Jaha or Khoja Nasreddin, and in Arab-Persian literature, Abu Nawas. In the literature of the Malay Archipelago, the Bataks are the most familiar with such humorous characters, including *Ama ni Pandir, Si Lahap, Si Bilolang dan Si Jonaha* and *Jonaka*. But, the best known of all comic characters is Kabayan in Sunda. He epitomizes all the characteristics of the comic tale. He is sometimes a fool, at other times cunning, and on still other occasions, simply lucky to escape the danger in which he finds himself. There is a lesser development of comic tales in Javanese literature, due perhaps to the presence of existing wayang (shadow puppet theatre) characters such as Semar, Nala and Petruk. The character *Gareng*, a lame knight in Javanese wayang, shares many similarities with other characters found in *jenaka* stories. However, the Javanese do have their fair share of comic characters, with the likes of Pak Banjir, Joko Bodo, Joko Dolog and Joko Lelur.

What follows is a summary and further commentary on nine comic characters found in Malay literature. Five of them, namely *Pak Kadok, Pak Pandir, Lebai Malang, Pak Belalang* and *Si Luncai*, have been featured in a collection entitled *Cerita Jenaka (Humorous Stories)* (MLS 6). Most of these stories, with the exception of the tale of Abu Nawas, are tales that hail from the Archipelago. R. O. Winstedt, nevertheless, maintains that virtually all of these *cerita jenaka* originated in India (Winstedt, 1920: 120).

1.4.1 *Pak Kadok*

Pak Kadok is an unfortunate character. A *seloka* or ditty about him goes like this:

> Oh unlucky Pak Kadok!
> His rooster triumphs, but he hocked his house!
> He throws away the rice he has,
> And goes home starving!
> Upstream he rows against the ebb
> Downstream against the tide!
> A wife he has but he kills her
> He starves himself to the brink of death,
> When he sails the wind dies!
> When he anchors the breeze blows!
> A house he has but becomes a guest in others' homes.

Pak Kadok is a very silly and foolish old man. One day he decides to take his rooster to the cockpit, believing that the bird will bring him luck. He asks his wife to sew him a shirt and pants out of paper. But because he is in such a hurry, she does not have time to sew the clothes, but simply glues them together. He then leaves for the cockpit.

The king is very attracted by Pak Kadok's rooster as he knows it brings a lot of luck. He wants to exchange roosters with Pak Kadok and tells him what a fine fowl his own rooster is and how Pak Kadok's cock doesn't look like it will bring him any luck. As a loyal subject, Pak Kadok obliges and exchanges his rooster with the king.

When his rooster wins, an elated Pak Kadok claps his hands, cheering and jumping up and down with joy to such an extent that his shirt and pants are ripped to shreds. Everyone breaks into laughter at the sight of Pak Kadok standing stark naked in full view of the crowd. He looks at himself and realizes he hasn't even a stitch on, and that the rooster that won the cockfight belongs to the king and is no longer his, as he made the exchange before the fight began. Pak Kadok runs home. The king proclaims loudly: "There goes Pak Kadok, his rooster triumphs, but he has lost his house."

In another incident, Pak Kadok receives invitations to two feasts (*kenduri*) on the same day. One invitation is for a feast at the hour of *zuhur* (just after noon), where meat from one buffalo will be served; the other invitation is for a feast held at noon, where meat from two cows will be served. Pak Kadok wakes up very early that day.

He doesn't eat his usual breakfast of soaked rice; instead, he asks that it be poured away on the ground for the chickens to eat. Because of his greed and eagerness to eat buffalo meat, he rows to the feast against the ebbing tide. When he arrives, it is well after noon; the feast is over and the guests have already gone home to their own villages. And so he rows to the next feast, this time against the rising tide. When he reaches there, it is already late in the afternoon, well after the hour of *ashar*, and the guests are starting to head for home. Pak Kadok doesn't even bother to stop by at the house where the feast is held but goes straight home. He reaches home at dusk. His wife greets him sarcastically. He loses his temper and hits her with a stick of firewood. As the will of God would have it, although he has only hit her once, she falls to the ground and dies.

Pak Kadok does not want to live in his house any longer. He decides to move in with a friend whose home lies at the rivermouth. The moment he prepares to set sail, however, the wind begins to die. And so he lets his boat drift in the river, waiting for the wind to pick up. He soon starts to tire and drops his anchor so he can rest and shake off his fatigue. Suddenly the wind picks up, but Pak Kadok is too tired to hoist his sail. He falls fast asleep in the boat. When he wakes up the next day, he weighs his anchor and rows to his friend's house. It is evening when he arrives. And he lives in his friend's home for the remainder of his life. It is from this story of Pak Kadok's misfortune that people have come up with the saying "*malang Pak Kadok*" or "unlucky Pak Kadok", which I quoted at the beginning of this section.

1.4.2 *Lebai Malang*

Besides Pak Kadok, there is another character in comic Malay tales whose bad luck is never-ending. This character is the wretched Lebai Malang.

Pak Lebai is a cleric; he reads the Quran fluently, is devoted in his worship, and is well-mannered and polite. Moreover he is kind, sincere and good-hearted. However, he is unremittingly beset with bad luck because of the one flaw in his character: his greed makes him indecisive.

One day, Pak Lebai receives three invitations: an invitation to pay his last respects to someone who has passed away; an invitation to a feast to mark a *khatam* Quran (completion of Quranic recital lessons) and an invitation to a feast to celebrate Prophet Muhammad's birthday. He thinks to himself: "Which invitation should accept? If I go to the funeral, I will be given a gift of white cloth and a mat; if I go to the *khatam* Quran feast, my belly will surely be full and I will go home with a gift of meat and rice; and if I go to the Prophet's birthday celebration, my belly will be filled with lots of snacks and goodies." He finally decides to attend the funeral because the Prophet teaches us, "do what is compulsory (*wajib*) before you do anything else."

But because he has deliberated for so long, he is too late for everything. On the way to the funeral, Pak Lebai meets the mourners who are already on their way back from the cemetery. He proceeds to the house where the *khatam Quran* feast is being held, but the guests are all about to leave. So he sets out for the house where the Prophet's birthday is being celebrated but the festivities are finished there as well. He receives only a packet of pancakes to take home.

When he reaches home, he remembers that he has not collected the juice from the palm tree. He climbs the palm tree and finds plenty of palm juice in the bamboo collection tube. But suddenly he sees a dog chewing the packet of pancakes he has left hanging on the ladder he used to climb the tree. Furious, he reaches for his cleaver to hit the dog but misses. He hurls the bamboo tube at the dog and misses again. He quickly jumps down from the tree and chases after the dog. The dog runs into a hole in a log to hide. As there is nothing else at hand, Pak Lebai strips off his pants, shirt and *songkok* (skull cap) in order to block the dog's exit. But this is to no avail and the dog still manages to escape.

Anon, two pigeons perch on Pak Lebai's arm, mistaking the stark naked Pak Lebai for a tree-stump. When Pak Lebai moves his hand to grab the birds, the birds fly away. Pak Lebai returns to the hole in the log to retrieve his clothes, only to find that they have gone. He returns home and recounts the events of the day to his wife. His wife, Mak Lebai, loses her temper and beats him. He runs under the mosquito net to find something to cover himself up with, and sits there ruefully reflecting on his misfortune. Mak Lebai sings a lament using a *syair* form:

> Oh the luck of the wretched poor man,
> He receves a gift of pancakes
> But loses his shirt and clothes
> His pancakes gone, eaten by a mutt
> After it, too tired for words, he ran,
> Hither and thither in a hustle,
> But the cleaver's gone, so too the palm juice
> So home he goes and gets an earful.

So goes the story of Lebai Malang.

1.4.3 *Si Luncai*

Si Luncai is a comic story that entered the Malay world in ancient times and today is considered an original comic tale. It probably originated in India.

It is said that in a particular city there lived a poor orphan boy nicknamed Si Luncai because he had a big belly and an enormous backside. When he walked, he never wore a shirt. He worked drying and milling paddy, and selling firewood. He very much wanted to meet the king but was never able to because he was so ugly.

One day, after grooming himself and donning beautiful clothes, Si Luncai summoned up courage to present himself before the king. The king had just shaven his head, Si Luncai broke down and cried when he saw the king's bald head. When asked why he was crying, Si Luncai replied that he was remembering his dead father. The king's bald head and wide forehead bore a striking resemblance to Si Luncai's late father. Upon hearing this, the king was furious and ordered that Si Luncai be arrested and executed.

The executioner took Si Luncai by boat to the river mouth, intending to throw him overboard. On the way, Si Luncai persuaded the executioner to give him a pumpkin to hug in the place of his mother. Then Si Luncai said he knew a way to relieve the rowers of their fatigue. He told the executioner and the boat crew to sing together: "Si Luncai has jumped overboard with his pumpkin!" with the chorus, "Let him go, let him go!" The executioner and boat crew did as they were instructed. When Si Luncai jumped into the river, the helmsman cried out: "Si Luncai has jumped overboard with his pumpkin!" The crew responded: "Let him go, let him go!"

Si Luncai, however, did not escape for very long. He was arrested, dumped into a gunny sack and tied up. The boat continued its way to the river mouth. Suddenly they heard the continuous bleating of a deer. Si Luncai told them that the sound was that of a deer caught in a trap he himself had set. Wanting to capture the trapped deer, the executioner landed the boat by the bank of the river, and went on foot to find the deer.

As the will of God would have it, a rich merchant sailed past. Si Luncai told the merchant that he had been thrown into the gunny sack for refusing to marry the king's daughter. The merchant was very keen to marry the princess, and agreed to take Si Luncai's place in the gunnysack. When the executioner returned empty-handed, his resentment towards Si Luncai grew even more intense. Believing that Si Luncai was still in the gunnysack, he vigorously hurled it into the river.

Not long after that, Si Luncai appeared again before the king, dressed in the lavish robes and turban of the merchant he tricked. He told the king that he was the spirit of dead Si Luncai whom the king had killed. Si Luncai claimed that he was now in heaven and that he had met the king's dead parents in the hereafter. If the king would like to see his parents, he should build a tall building. If the king recited the prayer Si Luncai taught him and looked up at the sky, he will be able to see his parents sitting on a throne in perfect bliss, surrounded by angels. But if anyone failed to see this vision, it meant that that person is not the legitimate child of their parents (*anak haram*). A tall building was then built as instructed. The king and his ministers all claimed they can see the king's late parents and the kingdom of Heaven, as they did not want to be considered bastards.

Si Luncai then promised to take the king to the nether world to meet his late father. A glass palanquin with an outer grilled covering was constructed for the journey. Si Luncai escorted the king to the opening of a very deep cave. The king stepped into the palanquin while Si Luncai sat under the grilled covering outside the palanquin. Both the king and Si Luncai were then lowered into the deep shaft. As the will of God would have it, Si Luncai saw an opening in the cave from which he could make his way back to the mortal world. He quickly jumped onto a rock at the edge of the hole. The palanquin, with the king in it, plunged down the shaft, straight into the mouth of a huge dragon, and he was swallowed by the dragon.

After seven days and seven nights, Si Luncai left the cave and reached home safely. The next day, he presented himself at the royal audience hall in the king's palace and was greeted with great reverence by his majesty's ministers and military commanders. Si Luncai was crowned king and married to the king's daughter, Princess Lela Kenda, in a ceremony solemnised by a *qadi* (senior religious official).

Anon when the time came for the marriage to be consummated, Si Luncai entered the princess's bed chamber. She burst into tears, repulsed at the sight of Si Luncai's ugly face. Despite the persuasion of her lady-in-waiting, she refused to go to bed, thinking of the fate of her poor father.

As dawn approached, Si Luncai dozed off and finally fell asleep. A thought crossed the princess's mind: "It's all because of this accursed Si Luncai that I have lost my father! If that is the case, then the best thing I can do is kill him." She took her father's dagger, stabbed Luncai in the throat and he died. The princess's then broke the news to her mother and the prime minister. Upon hearing the princess's account, the queen and the prime minister were outraged and deeply aggrieved at Si Luncai's deception. Subsequently, her Royal Highness Princess Lela Kendi ascended to the throne and succeeded her father, ruling the country justly. This is the story as it was told by the storyteller.

1.4.4 *Pak Pandir*

The story has it that Pak Pandir and his wife lived in the forest. Pak Pandir was not only very stupid, but a total nincompoop as well. One day the couple's daughter fell ill with *guam*[6] and became feverish. Mak Andeh asked her husband to catch some grasshoppers to use as bait for catching fish. Pak Pandir used a deer as bait instead.

Pak Pandir's foolishness is sometimes shocking. On one occasion, when asked to bathe his child in warm water, he placed the infant in a tub of boiling water. Even after the child has died, its skin flaking off and its gums exposed as if it were grinning, he could still remark: "Oh, my baby really enjoys a hot bath!" Only after his wife had pointed out to him that the baby was dead did Pak Pandir break down; he wailed, thrashing his head about like a madman. He was then asked to give the baby a burial. On the way to the cemetery, he did not notice the baby's body fall to the ground. However Pak Pandir stumbled upon the body on his way home. When he saw the body, Pak Pandir muttered: "It looks like I'm not the only one to suffer this misfortune!"

After some time has passed, Mak Andeh tells Pak Pandir to buy a buffalo to be slaughtered for a *kenduri* to commemorate their child's death. Mak Andeh describes the buffalo as something that grazes on grass. Pak Pandir buys a sickle instead. Fortunately for him, the seller whom he bought the sickle from agrees to give him a real buffalo when he returns to exchange it. Meanwhile, Mak Andeh is busy cooking rice and a variety of dishes by the potful. She sends Pak Pandir to invite a *haji* (a title given to someone who has made a pilgrimage to Mecca) and a *lebai* (a mosque cleric) to the feast. She describes them to him in this way: "The *haji* wears s turban on his head while the *lebai* has a beard under his chin." Pak Pandir 'invites' a sparrow and a goat instead. As a consequence, Pak Pandir has to endure Mak Andeh's yelling and cursing.

---

[6] *guam*, canker sores or oral thrush.

On another occasion, Pak Pandir is asked to call upon the benevolent spirit of a Muslim saint but instead he invokes a granny ogress by mistake. Nevertheless, his quickwittedness helped him save himself. When told to feed the ogre's children, he shoved buffalo bones down their throats until they choked to death. When the ogre parents tried to cross the river in pursuit of their children's murderers, he tricked the ogres into entering a large urn covered by a lily pad (*daun birah*). When the ogres punch through the lid of the urn, the leaf broke, allowing the water to rush in and drown them. With the ogres dead, Pak Pandir and Mak Andeh were able to help themselves to the treasure they found in the ogres' home.

On another occasion, Mak Andeh wanted to hold a *kenduri* (feast) in memory of her dead ancestors, family members and her deceased child. She had everything she needed for the feast, except salt. She sent Pak Pandir to the village to buy some salt. Having obtained a sack of salt, Pak Pandir made his way home. On the way home, he felt the urge to answer the call of nature. So, he looked for somewhere safe to hide the salt while he was doing his business. He searched high and low for a suitable spot to hide the salt, but couldn't find any and eventually hid it in a creek. Alas, when he returned to retrieve his sack of salt, he found that the salt had all dissolved.

Since then, Mak Andeh has stopped asking Pak Pandir to do anything at all. Pak Pandir has been left to himself and to do whatever suits him. One day, he cut down some bamboo to make a fish trap. He set the trap in a pond created by an embankment by the stream. Pak Pandir made a bountiful catch. He smoked the fish and ate it without rice, putting the remainder in a sack which he hung on a tree.

Since that day, Pak Pandir seldom ate at home. When asked why not, he told Mak Andeh he eats wild fruits and roots in the forest. Eventually, Mak Andeh discovered Pak Pandir's secret. One day, while Pak Pandir was sitting in a tree eating smoked fish, Mak Andeh made a noise: "tok-tok-kai". Frightened, Pak Pandir jumped down from the tree and ran helter-skelter home. His whole body was covered with thorns, and smeared with blood. His shirt was torn to shreds. And so Mak Andeh took all of Pak Pandir's smoked fish.

Not long after that, Pak Pandir ventured into the woods to trap birds. He took a bamboo cylinder containing sticky tree sap to coat the branches and twigs on a fig tree. Many birds became stuck to the sap and fell to the ground. Pak Pandir picked them up, bound them with string, and tied them around his waist. In this way, he had five to six hundred birds tied all over his body and he was soon completely covered with birds. The birds began to flutter and spread their wings, then flew into the sky taking Pak Pandir with them.

As the will of God would have it, the birds reached the village of King Shah Malim. Pak Pandir claimed to be *Raja Mambang* (King of the Sprites) and was subsequently given the hand of Princess Lang Lela in marriage. The princess, however, refused to share her bed with 'Raja Mambang'. In the end, Pak Pandir accidentally revealed his true identity and was cast out of the palace in disgrace. Shamefaced, Pak Pandir made his way home.

On another occasion, Pak Pandir helped his wife to build a house in the woods. When she asked him to go home to fetch fire, he asked her to grill him some bananas first. Annoyed, Mak Andeh gave him the bananas while they were still burning hot. Pak Pandir swallowed the bananas whole, without even peeling them. Choking on the hot food, he writhed on the ground in agony and died. Mak Andeh was left all alone, grieving over the loss of her husband. About three months later, she too fell ill and she passed away. And so goes the story of Pak Pandir.

1.4.5 *Pak Belalang*

There once was a farmer who lived with his wife and their son named Belalang (Grasshopper). Because of this, everyone called the farmer Pak Belalang (Father Grasshopper). The farmer and his family were very poor and had almost nothing to eat.

One day, Pak Belalang had an idea about how to get food. A neighbour's buffalo was ploughing on a nearby paddy field. He told his son to hide the buffalo, and then to spread the news in the village that he (Pak Belalang) could divine where to find the buffalo. Young Belalang did as he was told. For his 'success' in finding the buffalo, Pak Belalang was rewarded with rice, paddy, tobacco and fish. His fame as a clairvoyant soon spread far and wide.

One day, the king of the country lost seven chests containing gold, diamonds and other priceless treasure. Pak Belalang was summoned and ordered to find the missing treasure on pain of death. Pak Belalang walked home. As he rested in the centre of his house, he counted the pieces of bread his wife was making in the kitchen. He heard the sizzle of the bread as it hits the hot oil in the pan, and counted "one". By the will of God, at that very moment, the ringleader of a band of bandits had just broken into the compound of Pak Belalang's house. By the time Pak Belalang counted "seven", all seven bandits had sneaked into the compound. The bandits were afraid. They thought surely Pak Belalang knew they were the ones who stole the king's treasure. So they came in to Pak Belalang and confessed their crime. In this way, Pak Belalang escaped from his own impending 'doom' and was very handsomely rewarded by the king. His Majesty also conferred the title "Master Clairvoyant" upon him.

One day, two naval commanders came to see the king: one brought a duck and wanted to find out whether it is male or female; the other brought a smooth, circular piece of wood and wanted to determine where its beginning and end points were. Pak Belalang managed to solve both puzzles by pure coincidence. Rowing close to the ships in the middle of the night, he learnt the answers when he overheard a discussion between the two commanders. On another occasion, the wife of the prince of the kingdom of Askalan Rum was kidnapped by a genie seven days after their wedding day. Pak Belalang was summoned to the kingdom to find the prince's missing wife. With the help of Prophet Khidr, who appeared to him in a dream, he succeeded in his task and received a handsome reward.

Another time, Pak Belalang was threatened with death if he could not guess what the king had in his clenched fist. Pak Belalang could not guess the right answer. In his heart he thought he would surely die. Sobbing at the thought of leaving behind his son, Young Belalang, he moaned: "Death is upon me, goodbye my son, Belalang." Coincidentally, the king was holding a grasshopper in his clenched fist, and so Pak Belalang was once again spared. On his way home, he thought to himself: "If this is how things will always be, I had better set fire to my house so that I can say that all my astrological papers have been destroyed. Then I will be able to lead a peaceful life, without the king testing me all the time." And so, Pak Belalang stopped working and was granted an ample pension by the king in his retirement.

The *Tale of Pak Belalang* is also well-known among the Minangkabau and has been published by A. F. von de Wall; it is by and large similar to the summarised version given above. The main difference is a preamble at the beginning of the story that says that someone who has a piece of good fortune, or comes into possession of something without expecting it in the least, or if that something is obtained effortlessly, then that person can be said to have "the luck of Pak Belalang". Also, the idea of hiding something comes not from Pak Belalang, but from his son, Young Belalang. And the thing hidden is not a buffalo but clothes belonging to the child of the king's concubine. The story of the kidnapping of the prince's wife by a genie is also not present in this version.

There are two other well-known comic tales in Malay literature, namely the tales of *Mat Jenin* and *Musang Berjanggut* (The Bearded Fox). The stories are outlined below.

1.4.6 *Mat Jenin*

Mat Jenin is a well-known adaptation of a comic tale. This story is believed to have its origins in India, which then spread to the Middle East where it is told in the *Hikayat Seribu Satu Malam* (One Thousand and One Nights). By the 14th century, it had spread to the European world. In Malay literature, there are two versions of this story. One comes from a village headman in Perak, Mohamad Noordin bin Jaffar (JSBRAS Vol. 48, 1907), and another is found in the *Hikayat Pancatantera* (Tales from the Pancatantera) (story number 5), written by Munshi Abdullah. I will first outline the story of *Mat Jenin* as found in Perak.

Mat Jenin is an ordinary young man, but very adept at climbing coconut trees. One day, a plantation owner hires Mat Jenin to harvest coconuts in his plantation. The pay is two coconuts per tree, and there are twenty-five trees altogether. Mat Jenin starts to climb the trees and thinks to himself: "I will get 50 coconuts for climbing these trees. After I sell the coconuts, I will have a lot of money. I can then buy some cheap coconuts to turn into coconut oil. After I sell the oil, I can buy a rooster and a hen. I will keep both of them. The chickens will start laying eggs, and soon I will have a lot of chickens. After that, I will sell all the chickens and buy some ducks. In time, my ducks would also lay eggs and multiply. And I will then have a lot of ducks. My ducks will wander hither thither, saying Quack, quack". And the villagers will ask, 'Whose ducks are those?' To which others will reply: "Those are Mat Jenin's ducks." And people will say, "My, my, what a rich man Mat Jenin is."

"Then I will sell all my ducks. Next, I will buy some goats, two nanny goats and a billy goat. Over time, the goats would breed. Soon I will have lots of goats. I will sell them all. After that, I will buy a pair of buffaloes, a male and a female. In time, the buffaloes will also breed and I will have many buffaloes. And then I can sell all my buffaloes and buy a pair of elephants, a male and a female elephant. My elephants will give birth and in no time at all I will have lots of elephants.

"When I sell all my elephants for a lot of money I can then buy a ship laden with cargo and sail to another country. I will marry a beautiful princess. How blissful my life would be, making love to this woman of mine. During the day, I will play chess with the sons of kings. In the middle of playing chess, the court's ladies-in-waiting would be sent to call me to the royal bed chamber. Again and again they would call me, but I will ignore them. Finally, her royal highness the princess herself will come and call me, but I will ignore her too. She will tease me by tickling me on my right side. When I move away to the left, she will tickle me on my left side, and then on my right side when I move away again. As Mat Jenin wriggled to the right and left, he lost his grip on the coconut tree, fell to the ground and died.

This is the story of Mat Jenin as it has been told in the state of Perak. There is an incidental story in Munshi Abdullah's translation of the *Pancatantera* that is similar. One day, a poor Brahmin was offered dinner by a merchant. He told the merchant about his life of poverty. "I am a poor man with no brothers or sisters, and no roof over my head. Each day I have to struggle just to find enough food and drink to survive." The merchant felt sorry for the Brahmin and gave him a pot of flour. He told the Brahmin: "When you sell this pot of flour, you will receive a lot of money."

So the Brahmin took the pot of flour with him and went on his way. When the midday sun was at its highest in the sky, he put the pot of flour under a tree and lay down next to it. As he dozed off, he thought to himself, "When I sell this pot of flour, I will buy a goat. When the goat is fully-grown and has a young kid of its own, I will sell the goat and buy a cow. After I raise the cow for two or three years, then I will surely have four or five more cows.

"Then I would sell the cows' milk, and with the money I save, I can get married. Once I'm married, I would have a child. When my child is having a nap, my wife will do the housework. When the child cries, I will wake up and say: 'Hey wretched woman! How can you let my child cry? My blood will boil, and I will beat her with a a piece of wood." The Brahmin raised his hand as if to strike his wife, and as he did so, he hit the pot of flour. The pot broke and spilled its contents, mixing the flour with the sand on the ground. And so the Brahmin live to regret his actions.

In Malay, the expression "like Mat Jenin" refers to someone who likes to dream. But is it so wrong to dream? In actual fact, dreaming is like having ambitions. The difference is that an ambition is something that can possibly be achieved whereas dreams are hard to realize. "Hard to realize" does not mean "cannot be realized". If we are diligent and determined enough, our dreams can be achieved. But don't dream while you are doing something else, when you are studying for example, or the consequences may be disastrous. A person who doesn't dare dream or fantasise is seldom successful.

1.4.7 *Musang Berjanggut* (The Bearded Civet-cat)

Musang Berjanggut (Winstedt, 1908: 121-175) tells the story of a merchant's son, Kemala al-Arifin, who was adopted by King Syali Ariman. When he was mature and had completed reading the whole Quran, he was told that it was time for him to get married. But Kemala al-Arifin did not want to get married; according to him all the women in the kingdom were "bitches" (*betina*), and not one of them was a lady. The king was puzzled to hear his adopted son's words, but gave Kemala al-Arifin permission to look for a real lady who was not a bitch to be his bride. The young man was also given a sum of three thousand *ringgit* to help him in his quest and for his wedding expenses. But if Kemala al-Arifin failed in his mission, he would be executed, for he had insulted the dignity of all of the women in the kingdom.

Kemala al-Arifin set out on his journey, taking with him a bag of rice mixed with a variety of food stuffs such as spices, nuts, sugar, anchovies and coconut. Wherever he went, he always asked the people he met to cook his rice for him, but no one could. Finally, after six months of travelling, he arrived in the kingdom of Askalan Rum. He lodged with a farmer named Paman and handed to him the bag of rice, requesting that it be cooked for dinner. Dang Seri Arif Laksana, Paman's beautiful and intelligent daughter, poured the rice into a bamboo sieve and sifted the mixture so as to separate the rice, spices, sugar, fish and coconut into separate piles. Before long, a very tasty meal was served. Kemala al-Arifin was overjoyed that his search for a "real lady" had ended. That very night, Paman told his wife and daughter about Kemala al-Arifin and his peculiar behaviour, such as looking for a home with no kitchen and opening his umbrella in the middle of the forest. Dang Seri Arif Laksana was able to offer an explanation for each and every one of these seemingly bizarre acts. Kemala al-Arifin was so delighted when he heard her explanation that he felt a mountain of precious stones had fallen in his lap. The next day, he asked Paman for Dang Seri Arif Laksana's hand in marriage. His request was accepted. They were married in a magnificent and lavish wedding lasting for seven days and seven nights. Exactly three months after the wedding, Kemala al-Arifin remembered his promise to His Majesty the King to return home upon finding a lady to marry and he made his way back, accompanied by his new wife.

After some time, Kemala al-Arifin and Dang Seri Arif Laksana arrived at the palace, and were received by His Majesty. Everyone in the palace was completely stunned by Dang Seri Arif Laksana's beauty—she was like an angel from heaven. The *Raja Muda* (Crown Prince), *Bendahara* (Grand Vizier), *Toh Menteri* (Chief Minister), *Temenggung* (Security Chief) and *qadi* all secretly prayed for death or some disaster to befall Kemala al-Arifin so they could marry the beautiful Dang Seri Arif Laksana. The king too harboured the same malicious thoughts. One day, the king pretended to be ill and instructed Kemala al-Arifin to find the cure, the liver of a bearded civet cat. If he failed, he would be sentenced to death. With a heavy heart, Kemala al-Arifin returned home from the palace. Dang Seri Arif Laksana advised her husband to stay calm and suggested that perhaps the king only wanted to test his mettle, since he once said he would never marry a bitch and wanted to look for a real lady instead. She then asked him to hide at home and told everyone that Kemala al-Arifin had gone looking for the bearded fox. In his absence, the *Qadi*, the *Temenggung*, the *Bendahara*, the *Raja Muda* and the King, all wanted to pay Dang Seri a visit to try to seduce her. With great cunning, Dang Seri Arif Laksana arranged for them to visit her at different times, and thus was able to make fools of each one of them. The poor Qadi was locked up in a chest. The next day, Kemala al-Arifin brought the chest to the palace and announced that he had caught the bearded fox for which the king was looking. Everyone gaped in disbelief when they realised that the bearded fox in the chest was really the Qadi. The king now knew that Dang Seri Arif Laksana was indeed a real lady and not a *betina*. He bestowed the title Toh Puan Lela Mengerna upon her while Kemala al-Arifin received the title Datuk Seri Pada Arifin. The *Raja Muda, Bendahara, Temenggung* and the Chief Minister also showered the couple with gifts. The fame of Datuk Seri Pada Arifin and his wife soon spread far and wide throughout the kingdom and they were reknowned for their intelligence. Such is the story of *Musang Berjanggut* as told by Hadji Yahya bin Raja Muhammad Ali of Perak.

1.4.8 *Hikayat Mahasyodhak*

Hikayat Mahasyodhak, or *Masyhudulhak,* is also considered a comic tale. Only two copies of this *hikayat* have been found, and both are fairly 'recent'; they probably come from South India. The skeleton of the story, however, can be found in the earlier *Maha-Ummaga-Jataka* (Tale of the Great Tunnel), which is part of a collection of *jataka* stories on the Lord Buddha's previous reincarnations. The name *Mahasyodhak* probably came from *Mahosyoda,* which means "great cure" (from "*maha*" meaning "great", and "*usyada*" meaning "cure"). To the Achehnese, *Meudeuhak,* the protagonist, is regarded as the ideal leader, a model to which every leader should aspire. A synopsis of the story as provided by A. F. von de Wall (1916) is given below.

There once lived a merchant called Buka Sakti, who was childless. An astrologer advised him to remarry. Soon after his marriage to Ratna Kasina, the couple had a son who turned out to be wise and intelligent. From an early age, the boy was able to help his father administer the affairs of the village in a proper and just way, paying meticulous attention to every issue. The King wanted to make him a ministerial officer, but all four of his advisors disagreed with him. They insisted that Mahasyodhak was "a boy from the boondocks, untutored in the gentle ways of the court." In the meantime, Mahasyodhak continued to resolve more and more legal and administrative matters. For example, he persuaded a young woman who tried to elope with a Bedouin to return to her legal husband, a decrepit old man. He also managed to determine the real mother of a child by threatening to cut the child into half. He also arbitrated in a case to determine the rightful owner of a beautiful carpet.

When Mahasyodhak was seven years old, the king wanted to make him a state official. The king's four advisors asked that they first be given permission to test Mahasyodhak's intelligence. He was asked to determine the starting and end points on a piece of wood, then to differentiate between the skull of a man and that of a woman. He was also asked to coax a slow loris into the water, to weave a rope of sand, and finally to tie gemstones into a bracelet using the rope of sand. Mahasyodhak was able to complete all these tasks. Thus did Mahasyodhak begin his career as a state official.

The story then tells about a sage who had five disciples. One of them was a poor and wretched young man who, nevertheless, was a very dutiful pupil and served his master well. The story also goes that the sage had a daughter who was "beautiful in appearance, her face, was like the full moon, radiant and resplendent, her body was yellow-white in hue, like golden lacquer." The sage gave his daughter to his faithful pupil, Si Celaka (the Wretched One), to take as his wife. But Si Celaka never treated her properly; in fact, he always tried to run away from her. One day on the way home to his village, Si Celaka tricked his wife into climbing a tree and then left her stranded there. He barricaded the foot of the tree with thorns and branches of a fig tree. By the grace of God, the king happened to be strolling nearby, accompanied by his four advisors and Mahasyodhak. Mahasyodhak advised the king to marry the sage's daughter and to call her Putri Mereka Dewi. One day, Putri Mereka Dewi saw Si Celaka being flogged for taking too long to clear away some grass, and she smiled to herself. When asked why she was smiling, she disclosed her origins. The king was overjoyed to hear of his wife's noble lineage and sent lavish gifts to his parents-in-law. His father-in-law reciprocated by sending him a magic ring that would spin to warn its wearer if the food that he was about to eat is poisoned. As the king's fondness for Mahasyodhak continually increased so too did the jealousy of his majesty's four advisors. They detested Mahasyodhak and endlessly tried to devise ways of destroying him.

On one occasion, after he had explained to the king why the goat is good friends with the dog, his majesty asked Mahasyodhak: "Who is better: a wise man or a rich man?" Mahasyodhak suggested that it is much better to be intelligent than to be wealthy. A wise man can outwit his enemies and escape their malice and slander. But the four advisors retorted: "A rich man is better than a wise man because lots of wise people have made themselves slaves to the wealthy." The king then ordered that Mahasyodhak and the four advisors be locked up in two separate enclosures made of wood but done up in plaster to make them look like stone. Mahasyodhak's cell contained nothing but a chisel and hammer, while the cell of the four advisors contained not only a hammer and chisel but also gold, silver and other treasures. Near the two enclosures there was another enclosure full of delectable delicacies and various types of fruit. Using his wits, Mahasyodhak managed to break into the enclosure that was filled with food. The four advisors were very hungry and had to pay a high price to buy food from Mahasyodhak. When they were finally released from their enclosures, the four advisors were nothing but skin-and-bones while Mahasyodhak himself remained stout and healthy. The four advisors felt even more antagonistic towards Mahasyodhak. As a result of their campaign of calumny against him, Mahasyodhak was consequently exiled by the king.

The story goes that soon after, a deity—the tutelary spirit of the kingdom—manifested itself in human form. It presented four riddles to the king. If the king could not answer the riddles, he would be beheaded and his head hurled down from the highest point in the kingdom. The petrified monarch immediately summoned Mahasyodhak back to the palace. Mahasyodhak solved all the riddles with utmost ease. The deity told the king, "O king, you should never listen to slander. Instead, scrutinize carefully each deed and protect this realm, so that you do not fall into sin. For verily this world is ephemeral..."

When Mahasyodhak turned fourteen, the king decided that he should marry. Mahasyodhak asked the king for permission to choose his own bride. Dressed in the garb of a *darji* (tailor) and carrying a bundle containing patches of cloth, thread and needles, Mahasyodhak left the city. During the journey, he met a beautiful young woman about fourteen years old, whose beauty was radiant and resplendent. The girl's name was Citata. Mahasyodhak followed her home. In order to test her intelligence, Mahasyodhak gave her mother some low-quality broken rice (*beras gading*) to cook. Citata replaced the broken rice with similar-looking but better quality rice. Then, in order to test her patience, Mahasyodhak poured a bowl of curry over Citata's head, saying that it tasted terrible. Citata did not respond. She went down to the river to bathe and cleansed herself in scented water mixed with lime, herbs and flowers. Mahasyodhak was elated, and asked her parents for her hand in marriage. His proposal was duly accepted. Mahasyodhak sought permission to bring Citata back to his home country so that they could be married in the presence of his parents. This request too was granted.

A few days later, Mahasyodhak left for home together with Citata. When they reached a river bank, Mahasyodhak asked Citata if the water was deep or shallow. She asked him to test the water with the walking stick he had in his hand. They continued their journey and after some time, they reached Mahasyodhak's ancestral country. There, he asked her to wait while he went home to gather his family to welcome them. When he reached home, he ordered a young and handsome slave boy to meet and bring Citata home. The slave boy told Citata that Mahasyodhak was a slave trader who sold women and asked her to marry him. Citata remained steadfastly faithful to Mahasyodhak. The next day, Mahasyodhak sent ten women to bring Citata before him. Because Citata could not recognize Mahasyodhak, she was accused of lying and confined in a small hut. That night, Mahasyodhak ordered food and clothing be sent to her. The servant who brought food to Citata told her that the Interior Minister wanted to marry her, but she did not waver in her fidelity to Mahasyodhak. Mahasyodhak realised how faithful, intelligent and noble Citata really was. The next day, Mahasyodhak donned his tailor outfit, slung his bag over his shoulder, and went to claim Citata. Citata was absolutely delighted. He took her home, arranged for her to take a bath and dress in fine clothes. Soon, on one auspicious day, the king supervised Mahasyodhak's marriage to Citata.

That is how the story goes according to the storyteller. Mahasyodhak performed good deeds for the sake of God, and because of Him. He never discriminated between the powerful and the weak, but treated everyone as an equal. Moreover, he was patient in his dealings with the king's four advisors and their slanders. Not only that, he was good humoured, and refused to bear a grudge against his enemies. For these reasons, he was blessed by the Almighty in all his undertakings.

1.4.9 *Hikayat Abu Nawas*

The *Hikayat Abu Nawas* is a collection of comic tales. Although it originated from abroad, it became very popular in various parts of the Archipelago, especially among the *santri* (religious scholars), to the extent that the stories are considered to be part of the folklore of the region. Even so, there not many manuscripts of this *hikayat*, and the few that do exist are only be found in Jakarta and Singapore.

There are two versions of this story: one derives from Muslim India while the other has Persian-Arabic origins. The manuscript available in the National Library of Singapore was printed in Singapore by Sulaiman Mari, and comes from Muslim India. This manuscript is entitled *Hikayat Abu Nawas*. The Persian-Arabic version is called *Cerita Abu Nawas* (The Story of Abu Nawas) and was printed by Albrecht and Rusche in Batavia (now Jakarta) during the last century. Below is a summary of the story published in Singapore.

(1) The story tells that Abu Nawas and his father lived in Baghdad. Abu Nawas was very clever, much smarter than the average man. His father was a *qadi* (religious official). On one occasion, his father fell very ill and was close to death. He asked Abu Nawas to kiss his ears. His right ear smelled fragrant, but his left, in contrast, was foul. His father explained that when he arbitrated a dispute between two people, he only ever listened to one side of the story and ignored the other. That was why one of his ears smelled foul. He added that if Abu Nawas did not want to be a *qadi*, he should look for a way to escape such a fate.

(2) Soon after Abu Nawas' father passed away, Sultan Harun Ar-rasyid went to look for Abu Nawas to replace his father as *qadi*. Abu Nawas pretended to be crazy and acted as if he had lost his mind. One day, Abu Nawas said to someone close to him: "Hey herdsman, go and feed those horses some grass." The man went to the king and asked to be appointed as the *qadi*. The king granted his request and the man became the country's *qadi*. As for Abu Nawas, he spent his days teaching people the Quran.

(3) One evening a young Egyptian, who was in Baghdad on business, dreamed that he married the new *qadi*'s daughter. When the *qadi* heard about his dream, he ordered the young Egyptian to pay him the dowry. When the young man refused, all his possessions were confiscated and he was driven out of the city. The young Egyptian reported what had happened to Abu Nawas. Abu Nawas then instructed his students to destroy the *qadi*'s home. When he was brought before the king, Abu Nawas said he dreamed that the *qadi* had asked him to destroy the *qadi*'s home. He pointed out that the *qadi*'s law was, in effect, a decree based simply on a dream. This exposed the *qadi*'s cruel deed and he was subsequently punished by the king. Meanwhile, the young Egyptian continued to live in Baghdad and when the time was right, he returned to his own country.

(4) Abu Nawas was asked to raise two goats. He was to feed them both the same amount of food but after ten days one goat should be fat and the other one thin. Abu Nawas put a cat into one of the goats' pens. The cat kept jumping up and down, and making a lot of noise. The goat was too frightened to eat and so it became thin.

(5) Abu Nawas was asked to find six bearded cows that can talk, within seven days. Abu Nawas came up with were six bearded men who had no idea "what day it is today." People who don't know "what day it is today" are animals, and no longer human.

(6) On one occasion, Abu Nawas had no money. To earn some money, he asked Sultan Harun Ar-Rasyid to follow him to the home of a Bedouin. Then he sold the Sultan to the Bedouin. Sultan Harun explained to the Bedouin who he really was and was escorted back to the palace by the Bedouin.

(7) Sultan Harun ordered the arrest of Abu Nawas. Abu Nawas pretended to be dead and told his wife to publicly ask Sultan Harun to grant him a pardon. Once Sultan Harun had pardoned him, Abu Nawas began shouting from his grave, causing everyone to run helter-skelter home. From that day on, the Sultan would not allow Abu Nawas to go to the palace any more.

(8) Some time later, the Sultan wanted to see Abu Nawas and summoned him forthwith for an audience at the palace. Abu Nawas declined to come, saying he was having labour pains and was waiting for the midwife. And the midwife was none other than the Sultan himself.

(9) To test Abu Nawas's intelligence, the Sultan asked him to bring his deceased mother to the palace. Abu Nawas carried an elderly cake-seller to the palace, promising her half the reward he would be given. When Sultan Harun wanted to "reward" Abu Nawas with a hundred lashes of the cane, Abu Nawas refused and said that fifty lashes should be reserved for the old woman as she had been promised half of his reward. Because he felt sorry for the old woman, Sultan Harun decided not to whip Abu Nawas. Instead, Sultan Harun gave the old woman 50 dinars, and an equal amount to Abu Nawas as well.

(10) One day, Sultan Harun asked Abu Nawas together with ten ministers to enter a pool to look for chicken eggs. Anyone who failed to find an egg would be punished. But unknown to Abu Nawas, the sultan had already given the ministers an egg each. Obviously, Abu Nawas was never going to find a chicken egg in the pool but he managed to solve his predicament by claiming that he was a rooster. And he added: "How could the chickens lay eggs if there was no rooster?"

(11) One evening in Rabiul-awal, the third month of the Islamic calendar, Sultan Harun ar-Rashid held a celebration in his palace. The guests were sprinkled with rose water on arrival as was the custom. When Abu Nawas arrived, he was sprinkled with urine. Abu Nawas vowed to take revenge for this humiliation. One day, he pretended to be ill. When the Sultan came to visit him, Abu Nawas said that he was feeling much better after taking a particular remedy. Sultan Harun wanted to have some of that remedy too. When he tried it a bit, however, he realised it smelled of shit. Sultan Harun begged Abu Nawas not to tell anyone what happened. Abu Nawas promised that if the Sultan paid him a hundred dinars, he would not tell anyone what had happened.

(12) Abu Nawas was accused of indecent behaviour with one of the king's maids in the palace and thrown into a cage with a female tiger. He managed to distract the tigress long enough for it not to devour him. Meanwhile, Sultan Harun was suffering from a stomach tumour. Despite trying different types of remedies, the tumour simply would not go away. His physicians told the king, if he could be made to laugh, the tumour would burst and this would cure him. But no one in the palace could make Sultan Harun laugh. So Abu Nawas was released from his prison and was asked to tell the king a story. He told the king the reason why the tigress did not maul him and this made the sultan burst out laughing, causing his tumour to burst.

(13) One day, Abu Nawas was captured by a Bedouin, who wanted to slaughter him and cook him in wheat porridge. Abu Nawas managed to escape by promising the Bedouin that he would provide a fat man to replace him. The fat man was none other than Sultan Harun Ar-Rasyid. Sultan Harun told his captor that it would be better if he did not kill him but he made caps for the Bedouin instead.

Sultan Harun stayed at the Bedouin's house for six months. One day, Sultan Harun asked the Bedouin to take one of the fine caps he had made to sell to a minister. A secret message was embroidered on the cap which clearly indicated that it was from Sultan Harun. And in this way Sultan Harun was saved by his minister. The Bedouin was arrested and executed. Abu Nawas was arrested too. Abu Nawas explained that he only did what he did so that the sultan could see with his own eyes the cruel deeds of which his subjects were capable. If he were to merely tell the Sultan about such things, he might not have been believed. The sultan accepted Abu Nawas's explanation and pardoned him.

(14) Sultan Harun was having problems in the bedroom with his wife Siti Zubaidah. Abu Nawas taught him a secret and the sultan was able to satisfy his needs. When Siti Zubaidah found out that Abu Nawas had taught the sultan this secret, she was furious. She asked to be made king for a day, so that she could punish Abu Nawas. When asked to appear before Siti Zubaidah, Abu Nawas pretended to be crazy, he arrived sittng backwards on a female donkey, as he rode past the throne. Siti Zubaidah was shocked and ran off into her chambers.

N. St. Iskandar compiled a version of the *Hikayat Abu Nawas* based on several texts from the Jakarta Central Museum. It contains 20 stories and all of the stories in the *Hikayat Abu Nawas,* except the thirteenth, can be found in this collection. Still other stories can also be found in an old summarized version of the *Cerita Abu Nawas* (Winstedt, 1920a: 18-21). Most of those stories tell of the exploits of Abu Nawas in escaping the troubles in which he found himself. For example,

(1) When asked to stitch up a stone mortar, Abu Nawas asked for a stone thread.

(2) When asked to count the number of stars in the sky, Abu Nawas replied that there were as many stars in the sky as there were hairs on a goat.

(3) When asked to teach a cow to recite the Quran, Abu Nawas beat the cow to death in order to show that, no matter how long it lived, the cow would never be able to recite the Holy Book.

(4) When asked to find a bearded tiger, Abu Nawas tricked a headman who was lusting after Abu Nawas's wife into entering a cage.

(5) When asked to carry a mosque, he asked that the onlookers first place the mosque on his shoulders.

Abu Nawas also used his wits to help those who had suffered injustice. He helped a merchant fulfil a vow to sacrifice a big goat with horns a handspan long; he also helped a poor man who immersed himself in a pool of cold water to receive his reward. In his efforts to help the downtrodden, he outsmarted a cruel minister and also a Jew who demanded "a pound of meat". It is also true, of course, that he sometimes used his brains for his own benefit.

It should be noted that there are also stories which depict Abu Nawas as a poet, for example the two stories about Abu Nawas found in the unabridged and yet to be published version of the *Hikayat Bakhtiar*. The portrayal is both realistic and precise. According to historical sources, Abu Nawas was indeed a poet in the court of Sultan Harun Ar-Rasyid and his poems can still be read today. He used his poetry to make derisive remarks about people he disliked, and gave no quarter. He was also fond of making jokes. Abu Nawas was attacked many times by those who were offended at his poems and jokes. Finally, he was killed by a Baghdadi man in 810, at the age of 60.

1.5 *Cerita Pelipur Lara* (Folk Epics)

Another genre of folklore is described by R.O. Winstedt as "*folk-romances*". The Malays themselves call such stories "*cerita pelipur lara*" which literally means "tales to comfort your woes". What are these "*cerita pelipur lara*" actually?

According to its name, the *cerita pelipur* is a story that is used to soothe, or give comfort to someone from his woes or sorrows. In the old days, before the advent of the radio, TV or movies, these *cerita pelipur lara* were the only form of entertainment available to villagers. When the sun had set, and the villagers had finished their dinner and begun to relax, the storyteller would begin to tell his story. He would tell his story in a monotonous voice, as if he was reading from a book. The story would continue until late at night, and if not completed, would be taken up again on the following evening.

Even though the storyteller was illiterate, he never made any mistake in the recitation of his story. This was because he had heard these stories from a very young age told by his father and grandfather who were also storytellers. They were called the "*sahibul hikayat*", lords of the story. They earned their living by telling stories, and travelled from village to village. Their arrival was warmly welcomed by the villagers, who always paid them for their trouble (Winstedt, 1910: 1-2).

The story typically revolved around a magnificent palace. The king was the ruler of a vast realm. Sadly though, the queen could not have any children. This saddened the king and his life would be filled with sorrow. On the advice of an astrologer or shaman, his royal highness would begin to pray for a child. By the grace of God, the queen would become pregnant. During her pregnancy, many strange incidents would occur. And when the prince was born,

> Seven floor boards broke,
> Seven pillars snapped,
> The afternoon rain roared,
> Lightning flashed like fighting cocks,
> Thunderbolts clashed like arrows,
> Din and mayhem everywhere.

Often the child would be born together with magical beasts or weapons. In the *Hikayat Raja Budiman* for example, Lela Muda was born with a golden baby dragon. Raja Donan was born with a sword and *kris* (a Malay dagger), while Raja Muda entered the world with a *parang punting* (traditional Malay cutlass). The mother often died during childbirth or not long after (*Hikayat Awang Sulung Merah Muda*). And after the child had been born, he would fall victim to the treachery of a jealous court astrologer, and be banished to the jungle or set adrift at sea (*Hikayat Raja Donan*). Not uncommonly, the baby would then be adopted and raised by wild animals. Also more often than not, the child would be raised by a close relative such as an uncle or so on (*Hikayat Raja Donan*).

By the time he had become an adult, and sometimes even before then, the child would have embarked on his quest, either by land or sea. A magical weapon or amulet that grants him extraordinary power is often bestowed on him by God. The purpose of his journey is usually to carry out the divine injunction of a *Wali Allah* (a saint or holy man) received in a dream, which tells him to look for a beautiful princess. The princess usually possesses beauty beyond compare,

> Her body is slender like an areca palm;
> Her hair like unfurled palm flowers;
> Her face resplendent like the 14th day moon;
> Her eyebrows shaped like spurs;
> Her nose sharp like the jasmine;
> Her eyes like the Morning Star;
> Her ears like shells;
> Her mouth like a ruby-ripe pomegranate;
> Her teeth like two rows of pearls;
> Her chin like a hanging beehive;
> Her fingers like porcupine's quills;
> Her cuticles like the third day moon;
> Her thighs like a grasshopper's legs;

Her calves like ripe paddy;
Her heels like quail's eggs...

(H.B. Jassin, 1968: 142)

At times, the object of the quest is an elixir to cure an affliction suffered by a princess. In his search for the princess of his dreams or for the elixir, the prince will have to fight against wild animals, *jinn* (genies) or marry the princess who has the elixir in her possession. Thanks to the assistance of allies such as Nenek Kebayan, Si Kembang Cina, Bujang Selamat, or characters from the animal kingdom, as well as to the magical weapons he possesses, the hero always triumphs and his wedding immediately follows. Often he will marry more than one but no more than four princesses. Finally, he will return to his homeland and punish those who have wronged or betrayed him. He will then live happily ever after with his wives.

It should be mentioned here that Malays believe that these stories were actual historical events, which took place in the Malay Archipelago. The story of *Malim Deman* is set in Muar, *Anggun Cik Tunggal* in Tiku-Pariaman. And Benua Tua, which was ruled by a Crown Prince, was a village located near a river in Perak. According to R. O. Winstedt, Nyiur Gading was a name for Malaka, while Lindungan Bulan was the old name for Kedah (Winstedt, 1910: 183-188). However, Mohd. Taib Osman considers Winstedt's theory to be less than convincing as the reasons and evidence Winstedt puts forward are based on only a few stories and not the whole corpus of *cerita pelipur lara* tales (Mohd. Taib Osman, 1965: 20).

1.5.1 *Hikayat Awang Sulung Merah Muda*

Awang Sulung Merah Muda was the son of the king of Bandar Mengkalih. His parents died before he was born and he was raised by Datuk Batin Alim, together with his guardian's daughter, Putri Dayang Nuramah. When he was old enough, Awang Sulung Merah Muda was taken to a teacher to learn how to recite the Quran, as well as grammar and logic. Later, he also studied the traditional Malay martial art of *pencak silat*. He was a very quick pupil. His teeth were filed when he reached manhood, as was the custom. Some time later, Datuk Batin Alam asked Awang Sulung Merah Muda to pay the fee for the teeth-filing.

As he did not have any money, Awang Sulung Merah Muda was forced to do hard labour. Despite this, however, Datuk Batin Alam was still not satisfied and wanted to kill Awang Suluh Merah Muda. Awang Sulung Merah Muda ran away. He subsequently became the servant of Princess Dayang Seri Jawa. Meanwhile, Datuk Batin Alam's daughter, Princess Dayang Nuramah, who was in love with Awang Sulung Merah Muda, did not want him to slip into the hands of another woman.

And so the two princesses battled each other on the high ocean for seven days and seven nights to decide who should have Awang Sulung Merah Muda. Awang Sulung Merah Muda was concerned that one of them might be killed or hurt, so he separated them. Not long after, Awang Sulung Merah Muda married Princess Dayang Seri Jawa. Later he also married Princess Dayang Nuramah and two other princesses, that is, Princess Pinang Masak from Pati Talak Trengganu and

Princess Mayang Mengurai from Pasir Panjang. "The prince loved all his four wives very much, and was never separated from them."

1.5.2 *Hikayat Malim Dewa*

A king and his queen ruled Kuala Bandar Muar. In time, the queen gave birth to a beautiful baby boy named Gombang Malim Dewa. When he reached adulthood, Malim Dewa ascended to the throne (the elderly king having abdicated and left to undertake a pilgrimage to Mecca). One night, Malim Dewa dreamed of a holy man who asked him to look for a parakeet. The holy man told Malim Dewa that the parakeet would help him find a beautiful wife. True to the holy man's word, the parakeet persuaded three princesses to marry Malim Dewa: Princess Gentasari of Kuala Medan Baik, Princess Andam Dewi of Kuala Air Batu and Princess Nilam Cahaya from *kayangan* (the spirit world).

News of Princess Andam Dewi's beauty reached the ears of Maharaja Pertukal in Singa Tanjung Papan. He ordered his army to kidnap the princess. But his army perished at the hands of the princess' father. Maharaja Pertukal then cast a spell on Princess Andam Dewi that made her sick. The girl's father appealed to Maharaja Pertukal to cure the princess. He did, but his proposal for her hand in marriage was still rejected.

This so enraged Maharaja Pertukal that he enlisted his elder brother Maharaja Sianggerai to teach Kuala Air Batu a lesson. Maharaja Sianggerai sent a *garuda* bird to destroy Kuala Air Batu. Only the queen and Princess Andam Dewi survived the attack. When Malim Dewa heard what had happened, he quickly rushed to the scene. He was able to kill the *Garuda* but he himself succumbed to Maharaja Pertukal's evil spell and died. Fortunately, Princess Nilam Cahaya was able to bring him back to life by sprinkling him with rosewater. Malim Dewa then marched on Maharaja Pertukal's kingdom and managed to kill him in battle. His daughter, Princess Cahaya Laut, became a lady-in-waiting to Princess Andam Dewi. They travelled back to Kuala Bandar Muar. Thereupon, Princess Andam Dewi was crowned as Queen Indra Lela.

After some time had passed, Malim Dewa decided to undertake a pilgrimage to Mecca to seek God's forgiveness for the sins he had committed. On the way, he stopped at Kuala Medan Baik and married Princess Gentasari. Two years passed before he resumed his pilgrimage. This time, he stopped at Nyiur Condong, a country that had also been destroyed by the *garuda*. The sole survivor was Princess Santan Bertapis. Malim Dewa married the princess and lived at Nyiur Condong for twelve years. Eventually the Queen and Princess Gentasari came looking for him; only then did he return to Kuala Bandar Muar. Soon Malim Dewa again fell victim to Maharaja Sianggerai's evil spell and died. And once again, Princess Nilam Cahaya brought him back to life by sprinkling him with rosewater.

Restored to life, Malim Dewa launched an attack on Maharaja Sianggerai and killed him. Maharaja Pertukal's daughter, Princess Cahaya Laut, was of great service to Malim Dewa during the battle, and became another of his wives. After that, Malim Dewa went to the spirit world and married Princess Nilam Cahaya. Malim Dewa lived happily with his four wives. Every year, he visited each one of his wives' countries, one after the other.

1.5.3 *Hikayat Malim Deman*

Prince Malim Deman of Bandar Muar was wise and handsome. When he reached adulthood, he dreamed that a holy man told him to go to the house of a sorceress (*nenek kebayan*), who would help him marry Princess Bungsu of the spirit world. Accompanied by a throng of attendants, Malim Deman set out for Nenek Kebayan's house. On the way, his attendants died one after the other. Finally, he reached Nenek Kebayan's home. With the sorceress's help, Malim Deman managed to steal the magic clothes that gave Princess Bungsu the power to fly, and she could no longer return to her heavenly world. Nenek Kebayan then wedded them to each other.

Time passed and they eventually returned to Bandar Muar. A lavish banquet was held in their honour. Malim Deman was crowned king and not long after that, his father fell ill and passed away. After his father's death, Malim Deman neglected his duties as king and instead, passed his time at the cockfighting pit. It was in these circumstances that his wife gave birth to a son whom she named Malim Dewana. The baby soon grew up but Malim Deman never came back to the palace, even to see his son. Princess Bungsu's heart was filled with sorrow. By chance she then found her magic clothes. She flew back to the spirit world, taking her son Malim Dewana with her.

Once she had gone, Malim Deman began to regret his behaviour. For seven days and seven nights, he could not sleep, could not eat, and did nothing but weep. He vowed to retrieve his wife and son back. After many difficulties, Malim Deman reached Nenek Kebayan's house and asked her where he could find a *borak* (a mythical bird with a human face) to fly him to Paradise. With Nenek Kebayan's help, he learned that Princess Terus Mata, daughter of the King of Genies, owned such a bird. The King of Genies was willing to lend Malim Deman the *borak* on condition that he married Princess Terus Mata. Malim Deman agreed.

When he reached the spirit world, Malim Deman discovered that Princess Bungsu was about to be married to Mambang Molek. Malim Deman's rooster defeated Mambang Molek's bird in a cockfight. This was followed by a battle between the two men, in which Mambang Molek and his kin were killed. Malim Deman then married Princess Bungsu once again. Not long after, he returned to earth, bringing his wife and son with him. Later Malim Deman married Princess Terus Mata. Malim Deman thereafter ruled as a wise and valiant king. The king and his wives loved the young prince Malim Dewana very much.

The motif of a mortal marrying the fairy Princess Bungsu from the heavenly realm is found not only in Malay literature, but also occurs in Minangkabau and Achehnese literatures. The same story can be found in China too, although the story tells that an ordinary shepherd married Princess Bungsu. A strange twist in the plot exists in the Achehnese language version of *Hikayat Malim Deman,* in which the stories of Malim Deman and Malim Dewa have been merged. Here, Malim Deman was married to Princess Bungsu, as well as to two other princesses. These two other princesses suffer various misfortunes. One, Princess Alouih, is kidnapped after her country has been defeated by China; the country of the other princess, Princess Meureundam Dewi, is destroyed by a *Garuda*. It was Malim Deman who saved both women. When Malim Deman was later defeated by Raja Jawa, Princess Meureundam Dewi restored his life. She was the person who first called him Malim Dewa.

1.5.4 *Hikayat Raja Muda*

Sultan Degar Alam was the king of Benua Tua. He was married to Princess Nur Lela and their daughter was called Princess Lindungan Bulan. The king's brother, Raja Besar, was also married; his son was Bujang Selamat. In time, Raja Besar and his wife both died and the care of Bujang Selamat was passed to Sultan Degar Alam. Soon after, Princess Nur Lela became pregnant again and gave birth to a son who, at the time of his birth, was born bearing a cutlass (*parang puting*). After giving birth, Princess Nur Lela died. The baby was given the title of Crown Prince or Raja Muda.

Meanwhile, the king's nephew Raja Bujang Selamat had matured and completed his religious education. He married Princess Lindungan Bulan. Before long, she became pregnant and had a craving for coconut from a coconut tree that was so tall its branches almost touched the sky. Raja Bujang Selamat borrowed Raja Muda's cutlass and climbed the coconut tree. He soon reached a cluster of coconuts at the top of the tree. The nuts were protected by a snake; Bujang Selamat killed the snake, then crawled into its mouth. After seven days and seven nights, Raja Bujang Selamat eventually came to a clearing. An ornate palace stood majestically in the middle of the clearing. The palace belonged to Princess Telipuk Layu; she offered to give Raja Bujang Selamat the coconuts he wanted on the condition that: if his wife gave birth to a baby boy, the boy would become Princess Telipuk Layu's husband; if the child was a girl, she would become Princess Telipuk Layu's younger sister.

One night, Raja Muda dreamt that a holy man commanded him to marry Princess Bidadari Segerba, the youngest daughter of Maharaja Indra Dewa, ruler of the spirit world. Defying the wishes of his father and sister, Raja Muda went to find the princess. On Gunung Cinta Berahi (The Mountain of Passionate Love), playground of the fairy princesses, Raja Muda met Princess Bidadari Segerba and married her. Their union was blessed by Princess Bungsu's father. The story goes that Raja Bujang Selamat then went in search of Raja Muda. After some time, Raja Bujang Selamat arrived at the royal abode of Raja Muda and his wife. He was warmly welcomed by the royal couple. The two princesses made a pact that when they had children, the children would be betrothed to each other. Raja Bujang Selamat went back to his kingdom and was thereafter crowned king of the realm. His wife, Princess Putri Lindungan Bulan, became queen. She later had a baby boy named Raja Seri Mandul. At the same time, a large fish and a buffalo named Si Benuang were also born. Meanwhile, Raja Muda's wife, Princess Bidadari Segerba, also conceived a child.

One day, Princess Bidadari Segerba asked her husband to accompany her to Nenek Kebayan's house. After they arrived, the princess summoned her six sisters from the spirit world to come down to Nenek Kebayan's garden. Together they built a special chariot to fly Raja Muda to the spirit world. Raja Muda, however, refused to go with them because he had an ominous dream in which his body was encircled by a white snake. The meaning of the dream was that Raja Muda would marry someone more noble and beautiful than Princess Bidadari Segerba. She ignored the dream and flew to the spirit world with her six sisters. Raja Muda remained behind at Nenek Kebayan's house, feeling very sad. One day, while he was sorrowfully lying in the doorway of the house, a white elephant arrived to transport him to the country of Tanjung Bunga Sekaki, where the king had just passed away. Raja Muda was proclaimed the new ruler and was married to Princess Kuntum Ratna Sari.

The story tells that Princess Bidadari Segerba, upon learning that her husband had taken Princess Kuntum Ratna Sari as his new bride, immediately flew down to earth from the spirit world. She befriended Raja Muda's new bride and transferred the baby she was carrying into Princess Kuntum Ratna Sari's womb. Eventually, Princess Kuntum Ratna Sari gave birth to a baby girl who held a sword in each hand. The baby was named Princess Renek Jintan. She was destined to marry Raja Seri Mandul when she was old enough.

The story also tells that Maharaja Imbangan Jajar of Cempaka Sari ruled over a vast empire. When he heard of Princess Renek Jintan's beauty, he sent an emissary to ask for her hand in marriage. Because his proposal was rejected, the spurned emperor sent his army to attack Raja Muda's kingdom. A war ensued. Raja Seri Mandul came to Raja Muda's assistance, together with the buffalo that had been born with him. Maharaja Imbangan Jajar was defeated and killed. Raja Seri Mandul married both Princess Renek Jintan and Princess Telipuk Layu. A lavish banquet was held to celebrate the joyous occasion. Thereafter, Raja Seri Mandul received the title Seri Maharaja Besar Suri, King of Benua Tua, while his two wives became the queen of Benua Tua and Cempaka Sari respectively.

Before long, Seri Majaraja Besar abdicated in favour of his son Sultan Kemala Ajaib. During Sultan Kemala Ajaib's reign the country was peaceful and prosperous. Each year, the sultan and his wives visited his vassal states and the rulers of these vassal-states paid him their tribute of gold and treasures.

This is the story of *Hikayat Raja Muda*. The ending of this *hikayat* is somewhat confusing. No sooner have we been told of Raja Seri Mandul's marriage to Princess Renek Jintan, than we learn that he already has a son called Sultan Kemala Ajaib. Not only is Sultan Kemala Ajaib old enough to replace his father at the throne; he is already married as well. This particular story is only known on the Malay Peninsula.

1.5.5 *Hikayat Anggun Cik Tunggal*

The next story tells about king who ruled over a country called Tiku Pariaman. The king had eight children, four sons and four daughters:

> One named Alam Syamsuddin
> One named Pati Duraidin
> One named Si Megat Alang
> One named Paduka Raja
> One daughter named Warna Pinang Masak
> One daughter named Warna Pasah Embun
> One daughter named Si Mas Manah
> One daughter named Gondan Genta Sari

King Bedurai Putih of Telok Tambang Papan wanted to marry all four princesses. When his proposal was rejected, he declared war on Tiku Pariaman. Tiku Pariaman was destroyed in the war and nearly all the princes and princesses were captured. Only Princess Gondan Genta Sari and her niece Princess Gondan Genta Permai managed to escape. After the enemy retreated, the people of Tiku Pariaman gathered together once more and crowned the two princesses as rulers of the country.

After some time, Princess Gondan Genta Permai married a prince from the spirit world, who was named Si Tompok Alam. Soon after that, Si Tompok Alam returned to his own world, become gravely ill and died. Meanwhile, he had left Princess Gondan Genta Permai pregnant. After being pregnant for 12 months, Princess Gondan Genta Permai finally gave birth to something that was so tied up in a knot it was unidentifiable. The attendants had to borrow a magic knife belonging to Princess Gondan Gandar, the daughter of Raja Laksamana of Tiku Benua, in order to cut through the knot and the umbilical cord. The baby let out a deeply moving cry. At that very moment, Princess Genta Permai took her last breath and passed away.

The baby was called Raja Anggun Cik Tunggal. Time passed and he turned seven years old, and was sent to learn all manner of skills. First he learnt recite the Quran, then the martial art of *pencak silat*, courtly ceremonies and customs, as well as princely pursuits such as chess, checkers and *sepak raga* (a game between two teams using a rattan ball). Once he had mastered these skills, Raja Tunggal asked for permission to travel to Tiku Benua in order to amuse himself there.

He met a rich merchant in Tiku Benua, called Nakhoda Bahar. The merchant invited Raja Tunggal to "place wagers on his own skills". Raja Tunggal defeated Nakhoda Bahar at every game they played, including chess, checkers, *sepak raga* and cockfighting. Raja Tunggal also won when they fought with weapons. Incensed, Nakhoda Bahar challenged Raja Tunggal to free some of his ancestors who were still held captive by Raja Bedurai Putih, if he was brave enough to do so. Shocked, Raja Tunggal returned to princess Gondan Genta Sari to ask if Nakhoda Bahar was really telling the truth.

When Genta Sari confirmed the story, Raja Tunggal set sail to search for Raja Bedurai Putih. He borrowed the ship, the Dandang Panjang, from Raja Laksamana. Before leaving Tiku Benua, Raja Tunggal made a pact with Princess Gondan Gandariah, the daughter of Raja Laksamana and Princess Lindungan Bulan. They swore that if one of them broke their pact, that person would be turned into an animal; the princess would become a monkey while Raja Tunggal would turn into a gibbon; and only on Judgement Day would they again be reunited.

Raja Tunggal held a religious feast on board his ship to pray for a safe journey. One day, Nakhoda Bahar challenged Raja Tunggal to a wager to guess the depth of the sea. If Nakhoda Bahar lost the wager, he would divorce his concubine Princess Indah Di Karang. Nakhoda Bahar lost this bet too and had to divorce his concubine.

The story tells that Raja Tunggal wanted to continue his journey to Teluk Senai Tambang to capture Raja Pertukal as well as go to Bandan to have an audience with Raja Sianggerai. He instructed Nakhoda Bahar to take Raja Bedurai Putih's ship back to Tiku Pariaman. However, when Nakhoda Bahar reached Tiku Pariaman, the conniving merchant told everyone that Raja Tunggal had been killed by Raja Bedurai Putih.

Nakhoda Bahar added that before he died, Raja Tunggal's last wish was that Nakhoda Bahar be made king of Tiku Pariaman and marry Princess Gondan Gandariah. The merchant even claimed that he himself had killed Raja Bedurai Putih and was responsible for bringing Raja Bedurai's ship back. Unaware of Nakhoda Bahar's deception, Raja Laksamana and his courtiers made preparations for Nakhoda Bahar's wedding to Princess Gondan Gandariah. But as soon as the wedding ceremony was over, Putri Gonda Gandariah turned into a white monkey and lept up onto the roof shouting "*yu, yu, yu.*"

This took everyone by surprise. The princess's nanny, Si Kembang Cina, explained that Princess Gondan Gandariah had made a pact with Raja Tunggal and if the promise were ever to be broken, she would turn into a monkey. The fact that the princess had turned into a monkey was a sign that Raja Tunggal was still alive. The court's astrologer was summoned. He confirmed Si Kembang Cina's words and was able to predict Raja Tunggal's whereabouts. Raja Laksamana was furious when he realised Nakhoda Bahar's evil schemes. He ordered that Nakhoda Bahar be summarily put to the sword.

The story goes on to say that Raja Tunggal arrived in the kingdom of Teluk Tambang Papan. The king of Teluk Tambang Papan, Raja Pertukal, did not dare fight Raja Tunggal and welcomed him warmly instead. He released Raja Tunggal's grand-uncle, Raja Si Megat Alang, but told him that two other relatives were possibly being held in the kingdom of Bandan, which was ruled by Raja Sianggerai. Raja Pertukal also said that Raja Sianggerai's daughter, Princess Kaca Bertuang, had a special talking bird.

And so Raja Tunggal departed for Bandan where he succeeded in freeing his two relatives. While he was there, Princess Kaca Bertuang fell passionately in love with Raja Tunggal. A wedding was arranged. Raja Tunggal married Princess Kaca Bertuang and Bujang Selamat married the princess's nanny, Si Kembang Cina. As soon as the wedding was over, Raja Tunggal turned into a white gibbon. Princess Kaca Bertuang whipped the gibbon's body with the spine of a young coconut leaf and Raja Tunggal became human once more. Princess Kaca Bertuang warned Raja Tunggal that he must not to marry ever again. If he did, he would turn back into a white gibbon and never regain his human form.

After some time, Raja Tunggal decided to return to Tiku Pariaman. Afraid that he might turn into a gibbon again, he borrowed the young coconut leaf from his wife. After a long journey, he finally reached Kuala Tiku Pariaman. On the way, however, he learned that Princess Gondan Gandariah had turned into a monkey. One day, he saw a monkey leaping up and down over his ship. As the monkey refused to descend, they shot it. Raja Tunggal took the spine of the young coconut leaf and beat the monkey's dead body seven times. The monkey suddenly turned back into Princess Gondan Gandariah. Everyone was very happy.

The story of Anggun Cik Tunggal is extremely popular in the Minangkabau region of West Sumatra. The Malay version may have originated in the oral stories that came from Minangkabau. Balai Pustaka in Jakarta has also published the *Syair Anggun Cik Tunggal* which tells almost the same story but in verse. In the *syair*, however, Anggun Cik Tunggal defeats the skipper of a ship in various contests and then orders him take him to save his uncle who is being held prisoner by a pirate. Anggun Cik Tunggal kills the pirate, then orders the skipper to take his uncle home. The skipper again betrays Anggun Cik Tunggal but the *syair* ends somewhat differently. After conquering various kings and marrying their daughters, Anggun Cik Tunggal returns to his kingdom. The treacherous ship's captain is arrested and duly punished. Anggun Cik Tunggal is the only one who marries Princess Gandariah.

1.5.6 *Hikayat Raja Donan*

The story tells that there was once a king who ruled over a vast kingdom called Mandi Angin. His majesty was called Raja Besar, his wife Princess Lindungan Bulan. Sadly, the king did not have any children. And so the king made a covenant with God and gave alms to the poor in order to be blessed with a son. After some time, Princess Lindungan Bulan became pregnant. The king asked seven astrologers, all brothers, to forecast the future of the prince while he was still in the womb.

But misfortune came unexpectedly. The seven astrologers deceived the king and told him that if the prince were allowed to remain in the kingdom, the country would be ruined. That was why, as soon as Raja Donan was born, he was set adrift at sea. Although his birth was extraordinary—he was born together with a sword and a kris—it could not assuage his father's fears.

The story then tells of Bendahara Tua, the king's elder brother, who lived at the rivermouth. As if he knew his nephew's ill fortune, Bendahara prayed that God would let the baby drift to where he lived. And that was exactly what happened. But before Bendahara could lift the baby into his boat, the boat drifted out to sea. By the time Raja Donan had spent a year on the ocean he was able to talk, but he had still not returned to his birthplace.

One day, he encountered the naval forces of Raja Camar Laut who demanded he pay them a seafaring tax. Raja Donan refused. A battle ensued. Raja Camar Laut was defeated while his sister, Cik Ambong, became friends with Raja Donan and joined him on his voyage. More time passed. Raja Pertukal too wanted Raja Donan to pay him tax. Raja Donan again refused to pay him anything. Another battle erupted. This time Raja Pertukal lost. And his sister, Cik Muda, was persuaded to join Raja Donan in his voyage.

One day, Raja Donan asked Cik Ambong and Cik Muda where he could a find beautiful woman. The two women told him that the elders had said the most beautiful women were Princess Ganda Iran, the daughter of Bendahara Mangkubumi of Gendang Batu, and Princess Telipuk Cahaya, the sister of Raja Piakas from Beram Biru. On hearing this, Raja Donan promptly set sail for Gendang Batu.

When he reached the rivermouth, Raja Donan began to play his bamboo flute. Princess Ganda Iran heard the music and immediately wanted to meet the flute-player. Using an eagle as her envoy, the princess soon began exchanging messages with Raja Donan. In response to her request for a meeting, Raja Donan asked the eagle to convey a message telling her that: for the time being he was unable to meet her, but also promising that in three years, three months and ten days he would present himself before her. Raja Donan continued his journey and reached Goa Batu. With the help of a magic gemstone, he transformed Goa Batu into a vast country, complete with a moated city, its own chieftains and subjects. He also revived Raja Camar Laut and Raja Pertukal. After some time, Raja Donan held a feast to celebrate his conversion to Islam and circumcision. Remembering his promise to Princess Ganda Iran, he set out for Gendang Batu. Along the way, he met a bird named Mak Tonggang who told him that Princess Linggam Cahaya, who lived in the spirit world, would like to meet him. Raja Donan asked that the meeting be deferred for three years, three months and ten days and continued with his journey. He arrived at the cockfighting pit in Gendang Batu disguised as a repulsively ugly and disease-ridden aborigine. Those present not only abused him, they also beat and kicked him. Princess Ganda Iran heard his piteous weeping and summoned him to her palace. When she saw the bamboo flute tied at his waist, she asked him to play for her. As he played, the soul seemed to fly from her body and she fell down as though dead. Raja Donan vanished, then soon returned to revive her. He played his flute and the spirit returned to her body. She came back to life again.

Once again Raja Donan disappeared and re-emerged this time disguised as a very handsome slave boy. The boy was taken to the palace. Princess Ganda Iran fell deeply in love with the boy. He was so "sweet" she impatiently threw him to the ground and smothered him with hugs and kisses. The boy removed his disguise and revealed himself as Cik Tuakal, a comely and suave young man. When he told Princess Ganda Iran who he really was, she was thrilled. They made solemn oaths and promises to each other.

Cik Tuakal then went to the cockfighting pit. He asked a scruffy ragamuffin to hold on to his rooster, then gave the ragamuffin a large sum of money to take to the kingdom of Batu Goa. Cik Tuakal then proceeded to engage his rooster in a fight against Raja Piakas's bird. Because he did not have sufficient money, Raja Piakas wagered his country and his fiancée, Princess Ganda Iran.

Raja Piakas's rooster lost and he returned home in shame. Raja Donan married Princess Ganda Iran. Princess Telupuk Cahaya commanded all the animals in the animal kingdom to attack Gandang Batu but they were defeated by Cik Tuakal (Raja Donan). Raja Piakas then attacked Raja Donan, but he too was vanquished. When the war finally ended, all the warriors who had perished were brought back to life. A series of lavish weddings were held, all on a grand scale. Raja Piakas married Cik Ambong; Raja Bendahara married Putri Telupuk Cahaya; and the scruffy wastrel who ran errands for Raja Donan married Cik Muda.

Raja Donan returned to his homeland, Mandi Angin. The country had been overrun by jungle and his father and mother reduced to impoverished peasants. This was all the doing of the seven treacherous astrologers who had stolen the kingdom from the king and moved the capital to a new location. Raja Donan had the deceitful astrologers arrested and rebuilt his father's kingdom.

Thereafter, he made good his oath to the Princess Linggam Cahaya of the spirit world and ascended to the ethereal world to marry her. Seven months and seven days later, he returned to earth and was crowned king of Gendang Batu. (The composition of this version of the *hikayat* was completed in Singapore on third day of the tenth month of the Islamic calendar, Syawal, 1353.)

The the plot of the story of Raja Donan as retold by Esah binti Muhammad Ali and published in 1963 by Zaharah Khalid is more extensive. It tells the story of Raja Donan's parents and grandparents and ends with the story of Awang Merah Suara, Raja Donan's son. The stories are somewhat sketchy and disconnected. About Raja Donan himself, it is told that he was exiled from his country because he was betrayed by a treacherous astrologer. As a result, Raja Donan was taken to Sembilan Island and raised by Temenggung-Bendahara.

One day, Raja Donan received news that his mother was in danger and set out to prevent her being kidnapped by Mambang Bungsu, Raja Donan's stepfather. Raja Donan's parents then went in search of him but he hid himself from them. When his adopted siblings came looking for him, he killed them. Next, Raja Donan travelled to Goa Batu and founded a new kingdom, complete with a palace and its own subjects. Later, upon hearing from a bird that Princess Gandar Eran, the fiancée of Raja Perakas, was most incomparably beautiful, he set out to find her. Raja Donan won Princess Gandar Eran from Raja Perakas in a cockfight. Raja Donan and Princess Gandar Eran were then married. While the wedding ceremony was taking place, however, the bride was abducted by Raja Embong Bersokan. Fortunately, she managed to escape. This led to a war between Raja Donan and Raja Perakas and his brothers. The hostilies finally ended when Awang Merah Suara, the son of Raja Donan and Princess Gandar Eran, mediated between the two sides. And so, they all returned to their respective countries.

1.5.7 *Hikayat Raja Ambong*

Raja Ambong of Tanjong Bima, and his sister Princess Candra Rupa lost their father, and were raised by the Temenggung (Chief of Security of the Realm), the Laksamana (Admiral of the Realm) and members of the nobility. One night, when he was seven years and nine months old, Raja Ambong had a dream. He dreamt that an old man advised him to sail to every corner of the realm in a boat made of Merbau wood. According to the old man, Raja Ambong had to seek out seven craftsmen brothers, who lived at the tip of Tanjung Bima to help him build the boat. If they couldn't do it, Raja Ambong should ask his cousin Cik Alang Orang Linggi to enlist the help of Tukang Bongkok Bungsu. The next day, Raja Ambong told members of the court's nobility about his dream. The Temenggung was told to fetch the seven sibling craftsmen to build the boat that would be called the Bahtera Seludang Mayang (the Racing Palm-blossom). However, all seven siblings died attempting to build the boat. The Temenggung was then told to ask Cik Alang Orang Linggi to call Tukang Bongkok Bungsu. Tukang Bongkok Bungsu was a craftsman with extraordinary magical powers. He burnt some incense to drive out all the *jinn* and evil spirits from the timber, and then started to build the boat that Raja Ambong wanted. Within a short time, the boat was completed.

One night, without anyone knowing, Raja Ambong secretly set sail with Cik Alang Orang Linggi and Tukang Bongkok Bungsu. The next day, Princess Candra Rupa was sad to discover that her brother had already left. She set out after him in another boat. When she caught up with him, her brother was furious. The princess felt so crestfallen that she jumped into the sea. When they found her body, she was already dead. Raja Ambong then sent a letter to Princess Cahaya Intan to ask for a magic potion to bring his sister back to life. The princess was brought back to life, and they continued their voyage together.

The next story is a love story. One day, the son of the king of *jinn*s, Si Dewa Mambang, came to ask for the hand of Princess Candra Rupa. When the proposal was rejected, a battle ensued. During the fight, Si Dewa Mambang was decapitated. Raja Ambong then proposed to Princess Renek Jintan, Si Dewa Mambang's daughter. The princess agreed to marry him on the condition that he brought her father back to life. He agreed to this and they were married. The story then continues with an account of how Raja Ambong dived to the bottom of the sea and married Princess Cahaya Intan, the daughter of Raja Naga.

After three months Raja Ambong remembered his ship and his wife, Princess Renek Jintan, whom he had left behind on the ocean's surface. So he sought permission to return to his ship and then continued on his voyage. The ship passed by many states and finally arrived at Mayang Manggi. The crew was welcomed with great joy. Princess Mayang Manggi, the sister of Raja Mayang Manggi, fell in love with Raja Ambong and the two of them began to flirt by exchanging *pantun* (a traditional form of Malay quatrain). The princess possessed great magical powers and could make herself vanish. This astounded Raja Ambong. But the secret of her magical powers was revealed to him in a dream. From that day hence, Raja Ambong was able to beat Princess Mayang Manggi at all manner of fun and games. Not long after, the pairs were married. Their days together were spent amusing themselves in various ways. Then one day, Raja Mambang Bungsu, Princess Mayang Manggi's former fiancé, launched an attack on Raja Ambong. After a fierce fight, Raja Mambang Bungsu was killed.

One day, Raja Ambong suddenly wanted to return to Tanjung Bima which he had left three years and ten days ago. He set sail for Tanjung Bima and was warmly greeted by his ministers and subjects upon his arrival. Soon after that, Cik Alang Orang Linggi married Princess Candra Rupa. Raja Ambong lived happily with his two wives and his subjects lived in peace and harmony.

This *hikayat* was written in Singapore on 12 July 1886, or 10 Syawal 1302 according to the Islamic calendar.

1.5.8 *Hikayat Raja Budiman*

Raja Budiman of Serendah Sekebun Bunga had seven wives. Of the seven he most loved Princess Bungsu, the Queen Consort. One day, after she had been pregnant for seven months, Princess Bungsu gave birth to a very handsome boy whom they named Lela Muda, and a golden baby dragon. The baby dragon grew up very quickly. It was reared in a pond but the pond soon became too small. It was then kept in a big and wide river but that too proved too small and even small dinghies could not sail past him. So the golden dragon asked to be moved to the sea. The dragon also asked Raja Budiman's approval for him to be allowed to swim out from the palace. The dragon prayed for rain to fall for seven days and seven nights and the whole country was flooded. Before it left for the sea, the golden dragon presented his brother, Lela Muda, with a sword and a ring.

The story tells that the king, Raja Budiman, only played with Lela Muda, from the day he was born. The king's six daughters were jealous and tried to win back their father's affections. They asked Raja Budiman to summon seven astrologers to tell Lela Muda's fortune and paid the seven astrologers a thousand dollars each to say that Lela Muda would bring misfortune to the whole country. "The country will burn," said the astrologers. Only the youngest of the astrologers refused to be bribed by the princesses.

Meanwhile, Princess Tengah (the middle princess) was asked to feign illness, but the golden dragon made her seriously ill. The cure was for Princess Tengah to eat meat from a bird called Indra Bayu. Lela Muda was ordered to find the bird and threatened that if he failed he would be killed. So he set out to find the bird. He was given only one attendant, Selamat Tandang Desa. When they reached the jungle, they came upon Princess Syambulan Gunung and her husband, the ogre Mangku Bumi. The couple told Lela Muda that Princess Bungsu Kecil Selendang Cahaya of Gunung Dua Belas owned a Burung Indra Bayu. They were also warned to be careful of "the live pictures that can talk" at Padang Kecil. These "talking pictures" concealed many *jinn*s who could possess people. Lela Muda eventually reached Padang Kecil. The two men defaced any talking pictures they found there. Next, they forced a Nenek Kebayan (sorceress) to call Princess Bungsu Kecil Cahaya Bulan down to earth from her heavenly realm. Lela Muda won the princess's heart. While they were amusing themselves in Nenek Kebayan's garden, Princess Bungsu Kecil Cahaya Bulan's fiancé, Syaikh Ali, suddenly attacked them. In the fight that followed, Awang Sebuncul, the son of Selamat Tandang Desa, provided Lela Muda with invaluable assistance. Together with the princess, they flew to the spirit world, and spent three months and ten days there.

One day, Lela Muda asked leave to look for the Burung Indra Bayu in Gunung Dua Belas. Princess Bungsu Kecil Cahaya Bulan cautioned him against travelling on land. When the princess's father gave his approval, Lela Muda and his companion returned to earth, and set off for the country of Gunung Dua Belas by sea; sometimes they walked along the beach, at other times they swam. One day, just as Selamat Tandang Desa was too tired to continue swimming, they spied a ship belonging to Raja Pertukal and seized it. By summoning strong winds, they were quickly able to reach Gunung Dua Belas. Try as they might, they could not gain entry into Princess Bungsu Kecil Selendang Cahaya's palace. Her palace was tightly shut and there was no entrance of any kind to be found. One day, the princess felt hot and wanted to take a bath in order to cool down. The door of her palace was finally opened. Lela Muda transformed himself into a very fragrant *bunga tanjung* flower, while Awang Si Buncul—Selamat Tandang Desa's son—changed himself into a magnolia. The princess and her lady-in-waiting then each took a flower into her bed chamber. At midnight, the two men changed back to their human form and seduced the princess and her lady-in-waiting. They passed the night in pleasure. A relative of the princess guarding her quarters heard their laughter and immediately informed the king, Raja Tua. The army gathered to arrest Lela Muda. The king's subjects were also summoned. A fierce battle ensued. Initially Lela Muda and Awang Si Buncul were defeated and captured but then Lela Muda's golden dragon came to his assistance at the most critical moment in the battle. Raja Tua and his sons could not defend themselves against the dragon and surrendered. Lela Muda then married Putri Bungsu Selendang Cahaya. After a while, Lela Muda asked permission from the king to return to Serendah Sekebun Bunga. He was accompanied by Princess Bungsu Kecil Cahaya Bulan and Nenek Kebayan. The bird Burung Indra Bayu revealed his sisters' evil deeds to Lela Muda and the six princesses, together with the six astrologers, were captured and executed. The youngest astrologer, who refused to cooperate with the others, receieved a new title giving him authority over all the country's astrologers and traditional healers (*bomoh*). Lela Muda ruled over the realm for all time.

1.5.9 *Hikayat Terong Pipit*

This is the story of a Javanese prince named Raja Bungsu. Because he always quarreled with his cousin Raja Sulung Jawa, Raja Bungsu moved to the Malay Peninsula and founded a state called Johor Mengkalih Tanah Jakta. The story next tells that Raja Sulung Jawa traveled through the villages in his realm looking for a beautiful wife. He eventually reached the state of Lindung Bulan Kedah Tua and married Princess Ratna Juita. Not long after the wedding, the king died and Raja Sulung Jawa became ruler of Lindung Bulan Kedah Tua. Some time passed and Raja Sulung wanted to build a palace. However, no one dared cut down the Merbau tree he wanted to use to build his palace. No one, that is, except for a warlord named Wan Cik Long. For this service, Wan Cik Long received the title Datuk Maharaja Dinda and became the country's harbour master (*syahbandar*). His title was later changed to Wan Cik Antan Besi Antan Tembaga Selampit. Wan Cik was also granted a magic cannon by the king. Unfortunately, Wan Cik was slightly insane. He terrorised the merchants who called at the port so badly that no merchant ship dared ply its trade at Lindung Bulan Kedah Tua. When Wan Cik found out that he had incurred the king's wrath and that his majesty wanted to arrest him, he fled to Johor Mengkalih. Raja Bungsu also appointed him harbor master.

After some time, the queen, Princess Ratna Juita, gave birth to a son named Pekulun Duli Baginda. Both the king and queen were delighted to have a son and loved him very much. They invited Terong Pipit, a minister's son, Gelam, a warlord's son, and Jerun, the son of a village headman, to be his playmates. Some more time passed and Raja Sulung Jawa went in search of a magical garment for his son. His boat was stranded on the shores of Johor Mengkalih. Raja Sulung was apprehended and killed by Wan Cik, under the instructions of Raja Bungsu, Raja Sulung's cousin.

The story further tells that Tuan Putri Payung Mahkota, a cousin of Pekulun Duli Baginda, came down to earth. She took Pekulun Duli Baginda and his friends back to the spirit world and entrusted them to Maharaja Guru to study the arts of sorcery, invincibility and all types of weaponry. Once they reached the age of twelve, they returned to earth. They had a warship built and presently set sail to avenge the death of Raja Sulung. Encountering Wan Cik on an island, they fought him in a fierce battle. Wan Cik was defeated by Terong Pipit, but stubbornly refused to pledge allegiance to Pekulun Duli Baginda. Only after Terong Pipit threatened him with a powerful spear he had obtained from Maharaja Guru did Wan Cik finally pledge his loyalty to Pekulun Duli Baginda.

Wan Cik took Terong Pipit and his friends ashore. They met Tok Selamat, an opium seller, who was actually Raja Sulung's servant who had survived a previous attempt on his life by Wan Cik. The village headman's son, Jerun, meanwhile found himself in a comical situation. First, he lost all his money while gambling with the young men in the village. When he was forced by the young men to pay what he owed them, he robbed them instead. Later, when he was hungry he ate some Javanese fritters that had been cooked by three maidens. As he had lost all his money, the maidens took his shawl as payment for the fritters. Later, when they saw Jerun dancing in the centre of the market, they forgave him for taking their food without payment.

Raja Bungsu was aware of Wan Cik's treacherous nature and wrote a letter to Raja Belanda who was meditating in the forest, asking for help. He promised Raja Belanda half the country of Johor Mengkalih and the hand of his daughter if Raja Belanda were able to defeat Wan Cik. Raja Belanda came with his warriors. He defeated Wan Cik but in the end Raja Belanda himself was killed by Terong Pipit. Terong Pipit's army went on a rampage, setting fire to everything in town and killing everyone they met. They also captured Raja Bungsu and impaled him. His daughter Princess Sinar Bulan Gemilang Cahaya asked her grandfather Tok Rancang Besi for help. Wan Cik was no match for Tok Rancang Besi. Not only was he no match, even the sound of Tok Rancang Besi's voice made him quiver. So Terong Pipit went up to the spirit world to ask for help from Tok Maharaja Guru. With the aid of an iron net given to him by Tok Maharaja Guru, Wan Cik was able to capture Tok Rancang Besi and imprison him on an island. Tok Rancang Besi was then stoned to death.

Princess Sinar Bulan Gemilang Cahaya initially refused to accompany Pekulun Duli Baginda on his warship but was persuaded by Jerun to do so. One day, Terong Pipit suggested that they go and attack Tengku Sultan Maha Mulia, the king of Tanjung Pura who had been betrothed to Princess Sinar Bulan. If they did not attack him, he would surely attack them. And so they set out for the land of Tanjung Pura. In the ensuing battle, Sultan Maha Mulia defeated Wan Cik, Terong Pipit, Gelam and Pekulun Duli Baginda. Princess Sinar Bulan said she was delighted to meet her fiancé, Sultan Maha Mulia, and told him that the attack on Tanjung Pura was actually a ruse for her to that end. Sultan Maha Mulia was delighted when he heard this. The Princess then asked her fiancé to pick her some magnolias that were growing on a tree. Sultan Maha Mulia removed his belt and climbed up the tree. When he was up in the tree, Princess Sinar Bulan looked for the ivory box in his belt where Sultan Maha Mulia kept his soul and smashed it against the base of the tree. Sultan Maha Mulia immediately died. Wan Cik was trapped under some large boulders and Princess Sinar Bulan asked Jerun to release him. They then went in search of their other friends. When they were all together again, they returned to Lindungan Bulan Kedah Tua. Pekulun Duli Baginda was installed as the king and Wan Cik was reappointed as the harbor master once again.

One day, Princess Sinar Bulan learned from her lady-in-waiting that Pekulun Duli Baginda had another wife. She was so heartbroken that she decided to drown herself. When Terong Pipit found Princess Sinar Bulan, she was already dead. However, Princess Siti Dewi, Pekulun Duli Baginda's other wife, brought Princess Sinar Bulan back to life by sprinkling her with holy water taken from the Sari mountain ranges. From that day on, Princess Sinar Bulan and Princess Siti Dewi became the closest of friends.

The story also tells of the King of all the Jinns, Raja Jin Syamsul Alam from Antah Berantah. One day while he was circumnavigating the world, he saw the beautiful Princess Sinar Bulan and immediately kidnapped her. This provoked an uproar. Terong Pipit and his friends set off to fight the King of the Jinns but they could not kill him because his soul was not located in his body. One by one, the King of the Jinns defeated Terong Pipit, Gelam, Jerun and Pekulun Duli Baginda. Eventually only Wan Cik and the King of Jinns were left; neither could gain an advantage over the other. Wan Cik's wives knew that the King of Jinns' soul did not reside in his body and they tried to find out where it was kept from Dewi Hairani, the daughter of the King of the Jinns. With their assistance, Wan Cik was able to easily kill the King of the Jinns. Dewi Hairani was given to Jerun as a junior wife.

Next Terong Pipit and his brother went to search for a white elephant and the magical *ratna mala* flower as dowry for Princess Sinar Bulan. They were able to capture a white elephant but only with great difficulty. Then they fought the dragon Berma Sakti. The dragon failed to overrun Terong Pipit's warships and had to relinquish the magical *ratna mala* flower it kept in its mouth. They then returned to Lindungan Bulan Kedah Tua, where Pekulun Duli Baginda subsequently married Princess Sinar Bulan in a large and lavish wedding ceremony. During Sultan Pekulun Duli Baginda's reign, the fame of the kingdom of Lindungan Bulan Kedah Tua spread far and wide throughout the Malay Peninsula and Java.

The composition of the *Hikayat Terong Pipit* was completed on the 20th day of Jumadil Akhir (the sixth month of the Islamic calendar) in the Islamic year of 1341 (7 February 1923) by Panglima Ali Mudin bin Panglima Hasan in the village of Batas Liku, in Arau, Perlis, at the request of Major Farquhar of Pekan Kangar.

Finally, I would like to discuss two other well-known *hikayats* from the Minangkabau area, namely *Cerita Si Umbut Muda* (The Story of Si Umbut Muda) and *Sabai Nan Aluih* (The Tale of Sabai Nan Aluih). There is actually a very close relationship between Minangkabau and Malay literatures, due to the fact that a majority of Malays, especially those in Negeri Sembilan, can trace their origins to the Minangkabau region. And Malays who can read Jawi (the Arabic script) can easily read the Minangkabau stories. In one of his papers, Umar Yunus has observed that the Minangkabau texts could be recited either in the Minangkabau language or Malay (Umar Yunus, 1959: 14-17).

1.5.10 *Cerita Si Umbut Muda*

This story has been adapted into Indonesian by Tulis Sutan (Tulis Sutan Sati, 1961) and is as follows.

Si Umbut Muda was an extremely intelligent young man. He told his mother that he did not want to become a village headman, district chief, an officer or warrior. He only wanted to be a religious scholar. So he embarked on his religious studies under the tutelage of Tuanku Panjang Janggut in a mosque in Kampung Aur. After two years, he went to another mosque to study under Tuan Imam Muda. He studied many religious texts and learnt many religious songs. Si Umbai Muda had a wonderful singing voice. When he sang, passersby would stop their journey, birds would stop flying and perch in a tree, water would stop flowing downstream, all just to listen to him. When he had finished his studies, he returned to the village of Teberau.

One day, his former teacher, Panjang Janggut, invited Umbut Muda to a religious ceremony. Umbut Muda sang and his melodious voice captivated all present, including Panjang Janggut's daughter and his seven nieces. The youngest daughter, Putri Gelang Banyak, asked Umbut Muda to repeat a song that he had just sung. Seeing how beautiful Putri Gelang Banyak was—"her face like the moon on the fourteenth day, her eyebrows like the sharpened spurs of a rooster, her nose aquiline, her ears like spring snares, her lips like a slice of lime"—Umbut Muda became flustered. He was unable to continue singing, and his eyes could not even focus on the words written on the page. The seven sisters laughed at him. Ashamed and humiliated, Umbut Muda made his way home.

Si Umbut Muda asked his mother to request Putri Gelang Banyak's hand in marriage. At first Putri Gelang Banyak replied she was too young to marry but when she was further pressed, she insulted Si Umbut Muda. The girl said that if Umbut Muda was handsome, it was only the clothes he wore that made him so; if he was rich, it was only the gold he inherited from his father that made him so.

Umbut Muda was enraged by these insults. He asked his mother to look for some hollow driftwood at the river near Lubuk Mata Kucing. Because of her love for her son, Si Umbut Muda's mother carried out the perilous task of collecting the driftwood. Si Umbut Muda made a magic flute from the hollow driftwood. One day, Si Umbut Muda played his magic flute. Putri Gelang Banyak heard the sound of the flute and immediately felt her body becoming hot, as if she were on fire.

In order to cool off, she made her way to a spring. At the spring, Si Umbut Muda teased and made fun of her, which greatly upset the girl. In her anger she pelted him with the gourd, the pumpkin and the coconut shell she used as water containers. None of the things hit him, yet they were all broken. On seeing this, Putri Gelang Banyak began to cry. Si Umbut Muda approached the girl and tried to cheer her up by saying that all her water containers had broken when she saw a couple of buffaloes fighting in the middle of the road and tried to run away.

Two days later, Princess Gelang Banyak fell ill. She felt a shadow of her former self, her blood coursed through her veins and her heart raced. Many healers came to treat her but to no avail. Finally, the princess asked her father to look for a palm cabbage (*umbut*) in the village of Teberau. Thinking that she had asked him to look for river reeds (*umbut teberau*), her father went in search for them. Only after some time did he realise that she wanted him to find Si Umbut Muda. The father subsequently found the young man and asked him to marry Putri Gelang Banyak. But Umbut Muda refused, using the same insults which Putri Gelang Banyak had once made about him.

Once again, Si Umbut Muda left home to resume his religious studies, giving instructions as to what needed to be done should Putri Gelang Banyak pass away while he was gone. Some time after his departure, Putri Gelang Banyak died and was buried according to his instructions. Later Si Umbut Muda returned and used his learning to bring her back to life. Soon after that, the couple were married in a large and lavish ceremony.

Eventually, the couple succumbed to an incurable illness. Both Si Umbut Muda and Putri Gelang Banyak passed away and were buried side by side. "And so the story ends, the tale reaches its termination; the fire dies, its embers waft away, and there we shall leave it."

1.5.11 *Sabai Nan Aluih*

Sabai Nan Aluih is a very famous Minangkabau *kaba* (story) and has been translated into Malay by Tulis Sutan Sati (1954), in the form of a drama retaining the special characteristics of the Minangkabau language. The story is as follows:

> Sabai Nan Aluih was a very beautiful girl. Her skin was a rosy shade of gold, like ripe sugar cane amongst tall grass, like grilled shrimp. Her wavy hair was worn in three coils, her ears were shaped like spring snares, her eyelashes like a trail of ants, her nose like a single garlic clove, her chin like a hanging cloud. Her cheeks were smooth and full, her lips like a slice of lime, her brows shaped like a rooster's spurs, her tongue like a ripe mango. Her calves were like a swollen padi plant, her heels were smooth like quail eggs, her big toe like a gold nugget. Her body was slim and elegant, her eyes glowed in the dark, her fingers delicate and henna-painted, her grace and charm like a beautiful painting.

Word of her beauty reached Raja Nan Panjang in the region of Lima Puluh who promptly sent an emissary to ask for Sabai Nan Aluih's hand in marriage. However, Raja Babanding, Sabai Nan Aluih's father, rejected the proposal. Raja Nan Panjang was famous for his bad temper and immoral behaviour. Moreover, he was old and had many wives. Offended, Raja Nan Panjang challenged Raja Babanding to a duel in order to settle the dispute.

The night before the duel, Sabai Nan Aluih had a terrible dream. She asked her father not to meet Raja Nan Panjang but, undeterred, he interpreted her dream in a more positive manner. And so he left to confront Raja Nan Panjang. Once again Raja Nan Panjang demanded Sabai Nan Aluih's hand in marriage. And once again, his demand was rejected. And so, the duel began.

Raja Nan Panjang was on the verge of defeat in the fiercely fought battle; had the fight gone any further, he would surely have been killed or mortally wounded. To save himself, Raja Nan Panjang signaled to his friend, Raja Nan Kongkong, and the man shot Raja Babanding. Fatally wounded, Raja Babanding fell to the ground and his body was thrown into the bushes.

A herdsman found the badly injured Raja Babanding and quickly brought the news to Sabai Nan Aluih, who was weaving when word of her father reached her. Shocked and distraught beyond measure, she immediately rushed to her father's side. When she arrived, he regained consciousness and asked about her brother, Mangkutak Alam, his favourite. No one knew where Mangkutak Alam was. Soon after, Raja Babanding took his final breath and died. Sabai Nan Aluih was so consumed by anger over her father's death that she vowed to avenge him.

Sabai Nan Aluih went to Raja Nan Panjang and challenged him to a pistol duel. Raja Nan Panjang was killed in the duel by Sabai Nan Aluih. His wife, Narawatu, was told to take her husband's body home.

And that is the story of Sabai Nan Aluih. The tale seems to remind parents that they should not favour sons over daughters. Daughters can sometimes be braver and more devoted to their parents than brothers.

REFERENCES

Abujamin Rochman B.
1968. "Asal-usul dan Penjabaran sebuah Tjerita Rakyat," *Manusia Indonesia* II, I, 21-31.

Asdi S. Dipodjojo
1966. *Sang Kantjil, Tokoh Tjerita Binatang Indonesia*, Djakarta.

Atmani Hardja
1962. "Tindjauan Kesusastraan mengenal Tjerita Rakjat," *Pustaka Budaja*, III, 9, pp. 35-40.

Balai Pustaka
1963-1972. *Tjerita Rakyat I-IV*, Djakarta.

Brandes J.
1893-1894. "Dwerghert-verhalen uit den Archipel," *TBG*, pp. 37-8.

Cerita Abu Nawas,
n.d, Batavia, Albrecht dan Rusche

Clifford, H.
1896. *Hikayat Raja Budiman,* Singapore.

Coster-Wisjman, L.M.
1929. *Uilespiegel-verhalen in Indonesia in het bijzonder in de Soenda-landen*, Santpoort.

Demetrio Y. Radza, Francisco
1972. "Themes in Philippines Folk-tales," *Asian Studies*, X, pp. 6-17.

Dundes, A.
1966. *The Study of Folklore,* New York.

Dussek, O.T. (ed.)
1929. *Hikayat Pelandok: Iaitu Hikayat Sang Kancil, Hikayat Pelandok dengan Anak Memerang, Hikayat Pelandok Jenaka*, Singapore.

Geria, Ratnadi
1971. "Tjerita seekor Harimau dengan seekor Banteng," *Manusia Indonesia* V,1 & 2, pp. 245-257. *Hikayat Pelanduk,* Malay Literature Series, No. 13

Ismail Hussein
1967. "Sebuah Cherita Rakyat Melayu," *Tenggara*, I, pp. 60-75.

Jassin, H.B.
1968. *Tifa Penyair dan Daerahnya*, Jakarta.

Jumsari Jusuf.
1970. "Tjerita Jenaka,"*Manusia Indonesia*, IV (1& 2), pp. 77-78.

Klinkert, B.C. (ed.)
1885. *Hikajat Pelandok Djinaka of de Reinaert de Vos der Maleirs,* Leiden.
1893. *Hikajat Pelandok Djinaka*, Leiden.

Knapperti Jan
1976. *Myths and Legends of Indonesia*, Singapore.

Maxwell, G.W.E.
1881a. "Aryan Mythology in Malay Tradition," *JRAS*, new series 13, pp. 399 - 409.
1881b. "Two Malay myths: The Princess of the Foam and the Raja of the Bamboo," *JRAS*, New Series 13, pp. 498-523.
1886. "Raja Donan, a Malay fairy tale," *JMBRAS*, 18, pp. 241-269.
1887. "Raja Ambong, a Malay fairy tale," *JMBRAS*, 19, pp. 55-71.
1955. *In Malay Forest*, Singapore.
1971. *In Malay Forest*, Singapore.

Mees, C.A.
1927. *Hikajat Pelandoek Djinaka,* Santpoort.

Mohd. Taib Osman.
1965. *Kesusastraan Melayu Lama*, Singapura.
1970. "Kesusastraan Melayu dengan Chorak Masharakat dan Budayanya," *Penulis*, Tahun IV, 1 & 2.
1970. "The aims, approaches and problems in the study of folk literature or oral tradition with particular reference to Malay Culture," *The Brunei Museum Journal*, II, 4, pp. 17-28.
1975. *Tradisi Lisan di Malaysia*, Kuala Lumpur.

N. St. Iskandar
1964. *Hikayat Abu Nawas*, Djakarta.

Ng. Wirapoestaka.
1930. *Tjerita Kantjil Jang Tjerdik*, Batavia.

Radjab, M.
1971. "Kesusastraan Kaba di Minangkabau," *Pustaka Djaya* IV, 32, pp. 35-47.

Ramlan, M.
1972. "*Sekelumit Cherita Jenaka Nusantara,*" *DB,* 16, no. 8, pp. 356-362.
1973. "Berbagai Macam Cerita Binatang Nusantara," *DB,* 18, no. 4, pp. 160-163.

Skeat, W.
1958. *Fables and Folk Tales from an Eastern Forest*, Donald Moore, Singapore.
1900. *Malay Magic*, London.

Soetan Ibrahim, H.
1931. *Tjerita Si Kantan*, Batavia.

Syair Anggun Cik Tunggal,
n.d. Balai Pustaka.

Tulis Sutan Sati.
1954. *Sabai nan Aluih*, Djakarta.
1961. *Tjerita Si Umbut Muda*, Djakarta.

Umar Yunus
1959. "Beberapa Tjatatan tentang Transkripsi Bahasa Minangkabau," *Bahasa dan Budaya*, VIII, no. 1.

Voorhoeve, P.
1927. *Overzicht van den Volksverhalen der Bataks*, Dissertation Leiden.

Vries, Jan De.
1925.   *Volksverhalen uit Oost-Indie: Sprookjesen Fabels I & II*, Zutphen.

Wall, A. F. von de.
1900.   "De Pelandoek Djinaka," *TBG*, 42 (1), pp. 40-56.
1916.   *Hikayat Mashoeddoelhak*, Batavia

Winstedt, R. O.
n.d.   "De Pelandoek Djinaka," *TBG*, 42 (1), pp. 40-56.
            "De Pelandoek Djinaka," *TBG*, 42(1), p. 40-56.
1906.   "Some Mouse-deer Tales," *JSBRAS*, 45, pp. 61-69.
1909a.   "Awang Sulong Merah Muda," *JSBRAS*, 52, pp. 31-95.
1909b.   "Musang Berjanggut," *JSBRAS*, 52, pp. 121-172.
1910.   "Hikayat Seri Rama, romanised by R.O. Winstedt," *JSBRAS*, 55.
            "The History of Peninsula in Folktales," *JSBRAS*, 57.
1917.   "The Folk-tales of Indonesia and Indo China," *JSBRAS*, 7b, pp. 119-126.
1920a.   "Hikayat Abu Nawas," *JSBRAS*, 81, pp. 15-21; 83, pp. 94-95.
1920b.   "The Indian Origin of Malay Folktales," *JSBRAS*, 82, pp. 119-126.
1921.   "The Folklore of the Hikajat Malim Deman," *JSBRAS*, 83.
1927.   "The Tale of Trong Pipit," *JMBRAS*, 5 (3), pp. 373-591.
1943.   "Nature in Malay Literature and Folklore," *JRAS*, pp. 27-33.

Winstedt, R. O. & Sturrock (ed.)
1907.   *Papers on Malay Subjects: Malay Literature*, Part II.
1908.   "Musang Berjanggut," *JMBRAS*, Vol. 52, pp. 121-175.
1957.   *Awang Sulong Merah Muda* (edition I, 1908), Singapore.
1958.   *Hikayat Bayan Budiman*, Singapore.
1960.   *Hikajat Malim Deman* (edition I, 1908), Singapore.
1960.   *Hikajat Malim Dewa* (edition I, 1908), Singapore.
1960.   *Hikajat Anggun Che Tunggal* (edition I, 1914), Singapore.
1960.   *Hikajat Raja Muda* (edition I, 1914), Singapore.
1960.   *Hikajat Bayan Budiman* (edition I, 1920), Singapore.
1963.   *Cerita Jenaka* (edition I, 1908), Singapore.

Zahara Khalid.
1963.   *Raja Donan*, Kuala Lumpur.

2 The Indian Epics and The Wayang in Malay Literature

Two thousand years ago, trade relations were first established between India and the Malay world. Many Indian traders made a stopover in Sumatra and the Malay Peninsular on their way to China. The region along the coast of the Straits of Malaka was a vital lifeline for trade and commerce. A large part of the population were involved in these international trading activities. Under the influence of the Indian traders or the local populace who were themselves influenced by Indian culture, small kingdoms emerged in the area. Many of these kingdoms were located in the northern part of Malaya, such as Langkasuka and others. After Buddhism was founded in India, even larger numbers of Indians travelled to or stopped over in parts of the Malay world. Since Buddhism does not subscribe to a caste system, its followers were not hesitant about interacting with people of other races. Moreover, its followers showed a missionary zeal to spread their faith in all directions. Around 420 AD, a prince from Kashmir called Gunawarman travelled to Java and Sumatra. This explains why a large number of ancient relics found in these areas include Buddhist sculptures in the Amravati style from south India that date back to the second and third centuries CE. Many inscriptions etched in stone have also been discovered, including the famous stone tablet issued by King Mulawarman in the region around Kutai, Kalimantan in 400 A.D. Another stone tablet produced by King Purnawarman, the king of Taruma around Bogor, West Java, originated from a later period, circa 450 A.D.

Hindu influence, on the other hand, permeated throughout the Malay world over a longer and more sustained period of time, in a peaceful manner. A ship anchored at a Malay harbour. Its crew of Indian traders were astute enough to win the trust of the local Malay rulers. Some presented beautiful gifts to these rulers, others taught them the magic arts which could cure illnesses or defeat their formidable foes. Over time, some of the Hindu traders married the local princesses and became influential members of the community. The Brahmins amongst them were often invited to officiate at ceremonies where the local rulers were formally inducted into the caste of *ksatria* (the Hindu caste of kings, warriors and rulers). Eventually, the Hindu influence became so well-entrenched in the lives of the Malays, that it can be said, according to Winstedt, "till the 19th century, the Malays derived everything from India: religion, political system, astrology, medicine, literature, arts and crafts" (R. O. Winstedt, 1944b: 186).

This begs the question of who spread Indian culture in Southeast Asia? Many theories have been put forward. Some scholars assert that the traders, who belong to the *vaisya* (merchant) caste, were the ones who spread Indian culture in Southeast Asia. This theory, however, contradicts reality. The centres of Hindu culture in the Malay archipelago were not found along the coastal regions but in the more remote inland areas which were not frequented by traders; moreover, the culture found in the Archipelago was not that of the *vaisyas* but of the Brahmins, the religious elite. Other scholars, especially Indian scholars, on the other hand, maintain that the *ksatrias* were the ones who spread Indian culture in Southeast Asia. As a result of attacks by tribes from the north of India on them, an exodus of *ksatrias* fled to Southeast Asia and eventually it was they who propagated Hindu culture. This theory, however, is also disputed by other scholars. After all, such a large-scale migration across oceans would be far from easy. Moreover, had there been such a massive exodus of Indians to Southeast Asia, it would have certainly had an impact on the lineage or ethnic makeup of the inhabitants of Southeast Asia. But this was not the case.

More plausible theories have been propounded by J. C. Van Leur and G. Coedes. Van Leur argues that it was the Brahmins who were responsible for the expansion of Indian culture. The Brahmins were invited by the local rajas to officiate at ceremonies, either to inaugurate them as *ksatria* or to validate their power (Van Leur, 1955). According to G. Coedes, it was the local elites who pursued their studies in India who, upon their return to their homeland, were responsible for the spread of Indian culture in Southeast Asia. To corroborate this, he cites the example of the spread of Western culture in Asia in more recent times which, according to him, was the result of more and more Asians having gone abroad to study in the West rather than because of any direct action of Westerners themselves (Coedes, 1968: 26).

Before we discuss the role of the Indian epics in Malay literature, it would be useful to consider their position in India itself as well as to present a synopsis of the stories they contain. I will begin with the *Ramayana*.

2.1 *Ramayana*

The Ramayana is a famous Indian epic. It is a *kavya*, a poem used to pass on moral teachings to the young. The teachings are wide-ranging, encompassing: *darmasastra* (moral lessons); *arthasastra* (lessons on politics and warcraft) and *nitisastra* (lessons on how to lead a noble life). Besides these, the *Ramayana* provides an exemplar of the ideal Aryan way of life. Rama is a symbol of the obedient child; the cordial and benevolent brother; and the loving husband. He is also a courageous warrior and a paragon of the just and ideal king. Sita symbolises the faithful wife. Rama's brothers epitomise fraternal solidarity. On the other hand, Dasarata is a symbol of the weak king who is morally weak and unable to resist feminine wiles.

The general consensus among scholars is that the *Ramayana* was written by Valmiki. Or at least, he compiled the epic. However, there is still much dispute among scholars on the origins of the *Ramayana*. Lassen asserts that the *Ramayana* is an allegory of the conquest of South India by the Aryans. Jacobi holds the opinion that the *Ramayana* is a melange of history and myth. According to him, the palace intrigues which resulted in Rama's exile were founded on real historical events. This historical basis was then commingled with the story of the killing of Ravana taken from the *Rigveda*. In the *Rigveda*, Sita is the Goddess of Agriculture, while her husband Rama is the God Indra. The battle between Rama and Ravana is actually an allusion to the battle between Indra and Wirta, a demon. According to D. C. Sen, who studied the Bengali version of the *Ramayana*, the *Ramayana* derives from at least three sources, namely:

(i) the *Dasarata Jataka* (The Buddhist story of Rama),
(ii) myths about Ravana from South India, and
(iii) monkey worship.

Valmiki then combined these stories into one story with a single coherent plot.

This differs from Valmiki's own account, which claimed that the heavenly sage Narada had narrated the story of Rama to him. Brahma then came and asked Valmiki to compile the tale of Rama as Narada had narrated it and, in response to Brahma's request, Valmiki then committed the *Ramayana* to writing. When he had finished, Valmiki taught the *Ramayana* to Rama's sons, Lava and Kusa, who lived in exile with their mother in his hermitage. The *Ramayana* was first chanted at the ritual slaughter of a horse, presided over by Rama. Rama was reunited with his wife and sons as a result of this ceremony. Not long after, Lava and Kusa were crowned and Rama ascended to heaven (Haridas Bhattacharyya, Vol. II: 14-31).

The *Ramayana* is, in fact, a popular and ancient Indian folktale. In the *Mahabharata*, the story of Rama is told in the *Ramopakhyana*. Besides Valmiki's *Ramayana*, there are three other versions of the epic in India (see Sir George A. Grierson, 1927), namely:

(i) Yoga-Vasistha-Ramayana,
(ii) Adhiyat-Ramayana, and
(iii) Adbhuta-Ramayana.

The *Adbhuta-Ramayana* is particularly interesting as it clarifies a few things which were unclear in Rama's tale, for example, Sita's origin and how Rama came to be regarded as the avatar of Vishnu as he is portrayed in some versions (P. J. Zoetmulder, 1974: 227-228).

The *Ramayana* has had a profound influence. It has been an endless source of inspiration for India's poets and writers. In the fourth century, the great poet Kalidasa wrote a poem called *Raghuwansa* based on the story of Rama. In the sixth century, the poet Bhatti reworked the story of the *Ramayana* in a poem titled *Ravana-Wadha* (the killing of Ravana). This poem is better known as the *Bhatti-Kawya*. According to three Indian scholars, H. B. Sarker, Manomohan Gush and C. Bulcke, as well as an Indonesian scholar, Poerbatjaraka, the *Ravana-Wadha* is the source of the *Kakawin Ramayana* (a rendering of the *Ramayana* in Old Javanese language) and not Valmiki's *Ramayana*.

When Buddhism first appeared in India, the story of the *Ramayana* was again adapted to suit Buddhist teachings as the *Dasarata Jataka*. Many episodes from the *Dasarata Jataka* were taken from Valmiki's *Ramayana*. In the *Dasarata Jataka*, Rama is regarded as a *bodhisattva* (a potential Buddha) and Sita is Rama's sister, who later became his wife. The kidnapping of Sita and the events that happened thereafter are not to be found in this version.

The Jain religion also adapted the *Ramayana* story to suit its teachings. Rama is regarded as the eighth Baladeva (gentle hero). After killing Prativasudewa (the name the Jains gave to Ravana), Baladeva descended into hell. He was filled with so much remorse over the killing of Ravana that he decided to repent for his sin by becoming a sage in order to achieve *moksha* (enlightenment), in accordance with the Jain teaching of *ahimsa* (non-violence) which prohibits killing. In this version of the story, Baladeva is not a hunter, and Ravana and the other characters do not eat meat.

In 1100, the story of Rama was translated into Tamil by the poet Kamban. His work is called *Ramavatram* (the reincarnation of Rama). Kamban's rendition is considered the greatest and most renowned epic ever written in Tamil. Subsequently, various versions of the *Ramayana* emerged in Hindi, Malayalam, Telugu, Bengali and other languages. The best-known version is the Hindi volume compiled by Tulisi Das in 1560, the *Ramacaritamanas*. Hindus still greatly venerate the *Ramacaritamanas* and it is considered a sacred book. Rama is regarded as the reincarnation of Vishnu and very much revered as such.

The high esteem and veneration with which Rama is held by the Hindus are perhaps best encapsulated in the following story.

One day a wretched road-sweeper could be heard crying out in pain. His cries reached Hanuman. Hanuman felt that it was demeaning and unworthy for someone as abject as a lowly sweeper to invoke the name of his lord. He was furious and angrily kicked the road-sweeper. That afternoon, when he went before Rama, he was surprised to see a wound on his lord's chest. Seeing his disciple's puzzled look, Rama said: "Don't you know that whatever you do to my children, even to the lowliest amongst them, will be felt by me?" (Hooykaas,1947: 131).

To make it easier to understand the story and to make comparisons easier between different versions of the epic that are to be found in the Malay Archipelago and other places outside India, I will now provide a summary of Valmiki's *Ramayana*.

Summary of the *Ramayana*

Dasarata, the king of Ayodhya, had no children. In order to win the favour of the gods so that they will grant him an heir, he sacrificed a horse. While the ceremony was taking place, the gods were having their own meeting in heaven. The gods complained to Brahma, the Lord of Creation, that they were often troubled by the demon Ravana whom they could not destroy. Brahma told them that only a human being could kill Ravana. When Vishnu arrived, the gods promptly asked him to take a human incarnation so that he could kill Ravana. Vishnu agreed to their request by becoming Dasarata's son. Soon after the horse sacrifice, all three of Dasarata's queens became pregnant. Kausalya gave birth to Rama. Kaikeyi gave birth to Bharata, while Sumitra bore the twins Laksamana and Satrughna. Meanwhile, the gods created an army of warrior monkeys to help Rama kill Ravana. Among the legion of monkey warriors were Walin, Sugriva and Hanuman. Time passed and Dasarata's princes grew to become fearless warriors whose valour was unrivaled in their time. The most courageous of them all was Rama who was loved the most by his father as well as by his people.

One day, when Rama was 16 years old, a hermit by the name of Vismamitra came to see King Dasarata. The hermit had come to ask Rama for help to kill some demons who had been attacking his hermitage. Rama agreed to help and went with Laksamana to Viswamitra's sanctuary. After a fierce battle, Rama killed all the monsters.

On their way home, Rama and Laksamana stopped at the palace of King Janaka of Mithila who at that time was holding a contest to choose a husband for his daughter, Sita. Whoever could bend a special large bow would become Sita's husband. Sita had become Janaka's daughter when he found her between the furrows of the soil he was ploughing and adopted her. Many powerful kings and brave knights tried to bend the giant bow but none could even lift it, let alone bend it. No one, that is, except Rama who possessed such extraordinary strength that, with just one movement, he pulled the bow back and broke it into two pieces. So Rama came to be Sita's husband. A grand wedding was held and the whole country rejoiced. For not only was the joyous occasion to celebrate Rama's wedding, but also that of all his brothers. Laksamana married Urmila, Sita's sister. Bharata married Mandawi, King Janaka's niece, while Satrughna married Sruta-Kriti.

Several years passed. Dasarata decided that as he was growing old, the time had come for him to pass his throne to his son. Rama was the eldest and the mightiest of all his sons. So naturally his subjects were happy when he chose Rama to be his successor. Preparations for the coronation of the new king went on day and night. But amidst the festivities, one person—one of Kaikeyi's ladies-in-waiting—was secretly resentful. She wanted Bharata, Kaikeyi's son, to become king. With all the cunning that she could muster, she managed to persuade Kaikeyi to ask that Bharata should become king. The servant reminded Kaikeyi of a promise the king had made long ago to grant her two wishes, after she (Kaikeyi) had cured him from an illness. The lady-in-waiting insisted that Kaikeyi should ask for two things: firstly, that Rama be exiled in the forest for 14 years, and secondly, that Bharata be crowned king.

Finally, Kaikeyi yielded to her lady-in-waiting and made these requests to Dasarata. He was dumbfounded when he heard her demands. But what could he do? A king must fulfil his promises and Dasarata was famous for always keeping his word. The next day, when Rama came to see him, Dasarata was too sad to say anything. Rama was surprised to see his father's sorrow. Kaikeyi told Rama what had happened. With a willing heart, Rama acquiesced to her demands. Thereafter, together with Sita and his brother Laksamana, Rama left Ayodhya and went into exile in the forest.

Gloom descended over the whole country. Dasarata was the saddest of all. He recalled an incident which once happened when he was out hunting a long time ago. During the hunt, he had accidentally killed the son of a blind ascetic. Aggrieved, the blind ascetic had cursed him, saying that Dasarata would one day die from grief over the loss of his own son. In the end, the curse pronounced upon him came true and Dasarata died pining for his son, Rama.

After Dasarata's demise, Bharata and Satrughna, who had been staying with their grandmother at that time, were called home. Upon his arrival in Ayodhya, Bharata was shocked beyond words to find his father dead and Rama exiled to the forest. He rebuked his mother for what she had done and refused to take over the throne. He wanted Rama to be invited back home to Ayodhya and be crowned king. Bharata then left to look for Rama. After several days, he reached the forest where Rama had taken refuge in during his exile.

Leaving his entourage behind, he went on alone to see Rama. Bharata knelt in front of his stepbrother and begged Rama with all his heart to come back to Ayodhya and become its ruler. But no matter how fervently he begged, Rama refused to break his promise to his father that he would live in exile in the forest for 14 years. Bharata then said that he would rule the kingdom for just 14 years, after which, if Rama did not return, he would kill himself by self-immolation.

Rama agreed to Bharata's proposal and advised him to be kind to his mother. With a heavy heart, Bharata returned to Ayodhya. He placed Rama's sandals on the throne to indicate that Rama was the rightful king, and that he, Bharata, was only his proxy.

Rama in the meantime moved to the more remote Dandaka Forest. There he met a community of hermits and became their protector.

In one incident, the demon Wirada tried to kidnap Sita. Rama and Laksamana killed the demon. Again, Rama met the bird Jatayu who promptly became his close companion.

Suparnakha, Ravana's sister, fell in love with Rama, but he did not reciprocate her feelings. Neither did Laksamana. Suparnakha was enraged and vowed to kill Sita. Laksamana cut off Suparnakha's ears and nose. She complained to her brothers Khara and Dusana. They immediately deployed their army of demons and attacked Rama. He defeated them all. Dusana was killed during the battle but Khara managed to escape. Suparnakha's fury was further enraged. She fled to Langka and complained to Ravana about what had happened to her. She also told him how beautiful Sita was and that whoever possessed Sita would rule the world. Ravana decided to kidnap Sita. He sought help from the sorcerer Marica who could transform himself into different animals. Ravana and Marica then set out to kidnap Sita. Marica changed himself into a resplendent golden deer. When Sita saw the deer, she was enchanted by it and asked Rama to catch it. Laksamana warned Rama to be careful as the deer could well be an evil spirit in disguise who wished to harm Rama. Rama chased after the deer. Soon, they heard distant cries. "Sita, Laksamana, Sita, Laksamana!" The voice sounded like Rama.

Sita urged Laksamana to help Rama. Laksamana refused as he was suspicious of the voice he had heard. Surely Rama could capture a deer. Sita, however, persisted and even accused Laksamana of not wanting to help Rama because he wanted her for himself. In the end, Laksamana felt he had no choice but to go to Rama's aid.

The moment he was gone, Ravana, disguised as a hermit, approached Sita and asked her to be his wife. When Sita refused, Ravana assumed his true form and abducted Sita. Sita shouted for help. Jatayu heard her cries and he came to fight Ravana. Defeated, Jatayu fell to the ground. Ravana then took Sita to his palace in Langka. There, he tried to persuade Sita to marry him, and when that failed, coerced her into becoming his wife. Sita refused and swore that Rama would kill him.

When Rama and Laksamana returned, they discovered that Sita was missing. They had no idea whether she was alive or dead. Although they searched everywhere for her, they could not find her. Finally, they found the mortally wounded Jatayu, who before drawing his last breath, told them what had happened. Rama and Laksamana at once started out for Langka. During the journey, they met a headless demon called Kebandha whom they killed. It turned out that Kebandha was actually the son of a deity who, because of a spell cast on him by another deity, had been turned into a headless monster. Kebandha was deeply grateful to Rama and Laksamana because by killing him, they had freed him from this curse. He advised Rama to seek help from Sugriwa, the son of Surya the sun, who had been banished from his kingdom by his brother, Balin.

Finally, they reached the mountain where Sugriwa lived. They straight away made a pact with each other: Rama would help Sugriwa reclaim his kingdom and wife from his brother Balin; and Sugriwa in turn would assist Rama look for Sita. Balin was quickly defeated and Sugriwa reinstated as king of the monkeys. Sugriwa assembled all his monkey subjects and sent them to the four corners of the world to look for Sita.

Hanoman was a renowned monkey warrior. He was, in truth, the nimblest and most fleet-footed son of the wind god. Bearing Rama's ring, Hanoman headed south to look for Sita. There he met Sampati, an older sibling of the bird Jatayu, who told him that Ravana lived on the island of Langka. Hanoman swiftly made his way there. When he reached Ravana's palace, he found a woman being threatened and tormented by Ravana. The woman staunchly refused to submit to Ravana's demands. The woman was none other than Sita.

When Ravana left her side, Hanoman approached her. Sita only believed what Hanoman had to say to her when he showed her Rama's ring. Even then, she refused to go with him because she had sworn never to touch anyone but her husband, and instead gave Hanoman her ring for him to take back to Rama.

To test the enemy's strength, Hanoman challenged all of Ravana's demon warriors in the palace to a fight. Unfortunately, Hanoman was eventually captured and sentenced to be burnt alive. He managed to escape however and created an enormous fire in Ravana's palace. He then returned home to convey news of Sita to Rama.

Ravana eventually heard that Rama was preparing to launch an attack on Langka. His brother, Wibhisana, advised Ravana to return Sita to Rama. But this advice went unheeded. Wibhisana decided to join Rama's side instead. He suggested that Rama ask the sea god for advice. The sea god told him that there was a monkey named Nala, who could help them build a bridge across the sea to Langka. Rama summoned Nala and ordered him to build the bridge. The bridge was completed in just five days.

Soon Rama's army began to surround Ravana's palace. Ravana's second brother, Kumbakarna, did not approve of Ravana's actions but was prepared to fight alongside him. Ravana's son, Indrajit, was the only one not to criticize his father's actions.

A fierce battle ensued. Ravana's brothers and relatives perished, one after another. In the end, Ravana's favorite son, Indrajit, also fell in battle. Ravana had no choice but to cotniue to fight alone. The clash between Rama and Ravana was ferocious; they fought like two savage lions. Rama found it extremely hard to defeat Ravana. He soon realised that no ordinary weapon could kill Ravana. He then used an arrow given to him by the God Indra. The moment Ravana was struck by the arrow, he fell to the ground and died.

Peace was restored to the world. No monsters disturbed the peace and good order of men and the gods. Wibhisana ascended the throne in Langka, and Rama was reunited with Sita. Rejoiced at the turn of events, Rama returned to Ayodhya and was crowned king. Nevertheless, Rama still had doubts about Sita's chastity as she had lived in Ravana's palace. To prove her innocence, Sita walked through a blazing fire. She emerged untouched, proving herself to be a chaste and faithful woman.

Rama ruled for a thousand years. Many of his righteous deeds are recorded in the *Ramayana*. However, he later became influenced by malicious rumour-mongers who continued making insinuations about what might have happened during Sita's stay in Ravana's palace, thus casting aspersions on her chastity. In order to save his own honour, Rama, with a heavy heart, was forced to ask Laksamana to take Sita to a distant place of exile on the other side of the Ganges. There, Sita met Valmiki, the chronicler of the *Ramayana*, and stayed at his house.

Not long after, she gave birth to two sons, Kusa and Lawa. Valmiki taught Rama's two sons to sing many songs, including the *Ramayana*.

One day, Rama held a sacrificial slaughter of a horse (*asmaweda*). Kings, Brahmins and singers, all gathered in the city of Ayodhya. Rama's two sons sang songs about Rama. Upon hearing the songs, Rama was reminded of his wife, Sita, whom he had banished. He sent a messenger to invite Sita and Valmiki to Ayodhya.

Valmiki explained to Rama that in truth Sita had remained as virtuous and chaste as she had always been, and that the two boys who sang at the ceremony were none other than Rama's own sons. But Sita's life was coming to an end: from the earth she came and to the earth she would return. Mother Earth had come to claim Sita. Rama wept, overcome with grief. The world seemed empty. Vishnu consoled Rama and advised him not to be sad, as Rama was himself also an incarnation of Vishnu. Furthermore, Rama would be able to meet Sita in the heaven. Rama and his three brothers then merged and became Vishnu once more. The gods welcomed their return.

And this is how the *Ramayana* ends:

Whoever is childless, will be blessed with a child by reading the *Ramayana*. Reading or listening to the epic can cleanse a person of all sins. A person who memorises it will be blessed with livestock aplenty as well as showered with gold and diamonds. Whoever reads the *Ramayana* will be forever honoured in this life and, together with his descendants, secure a place of distinction in heaven.

It is with this mindset that the *Ramayana* is read in India.

2.1.1 The *Ramayana* Outside India

The story of Rama is also very popular outside India. In Thailand, six of its kings were called Rama and the Thai monarch was considered to be an incarnation of Vishnu. The capital of the ancient Thai kingdom, Ayuthia (or Ayutthaya), also brings to mind the Ayodhya found in the *Ramayana*. In Laos, Rama's story is told in the *Rama Jataka* that was inspired by the *Dasarata Jataka*. The *Rama Jataka* has quite a peculiar storyline. In this story, Rama and Ravana are cousins. In the end, both of them are reconciled and Sita (known as Cantha in this story) is given to Ravana to be his wife. In Champa (now South Vietnam), the story of Rama has become a popular folk epic; all the events described are said to have taken place in Champa (Hari Das B, Vol.11: 20). In Burma, Rama's story is also well-known. And finally, the story of Rama is also the source of *wayang lakon* (traditional plays) in various parts of Southeast Asia, including Thailand, Laos and Indonesia.

2.1.2 The Story of Rama in Indonesia

The story of Rama has long been known in Indonesia. About a thousand years ago, during the reign of King Daksya (910-919 A.D.), bas-reliefs telling the story of the *Ramayana* were carved on the walls of the Loro Jonggrang complex of the Hindu temple in Prambanan, Yogyakarta. Not long afterwards, around 925 A.D., an unnamed poet transcribed the *Ramayana* into Old Javanese, as the *Kakawin Ramayana*. The plot of this *kakawin* is similar to Valmiki's *Ramayana*, but the work is not a translation of the Sanskrit original. Scholars such as Poerbatjaraka and Hooykaas assert that the source of the *Kakawin Ramayana* was a Sanskrit poem entitled *Ravana-vadha* (The Death of Ravana) composed by the poet Bhatti. The *Ravana-vadha* is also called the *Bhattikavya*.[1] Five hundred years later, the *Ramayana* was again the inspiration for the reliefs of the Panataran Hindu temple complex in East Java.

The *Kakawin Ramayana* is a work of art of the highest order and has been translated time and again into relatively newer languages. In the second half of the 18th century, a court poet by the name of Yasadipura I arranged the *Kakawin* into *kawi miring*,[2] a Javanese verse style in *macapat*. Poerbatjaraka considers the *Serat Rama* an important work of Javanese literature and it has also been translated into Balinese and Madurese.

Besides the *Serat Rama*, which is still quite faithful to the original *Kakawin Ramayana*, there are other versions that are very different. One such work is the *Serat Kanda Ning Ringgit Purwa* (*The Book of Kanda Ning Riggit Purwa*), or simply the *Serat Kanda*. It was written after the *Serat Rama* but contains elements that are much older and is often performed in *wayang purwa* (shadow puppetry). The *Serat Kanda* is a uniquely Javanese version of Rama's story that contains Islamic elements, the story of the Pandavas, and Javanese tales. There is also a version of the *Ramayana* called the *Raja Keling* (The Tamil King)[3]; the storyline is almost the same as that in the *Hikayat Melayu*. I will now summarize the *Serat Kanda* and the *Raja Keling*.

2.1.3 *Serat Kanda Ning Ringgit Purwa* (Juynboll, 1911)

The story begins with an argument between Adam and Eve as to who would incarnate as a child.

This is followed by the story of Watu Gunung. After killing Watu Gunung, Vishnu heard a supernatural voice announcing that in another incarnation, his wife would be kidnapped by an avatar of Watu Gunung. Vishnu left his wife Sri and went to meditate in a cave. While meditating, he felt an urge to enter into the earth. So he did and married Dewi Pertiwi, the daughter of Antaboga. Not long after, Pertiwi gave birth to a son named Boma. Vishnu had two children with his first wife, Gunadeva and Gunadewi.

Srigati's wife gave birth to an elephant called Gajendra. Gajendra became king of Champa and wanted to marry Indradi, daughter of the Supreme God, Batara Guru. However, Indradi did not like Gajendra and asked Gautama to kill him.

From here, the plot is almost the same as the *Arjuna Wijaya*. Arjuna Sahasrabahu defeated ten kings and married their consorts. Giling Wesi, the king of Tritusta, had two sons, Manumana and Manumada, and a daughter, Sardi. Princess Sardi married Resi Tama from Langka and gave birth to Sarwa, who became king of Sunggala. Sarwa's chief minister was Citrabaya.

---

1   The general view that the *Kakawin Ramayana* was written by the poet Yugiswara is disputed by Hooykaas (1955) and Poerbatjaraka, (1957: 2-3).
2   *Kawi miring* is a textual style that is intermediate to traditional and modern styles.
3   *Keling*, according to Pigeaud, is the name of a place in the Berantas Delta. But surely there is a connection with the fact that South Indians are referred to as "*Keling*s" in Malay?

We continue with the story of Subana. Subana had two sons, Sumangli and Mangliawan. Sumangli had a daughter, Sukesi, and a son, Prahasta. Mangliawan wanted Vishnu's wife, Sri, so he launched an attack on Vishnu's heavenly realm but was killed by Vishnu and his son, Gunadewa. A supernatural voice told Vishnu that in another incarnation, his wife would be kidnapped by Dasamuka.

King Sarwa fell in love with Sukesi, who was engaged to his son, Bisawarna. Trying to protect herself from Sarwa, Sukesi slapped him ten times. Soon, Sukesi gave birth to a son with ten heads whom she named Dasamuka. This was followed later by the births of two more sons, Kumbakarna and Sarpakanaka. Prince Bisawarna, King Sarwa's son, accused Sukesi of being unfaithful and left the palace to meditate.

Subsequently, another son, Wibusanam, was born to Sukesi. Sumangli and Prahasta wanted to kill King Sarwa for violating his own son's fiancée. Batara Guru sent Narada with a steed for Prince Bisawarna. Dasamuka tried to steal the horse for himself. A fight ensued between Bisawarna and Dasamuka. Their father, King Sarwa, intervened and revealed that they were actually brothers. Dasamuka became dissatisfied with merely being the king of Sunggala. He wanted to rule Langka as well. He launched an attack on Langka but he was unsuccessful. Dasamuka then fled to Bali. He overheard a conversation between Bisawarna and his wife in which he told her about the one part of his body where he was vulnerable. Dasamuka finally succeeded in killing Bisawarna.

Darmayati, the king of Tanjung Pura, had a daughter called Citrawati. Dasamuka asked for her hand in marriage. The dowry was that Dasamuka had to produce the heads of 1,000 *rishi* (holy men). Dasamuka commanded Gemuka to cut off their heads. The *rishis* begged Kertanadi to protect them. Kertanadi was able to fight Gemuka and save the *rishis*. Arjuna Sahasrabahu came to the aid of Gemuka and in turn managed to kill Kertanadi. Arjuna then married Citrawati, the princess of Tanjung Pura. This angered Dasamuka and a fight erupted between Dasamuka and Arjuna. Dasamuka proved to be no match for Arjuna and was killed. In the end, Arjuna himself was killed by Bali, a *rishi* from Argapura.

Finally we come to the story of Rama and Laksamana. Dasamuka forced Dasarata, Rama's father, to give up his queen Lesmanadari to him. Keikayi was enthroned as queen n her place. The story then tells how Rama won Sita in a contest held by Kala. The manuscript ends abruptly with a scene in which Rama and Sita were bathing in a pool together and were suddenly transformed into a pair of monkeys.

2.1.4 *Rama Keling* (Juynboll, 1911: 57)

Van der Tuuk gave the title, *Rama Keling* to this version of the *Ramayana*. According to Brandes, this manuscript is called *Serat Kanda Ning Ringgit Purwa*. Broadly speaking, the story is similar to *Hikayat Sri Rama*. The story begins with Ravana's forefathers, followed by a story about how Dasamuka wanted to attack the sun (because he was too hot); then how he wanted Dasarata's wife, Lesmanadari, for himself. Lesmanadari created a life-like clone of herself. The false Lesmanadari gave Dasamuka a son named Trinetra.

Gutama had a daughter, Anjani, and two sons, Bali and Sugriwa. Maesasura wanted to steal a heavenly nymph but he was foiled by Bali.

Sukmapapa (Rama) and Sukmarasa (Laksamana) returned to the palace, after they had finished studying with Begawan Sayak. The following episodes of the bridal contest held by Rishi Kala, and Dasamuka's kidnapping of Sinta, are similar to that of the *Hikayat Sri Rama.*

Other episodes include the story of how Hanoman was burnt by a red ball (the sun) which he mistook for a fig; the birth of Tunggangan, Hanoman's son; followed by an episode about how Hanoman became Rama's warrior and how he was ordered to leap over to Langka to see Sinta; the burning of Langka; the battle between Rama and Ravana—all of which are identical to episodes in the *Hikayat Sri Rama.*

Sinta had to walk through fire to prove her innocence. In the end, it was revealed that Sinta was actually the daughter of Ravana and Banodari. Laksamana did not want to accept Banodari as his mother. Banodari disappeared. Wibusanam became king of Langka while Sugriwa ruled Agrastina.

At Ciyata's request, Sinta drew a picture of Ravana on her fan. Angered, Rama commanded Laksamana to kill Sinta. Laksamana slayed a deer instead and sent Sinta back to her father, Rishi Kala. Sinta had a son who later went missing. The Rishi created another boy to replace Sinta's lost child. Subsequently, Rama and Sinta reconciled. This manuscript ends with a rebellion led by Anggada who set fire to the entire town, killing all the monkeys there. Rama and Laksamana themselves perished in the fire.

In Javanese literature the various stories of Rama include the *Ramayana Sasak, Rama Tambak* and *Rama Nitis*. The *Ramayana Sasak* is more complete than the other two. It includes the battle between Rama and Ramaparasu, the story of Sahasrabahu, and continues through to the story of Sinta's trial by fire and her reconciliation with Rama. The other two only contain parts of the original epic. The *Rama Tambak* only describes the end of the war in Langka, whereas the *Rama Nitis* focuses on Anggada's rebellion. A unique feature of these Javanese versions of the *Ramayana* is that the story of the Pandavas had been interwoven into them to form one single story.

2.1.5 The *Ramayana* in Malay

The *Ramayana* is known in Malay as the *Hikayat Sri Rama*. There are two different versions of the *Hikayat Sri Rama*. The first version was published by Roorda Van Eysinga in 1843; the second by W. G. Shellabear in 1915. Roorda's version, though not dated, is believed to be the oldest manuscript in Malay. Its plot is close to Valmiki's *Ramayana* even though it contains many episodes not found in Valmiki's version. The original manuscript of the Shellabear version of the *Ramayana* was presented to Archbishop William Laud in 1633 and was preserved in the Bodleian Library, Oxford. Compared to Roorda's version, the Shellabear text bears a strong Islamic influence and deviates substantially from the Valmiki *Ramayana*. The story begins with a young Ravana banished from his homeland, living in exile in Serendib Hill where he spent his days in strict ascetic practice. Moved by Ravana's earnest supplications, the Prophet Adam bestows upon him kingdoms in all four worlds, on the condition that he ruled over them justly. This story is not found in Roorda's version.

According to Dr. A. Zieseniss (1963), both Roorda's and Shellabear's versions originated from the same oral source. Except for the story depicting Ravana's youth which is not found in

Roorda's rendition, the stories found in the two versions generally complement one another. An episode or a story narrated at great length in the Roorda version will sometimes be given a very cursory depiction in the Shellabear version and vice versa. When we combine these two versions, we have an organic narrative with a clear plot. In general, Roorda's version is more detailed until the building of the bridge to Langka; after that, Shellabear's version is the more complete.

Beside the Roorda and Shellabear versions, which are regarded as 'literary' versions, there are two other versions, which are 'folkloric' (or 'rhapsodic') versions. These are the *Cerita Sri Rama* (*The Story of Sri Rama*) published by Maxwell in 1886, and the *Ramayana-Patani* (Winstedt, 1929). Maxwell's *Cerita Sri Rama* is derived from a folk story recited by Mir Hassan, a traditional storyteller from Kampar, Perak. There are changes in the plot and the names of the characters. Sita is known as Sekuntum Bunga Setangkai (Blossom), Hanoman is called Kera Kecil Imam Tergangga (Tiny Topsy-Turvey Monkey of Great Faith), whereas Ravana is known as Buana. The presence of Minangkabau and Arabic influences is also unmistakable. The *Ramayana-Patani*, on the other hand, was originally written for G. M. Laidlaw, an assistant district officer in Kroh, Perak, in 1911. The story contained in this manuscript is incomplete and departs greatly from the story of Rama with which we are familiar, especially in the first part. Winstedt has written an English summary of this Patani version of the *Ramayana*. The *Cerita Sri Rama* has more recently been published by Dewan Bahasa dan Pustaka (Farid Mohd. Onn, 1965).

Below are three summaries: the first of the *Hikayat Sri Rama,* based on Roorda and Shellabear's versions; followed by a summary of Maxwell's manuscript of the *Cerita Sri Rama*; and lastly a summary of the *Ramayana-Patani*.

2.1.6 The *Hikayat Sri Rama*

Emperor Ravana was banished to Serendib Hill, where he practised an extreme form of asceticism which involved hanging upside down by his feet. For twelve long years he meditated in this position. Taking pity on him, God sent the Prophet Adam to ask Ravana what he wanted. Ravana asked for four kingdoms: a kingdom on earth, a kingdom in the spirit world, a kingdom under the ground, and a kingdom in the sea. God granted him his request on condition that Ravana ruled justly and that he did not do anything prohibited by God. In another version, it is said that God also warned him not to meddle with other people's wives and daughters.

In his kingdom in the spirit world, Ravana married Princess Nila Utama and had a son, Indra Jat. When his son reached the age of twelve, he made Indra Jat king of the spirit world. In the underworld, Ravana married Princess Pertiwi Dewi who gave him a son, Patala Maharayan. When Patala Maharayan came of age, he was crowned king of the underworld. In his kingdom in the sea, Ravana married Gangga Maha Dewi and fathered a son, Gangga Maha Suri, who, upon reaching adulthood, was installed as king of the sea. On earth, Ravana built a most magnificent kingdom, Langkapuri. Ravana ruled justly over his domain. Every kingdom in the world paid homage to Ravana. Only four refused to pay court to him, namely: Indrapuri, Biruhasa, Lekor Katakina and Aspaha.

It is told that Berma Raja, Ravana's grandfather, had died in Indrapuri. Upon his death, his eldest son, Badanul, succeeded him to the throne. Badanul in turn was succeeded by Citra-Baha who had three children: a son named Kamba Kama, another called Bibusanam (Vibhishana) and a daughter named Sura Pandaki. Naranda, the younger brother of Jama Mantri, King Badanul's son, became king after Citra-Baha. He was succeeded by Mantri Sakhsah as king.

Maharaja Balikasa, the king of Biruhasa Purwa, made preparations to attack the country of Indrapuri, because his kingdom had once been conquered by Citra-Baha who had also killed Balikasa's father. Balikasa sent an ogre (*raksasa*) with magical powers to Indrapuri. The ogre killed many citizens of Indrapuri and a large number of her ministers. A war eventually broke out between Maharaja Balikasa and Mantri Sakhsa of Indrapuri. News of the war reached Ravana who came and made peace between the two rulers. Ravana then remained in Langkapuri. He gave Jama Mantri the title of Mangkabumi (Prime Minister). Kamba Kama became head of the military. Bibusanam was made chief of the astrologers, members of the literati and clergy of the realm. Barga Singa, Ravana's son, was in charge of gathering intelligence about other kingdoms. (These stories about the young Ravana are only found in the Shellabear version.)

Dasarata Maharaja, a valiant king and warrior in the country of Isafa, had no children. On the advice of a Brahmin, the king performed the religious ritual of *Homam* (making offerings into a consecrated fire). Not long after, his queen, Mandudari, became pregnant. (In the Shellabear version, she became pregnant after swallowing a magic stone from a Brahmin.) Mandudari, who herself was a princess born in magical circumstances in a clump of bamboo, begot Rama and Laksamana. Dasarata also fathered three children with Baliadari, his concubine: Bardan, Citradan and a daughter Kikewi Dewi. (The daughter is not mentioned in Shellabear).

Sri Rama was a very brave and handsome prince, but he was also very mischievous. Because of this, the ministers preferred one of Baliadari's other sons, Baradan or Citradan, to be the next king. Dasarata himself promised on two occasions that he would choose one of Baliadari's sons to succeed him as reward for the years of devotion his concubine had given him.

When Ravana learnt that Dasarata had taken a very beautiful princess as his wife, he wanted her for himself. Ravana then came to see Dasarata and demanded that the princess be given to him. Dasarata agreed to this. News of his decision was immediately conveyed to Mandudari who, upon hearing this, retired to her chamber. Not long after, a princess resembling Mandudari appeared from the chamber. Her name was Mandudaki. Ravana left with Mandudaki. After they had left, the real Mandudari emerged from her chamber and explained what had actually happened. The princess Ravana had taken with him, she revealed, was a model of herself, conjured from the dead cells of her skin (*daki*). Realising that he had not lost his wife after all, Dasarata was overjoyed. Dasarata asked an old woman to smuggle him into Ravana's palace and slept with Mandudaki, thus becoming the biological father of Ravana's child.

In due time, Mandudaki, having fallen pregnant, gave birth to a beautiful princess whose name was Sita Dewi. Fortune-tellers predicted that Sita Dewi's husband would one day kill Ravana. Enraged, Ravana wanted to kill Sita Dewi there and then. Moved by Mandudaki's pleas, he had the girl put in an iron chest and set her adrift on the sea.

One day, Maharesi Kali, king of Darwati Purwa, found the iron chest while meditating by the sea. He rescued Sita Dewi and raised her as his own child. Before long, it became well-known far and wide that Maharesi Kali had a very beautiful daughter. When Sita Dewi reached her twelfth birthday, Maharesi Kali held a contest to choose a suitable husband for her: whoever could lift the magic bow the Maharesi kept in his front yard and was able to shoot a single arrow through forty *lontar* (palm) trees would win Sita Dewi's hand.

A great many high-ranking princes eager to be Sita's husband gathered in Maharesi Kali's kingdom. The only ones who did not come were King Dasarata's sons. Maharesi then went to personally invite them. With considerable reluctance, King Dasarata finally allowed Sri Rama and Laksamana to follow Maharesi Kali back to the kingdom of Darwati Purwa. During the journey, Rama showed to one and all proof of his courage when he defeated and killed the *raksasa* Jagina (referred to in the Shellabear version as Jekin), a rhinoceros and a *naga* (serpent), which had been terrorizing travellers on their journey.

The contest began. Not one of the princes could shoot a single arrow through forty palm trees. Ravana himself only managed to shoot through thirty-eight trees (only according to Roorda's version). Finally, Rama calmly made his way into the arena. With a single arrow, he pierced all forty trees. The princes gathered there were amazed. With that, Rama won Sita Dewi as his wife.

To test Rama's intelligence, Maharesi Kali hid Sita Dewi among the idols in a temple. He told Rama that she had vanished. Rama easily found Sita. During his journey home, four of the disappointed princes ambushed him and try to abduct Sita Dewi. Rama defeated them all.

Preparations were made for Rama's coronation. A hunchback servant encouraged Baliadari to insist that Dasarata fulfill his promise by making one of her sons king. Alas, a promise made by a king can not be broken. Dasarata had no choice but to agree to Baliadari's demands. Rama and Sita, accompanied by Laksamana, then left the kingdom and made their way into the forest to lead a life of contemplation.

While they were wandering in the wilderness, the three met several Maharesis who treated them kindly. Anggasa Deva, Kikukan and Wirata Sakti fed them and invited Sri Rama to stay with them. Rama declined and continued until he reached Indra Pavanam hill. A *raksasa* called Purba Ita tried to kidnap Sita. Rama killed the demon and settled there.

According to the Shellabear version, after defeating the four princes who tried to ambush him, Rama decided not to continue on his journey home because his father had chosen Baradan as his successor. Rama and Sita, together with Laksamana, then entered the forest to find a suitable place in which to meditate. They met a holy man, Maharesi Astana, who informed Laksamana about two strange ponds in the forest. The first pond contained clear water, but anyone who bathed in it would turn into a monkey. The other pond was murky. Rama and Sita bathed in the clear-water pond and instantly turned instantly into monkeys. Fortunately, Laksamana was there to save them. Rama then had Sita's throat massaged and she spat out his sperm. Bayu Bata took the sperm and placed it in Dewi Anjani's open mouth. Dewi Anjani became pregnant and gave birth to Hanoman. Rama then made his residence in a secluded spot in the forest.

Ravana wanted to attack the sun as he felt that it was always disturbing his peace. Upon his return from his futile campaign, he found his city surrounded by, what looked to him, a serpent-like monster. He hacked at the monster, only to realise too late that what he had actually severed was not a serpent but the tongue of his kinsman, Berga Singa. Meanwhile, Sura Pandaki was afraid that her son, Darsa Singa, might be killed by Ravana, so she took him into the forest and told him to take refuge and meditate in a clump of bamboos. Laksamana eventually killed Darsa Singa. Enraged, Sura Pandaki vowed to take her revenge. She transformed herself into a beautiful woman and approached Rama with the intention of kidnapping him. When Rama spurned her advances, she turned her attention to Laksamana but he cut off her nose.

Sura Pandaki's brother, Darkala Sina, attacked Rama, but he too was defeated. Sura Pandaki then urged Ravana to fight Rama and Laksamana. Flanked by two magical *raksasas*, Ravana came to the forest where Rama was meditating. One of the *raksasas* turned himself into a golden deer while the other turned into a silver deer. Sita Dewi was fascinated by the deer and implored Rama to catch them. Rama went to capture them.

Soon, they heard Rama calling for help. Sita insisted that Laksamana leave her and go to Rama. When Laksamana refused, Sita accused him of wanting her for himself should Rama die. The accusation left Laksamana with no other choice. Before he departed, he drew a magical line in the ground with his forefinger to ward off any potential intruder.

After Laksamana left, Ravana approached Sita disguised as a poor Brahmin begging for alms. Sita innocently stepped across the line Laksamana had drawn in order to give alms to the false brahmin. The moment she did, Ravana captured her. The bird Jentayu tried to help Sita but was itself killed by Ravana.

Rama and Laksamana were frantic when they returned and found Sita missing. Rama, collapsed at the very spot where his beloved used to sit and remained unconscious for several days. Rama recovered and the two brothers set out to find Sita.

They first met the bird Jentayu who told them that Ravana had kidnapped Sita. They then met the monkey king Sugriwa who had been driven out of his kingdom by his brother Balya. Rama and Laksamana helped Sugriwa to regain his kingdom. Before he died, Balya asked Rama to look after his wife and two sons, Anggada and Anila. Balya also told Rama that his nephew, Hanoman, could help him reunite with Sita.

Meanwhile, saddened by Rama's departure and the news that he had lost his wife, Rama's mother, Mandudari, was overwhelmed with grief and died (according to Shellabear's version, Dasarata died). Beradan and Citradan went to look for Rama to ask him to return and become the new king. Rama refused but gave them his sandals to take back to Ayodhya as a symbol of his rule.

Sugriwa gathered his monkey troops. None of them dared make the leap across the sea to Langka. Only Hanoman was prepared to take on the task on condition that he was allowed to share a meal of a single leaf with Rama. Rama agreed on the condition that Hanoman first take a bath in the sea. After they had their meal together, Rama gave Hanoman a ring to bring to Sita as a sign that he had really been sent by Rama.

Hanoman disguised himself as a Maharesi and met Sita Dewi in Ravana's palace. In the course of their conversation, Hanoman told Sita about his origins and Sita acknowledged him as her son. Tempted by the many mangoes he found growing in the palace grounds, Hanoman was captured and set on fire. But Hanoman jumped this way and that, causing the fire to spread throughout the city. Hanoman wanted to take Sita back to Rama, but she refused. Firstly, because she did not want to be 'touched' by any other man but Rama; and secondly, she wanted Rama to have the honour of rescuing her.

Meanwhile, the bridge to Langka had almost been finished, despite the efforts of Gangga Mahasura, Ravana's son, to destroy it. Hanoman had easily disposed of the fishes and crabs Masura sent to undermine the bridge. Ravana was becoming anxious and conferred with his brothers and ministers how best to prepare against Rama's imminent attack. Bibusanam, the elderly minister, suggested that Sita be returned to Rama.

This made Ravana so furious he wanted to kill Bibusanam. To save himself, Bibusanam fled and surrendered himself to Rama. Ravana's sons, Indra Jat and Kumbakarna, also advised their father to return Sita. But Ravana refused. Finally, the war began. Ravana's sons perished in battle, one after the other. First, Buta Bisa fell; then Patala Maharayan, Indra Jat, and finally, Mula Patani. After that, Ravana took to the battlefield. Following a fierce exchange of arrows, Ravana was defeated. The war between Rama and Ravana was over.

Rama entered the city of Langkapuri. Afraid that his wife's honour may have been tainted by Ravana, Rama refused to take Sita back. Sita proved her chastity by throwing herself into a raging bonfire and emerging from it unscathed. In the end, Rama and Sita were reunited. Many great princes presented themselves before Rama once he had returned to Langkapuri. So did Rama's brothers, Beradan and Citradan.

Maharesi Kala also came and told Rama the story of Sita's true parentage. Sita learned that Mandudaki was her mother, and Ravana her father. Soon after, Rama founded a new city on top of a hill, Durja Pura Negara.

After taking a special potion made by Maharesi Kala, Sita became pregnant. During her pregnancy, Rama's sister Kikewi Dewi came to visit Sita and asked her to draw an image of Ravana on a fan. Rama found the fan. Kikewi lied, saying that Sita had drawn the picture and taken it to bed with her. Rama was angry and ordered Sita to leave the palace. Sita went back to Maharesi Kala's home. Before she departed, Sita swore that whoever told the lie about her, would be struck dumb for ever more. And, if she were innocent, all the animals in the land would mourn for her after she left the kindom.

In Maharesi Kala's home, Sita gave birth to a son, Tilawi (Shellabear: Lawa). One day, Maharesi Kala took the boy for a walk. Tilawi became lost but managed to find his way home to his mother. The maharesi was afraid the boy had gone and made a spell over some *lalang* grass. In an instant, a boy who looked exactly like Tilawi appeared. The boy was named Kusa (Grass). Tilawi and Kusa grew up to be brave and strong young men. They killed many *raksasas*.

After some time, Rama realised he had wronged Sita and begged her to come back to him. Upon her return, the animals began to make their various noises again. Kikewi Dewi also asked Sita to forgive her. Sita's son, Tilawi, married Princess Indra Kusuma Dewi, Indra Jat's daughter, and became the king of Durja Pura. Kusa, in the meantime, married Gangga Surani Dewi, daughter of Gangga Mahasura, and ruled Langkapuri.

After a number of years, Rama founded a city at the site of a hermitage and called it Ayodhya Pura Negara. Finally, after living forty years happily with Sita, Sri Rama left this mortal world for a world everlasting.

This is the story of the *Hikayat Sri Rama*, according to Roorda and Shellabear.

2.1.7 The Story Of Sri Rama

This story was told by Mir Hassan (from Kampar, Perak) and published by Maxwell (*JSBRAS* June, 1886).

Sri Rama, the king of Tanjung Bunga, had been married to Princess Sekuntum Bunga Setangkai for three years, but they had no children. Day and night the thought of him being childless constantly disturbed him, making him seethe with fury. One night, he sounded the sacred drum (*tabuh larangan*). The Temenggung and all the other high-ranking court officials in the kingdom quickly assembled. Sri Rama announced to his subjects that he was calling his brother Laksamana, who was a shaman (*pawang*). Laksamana arrived and predicted that a son would be born to Sri Rama. But before that could happen, Sri Rama had to build seven boats and go on a voyage. The one thing he must not do was to bathe in a crystal-clear pond which he would find at the top of a mountain.

Sri Rama and his princess went on a cruise at sea. But they forgot Laksamana's warning and bathed in the pool of clear water. The moment they did, they turned into monkeys. Laksamana arrived and quickly immersed them into another pool—one filled with murky water, and they reverted to their human form. Not long after their cruise, Sri Rama's wife became pregnant. When the pregnancy reached its full term, the child they had desperately longed for was finally born. Their newborn son was a monkey. Rama was dumbfounded. The midwife thus named the baby monkey, Kera Kecil Imam Tengganga (The Tiny Topsy-Turvey Monkey of Great Faith).

Kera Kecil grew quickly. In just seven days, he could already walk to the audience hall and in 44 days, he could run from one end of the kingdom to the other. But Rama was still unhappy. He was embarrassed to have a monkey for a child. Kera Kecil was taken to the middle of the forest and left there. At first the little monkey was happy to have the freedom of exploring the massive forest. But he soon became bored and decided to venture outside the forest. He arrived in Syah Noman's country. (In this story, all of Hanoman's adventures are given to Kera Kecil).

Syah Noman, who knew Kera Kecil's background, invited the monkey to live with him. But after he discovered that Kera Kecil ate so much food—44 baskets of green leaves in just one meal—Syah Noman was no longer willing to feed Kera Kecil and asked him to go to Gunung Inggil Beringgil, where he would find many types of fruit. Kera Kecil could eat as much as he wished, on one condition: he must not eat any red fruit.

Kera Kecil did not heed Syah Noman's warning and tried to eat the red fruit, which turned out to be the sun itself. Due to the extreme heat, Kera Kecil collapsed in Bandar Tahwil. Fortunately, Princess Renik Jintan, daughter of Syah Kobad, the king of Bandar Tahwil, felt sorry for him and looked after him. Not long after, Syah Noman set out to search for Kera Kecil. The sun told him what had happened and told Syah Noman that the monkey was being treated in Bandar Tahwil. Syah Noman took Kera Kecil and made him king of all the monkeys in Antah Berantah forest.

Raja Duwana from the island of Kaca Puri heard of Princess Sekuntum Bunga Setangkai's beauty and fell in love with her. With his extraordinary powers, he flew to Tanjung Bunga and turned himself into a golden goat. The princess wanted the golden goat. Rama and his subjects chased the goat. When it entered the forest, Rama continued the chase.

Night fell. Rama had still not returned. Meanwhile, Duwana approached the princess. After an exchange of poems, Duwana took the princess back to Kaca Puri. However, it became clear that the princess was his own daughter who was previously thought to have been lost.

When he returned to the palace, Sri Rama was shocked to find the princess gone. He immediately informed Laksamana. Laksamana discovered that the king of Kaca Puri had kidnapped the princess. The two brothers then left together to look for the princess. Along the way, they met Kera Kecil in the forest of Antah Berantah. The monkey king was willing to look for the princess if he was allowed to eat a leaf with Rama. Rama decreed that if Kera Kecil could successfully bring the princess home, Rama would accept him as his own son and take him home to Tanjung Bunga.

After several failed attempts, Kera Kecil finally managed to leap across to Kaca Puri with the help of a genie. When he found the princess, she admitted that Raja Duwana did wish to marry her at first. But when he realised that she was his daughter, he wanted to send her home but delayed this to test Sri Rama's loyalty.

Princess Sekuntum Bunga Setangkai wanted to get King Duwana's permission first before leaving but Kera Kecil simply took his mother away by force back to Tanjung Bunga. King Duwana chased after them and a fight started between him and Kera Kecil. King Duwana was, however, no match for Kera Kecil and admitted defeat. He soon returned to Kaca Puri.

Sri Rama accepted Kera Kecil as his son. Soon after, the young man asked his father to seek Princess Renik Jintan's hand in marriage for him. Syah Kobad was afraid to reject the proposal and comforted himself with the thought that it must have been his fate to have a monkey for a son-in-law. And so Kera Kecil married Princess Renik Jintan. Every night, Kera Kecil shed his monkey skin. One night, the princess asked her old lady-in-waiting to burn Kera Kecil's monkey skin. After that, Kera Kecil lived as a man, with the name of Mambang Bungsu. After some time, Mambang Bungsu was crowned as king of the realm.

Raja Jin also came to propose to Princess Renik Jintan. But since the princess was now the wife of his friend, Kera Kecil (Mambang Bungsu), the king of genies returned home. Thereafter, Mambang Bungsu continued to rule the kingdom of Bandar Tahwil in peace.

2.1.8 The Patani *Ramayana*

Tuk Mahasiku was 128 years old. To atone for his sins, he meditated in a hole at the top of a tree. One day, a bird asked its mother why Tuk Mahasiku was meditating. The mother replied that the old man was doing penance. It added that it would be impossible for the old man to eradicate his sins as he had no children to pray for him. Tuk Mahasiku overheard this conversation and immediately decided to marry. But no princess was willing to become his wife. And so, Tuk Mahasiku created a princess from sandalwood and called her Princess Cendana (Sandalwood). He took her as his wife. The couple was blessed with a child. Tuk Mahasiku went away again to meditate. Before departing, he gave his wife a magic flower. With this flower, Princess Cendana would be able to summon her husband. After Tuk Mahasiku left, Princess Cendana became lonely and asked her magic flower to help her. The Sun God appeared, and together they produced a son. Not long after, the princess summoned the Moon God and conceived another child. When she met the Monkey King, she bore a child with him too. Tuk Mahasiku soon heard about his wife's infidelity and turned her back into sandalwood. He also turned her illegitimate children into monkeys although they were later allowed to take on human form once again. The Sun God's son was named Maharaja Bali; the Moon God's son was named Sri Gua while the son of the Monkey King was given the name Maharaja Bilok.

Forty-nine princesses lived in the country of Selimbah Seladang. The eldest was called Bisnu while the youngest was Hulubalang Bisnu. One day, all the princes were swallowed by a dragon. But Maharaja Bali and Sri Gua managed to save them.

Buta Lohok of Langgapuri had four sons – Sri Maharaja in the furthest corner of the sky; Sri Maharaja, the husband of Princess Mutu Giri; Pedang Wana and Buta Anatok. Buta Anatok married Princess Kelopak Betung and had two children, Sri Acak and Pak Samat.

Sri Acak fell in love with Princess Mutu Giri, his uncle's wife. His uncle was willing to surrender Princess Mutu Giri to his nephew, but the young man first had to study the magic arts under the god Bisnu. And so Sri Acak went up to the celestial world, where he married a nymph. Bisnu wrote a *mantra* on Sri Acak's index finger. With this mantra, Sri Acak killed all the gods who had given him trouble in the past. Bisnu became worried that Sri Acak would use the mantra to kill all the princes in the world, so he ordered his warriors to cut off Sri Acak's index finger.

Sri Acak returned to see Bisnu. That night, he dreamt that he was embracing a beautiful princess and ejaculated in his sleep. Bisnu kept the sperm. Forty days later, a princess was born from this sperm. Bisnu turned the baby into a flower and set it adrift in a river. The flower changed into a grasshopper. The grasshopper was eaten by a frog.

One day, the frog found itself pursued by a snake. Bisnu saved the frog. This angered the snake which wanted to take revenge on Bisnu and poisoned the milk he was about to drink. The frog, however, knew about the snake's plan and drank the poisoned milk in order to save Bisnu. The frog died. Bisnu cut the frog's stomach open. There he found a beautiful baby girl. Bisnu took the baby and brought her up well. When she turned 15, Bisnu named her Mandum Daki and organised a competition to find a suitable husband for her.

Sri Maharaja suggested that Sri Acak should ask for Mandum Daki's hand. On the way to Mandum Daki, Sri Acak married the daughter of King Markum Berhad. Mahasiku crowned Sri Acak and named him Maharaja Wana. Mahasiku also told Sri Acak (Maharaja Wana) to visit his father, Maharaja Bali. But Wana refused. Hulubalang Sri Gua kidnapped Mandum Daki and took her to Maharaja Bali. This led to a battle between Maharaja Wana and Maharaja Bali. Maharaja Wana was captured and imprisoned. Mahasiku arrived and made peace between Maharaja Wana and Maharaja Bali. The princess was returned to Maharaja Wana.

Princess Mandum Daki gave birth to a baby girl but the baby was said to be cursed and was thrown into the river. A dragon saved her and placed her into a frangipani flower in Mahasiku's garden. Mahasiku found her, named her Princess Seroja and brought her up. One night, Hulubalang dreamed about Princess Seroja and ejaculated. Seven months later, a baby was born from his sperm. Due to his fear of Bisnu, he disposed of the baby but the child was later rescued by Mahasiku who named him Serawi. When Serawi reached adulthood, he was discovered flirting with Princess Seroja and banished to a country ruled by an ogre. After killing Maharaja Burung, Serawi married the ogre's daughter.

Mahasiku renamed Princess Seroja 'Siti Dewi'. Another bridal competition was held. Serawi won the princess. He was given the name Sri Rama; his companion was called Laksamana.

The rest of the tale is very similar to *Hikayat Sri Rama*. Siti Dewi was kidnapped by Maharaja Wana. Sri Rama and Laksamana did all they could to get her back. They were helped by Hanoman, Rama's son. The story ends with the reunion of Siti Dewi and Rama. Bibbusanam was crowned king and replaced Maharaja Wana, while Lela Anggota was made the Crown Prince. Finally, Rama made the decision to return to his own kingdom.

2.1.9 Other Versions

We have discussed the best-known versions of the *Ramayana*, but there are lesser-known ones. One of these is the *Hikayat Maharaja Rawana,* which is kept in a library in Berlin, the Preussische Staatsbibliothek (Overbeck, 1933). This manuscript is undated and was copied from other manuscripts by someone who was not fluent in Malay, which has resulted in the numerous errors in the manuscript. Here and there are Javanese words such as *anom, likur, ilat, siwalan, ratu mas, raden* and others. The spelling is influenced by Minangkabau, thus the word "beri" is spelt as "bari". The story is similar to *Hikayat Sri Rama*. But the hikayat ends strangely with the rebellion of Anggada, Maharaja Bali's son, who was upset by what he considered Rama's neglect of him. No one could defeat Anggada. In the end, Maharaja Bali had to be brought back to life in order to restore peace. Anggada then returned to Likur to rule there. Jangga Pulawa, Rama's son, occasionally visited his father.

Winstedt and E.C.G. Barrett have both discussed versions of the *Ramayana* that have not yet been published (Winstedt, 1944a; Barrett, 1963). The version discussed by Winstedt, the Raffles 22 manuscript, is similar to the manuscript discussed by Barrett, the original Wilkinson manuscript. Both begin with the tale of Si Rancak. The Raffles 22 version is in poor condition, while the Wilkinson version has been much better preserved. Both provide a clearer understanding of Ravana's early life.

One day, Si Rancak saw a very beautiful princess. When he tried to capture her, she vanished. Si Rancak realised that the princess was actually an incarnation of Mahabisnu. Angrily, he began a period of meditation in order to earn magic powers from Dewata Mulia so that he could fight Mahabisnu. When he returned to the celestial world, Mahabisnu related this incident to Paratusura (one of Siwa's names), who also wished to see Mahabisnu in his incarnation as a beautiful princess. Mahabisnu then changed himself once more into the princess and danced in front of Paratusura. Paratusura felt so much desire for the princess that he ejaculated. Raja Bayu placed the sperm in the mouth of Dewi Anjani who had been meditating for a thousand years.

Si Rancak teased the wives of Begawan Bisparupan. Mahabisu struck Si Rancak so hard that the seven levels of heaven fell to earth. Then Mahabisnu had a meeting with Batara Guru, the gods and other celestial beings about Si Rancak's prayer for magic powers. Mahabisnu and Kisna Dewa decided to strengthen themselves through meditation so they could fight Si Rancak.

Acccording to another story, Maharaja Bramaraja had seven sons. The second son was a warrior named Citrabaha. Maharaja Bramaraja sent Citrabaha to attack a city ruled by an ogre Dati Kuaca. Citrabaha killed the ogre and married the ogre's daughter, Raksagandi. After a pregnancy that lasted 100 years, the ogre princess gave birth to a massive baby, Rawana (the incarnation of Si Rancak). By the time he was 12, Rawana had developed the evil habit of killing his playmates. His grandmother was angered by his behaviour and ordered that Rawana be banished to Serendib Hill.

Thereafter the story develops in a similar way to Shellabear's version of *Hikayat Sri Rama*.

The Raffles manuscript is perhaps older than the Roorda and Shellabear versions. It is often used as a reference to correct inaccuracies in those two versions. Furthermore, the Raffles manuscript also contains stories of Vishnu's experience in his incarnation as Rama that are not found in Shellabear's version.

2.1.10 Other Manuscript Versions of the *Ramayana*

According to Achadiati Ikram who has examined 17 manuscripts of the *Hikayat Sri Rama*, there are four separate rescensions of the hikayat (Achadiati Ikram, 1978: 91-105). Version I begins with the story of Dasarata founding a state; version II starts with the origins of Ravana; version III with banishment of Ravana to Serindib Hill, while version IV starts with a scene that is usually to be found near the end of the story, when Hanoman leaves for Indrakila mountain. Besides these four versions, there are two other manuscripts that begin with the story of Si Rancak as discussed above, the Wilkinson and Raffles 22 versions. These two manuscripts are bundled together by Achidiati Ikram into a mixed version that is close to version I.

Generally, there are no major differences between one manuscript and the next with regard to the ending of the story. An exception is to be found in one manuscript that is kept in the library of the Central Museum, the *Serat Kanda* (Bat. Gen. 209); it has been embellished with various Javanese stories. Vishnu is incarnated as Arjuna Vijaya, while Dewi Sri is portrayed as Dewi Citrawati. Strangely, Ravana also fights with Dasamuka in this story. Another unusual characteristic of this manuscript is the presence of traditional clown figures such as Semar and Nurugareng. The ending suggests that Rama considered himself very advanced in age and wished to return to the celestial realm by death through self-immolation. Many others were willing to support him or to die together with him but Sita requested a delay of three days. Rama was angry and became suspicious of Sita's faithfulness. Batara Guru came down and took Sita. No one dared stand in their way. Rama ascended the *pancaka* funeral pyre and returned to his celestial abode.

2.1.11 Origins of the *Hikayat Sri Rama*

The Rama stories found in the Archipelago contain similar central themes, but there are also some different elements, especially in the relationships among the primary characters. Where do these differences come from? Following the archaeological work done at Candi Prambanan and the uncovering of relief sculptures showing different episodes from those at Candi Penataran, scholars have attempted to explain these differences in a more theoretical manner. Among the theories to be considered are those of Juynboll, Rassers, W. F. Stutterheim and A. Zieseniss.

Juynboll argues that the Rama stories came to Indonesia along two different routes. The Valmiki *Ramayana* came first and was rewritten as the *Kakawin Ramayana*. The *Serat Rama Jasadipura* also used the Valmiki version as its source, as did the Balinese shadow plays. Several centuries later the story of Rama that had been popular in South India arrived in Indonesia. That these stories were indeed well-loved could be surmised from names of characters such as Parwadam,

Bibusanam, Beradan, Citradan and others. These stories first arrived in Malaya, and were then brought to Java where they inspired the *Raja Keling* and Rama shadow plays[4] (Juynboll, 1902: 546).

Rassers believed that the *Hikayat Sri Rama* was actually a collection of stories of Pandji (a legendary prince from East Java), but which borrowed the names of the characters from Indian epics (Rassers, 1922: 265).

W. Stutterheim (1925) disagreed with both Rassers and Juynboll. Stutterheim noted that differences already existed in India among the various accounts of Rama's life. The *Hikayat Sri Rama* is the product of these different influences, and of other oral stories which suited the style of Indonesian storytelling.

Further, the Bengali scholar, Rai Saheb Dineschandra Sen, also agreed that these variations were already present in India. The differences emerged because the *Ramayana* was a blend of three different stories which subsequently had a life of its own. The three stories are as follows:

(1) The story of Rama leaving the palace with his brother Laksamana and sister Sita due to a power struggle. This story is found in Jataka stories of northern India;
(2) The story of a devout Ravana who won power and extraordinary strength by practising asceticism;
(3) The story of Hanoman which arose from the ancient practice of monkey worship in India which still exists to this day.

A Rama story consisting of three parts emerged from a combination of these three stories:

(1) Rama was close to being crowned king but was banished by a usurper. He was accompanied by his queen Sita (who was not his sister).
(2) During their wanderings in the forest, his wife was kidnapped by the ogre Ravana.
(3) Rama succeeded in rescuing Sita but only after getting help from the monkey king Sugriva, and especially from his general, Hanoman.

In order to produce a single story on the basis of these three independent stories, it is vital to create relationship among the main characters. As there was no link among the three stories in the beginning, each author determined his own structure or plot, and thus there emerged different versions of Rama's story.

The relationship among the three characters can be illustrated through the following diagram.

---

4   Singaralevu (1968), a lecturer in the Universiti of Malaya, studied the origins of the *Hikayat Sri Rama*. He maintained that both the *Hikayat Sri Rama* and the *Romakian* are based on popular Indian Rama stories. This story had been narrated by a Tamil priest who was not only conversant with the Tamil *Kamparamayan* but was also familiar with Valmiki's *Ramayana* and other versions of Rama stories. Singaralevu also pointed to the Tamil form of the characters' names. *Am* is the neutral singular suffix while *an* is the masculine singular suffix.

THE INDIAN EPICS AND THE WAYANG IN MALAY LITERATURE

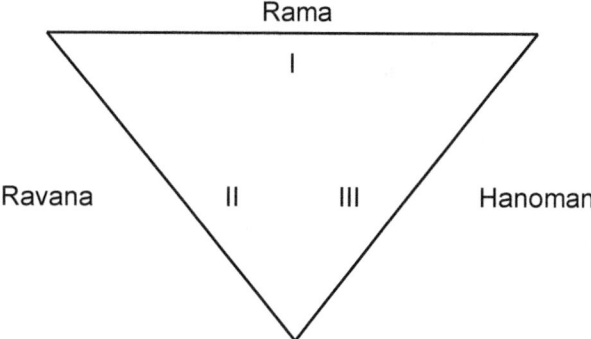

The structure of the Rama story can connect the three characters in the following ways:

I and II
II and III
I and III

In the beginning, it was most likely that the connection among the three characters was done in various ways. But two particular ways that became popular and before long two sets of stories that encompassed all the other variations of the Rama story soon emerged. We can refer to the two ways as A and B.

The relationship between I and II is as follows:

A. Surpanakha, Ravana's sister, fell in love with Laksamana, Rama's brother. She was spurned. To take revenge, Ravana kidnapped Sita, Rama's queen, King Janaka's daughter.

B. The *Hikayat Sri Rama* and *Rama Keling* connect the characters in the following way: Ravana wants to have Mandudari, Rama's mother, and instead obtains a woman who bears an exact resemblance to her. Rama's father seduces the pseudo-Mandudari and becomes the father of Mandudari's baby girl, Sita. Thus, when Rama later marries Sita, he was actually marrying his own sister.

The relationship between I and III:

A. Rama helped the monkey king Sugriva who later directed his general Hanoman to assist Rama.

B. Hanoman is the son of Rama and Anjani, Sugriva's sister.

The relationship between II and III:

A. There is no relationship between Hanoman and Ravana.

B. Hanoman had a son, Hanoman Tunggal, who was raised by Gangga Mahasura, Ravana's son.

The connection between the characters found in both streams of the Rama story can be structured in the above ways. The connections in version B are older but less logical.

On this basis, the Rama stories that belong to A are:

(a) *The Ramayana* by Valmiki
(b) *Kakawin Ramayana*
(c) Stories depicted on the temple reliefs of Candi Panataran in East Java
(d) *Serat Rama* by Jasadipura I

Those that belong to B are:

(a) Popular Rama stories in India
(b) *Hikayat Sri Rama*
(c) Stories depicted on the temple reliefs of Candi Prambanan, Central Java
(d) *Serat Kanda Ning Ringgit Purwa* (wayang stories)
(e) *Serat Rama Keling* in Java and Madura

Besides the different relationships between the characters, there are also differences among the various versions of Rama's tale.

1. Sita is considered to be Rama's sister in the Malay version, the *Serat Rama Keling*, and the wayang stories of Yogyakarta. In this respect, the Malay version matches the *Jataka*.

2. The *Serat Rama, Hikayat Sri Rama*, as well as *Jain Ramayana* (written by Hemcandra Acarya, 1089-1173) begin with the story of Ravana. Javanese wayang stories start with the *Arjuna-Sasra-Bahu* cycle that tells the story of Ravana's adventures before he met Rama, whereas the Malay version puts much more stress on the superpowers Ravana acquired through asceticism.

3. The reason Rama gave for leaving the palace varies according to the different texts. In the Jataka, he left home on the advice of his father who was worried that Rama and Laksamana might possibly suffer as a result of Kaikeyi's jealousy. According to Valmiki and the *Serat Rama* of Jasadipura I, Rama was banished from the kingdom at the request of Bharata's mother. In the Malay version, Rama is said to have left the palace by his own free will, after it became clear that Bharata was going to be crowned king, whereas in Javanese wayang stories, Rama's departure was the result of false accusations against him by Bharata's mother.

4. In the Malay version and Javanese wayang stories, Hanoman had a son, Tunggal, who was raised by Ravana's son. Tunggal did not meet his father until he was an adult.

5. In several Bengali versions, Rama had a sister from a different mother, Kukua. After Sita returned from Ravana's dungeon, Kukua persuaded Sita to draw Ravana on a fan. When Sita was asleep, Kukua reported to Rama about the fan. This incident is not found in Version A. But in the Malay version, Kikewi Dewi was the mastermind of the evil plot to discredit Sita. Banished from the palace, Sita went to take refuge with Kala, and this was where she gave birth to Tabalavi. She later adopted a boy she named Gusi.

In the modern Javanese version, Rama became suspicious about Sita's fidelity during her stay at Ravana's palace. Sita was ashamed and wanted to set herself on fire. She entered the pyre but the fire could not burn her, and the gods came down from heaven to assert her innocence.

The Indian version of the *Ramayana* narrates the episode in a poem. In the poem, Rama was so suspicious of Sita that he sent her away a second time. In Valmiki's ashram, Sita gave birth to two sons, Kusa and Lava.

6. The *Jain-Ramayana* tells the love story of Laksamana and Princess Vanamala. Perhaps this is the source for the story in Yogyakarta wayang in which the monkey, Jambawan (in the form of Laksamana) went to meet a beautiful princess.

7. In Yogyakarta, a wayang story tells that Antraka Wulan, wife of Branta (Bharata) did not love her husband. But she was willing to love him if he could solve a difficult riddle. Laksamana helped Bharata find the solution and Bharata won the love of Antraka Wulan. The *Hikayat Sri Rama* tells that Sandar Dewi hated her husband. Rama sought help from Hanoman who was immediately attracted to Sandar Dewi and, taking on the form of Tabalavi, made love to her.

The above points are the view of W. F. Stutterheim as summarised by J. Kats. These views are supported by A. Zieseniss (Zieseniss, 1963). According to Zieseniss, all these differences can also be found in India, for example in the *Padmapurana* and the *Jaina Ramayana*. There are original elements but they are not significant and do not detract from the further characteristics of the Hindu narrative. Further, Zieseniss suggests that *Hikayat Sri Rama* was a folk tale that reached Indonesia in different forms by oral transmission from different parts of India, especially the eastern and western parts. Once in Indonesia, the basic story combined with other elements to become one with a unified plot.

Santosh N. Desai also agrees that these differences were already present in India. He argues that in India the stories can be divided into two groups, the Valmiki group and the non-Valmiki group (Santosh N. Desai, 1979: 13-15). The Valmiki group, found in northern India, deals with the life of Rama as a prince of Ayodya and his exile, while the non-Valmiki group focuses on the *raksasa*s, especially Ravana, and their war against the Wanaras (monkeys). Valmiki combined these two groups into a unified literary work that became known as the *Ramayana*. In his composition, Valmiki did not include all the aspects of the story; those aspects of the story which contradicted Hindu teachings were omitted. That explains why there are many versions of Rama's story in India. Moreover, Santosh N. Desai adds that the Valmiki group particularly exalts Rama as a just ruler.

To be such a ruler, the individual has to be a person of excellent qualities and observe an exemplary lifestyle. He must have experienced sorrow, suffering, and tests of inner strength, but still retain his convictions and integrity. In contrast, the non-Valmiki group focuses on Ravana more prominently and regards him as a heroic warrior. His knowledge and powers are also much admired.

2.1.12 The status of *Rama* in Southeast Asia

In the literature of Southeast Asia, Ravana occupies a higher status than he commonly does in India. *Ramakirti,* the Thai story of Rama, insists that Ravana really loved Sita. Because of his love for Sita, he is prepared to sacrifice his family, kingdom and wealth, and finally, even his own life. Such is the power of love. In Malay literature, we find some texts that begin with the tale of Ravana, and there is even story entitled the *Hikayat Maharaja Rawana.*

In the *Hikayat Sri Rama,* Rama is depicted as being the great-grandson of Adam, with the power of invincibility—no weapon could injure him. Besides that, Rama was portrayed as a child who was mischievous, poor, wretched and incapable of protecting his one and only wife. He was also not a valiant prince. He fainted when he heard that Sita had been kidnapped. He also fainted when he heard rumours spread by Ravana that Sita had died. He was even ready to serve as a general in Ravana's army on the condition that Ravana did not take his wife away.

According to H. Overbeck, the real hero in Malay literature is Laksamana and not Rama (Overbeck, 1938: 292-333). Rama is weak and gives up too easily. On the other hand, Laksamana is a courageous warrior and always rescues his brother when he faces difficulties. In folk romances, Laksamana is even depicted as a knowledgeable shaman. And that could be the reason why, during the Malaka Sultanate, Laksamana was the title given to a naval commander, while Sri Rama was the nickname given to a person who looks after elephants who is always drunk. Hang Tuah, the true Malay warrior, was also awarded with the title "Laksamana" by the Sultan of Malaka.

2.2 The *Mahabharata*

The *Mahabharata* is actually the history of the Bharata race, told in 24,000 verses. But with the passage of time, all sorts of folktales have been included, such as myths about Vishnu, Siva, and the Brahmin caste. Other added material includes philosophy, the Brahmanic code of law, didactic folktales and sacred verses, all of which resulted in the text becoming an enormous literary work. It is not just an ordinary epic; it has become a major Hindu sacred text—a sacred text which outlines the Hindu way of life, the Hindu social and political order, as well as Hindu culture and way of thinking. So it not surprising to hear Hindu scholars say "Everything that can be found in India, can be found in the *Mahabharata*".

The *Mahabharata* is also regarded as the fifth Veda, but one that can be read by anyone, even women and the members of the lowest caste in Hindu society (*sudras*). Women and *sudras* are forbidden to read the other Vedas. As a result of this opportunity, there are many uneducated Hindus who have learned abour their own culture from the *Mahabharata*. Not only that, the *Mahabharata* has become a book of *dharmasastra* or ethical and social instruction, whether one be a king, warrior, brahmin or a member of another caste. An understanding of *dharma*, righteous social behaviour, is strongly emphasized. Before the great war begins, Arjuna is worried and reluctant to fight against his teacher, uncles and cousins in the impending battle. In the well-known poem, the *Bhagavadgita*, Krisna explains that the duty of a warrior is to fight. A person who fulfills his duty is not only sinless, but in fact earns merit from God. On the other hand, a warrior who is cowardly and does not dare kill his enemy in battle is considered to have committed a sin. Krisna adds that the spirit (*atma*) cannot be destroyed and pervades the whole universe.

As a person sheds shabby clothing and dons new attire, the spirit casts off the old physical body and moves into a newer one. "Each birth will meet its death and each death means rebirth. If something cannot be avoided, why are you sad?" Krisna asks Arjuna. Finally, Krisna urges Arjuna to free himself from both joy and sorrow. "A person who can detach himself from all desire and wanders without needs, without thinking of reaping profit for himself, will attain peace in his soul."

According to tradition, the composition and arrangement of the *Mahabharata* is attributed to the poet Vyasa. After the epic was completed, Vyasa taught it to his son, Suka, and his students. It is estimated that the *Mahabharata* finally reached its present form in the 15th century C. E.

Scholars who have studied the epic have presented many theories regarding the *Mahabharata*. Some believe that the epic has a historical foundation and tells the story of splendid characters and of wars that claimed a great many lives. Others believe that the *Mahabharata* is a symbolic poem and portrays the battle between day and night. Still other scholars state that the epic is a battle between two opposites—*dharma* and *a-dharma*, good and bad, justice and evil—in which the ultimate victory belongs to the good side.

The *Mahabharata* has also been a source of inspiration for Sanskrit poets. In the sixth century, Bharavi composed the poem *Kiratarjuna* which recounted how Arjuna meditated in order to obtain a magic weapon. The stories of Nala, Damayanti and Savitri, are among the *Mahabharata* episodes which have often been rewritten by the greatest poets.

The *Mahabharata* had also been translated into the regional languages of India. In the tenth century, the epic was translated into Tamil and given the title *Perundevanar*. In the eleventh century, translations were made into Telugu. For a thousand years, the *Mahabharata* has been continuously rewritten. During this time, almost all the Indian languages have developed their own version of the *Mahabharata*.

Below is summary of the *Mahabharata* based on P. Thomas (1973, 49-65).

A Summary of the Mahabharata

Syantanu, the king of Hastinapura (Delhi), was out hunting when he met a very attractive woman by a river. He married her and promised not to ever criticize any of her actions. In due time, she gave birth to various children but each time, she set the baby adrift in the river. When she was about to do this to her eighth baby, Syantanu stopped her. His wife then explained that the other seven babies had been "liberated" but this eighth one had been cursed by a holy man (*rishi*) to live as a human being. She asked Syantanu to raise the baby properly but explained that she could no longer stay with him. Once she had uttered those words, she vanished. And the baby was none other than the mighty Bhisma.

On another occasion, Syantanu was also out hunting again. This time he met Satyavati, the daughter of the king of fishermen. The fisherman was willing to give his daughter to Syantanu if Syantanu promised to crown Satyavati's son as king in due course. Syantanu, however, loved Bhisma very much and this condition greatly saddened him. Bhisma was aware of Syantanu's dilemma and brought Satyavati to his father, vowing that he would never marry.

In time, Syantanu passed away and so did his son. His son left behind two wives, Ambika and Ambalika. To beget heirs to the throne, both women were instructed to sleep with a sage with magical powers. That sage was Vyasa whose beard reached the ground and whose body stank. When he embraced Ambika, she closed her eyes so tightly that their baby, Dhretarastra, was born blind. Ambalika turned pale in Vyasa's embrace and so her son, Pandu, was born with pale skin. When they were of age, Pandu was crowned king as his elder brother, Dhretarastra, was blind.

Pandu had two wives, Kunti and Madri. Because of a curse by a holy man, Pandu could not have sexual intercourse with his wives. Once, however, Kunti had received a divine favour by the gods. All she had to do was pray, and she would be granted five children. To test the blessing, Kunti prayed to Surya, the sun god, and was granted a child. As she was unmarried at that time, she immediately disposed of the baby. Kunti then told Pandu about the special divine favour she had obtained from the gods and asked his permission to again invoke the deities. By summoning Dharma, she begot Yudhistira (Dharmawangsa). By invoking Vayu (God of the Winds), she gave birth to Bima. Invoking Indra, she conceived Arjuna. She then lent her blessing to Madri, who invoked the twin gods (Ashvin), and was granted twin sons, Nakula and Sadeva.

One day, after the birth of these babies, Pandu went to the celebrations in the forest. Dazzled by the beauty of nature around him, he became overcome by sexual desire. He tried to embrace Madri and fell down dead. Madri committed suicide to atone for her husband's death.

After Pandu's death, Dhretarastra became king. He wanted to engage an accomplished tutor for his sons, the Kauravas, as well as his nephews, the Pandavas. The tutor he had been waiting for was Drona, son of Bhradvaja. It was said that in the past, when he was married and living in poverty, he had asked a close friend Drupada, king of Pancala, for help. But Drupada turned him away. Angered by this rejection, Drona's decided to pass on his knowledge to his students so they could help him take revenge on Drupada.

One day, Drona gathered his students and asked them if they could carry out a task for him after they had learned to use their weapons. None of them answered him. Only Arjuna, the third son of the Pandava clan, was willing to help his teacher. Arjuna became Drona's favourite student. More and more students came to Drona from other areas, including Karna, the son that Kunti had been granted by Surya, the Sun God, before her marriage to Pandu. No one knew Karna's background. Karna was often chose as Arjuna's sparring partner. He always chose to be on the Kauravas' side, pitting himself against the Pandavas.

Arjuna became an excellent archer. But one day, he met a young man who was an even better archer than he was. The young man was Eklavya. Arjuna told Drona about this. Drona asked Eklavya who his teacher was and the young man pointed to a clay statue of Drona. Drona understood what had taken place and asked Eklavya for his payment. The payment he asked for was Eklavya's thumb. Without his thumb, Eklavya lost his prowess. And so, Arjuna became the finest archer in the land.

One day, King Dhretarastra held a bridal contest. The Pandavas—Yudhistira, Bhima, Arjuna, Nakula and Sadeva were already in the arena. And so were the Kauravas under the command of Duryodhana. The fight between Bhima and Duryodhana became so intense that Drona felt he had to break it up, before it became too extreme. Then Arjuna displayed his prowess with different types of weapons. After he was done, Karna came forward, also wanting to show his mastery over weapons. But as no one knew anything about his background, he was forbidden from taking part. However, the Kauravas supported him and even gave him a country to reign over. And so, Karna and the Kauravas became close allies.

As payment for his lessons, Drona ordered his students: "Arrest Drupada, the King of Pancala, and bring him to me."

The Kauravas, assisted by Karna, tried to capture Drupada but failed. Then it was the Pandavas' turn. Arjuna easily captured Drupada and brought him before Drona. Drona released Drupada, as he had only wanted to embarrass him. Drupada was angry and vowed to take his revenge on Drona.

Dhreterastra planned to make Yudhistira his heir to the throne, as the throne had rightfully belonged to Yudhistira's father, Pandu. Furthermore, the Pandavas had already won widespread fame for their military expertise. Duryodhana, Dhretarasta's son, was jealous of the Pandava brothers. Soon, Dhretarasta himself also became envious of his nephews. Together they both began to devise plans to get rid of the Pandavas. Duryodhana built a magnificent castle in Varnavata using highly combustible materials. He described how beautiful the castle was and persuaded the Pandavas to live there. A faithful minister, Vidura, revealed Duryodhana's evil plan to the Pandavas and warned them to be careful. Because of that, when a fire broke out in the castle some time later, the Pandavas were able to save themselves. After their escape, the brothers lived like Brahmins.

Drupada, the king of Pancala, organised a competition to choose a husband for his daughter, Draupadi. The man who could shoot his ancient arrow would win the hand of his beautiful daughter. All the noblest kings tried their luck, with no success. So did the Pandavas. But none of them met with any success. When Karna was about to take his turn, Drupadi cried out: "I refuse to marry the son of a stable hand!"

Karna had no choice but to withdraw. Arjuna then stepped forward. He shot the arrow five times, and each time his arrow hit the target, a ring that had been tied high up in the air. The Brahmins cheered. But the other suitors were incensed. How could a homeless Brahmin be accepted as a king's son-in-law? The suitors attacked Drupada. Bima bravely defended Drupada. Krisna then revealed to the dissatisfied suitors Arjuna's real identity—far from being just a wandering ascetic, he was the son of Pandu. Peace was restored. The Pandavas took Drupadi back to their home. They told their mother Kunti that they had just won a big prize. Kunti replied: "Share the prize equally among yourselves."

Later Kunti discovered that the prize was a young woman. But a mother cannot take back her words. And so, Drupadi became a wife to all the five brothers.[5]

Duryodhana realised that his plan to exterminate the Pandavas by trapping them in a blazing castle had failed, and that the Pandavas had now won a powerful ally in Draupada, king of Pancala.

---

5   According to Romesh C. Dutt, the practice of several brothers sharing one wife is common among ethnic groups living in Tibet and the mountain regions of the Himalayas, but was unpopular among the Hindus. This practice was in fact forbidden by Hindu laws and customs. Taking into account several other incidents in the *Mahabharata,* Drupadi can be considered the wife of Yudhistira. Bima was already married to the Queen of the Jungle and had a son Gatotkaca. Arjuna was married to Rukmini, Krisna's sister, and they had a son Abhimanyu. Only Yudhistira had no wife. And although Arjuna had won Drupadi's hand in the competition, we can regard Drupadi as Yudhistira's.

So Duryodhana was left with no choice but to surrender part of his kingdom to the Pandavas. He kept for himself the arable portions of the land, while giving away the thick uncleared forests to the Pandavas. Even then, the Pandavas were contented.

The Pandavas built a resplendent palace in the woods, and gradually the inhospitable and impenetrable forest became a thriving and prosperous country. Yudhistira decided to hold a coronation sacrifice (*rajasuya*). The most powerful kings were invited by the Pandavas to attend the ceremony. On the day of the coronation, Krisna was invited to sit in the highest position; this was greatly resented by one of the guests, Sisupala. Sisupala's disapproval angered Yudhistira and Bima. Bhisma told those present that it had been predicted that Sisupala would die at Krisna's hand as he had insulted Krisna more than a hundred times. Sisupala became even more incensed and tried to strike Krisna again. This was his 101th offence against Krisna, and Sisupala immediately died as had been predicted.

Duryodhana was also present at Yudhistira's coronation. He stayed at Yudhistira's palace and saw its exquisiteness with his own eyes. This further intensified Duryodhana's hatred of the Pandavas. Once he had returned home, Duryodhana tried to think of other ways in which he could destroy the Pandavas. He knew that Yudhistira was honest and true to his word but he also had one weakness: he liked to gamble.

King Sakuni was a superb gambler and agreed to help Duryodhana. Yudhistira wagered all his possessions gambling against Sakuni and Duryodhana and lost everything. Finally, he even wagered himself, his brothers and even his wife, Draupadi, and still lost. The Pandavas were now reduced to mere slaves. Dhretarastra, who was anxious to prevent further conflict, released the Pandavas, on condition that they exiled themselves in the forest for twelve years. This was to be followed by another year when they were to live in disguise. If their identities were discovered during that year, they had to undertake another twelve years of exile in the forest.

Their twelve years in the forest were filled with interesting events. Krisna's presence reduced their grief and loneliness. A rishi, Vyasa, came and advised Arjuna to meditate, which Arjuna did. Arjuna met a hunter, who was an avatar of the god, Siva. Duryodhana also sought them out, but only to hurl insults and abuses at the brothers.

On one occasion, while Duryodhana was in the forest where the Pandavas lived, he became embroiled in a fight with certain spirits (*gandaras*) and was captured. Fortunately, the Pandavas came to Duryodhana's rescue, but not only did Duryodhana show no gratitude, his hatred towards his cousins increased. Many other sages and holy men came to visit and honour the Pandavas. They narrated many old folktales and stories about ancient kingdoms to the exiled brothers. Among these were stories of Nala and Damayanti; Agastya and how he drank all the water in the land to the very last drop; the story of the Brahmin Parasu Rama who wiped out all the ksatriyas on earth; the tale of Bhagiratha who brought the Ganges River to earth; Manu and the great flood; stories of Vishnu and other gods; Rama and his deeds; and the tale of Savitri, a faithful wife.

Twelve years of exile passed. During their year of living in disguise, the Pandavas served Wirata, king of Matsyas. The year passed. It was time for the Pandavas to reclaim their kingdom and they sent Krisna to make their representation to the Kauravas. Among the Kaurava clan, Dhretarastra, Bhisma and Drona all urged Duryodhana to return the throne to the Pandavas.

However, Duryodhana stubbornly refused. This led to a fierce battle between the Pandavas and the Kauravas, which lasted for 18 days.

Arjuna's heart was heavy with dread at the thought of fighting his own kin, friends and teacher. The wise Krisna was able to put his fears to rest through the well-known discourse, the *Bhagavadgita*. Krisna explained that each person had his own purpose and destiny, regardless of his caste, and performing one's duty in life was one's most vital task.

When the battle began, Bhisma led the Kauravas' army. For nine days, he defended the Kauravas. Unless Bhisma died, there would be no possibility of the Pandavas winning. Meanwhile, Arjuna was still pondering the dilemma of fighting the Kauravas and was reluctant to challenge Bhisma. Bhisma himself was in a difficult position as he loved the Pandavas as if they were his own children. But nothing could be done about this, as Duryodhana would not stop the war, and so Bhisma had to continue to fight. He promised the Pandavas that he would not strike any wounded adversaries or any transsexual. Draupadi's brother had been born as a woman, Sikandhi. The Pandavas placed him at the head of their army and instructed him to attack Bhisma. Bhisma, faithful to his promise to drop his weapons before a woman, was finally defeated. After Bhisma's death, Drona became commander of the Kauravas. For five days, he proved to be unbeatable. Arjuna was also unwilling to fight against his former teacher.

Finally, the Pandavas used a trick to unsettle Drona. When an elephant named Aswathaman was killed, the Pandavas cried out: "Aswathaman, Drona's son, has been killed." Drona heard the news and thinking that his own son, Aswathaman, had been killed, immediately lost the will to fight and was killed by Drupada's sons.

Karna then took over as the Kauravas' commander. Two days later, after a ferocious battle, Karna was killed by Arjuna. Finally, Salya led the Kauravas' forces. One day later, he was defeated by Yudhistira. That night, Drona's sons protested in the Pandava camp that the Pandavas had deceitfully caused their father's death. Duryodhana heard this and died happy.

The Pandavas had won the war. Yudhistira was crowned king of Hastinapura.

But the *Mahabharata* does not end there. It was said that before he breathed his last, Bhisma passed down to Yudhistira all he knew about kingship, the duties of each caste, and the life stages that each person should experience. Krisna also taught Yudhistira about the soul, emancipation, creation, the Wheel of Life and so on. Yudhistira, who was feeling guilty over the war, held a horse sacrifice to proclaim himself Paramount Sovereign, unchallenged by any other king.

After some time, the Pandavas heard that their uncle Dhretarastra had passed away in the forest. They were saddened by the news. And then came word that Krisna had also died. The Pandavas realised that their end was near and embarked on a long journey to Mount Meru in the Himalayas. One after another, the Pandavas died along the way. First Draupadi, then Sadeva, Nakula, Arjuna and lastly, Bima. Only Yuhistira reached heaven in his mortal form. In heaven, he was tested by the gods. After he passed the test and entered heaven, he was joined by his brothers and Draupadi.

Pariksit, Arjuna's grandson, inherited the kingdom of Hastinapura. But before long, he died from a snakebite. His son held a snake sacrifice to kill all living snakes. While the ceremony was underway, the famous poet Vyasa arrived and sang about the lives of his forefathers. This story was called the *Mahabharata*.

2.2.1 The *Mahabharata* in Javanese literature

The *Mahabharata* had a great influence on Javanese literature, probably even greater than the *Ramayana*. About a thousand years ago, during the rule of King Dharmawangsa, a prose summary of the 18 books (*parva*), of the *Mahabharata* was written in the Javanese language. This translation in prose became a rich source of inspiration for later Javanese poets. Among the well-known parvas were the *Adiparva, Wirataparwa* and *Bhismaparwa*. The influence of the *Mahabharata* was so strong that the Javanese considered the warriors of the Indian epic as their forefathers. The ruling monarch was also regarded as an incarnation of an Indian warrior. Furthermore, the *Mahabharata* was considered as having magical powers. The translation was not only said to honour the forefathers, it could also confer special powers to the rulers. So it is not surprising then that the *Mahabharata* continued to be adapted by Javanese poets, often at the order of the king.

The *Mahabharata* soon became ingrained in the life of the Javanese. An early form of the shadowplay, the *wayang kulit*, took its stories from the Indian epics, especially from the *Mahabharata*. Many Javanese stories which are considered original, such as the *Suda Mala* (an exorcism of the goddess Durga by Sadeva) and the *Nawa Ruci* (the story of Bima's search for the elixir of life), also feature characters drawn from the *Mahabharata*. It is correct to say that the *Mahabharata* has become an integral part of Javanese mythology.

The story of the Great War was composed in a poetic form suitable for singing as the *Kakawin Bharata Yudha* in 1157 by Mpu Sedah during the rule of Jayabaya, king of Kediri. The author, Mpu Panuluh, was a very productive Javanese poet. Besides the *Kakawin Bharata Yudha,* he also wrote the *Kakawin Hari Wangsa* which tells the story of Krisna's marriage to Rukmini. In his later years, he also composed *Kakawin Ghatotkacasraya* about the marriage of Abhimanyu, Arjuna's son, to Dewi Sundhari, Krisna's daughter. The *Ghatotkacasraya*, the subject of a dissertation by Sutjipto Wirjosuparto in the University of Indonesia, was a very important work in the development of Javanese literature. The *Kakawin Ghatotkacasraya* introduced *punakawan* (clown servants) for the first time. Based on the presence of punakawan, Dutch scholar Stein Callenfels, a wayang expert, declared that wayang stories must be older than the kakawin form.[6] When Old Javanese was no longer widely understood, the *Kakawin Bharata Yudha* was translated into modern Javanese by the kraton poet, Yasadipura I, during the reign of Paku Buwana III. Yasadipura I's translation, called *Brata Yudam* or *Kakawin Bharata Yudha,* became an important source for further wayang performances.

Arjuna has always been one of the most popular characters. As a result, works featuring Arjuna are more abundant than those featuring other characters. Arjuna's period of meditation undertaken in order to earn a magical weapon is the theme of the *Kakawin Parta Yajna*. The hero's marriage is told in the *Kakawin Arjuna Wiwaha*, written by Mpu Kanwa at the beginning of the 11th century. This popular kakawin was translated in modern Javanese by Yasadipura I during Paku Buwana III's reign as well. Yasadipura I's translation was titled *Minta Raga*. The story of Arjuna's marriage can also be found in temple reliefs at Surawa, Jago, Kedaton and Selamangelang.

The *Mahabharata*'s biggest influence has been on *wayang* stories. The number of wayang stories that take their plots from the *Mahabharata* is too vast to count. According to some scholars, the Malay *hikayat* which depict the exploits of these epic warriors are actually translations of

---

6   Pigeaud disagrees with this view, claiming that the wayang did not yet exist in the 12th century (Pigeaud 1967-1970, Vol 1: 186).

wayang stories. Several of these stories were translated into Malay, including the *Hikayat Pandawa Lima, Hikayat Sang Boma* and so on.

We will now look at the place of the *Mahabharata* in Malay literature.

2.2.2 The *Mahabharata* in Malay Literature

In Malay literature, the *Mahabharata* is known as the *Hikayat Pandawa*, a very popular work at one time. This can be seen by the abundance of manuscripts of this hikayat, variously called the *Hikayat Pandawa, Hikayat Pandawa Lima, Hikayat Pandawa Jaya*, and *Pandawa Panca Kelima*. There are also stories of the Pandavas which deviate from the usual narratives, such as the *Hikayat Pandawa Lebur, Hikayat Darmawangsa* and the *Hikayat Angkawijaya*.

According to some scholars, these Pandava stories have been freely translated from *kakawin*, ancient Javanese poems. The *Hikayat Sang Boma* is a free adaptation of *Kakawin Bhomakawya*; *Hikayat Perang Pandawa Jaya* a free adaptation of *Kekawin Bharata Yudha*, while *Kakawin Ghatotkacasraya* and *Kakawin Arjuna Wiwaha* can be traced back to the *Hikayat Pandawa Lima* or *Hikayat Panca Kelima*.

2.2.3 *Hikayat Pandawa Lima*

Van der Tuuk has summarised a manuscript of the *Hikayat Pandawa* that is now part of the collection of the Royal Asiatic Society (No. 2). The manuscript (Van der Tuuk 1875b: 1-90) consists of 288 chapters and is divided into three parts. The first part is a collection of beautiful scenes. The second presents the main battle and is entitled *Hikayat Pandawa Jaya*. This portion is a translation from the *Kakawin Bharata Yudha* of Mpu Sedah. The third part is a narrative not found in the *Kakawin Bharata Yudha*. From page 44 onwards, the plot of the manuscript is similar to the *Hikayat Pandawa Lima* published by Khalid Hussain.

2.2.4 Summary of the Story (Royal Asiatic Society Manuscript No. 2)

1. Barma Sakti and Brahma fought each other. Barma Sakti invaded the palace of Dewi Puspa Maniaka and took her as his wife. They had two sons. When one of their sons, Sang Mangunang, grew up, he took the country of Marcu Jantaka from the hands of Maharaja Dewa and called himself Warga Dewa. The defeated Maharaja Dewa sought refuge with the Kauravas.

    Kadatadastara, prince of Warga Singa, fell in love with Dewi Araskandi, one of Warga Dewa's concubines, but failed to capture her. Sang Mangunang (now called Warga Dewa), attacked the country of Mercu which was ruled by Wirsapati. Warga Dewa also attacked the sanctuary at Gua Imagunah. The ascetics asked Warga Singa for help. Warga Singa sent his eldest son Kadatadastara to help them but he failed. Warga Singa then appealed to Barma Sakti for assistance. Barma Sakti arrived and restored peace between Warga Dewa and Warga Singa. Kadatadastara became angry and pledged to take revenge for the murder of his brother by Warga Dewa. He began taking secret lessons in magical powers from Batara Durga.

Kadatadastara professed his love for Dewi Araskandi, Warga Dewa's wife. Dewi Araskandi planned to kill Kadatadastara by asking him to find hibiscus flowers and firewood.

The fire was lit and they both perished in the blaze. Dewi Araskandi's soul entered the womb of Maharaja Wangsapati's wife, who was pregnant. Eventually, Wangsapati's wife gave birth to twins, a son called Sang Utara and a daughter called Dewi Utari.

Warga Dewa ordered a search for his missing wife. The home of Warga Singa was destroyed in the search. Dewi Asmarakandi, Kadatadastara's sister, committed suicide and her soul entered the body of Batara Kresna's wife, who was pregnant. Batara Kresna's wife had a baby girl who they named Dewi Siti Sundari. When she was older, Dewi Siti Sundari was given to Baladewa who raised her as his own daughter.

Warga Dewa wanted to marry Langga Satra's daughter. Langga Satra's condition was that Warga Dewa had to find 40 heavenly nymphs. The god Indra provided Warga Dewa with the nymphs and thus he was able to marry Puspa Indra Dewi, Langga Satra's daughter.

Darmawangsa gambled against Duryodhana. Duryodhana cheated and Darmawangsa lost everything. First, he lost his possessions, then his palace. Then he staked his brothers and wife, Draupadi, and lost them too. The Pandavas, except for Draupadi, were now slaves to the Kauravas. In the Kauravas' palace, the Pandavas bore much abuse and many insults. The Kauravas were still not satisfied and decided to exterminate the Pandavas.

One day, Duryodhana ordered the Pandavas to retrieve an arrow that had fallen into the underwater lair of a dragon, with the promise that half the kingdom would be handed over to the Pandavas if they succeeded. The Pandavas dived into the depths and were swallowed by the dragon. Believing that the Pandavas had all perished, the Kauravas rejoiced. But they were wrong. The Pandavas were alive; the dragon died.

After they escaped from the dragon's body, the Pandavas travelled and arrived at the country of Mardu Nagara. They adopted new identities and served Warga Dewa. Batara Kesna tried to visit them at Indrapasta, but found that the Pandavas were already gone. He took Dewi Subadra and Abimanyu with him to Darawati. Abimanyu, Arjuna's son, was a handsome young man and much loved by Kesna. Kesna wanted his daughter Siti Sundari to marry Abimanyu. Siti Sundari was also loved by Baladeva and was adopted by him as his own daughter. Without Kesna's knowledge, Baladeva betrothed Siti Sundari to Laksamana Kumara, Duryodhana's son.

Abimanyu and Siti Sundari fell in love. With the help of Batara Marpata, Abimanyu went to meet Siti Sundari and they exchanged kisses. Baladeva was infuriated when he found out and wanted to kill Abimanyu. Subadra and Rukmini told this to Abimanyu. The young man escaped into the forest where he encountered an ogre, Kala Waktra who took him to Durga's abode. The goddess Durga told Abimanyu that her cousin, Gatotkaca, would be able to help him. Abimanyu was then taken to Purabaya to meet Gatotkaca. Together, Gatotkaca and Abimanyu went to kidnap Siti Sundari. The Kaurava clan attacked Darawati. Gatotkaca came and drove out the Kauravas. The battle intensified. Batara Kesna, when informed of the raging battle, left his place of meditation to mediate between the two opposing sides. He decreed that Siti Sundari could choose the man she loved. Siti Sundari chose Abimanyu. With the dispute ended, Gatotkaca returned to his own country.

Narada asked the Pandavas to return to Indrapasta. The people were overjoyed to see them. Not long after, Darmawangsa sent Arjuna to invite Batara Kesna, Baladeva and Wangsapati to come to Indrapasta. A huge festival was held. Kesna advised the brothers to delay declaring war on the Kauravas until they had amassed a sufficient number of powerful weapons. The only way to obtain such weapons was by going through a period of meditation and asceticism. But of the five brothers, only Arjuna was willing to undertake the rigours required to win such magical weapons.

Duryodhana sent Karna (Ambakarna) to Indrapasta to invite the Pandava brothers to their home. Karna was surprised to see that the Pandavas had returned to Indrapasta, and brought this news to Duryodhana.

Abimanyu fell in love with Utari, the daughter of Wangsapati, and married her. Siti Sundari was displeased but she was placated when she recited a mantra.

The Pandava brothers discussed the impending war and their chances of victory. Sang Aryu Darbala was sent to Duryodhana to ask for their rightful half of the kingdom which had been promised by Duryodhana as a reward for retrieving an arrow from the dragon's lair. Duryodhana was willing to grant them their share of the kingdom on condition that they exile themselves for twelve years, twelve months and twelve days. On Kesna's advice, the Pandavas agreed.

Dewi Anggara Mayang and Dewi Tunjung Tutur wished to return to the celestial realm. But so long as Warga Dewa was still alive, that was impossible. The two women looked for a way to kill Warga Dewa. They told Warga Dewa that Rajuna's two wives, Siti Sundari and Dewi Utari, were incarnations of Warga Dewa's wife and encouraged him to win her back again. Warga Dewa believed them. A fierce battle took place between Warga Dewa and the Pandavas. In the battle, many men perished on both sides. Begawan Narada and Barma Sakti came down to earth to arbitrate between the two warring factions and peace was restored. The men who had lost their lives in battle were brought back to life. Dewi Anggara Mayang and Dewi Tunjung Tutur and other celestial beings were ordered to go back to the celestial world, which was, after all, where they belonged.

2. This part deals with the Great War. Batara Kesna was sent to Astinapura to ask Duryodhana for the return of half the kingdom as he had earlier promised. Duryodhana refused, and was supported in this by Karna. And thus the famous battle, the Bharatayudha, began. The Kauravas fell in one battle after another. Begawan was the first to meet his death, followed by Bisma, Drona and Karna and lastly, Salya. Finally, Patih Sangkuni and Duryodhana were also killed. The Pandava forces also lost many lives, most notably those of Abimanyu and Gatotkaca. The war ended in victory for the Pandavas.

According to Van der Tuuk, Part Two is adapted from the *Kakawin Bhratayudha* by Mpu Sedah, itself adapted from Sanskrit.

3. After being killed by Bima, Patih Sangkuni came back to life again thanks to a superpower known as Panji Suata. Patih Sangkuni gathered the scattered subjects of the Kaurava and formed a new state in Imaguna forest. When Kesna heard this, he urged Darmawangsa to send a spy to see if this was true. Kesna offered his own son, Prajamena, to do this as he was still only a child. Had someone else gone, Sangkuni would run away. At first, Prajamena

refused. Kesna was annoyed and recounted stories of his bravery as a child to motivate Prajamena. Finally, Prajamena agreed to go, after borrowing weapons from Rajuna, Bima, Sadeva and Nakula. The Kauravas' men fled even before Prajamena's army arrived, leaving Patih Sangkuni alone on the battlefield. After seeing Rajuna's weapon in Prajamena's hand, Patih Sangkuni also ran away and turned himself into a mountain. Prajamena returned home and reported on Patih Sangkuni's disappearance and that Imaguna Mountain had now become two hills. Kesna found this hard to believe but agreed to go and see this second mountain. The Pandavas encountered much danger when they reached the mountain. Firstly, Patih Sangkuni changed himself into a river and almost drowned Bima and Rajuna. Then he swooped on Darmawangsa's shadow, causing Darmawangsa to lose consciousness. Patih Sangkuni stabbed Darmawangsa's shadow and yelled out, as if Darmawangsa himself was calling for help. Blood rained onto the earth. Bima, Rajuna and Nakula lost their will to live, believing that their brother Darmawangsa had died. Fortunately, Sadeva arrived and exposed Patih Sangkuni's trick. Sadeva also recaptured Darmawangsa's shadow and killed Patih Sangkuni. His body was cremated and his ashes scattered at sea.

Bima killed the wives of the Kauravas: Dewi Karnawati, Nilawati and Irnawati. Rajuna captured Duryodhana's wife, Banuwati. Not long after, Dewi Utari gave birth to a son, Parikasti, who was much loved by his grandfather, Rajuna.

A short time after Rajuna had taken Banuwati as his wife, his body was possessed by Duryodhana's spirit. From that moment on, he refused to regard Parikasti as his grandson and refused to be part of the Pandava clan. He even wanted to kill them. His enmity towards the Pandavas led to a battle. In the end, his brother Darmawangsa stood before him. Darmawangsa saw that Rajuna was possessed by Duryodhana and the reason for Rajuna's rebellion became clear to him. Darmawangsa hurled seven blades of wild grass at Rajuna's body. Duryodhana's spirit was so shaken by this that it flew out of Rajuna's body. Rajuna regained consciousness and realised his wrongdoing. He asked Darmawangsa for forgiveness. Darmawangsa rebuffed him and even cursed him till Rajuna fell ill with a strange disease. He withdrew into the jungle, accompanied by Banuwati.

When Batara Kesna came to visit Darmawangsa, he found that Rajuna had already left the palace due to his guilt for the sins he had committed against his family. Kesna urged Darmawangsa to forgive Rajuna; otherwise Kesna himself would go into exile in the forest. Darmawangsa relented. Kesna went to fetch Rajuna but Rajuna refused to return home until he found a wife resembling Srikandi. Kesna told Rajuna that the wife of Arjuna Sasrabahu, Dewi Ratnawati, not only resembled Srikandi but had special powers and excelled at wielding weapons. And so Rajuna (now called Arjuna Wijaya) fought against Arjuna Sasrabahu. He killed Arjuna Sasrabahu and took Ratnawati as his wife. Begawan Narada revived Arjuna Sasrabahu and urged him to pay his respects to Kesna and Rajuna. Not long after, Kesna, Rajuna, Banuwati and Ratnawati returned to Mertawangsa, where Rajuna was forgiven by Darmawangsa.

The Pandavas went for an outing at the seaside. They dried up the sea in order to harvest its contents. The sea ogres (*bota*) emerged from the ocean and in order to take their revenge, they kidnapped Parikasti. Rajuna turned himself into a bird and snatched Parikasti back. He killed the king of the *bota*s. Soon after, Parikasti was enthroned as king.

Begawan Narada came to take the Pandavas back to the celestial world as their time on earth was drawing to a close. The Pandavas met their mortal death in different ways. Darmawangsa died in his sleep. Bima died a slow and awful death, as he had been cruel towards his enemies. Rajuna, Nakula and Sadewa stabbed themselves in the chest. After their demise, all the gods and celestial beings came to scatter the most fragrant flowers over their remains. The wives of the Pandava brothers killed themselves. Parakasti had their bodies cremated and kept their ashes in five large, tall candis (temples). Parikasti returned to his kingdom. Kings of his vassal states came to pay tribute to him. Under his rule, the kingdom enjoyed much peace.

"And thus ends the *Hikayat Pandawa Lima,* composed by the erudite author. Those who read or hear it will become wise."

2.2.5 Other Manuscripts

There are many manuscripts of the *Hikayat Pandawa;* eight in the Jakarta Museum and three in the Leiden Library. They bear different titles—some are called the *Hikayat Pandawa Lima,* the *Hikayat Pandawa Jaya* and so on. Others deviate from the general Pandava stories: the *Hikayat Darmawangsa, Hikayat Pandawa Lebur* and *Hikayat Angkawijaya* (the Javanese name for Arjuna). The *Hikayat Darmawangsa* has the same plot but, due to its many deviations, it can be considered a corrupted *Hikayat Pandawa*. The *Hikayat Angkawijaya* tells how Krisna and Arjuna went to Merbabu Mountain to pray for a son. Below I present summary a summary of the Hikayat Pandawa Lebur (v. d. Wall collection 144) for your information.

Summary of *Hikayat Pandawa Lebur*

Raja Beraja Nila asked if there were still kings he had not yet conquered, and was told "King Orga Sina of Mandapura Nagara". Raja Beraja Nila then ordered his troops to attack Mandapura and capture its king. Orga Sina was startled. Arjuna, incarnate as Cekel Sukma Diluh, and his faithful followers, Semar and Cemuris, came to Mandapura. When he heard of the invasion, Arjuna pitted himself against Raja Beraja Nila. Arjuna proved himself much too powerful for the raja and killed him. Arjuna then married a princess from Mandapura named Kusumananti. Henceforth, Arjuna was called Prabu Anom Mangku Nagara.

At Dewi Sambadara's request, Kresna went to look for Arjuna as the Kurawas were about to attack against Martawangsa. He hoped to be able to bring the women and children to the safety of Purawati. In Dewalwati, Krisna fought against giants who had surrounded the city. Gatotkaca witnessed this battle from heaven and came down to help Kresna. Krisna renamed him Kiprabaya. The Pandawa brothers—Darmawangsa, Bima and Nakula—went with Narada to Martawangsa, where all the women and Krisna were gathered together.

Krisna failed to find Arjuna. So did Suyudana. The Kurawas prepared to declare war on the Pandawas. The Pandawas lost the first battle but Bima managed to hold off the Kurawa attack. There was a king in Indra Puspa called Panca Wira Jaya, who wanted to possess the world's most beautiful women. He heard that the wife of Sastra Wijaya (Krisna's brother) was very stunning and insisted that she be handed over to him. When his demand was rejected, Panca Wira Jaya attacked the Pandawas. At the same time, the Great War was still continuing.

Krisna found Arjuna in Mandapura. Orga Sina was shocked to discover the identity of his ally. They all went to Martawangsa. A fierce battle was raging. Arjuna quickly entered into the thick of the battle but was killed by Karna. However, he was revived by the Wijaya Kusuma flower. Purabaya (Gatotkaca) heard that Dewalwati had been surrounded by Panca Wira Jaya and offered his assistance. He killed Panca Wira Jaya. Raden Samba was also killed but was sprinkled with holy water and revived again.

Widadari Indra Sati had to undertake penance in order to atone for a past mistake. While she was meditating, Gatotkaca's sperm fell from the sky into her mouth. Soon after, Widadari Indra Sati became pregnant and gave birth to a boy who looked exactly like his father. The baby was raised by Durga and named Tunggal. Tunggal grew up quickly in heaven. He is most commonly known as Adi Bramu. Adi Bramu wanted to find his father but first he had to meditate for three years. After three years, he returned to earth.

Pancawati was under siege from a giant, who could only be defeated by Adi Bramu. Many men had tried to kill the ogre in order to marry the princess who had been promised to the victor. Purbajaya and Arjuna also tried but even these mighty warriors failed. Finally Adi Bramu arrived and killed the ogre with the help of the gods. Adi Bramu then married Princess Puspa Seri Jati. Soon after, he departed for Astinapura. During the journey, he thwarted many attempts to kidnap his wife. Adi Bramu met Gatotkaca. A misunderstanding arose which escalated into an intense battle between the two, during which both changed their forms many times. Havoc swept through the world, and the celestial world was almost burnt to ashes. Narada came down from heaven and revealed everything to Adi Bramu. The battle came to an end. Adi Bramu knelt before Gatotkaca. Martawangsa held a lavish celebration. The manuscript ends at this point.

Other than *Hikayat Pandawa Lima*, one other Malay hikayat has been published, the *Hikayat Sang Boma*.

2.2.6 *Hikayat Sang Boma*

Scholars disagree on the origins of this hikayat. Windstedt states that this hikayat derives from the *Kakawin Bhomakawya*. A. Teeuw, who studied the story of Boma for his dissertation, largely agrees with Winstedt. According to Teeuw, the *Hikayat Sang Boma*, is largely, if not completely, based on the *Bhomakawya*. Teeuw also compared the *Bhomakawya* with other Boma stories which are well-known in India, including the conflict between Boma and Krisna, the love story of Samba and Januwati, as well as the rivalry between Vishnu and Brahma. But the details of these stories are very different indeed.

Teeuw (1946) further believes that the hikayat has a single plot, the whole text focuses on Samba. This is not the case with the *Bhomakawya*, which consists of two parts. The first part is the love story of Samba and Januwati. The second part recounts the slaying of Boma by Krisna (in *Hikayat Boma*, Boma is killed by Hanoman). Samba does not play any role in the second part. His story can be said to end when he marries Januwati in the middle of the story. Teeuw concludes that *Kakawin Bhomakawya* is synthetic in nature while the hikayat is analytical. What he means is that many incidents in the kakawin, such as the birth of Boma and his background, the previous incarnations of Samba and the kidnapping of Januwati, are all narrated by the various characters. In Malay hikayat, these are separate incidents. Perhaps this explains why some scholars believe that the *Hikayat Sang Boma* is actually a collection of wayang stories, especially when such episodes are easily performed on their own. C. Hooykaas suggests that the *Hikayat Sang Boma* is a handbook for *wayang purwa* performances.

2.2.7 *Hikayat Sang Boma* (Raffles 15 Manuscript)

One day, Brahma paid a visit to Vishnu in the celestial world and asked him which one of them had been created by Dewata Raya Mulia. They both played a game of hide and seek. Brahma could not hide from Vishnu. Then it was Vishnu's turn to hide. He changed himself into a pig and burrowed into the earth. While underground, he met a beautiful maiden called Dewi Pertiwi and married her. Vishnu told her that if she should have a baby, she was to give the infant the Wijaya Kusuma flower.

Dewi Pertiwi then gave birth to an extremely ugly baby. Too embarrassed to keep the child, she threw the baby into the sea. Brahma saw this and, knowing that the baby was Vishnu's, adopted him. Brahma and Vishnu both taught the child to be invulnerable and the ways of winning at war. Vishnu advised him not to offend any ascetics. Brahma predicted that Boma would "become such a powerful king that no one would dare challenge him, even the gods would fear him" and "if he died, he would revive as soon as he fell to the ground". Only Vishnu would be able to kill him, said Brahma.

Boma entered the earth to obtain the Wijaya Kusuma flower from his mother, Dewi Pertiwi. As long as the flower was in his hand, Boma would not die; if he did, he would be able to come back to life. Shortly after, Boma received a horse called Wilmana from Baruna. Riding Wilmana, Boma flew to the country of Prajotasena and snatched the kingdom from Danusara (Daneswara). Boma killed Danusara but retained his ministers and commanders. The buffalo Aria Karia retained his position as governor; Patih Mudra (Karna) became king. And so Boma enjoyed himself for forty days, eating and drinking. From then on, the kingdom thrived.

On one occasion, Vishnu and Brahma were amusing themselves on Tenunan Mountain. Vishnu saw *nagasari* flowers scattered around the plain and picked one. He prayed over the nagasari flower and a handsome young man appeared, named Darma Dewa. Brahma prayed over the flower once again and a beautiful woman emerged. She was named Darma Dewi and was married to Darma Dewa. The couple lived happily on the mountain.

Vishnu incarnated himself as Krisna and asked Darma Dewa to accompany him. They descended from the mountain and entered the womb of the wife of Pasu Dewa (Basu Dewa). Shortly after, Pasu Dewa's wife gave birth to beautiful twins. One was called Bala Dewa; he ascended the throne at Madura. The other was also called Krisna and he ruled Daruwati Pura. After becoming king, Krisna married two women, Dewi Rakmi (Rukmini) and Dewi Jambuwati. Dewi Jambuwati became pregnant.

Darma Dewa left his wife with a heavy heart and entered the womb of Dewi Jambuwati. She soon gave birth to a handsome boy. The boy was named Raden Samba Prawijaya. Abandoned by her husband, Darma Dewi pined and eventually immolated herself. Later, she entered the womb of the wife of Jantaka, Dewi Dusila, who gave birth to a baby girl. The baby was named Dewi Januwati and was given a governess who was the daughter of a nymph. Dewi Januwati soon grew up to become a peerless beauty and the fairest maiden in the whole world.

Boma ordered his two governors, Mudra and Aria Karia, to ask for Dewi Januwati's hand in marriage. As the two representatives behaved crudely, the proposal was rejected. Boma declared war on the king of Jantaka and killed the king with hs arrow named Samoga-moga. Boma took Januwati back to his palace by force. She would not stop crying and refused to be consoled by Boma. Finally, Januwati confessed to her governess that she was actually Darma Dewi. The governess, Puspa Wati, told her that only a fairy called Nila Utama could arrange for Januwati to be reunited with Darma Dewa. Upon learning this, Januwati laid down a condition for Boma: If he really wanted her, he had to provide her with two ladies-in-waiting, specifically the nymphs Dewi Nila Utama and Dewi Supraha. In order to fulfil her wish, Boma declared war on the celestial world and quickly proved to be too powerful for the gods. The king of the gods, Indra, was forced to hand over Dewi Nila Utama and Dewi Supraha to Boma.

Boma then attacked the hermitages at Jangga Baru Mountain and Arkasa Mountain. The ascetics who managed to escape asked Begawan Karanda Dewa (Kawi: "Gunadewa") and Begawan Anggi (Kawi: "Angkari") for help. Karanda Dewa and Anggi quickly went to see Batara Guru. Marami, Jarakesti, Narada and the other gods were all present when the envoys arrived. Batara Guru then sent Narada to ask Krisna for help. Krisna deputed his son Samba and two warriors, Surata and Surana, to lead the army against Boma. On the way, they were attacked by ogres. They killed the *raksasa*s one after the other. Aria Pakitu perished at the hands of Surata, Samoga was killed by Surana, while Irangkasa was destroyed by Samba himself. Shortly after, Samba and his men reached the hermitage and were welcomed by Katambara. After some time, the men reached Prejuta Hill. In one of the gardens on the hill, they encountered three nymphs: Tanjung Maya, Tanjung Biru and Tanjung Sari. Samba captured the three nymphs. Samba and his companions fell in love with the nymphs.

Soon after, they were attacked by a *raksasa* called Pralemba. They managed to kill the ogre. Eventually they reached Wisa Dewa's hermitage, which was surrounded by splendid fruit trees. Wisa Dewa welcomed them and served them a magnificent feast. Samba then continued his journey and finally reached Tenunan Mountain. Nila Utama told Samba that Darma Dewi had incarnated as Januwati and been kidnapped by Boma. Samba put on the magical jacket called Antakesuma; in this way, Samba and Nila Utama were able to fly to Boma's palace. Surata and Darga followed behind them, leading the citizens of the kingdom. Surata and Darga told Samba that the ascetics and holy men had advised them not to stay too long in Boma's palace. On hearing human voices, the guards at the Nila Suri Dewi palace (Kilasuridewi) and the ogres, surrounded Samba's men.

Narada descended from heaven and told Samba the story of Januwati. He advised him to return home and fetch his father, Krisna. Shortly after, Narada came once again to convey the news that Januwati had been hidden by Kilasuri in a golden pond on a golden hill. Samba was appointed to attack Prajotaksana (or Traju Trisna). Prajotaksana's city was burned to the ground and Januwati rescued. Kilasuri escaped to the celestial realm to report to Boma what had happened. Samba was attacked on Magadha Hill by Jarasanda, who wanted to revenge his son's death at the hands of Arjuna. Jarasanda beat Samba so badly that he lost consciousness. Fortunately Begawan Wisa

Dewapati found Samba and treated his injuries. After making a full recovery, Samba declared war on Jaraksana and captured one of his sons. Samba left Wisa Dewapati and returned to Darawati, where he met Krisna's three wives: Satiabana, Rakmi and his own mother, Jambuwati.

Fearing an attack from Boma, Derma, Gatotkaca's grandfather, sought the protection of Pasudewa. Gatotkaca and Bima were absent, as they had decided to meditate on Kandarana Mountain. Derma and Pasudewa then went to fetch Krisna. All the Pandawa warriors gathered in Darawati Purwa as Krisna was preparing to counter an attack from Boma. Arjuna was the first to arrive.

While Boma was waging war on the celestial world, Nila Suri informed him that Samba had defeated the state of Traju Trisna and captured Januwati. Angered, Boma immediately wrote to Krisna, demanding that Samba and Januwati should be tied up and handed over to him. If not, Boma threatened to turn Darawati Purwa into an ocean of blood. Krisna, however, refused to meet Boma's demand. The incensed Boma ordered Kirana and Mudra to kidnap Samba and Januwati. Bala Dewa and Arjuna looked everywhere for Samba and Januwati but failed to find them. They encountered Palarasa who had assumed the form of Narada. Palarasa told Bala Dewa and Arjuna they could stop their search, as Kamajaya had taken Samba and Januwati to heaven. Unaware of Palarasa's deceit, Bala Dewa and Arjuna were completely tricked. Boma was about to throw Samba into the fire, when suddenly, Hanoman, who had been meditating in Tursina, appeared and snatched Samba away. And so, a terrible war took place between the *raksasa*s and Hanoman's monkey warriors. By this time, Krisna had discovered that Boma had kidnapped Samba and Januwati, and he attacked Boma. Hanoman reunited Krisna and Samba. In the battle, there were many casualties on both sides. One night, Samba and Arjuna sneaked into Boma's palace and rescued Januwati. Discovering that Januwati had gone, Boma fought against Samba and Arjuna and killed them both. Krisna himself dealt terrible blows to Boma but failed to kill him. Finally, Hanoman arrived and after a terrible battle, succeeded in capturing and killing Boma. Narada and Indra descended from the heavens with the holy Utama Jiwa water and revived all of the dead Pandawas except for Samba who had caused Boma such agony. The Pandawas returned to Darawati and made preparations to bury Samba. Januwati and Tanjung Sari, who loved Samba with all their hearts, pledged to avenge his death.

Darmawangsa, Bima and Gatotkaca arrived in Darawati and found out that Samba had died. They too were overcome with grief. Semar was saddened by Narada's refusal to revive Samba and went to Batara Guru to express his dissatisfaction. Batara Guru had to defer to Semar's wishes, as Semar was his elder brother, Ingkang Sinuhun Sang Hyang Tunggal (the god Batara Ismaya). Narada and Indra then had no choice but to descend to earth to revive Samba. The Pandavas and their subjects were overjoyed. Samba, Januwati and Tanjung Sari were honoured by being taken in a procession around the country. Shortly after, Samba became king of Darawati. The story tells that under his rule, there was never a lack of food and his fame spread far and wide throughout his realm.

2.2.8 Other Manuscripts

There are many manuscripts of the *Hikayat Sang Boma:* five in the Jakarta Museum, and two at the Leiden University Library. The contents of the manuscripts are similar to the summary given above. The only difference is the name of the flower given to Sang Boma. In one manuscript, it was called Wijaya Mala and in another, Mulia. The *raksasa* who was born together with Boma is also given different names in the various manuscripts.

2.2.9 *Wayang Kulit*

Apart from the Panji tales, the major Javanese influence on classical Malay literature derives from *wayang kulit* (shadow puppetry). Based on their contents, there are four types of *wayang kulit*:

1. *Wayang Purwa*. This is the oldest type of wayang. The stories are based on myths and stories that originate in India.
2. *Wayang Gedog*. This type of wayang was created by Sunan Giri in 1553. The stories revolve around the Panji stories, which narrate the adventures of a Javanese prince in his search for his lost fiancée.
3. *Wayang Klitik* or *Kerucil*. This wayang uses wooden puppets to tell the story of Damar Wulan and the history of the Majapahit Kingdom.
4. *Wayang Golek*. This form of wayang was created by Sunan Kudus in 1584. It uses three-dimensional puppets on rods—the male characters are dressed in robes, turbans and shoes, while the female characters are dressed in kebaya, making them look like miniature people. The performances narrate the story of Amir Hamzah (uncle of the Prophet Muhammad), as adapted into Javanese.

Only the *wayang purwa* will be discussed in this chapter.

2.2.10 Origins of *Wayang Purwa*

The *Wayang Purwa* is the oldest form of wayang; its influence is such that when people speak of "wayang", they are usually referring to wayang purwa. There are several interpretations of the meaning of "*purwa*". Some scholars believe "*purwa*" means "origin" or "ancient", as *wayang purwa* derives its stories from the beginning of time. Others suggest that "purwa' derives from "parwa" (or "parwan") which means "part", as the *wayang purwa* derives its stories from the *Mahabharata* which consists of 18 *parwa* (parts).

From both of these interpretations, it is clear that wayang purwa is indeed very old. In *Arjuna Wiwaha,* written by Mpu Kanwa for Raja Airlangga in 1030, there are already references to wayang performances: "When watching wayang, some people become sad and cry, although they know it is only a play performed by hand-held puppets..."

This is clear proof that wayang already existed in the eleventh century. And long before that, the existence of wayang can already be seen in two inscriptions. The first, by King Lokapala in 840, records that "*aringgit*" (wayang performers) took part in wayang performances. The second inscription, by King Balitung in 907, says, in part, that: "*Si Galigi mawayang*" which means "Galigi held a wayang" (Ras, 1976).

Despite this, scholars still do not agree on the true origins of the wayang. Some scholars believe that the wayang was created by the Javanese. Many other scholars maintain that the wayang had its roots in India. According to Brandes, the wayang is definitely a Javanese creation. Firstly, there is no form of puppet performance in India that uses leather puppets, and the acting style is very different. Secondly, the terms used in the *wayang* are Javanese terms and not Sanskrit words.

G. A. J. Hazeu supported Brandes' view. He argued that the performance arts in Java were not merely for entertainment but were strongly linked to ancestor worship. The ancestors are regarded as spirits who can protect living family members, if those spirits are fed and worshipped. In the beginning, the head of the family was responsible for praying to, and summoning, the spirits. Then this responsibility was taken over by healers or shamans. Moreover, Hazeu shows that several ethnic groups in the Archipelago still retain the tradition of displaying pictures of their ancestors so that their spirits can descend to earth. From this tradition arose the habit of making pictures or shadows against a white screen. The *wayang* was, thus, born as a form of ancestor worship. It can further be said, in other words, that the *wayang* is the surviving vestige of religious rituals that were practised even before Hinduism and Buddhism arrived in this part of the world (Hazeu, 1897: 41-43).

Hazeu's view received strong support from J. Kats. Kats pointed out that the clowns—Semar and his sons, Petruk and Nalagareng—are not found in the Indian epics. Kats states that Semar is much more than a clown. He protects his masters, the Pandavas, and offers them advice when they are in difficulty. On many occasions, he shows that he knows more about the deception and trickery of men and gods than his masters do. He also argues with the gods. He is Sang Hyang Asmarasanta (or Batara Maya), and has been given the task of protecting the descendants of Brahma and Wisnu. It is highly likely that Semar is considered the true ancestor of the Javanese (Kats, 1923: 40-41).

W. H. Rassers' position was not as consistent as those of Brandes and Hazeu. At first, he argued that the *wayang* developed from totemic initiation ceremonies. The illuminated white screen (*kelir*) was a symbol of the community or the ethnic group itself, while the individuals on the right and left of the stage depicted two sections of the community. The initiate had to endure different challenges and painful initiation rites in order to win a wife from the other moiety of the clan. Later, in his following work, *Tentang Makna Lakon Jawa (On the Meaning of Javanese Theatre,* 1931), Kats writes that it was also possible that the *wayang* originated from India. At the very least, there is a clear link between Javanese plays and the *wayang* found in India.

N. J. Krom (1931) disagreed with the view of Brandes and Hazeu that the *wayang* was created by the Javanese. He maintained that the fact that the terms relating to puppetry are all Javanese did not prove anything. He also cited Pischel's research, which postulated that *cayantaka,* a form of performance similar to the *wayang,* had been practised in India after the second century BCE. Krom pointed out that the *wayang kulit* is prominent only in areas which had been strongly influenced by Indian culture, such as Bali and Java. Moreover, the themes of the plays are also derived from the *Mahabharata*. Even so, Krom also accepted that the Javanese did have a role in the creation of the *wayang*. Krom concluded that although the *wayang* came from India, it showed uniquely Javanese characteristics from the beginning. At first, the *wayang* was only performed for royalty. Gradually, it spread to the general populace and was adapted to suit the event or ceremony that was being held at that time. In this way, the *wayang* developed a Javanese form, although it still retained the Hindu stories as well. As a result, the *wayang* can be said to be a "Hindu-Javanese" creation.

More recently, J. J. Ras too has argued that the *wayang* came from India. He notes studies by Stan Harding, H. Meinhard, and especially F. Seltmann, who indicate that there are many forms of shadow theatre in India. According to Seltmann, performances usually take place during spring and harvest time. In Kerala, performances have strong religious elements. Seltmann adds that in Mysore and Andhra, shows also feature an ugly-looking clown with a protruding stomach, called Killekyata (Ras, 1976: 53-54). Amin Sweeney accepts that Pischel's research has already shown the existence of classic shadow theatre performances in India and the newer studies have shown that the form still live and thrive in various areas there. All of these arguments add to the possibility that we must look to India for the original source of the *wayang kulit* of Southeast Asia (Sweeney, 1976: 31).

Apart from these proposals, there is a further theory that the *wayang* actually came from China. James R. Brandon pointed out that if that the *wayang* developed from ancestor worship and the need to communicate with one's ancestors, then it should be to China, or at least, Central Asia, that we should look for the source of the *wayang kulit* in Asia. He refers to B. Laufer's statement that *wayang kulit* in China was based on animism (ancestor worship). A folktale tells in 121 BCE, the Emperor of China was so saddened by the death of his queen that he ordered his people to display her shadow on a white screen. Laufer concludes that: "the shadows of the puppets are the shadows of the dead who have returned to earth", and the belief that ancestors manifest themselves as shadows or spirits is a uniquely Chinese belief. This shows that the puppet play still occupies a vital position in Chinese life (Brandon, 1974: 42-43).

It should be said here that Laufer's views actually derive from those of the German scholar G. Schlegel, whose analysis had already been rejected by Hazeu. Hazeu admits that there are similarities between the *wayang* of the Javanese and that of the Chinese, but he also insists that their techniques are very different from each other. Moreover, there is no evidence that there were sufficiently large numbers of Chinese people living in Java long ago for the Javanese to want to imitate their practices. Furthermore, shadow theatre has never been very popular in China (Hazeu, 1897: 27-28). Nevertheless, B. M. Goslings also believed that Javanese shadow theatre may have been inspired by a Chinese form called "*Ying-hi*", or "shadow performance". Goslings suggested that the very formal Javanese term for wayang, "*ringgit*" is derived from *yinggih*, as it is easier to pronounce the term in that way (Bezemer, 1928: 369-370).

Narratives

There are 179 complete *wayang purwa* narratives (*lakon*). They can be divided into four categories or cycles. The first category contains seven narratives. Three relate how a *raksasa* attacked Batara Guru's realm and demanded the surrender of a particular nymph to him on the threat that he would otherwise destroy heaven. Batara Guru could do nothing to counter the attack. Fortunately, a sage (*rishi*) was able to repel the *raksasa*. Three other lakons tell how Dewi Sri, the Goddess of Agriculture, exterminated all small animals that ruined the crops. The last lakon is performed during an exorcism, to save an infant from the possibility being eaten alive by Batara Kala.

The second category is the Arjuna Sastra Bahu Cycle of five lakons. They deal with the death of Dasamuka who was later reincarnated as Rawana. Arjuna Sastra Bahu undertook a period of meditation to obtain special powers and finally became king. He killed Dasamuka but was later defeated by Rama Bargawan.

The third category, the Rama Cycle, contains 18 lakons. Four lakons describe the birth of Sinta and her marriage to Rama. Rama's exile into the forest and the kidnapping of Sinta by Rawana fill a further two lakon. Rama's grief and his encounter with the monkey warriors Hanoman and Sugriwa take up two more lakon. The battle that ends with the death of Rawana, and Rama's reunion with Sita, is told in 10 lakons. Almost all the lakons in the Arjuna Sastra Bahu and Rama cycles are based on episodes in the *Ramayana*. Yet, the details differ. In the Rama Cycle, Rama is already an adult and an avatar of Vishnu. At the end of the story, he even becomes incarnate as Krisna and then plays an important role in the Pandawa Cycle.

The fourth category, the Pandawa Cycle, contains 150 lakons. This widely admired Cycle covers a long span of time, starting with Wisnu, the forefather of the Pandawa clan, and ending with Parikesit, regarded as the father of the first king of Java, Yadayana. The stories revolve around Pandu's sons, Yudhistira, Bima, Arjuna, Nakula and Sadewa and their rivalry with their cousins, the ninety-nine Kurawas, especially Duryudana, Sursana and Durgadasena. Yet, the conflict that led to the Great War and the heavy casualties the war inflicted on both sides, takes up only thirty-two lakons. Ninety-four lakons portray events in the Pandawas' Amarta palace in the forest. The most popular narratives relate to the marriages of the Pandawas, especially those of Arjuna and his sons, Abimanyu and Irawan. The twenty-three remaining lakons present the marriages of the Pandawas' forefathers (Brandon, 1970: 10-14).

2.2.11 The Social Functions of *Wayang*

For the Javanese, the *wayang* is not merely a form of entertainment. It plays a social role as well. *Wayang* performances are often held when a woman is expecting a child. If her husband hopes that the baby will turn out to be well-mannered and refined, he will stage the lakon entitled "The Birth of Arjuna". If he wishes for the child to be strong and courageous, then he will ask for a story of Bima, the Bima Bungkus, to be performed. If the couple wishes for a polite and beautiful daughter, then there are other appropriate lakon. The occasions of the completion of Quranic recital lessons (*khatam Quran*), a marriage, winning an award, or receiving blessings from God, are all celebrated with specific plays. It is perhaps for this reason, Tjan Tjoe Siem states that the *wayang* is not mere performance but is a religious ritual based on spiritual beliefs (Tjan Tjoe Siem, 1952: 17).

2.2.12 The Philosophy of *Wayang*

The *wayang* also symbolizes the development of the individual mind and soul in society. In an opening scene (*jejer*), the King commonly discusses the state of the country with his ministers and commanders of his army. This symbolizes the young child growing to adulthood. The armies sent to the battlefield and the initial failure, portray the struggles of the young man as he begins to navigate life in society. This incident is followed by an escalation of war in which we see a knight engaged in battle with various ogres. This battle signifies the struggle between good and evil inside every human being. The battle ends in victory for the warrior. This phase epitomizes the meaning of life and its trials and tribulations. Finally, there is sometimes a scene in which wooden puppets are dressed as dancers, the *tarian golek;* "*golek*" is linked to the term "*goleki*", seeking, encouraging the audience to search for the meaning and message of the play they have witnessed (Mangkunegara, 1957: 3-4).

It should be emphasized that the battle of the *wayang* is the eternal struggle between good and evil. This battle is ever present. When one form of wickedness is eliminated, another arises. When Rawana is killed, he will come to life again. When the world no longer contains evil, it will no longer be in balance.

2.2.13 Malay *Wayang* Stories

The *wayang kulit* is also very popular in the outlying regions influenced by Malay culture such as Palembang, Jakarta and Banjarmasin in Indonesia, as well as Kelantan in Malaysia. According to A. Ikram (Ikram, 1975: 15-17), Javanese plays are likely to be the source for Malay *wayang* stories such as: *Wayang Pandu* (Bat. Gen. 241) which traces the ancestry of the Pandawas; *Hikayat Arjuna Mangunjaya* (Bat. Gen. 191) which follows the adventures of Arjuna in his search for his wife, Kawintarsah, who had been taken by a giant eagle (*garuda*); the *Lakon Jaka Sukara* (Bat. Gen. 246), which relates the efforts of two of Arjuna's sons born to the daughters of holy men to find their father; and the *Hikayat Maharaja Garebak Jagat* (Bat. Gen. 251 atau MI 251), which tells the story of how the clowns changed their appearance as Rajuna was about to kill them at the order of the priest Drona, despite the fact that the punakawan were carrying out a task set by the Pandawa Queen to return Batara Narada's ring to heaven.[7] The Pandawas saw Arjuna as their enemy and eventually beheaded him. But his death led to such a serious drought that the gods were forced to revive him.

According to Van der Tuuk, the majority of Malay *wayang* stories were adapted from the Old Javanese translation of the "Adiparwa", the first part of the *Mahabharata*. Their contents are very different from Modern Javanese *Mahabharata* stories, such as *Lakon Obongan Bale Si Galagala*. The forms of many words and the names of the characters also show that Malay *wayang* stories were derived from old Javanese. For example, Malay *wayang* used the word "*merumrum*" to describe the efforts of a man to flatter his beloved. In Old Javanese, the word is "*angrumrum*" or "*mengrumrum*", while Modern Javanese uses the form "*ngrungrung*". Pandu's eldest son is called Darmawangsa and not Damakusuma as in Modern Javanese. Pandu and Drupadi's son is named Pancakurmara and not Pancawala, as in the Modern Javanese *Brata Yuda*.

Van der Tuuk has summarised a manuscript containing nineteen *wayang* stories. The manuscript, *Hikayat Pandawa* (Bat. Gen. 15) is held by the Central Museum Library, Jakarta. The plot is similar to the Leiden manuscript, codex 3377, although H. H. Juynboll has shown that there are differences between the two texts. Two of nineteen stories have been translated to English by Winstedt. Below are summaries of the nineteen stories, as published by Van der Tuuk (1879: 489-552).

1. Bismaka, the king of Mandipura, had three daughters: Amba, Ambawati and Ambalika. He promised to marry one of them to whomever could slay two *raksasa*s in a contest. All the great kings were invited to take in the contest. Dewabrata, the eldest son of Dewi Sayojana Sugandi, the widow of the king of Astina, was also invited. At that time, Bismaka was a student of Bagawan Rama Parasu. Dewabrata accepted the invitation. Thirty-nine kings had gathered

---

7 This manuscript was the primary text studied in the thesis written by Nikmah Sunardjo in 1980 for the Faculty of Letters, University of Indonesia (published by Balai Pustaka in 1989).

in the arena by the time Dewabrata arrived, but not one of them could overcome the two *raksasas*. Dewabrata succeeded. He was asked to choose which one of the three princesses he preferred, but he ran away with all three of them. As he fled, he was intercepted by the other suitors but he managed to defeat them all. When he reached home, Dewabrata and his two brothers married the three princesses. But since he had to remain chaste in order to continue practising meditation, Dewabrata did not dare consummate his marriage. One night, he left his home quietly. His wife, Amba, aware of his departure, followed him. Dewabrata was angry with her and shot her with an arrow. She died. He immediately regretted his action and made a solemn vow that when he died, it would be at the hands of a woman. His wife's soul rejoiced at this proclamation. Dewabrata became an ascetic and called himself Bagawan Bisma.

The gods in heaven attacked Bagawan Bisma's brothers, as they had taken names identical to those of the gods. But the gods failed. Only after Batara Guru intervened did Bisma's two brothers fall in battle.

When Bisma visited his mother, she urged him to marry his brothers' widows. Bisma refused, but suggested that the widows send for Bagawan Biyasa. When Bagawan Biyasa came to his wives, they were afraid. Ambawati closed her eyes, Ambalika concealed her body, while the third wife, Widura Sukma, raised one of her legs. As a result, their babies were all born with deformities. Ambawati's son, Destara, was blind. Ambalika's son, Pandu, had pale skin, while Widura Sukma's son was lame. By the age of seventeen, Pandu had become a capable young man, learning about warfare from his father, Biyasa.

2. Basukwesti, the king of Bodinagara, had a daughter, Kunti Nalibrata and two sons, Basudewa and Arya Prabu. Basukwesti wished to find a husband for Kunti and sent his sons to invite the noblest kings to attend a bridal contest.

Kunti Nalibrata was saddened by the news that she was to be married, as she was carrying Dewa Surya's baby, conceived in a rather strange way. When he found out about her pregnancy, her father so furious he wanted to kill her. The god Surya appeared and explained everything. The baby in Kunti's womb was born through her ear and blown to a distant place by Dewa Surya. When the baby fell to the ground, he was found by a holy man named Bambang Radeja. The baby's placenta fell at the foot of Wilis Mountain. A second meditating sage found the placenta and recited a divine mantra, and another baby was born from the placenta, called Jayadrata.

Basukwesti was relieved to have been spared the shame of Kunti's pregnancy. Many kings attended the contest, the most famous being Salya and Pandu. Pandu was accompanied by Biyasa and Semar, together with Semar's sons.

3. Salya defeated the other kings and was about to take Kunti's hand in marriage. However, Pandu arrived and defeated Salya. Salya was forced to also give away his sister, Mandurani, to Pandu. Pandu departed for home with his two new wives. During the journey, their way was blocked by Gandarsena who wanted to kidnap Pandu's wives. Pandu defeated Gandarsena and forced him to surrender his two daughters, Arya Gandarsena dan Dewi Anggandari. Pandu gave Dewi Anggandari to the blind Destarata. She vowed that her children would become the bitter enemies of Pandu's children.

4. Basudewa had two wives, Dewi Araswati dan Dewi Andanu. One day, he went hunting with his first wife, Dewi Araswati, but forgot to bring Dewi Andanu. A *raksasa*, Buwasanggara, whose previous proposal to Dewi Andanu had been rejected, took on the form of Basudewa and made love to Dewi Andanu. When Basudewa heard that his wife had been unfaithful, he wanted to kill her. But he was stopped by Arya Prabu. Dewi Andanu gave birth to a baby which was immediately taken to Wilis Mountain and left there. The baby was none other than the *raksasa*, Kangsa.

   Buwasanggara invited Kangsa to come to Wilis Mountain. Kangsa had become a powerful king and had conquered many countries. He sent an elephant to his father.

5. Dewi Kunti and Dewi Mandurani had discussed why Pandu was unable to give them children. One day, Pandu and his two wives went hunting. Batara Guru and Narada changed themselves into a pair of antelopes and mated in front of the two women, who found the animals' behaviour deeply disturbing. Semar tried to chase the antelopes away but they would not budge. Pandu became angry and shot them with a single arrow. Batara Guru and Narada changed back into their true selves.

   Batara Guru was incensed and vowed to take revenge on Pandu. A god was sent to kidnap Pandu and take him to the field of Si Jampang Ruji where he was beaten to death. Pandu's death was kept a secret and Widura was invited to replace him as king.

   Dewi Kunti wished to have children. With Biyasa's help, she then gave birth to three sons who were the incarnation of gods. The first one was named Darmawangsa, the second Bima and the third Arjuna. Arjuna was the incarnation of the God of Love who, at the time he was born, was already giving his own mother a flirtatious glance. Dewi Mandurani gave birth to twins, Sang Nakula and Sang Sadewa.

   One day, four of Pandu's sons were playing chasing, while Bima hid under a shell. Semar asked the boys if they would like to play at Mamantang Mountain, hoping that the elephant Sena would kill Bima. When they reached the mountain, they were set upon by Sena. The four boys climbed trees to escape, leaving Bima behind on the ground. The elephant charged at Bima, breaking the shell around him. Bima stepped out of the shell and killed the elephant. From then on, Bima was known as Sang Sena.

   In Astina, the people had a huge celebration. Destarata had fathered 108 sons. The eldest was Duryodana, followed by Dursana, Burisrawa and the others. Gandaradesa was invited to raise the boys and given the name Arya Sangkuni.

6. Basudewa of Darawati Purwa had two children called Kakarsana and Ajarana (in the Javanese lakons, the latter is called Narajau). They were capable and very strong princes. Kangsa lived in Wilis Mountain was told that he would meet his end as the hands of two sons of a mighty king. Angrily, he invited the two princes to play with his pet elephant. The elephant was no match for the valiant princes and they killed it. Kangsa also tried to kill the two princes but he too was defeated.

   Meanwhile, Basudewa had a daughter, Subadra. He heard a divine voice saying that Ajarana was the incarnation of Wisnu and should be renamed Kresna, while Kakarsana should be renamed Baladewa. Kresna replaced his father as king of Darawati. Baladewa married Satyawati, Salya's daughter, and became king of Mandura.

7. The Kurawas, led by Duryodana, tried all sorts of cunning strategies to wipe out the Pandawas. But their evil plans were always thwarted by Bima, who was always warned in advance by Semar of what was happening. Duryodana complained to Sangkuni that Bima was a malicious person. Sangkuni went to meet Biyasa, who cautioned Sangkuni that his actions would only lead to a war between the Kurawas and Pandawas. Biyasa predicted that the Pandawa side would triumph. Sangkuni refused to believe this. Destarata wished to poison Bima but to no avail.

Sangkuni tried everything he could think of to ensure that the kingdom remained in the hands of the Kurawa. He invited the Pandawas to a cockfight. His rooster was Dursasana, Duryodhana's brother. Bima also spoiled this ruse. Frustrated, Duryodhana insulted the Pandawas by saying that they did not know who their father was or where he was buried. So, the Pandawas went to ask their mother, Kunti.

Worried, Kunti took her sons to look for Biyasa. Bima forced Biyasa to tell the Pandawas that Pandu had been taken away by Batara Guru. Batara Guru lived in heaven and only those who had died could visit him there.

Bima did not care about the advice and insisted on going to look for their father. Semar and his sons acted as guides. Before long, they reached Mount Mahameru, the abode of the gods.

Bima ran amuck in heaven, causing a battle among the Pandawas and the gods. Neither side won or lost. In the end, Batara Guru had to give Pandu's body to the Pandawas. The Pandawas returned to their home and decided to build a temple for Pandu's final resting place.

After hearing of Pandu's death, kings came from all lands to Mertawangsa. Biyasa advised the Pandawas that they must always heed Kresna's advice. Biyasa also revealed to the Pandawas that the temple could only be built by the ascetic Pusaragam. Bima was asked to fetch Pusaragam, and he helped the Pandawas build the mausoleum. As soon as he had finished, Pusaragam vanished before their very eyes. The kings returned to their own lands. Biyasa went back to his hermitage. Widura was appointed to take care of the Pandawas.

8. Bagawan Kumbayana travelled from India to Java. He called himself Dangyang Drona and married Bagawan Kerpa's sister. His fame spread far and wide. The greatest kings came to learn from him, as did the Kurawas and Pandawas. Of all his students, Arjuna proved to be the best. Duryodana complained about this to Sangkuni. Sangkuni urged Drona to destroy Bima, promising him half the kingdom of Astina as a reward. Drona asked Bima to bring back the elixir of life from Sakuranga Ocean. Drona promised to teach Bima all types of magical powers if he succeeded. Bima killed the dragon (naga) that guarded the ocean and returned with the elixir. Drona refused to accept the elixir, saying that it had been contaminated by the blood of the dragon. He ordered Bima to go back to the ocean again, this time to its very centre. Widura warned Bima to be careful.

While passing through the forest, Bima killed an ogre. The *raksasa* was actually Indra, the King of Gods. Indra thanked Bima for releasing him from a curse and revealed Drona and Duryodana's wicked plan. As he was crossing a river, Bima was almost swept away by the waves. Batara Guru felt pity for Bima and saved him. Bataru Guru told Bima that Drona had tricked him into carrying out the difficult task to have him killed. Bima quickly returned home and forced Drona to reveal the truth. At the request of Drona and Darmawangsa, the Kurawas and Pandawas made peace with each other. The Pandawas returned to Widura, the home of their uncle. The Kurawas returned to their own country. Duryodana was crowned king of Astina and married Banuwati, Salya's daughter.

9. No one could cross Mount Indraguna without being attacked by a ferocious lion. Ugrasena wanted to kill the beast, but it killed him instead. His wife, Ciptawati, sought protection from the monkey Bagawan Kapi Jembawa. Ciptawati promised Kapi Jembawa her kingdom and daughter Ugrawati if he could kill the lion. Kapi Jembawa not only killed the lion, he also revived Ugrasena. Kapi Jembawa married Ugrawati, who quickly discovered that her husband was not actually a monkey at all. Ugrawati gave birth to a girl named Jambuwati. Kapi Jembawa left his wife and daughter, and became a hermit once more.

10. Kesna refused to marry a princess chosen for him by his father, Basudewa, and was banished from the kingdom. He went to Mount Indraguna, wanting to be eaten by the lion that roamed the mountain. He did not meet the lion but instead found himself in a beautiful garden. Jambuwati also entered the garden. Kesna immediately fell in love with her. Her father accepted Kesna's proposal as he knew that Kesna was an incarnation of Wisnu.

11. Kesna arrived in Malya Pura and saw Princess Satyabama, whom he kidnapped. The princess was actually the woman Basudewa had chosen to be Kesna's wife. When he reached home, Kesna was warmly welcomed by his parents and his sister, Subadra. Princess Satyabama's father was quickly informed, and a lavish wedding was held in Darawati.

12. Kunti wanted her children to inherit the throne and asked Kesna for advice. Bima was sent to negotiate the return of half of Astina from the Kurawas. The Kurawas set a condition that the Pandawas had to dig a river to the sea, and they had to dig faster than the Kurawas. Due to the extraordinary strength of Bima, the Pandawas won again. However, the Kurawas still refused to surrender the half of Astina that rightfully belonged to the Pandawas.

Sangkuni tricked Bima, saying that half of Astina was worthless; it would be much better to clear new land on a mountain. Sangkuni also indicated that the Kurawas would send two hundred people each day to help the Pandawas. Kesna and the Pandawas were furious because Bima swallowed Sangkuni's lies. No one had ever lived in the jungle because it was the home of Arya Sapujagat, king of the spirits. The subjects who were sent to the mountain never returned. Bima fought Arya Sapujagat, defeating him only after an intense battle.

The Pandawas settled in the forest and started a new kingdom. Darmawangsa became king, Bima was chosen as *arya* (regent) while Arjuna was given a new title, *dipati* (lord). Their twin brothers became ministers. They called the kingdom Martapura; it soon became famous and many people settled there.

The Kurawas invited Bima and his servants to a festival. They poisoned Bima and his companions, then threw them into the deepest part of the ocean, where the serpent, Naga Arya (also known as Antaboga), lived. Naga Arya brought Bima and his companions back to life. Bima married Naga Arya's daughter, Naganini. Shortly after, Bima felt homesick and said goodbye to his serpent family. Naganini gave birth to a son named Raden Antaraja.

During the journey home, Bima fought with *raksasa*s and wild beasts. Due to his extraordinary strength, he not only defeated them but earned various magical weapons as well. Batara Guru and Hanoman were among those who gave these superweapons to Bima. When Bima arrived in Astina, he found that Arjuna was being attacked by the Kurawas for sleeping with Duryodana's wife, Banuwati. Bima overpowered the Kurawas. Together with the other Pandawas, Bima made his way home to Martawangsa.

Destaraja felt disconsolate when he heard about these incidents. He decided to destroy the Pandawas. Destarata built a highly inflammable palace and invited the Pandawas to live there. One night, the palace was set alight. The Kurawas rejoiced, for they were sure that the Pandawas had perished in the fire.

In fact, the Pandawas had managed to escape. They fled to the country of Pring Gendani, ruled by king Arimba. The king's sister, Arimbi, was the governor. Bima and Arimba fought an intense battle that Bima won thanks to Semar, and he married Arimbi. Arimbi gave birth to a baby; no one could cut the baby's umbilical cord, even with the sharpest knife.

Batara Guru was in difficulty. King Naga Percona threatened to attack heaven if Batara Guru did not hand over the nymph Bidadari Sakerba. The serpent king could only be defeated by an infant who had not yet lost its umbilical cord. Batara Guru sent Narada to find such a baby, and gave him the divine *konta* arrow to take with him.

Bambang Radeja was expelled from home by his adopted father, a *maharesi* (sage), because he loved killing animals. The maharesi told Bambang Radeja that he had a brother, Jayadrata. While wandering in the forest, Narada thought Radeja was Arjuna and gave him the konta arrow. Later Narada realised his mistake but Radeja was unwilling to return the arrow. Narada chased Radeja, and when Arjuna and Semar arrived, they too joined the chase. Arjuna only managed to catch the quiver that held the arrow, but Narada was able to use the quiver to cut Bima's baby son's umbilical. Bima named the boy Gatotkaca. Narada immediately took the baby to heaven.

Bima was angry, even though he knew why he had lost his son. Gatotkaca grew quickly. By the time he reached heaven, he was able to fight and he easily defeated Naga Percona. When he returned home, no one recognized him because he had been only a child when he left; now he was an adult. Gatotkaca became king of Pring Gendani.

13. Bambang Radeja visited Bagawan Sampani and met his brother, Jayadrata. Bagawan gave Radeja a new name, Karna. Jayadrata told Radeja that he and the Pandawas actually shared the same mother. Taking Jayadrata with him, Karna went in search of his real brothers, the Pandawas. When he reached Astina, he heard from the Kurawas that the Pandawas had perished in a fire. Karna and Jayadrata then stayed to serve the Kurawas. Karna was given the title of "lord" (*dipati*) and made a member of the Kurawa clan. Karna married Dewi Sutrikandi. Jayadrata was appointed chief of security (*temenggung*) and married Sutikawati, Salya's daughter.

14. The Pandawas set out for Martapura, leaving Gatotkaca to stay behind in Pring Gendani together with his mother and uncle. During the journey, they paused at Pancalapura. The king was holding a bridal contest; the victor would win the hand of the Princess Drupadi. Arjuna disguised himself as a mountain-man and won the contest. The Pandawas returned

home with Drupadi. Arjuna and Bima both wanted to marry her, but finally Biyasa arrived and decided that Drupadi should go to Darmawangsa as he was the eldest. Arjuna then left for his teacher's home.

15. Sang Ekalaya (known in Javanese shadow theatre as Palgunadi) wished to study with Drona and learn how to gain magical powers. Duryodana refused to allow Ekalaya to study with Drona as he was a commoner. Ekalaya then made a clay statue of Drona and practised in front of the statue. Batara Guru admired the youth and presented him with a ring. Ekalaya became a very skillful archer. He hunted all the animals in the jungle until there was none left. One day, Drona sent Arjuna to hunt in the forest. Arjuna discovered that all the animals in the forest had been killed; Ekalaya even shot Arjuna's dog. Arjuna and Ekalaya began firing arrows at each other. Arjuna could not defeat Ekalaya and demanded to know the name of his teacher. "Drona," Ekalaya replied. Drona came and cut off the finger on which Ekalaya wore the ring Batara Guru had given him. Ekalaya died. Before Ekalaya died, his spirit warned them that he would have his revenge in the coming Great War.

    Drupadi gave birth to a daughter whose habits and mannerisms were the same as a man's. Her name was Srikandi. She even wished to marry a woman and took Princess Nilawati as her wife. As she lacked a man's genitals, she felt ashamed at being unable to consummate the marriage and fled to the forest. The goddess Durga advised Srikandi to trade genitals with a *raksasa*, Bagawan Binum. Using the *raksasa*'s genitals, Srikandi successfully fathered two children. Bagawan Binum kept waiting for Srikandi to return his sexual organs as he could no longer tolerate the pains of monthly menstruation. Srikandi refused and wanted to run away again. Batara Guru forced her to give back what she had borrowed. Srikandi returned home to her father's home and resumed life as a woman, waiting for a king to marry her.

16. Raja Seta of Kalanggana stole Kano's extraordinary elephant. Worried, Kano asked Arjuna for help. Arjuna could not help him as he had no weapons. But he felt so sorry for Kano that he stole back the weapon he had previously given to Darmawangsa. But Darmawangsa discovered the theft and banished Arjuna for twelve years. Arjuna defeated Seta with this weapon. He then married Seta's sister, Sriwati. Kano also gave Arjuna his sister, Kanowati, to be his wife.

17. Dursasana asked for the hand of Subadra, Kesna's sister. The proposal was accepted by Baladewa but he was unaware that Kesna had already promised Subadra to Arjuna. Dursasana arrived in Astina, behaving in a very arrogant manner. Kesna sent his youngest brother to look for Arjuna. He found Arjuna almost dead, as he had suffered greatly during his twelve years of exile. However, Arjuna was quickly restored to health.

    Arjuna fell in love with Subadra and kidnapped her. The Kurawas pursued Arjuna, assisted by Karna and Jayadrata. An intense battle ensued. The Kurawas was helpless against Arjuna. Arjuna returned to his land and was warmly welcomed by his family.

    Drona fell in love with Srikandi. Srikandi was willing to marry Drona on condition that Drona defeat her uncle, Gandasukma. The Kurawas' efforts were of no avail. Drona appealed to Arjuna for help. Arjuna defeated Gandasukma who then disappeared. Srikandi, however, still refused to marry Drona. Bima challenged Drona to a fight but Drona declined. Arjuna was afraid that a calamity would befall them as it was most disrespectful to challenge a teacher. Arjuna fled and disguised himself as a monk. Everyone in Martapura looked for Arjuna but he was nowhere to be found. Gatotkaca had also gone away to meditate.

Naga Arja of Saptapatala wanted to crown his grandson Antaraja. But Antaraja was only willing to be king if he could first meet his father. Antaraja then left to look for his father. Gatotkaca took Antaraja to see their father, Bima, and the other members of his family. Gatotkaca and Antaraja then went to find Arjuna. They searched for seven days but still had not found Arjuna. Gatotkaca too vanished and went to meditate.

18. Sasawarna heard about Subadra's beauty and wanted her for a wife, although Subadra was already married to Arjuna. He sent his governor, Dumaraksa, to bring a letter to Martapura. Kesna dreamt that the sea had flooded Martapura and its mountains had collapsed. He also heard that Arjuna was missing. He immediately departed to Martapura. There he found the Pandawas shrouded in gloom. At the same time, Sasawarna's governor arrived. Kesna was willing to let Subadra go with Sasawarna on condition that Sasawarna produced the head of a priest (Arjuna in disguise) as a gift, as well as a white elephant (an incarnation of Antaraja) and a buffalo (an incarnation of Gatotkaca) as escorts.

As a monk, Arjuna was unwilling to engage in combat and he allowed Sasawarna to cut off his head. If not for the help of Batara Guru, Dumaraksa would have been killed by the two animals he had to hunt to fulfil Kesna's condition. Accompanied by a large entourage, Sasawarna arrived in Martapura. Arjuna's head was placed in a temple. Arjuna came back to life. Sasawarna then had to fight Arjuna to win Subadra. He failed and fled. When he reached home, he found his wife in an embrace with Arjuna. Furious, he wanted to kill her, but Sasawarna was told that this was his punishment for wanting to take away someone else's wife.

The Kurawas and Sasawarna discussed possible ways to fight Arjuna. Two of Ekalaya's brothers, Sang Kesna and Malangdewa, came to take revenge on Arjuna for the death of their brother. Drona pacified the two brothers and persuaded them to serve the Kurawas.

Ekalaya's brothers went looking for the Pandawas. They found the Pandawas busy building a temple on Mount Botar. Sang Kesna cunningly stole the heirloom amulet that was the source of the Pandawas' power. Malangdewa also managed to defeat Arjuna in a battle. He took Arjuna's head to Astina, much to the delight of the Kurawas. Arjuna, however, came back to life and seduced Banuwati, Duryodhana's wife. Arjuna and Malangdewa again clashed on the battlefield. This time, Arjuna emerged the victor. Sang Kresna too was killed by Kesna. Bima wanted to destroy Astina but was stopped by his brother, Darmawangsa. To celebrate their victory, a lavish festival was held in Martapura.

2.2.14 Thai *Wayang*

There are two well-known forms of *wayang* in Kelantan—*Wayang Jawa* (Javanese *wayang*) and *Wayang Siam* (Siamese *wayang*). The *Wayang Jawa* portrays many stories from the Panji cycle; the stories of the Pandawas are rarely performed now. The reason for the decline is that the bangsawan theatre performers who play the main roles in the *Wayang Jawa* are no longer popular, whereas the *Wayang Siam* is thriving. In Kelantan itself, there are at least three hundred puppet masters (*dalang*) performing the *Wayang Siam*. And it goes without saying that *Wayang Siam* dalangs can also be found in Trengganu, Patani, Kedah and Perak, which are also close to Southern Thailand.

According to Amin Sweeney, *wayang* performances often open with an *upacara* (ritual) called a *kenduri* (feast) (Sweeney, 1972b: 273-279). The *dalang* will call various types of spirits, angels and demons to descend to earth, informing them that the purpose of the feast is to avoid conflict and to guarantee that the performance will proceed smoothly. After the feast comes the *upacara buka panggung* (ritual to prepare the stage), in which the dalang recites mantras to enchant the audience. Next is the story of *Tok/Wak Peran Hutan*. In this short piece, Maharesi Kala Api or Sri Rama ask Peran Hutan to find meat of a white mousedeer. While he is hunting, a tiger attacks him. As the tiger is about to eat him, Peran Hutan has a vision of his teacher and receives a new burst of strength. He kills the tiger. But he had no energy left to repel the negative force (*badi*) that the dead animal pours out. He consults his teacher, who teaches him some mantras to counter the animal's malignant energy. It is clear that this performance is meant to repel any negativity around the stage. This is followed by a song of praise, in which the dalang formally invites all the angels and *jinn*s to attend the feast that is about to be served.

The second part of the show is the *Story of Batara Kala*. This performance is considered dangerous and children are forbidden from sleeping near the stage when the play is being enacted. The climax of the story is when Kala, hungry for blood, chases Mak Babu until they reach a *wayang* stage. Wak Long, the dalang, challenges Kala. A debate ensues between Wak Long and Kala. Kala is satisfied and is asked to wait briefly for the feast that will soon be served to him. The white screen is then rolled up and the dalang acts like a man possessed as he serves food to the newly arrived *jinn*s and angels.

The final part of the opening ritual is the dismissal (*pelepas*), in which the dalang farewells all the *jinn*s and angels who had been present at the feast. This is the final step taken in order to remove any negative energy from around the stage.

Although the story of Rama is the most important play in the *Wayang Siam,* stories from other sources are also performed. These include stories of the Pandawas; folk stories, such as *Hikayat Terong Pipit;* stories taken from *Mak Yong* dance-drama; and *Tarik Selampit* in which stories are narrated using a combination of rhythmic prose and song. Sometimes *Hikayat Indra Bangsawan, Hikayat Saiful Lizan* and *Hikayat Hang Tuah* are also performed. I present below a well-known *Wayang Siam* story, *Cerita Maharaja Wana* (*The Tale of Maharaja Wana*) (Sweeney, 1972: 89-126; 295-337).

1   The demon Bota Dati Kuaca tried to attack the land of Birma and was killed. Bentera Baha, a prince of Birma, inaugurated himself as ruler of Bota Dati, Kuaca's country, and married his widow.

2   The demon Bota Seranjuk Dewa, from the celestial realm at the side of the world where the sun sets, wanted to seduce the beautiful wife of Dewa Berembun who lived in the celestial abode where the sun rises. One day, while Dewa Berembun was absent from home, Bota Seranjuk Dewa assumed the form of Dewa Berembun and made love to Siti Andang Dewi, Dewa Berembun's wife. After his wish had been fulfilled, Bota Seranjuk Dewa descended to earth and incarnated through the mouth of Bentera Baha's wife. Shortly after, Dewa Berembun

returned to his celestial home. From her husband's words, Siti Andang Dewa realised that she had been deceived by Bota Seranjuk Dewa. Feeling embarrassed and ashamed, she descended to earth in a newly incarnated form to look for Bota Seranjuk Dewa and take her revenge.

3   Dewa Berembun, a teacher, lost the desire to teach as he was feeling too nervous. He handed over his teaching tasks to Dewa Sayang Kenung. Soon, all his students completed their studies, except Bota Kemang who was stupid although he worked hard and respected his teacher. Out of his affection for this one student, Dewa Sayang Kenung gave him a magic torch. Just by pointing the torch, he could destroy whatever he chose. Bota Kemang wreaked havoc in heaven and on earth using his torch. He destroyed all the forests, hills and valleys.

Dewa Berembun was furious to hear of Bota Kemang's actions. He ordered Dewa Sayang Kenung to give back the magic torch. Dewa Sayang Kenung took on the form of a beautiful girl and traversed all corners of the forests and fields in his search for Bota Kemang. Bota Kemang was instantly smitten by the beautiful maiden, and was willing to dance for her if she would become his lover. And so, Bota Kemang danced, wielding the torch and pointing it to his face, causing him to disintegrate immediately. Dewa Sayang Kenung took the torch and returned to heaven.

Dewa Berembun embraced Dewa Sayang Kenung, who was still in a female form, thinking that she was his wife. When he realised his mistake, his seed had already been spilled, and so, he instructed one of the deities to blow it into Maya Angin's mouth, which was constantly open. As soon as the sperm entered her mouth, she closed it and became pregnant.

Two birds made a nest in the beard of an ascetic, Maharesi Buring Jerijit. One day, the birds fought so hard that they became entangled in the maharesi's beard. When he chided them, they taunted him, saying that his mediation was in vain, for he had no son to carry on his name. And so, the maharesi formed a desire to have children. He took the pith of a sandalwood tree (*cendana*) and prayed over it; a woman appeared, called Tuan Putri Siti Cendana. He took her as his wife. Shortly after, the woman gave birth to a baby girl. The maharesi resumed his meditation. Before leaving, he showed her a certain gesture. Whenever she made that gesture, he would come. On one occasion, she made the gesture and he came and sported with her. However, she also used the same gesture to invite Dewa Matahari and Dewa Cahaya Bulan to come and later gave birth to two boys. Her secret was revealed to the ascetic by her elder daughter. The maharesi was so infuriated that he forced her back into a sandalwood tree once more. He cast a spell on the two boys and changed them into monkeys. But the maharesi's wife also cast a spell on her daughter and the girl was forced to meditate on Gunung Angin hill with her open mouth as a punishment. She became Putri Maya Angin. Dewa Matahari came down to earth and built a city called Akian for his son, Raja Bali. Dewa Cahaya Bulan also came down to earth and named his son Raja Sekerba or Sagariwa.

4   Sirat Maharaja of Siusia Mendarapura, and his queen Cahaya Bulan, had two sons, Tengku Sri Rama and Laksamana. He also had two sons from his concubine Mandudari, named Semardan and Cardan. When they grew up, Sri Rama and Laksamana went to study with a teacher in Gunung Sahpian.

5   Queen Bentera Baha of Dati Kuaca had three children—Maharaja Wana, Mah Babu Kenung and Mah Prabu Anam. Because Maharaja Wana was so mischievous, he was banished to the island of Pulau Langkapuri. On the island, Maharaja Wana undertook an extremely arduous form of meditation. The Prophet Adam visited him and granted him power over the four worlds, on the condition that he did not disturb the countries in the East.

   Maharaja Wana built a state on the island. After that, he went to visit his vassal states, to look for a wife. Maharaja Wana also conquered Gua Singa Maling, which was ruled by Kepan Putih, and Gunung Tiga that was ruled by Raja Gagak. He married one princess from each of the four worlds. The princesses all had children—Putri Naga from the sea gave birth to Gangga Masur, who had the body of a boy but the head of a sea serpent; Putri Maya Bumi from earth gave birth to Putri Mata Api; Princess Mayang from the air gave birth to Nerajit, who had six heads and ten hands. Maharaja Wana even had sexual relations with an elephant and a tiger; they too gave birth to his offspring. The babies asked their mothers who their father was, and were told that Maharaja Wana was their father. Again Maharaja Wana came to Maya Bumi and they had another son, Maula Tani; the boy was born with five hundred heads and five thousand hands.

6   Maharaja Wana decided that none of his wives were fit to be his queen. He defeated Sirat Maharaja and demanded that Sirat Maharaja's wife, Princess Cahaya Bulan, rub the dead skin from her body and that this dirt (*daki*) be made into her double. The double was then given to Maharaja Wana and named Mandudaki.

7   Siti Andang Dewi entered Mandudaki's body, and Mandudaki became pregnant. While Mandudaki was expecting her baby, Maharaja Wana saw many ill omens in his dreams. Maharaja Babu Sanam, Maharaja Wana's brother, was a very learned astrologer; he predicted that the birth of the baby would bring about great disaster to the country. Mandudaki was taken to the beach. Maharaja Babu Sanam aborted the foetus, placed it in a jar, and threw the jar into sea. Maharesi Kala Api found the jar and raised the child, who grew to become the beautiful Putri Siti Dewi.

8   Maharesi Kala Api held a contest to choose a husband for Princess Siti Dewi. Various spirits, elves, demigods, demons and ogres gathered at his temple. With Laksamana's assistance, Sri Rama emerged victorious and traveled to the east with her.

9   After enthroning Batara Guru as the king of heaven, the one supreme god Sang Hyang Tunggal came down to earth. He created a comically ugly creature, Pak Dogol, as his companion. Then, from the dirt on his body, he created Wak Long. Pak Dogol and Wak Long went to Langkapuri to work as servants.

10 After a pregnancy of nine months and ten days, Princess Maya Angin gave birth to a monkey named Kera Putih. The monkey had such a huge appetite that Princess Maya Angin could not provide him with enough food. She sent him to forage for fruit in the forest. Kera Putih met Dewa Matahari, who told him his origins. He was then taught various forms of knowledge and renamed Hanoman Kera Putih. Hanoman Kera Putih went to Pakiam to look for his father and was warmly received by his uncle, Bali.

11 Maharaja Wana tried various tricks to kidnap Siti Dewi. Finally, he succeeded and took Siti Dewi home to Langkapuri. The bird Jentayu witnessed the kidnapping, but was mortally wounded trying to save Siti Dewi. Before the bird died, it told Sri Rama who had kidnapped his wife.

12 Raja Bali obtained a wife from his father, Dewa Matahari. Later, Dewa Cahaya Bulan chose a girl for his brother, Sagariwa, and Raja Bali also took her. Finally, his teacher created a third wife for him.

13 Hanoman met Sri Rama again and was acknowledged as his son. Together they left for Langkapuri.

14 Bapak Sapi liked to marry his own daughters. If his wife gave birth to male children, he killed them. One day, she gave birth to a boy and looked after him in secret. When he grew up, the child, who was named Anak Amuk (Chaos), killed his father and proceeded to wreak havoc throughout the country. He challenged Raja Bali. Raja Bali suggested that they fight in a cave. Before he left, he gave his brother Sagariwa the following instructions: if white blood flowed from the cave, that meant that he had been killed and Sagariwa must seal the cave to prevent Anak Amuk from creating more pandemonium in the country. But if red blood flowed, then that was a sign Raja Bali had been victorious and the cave should be opened. After some time, Sagariwa saw foam coming from the cave. Thinking that Raja Bali was dead, he sealed the cave. Sagariwa married Raja Bali's wives. Raja Bali managed to escape from the cave and return home. He banished Sagariwa to the forest, where he met Sri Rama. Sagariwa was willing to help Sri Rama look for Siti Dewi if Sri Rama would help him kill Raja Bali. Sri Rama agreed to this request.

15 A decision was made to build a bridge to Langkapuri. Sagariwa asked his brothers and nephews to help in the construction but they could not complete the task. Finally, Hanoman Kera Putih succeeded in finishing the bridge. When the bridge was subsequently destroyed by the fishes and the turtles under the command of Tuan Putri Ikan and Raja Labi on the order of Maharaja Wana, Hanoman Kera Putih repaired it. Next, Hanoman Kera Putih was sent to Langkapuri where he spread an enormous fire. He found Siti Dewi and she accepted him as her son. But he declined to rescue her, as he believed the honour of saving her should fall on Sri Rama.

An intense battle took place. One after another, Maharaja Wana's allies and sons fell on the battlefield. The first to die was Raja Gagah, followed by Raja Rimau and then Kapan Putih.

The battle became even more intense. Hanoman Kera Putih played an important role in the war, killing many of Maharaja Wana's allies and sons. He married the queen of the fishes, Tuan Putri Ikan, so that she would no longer help Maharaja Wana. When Raja Labis kidnapped Sri Rama and Laksamana, Hanoman rescued them. Because Maharaja Wana's younger brother, Mah Babu Sanam, had not approved of Maharaja Wana's actions, he had been banished from Langkapuri. Mah Babu Sanam contributed much to Sri Rama's efforts by advising him about the size of Maharaja Wana's forces and the expected time of their arrival on the battlefield. He also knew all about the treacherous plans of Maharaja Wana's allies and sons, and warned Sri Rama to take adequate counter-measures against them. Unfortunately, Sri Rama did not heed the advice and his army was almost defeated by Maharaja Wana's son, Nerajit. But in the end, Maharaja Wana's army was defeated.

16   Maharaja Wana was terrified: all his children, family members and friends were dead. He hid his soul in Maharesi Kala Api's house and refused to come out to continue fighting. Hanoman stole Maharaja Wana's soul and tricked him into resuming the battle. Maharaja Wana was killed by an arrow from Sri Rama's bow. Mah Babu Sanam was crowned king of Langkapuri. Sri Rama returned to his home country, together with Siti Dewi and his entourage. The story ends with a rebellion by two sons of Maharaja Wana who were not killed during the invasion of Langkapuri as they were still children at that time. The rebellion was quelled by Sri Rama and Laksamana.

REFERENCES

Anderson, Benedict R. O.
1965. *Mythology and the Tolerance of the Javanese,* Ithaca.

Attagora, Kingkeo
1963. "The *Ramayana* Epic in Thailand and South East Asia," *Assam Research Society Journal,* 15, pp. 3-21.

Balai Pustaka
1959. *Hikayat Sang Boma,* Djakarta.

Barret, E. C. G.
1963. "Further Light on Sir Richard Winstedt's undescribed Malay Version of *Ramayana,*" *BSOAS,* 26, pp. 531-543.

Basham. A. L.
1959. *The Wonder that was India,* New York.

Bezener, T. J.
1928. "Over Gorsprong en Beteekenis van de Wajang," in *Kolonial Tijdschrift,* 17.

Brakel, L. F.
1980. "*Two Indian Epics in Malay,*" *Archipel* 20, pp. 143-160.

Brandon, James R.
1970. *On Thrones of Gold, Three Javanese Shadow Plays,* Massachusetts.
1974. *Theatre in Southeast Asia,* Massachusetts.

Cadet, J. M.
1971. *The Ramakien, the Thai Epic,* Tokyo.

Callenfels, Stein
"De Sudamala in de Hindu Javaansche Kunst", *VBG,* 66.

Chambert-Loir, Henri
1977a. "A propos du *Mahabharata* Malais," *BEFEO,* 64, pp. 265-291.
1977b. "Notes sur une Epopee malaise: Le Hikayat Dewa Mandu," *BEFEO,* 64, pp. 293-302.

Clara van Groenendael, Victoria M.
1985. *The Dalang behind the Wayang,* (*VKI* 114), Dorhrecht.
1987. *Wayang Theatre in Indonesia: An Annotated Bibliography,* Dordrecht.

Coedes, G.
1968. *The Indianized States of South East Asia* (translated into English by Susan Brown Cowing), Kuala Lumpur.

Cuisinier, Jeanne
1957. *Le Theatre D'Ombres a Kelantan,* Paris.

Darasuprapta
1969. "Titik-titik hubungan pada tjerita Ardjunasasrabau – Rama-Mahabrata-Panji-Damarwulan-Menak dalam khazanah kesusteraan Djawa," Bull, Fak. Sastra Kebudayaan Univ. Gama I pp. 61-70.

De Zoete, Beryl and Walter Spies
1938. *Dance and Drama in Bali,* London.

Dhani Nivat, Prince
1946.   "The Rama Jataka, A Lao version of the story of Rama," *JSS*, 36 (I), pp.1-2.
1956.   *The Nang*, Bangkok.
1967.   "Hide Figure of the Ramakien," *JSS*, 53 (1), pp. 1-30.

Dhanit Yupho
1952.   *Classical Siamese Theatre*, Bangkok.
1963.   *The Khon and lakon*, Bangkok.

Dowson, J.
1950.   *A Classical Dictionary of Hindu Mythology and Religion, Geography, History and Literature*, London.

Dutt, Romesh C.
1961.   *The Ramayana & The Mahabharata*, London.

Ensink, J.
1967-1968. "Rekhacarma. On the Indonesian Shadow-play with special Reference to the island of Bali," *Adyar Library Bulletin*, Vol. 31-32, pp. 412-441.

Eysinga, Roorda van
1843.   *Geschiedenis Van Sri Rama, beroemd Indisch heroisch dichtstuk*, Amsterdam.

Farid Mohd. Onn
1965.   *Cherita Seri Rama*, Kuala Lumpur.

Francisco, Juan R.
1962.   "The Rama Story in the Post Muslim Malay Literature of Southeast Asia," *The Sarawak Museum*, Journal 10, no. 19-20.

Fretz, A. Wagner
1959.   *Indonesia. The Art of an Island Group*, London.

Gerth Van Wijk
1891.   "Iets over verschillende Maleische redactien van den Seri Rama," *TBG*, 34, pp. 401-433.

Goslings, B.M.
1938.   *De Wajang op Java en op Bali in het verleden en heden*, Amsterdam.

Grierson, Sir George A.
1927.   "The Adbhuta-*Ramayana*," *BSOAS*, IV/3.

Haridas Bhattacharyya
1953-1962. *The cultural Heritage of India* (2nd edition). Calcutta.

Hazeu, G. A. J.
1897.   *Bijdrage tot de kennis van het Javaansche tooneel*, Leiden.

Hardjowirogo, R.
1952.   *Sedjarah Wajang Purwa*, Djakarta.

Hikayat Sang Boma
1957.   *Hikayat Sang Boma* (no, 297), Djakarta, Balai Pustaka.

Hill, A. H.

1949. "Wayang Kulit Stories from Trengganu," *JMBRAS,* 16 (3), pp. 85-105.

Holt, Claire.
1967. *Art in Indonesia Continuity and Change,* Ithaca.

Hooykaas, C.
1947. *Over Maleise Literatuur.* E. J. Brill, Leiden.
1955. "The Old Javanese Ramaya Kakawin," *VKI,* 16.
1958. "The Old Javanese *Ramayana,*" *Majalah Ilmu Bahasa, Ilmu Bumi dan Kebudayaan Indonesia,* 76, pp. 501-518.
1966. "A Note on the Maha-Bharata in Malaysia and Indonesia: Sabha-parva found in Bali," *JMBRAS,* 38(2).

Ikram, A.
1975. "Memperkenalkan naskah-naskah wayang dalam bahasa Melayu," *Bahasa dan Sastra* 1 (2), pp. 12-18.
1978. *Hikayat Sri Rama Suntingan Naskah disertai Telaah Amanat dan Struktur,* disertasi, Jakarta.

Jones, Mrs. J. M. F.
1957. "The Wayang Kulit of Java and Bali," *Man* 57, pp.131-133.

Juynboll, H. H.
1902. "Indonesische en Achterindische Tooneelvoorstellingen uit het Ramajana," *BKI* 54.
1915. *Het Javaansche Tooneel,* Baam.
1911. *Supplement op den Catalogus van de Javaansche en Madoereesche Handschriften,* Leidsche Universiteits-bibliotheek I-II, Leiden.

Kats
1923. *Het Javaansche Tooneel* Dell I. *De Wajang Poerwa,* Weltevreden.
1926-1928. "The Ramajana in Indonesia," *BSOAS,* IV, pp. 579-585.
1931. *Tentang Makna Lakon Jawa.* Batavia.

Khalid Hussain
1964. *Hikayat Pandawa Lima,* Kuala Lumpur.

Koentjaraningrat (ed.)
1959. *Tari dan Kesusastraan di Indonesia,* Jogjakarta.
1931. Krom, N. J. *Hindoe-Javaansche Geschiedenis.* Martinus Nijhoof.

Kunhan Raja, C.
1962. *Survey of Sanscrit Literature,* Bombay.

Leur, J. C. van
1955. *Indonesian Trade and Society,* The Hague.

Maha Vajeravudh
1967. "Notes on the Siamese Theatre," *JSS,* 55 (1), pp. 1-30.

Mechelen, Ch. te
1879. "Een en ander over de wajang," *TBG* 25, pp. 72-107.

Mangkunegara VII
1957. *On the Wayang Kulit (Purwa) and its symbolic and mystical elements* (translated from the Dutch by Claire Holt), Cornell.

Maxwell, W. E.
1886. "Sri Rama, a fairy tale told by a Malay rhapsodist," *JSBRAS*, 17, pp. 87-115.

McPhee. Colin
1936. "The Balinese Wajang Koelit and its Music," *Djawa* 16, pp. 1-50.

Mellema, R. L.
1954. *Wajang Puppets, Carving, Colouring and Symbolism*, Amsterdam.

Nikmah Soenardjo
1993. Hikayat Maharaja Garebag Jagat: Suntingan Naskah disertai Tinjauan Tema dan Amanat Cerita serta Fungsi Punakawan di dalam Naskah. Jakarta, Balai Pustaka.

Noorduyn, J.
1971. "Traces of old Sundanese *Ramayana* tradition," *Indonesia*, 12, pp. 151-158.

Overbeck, Th.
1933. "Hikayat Maharaja Ravana," *JMBRAS*, 11 (2), hlm. 111-132.
1938. "Boekbespreking: Over Maleische Literatuur," *TBG* 78 (2), pp. 292-333.

Pigeaud, Th.
1938. *Javaansche Volksvertooningen*, Batavia.
1967-1970. *Literature of Java I-III*, The Hague.

Poerbatjaraka, R. M. Ng.
1957. *Kepustakaan Djawa*, Djakarta.
1965. *"Ramayana Djawa-Kuna,"* Madjalah Ilmu-ilmu Sastra, Indonesia, III-1, pp. 1-10.

Raghaven, V. (ed.)
1963. *The Indian Heritage*, Bangalore.
1980. *The Ramayana Tradition in Asia*, New Delhi.

Ras, J. J.
1976. "The Historical Development of Javanese Shaddow Theatre," *RIMA*, vol.10 (II).

Rassers. W. H.
1922. *De Pandji Roman*, Antwerpen.

Ray A. Olsson, M. D.
1968. *The Ramakien, A Prose Translation of the Thai Ramayana*, Bangkok.

Rentse, Anker
1936. "The Kelantan Shadow-play," *JMBRAS*, 14 (3), pp. 283-301.
1947. "The Origin of the Wayang Theatre," *JMBRAS*, 20 (1), pp. 12-15.

Resink-Wilkens, A. J.
1939. "Eenige opmerkingen over de wajang-koelit voorstellingen," *Djawa*, 19 pp. 38-41.

Richman, Paula
1991. *Many Ramayana*, Berkeley.

Roedjiati, S. W.
1961. "Tjerita Tabut," *Bahasa dan Budaja*, 9 (3 dan 4).

Ronkel, Ph. S. van
1919. "Aanteekeningen op een oude Maleische *Ramayana* tekst," *BKI,* 75, pp. 379- 383.
1929. "The *Ramayana* in Malaya," *Acta Orientalia,* 7, pp. 319-324.

Santosh N. Desai
1979. "*Ramayana* - An instrument of historical contact and cultural transmission between India and Asia," *Journal of Asian Studies,* 30 (1), pp. 5-20.

Sachithanantham, Singaavelu
2004. *The Ramayana Tradition in Southeast Asia,* Kuala Lumpur.

Sarkar, H. B.
1934. *Indian influences on the literature of Java and Bali,* Calcutta.
1966. "The language and literature of ancient Indonesia and Malaysia," *Journal of Indian History,* 44 (3), pp. 647-681.

Sarkiman
n.d. *Wayang Purwa Asal-usul dan perkembangannya,* Jakarta

Scott-Kemball, Jeune
1959. *The Kelantan Wayang Siam shadow puppets, Man* 108, pp. 73-78.
1970. *Javanese Shadow Puppets,* London.

Sears, Laurie Jo
1979. *The transmission of the epics from India to Java,* Madison.

Seno-Sastroamidjojo, A.
1964. *Renungan tentang pertunjukan Wajang Kulit,* Djakarta.

Serrurier, L.
1896. *De Wajang Poerwa, eene ethnologische studie,* Leiden.

Shellabear, W. G.
1915. *Hikayat Seri Rama, JMBRAS,* no. 71.
1964. *Hikayat Seri Rama* (1915 Romanised Version), Singapore.

Sheppard, Haji Mubin
1963. "Malay Shadow Play Figures in the Museum of Archaelogy and Ethnology, University of Cambridge," *Federation Museums Journal,* 8, pp. 14-17.
1968. "The Khmer Shadow Play and its links with ancient India," *JMBRAS,* 41 (1), pp. 199-204.

Singaravelu, S.
1968. "A Comparative study of the Sanscrit, Tamil, Thai and Malay version of the story of Rama," *JSS,* 56 (2), pp. 137-185.
1981. "The Rama Story in the Malay tradition," *JMBRAS,* 54 (2), pp. 131-147.

Soedarsono
1969. "Classical Javanese dance: history and characterization," *Ethnomusicology* 13 (3), pp. 489-506.

Stutterheim, W.
1925. *Rama-Legenden und Rama-Reliefs in Indonesien,* I-II, Munchen.

Sutjipto Wirjosuparto, R. M.
1968. *Kakawin Bharata Judha,* Djakarta.
1969. *Rama Stories in Indonesia,* Djakarta.

Swami Satyananda Puri & Charoen Sarahiran
1948.   *The Ramakirti (Ramakien) or the Thai version of the Ramayana*, Bangkok.

Sweeney, Amin
1969.   "The Rama Repertoire in the Kelantan Shadow-play," *Tenggara* 5, pp. 129-138.
1970.   "The Rama Repertoire in the Wayang Siam," *Raghavan Felicitation Volume, Sanskerta Rangga*, Madras.
1971.   *Malay Shadow-puppets*, London.
1972a. "The Shadow-play of Kelantan," *JMBRAS*, 43 (2), pp.53-80.
1972b. *The Ramayana and the Malay Shadow-play*, Kuala Lumpur.
1976.   "The Malay Shadow Play with Special Reference to the Wayang Siam," in *An International Seminar on the Shadow Plays of Asia*, Tokyo.

Teeuw, A.
1946.   *Het Bhomakawya Een Oudjavaans Gedicht*, Groningen.

Thomas, P.
1973.   *Epic, Myth and Legends of India (13th edition)*, Bombay

Tjan Tjoe Siem
1938.   *Hoe Koeroepati zich zijn vrowo erwerft; Javaansche Lakon*, Leiden.
1952.   "Sedikit tentang arti wayang dan goenanya untuk pembangunan kita," *Bahasa dan Budaya*, vol. I no. 1.

Tuuk, H. N. van der
1875a. "Geschiedenis der Pandawa's naar een Maleisch handschrift der Royal Asiatic Society," *TBG*, 21, pp. 1-90.
1875b. "Geschiedenis van Boma naar een Maleisch handschrift der Royal Asiatic Society," *TBG*, 21 (1), pp. 91-101.
1879.   "Enige Maleische wajang verhalen toegelicht," *TBG*, 25, v-vi, pp. 489-552.

Ulbricht, H.
1970.   *Wayang Purwa*, Kuala Lumpur.

Wahjono
1973.   "Epics that inspire," *Hemisphere*, 17 (8), pp. 7-11.

Winstedt, R. O.
1910.   "Hikayat Seri Roma, romanised by R. O. Winstedt," *JSBRAS*, 55, pp. 1-99.
1929.   "A Patani version of the *Ramayana*," *Feestbundel Koninkijk Bataviaasch Genootschap* ii, pp. 423-434.
1944a. "An undescribed Malay version of the *Ramayana*," *JRAS*, pp. 62-73.
1944b. "Indian influence in the Malay World," *JRAS*, p. 186.

Zieseniss, A.
1963.   *The Rama Saga in Malaysia* (translated from the German by P.W. Burch), Singapore.

Zoetmulder, P. J.
1971.   "The Wajang as a philosophical theme," *Indonesia*, 12, pp. 85 - 96.
1974.   *Kalangwan: A Survey of Old Javanese Literature*, The Hague.

3 Javanese Panji Stories

3.1 The Panji stories

Panji stories were a product of Javanese literature. They were very popular among Indonesians, especially among the Javanese and Balinese, but also among the Malays who adapted them into a prose form known as the *hikayat* intended for recitation to an audience by a storyteller. The enduring popularity of the Panji tales is evidenced by the many old Panji manuscripts that can be found in various libraries in London, Leiden, Jakarta and Kuala Lumpur. Its prevalence may be attributed to the fact that, like the much-loved *penglipur lara* (soother of woes) tales, they often tell stories of adventure and war. Perhaps what makes the Panji stories even more widespread is that they sometimes contain erotic love stories and comical tales depicting the antics of *punakawan*s (court jesters or clowns) which can, at times, be downright bawdy and risqué—something that cannot be found in the tales of the *penglipur lara*. The spread of Panji stories could also be partly due to propaganda purveyed by the Javanese themselves.

A number of in-depth studies have been done by scholars on the Panji stories. Among these, the one that most deserves our attention is the work of Dr W. H. Rassers. In his dissertation, *De Pandji Roman,* Rassers explicates the origins of the Panji stories at great length. According to him, the Panji stories may have had their origins in an ancient myth about the moon and sun, as found in the story of Kalangi and Manimporok of the Minahasa (Sulawesi) region. The myth tells of two gods, Kalangi and Manimporok, who were good friends. One day, Manimporok called on Kalangi who was not at home at the time. Seeing Kalangi's wife, Kalongkopan, alone at home, lust got the better of Manimporok and he abducted her. Upon returning home, Kalangi was devastated when he found his wife gone. Pining for her, he spent his days making a figurine that looked like her. In the end, the figurine came to life and became Kalangi's new wife. It is through this myth, according to Rassers, that the Minahasans account for the waxing and waning of the moon. Kalangi is believed to be the symbol of the waxing moon; Manimporok the waning moon, while Kalongkopan is the full moon.

Such myths about the moon and the sun, Rassers goes on to elaborate, reflect the structure of an ancient society. According to him, ancient Javanese society was divided into two distinct groups. The Panji stories depict the lives and conduct of these two conflicting groups and the tension and rivalry that characterised their relationship. The experiences of the heroes and heroines in these stories, for example in the initiation rites they had to go through before marriage, are not ordinary experiences. In marriage, exogamy is practised, which means they had to look for prospective spouses from outside their own group. They cooperated with, but also at the same time, competed against each other. Each group, in turn, was sub-divided into two further halves, forming four distinct social groups in all. According to their totemic belief, each of the four sub-groups identified itself with a spirit-being, such as an animal or plant, to which they believed they had a mystical kinship, and which served as their guardian spirit. As part of a totemic ritual, an initiation rite was held whenever a prospective bride or bridegroom sought to marry into another clan. This initiation was usually held in a *rumah haram* (forbidden house)—the hub of cultural and ceremonial activities in the community, located in the forest. The existence of two moieties in Javanese society gave birth to these two figures symbolising marriage and initiation.

This is Koentjaraningrat's summary (1959: 36-38) of Rassers explanation of the origins of the Panji stories. Such a social order also influenced other literary works—for example, Rassers argues that the *Ramayana* and *Mahabharata* are also Panji tales. Rama and Dasaratha can both be regarded as the waning moon; Sita symbolises the full moon, while Rawana the waxing moon. By possessing Sita, Rama also possessed power over the earth. By extension, the battle between the Pandawas and the Kurawas can be seen as being the struggle between the waning and the waxing moon.

Many scholars, however, have postulated various arguments to refute Rassers' theory. K. A. H. Hidding argued that the struggle between the two forces depicted in Indonesian mythology, and then retold in the Panji stories, symbolised the eternal battle of good and evil inherent in man. T. G. Th. Pigeaud rejected the notion of moieties, the division of primitive Indonesian society into two groups, as asserted by Rassers; B. M. Goslings disagreed with Rassers who referred to the Panji as sacred stories; while W. F. Stutterheim disputed Rassers' view that all successive Javanese literary forms are based on the Panji story motifs. H. B. Sarkar, a scholar from India, furthermore maintained that the Panji stories are nature-myths and bear no relation to totemism or exogamy (Koentjaraningrat, 1975: 135-142).

The Javanese scholar Poerbatjaraka took issue with Rassers on several points. He noted that the Panji manuscript on which Rassers based his comparison, i.e. the *Hikayat Cekel Waneng Pati*, is a relatively new version of the story. In older versions, such as the *Hikayat Panji Kuda Semirang*, Panji is always portrayed as having two lovers; and it was his first lover, a *patih* (regent)'s daughter, who was killed by the queen. In many versions, the status of this first lover is often elevated so that she came to be portrayed eventually as none other than the princess of Daha, Candra Kirana. Poerbatjaraka contends that the Panji stories emerged at the end of the Majapahit era, at a time when there was a demand for reading material. The Javanese could no longer read Sanskrit and there was no fresh material available from India. They were, moreover, not yet prepared to accept Islamic texts written in the Malay language (Poerbatjaraka, 1940). In his edition of the *Suluk Wujil*, Poerbatjaraka also attacks Rassers' view that the *wayang* is a remnant of ancient Javanese initiation rituals.

Another viewpoint that deserves our attention is that of J. J. Ras (1973: 436-440). According to Ras, the Panji stories retell an episode in the legendary history of Java. That is why this tale can also be found in historical texts such as the *Babad Tanah Jawi*, the *Serat Kandi*, the tale of *Jaya Lengkara*, and several others. The story, in its most basic form, can be found in the *Babad Daha-Kediri*, as follows:

King Sri Gentayu from Janggala had five children, namely:

(1) Dewi Kili Suci, a nun living in a hermitage on Mount Kapucangan;
(2) Raden Dewakusuma, also known as Prabu Lembu Amiluhur, who took over the throne of Janggala from his father;
(3) Prabu Lembu Amerdadu, ruler of Daha;
(4) Prabu Lembu Pengarang, ruler of Urawan; and
(5) Prabu Amerjaya, ruler of Singasari.

Lembu Amiluhur wanted his son, Panji Kuda Rawisrengga, to marry Candra Kirana, a princess of Daha. Against his father's wishes however, Panji had already fallen in love with Dewi Angreni, the daughter of the *patih* (regent) of Daha, and wanted to marry her instead. Believing that her nephew Panji (also known as Raden Inu) was the embodiment of the god Wisnu, his aunt, Kilisuci the nun, felt it was her duty to intervene to ensure that Wisnu did not marry the wrong person. She believed that by killing Angreni, Dewi Sri's spirit (Javanese: *titisan,* incarnation, avatar) would transfer itself from Dewi Angreni into Candra Kirana, thereby facilitating the union of Wisnu and Dewi Sri through the marriage of Raden Inu and Candra Kirana. Dewi Angreni was put to death, but Panji still refused to marry the princess of Daha, thus incurring the wrath of his father who banished him from the kingdom. His wanderings brought him to the kingdom of his uncle, the Ratu of Urawan. There, his uncle took pity on him and gave him his daughter's hand in marriage. Meanwhile, a king from Hindustan came to Daha to ask for Candra Kirana's hand in marriage. When his request was refused, war broke out. Panji was sent by his uncle to help Daha. The Hindustani king was eventually defeated. With Panji back in Daha, his aunt Kili Suci seized the opportunity to arrange a marriage between him and Candra Kirana, in order to fulfil the latter's function as the true incarnation of Dewi Sri pre-ordained to marry Wisnu in his manifestation as the prince of Janggala. (In this story Panji was the grandson of Erlangga, who was regarded as the incarnation of Wisnu).

It is evident from the story above that the tale of Panji is the story of a marriage. That is why many Panji stories, such as the *Hikayat Cekel Waneng Pati*, are often enacted in shadow theatre form at royal wedding ceremonies. By regarding the prince of Kuripan as the incarnation of Wisnu, and the princess of Daha as Sri, the story symbolised in an alegorical way the marriage of Wisnu and Dewi Sri.

Ras then goes on to make a case for the social role of Panji stories. The fact that the Panji stories were often re-enacted during royal wedding ceremonies from the 12th to the 14th centuries explains why a large number of Panji manuscripts exist both in and outside of Java. Ras suggests that it was common practice at that time for Javanese princess and princesses to be sent abroad to marry into other royal families in the region, as a means of forging alliances between kingdoms. The royal entourage would usually consist of a *dalang* (puppeteer) accompanied by a *wayang gedog* ensemble. As part of the festivities, the Panji story would be staged in the required form, and translated into Malay, Balinese, Cham or Thai as the circumstances dictated, for the benefit of the audience. In the plays, the Javanese prince would usually call the country of the foreign princess he was going to marry Daha, whereas a Javanese princess would refer to the country of her foreign royal husband-to-be as Kuripan. This is the reason why we can often find places in Kalimantan,

Bali, Lombok and Sumatra named Daha and Kuripan. The king of Banjarmasin often referred to himself as Raden Putra, one of the names of Raden Inu. The tale of Panji then spread to Bali where it was known as the *Tale of Malat*, to Makassar where it became the *Hikayat Cekela*, and to Sumatra and the Malay Peninsula, where the Panji story is well-known by various other names. In Java, the Panji story became material for *wayang gedog* and *wayang topeng*.

The chronology of the spread of the Panji stories in the Malay Archipelago has been a source of debate between Dr. C. C. Berg and Dr. Poerbatjaraka. According to Berg, the Panji story emerged in East Java between 1277, the time of the Pamalayu campaign, and circa 1400, that is, the 13th and 14th centuries. The spread of the Panji stories, he contends, coincided with the golden age of the Majapahit empire as a result of Javanese political expansionism (Berg, 1928). Poerbatjaraka disagreed with Berg for several reasons. Firstly, during the Pamalayu expedition (1277), memories of Singasari (1222-1292) were still fresh. It would be ridiculous for the audience to consider Singasari and Kediri Daha (1045-1222) as belonging to the same era. Secondly, the language in which the Panji stories were first written was Middle Javanese, and not Old Javanese as postulated by Berg. Thirdly, the Panji stories were written in *macapat* or *tengahan* (traditional Low or Middle Javanese verse), and not in Indian metres. Fourthly, the names of places in the Panji stories are similar to those mentioned in the *Pararaton* and the *Babad* (historical texts of Majapahit). Fifthly, appellations such as *kuda, jaran, undakan, lembu,* and *kebo* used in character's names in the Panji stories can also be found in the *Pararotan* and *Negara Kretagama* (written by Mpu Prapanca in 1365). Finally, based on a relief depicting an episode from the Panji story, dated 1365 in the Saka calendar (or 1413 AD), Poerbatjaraka concluded that the original Panji stories were composed on or after the golden age of the Majapahit empire (1293-1520) (Poerbatjaraka, 1940: 363-369). It needs to be mentioned that Berg's views remained unchanged in his later work (Berg, 1954)

Here are seven well-known Malay Panji stories.

3.2 *Hikayat Galuh Digantung*

According to Poerbatjaraka's comparative study of eight different versions of the Panji stories, this *hikayat* is one of the older versions of the Panji tale. It tells the story of Ratu Kuripan's sister, Kili Suci, meditating on Mount Pucangan. H. Overbeck is of the opinion, however, that the *hikayat* was probably written at a later period, as it exhibits influences from the *Hikayat Sri Rama* and the *Mintaraga*. It also contains, he points out, many Javanese words, especially in episodes that take place in the *kraton*, and in scenes depicting ceremonial festivities or describing traditional costumes. Even the riddles or *wangsalan* are in Javanese.

The *hikayat* was copied in 1300 AH (1882 AD) in Palembang. However, according to a *syair* written as its prologue, the *hikayat* was copied in 1283 AH (1886 AD). The following is a summary (Overbeck, 1932).

The tale begins with a genealogy of Pandu Dewata, from Raden Arjuna to Bambang Selaka. Bambang Selaka, the last in the line of divine kings to rule the world, returned to the celestial world to become a god again. There, he married a *bidadari* (an angel-like heavenly spirit) called Batara Naya Kesuma. Meanwhile, the mortal world he left behind had become quiet and empty, with no great kingdom remaining.

Ruing a world now devoid of human drama, the gods Batara Kala and Batara Narada sent Batara Naya Kesuma and her husband down to earth. Batara Naya Kesuma was told she could return to heaven only if she bore children who, when they grew up, would become great kings on earth. Naya Kesuma became ruler of Kuripan, and Kuripan became a vast and mighty kingdom. She bore five children; the first became king of Kuripan; the second, king of Daha; the third, king of Gagelang; the fourth, king of Singasari; and the fifth, a daughter, lived with her grandfather in Daha.

The king of Kuripan went to the island of Nusa Sari to make an offering to the gods in the hope of being granted a child. There, he met his brother, the king of Daha, who had also come to the island to ask the gods for the same favour. The two made a pact with the gods that if they were each granted a child, they would betroth them to each other.

Before very long, the king of Kuripan had a son with Paduka Mahadewi, named Raden Kertabuwana. The queen later gave birth to two other sons and two daughters. The two younger princes were named Raden Inu Kertapati (Panji) and Raden Carang Tiningal; the two princesses were named Raden Mertaningrat and Raden Retna Wilis. Meanwhile, in Daha, the royal couple too was blessed with children. The queen bore a son, Raden Perbatasari Gunung Sari, and a daughter, Raden Gala Candra Kirana. Around the same time, the king of Gagelang also received a son and a daughter. The king of Singasari's wife too gave birth to a princess.

The kings of Kuripan and Daha betrothed Inu (Panji) to Candra Kirana. However, it was said that Inu was too fond of his weapons and had no respect for human life. He did little else with his time apart from hunting and this raised doubts in his father's mind that he might not make a good king. Inu was well-aware of his father's misgivings, so, one night, he left the palace accompanied by his servants, Jurudeh (senior) and Persanta, to meditate on Mount Sila Merju. Fearing the king's wrath if he found out about Inu's escape, his other *punakawans* Punta, Kertala and Jurudeh (junior), decided to leave for another mountain, Mount Arga Jembangan, to meditate there.

News of Inu's disappearance quickly reached Daha. Upon learning this, six princes from six kingdoms came to ask for Candra Kirana's hand. Meanwhile, a deity who had been cursed by Batara Guru, arrived in Daha disguised as Kelana Jeladeri. He presented a riddle to the people of Daha; if they could not solve the riddle, Candra Kirana would be his. No one could solve the riddle. The king of Daha asked for a reprieve of three months, and sent his *patih* to scour the kingdom to find someone who could solve the riddle. On Candra Kirana's request, he was also instructed to look for a female *dalang*.

In the meantime, Inu had achieved self-realisation. Batara Guru sent the beautiful nymphs, Segerba and her sister, to seduce Inu but he was not in the least distracted by them. Batara Guru then cast a spell and transformed Inu and his *punakawan*s into women. Inu became a female *dalang* named Kin Penggoda Asmara and was ordered by Batara Guru to go to Daha. Inu was a very skilful *dalang* and endeared himself to everyone. When Kelana Jeladeri returned, Inu told him that the riddle he set was very difficult indeed and asked that he be allowed to retire to Mount Arga Sila Mercu to ponder its solution. On the mountain, Inu succeeded in solving the riddle and broke the spell on Kelana Jeladeri, changing him back into a god again. At the same time, Inu and his *punakawans* were also turned back to men.

Back in Daha, Princess Candra Kirana had fallen ill from a mysterious illness which could only be cured by the *gandarapuraloka* leaf. The king of Daha announced that whoever found the leaf would win Princess Candra Kirana's hand. After fourteen days searching with Princess Nantaloka, Batara Guru's daughter, Inu finally succeeded in finding the leaf. Princess Candra Kirana recovered from her illness after being given the leaf, and the king, in gratitude, gave Inu the title Adipati Tambak Baya. When the princess wanted a dove she saw flying in the palace's *pendopo* (pavillion), Inu caught it for her. Before long, Inu and Candra Kirana were married. The six princes whose offers of marriage to Candra Kirana were earlier spurned, attacked Inu to try to wrest his bride from him, but were easily defeated.

The king of Mengawan-awan too sent a delegation to Daha to ask for Candra Kirana's hand, threatening to wage war on the kingdom if his suit was rejected. He also instructed one of his emissaries to bewitch the princess. Candra Kirana refused to see Inu when he arrived at the *kraton* and started screaming that she wanted to see only Ratu Mengawan-awan. Humiliated, Inu left Daha that very night. Fortunately, Raden Perbatasari, Candra Kirana's brother who was skilled in magic, managed to break the spell that had been cast on his sister. Inu, in the meantime, was able to defeat Ratu Mengawan-awan's army and crush the attack on Daha.

Inu sent all the spoils of war to Daha, but he himself chose to remain in the forest to lead a nomadic life as a wayfarer. Meanwhile, the people of Daha were beginning to realise that Adipati Tambak Baya was actually Inu of Kuripan. This realisation further added to Candra Kirana's torment and shame. Wrecked by guilt for having hurt Inu's feelings, and no longer able to bear the scorn and contempt of her parents and brother, Candra Kirana left the *kraton* one night with two of her ladies-in-waiting, Ken Bayan and Ken Sandak, to look for Inu. Wandering in the forest, they were later found by Inu under a *randu* (kapok) tree. He was overjoyed to see Candra Kirana, held her in his lap and kissed her. But when Candra Kirana in her remorse asked that he kill her for the pain she had caused him, Inu was again reminded of the humiliation she put him through. He ordered his *punakawans* to tie up the princess and her ladies-in-waiting, and hang them from the *kapok* tree.

Batara Kala happened to be making his rounds of the world at that time; he found the three women and changed them into men. Candra Kirana became a man by the name of Mesa Cidera Asmara, while her ladies-in-waiting became Jaran Kembang and Jaran Sari. The three women, in their new incarnations, were destined to be indomitable warriors. They were given weapons by Batara Kala and an army created from the branches and leaves of the kapok tree. Thereafter, Candra Kirana embarked on a campaign of exploration and conquest. She sacked the kingdoms of Pekambangan and Cemara, killing their rulers and their royal households. Next, she marched on Lasem and Janapura, subdued the kingdoms, and forced their rulers to capitulate and join forces with her. Candra Kirana then took the name of Pangeran Kesuma Agung and pledged her allegiance to the king of Gagelang whose son, Raden Sarikin, soon became her boon companion.

Meanwhile, Inu, after defeating Ratu Pamotan and his brothers, arrived in Gagelang under the name Kelana Edan Asmara Sira Panji Lara Branti. There, Inu formed a close friendship with Candra Kirana, although he was unaware of her true identity. Not long after, the king of Mentaun asked for the hand of Princess Raden Kemuda Agung, the princess of Gagelang. The king of Mentaun threatened to invade Gagelang with help from his brothers if his proposal was not accepted. His proposal was rejected, and an intense battle ensued. Inu and Candra Kirana came to the aid of the king of Gagelang. Coincidentally, Raden Gunung Sari, who was looking for Candra Kirana, and Carang Tiningal, who was looking for Inu, happened to arrive in Gagelang at the same time and joined forces to help Gagelang. The king of Mentaun and his brothers all perished on the battlefield. The king of Gagelang was overjoyed and rewarded Inu, Candra Kirana, Carang Tiningal and Gunung Sari with new titles. A lavish feast was held. As part of the celebrations, a *wayang kulit* performance was held, with Candra Kirana as *dalang*.

Jenggala/Kuripan was being attacked by a legion of talking animals, led by a *raksasa* called Sang Sukma Indra and an ogre, Sang Sukma Ledera. Sang Sukma Indra and Sang Sukma Ledera were actually gods who had once lived in *kayangan* (the heavenly celestial world) but were cursed because of their scandalous dalliances with the heavenly nymphs and transformed into their present wretched forms. A mysterious voice told the king of Kuripan to ask for help from the king of Gagelang. Inu and his brothers arrived in Kuripan and he was touchingly reunited with Candra Kirana. War broke out between the legion of talking animals and Kuripan. Sang Sukma Indra and Sang Sukma Ledera were both killed and returned to heaven. Batara Kala, who witnessed the battle, created a huge typhoon; Candra Kirana and her ladies-in-waiting flew to safety and were changed back to women. A city, Perjuwita Indra, was created for Candra Kirana (now known as Ratu Emas). When the typhoon died down, Inu discovered that Candra Kirana was nowhere to be found.

Inu and his brother Gunung Sari went to meditate on Mount Mercu Sakti. After twenty-one days of meditation, Batara Kala revealed Candra Kirana's location. With the help of Sang Sukma Ledera, Inu and Gunung Sari arrived in Perjuwita Indra. Candra Kirana, however, refused to see Inu, for she had still not forgiven him for the wrong he had done her. The kings of Kuripan and Daha were told about the lovers' quarrel and stepped in to mediate. Finally, with persuasion and exhortation from all parties concerned, Candra Kirana was reconciled with Inu.

The kings of Kuripan, Daha, Singasari and Gagelang abdicated to make way for their heirs to rule over their respective kingdoms. A number of splendid weddings were held. Though Inu chose Candra Kirana to be his queen, he also married six other princesses from the countries he had invaded. The other princes, Raden Gunung Sari, Raden Carang Tiningal, Raden Kertabuwana and Raden Sarikin also married the respective princesses of their choice.

When news of Inu's and Candra Kirana's wedding reached the ears of the Belambangan king, he came to Kuripan with his army. He demanded that Candra Kirana be surrendered to him, prompting another war. Inu and his family crushed their enemies. The ruler of Belambangan and his allies were defeated, their wives and children were enslaved and their riches plundered. Peace was once again restored. The elderly king of Kuripan retired into the mountains to meditate and Inu became the ruler of Kuripan, reigning over his kingdom justly, and earning the love and respect of all of his subjects.

3.3 *Hikayat Cekel Waneng Pati*

The *Hikayat Cekel Waneng Pati* is a well-known Panji story. In his 1866 report on the Malay manuscripts kept in the Royal Asiatic Society in London, Van der Tuuk stated that, "The *Hikayat Cekel Waneng Pati* is one of the most important Malay texts and has influenced almost every other work of literature." This view was supported by R.O. Winstedt who argued that the humorous tales found in the *cerita jenaka*, the use of fancy titles for characters in Malay animal tales, the episode of the marriage proposal to the Princess of Gunung Ledang in the *Sejarah Melayu*, and some additional stories in the *Hikayat Hang Tuah*, were all modelled after the Panji stories.

There are many manuscripts of this *hikayat*. Twelve can be found in the Jakarta museum library; seven in Leiden; and eleven in various British libraries. Even so, a complete edition of this *hikayat* has yet to be published. Its origins are not very clear. Only one manuscript, that is kept in the library of the Museum of Jakarta, mentions Sumirada as the *dalang* who is said to have composed this story as a 'soul-soothing' tale for the love-struck or for those pining for romance; another manuscript attributes it to Surengrana as the *dalang* who wrote it for the benefit of other Javanese *dalang*s who had run out of stories to tell. It should also be pointed out here that the version of the *Hikayat Cekel Waneng Pati*, edited by Baharuddin Zainal and published by Dewan Bahasa dan Pustaka, is not a complete version. The plot is not faithfully adhered to, and the stories are often hard to follow.

A Summary of the *Cekel Waneng Pati*

This summary is based on three manuscripts found in the Leiden Library, Cod. 1709, Cod. 2283 and Cod. 2284; a more detailed summary can be found in Rassers' dissertation.

1. Cod. 1709

The god Batara Naya Kusuma married Dewi Nila Utama, the daughter of Batara Kesna Indra. Soon Dewi Nila Utama became pregnant and gave birth to two beautiful children. The boy was named Dewa Indra Kamajaya while the girl was called Dewi Nila Kencana. When they grew up, they fell in love with each other and vowed to be together in life and in death. However, Batara Naya Kusuma ordered his children to live on earth as mortals if they wished to be together.

The story tells that the Lord of Kuripan had four siblings: one brother was ruler of Daha, the second the ruler of Gagelang. He also had two daughters, one became queen of Singasari while the other, Ni Rara Suci, led a life of meditation on Mount Pucangan. One day, Batara Kuripan saw a fawn crying over the body of its mother, which had just been shot dead by an arrow. Moved by what he had witnessed, Batara Kuripan felt a sudden longing to have a son. So together with his queen and a retinue of his consorts and concubines, Batara Kuripan set sail for the island of Nusa Sari. His intention was to make an offering to the gods to ask for a son. In this he was not alone, for his brother, the ruler of Daha, had also come to the island to make a similar request. Not long after his return from Nusa Sari, his queen, Paduka Mahadewi, gave birth to a boy named Raden Karta Buwana. Meanwhile, Indra Kamajaya had incarnated as the son of Paduka Kamajaya, the queen of Kuripan, and was named Ino Kertapati (another of Panji's titles) or Undakan Rawiserengga. Ino Kertapati had five *punakawans* – Jurudeh, Punta, Kertala, Prasonto and Turas – who were incarnations of Dewa Indra Kamajaya's courtiers in the celestial world. Ino grew up into a handsome young man. The queen became pregnant again and gave birth to another handsome boy, whose name was Carang Tinangluh. Soon after, she gave birth to a baby daughter.

120

The queen of Daha too became pregnant and gave birth to a very beautiful baby girl. The baby was an incarnation of Nila Kencana, and named Kencana Ratna. She was also known as Raden Galuh Candra Kirana Lesmi Ning Puri. Not long after, the queen had another son, Raden Gunung Sari, also known as Raden Perbata Sari.

The betrothal of Raden Inu and Candra Kirana was celebrated on a grand scale. On that day, the people of Kuripan and Daha were entertained with a *wayang topeng* performance and all manner of entertainments. Sang Nata of Kuripan and Sang Nata of Daha had both forgotten the vow they had made to the gods, thus incurring the wrath of Batara Kala. Wanting to punish them, Batara Kala went to visit Ratu Soca Windu, the ruler of a vast kingdom.

One night, Ratu Soca Windu dreamt that his realm and the whole of Java would fall into the hands of the prince of Kuripan. In order to prevent this happening, he sent two of his viceroys to kidnap Ino in the depth of the night. Ino's *punakawans*, Jurudeh, Punta and Kertala, could not save him from his abductors. Afraid of the punishment that awaited them, the three servants did not dare return to Kuripan. Instead, they went to meditate on Mount Sela Mangling. The king demanded that Raden Inu marry the princess of Soca Windu. However he staunchly refused and was, as a result, tortured; his half dead body was then thrown into the river. But luck was on his side. His body was found by two of his other *punakawans*, Prasonto and Turas. Raden Inu recovered from his ordeal and changed his name to Cekel Waneng Pati. His *punakawans* also gave themselves new names. Cekel Waneng Pati then travelled to Daha in disguise. There, he learned that Candra Kirana had been kidnapped by an ogre. The king of Daha announced that whomever could kill the ogre and bring his daughter back would be given her hand in marriage. Cekel Waneng Pati managed to kill the ogre, who turned out to be the god Siva. Lord Siva was grateful to Cekel Waneng Pati for breaking the evil spell that had turned him into an ogre, and rewarded Cekel Waneng Pati with magic powers. Upon his return to Daha, Cekel Waneng Pati was not allowed to marry Candra Kirana. The king of Daha, who was under the impression that Cekel Waneng Pati was just a commoner without a title to his name, nonetheless permitted him to stay at the palace. During his stay there, Raden Galuh (Candra Kirana) treated Cekel Waneng Pati with tender loving care.

Against their father's wishes, Carang Tinangluh and his sister Angling Karas went in search of Raden Inu. Their defiance incurred their father's wrath; he cursed Carang Tinangluh to have a hideous face and a croaky voice. Accompanied by his sister, Carang Tinangluh went to Mount Arga Sela and met three of Raden Inu's *punakawans* who were meditating there. Together with the *punakawans*, Carang Tinangluh and his sister remained in meditation on the mountain. After sixteen months, the god Batara Indra appeared and presented them with magic weapons. Armed with these weapons, Carang Tinangluh conquered every kingdom he came across on his subsequent journey, and took the princesses of those kingdoms as his wives. Carang Tinangluh changed his name to Kelana Prabu Jaya; his sister took on the name Raden Ratna Wilis.

Meanwhile, the king of Manggada asked for Candra Kirana's hand in marriage, threatening to crush Daha if his proposal was rejected. The king of Daha asked Manggada for a delay of three months as Candra Kirana was still in love with Raden Inu. To console Candra Kirana, the king of Daha and his courtiers undertook a hunting expedition. The god Batara Kala created a majestic golden deer that immediately caught Candra Kirana's attention. The king of Daha promised to give her in marriage to anyone who could catch the deer alive. The king of Manggada tried but failed. Cekel Waneng Pati succeeded on his first attempt. The king of Daha however broke his promise and refused to let Cekel marry his daughter. Cekel Waneng Pati then left with his *punakawans* to bathe in the garden of solace. Raden Galuh (Candra Kirana) also went to bathe in the pond. The manuscript ends with the words, "When finished, Raden Galuh left the garden forthwith." The language of the manuscript is very good.

2. Cod. 2283

The first one hundred and thirty pages of this manuscript contain the same story as above. Page 131 continues the Cod.1709 manuscript.

Kelana Brahmana, a poet, having conquered many mighty kingdoms, arrived in Daha. He presented the king with two riddles. If the king failed to answer the riddles, he would have to marry his daughter Candra Kirana to Kelana. The king of Manggada could not solve the riddles. Cekel Waneng Pati could, but, yet again, the king of Daha broke his promise and refused to let Cekel Waneng Pati marry his daughter, Candra Kirana.

Kelana Prabu Jaya was also travelling and conquering all the countries that he came across. His army was making its way to Daha. The king of Daha was worried. The king of Manggada offered to fight Kelana Prabu Jaya on condition that Cekel Waneng Pati first be banished from the kingdom. At Perbata Sari's insistence, Cekel Waneng Pati remained in Daha. Meanwhile, the king of Maggada was defeated by Kelana Prabu Jaya. Cekel Waneng Pati, now bearing the title Adipati Tambak Baya, was summoned to the battlefield. Kelana Prabu Jaya was no match for Adipati Tambak Baya and was killed by him. Afterwards Adipati Tambak Baya discovered that he had killed his own brother, Carang Tinangluh. Horrified, Adipati Tambak Baya fainted. Batara Kala brought the two brothers back to life and they returned to Daha.

When Candra Kirana heard that Adipati Tambak Baya had been killed on the battlefield, she ran away from Daha. In the forest, she changed her name to Ken Sela Brangti. There she was found by the king of Lasem who adopted her as his own child. Meanwhile, her brother, Perbata Sari, also known as Mesa Ulun Sira Panji Pandu Rupa, went to find her. He set sail for Tuban and later captured the city of Tanjung Pura. He then called on the king of Lasem, who wanted to betroth him to Ken Sela Brangti. When they met, they discovered that they were actually brother and sister.

Adipati Tambak Baya went to find Candra Kirana. After subjugating the city of Mount Kendang, he and his brother, Kelana Prabu Jaya, arrived in Gagelang and were warmly greeted by the king. Adipati Tambak Baya was given a new title, Temenggung Arya Wangsa, while Kelana Prabu Jaya was now known as Arya Prabangsa.

Mesa Ulun and Sela Brangti also arrived in Gagelang. Mesa Ulun, now called Demang Urawan, became Arya Wangsa's good friend. However, not long after, the two friends had a disagreement. Demang Urawan was angry that the king of Gagelang wanted Arya Wangsa to marry Sela Brangti. Ken Sala Brangti then fell ill. A traditional healer (*dukun*) foretold that only Arya Wangsa could cure Ken Sela Brangti. In fulfilment of the prediction, Arya Wangsa brought Sela Brangti back to health and married her. He subsequently also married two other princesses.

Kelana Guling Patirat attacked Gagelang. His attack was repelled by Arya Wangsa who by now had become the minister in charge of law and order (*temenggung*). Arya Wangsa was given a new title, Pangeran Adipati, and married the princess of Gagelang, Raden Galuh. Raden Galuh was jealous because Adipati loved Ken Sela Brangti so very much. She spread a rumour that Ken Sela Brangti had been unfaithful to her husband. Pangeran Adipati was deceived by the rumour and banished Ken Sela Brangti to Kasetraan. Before long Pangeran Adipati realised his mistake and fell ill. Ken Sela Brangti was warmly received in the underworld and soon gave birth to a son whom she named Mesa Tandraman. The princess of Gagelang also gave birth to a son, whom she named Citra Angling Baya. Arya Prabangsa set out to obtain a potion to cure Pangeran Adipati; he went to Mount Indraloka, where a hermit with extraordinary supernatural powers lived. The hermit asked Arya Prabangsa to seek help from Batara Kala. Batara Kala told him that the only remedy for Pangeran Adipati's ailment was the Gandapura Wangi flower, and that the only person who could find this flower was Ken Sela Brangti's son. Together with Citra Angling Baya, Mesa Tandraman went to an island, where he was confronted by an ogre. He killed the ogre. In gratitude, the ogre revealed to Mesa Tandraman that the Gandapura Wangi was actually not a flower but the breast-milk of a celestial nymph, Dewi Sukarba. Mesa Tandraman immediately flew to the garden of Banjaran Sari and married Dewi Sukarba. The Gandapura Wangi now in his possession, he then set out to meet Citra Angling Baya.

Citra Angling Baya killed Mesa Tandraman and returned to his father's palace with the Gandapura Wangi. Batara Kala revived Mesa Tandraman, who promptly set off to Kasetraan and then, together with his mother, left for Daha. Meanwhile, Citra Angling Baya could not open the box that contained the Gandapura Wangi. Pangeran Adipati realised Mesa Tandraman had found the flower, not Citra. He sent for Mesa Tandraman, who immediately opened the box and cured Pangeran Adipati. During Mesa Tandraman's absence, Dewi Sukarba had given birth to a boy, whom she named Mesa Dewa Kusuma Yuda. The king of Manggada arrived and asked for Candra Kirana's hand in marriage, threatening war if his demand was refused. The threat was averted. Pangeran Adipati arrived in Daha and was reunited with Candra Kirana. Arya Prabangsa and Mesa Tandraman also returned to Daha under new names, disguised as *gambuh* dance-drama players. Demang Urawan also returned to Daha.

The king of Daha heard that a man had entered Candra Kirana's palace. Infuriated, he dispatched one of his *patihs* to seek and kill the thief but without success. The king of Manggada too sent his guards to capture the intruder but to no avail. Finally, the task fell to Arya Prabangsa. Candra Kirana revealed that the intruder was his brother, Pangeran Adipati.

3. Cod. 2284

The king of Soca Windu who had abducted Raden Inu in the past, returned again with his army. His aim this time was to kidnap Candra Kirana. This troubled the King of Kuripan who abdicated in favour of his son, Raden Inu, now called Ratu Anom Kusuma Yuda. The king's grandson, Mesa Tandraman, or Ratu Wirabumi, acquired the new title of Raden Arya Mangku Negara. Perbata Sari became Queen of Daha. Carang Tinangluh became Prabu Anom of Singasari. Almost every prince and his retinue of royal personages received new titles. The plan to kidnap Candra Kirana was unsuccessful. The king of Soca Windu was defeated by Ratu Anom Kusuma Yuda and forced to give up his daughter, Ratna Komala, to Arya Mangku Negara, who then became the new king of Soca Windu.

All the great kings, their queens and consorts went for an outing at the beach. They were having a lively time, when the goddess Dewi Sukarba suddenly appeared with a group of celestial nymphs (*bidadari*) to join them in their revelry. Dewi Sukarba was angry because Ratu Wirabumi (Mesa Tandraman) seemed to neglect her. Using her magical powers, she created an Indian prince named Sukma Wijaya and had him fall in love with Ratna Komala. Sukma Wijaya proceeded to conquer many mighty kingdoms before advancing on Kuripan. Upon reaching Kuripan, he demanded Ratna Komala's hand in marriage. War broke out. Kidnappings ensued on both sides. The war was without end. Batara Kala commanded Dewi Sukarba's son, Mesa Indra Dewa Kusuma, to go down to earth to help his father and grandfather. Powerless, the Indian prince sought help from his *guru* in the celestial world, Dewa Sukmanasa. Dewa Sukmanasa appeared and the battle intensified again with still no end in sight. Finally, Batara Kala intervened and scolded Dewa Sukmanasa because of his involvement in the war. Batara Kala arranged a peace between the two warring sides. A large-scale wedding celebration was held in Kuripan. A few days later, the Indian king returned to India. The other kings also returned to their own countries. In the version of the *Hikayat Cekel Waneng Pati* published by Dewan Bahasa dan Pustaka (1965), the plot is carelessly constructed. The story of the birth of Ino and Candra Kirana is also omitted. The ending is also different.

3.4 *Hikayat Panji Kuda Semirang*

R.M. Ng. Poerbatjaraka has examined a manuscript of this *hikayat* kept in the library of the Central Museum in Jakarta: the *Hikayat Panji Kuda Semirang* (from the collection of Cohen Stuart no. 125). Copied in the Muslim month of Safar in 1248 Hijrah (September 1832), this hikayat is actually titled *Kuda Semirang Panji Pandai Rupa*. According to Poerbatjaraka, this *hikayat* derives from an old Panji story. It begins with the story of Arjuna and Samba's reincarnation on earth. In this *hikayat* Panji has two wives; according to Poerbatjaraka, there is a tendency to raise the status of Panji's first wife to such an extent that she becomes virtually identical with the princess of Daha, Candra Kirana.

Poerbatjaraka believes that this *hikayat* was directly transcribed from Javanese. Many Javanese words, phrases and sentences are to be found in this text. These words and turns of phrase, although corrupted, can still be traced back to their original Javanese forms. The original text, Poerbatjaraka explains, was written in Middle Javanese. A summary of the story is given below.

This is the tale of four kings, who lived in Java. They were brothers. The eldest was the ruler of Kuripan; the second the ruler of Daha; the third, the ruler of Gagelang and the youngest, the ruler of Singasari. The king of Kuripan already had a son, Brajanata, with his consort, Maha Dewi, but had not yet been granted a son with his first wife, the queen. He prayed to the gods that the queen bear him a son. Batara Kala happened to be hovering over the island of Java while the king was praying. He smelled the incense lit by the king and carried his request to Batara Guru. Batara Guru decided to send Arjuna and Samba, together with their wives, down to earth. Arjuna and Januwati, Samba's wife, were incarnated in Kuripan, while Samba and Arjuna's wife, Subadra, manifested in Daha. Not long after, the queen of Kuripan gave birth to a son. The prince was named Inu Kertapati and given the title Kuda Rawisrengga. Four of Kuripan's highest office bearers—the

Patih (chief minister), *Demang* (district chief), *Rangga* (military commander) and *Jaksa* (chief justice) also had sons at about the same time as the king. Their sons, Jurudeh, Punta, Semar and Gemuris respectively, were presented to the king of Kuripan to be the young prince Inu Kertapati's playmates. After some time, the King of Kuripan had another son, Carang Tinangluh, whose title was Pangeran Anom. Then a daughter was born to the king and he named her Ratna Wilis.

The story continues that the King of Daha too prayed to the gods for a child. His wish was granted and he was blessed with a daughter called Galuh Candra Kirana. Two little girls were found to be her playmates, Bayan and Sanggit. After some time, a boy was born to the royal couple; he was given the name Perbata Sari and the title of Gunung Sari, as he lived in the mountains. The King of Gagelang meantime also had a daughter, named Ratna Kumuda Agung, and a son, Singa Menteri.

After some time, Inu grew up and was betrothed to Candra Kirana. Celebrations lasting many days and nights were held in Kuripan and Daha. The rulers of Kuripan and Daha neglected to pray to the gods. Angered, Batara Kala received permission to punish the two royal families by separating Inu and Candra Kirana.

The story tells that the goddess Dewi Anggar Mayang fell in love with the god Dewa Jaya Kusuma, who loved her too. Their love for each other, however, was regarded as sinful and they were cursed to be cast out of their celestial abode and exiled to earth. Anggar Mayang could only return to the heavenly world after she had been killed on earth, as could Jaya Kusuma. On earth, Anggar Mayang took the form of Marta Langu, the daughter of the village headman of Pengapiran. Jaya Kusuma took the form of a giant (*raksasa*) called Kumbakarna.

One day, while he was out hunting, Inu met Marta Langu. Attracted by her beauty, he took her back to his palace. From then on, he spent all his time with her and was no longer interested in going to Daha to marry Candra Kirana. His mother the queen was furious and tried to find a way to kill Marta Langu. One day she pretended to be ill and asked Inu to look for a mother tigress so that she could eat its heart. Inu set out for the forest. Once in the forest, Inu sensed that something was wrong; there was not a single animal in sight, not even a mosquito or beetle, let alone a tiger. He could not hear a single bird. Inu felt there was something ominous about the silence and returned immediately to the palace. To his horror, he found that while he was away, Marta Langu had been killed by the queen and her body disposed of in some unknown location. Inu was very sad. His face turned ashen and he became thinner and thinner with each passing day. (The same story can be found in the *Syair Ken Tambuhan*). Inu left in order to meditate on a mountain.

Batara Kala unleashed a typhoon, which, in the ensuing confusion, carried Candra Kirana and her two ladies-in-waiting to Mount Jambangan. Candra Kirana stayed on the mountain under the name Endang Sangu Lara. Her two ladies-in-waiting also took on new names: Sangit and Maya Branti.

News of Candra Kirana's disappearance reached Kuripan. Inu received the news calmly. That night, accompanied by his four clown servants, Inu quietly left Kuripan. The group reached the summit of Mount Danu Raja and meditated there. A monkey ascetic told Inu that Candra Kirana was still alive. During his sojourn on the mountain, Inu was taught all sorts of knowledge by the ascetic. Before long, Inu continued his journey, now known as Mesa Angulati Sira Panji. His servants also changed their names. When they reached Mataun, Inu conquered the country and married its princesses.

The story further tells that Carang Tinangluh went to meditate on Mount Lewihijau, calling himself Wirpati. On the summit of the mountain, he practised an extreme form of meditation and was granted a magical strand of hair that could change into an arrow at his command. Armed with this weapon, Carang Tinangluh resumed his journey. On another mountain, he killed a *raksasa* who turned out to be god. The *raksasa* was thankful to Carang Tinangluh for setting him free from the curse, and in return, handed him Ratna Wilis, whom he had earlier kidnapped, together with untold riches. Carang continued his journey with Ratna Wilis. Meanwhile, Brajanata had also left Kuripan to find his brother, Inu. He conquered the kingdom of Madiun, and married its princesses.

Next the story tells that Perbata Sari went in search of Candra Kirana and finally found her on Mount Jambangan. Together with his sister, Perbata Sari resumed his travels. He conquered the kingdom of Pandan Salas and married the king's daughter. Perbata Sari then travelled to Lasem, leaving Endang Sangu Lara in Pandan Laras. Meanwhile, Inu, now known as Mesa Angulati Sira Panji, arrived in Pandan Salas and immediately conquered it. There he met Endang Sangu Lara, without realising, however, that she was Candra Kirana, the beloved for whom he was searching. On hearing about Inu's invasion of Pandan Salas, Perbata Sari attacked Inu's army. Perbata Sari was defeated in the fierce battle that followed. Only then did Inu discover that Perbata Sari was actually "Pangeran Daha," Candra Kirana's brother. Mourning his death, Inu placed Perbata Sari's body on a raft, together with those of his wives who had come to avenge him, and set the raft adrift on the river. The raft eventually washed ashore at Tanjung Pura, and the bodies of Perbata Sari and his wives were subsequently brought back to life by Batara Guru. At the riverbank, Inu and Candra Kirana fell unconscious. Batara Kala flew Candra Kirana back to her kingdom and changed her into a man named Kuda Semirang Sira Panji Pandai Rupa. When Inu regained consciousness, he discovered that Candra Kirana was no longer in the kingdom. Determined to find her, Inu continued his journey, under the name of Kelana Edan Sebanjar Sira Panji Marga Asmara. In his quest, he conquered many kingdoms and took the vanquished princesses to be his wives. Finally, he reached Gagelang, where he was adopted by the queen of Gagelang. In Gagelang he was reunited with Carang Tinangluh and Ratna Wilis. They exchanged stories of their adventures.

The story continues that Brajanata also sought permission to look for his brother. In Madiun, he wrested power from the king and married his daughter. Calling himself Misa Kuda Panji Kusuma Indra, Brajanata then resumed his travels. After conquering Tanjung Pura, he reached Gagelang and served under the King of Gagelang. There Brajanata was eventually reunited with his brothers, although they all acted as if they did not know one another.

It is then told that Candra Kirana was in Tumasik. Soon, she resumed her journey and reached Gagelang. There, she met Inu once more. Inu seemed to recognise her and tried to win her heart, but she pretended to ignore Inu and snubbed him. Meanwhile, Perbata Sari arrived in Gagelang in the guise of a puppeteer. Because of his skillfulness and talent, he received many invitations to perform.

One day, the King of Soca Windu sent an emissary to ask for the princess of Gagelang's hand in marriage for one of his sons. The proposal however was rejected. Offended, Soca Windu attacked Gagelang. Fortunately, the assault was rebuffed by Inu and his brothers, who happened to be in Gagelang at the time. When the war concluded, Candra Kirana and her brothers decided to withdraw to Mount Dana Raja, where they established a new kingdom. Candra Kirana changed back to a woman, calling herself Ratu Dewi Kusuma Indra. After Candra Kirana's departure, Inu felt there was no reason for him to stay in Gagelang any longer, and so he too embarked on a sea-vogage. He came to a mountain and was told that he would soon be reunited with his sweetheart; but before this could happen, he would have to meditate for forty days.

The story next tells of Ratu Panggala Jawa's request to marry Ratu Danu Raja (Candra Kirana). In response, Ratu Danu Raja set him a number of conditions: the wedding ceremony must be held under the Tenjo Maya pavillion and witnessed by seven *bidadaris* from heaven; and Ratu Penggala Jawa must give her two white elephants. The king of Panggala Jawa refused to comply with her demands, and attacked Daha. Inu had just completed his period of meditation, and came to Ratu Danu Raja's aid. The attack on Daha failed. It was now Inu's turn to ask for the hand of Ratu Danu Raja. The queen laid out to Inu the same conditions she set her earlier suitor. Carang Tinangluh volunteered to help his brother. Together with Semar, they set out for Mount Indrakila on whose summit, it was said, lay the portal to the celestial realm. During his journey, Carang Tinangluh killed a giant who was the avatar of a fairy (*peri*). The *peri* was grateful to Carang Tinangluh and rewarded him with two white elephants. Soon after this, Carang Tinangluh reached the gateway to the celestial kingdom. To gain entrance into the celestial world, Semar ran amuck, forcing Batara Guru to order the gates of heaven opened, because Semar was none other than the Supreme Deity Sang Hyang Tunggal. Carang Tinangluh obtained the Tenjo Maya pavillion and returned to earth with seven *bidadaris*.

Raden Inu was overjoyed when he learned that Ratu Danu Raja was his fiancée, Candra Kirana, the princess of Daha. The kings of Kuripan and Daha were informed and a number of weddings were celebrated. Inu marrried Candra Kirana, Carang Tinangluh married the princess of Gagelang, Perbata Sari married Ratna Wilis, Singa Menteri married the princess of Singasari, and Brajanata married one of Soca Windu's daughters. The wedding ceremonies over, the princes were all crowned kings: Inu in Kuripan, Perbata Sari in Daha, Singa Menteri in Gagelang, Carang Tinangluh in Singasari and Brajanata in Wirabumi. The former kings retired to the mountains to lead lives of asceticism and eventually returned to the heavenly world. The five new kings reigned justly and each of their kingdoms prospered. Many kings willingly sent tribute to the five young kings of Java. So the story ends.

3.5 *Hikayat Panji Semirang*

Since its first publication in two volumes by Balai Pustaka in 1911 and 1912, this *hikayat* has been reprinted many times and has proven to be very popular with the reading public. It has also been rewritten for adolescent readers by S. Sastrawinata. It is also highly probable that the version of the *Hikayat Panji Semirang* published by Pustaka Antara, Kuala Lumpur, is the same text, although this is not acknowledged by its publishers.

According to Poerbatjaraka, this *hikayat* is a more recent version of the Panji story. The words *"Cekel Waneng Pati Berahi kepada Ken Beranti,"* ("Cekel Waneng Pati was enamoured of Ken Beranti") are to be found in this version of the Panji story, proving that this *hikayat* is not as old as the *Hikayat Cekel Waneng Pati* discussed by Rassers.

It should be mentioned here that the title *Hikayat Panji Kuda Semirang* (Bat. Gen. 177), is probably a mistake. Its contents are different from those of the work discussed by Poerbatjaraka, and are similar to those published by Balai Pustaka. Similarly, the title *Hikayat Panji Semirang* for the work published by Dewan Bahasa dan Pustaka in Kuala Lumpur, is also incorrect. Its contents are not those of the *Hikayat Panji Semirang*, but of the *Hikayat Panji Kuda Semirang*. Moreover, this is not the original text but a summary based on a manuscript kept at Leiden. However, the *Kuda Semirang Seri Panji Pandai Rupa I*, published by Ahmad bin Muhammad Thaib in Kota Baharu, Kelantan, is the same as the *Hikayat Panji Semirang* (Winstedt, 1948: 53).

A summary of the *Hikayat Panji Semirang*, based on the text published by Balai Pustaka, is presented below.

The story has it that the inhabitants of heaven descended to earth and became the kings of Kuripan, Daha and Gagelang, while another became the Princess Biku Gandasari of Mount Wilis. The King of Kuripan ruled over a vast kingdom with a firm but just hand, and was much loved by his subjects and courtiers alike. It is said he had a son who was very handsome, absolutely resplendent. The prince was named Raden Inu Kertapati, and was known to his subjects as Raden Asmara Ningrat. When he grew up, Raden Inu was tutored in the ways of the magic arts and in the other skills a royal prince would need. He was also served by four foolish servants - Jerudi, Puntah, Karta and Persanta - whose duty was to be his companions and to amuse him.

The story tells that the King of Daha had a queen and two consorts. The queen was called Tuan Putri Puspa Ningrat; the consorts were Maha Dewi and Paduka Liku. The King of Daha, it is said, was ruled by his appetites, and submitted to his wives' every demand, especially those of Paduka Liku. The king had two daughters, the elder being Galuh Candra Kirana, the daughter of the queen:

> her beauty was beyond words: her nose was pointed, her eyes were as bright as the blade of a sword and glinted like glass; her eyelashes were curled, her fingers looked as if they had been honed; her calves were like ripe padi, her heels as smooth as peeled eggs; her cheeks were round like a durian; her eyebrows were like the new moon and curved like the rainbow, her lower lip was round, as if it had just been bitten.

Galuh Candra Kirana had two very devoted ladies-in-waiting, Ken Bayan and Ken Sanggil. The other sister was Galuh Ajeng, the daughter of Paduka Liku; she resented Galuh Candra Kirana, and was inclined to cry and roll about on the ground over even the most trivial matters.

The story further tells that the King of Gagelang ruled over a prosperous and peaceful kingdom. Many traders and merchants came to Gagelang on business. Sages, spiritual taechers, priests and Brahmins also left from their mountain abodes to settle in the kingdom. The king had a son, Raden Singa Menteri, who was uncouth and arrogant. Sometimes he behaved like a madman; he had been known to give the belt he was wearing or a ring to anyone who flattered him.

It is said that the three kings had a sister called Biku Gandasari, a beautiful woman who led a strict religious life. Gandasari's spiritual observances had endowed her with great supernatural powers and insight. Every ascetic, animal and spirit feared her and bowed down before her.

One day, the King of Kuripan asked for Candra Kirana's hand in marriage on behalf of his son, Raden Inu Kertapati. The betrothal of Raden Inu and Candra Kirana made Galuh Ajeng very jealous. It also stirred resentment in Paduka Liku, who saw that her husband, the king of Daha, was even more fond of Candra Kirana than ever before. She decided to find a way to get rid of the queen and instructed her brother, Menteri, to look for a magical potion that would make her the object of the king's affections. Her evil scheme went as planned. She poisoned the queen, who subsequently died. The king at first wanted to kill Paduka Liku, but instead became completely enamoured with her. Now an orphan, Candra Kirana sat weeping at her mother's grave day after day, becoming a shadow of her former self. Her eyes were puffy and red, and her once beautiful hair was dishevelled. Only Maha Dewi, the king's other consort, tried to comfort her.

The King of Kuripan heard the news of the queen of Daha's death and of the suffering this had caused Candra Kirana. He sent two dolls to Daha to comfort Candra Kirana. One was made of gold but wrapped in rags; the other was made of silver and wrapped in a silk cloth embroidered with gold thread. Galuh Ajeng chose the silver doll. When she found out that her doll was ugly, whereas Candra Kirana's golden doll was beautifully-crafted, she demanded that Candra Kirana give her the golden doll. Candra Kirana refused, ignoring her father's commands. To punish her for her stubbornness, Candra Kirana's hair was forcibly cut. As her hair was being cut, Candra Kirana fainted. The earth began to shake as if it were angry at the king's actions; rain began to drip down from the sky as if it was crying over Galuh Candra Kirana's fate; the roosters crowed as if they were haranguing the king; the birds and all the animals in the forest were aggrieved by what the king had done.

Galuh Candra Kirana could not bear to live in the kingdom any longer. One day, she left Daha, accompanied by her two ladies-in-waiting, Maha Dewi the king's consort, and a loyal minister, Galuh. After some time, they reached a place near Kuripan. Candra Kirana built a city and became its ruler, dressing herself up as a man and changing her name to Panji Semirang Asmaran Taka. Her two ladies-in-waiting also took new names: Kuda Perwira and Kuda Peranca respectively. And so, Galuh Candra Kirana lived in her newfound city. She captured all who passed through her domain and forced them to live there. Only the people of Gagelang were spared. In time, the new kingdom became well-populated and was filled with activity day and night.

Once, Panji Semirang attacked the King of Mentawan. The king could not repel the attack, and surrendered all his lands and family to the victor. The two princesses of Mentawan initially wept over the misfortune that had befallen the royal family, but after meeting their handsome, gentle and well spoken captor, they soon fell in love with him. They begged him not to leave them behind in Mentawan but to take them back to his kingdom instead.

One day, the King of Kuripan sent treasure to Daha. On the way, however, the treasure was stolen by Panji Semirang, who promised to return it to Raden Inu if he came to claim it. Raden Inu came and the pair soon became fast friends. When he held Panji Semirang's hand and wrist in a handshake, he found them to be as smooth and delicate as a woman's, but he did not realise that Panji Semirang was in fact Candra Kirana. Thereafter, Raden Inu continued his journey to Daha and married a princess. Only after the wedding did he find out that the princess was not Candra Kirana, but Galuh Ajeng. Raden Inu found himself unable to stop thinking about his new friend, Panji Semirang. Before long, he could no longer bear Galuh Ajeng and her endless demands.

So one day, Raden Inu left Daha to look for Panji Semirang, only to discover that he was no longer in the country. Maha Dewi also told him that Panji Semirang was actually Candra Kirana. Changing his name to Pangeran Panji Jayeng Kesuma, Raden Inu continued his search for Candra Kirana. He conquered the lands he came upon and married their princesses. Before reaching Gagelang, he married two more princesses: Princess Galuh Nawang Candra from Sedayu and Princess Nila Wati from Jaga Raga.

The story tells that Candra Kirana was afraid Raden Inu would discover her secret. So, before he could find her, she dismantled the city and set out to wander around the country. Her only companions were the two ladies-in-waiting and the two princesses of Mentawan. After some time, she reached Mount Wilis, where her aunt Biku Gandasari lived as a hermit. Her aunt cordially welcomed her. Soon, Biku Gandasari asked Candra Kirana to go to Gagelang disguised as a *gambuh* singer. Candra Kirana made her way to Gagelang, in the guise of Gambuh Warga Asmara, accompanied by her two ladies-in-waiting and the two Mentawan princesses. The arrival of the *gambuh* players caused great excitement in Gagelang. They performed *Raden Cekel Waneng Pati Berahi Ken Sila Beranti* and *Panji Semirang*. Their audiences were so deeply moved it was as if they were drunk. Raden Inu (Raden Panji Jayeng Kesuma) was fascinated by the lead player, Gambuh Warga Asmara, and regularly invited him to take a stroll together. Their appearance and demeanour were so alike that they might have been born of the same mother.

The story now tells that the King of Lasem and the King of Pudak Setengal, who were the brothers of the King of Jaga Raga, launched an attack on Gagelang. Raden Panji and his clown servant Semar met their attack. The two kings could not withstand their assault and surrendered. They gave their two daughters to Raden Panji.

In the meantime, Nila Wati, one of Raden Panji's consorts, suspected that Gambuh Warga Asmara was actually a woman, and asked him to investigate the matter. One night, after a performance of *Lakon Panji Semirang*, Raden Panji went to peep at Gambuh Warga Asmara from behind the curtain of her bedroom. He saw Gambuh Warga Asmara play with her golden doll, cradle it and throw it in the air while talking to herself. Raden Panji could no longer control himself and leapt out into Warga Asmara's bedroom. He held her hands and kissed her, as he whispered sweet words into her ears. Raden Panji and Gambuh Warga Asmara delighted in each other's company day and night. Raden Panji forgot the world around him and his other wives. After some time, Raden Panji invited Candra Kirana and the other princesses to return with him to Kuripan.

The narrative then moves back to the story of Paduka Liku and Galuh Ajeng. The potion they had given the King of Kuripan lost its potency, and he no longer cared about them. Paduka Liku asked her brother, Menteri, to look for a quid of betel leaves. This time, Menteri was struck by lightning and died in the forest. Paduka Liku was so grief-stricken that she fell gravely ill and died not long thereafter. Galuh Ajeng was forced to marry Raden Singa Menteri, a hideous man with a short neck and very crooked teeth.

The king greeted the return of Raden Inu to Kuripan with great joy. Soon Inu was crowned the new king and given the title Sang Ratu Prabu Anom. Candra Kirana became his queen; Princess Nila Wati became his chief consort, Maha Dewi; while the two princesses of Mentawan, Galuh Nawang Candra and Princess Puspa Juita, assumed their roles as minor consorts. The old king, having relinquished his throne, departed for Mount Wilis to live as a sage. More and more visitors came to Mount Wilis, as scholars, teachers, Brahmins, ascetics and priests travelled there to pay their respects to the old king. Subsequently, the King of Gagelang also abdicated, passing his throne to Raden Singa Menteri, and he too retired to a mountain to lead the life of a holy man.

Thereafter, the kingdoms of Gagelang and Kuripan continued to prosper; many traders and merchants stopped there to conduct their business.

3.6 *Hikayat Misa Taman Jayeng Kusuma*

This *hikayat* was edited by Abdul Rahman Kaeh, from a manuscript kept in the National Library of Malaysia. Not much is known about it. According to Abdul Rahman Kaeh, this *hikayat* might have been transcribed between 1860 and 1870. Another manuscript, Add. 12387, *Hikayat Misa Taman Sira Panji Jayeng Kusuma*, exists in the library of the British Museum, bearing the same storyline. There are, however, some differences: for example, in Add. 12387, Raden Inu is said to have died in a battle against the King of Lasem. This incident is not found in the other *hikayat* (Abdul Rahman Kaeh, 1977: 69-81). Furthermore, it is not clear whether this *hikayat* is the same as the *Hikayat Misa Taman* mentioned by Werndly in 1736. Below is a summary of the *hikayat*.

The story tells that Betara Naya Indra descended to earth and became the King of Kuripan. Before long he was blessed with five children: his sons became the rulers of Kuripan, Kediri, Gagelang and Singasari, while his daughter married the King of Majapahit. Betara Naya Indra then returned to the celestial world, leaving his sons to rule the world and in turn they begat their own children. And when their children grew up, they were betrothed to suitable partners.

Raden Inu Kertapati, the prince of Kuripan, was betrothed to Candra Kirana, the princess of Daha. However, after seeing a portrait of her painted by Semar, he refused to marry Candra Kirana. (While Semar painted the portrait, Candra Kirana was attended by a goddess disguised as a hideous woman. The foolish Semar painted this ugly woman instead.) Not long after, Inu married a different princess of Daha. Only after the marriage did he discover how truly beautiful Candra Kirana was. Candra Kirana, in the meantime, had been engaged to marry Raden Singa Persatu, the prince of Belambangan. Inu had fallen deeply in love with her and could not control his longing; he wanted to be near her all the time. To prevent any untoward incident, Batara Kala flew Candra Kirana to a forest in Segara Gunung. She was found by the King of Segara Gunung who adopted her as his own daughter, changing her name to Ken Segerba Ningrat.

Raden Inu and his brother, Raden Carangluh, went in search of Candra Kirana. They reached Mount Jamurdipa and spent time in meditation there. After some time, Batara Indra appeared before them and presented them with a magic ring. He also taught them the magic arts. Thus equipped, they continued their search for Candra Kirana, assuming new names: Raden Inu called himself Misa Jayeng Kusuma Sira Panji Jayang Seteru, his brother's new name was Kelana Anom Perwira. They defeated four kings, brothers, who had set fire to the guest-house at the foot of Mount Jamurdipa, which belonged to a nobleman from Raden Inu's court. After their victory, Raden Inu and his followers settled in Kembang Kuning, the kingdom previously ruled by the four kings.

Candra Kirana's brothers, Raden Asmara Agung and Raden Gunung Sari, were also looking for her. Raden Asmara Agung defeated a deity and thus freed the god from an evil curse; he too was rewarded with a magic ring. Armed with this ring, Raden Asmara Agung continued his travels. He and his brother assumed the names of Kelana Wirapati Kusuma Agung and Kelana Kusuma Anom. They conquered many countries and married the princesses of each of the lands they vanquished. Finally, they reached the Malay Peninsula. The Malay king welcomed them and arranged a marriage between his daughter and Kelana Wirapati Kusuma Agung.

Meanwhile, Raden Inu continued searching for Candra Kirana and eventually reached Segera Gunung. The King of Gunung surrendered to Raden Inu and gave up his daughters—one of whom was Candra Kirana—to Raden Inu. Raden Inu was immediately attracted to Ken Segerba Ningrat, and eventually married her, not knowing she was Candra Kirana.

After their sojourn in the Malay Peninsula, Raden Asmara Agung and his brother carried on their journey until they reached Lasem. They entered the kingdom disguised as puppet masters. The King of Lasem invited them to hold a *wayang* performance in the palace. The king also asked Raden Gunung Sari to encourage the princess of Lasem to love her husband, the prince of Tumasik. Of course, Raden Gunung Sari and the princess of Lasem fell in love with each other instead. The King of Tumasik was furious. A fight broke out. The King of Tumasik was killed while his son fled into the forest. Raden Gunung Sari married the princess of Lasem.

The tale continues with Raden Inu who loved his new wife, Ken Segerba Ningrat, so much he continually doted upon her. This aroused a great deal of jealousy in his concubine Ratna Lango, who spread a rumour that Ken Segerba Ningrat had been unfaithful to her husband. Believing the rumour, Raden Inu beat his wife. Ken Segerba Ningrat refused to be treated in this way and decided to leave the palace, together with two of her ladies-in-waiting. During her flight from the palace, she was carried to Mount Wilis by Batara Kala. Under the name of Endang Kusuma Jaya, she sat in meditation on the mountain.

Raden Inu went looking for the man who had supposedly betrayed his wife. Batara Kala revealed the truth to him — Ken Segerba Ningrat was none other than Candra Kirana, his fiancée. Realising his mistake, Raden Inu became seriously ill. To cure him, Raden Inu was eventually taken to the mountain where Ken Segerba Ningrat was meditating. Afraid that Raden Inu would discover her secret, Ken Segerba Ningrat left the mountain before he could find her. This time, Batara Kala changed her into a man and gave her the name Misa Jejujuk Sira Panji Maling Daha. Raden Inu continued his search. He conquered many countries along the way. Not long after, Raden Inu, disguised as a wayfarer named Misa Edan Sira Panji Jayeng Kusuma, and his brother, Carang Tinangluh or Misa Kelana Jaya Wirasuka, arrived in Gagelang where they were cordially received by the king.

Meanwhile, Misa Jejujuk (Candra Kirana) arrived in Belambangan Jaya where she found the King of Belambangan and the King of Pandan Salas had been captured and imprisoned by the

King of Astina Jajar. Misa Jejujuk defeated the King of Astina and freed the two kings. Misa Jejujuk had also been ordered to take Ratna Wilis, Raden Inu's sister, with her. Raden Kerta Buana set out to rescue his sister, despite his father forbidding him to do so. For his disobedience, he was turned into a *raksasa*, and in this ogre form rescued Putri Nawang Kusuma, who had been kidnapped by Raden Nawang Kusuma, a recluse. Thereafter, Raden Kerta Buana built the city of Tambak Kencana and settled there.

After a period in Lasem, Raden Agung and Gunung Sari continued their travels and reached Gagelang. At the same time, Misa Jejujuk arrived in Gagelang in the guise of a vagabond; she was reunited with her brothers and, more importantly, with her fiancé, Raden Inu, although they were all still in disguise. Raden Inu began to suspect that Misa Jejujuk was Candra Kirana. Unwilling to reveal her true identity, Misa Jejujuk (Candra Kirana) left Gagelang. During her journey, she arrived in Tambak Kencana where she killed a *raksasa* who turned out to be none other than Raden Kerta Buana. Misa Jejujuk was subsequently crowned ruler of Tambak Kencana and took the title Sang Prabu Anom.

The tale continues with the story of King of Mengganda. Accompanied by his brothers, the King of Mataram and the King of Soca Windu, he asked for the hand of the princess of Gagelang. His proposal was rejected and a ferocious war broke out. In the ensuing battle, Raden Inu and his brothers, aided by Prabu Anom (Candra Kirana), defeated the king and his brothers. Raden Inu then learned that Prabu Anom had previously rescued Princess Nawang Kusuma (from Daha) and Galuh Majapahit, and he asked that the two princesses be returned to their fathers. However, Prabu Anom refused and another battle erupted. This time, Prabu Anom assisted by Batara Kala, emerged victorious. Raden Inu and his brothers were taken prisoner. The king of Gagelang intervened and secured the release of Raden Inu. Rulers from far and wide paid homage to Prabu Anom. A few days later, to everyone's surprise and delight, Batara Kala changed Prabu Anom back to a woman. And thus, the two sweethearts were finally reunited after their long separation. A lavish festival was held. The kings of Kuripan, Daha, Singasari and Gagelang made their way to Mount Segara Kidul to fulfil their vows to the gods, then abdicated so that their sons could ascend the thrones of their respective kingdoms.

3.7 *Hikayat Dewa Asmara Jaya*

Acccording to Harun Mat Piah's study of a manuscript of this *hikayat* for his Master of Arts degree from the University of Malaya in 1972, this *hikayat* is more complete than any other known *hikayat* (Harun Mat Piah, 1980: 34). Nothing, however, is said about the *hikayat*'s origin, except that the manuscript belongs to the M. Niemann Collection kept in the Royal Library of Belgium and was copied in July 1872. Mat Piah claimed that the manuscript of the *Hikayat Dewa Asmara* comprises two parts. The first part is the *Hikayat Dewa Asmara Jaya;* its contents are almost the same as another manuscript of the same title kept in the library at Leiden University. The second part consists of the *Hikayat Cekel Waneng Pati* text, which has already been discussed above. Below is a summary of the first part.

Dewa Asmara Jaya descended to earth in order to become the ruler of Kuripan. His queen ate a lotus flower and bore a daughter named Ratu Candra Kirana. The royal couple later had four sons: Kuda Rawi Serengga, Kuda Mengsari, Kuda Wirajaya and Kuda Wirasani. Meanwhile, the King of Majapahit had a son, Raden Bambang Sukma Indra, and four daughters: Raden Ayu Kusuma, Raden Candra Kirana, Raden Dewi Kusuma and Raden Nila Kusuma. Raden Bambang Sukma grew to be a brave prince. He defeated a weretiger (*harimau jadian*) and a rogue ascetic. The ringleader of a band of marauding bandits surrendered to him. When his daughters reached their maturity, the king of Majapahit sent a messenger to Kuripan, inviting the kingdom's princes to offer proposals of marriage.

Kuripan at that time however was in turmoil. Kuda Rawi Serengga and Kuda Wirajaya had both fallen in love with the same girl, Ken Maya Sari, the daughter of a district chief (*demang*). Because of his jealousy, Kuda Wirajaya stabbed the girl, thus incurring the wrath of the King of Kuripan. Kuda Rawi Serengga refused to forgive his brother. Wracked with guilt, Kuda Wirajaya, accompanied by a faithful *punakawan*, went to Mount Imagiri to atone for his sin. At the same time, Kuda Rawi Serengga and Kuda Mangsari departed for Majapahit to marry the princesses of Majapahit.

Sukma Wijaya, the son of Begawan Derpa Sena, had been raised by a farmer. The sage asked him to help Kuda Wirajaya. Sukma Wijaya took the name Sang Sura Kelana and elevated the farmer who had raised him to the status of village chief (*dipati*). At the same time, Batara Kala also ordered Kuda Wijaya to look for Sang Sura Kelana and to go with him to Majapahit. Kuda Wijaya then changed his name to Bambang Negara.

While on their way to Majapahit, Kuda Rawi Serengga and Kuda Mangsari were trapped by an army led by the King of Jajar Cemara. Fortunately, Sang Sura Kelana and Bambang Negara arrived in time to rescue them. The princes of Kuripan arrived in Majapahit. Kuda Rawi Serengga subsequently made peace with his brother, Kuda Wirajaya (Bambang Negara). The Kuripan princes then married the Majapahit princesses.

The king of Jajar Cemara and his allies once again ambushed the princes of Kuripan as they made their way home to Kuripan. A terrible war ensued. The king of Jajar Cemara was defeated and his kingdom fell into the hands of the Kuripan princes. Upon their return to Kuripan, the princes became the kings of Kuripan, Daha, Gagelang and Singasari respectively.

Sang Sura Kelana returned to his own country, Jajar Angsoka, and married Princess Raden Ratna Kusuma. He built a beautiful city and spent the intervening years there with his beloved wife. Eventually, he left her and returned to the mountain to resume his life as a hermit. When he was old, Dewa Asmara Jaya departed the mortal world to return to his celestial abode. His unmarried daughter, Princess Candra Kesuma, went to the mountain to take up a life of meditation, calling herself Kili Suci and taking the title Nila Rajapati.

That is the gist of the first part of the *Hikayat Dewa Asmara Jaya*. Judging by a summary of the *hikayat* given by Harun Mat Piah in his study and comparing this to the contents of the Leiden manuscript found in the catalogue of H.H. Juynboll, there are obvious similarities between the two manuscripts. There are variations in the names of the characters, but this is due perhaps to the different way in which they have been transcribed. The greatest difference, however, probably lies in the story of Sang Sura Kelana. In the Leiden manuscript, it is said that, upon his arrival in Majapahit, Sang Sura Kelana was made a regent of the Majapahit with the title Adipati Kawan Cara. Then, after his victory against a second attack from King Jajar Cemara, he was adopted as a son by the King of Majapahit and given the name Pangeran Jaya Kesuma.

3.8 *Hikayat Undakan Penurat*

Acccording to S. O. Robson, the only extant manuscript of this *hikayat* is the Cod. Or. 1935, copied in 1825 in Solo (Central Java) and kept at the Leiden University library. This *hikayat* nevertheless is one of the best-known versions of the story of Ken Tambuhan and Raden Menteri, and bears a close relationship with the *Syair Ken Tambuhan*.

One problem that arises is this: can this *hikayat*, or the *Syair Ken Tambuhan* for that matter, be considered a Panji story? The Panji story often tells of Indian warriors such as Arjuna, Samba or Naya Kusuma being reincarnated on earth as kings of Java. This, however, is not what this *hikayat* is about. There is no mention of Kuripan, Daha, Singasari or Gagelang. The hero and heroine are not called Raden Inu or Candra Kirana. The protagonists do not undertake quests disguised as itinerant wanderers, neither do they conquer the lands they come across during their travels. According to these conventions, therefore, the *hikayat* cannot be considered a Panji story. Furthermore, it is worth noting that this *hikayat* also serves as a preface to some of the Panji stories, for example to the *Hikayat Panji Kuda Semirang*, discussed above, or to the *Panji Angreni* which originates from Palembang.

According to A. Teeuw, the story of Ken Tambuhan and Raden Menteri probably originated from a folktale about the love between a prince and a commoner. Their romance incurred the wrath of the queen who ordered that the girl be killed. The prince avenged the girl's death. This tragic love story was incorporated into the Panji story and adapted to suit its general characteristics. It was then further developed and became a separate story in its own right, resulting in what we now know as the *Hikayat Undakan Penurat*[1] and the *Syair Ken Tambuhan* (Teeuw 1966: xxii-xxiii). The following is a summary of the tale based on the text compiled and translated by Robson (1969).

This is a *hikayat* about Ratu Pura Negara, who was famous throughout Java and the Malay world. One night the king dreamed that the moon fell into his lap. In his dream, he picked up the moon, cradled it in his arms and gave it to the queen, who wrapped it in a cloth. Not long after, the queen became pregnant and on an auspicious day, gave birth to a son. The boy was extremely handsome, his complexion was radiant, and his disposition was sweet and tender. The baby was named Raden Undakan Penurat but he was better known as Raden Menteri. Punta Wirajaya, the son of one of the king's ministers, was chosen to be the young prince's tutor.

In time, Raden Menteri grew up and was betrothed to the princess of Banjar Kulon. One day, Raden Menteri went hunting for birds with his blowpipe. He unwittingly ventured into a forbidden garden called Taman Penglipur Lara, The Garden of Consolation. There he met the most beautiful princess he had ever seen. Her name was Ken Tambuhan and she was the daughter of the King of Wengger. The king held her prisoner. Raden Menteri was overwhelmed by Ken Tambuhan's beauty and took her home. He then married her.

When she found out, the queen was furious. She devised a plan to kill Ken Tambuhan. One day, the queen sent Raden Menteri to hunt for a buffalo. Palembaya took Ken Tambuhan to the forest and killed her. Ken Bayan, Ken Tambuhan's lady-in-waiting, tried to save her mistress and was also killed. Raden Menteri couldn't find a single buffalo to bring back to the queen. Not only

---

1 According to Teeuw, "*Andakan Penurat*" should actually be '*Undakan Penurat*', *undakan* means 'horse', part of Panji's name, whereas *andakan* has no meaning (Teeuw, 1966: xxii).

couldn't he find a buffalo, he couldn't even see a grasshopper. He decided to return to the palace. On the way, he came across Ken Tambuhan's dead body. Shocked and saddened, he unsheathed his keris and stabbed himself, his body falling onto the corpse of Ken Tambuhan. Punta Wirajaya also stabbed himself.

News of the deaths of Ken Tambuhan and Raden Menteri reached the king, who collapsed in shock. When he revived, he asked his men to bring home the bodies of Raden Menteri and Ken Tambuhan to be cremated and their ashes kept in two golden mausoleums. After the loss of his son, the king paid no attention to the queen. While travelling around the earth, Batara Kala took pity on the king and predicted that Raden Menteri would eventually be reunited with his wife, Ken Tambuhan.

One day, the queen discovered that the mausoleums had turned into two *bunga tanjung* flowers—one in full bloom, the other curled shut. Each day, once in the morning and again in the afternoon, Sang Nata and his queen would come to look at these flowers. Not long after, Sang Nata dreamed that Batara Kala, disguised as an old man, asked him to pick the two flowers. He was instructed to give the furled flower to the queen and have her burn incense over it, while he was to do the same with the flower in bloom. Both the king and queen carried out Batara Kala's instructions. As they did so, Raden Menteri suddenly emerged from the furled flower, and Ken Tambuhan appeared from the flower in bloom. Sang Nata and the queen were overjoyed. A grand celebration was held. Soon after, Raden Menteri and Ken Tambuhan were married. After the wedding, Raden Menteri replaced his father on the throne of Pura Negara. He was an excellent king, the population of the state continually increased, and many merchants came to trade. He was greatly loved by his subjects.

Haji Zain al-Abidin of Petojan Pengukiran village finished copying the *hikayat* on 11 December 1825.

3.9 Javanese Panji Stories

The Panji stories are essentially of Javanese origin and because of this there are a great many Panji manuscripts. The best known are the *Malat* and the *Panji Angreni*. The *Malat* is named after its hero, Panji Amalat Rasmi, meaning "the conqueror of beauty". The heroine's name, Putri Anrang Kesari, means "the princess who rivals the saffron *kesari* flower". The *Malat* is famous for its long and complicated plot. According to Dr Poerbatjaraka, the *Malat* is actually a very new Panji story, whose apparent antiquity is contrived. The *Panji Angreni* from Palembang, by contrast, is a much older and typical Panji story. The characteristics of a prototypical Panji story are as follows:

(1) There are four royal siblings (their names are not mentioned). The sister becomes a nun (*biku*).
(2) Gagelang is the fourth kingdom, not Urawan.
(3) Its prelude tells the story of Indian warriors (such as Arjuna, Samba and others) being reincarnated as mortals on earth. A tale that tells the story of Naya Kusuma's reincarnation should be regarded as a new version of the Panji story (Poerbatjaraka, 1940: 157-215).

A Summary of the *Panji Angreni* (from Palembang)

Part I

The story tells that Ratu Keling (the king of Janggala or Kuripan) had four children. The eldest, an unmarried woman named Rara Sunti, became a nun. The others ruled Mamenang (Daha-Kediri), Urawan and Singasari respectively. The king of Janggala had four sons, named Waneng Pati, Brajanata, Carang Waspa, and Onengan.

Panji Waneng Pati (also known as Raden Mantri, or Raden Putra) was betrothed to a princess from Daha named Sekar Taji (Candra Kirana). One day, the prince decided to go sightseeing in order to console his longing heart. In a certain district, he met Angreni, the daughter of a regent. He took her home and married her. Panji was so happy with his new bride that he no longer wanted to marry the princess of Daha. His father was furious and looked for a way to separate them. Panji was ordered to pay his aunt a visit at her mountain hermitage. While he was away, Brajanata killed Angreni on the king's orders. When Panji returned and found his wife dead, he was completely distraught.

Life in the palace without his wife became unbearable. One day, Panji left the palace, together with his brothers and *punakawans*, and set out on a voyage. He changed his name to Jayengpati; his *punakawans* also assumed new identities. During his voyage, Panji reached the island of Bali; he conquered the king of Bali and took the beautiful Balinese princess, Andayaprana, as his wife. Thereafter, Panji continued on his journey. He defeated the king of Belambangan and many other kings on the eastern seaboard, and married their daughters as well. Even so, he still pined for his beloved Angreni.

While he was in Wirasaba, an envoy arrived from Daha, asking his assistance to repel the forces of the King of Matuan. As a reward, he was promised the hand of the princess of Daha, Sekar Taji. Panji was immediately attracted to Sekar Taji because of her resemblance to Angreni. He completely forgot about his beloved. Meanwhile, Gunung Sari, another Daha princess, had fallen in love with Onengan, Panji's youngest brother. After they had defeated Daha's enemies, Panji married Sekar Taji.

News of Sekar Taji's wedding to Jayeng Sari (Panji) spread and eventually reached Janggala. Not knowing that Jayeng Sari was his own son, Panji, the King of Janggala was furious when he heard the news. To honour the promise he had made to the Daha king to wed Panji to his daughter, he had schemed to have the rival for Panji's affections killed, and because of this, Panji had run away. But now, Daha had the audacity to marry the princess to someone else. The king of Janggala sent an army to Daha under the command of Rajanata. The next day, an envoy from Janggala also arrived in Daha. It was revealed that Jayeng Sari was really Panji, the prince of Janggala. Everyone rejoiced greatly.

Part II

The story is told of the brave and valiant Kelana Tunjung-Seta, ruler of Nusakencana. The king had a half-sister, Angrenasari, who was an incarnation of Angreni. The king loved neither the queen nor his various concubines. Instead, he was very much in love with his half-sister Angrenasari. She rejected him, insisting that it was improper for a brother and sister to be so close.

The king of Nusakencana wanted to conquer Kediri. Not only that, he wanted to move his palace to Java. The heavenly messenger Batara Narada descended to earth to warn Panji about the king of Nusakencana's evil plans. He also advised Panji to move elsewhere. Soon, the king of Nusakencana arrived in Kediri and told the king of his wish to serve under him as his vassal, in fulfilment of a vow he made to the gods during a previous illness. The king of Kediri granted his request. In the meantime, Panji prepared himself for whatever might happen.

One day, on her way back from a feast, the queen of Nusakencana lost her way and found herself at Panji's residence. She succumbed to his charms and they became lovers. Panji advised her to tell the king of Nusakencana that she had been raped. The king was enraged. A ferocious war ensued. The king of Nusakencana was defeated, but Panji himself was mortally wounded. Batara Narada came down to earth and brought Panji back to life. Angreni and Sekar Taji were reunited in the one body as Candraswara.

And thus ends the second part of *Panji Angreni*. This is similar to the Panji story published by Roorda. There is, however, a further tale of Bambang Swatma, who disguised himself as Panji. His disguise was so convincing that the king of Daha could not tell who was the real Panji and who was the impostor. Finally, the real Panji confronted the impostor and killed him. Everyone was overjoyed and large scale celebrations were held. The Brussels library has two Panji manuscripts which are the same as the Panji (Angreni) Palembang.

3.10 Cambodia and Thailand

Stories of Panji have spread as far abroad as Cambodia and Thailand, probably through Malay manuscripts written in the Arabic script. The hero in the Cambodian Panji is called Eynao, which reminds us of the way *Ino* is spelt in Jawi. The Thai scholar, Prince Dhani Nivat (1956: 113-136), has suggested that the Cambodian version of the Panji story on which Dr Poerbatjaraka based his study was actually an adaptation of a modern Panji story written in Thai by King Rama II (1767-1824). Furthermore, there are two versions of the Panji tales in Thai: the first is known by the name *Dalang*, and the second as *Ari Negara*. Based on the *Dalang* summary provided in Prince Nivat's paper, it appears that the *Dalang* is really a collection of miscellaneous stories from different versions of the Panji tales. For example, Ino is said to have three lovers (beside his many lovers). The first, Busba Desa, is different from Busba Daha, the Daha princess who is said to be his second lover. Furthermore, Ino, so the story goes, also abducted Busba Sari, the daughter of a village headman. His first lover was killed by the king, whereas the story of the third lover is not elaborated. Ino or Panji, the story continues, was tricked and then set adrift in a boat to an island inhabited only by women. After escaping from the island, Panji became a *dalang* whose fame soon spread far and wide. Busba Daha, the princess of Daha, was spirited away by an ancestral spirit and forced to disguise herself as a man. The rest of the story revolves around the lovers' search for each other, accompanied by innumerable and often convoluted stories of wars and romances. Finally, Panji is reunited with Busba Daha in Kalang. For comparative purposes, a summary of the Cambodian Panji story as presented by Poerbatjaraka (1940: 37-67) is given below.

Summary of the Cambodian Panji story

Eynao, the prince of Kuripan, broke off his engagement to Bossaba, the princess of Daha, and married another princess. He soon regretted his decision. But it was too late. Bossaba was already betrothed to another man, the prince of Carika and the day of the wedding had been set. Bossaba was especially angry at Eynao for cancellling their engagement. Siyatara, her brother, tried to placate her, but to no avail.

Upon hearing of Bossaba's forthcoming wedding, Eynao fainted. His brother-in-law, Sangkha-Marita, suggested that they kidnap Bossaba and hide her in a cave. Not only did they succeed in kidnapping her but they were also able to convince Carika, Bossaba's fiancé, that another prince had kidnapped Bossaba, not Eynao.

Eynao's terrible deed angered Pattarac-Cala, the ancestral spirit of both Eynao and Bossaba. She carried Bossaba away to a faraway place. Bossaba was changed into a man and given a new name, Onacan. He was also given a magic weapon. Armed with the magic weapon, Onacan embarked on a journey and was adopted by the King of Pramotan as his son. He then continued on his travels. At a hermitage at the foot of a mountain, he met a handsome young ascetic, who was none other than Panji, that is, Eynao himself. Eynao suspected Onacan (Bossaba) and kept a close eye on him wherever he went. They reached the kingdom of Kalang where both of them pledged their allegiance to the king. Their prowess in wrestling and handling weapons impressed the king. Onacan and Eynao soon became close friends.

The King of Calapan asked for the hand of the King of Kalang's eldest daughter on behalf of his younger brother, the King of Camara. But as the princess was already betrothed to someone else, the proposal was rejected. The King of Calapan led his army against Kalang. Eynao and Onacan, broke his attack. After their victory, Onacan retreated to Mount Enang, where he was visited by Pattarac-Cala, his ancestral spirit. Pattarac-Cala changed Onacan back into a woman and named her Ci Enang. The spirit also predicted that Ci Enang would meet Eynao on Mount Enang.

Meanwhile, his sister Bossaba's disappearance had left Siyatara in a state of despair. To cheer himself up, he went hunting. During his hunt, he came across a beautiful golden peacock and gave chase. His pursuit eventually led him to Kalang, where he took the name Jaran. In Kalang, he met Eynao and Vyada, Eynao's sister, his fiancée. The couple were overjoyed to see each other.

Eynao's fame aroused the jealousy of the King of Preah-bat-meang-roda, who sent four sorcerers to abduct him. Unsure where they could find him or what he looked like, the sorcerers kidnapped Jaran instead. Fortunately, Princess Daravan, King Meang-roda's daughter, took pity on Jaran and saved him from various tortures. Eynao was baffled by Jaran's disappearance, and set out to find him. Following a great battle, Eynao found Jaran and set him free. They also found Ci Enang, alias Onacan, alias Bossaba. Everyone rejoiced. Their weddings were celebrated in Kalang with many festivities, and attended by both the kings of Kuripan and Daha. Not long after this, the newly-married princes ascended the thrones of their respective kingdoms.

REFERENCES

Abdul Rahman Kaeh
1975.   "Naskah-naskah Panji: satu huraian," *DB*, 19, no. 2, pp. 76-93.
1977.   *Hikayat Misa Taman Jayeng Kusuma*, Kuala Lumpur.

Baharuddin Zainal
1956.   *Hikayat Chekel Waneng Pati*, Kuala Lumpur.

Baroroh Baried et al.
1982.   *Panji Citra Pahlawan Nusantara*, Jakarta.

Berg, C. C.
1928.   *Kidung Soendayana*, Soerakarta.
1954.   "Bijdragen tot de kermis der Pandji verhalen," *BKI*, 110, pp. 189-216; 305-334.

Dhani Nivat, Prince
1956.   "The Dalang," *JSS*, XLIII, 2, pp. 113-136.

Harun Mat Piah
1980.   *Cerita-cerita Panji Melayu*, Kuala Lumpur.

Hikayat
1917.   *Hikayat Pandji Semirang*, Batavia.

Klinkert, H. C.
1897.   *Hikajat Mesa Kagungari Seri Pandji Wira Kusuma*, Leiden.

Koentjaraningrat
1959.   *Tari dan Kesusastraan di Jawa*, INTI, Jogjakarta.
1975.   *Anthropology in Indonesia*, 's-Gravenhage.

Nafron Hasjim.
1984.   *Hikayat Galuh Digantung*, Jakarta.

Nikmah Sunardjo
1993.   *Hikayat Maharaja Garebag Jagat: Suntingan disertai Tinjauan Tema dan Amanat Cerita serta Fungsi Punakawan di Dalamnya*, Jakarta, Balai Pustaka.

Overbeck
1932.   "Java in de Maleische litenatum (*Hikayat Galuh Digantung*)," *Djawa*, 12, pp. 209-217.

Poerbatjaraka, R. M. Ng.
1940.   *Pandji-verhalen Onderling Vergeleken (Tjerita Pandji dalam Perbandingan*, (translated by Zuber Usman and H. B. Jassin, 1968), Bibliotheca Javanica.

Pustaka Antara
1963.   *Hikayat Panji Semirang*, Kuala Lumpur.

Ras, J. J.
1973.   "The Panji roman and W. H. Rasser's analysis of its theme," *BKI*, 129 (4), pp. 411-459.
1976.   "The historical development of the Javanese shadow theatre," *RIMA*, 10 (2), pp. 50-76.
1982.   "The social function and cultural significance of the Javanese wayang purwa theatre," *Indonesian Circle*, 29, pp. 19-32.

Rassers, W. H.
1922. *De Pandji-Roman,* Antwerpen.
1959. *Panji, the Culture Hero: A Structural Study of Religion in Java,* The Hague.

Robson, S. O.
1969. *Hikayat Andakan Penurat,* The Hague.
1971. *Wangbang Wideya, a Javanese Panji Romance,* The Hague.

Sastrawinata, S.
1963. *Panji Semirang,* Djakarta.

Teeuw, A.
1966. *Shair Ken Tambuhan,* Kuala Lumpur.

Winstedt, R. O.
1941. "The Panji Tales," *JMBRAS,* 19 (2), pp. 234-237.
1948. "A Panji Tale from Kelantan," *JMBRAS,* 2, 2 (1), pp. 53-60.

Zoetmulder, P. J.
1974. *Kalangwan, a survey of old Javanese literature,* The Hague.

4 Literature Belonging to the Period of Transition from Hinduism to Islam

It is very difficult to determine which literary works belong to the period of transition from Hinduism to Islam in the Malay Archipelago. Firstly, traditional Malay literature is generally not dated and does not bear the name of its author. Secondly, it is written in the Arabic alphabet. This means that it was the advent of Islam in the Malay Archipelago and the ensuing use of the Jawi script that heralded the birth of traditional Malay literature in general. Thirdly, one can find evidence of Islamic influence even in the very oldest known Malay literary work, the *Hikayat Sri Rama*. For example, there is mention in one version of the *Hikayat Sri Rama* of the prophet Adam bestowing supernatural powers upon the meditating Rawana. In the folktale *Hikayat Pelanduk Jenaka*, the animal protagonist, the mousedeer, is often referred to as a servant of the prophet Sulaiman (Solomon) and of Syaikh Alim (a holy man) who lived in the forest. Fourthly, all literary works produced during the transition period were called *hikayat*s, and the word *hikayat* is an Arabic word that means "story". According to L. Brakel, the word *hikayat* was initially used to mean a "short story", and was only used to denote a story of greater length after the publication of the *Hikayat Muhamad Hanafiah* (L. Brakel, 1979: 6). So which literary works belong to the transitional era?

Malay literature of the transitional age is a coming together of Hindu-inspired literature and Islamic influence. In other words, works which are patently Hindu but also contain Islamic elements, such as the *Hikayat Sri Rama*, are not considered literature of the transitional period. The characteristics of transitional age literature are as follows. The supreme deity in such works is initially referred to as "Dewata Mulia Raya" or "Batara Kala", and then later replaced by "Raja Syah Alam" or "Allah Subhanahu wa Taala" (Allah, Glorious and Exalted). The plot usually tells of gods and goddesses (or *bidadari*s) who descended on earth to become kings or princes and princesses. If they are reincarnated as the children of royalty, their births are usually heralded by a mysterious or extraordinary phenomenon. Sometimes they are born together with magic arrows or swords *(Hikayat Indra Bangsawan)*. Their birth is a harbinger of prosperity and abundance in the kingdom. But due to the treachery of either evil sorcerers *(Hikayat Si Miskin)* or perfidious relatives *(Hikayat Jaya Langkara)*, our hero will be banished from the kingdom. The banishment is in itself perhaps unavoidable. The hero in *Hikayat Indra Putra* is carried off by a peacock, while the hero in *Hikayat Syah Kobat* is kidnapped by his own ancestor. Sometimes our hero himself goes on a self-imposed exile, in search of a princess who appears in his dream (*Hikayat Langlang Buana*), to find a magic bamboo flute (*Hikayat Indra Bangsawan*) or a potion to cure an ailment (*Hikayat Jaya Langkara*).

During their exile, the heroes learn a gamut of magic skills that could help them in a battle. They may also procure magical weapons or objects that grant them extraordinary powers, such as a machete that can cut down an enemy by itself (*Hikayat Parang Punting*), a gemstone that can summon a *jinn* to come to the aid of its owner in battle (*Hikayat Langlang Buana*), or a magic stone that can create a city, complete with everything in it (*Hikayat Indra Bangsawan*). With the help of such magic weapons, the hero is able to rescue a princess held captive by a dragon (*Hikayat Parang Punting*) or a *raksasa* (*Hikayat Indra Bangsawan*), and later marries her. After marrying her, our hero would then have to fight off attacks by nine, sometimes forty-nine, or even ninety-nine, angry princes whose efforts to win the princess' hand in marriage she had spurned. And not surprisingly of course, our hero always wins.

As time went on, the Islamic elements became more and more obvious. Though Hindu motifs can still be found in the literature of this period, such as rescuing a princess held captive by a *garuda* (a large mythical eagle-like creature), magical cures or transferring a human soul into to the body of an animal, these are usually intermingled with Islamic elements. Indera Jaya, for example, answers his wife's questions on Islam, while Lukman Hakim also appears later in the same story to expound the difference between *sembahyang* (worship) and *salat* (Islamic ritual prayer), as well as the meanings of *syariat* (law), *tarikat* (mystical company), *hakikat* (reality) and *makrifat* (spiritual knowledge) (*Hikayat Syah Mardan*). Isma Yatim explains to the king the terms and provisions of sovereignty in relation to Allah's laws (*Hikayat Isma Yatim*). Furthermore, elements of Persian literature are also imitated, such as the way in which chapters are divided under individual titles (*Hikayat Isma Yatim*). In time, the literature of the transition period gradually evolved to become a fully Islamic literature.

Another feature of works written during the transitional era is that they are often known by both Hindu and Islamic titles—the latter being usually better known than the former. For example, we know the *Hikayat Si Miskin* better by that title rather than by its Hindu name, the *Hikayat Marakarma;* likewise the *Hikayat Syah Mardan* better than the *Hikayat Indra Jaya* or *Hikayat Bikrama Datya;* and the *Hikayat Ahmad Muhammad* better than the *Hikayat Serangga Bayu*.

In the following sections, I will discuss fourteen *hikayat*s written during the transitional Hindu-Islamic era, namely:

Hikayat Puspa Wiraja
Hikayat Parang Punting
Hikayat Langlang Buana
Hikayat Si Miskin
Hikayat Berma Syahdan
Hikayat Indra Putra
Hikayat Syah Kobat
Hikayat Koraisy Mengindra
Hikayat Indra Bangsawan

Hikayat Jaya Langkara
Hikayat Nakhoda Muda
Hikayat Ahmad Muhammad
Hikayat Syah Mardan
Hikayat Isma Yatim

4.1 *Hikayat Puspa Wiraja*

The *Hikayat Puspa Wiraja,* or *Hikayat Bispu Raja,* is a very popular tale. Save for some slight variations, its plot can also be found in the *Hikayat Bakhtiar* and *Hikayat Maharaja Ali.* The tale also bears some resemblance to parts of the *Hikayat Seribu Satu Malam (Tales of One Thousand and One Nights,* or as it is better known in English, the *Arabian Nights),* as well as to folktales found in Kashmir and Sri Lanka. However, there are not many manuscripts of this *hikayat.* The most notable manuscript is the Leiden manuscript (Cod. Or. 1401), copied on 3 Rajab 1237 H (1821) by Muhammad Cing Said (?). According to scholars, this Leiden manuscript contains several lexical archaisms such as *persembah, persalin* and so on. A discernible Javanese influence is also present, as evidenced in the use of Javanese-inflected conjugations such as: *masang* for *memasang,* and *merintahkan* for *memerintah.* There are no Portuguese words whatsoever. God is still referred to here as *"Dewata Mulia Raya".*

This *hikayat* is said to have come from Thailand. Van der Tuuk and R. O. Winstedt, however, do not subscribe to this view. Firstly, there are no Thai words or aristocratic titles/designations used in this *hikayat.* Secondly, it bears a close resemblance to an Indo-Persian version. Thirdly, a story in the *hikayat* about the misfortune that befell a king after he took a baby bird from its nest may have originated from a story written in Pali. Van der Tuuk further argues that what was regarded as a Siamese term found in the *hikayat,* transliterated as "Astana Pura Negara," might have instead been "Tatsyasila", a well-known Buddhist centre of learning featured in Indian literature (Winstedt, 1921a: 96-103).

This *hikayat* has been published twice—first in Leiden in 1849 by J. C. Fraissinet under the title *Hikayat Bispu Raja*; and then by the Singapore Government Press in 1899. Below is a summary of the *Hikayat Bispu Raja* published by J. C. Fraissinet.

There was once was a kingdom called Astana Pura Negara. Its king was called Bispu Raja; its queen, Kemala Kisna Dewi. The royal couple had two sons: the elder one was Jaya Indra, the younger—still a baby—was called Jaya Cindra.

One day, the king heard that his younger brother, Antaraja, was plotting with a band of young nobles and warriors within the palace to overthrow him. The king was gravely troubled by the news. He realised that if he was drawn into a civil war against Antaraja, many of his subjects would die and there would be much bloodshed. To avoid this, the king decided to relinquish his throne and leave the kingdom. "Take me with you, Your Majesty," said the queen to her husband. "I am like a pair of stockings; without them, the feet suffer." That night, the royal couple and their children left Astana Pura Negara under the veil of darkness. They journeyed through thick forests and across vast plains. When day broke, they found themselves beside a river and after many hours of walking, took their rest under a tree. A while later, the king heard the sound of a baby parakeet

LITERATURE BELONGING TO THE PERIOD OF TRANSITION FROM HINDUISM TO ISLAM

in a tree calling for its mother. On hearing this, the king's son began to cry as he wanted to have the baby bird. Despite knowing that whoever separates a baby bird from its mother will become a pauper, the king, out of love for his son, took the baby bird from its nest. After a while, he returned the chick to its nest. When the mother bird returned, she smelled human scent on her baby and pecked at it.

The king then carried his wife across the river. When he returned to get his sons, he found they were missing. Overwhelmed, the king fainted. When he regained consciousness, he frantically scoured the riverbank but his sons were nowhere to be seen. The king then crossed back over the river to his wife, only to find that she too was missing. He searched for her around the trees, without success. In the end, the king had to come to terms with the loss of his family and plodded on through the thick forest. After some time, he reached a city. Completely exhausted, he fell asleep in a hall at the edge of the city. When he awoke, he found himself on an elephant.

A minister from the palace announced to him that the elephant had chosen the king to be the next ruler of the kingdom, as the reigning monarch had passed away without leaving an heir. And so the king became ruler of his new kingdom and ruled over his realm justly and benevolently. News of his ascension was announced to all of the kingdom's vassal states and their rulers who came bearing many gifts to pay homage to the new king. This change of fortune however did not bring the king happiness, for he was still beset by sorrow day and night as he thought of his wife and sons. Beseeching Dewata Mulia Raya for divine help to reunite him with his family, he ordered that alms be given to the ascetics and poor persons in his kingdom. This made the previously impoverished persons well-off.

The story says that the king's two young sons were not actually missing but had been taken home by a kind fisherman who had found them by the riverbank. The fisherman looked after the young princes well. His day, he presented his two charges to the king in the hope of that this would please His Majesty and gain him the king's favour. The king took a liking to the two "fisherman's sons", as they bore an uncanny resemblance to his own lost sons. They were taken into service in the palace—first as pages, then later as heralds. The king rewarded the fisherman with new clothing and a large sum of gold.

One day, a ship's captain arrived from Bijaya Nekerma and he was invited to a dinner in the palace. The two princes, acting as junior courtiers, were assigned to look after the captain's ship. The younger page felt sleepy and dozed off. His elder brother woke him up and told him how they had come to be the king's pages. A woman, who happened to be sleeping in the ship's cabin, overheard Jaya Indra's story. The woman was their mother, Putri Kemala Kisna Dewi, who had been abducted by the ship's captain. Overjoyed that she was finally reunited with her long-lost sons, Putri Kemala Kisna Dewi came out to greet her children and began hugging and kissing them. This was seen by the ship's crew who, not knowing that the two pages were Putri Kemala's sons, were scandalized by her public show of affection. They accused the two pages, who had been appointed to guard the ship, of inappropriate behaviour with the captain's wife. The king was furious and sent an executioner to arrest the errant pages and take them out of the kingdom where they were to be beheaded. Putri Kemala Kisna Dewi sobbed and tried to explain to the king that the two pages were actually her long-lost sons, but he ignored her.

The story next tells that when the executioner reached the city's eastern gates, the gatekeeper refused to open the gate as he did not believe the two pages were guilty. Moreover, it was not customary at that time to execute people in the middle of the night. The gatekeeper then began to tell him a tale about someone who acted rashly without getting to the heart of things. The executioner, unable to pass through the eastern gate, had no choice but to find another way out of the city. However, when he reached the southern, northern and western gateways, he received the same response from the respective gatekeepers. The stories they told him went like this:

1. A king who ruled over a vast kingdom was once waiting for an opportune time to build his palace. An astrologer had told him that if he built his palace on a certain day and month, it would turn to gold. When the auspicious moment arrived, the astrologer struck his gong. But the palace did not turn to gold as the astrologer had predicted. The king was furious and had the astrologer killed. Not long after this incident, a farmer came to see the king to present him with a bunch of "golden bananas" (*pisang emas*) which the farmer had planted when the gong was sounded. Only then did the king realise how foolish he had been.

2. A king, it was said, once kept a pet parakeet. One day, the parakeet brought a mango to the king. The bird told him that anyone who ate the fruit would turn the colour of gold. Upon hearing this, the king planted the mango so that it would produce many fruits. After some time, a mango tree grew and started to bear fruit. A ripe mango dropped from the tree and fell near a hole where a cobra dwelled. One of the king's gardeners found the mango and presented it to the king. The king gave the fruit to an old man who ate it and died. Thinking that his parakeet had betrayed him, the king killed the bird. The king then took another mango to feed to one of his prisoners. It was later reported that the pirate had eaten the mango and his body had immediately turned a golden hue. In order to get to the bottom of the matter, the king asked his men to investigate. It transpired that the mango the king gave to the old man had fallen into a cobra's hole. The king deeply regretted killing the parakeet without first finding out the truth of the matter.

3. Another story told of a poor couple who kept a pet mongoose they loved very much. One day, the couple went to work in their padi field, leaving the mongoose to guard the house and look after the couple's baby. In their absence, a large poisonous snake slithered into the house and fatally bit the baby from under the baby's cradle. When the mongoose saw the snake, it pounced on the creature and killed it. With its mouth covered in the blood of the snake, the mongoose then waited by the door for the couple to return. When the farmer discovered that the baby was dead and saw the mongoose with blood around its mouth, he killed their beloved pet. Not long after this, he stumbled upon the remains of the snake. He realized what had happened and regretted his actions.

4. A poor couple had a dog which they loved very much. One day, the husband set out on a voyage; he instructed the dog to guard the house and to look after his wife while he was away. During her husband's absence, the wife began an affair with a younger man. One night, while the husband was out on his boat waiting for fresh cargo to arrive, the dog attacked the wife's lover and killed him. When the woman tried to flee, the dog pounced on her and killed her too. When the husband returned, he found his wife sprawled in the doorway and the dog standing over her dead body with its mouth covered in blood. Without

a moment's forethought, the man grabbed his spear and killed his dog. On entering his house, he discovered the body of his wife's lover in the bedroom. Only then did the poor merchant realize what had happened and he deeply regretted his actions.

By the time the gatekeepers finished telling their stories, daylight had broken. The four men went to consult the greatest astrologer in the land and told him that the king wanted to execute the two royal pages. The chief astrologer then brought the four gatekeepers to the king and appealed to him to investigate the accusation further before passing sentence on them. The two pages were summoned. After hearing Jaya Indra's testimony, the king realized that the two pages were in fact his long-lost sons. Relieved and elated, the king lept from his throne and tearfully rushed to embrace and kiss them. At his command, the ship's captain was summoned to present Putri Kemala Kisna Dewi to the king. The captain swore that he never had any sexual relations with the princess, or even came close to her; each time he tried to approach her, his body felt as if it was on fire. The king was happy to hear the captain's assurances. The royal orchestra played and the news was greeted with great merrymaking throughout the kingdom. Putri Kemala Kisna Dewi became his queen. During the king's reign, his subjects lived peacefully under his protection. After a long time, the king abdicated to devote himself to worship, piety and charity in the service of "Dewata Mulia Raya", and he installed his son, Jaya Indra, as the new king of Semanta Pura Negara.

The story has it that Jaya Indra's uncle, Antaraja, who reigned in Astana Pura Negara, fell ill one day and suddenly died, leaving the kingdom without a monarch, successor or heir apparent deemed fit to succeed him. A messenger was sent to Semanta Pura Negara to seek the king's advice on how to resolve this situation. The king sent his younger brother, Jaya Cindra, to Astana Pura Negara to be its next ruler. Before his brother's departure, Jaya Indra instructed him not to tamper with age-old customs and traditions, to govern according to the just rule of law, and to treat all his ministers, military chiefs and those who would serve under him, with love and dignity. Adhering to these precepts, the two brothers enjoyed long and successful reigns over their respective kingdoms.

Although its details may vary, the *Hikayat Maharaja Ali* can be considered to be a version of the *Hikayat Puspa Wiraja*. According to C. O. Blagden, the manuscript of the *Hikayat Maharaja Ali* kept by the Royal Asiatic Society in London comprises two stories—the first is a version of the *Hikayat Puspa Wiraja,* the second a shorter version of the *Hikayat Raja Jumpah*. The manuscript came from the wife of Encik Husin who presented it as a gift to one Encik Muhammad ibnu'l-haji Abdul Fatah. Below is its summary (Blagden, 1929: 415-436).

There once was a king by the name of Maharaja Ali, the king of Badagra, who ruled over a vast empire. After having been on the throne for a considerable period of time, the king still had no heir. His astrologers however prophesied that His Majesty would soon have three sons. They foretold, however, that, unfortunately, the eldest son would bring the king untold hardship. Not long after that, the king's wife became pregnant and gave birth to a fine baby boy whom they named Baharum Syah. The king subsequently had two more sons, named Raja Tahir and Raja Badar Syah.

The boys grew as the months passed, becoming more and more good-looking. The eldest son, Baharum Syah, however, increasingly showed signs of a bad disposition; he was abusive and cruel towards the king's ministers and generals, beating and even killing several of them. He was also known to take liberties with other people's wives and daughters. The king did not rebuke him because he loved him so much.

One day, the king's ministers agreed to demand that the king relinquish his throne and leave the kingdom. If he refused, they threatened that they would desert the kingdom themselves. On his wife's advice, the king and his family departed, taking their belongings with them. Along the way, they were set upon by twelve highwaymen who robbed them of all their possessions. Raja Baharum Syah was separated from the rest of his family and became lost. Each Friday, the queen and her two sons would beg for alms at the mosque.

The prime minister of the country gave her alms one day and promptly reported her beauty to the king of Kabitan, Raja Serdala. The king immediately desired her and tricked her into coming to his palace. When he heard of this, Maharaja Ali became despondent and resigned himself to leaving his wife's fate in God's hands. He left Kabitan, together with his two sons. After walking for some time, they came to a river. Maharaja Ali tried to help his sons swim across the river. Unfortunately, when they were in the middle of the river, Maharaja Ali was eaten by a crocodile. A boatman rowing nearby heard Maharaja Ali's two sons weeping, and hurried to rescue them. The boatman took the boys home and raised them as if they were his own sons.

Meanwhile, Maharaja Ali's wife, Putri Hasinan, was being urged by the king to marry him. But she refused and tried to distract him instead by telling him a story that went like this:

During the time of Allah's prophet David (Daud), there lived a very handsome prince, the son of King Nursyirwan. One night, the prince dreamed that he met the most beautiful maiden he had ever seen. The next day, he asked his father to look for the girl he had seen in his dream. Every effort by the king to find her came to nought; his search was in vain. The prince then sought his father's permission to look for the woman himself. After some time, he came to another country and headed for its mosque. By the will of Allah, he met the muezzin who was just leaving the mosque, and was invited to his home. Imagine his surprise and joy when he reached the muezzin's house and saw that his host's daughter looked exactly like the beautiful maiden who had appeared in his dream. The prince immediately asked the muezzin for his daughter's hand in marriage. His proposal was accepted and the two were soon married before a religious official (*kadi*).

Not long after they were married, the prince decided to take his wife back to his home country. During the journey, seven outlaws waylaid them and threatened to kill the prince and kidnap his wife. In response to his wife's pleading, the robbers buried the prince waist-deep in the ground and took her with them. When the outlaws had escaped, the prince managed to free himself and chased after them till he reached the city. There the prince sought an audience with Prophet David to report his ordeal. One of the criminals was soon apprehended but produced four witnesses who swore that the woman was his wife, so he was eventually released. The Prophet David was furious and ordered that the prince be impaled. By the will of Allah, the prince's wife saw her husband just before he was about to be put to the stake, and quickly ran to the Prophet Solomon (Sulaiman), the son of the Prophet David, who happened to be playing in the street at the time. The Prophet Solomon begged his father's permission to investigate the matter further. He interrogated the witnesses one at a time and discovered that none of them could tell him the exact day on which the woman was married to the man who kidnapped her. The lie was exposed and it was revealed that the prince had been telling the truth. Prophet Solomon allowed the prince to continue on his journey home with his wife. The bandit and his false witnesses were duly punished. The Prophet David handed over his kingdom to his son, Solomon, who was only seven years old at the time.

The story however only managed to temporarily divert Raja Serdala's evil intentions. When it ended, he tried to embrace Putri Hasinan but she resisted him, tearfully imploring Allah for help. At that very moment, Raja Serdala's arms miraculously shortened.

Meanwhile, a skull washed ashore. The Prophet Jesus (Isa) was walking along the beach. Maharaja Ali's skull greeted the prophet and beseeched him to bring him back to life so that he could be reunited with his wife. Maharaja Ali was miraculously resurrected by the Prophet Jesus' earnest supplications. Maharaja Ali returned to his kingdom, together with Prophet Jesus.

Upon his arrival, Maharaja Ali found his kingdom in turmoil; his ministers were squabbling with each another to determine which one of them should become king. When they saw the Prophet, the ministers asked him to choose one of them to be king. Jesus chose Maharaja Ali. Without anyone recognizing who he really was, Maharaja Ali once again became ruler of his kingdom. He was a just and munificent king. Every day without fail, he gave alms to the poor and prayed that God would reunite him with his wife.

Meanwhile, Maharaja Ali's two sons had grown up to be fine, handsome, well-mannered and intelligent young men. When they heard what a wonderful king Maharaja Ali was, they presented themselves at his court and asked the ruler to bestow his favour upon them. Maharaja Ali liked the brothers and made them royal pages in his palace.

The story next tells that Raja Serdala made his way to Maharaja Ali's kingdom to seek treatment. He told Maharaja Ali how his arms had become short and requested the maharaja to assign two of his trusted men to guard his ship as he wanted to spend the night on land. Maharaja Ali sent the two young princes to guard the ship. By the will of Allah, two birds flew on board the ship and started to fight over a fish that one of them had caught. Seeing their antics, the younger prince burst out laughing. His elder brother chided him and began to tell about their childhood and early life. Putri Hasinan, their mother, overheard the story. Delighted, she rushed out of her cabin and tearfully hugged her two sons. Everyone on board was shocked by what they saw. Maharaja Ali was furious and ordered that the two pages be arrested and executed. They were brought before the jail keeper who, as it turned out, was their eldest brother, Baharum, who had lost his way in the jungle so many years ago. Baharum took them to Maharaja Ali. The king summoned Princess Hasinan. And so Maharaja Ali was finally reunited with his wife and children. Having witnessed the greatness of Allah, Lord of the universe, as He ruled all creation, Raja Serdala was awestruck and turned pale. He was not punished, however, but was allowed to marry the daughter of a minister. Maharaja Ali continued to reign over his kingdom with justice and benevolence.

4.2 *Hikayat Parang Punting*

The *Hikayat Parang Punting* bears a strong Hindu influence. Almighty God is referred to as Batara Kala; the world is ruled by kings who have descended from heaven; and a *sayembara* (contest) is held in order to find a suitable husband for the princess. The manuscript of the *hikayat* available to us, however, is relatively recent, having been copied in Singapore in 1920 (Winstedt, 1922e: 62-66). Dewan Bahasa dan Pustaka have also published a version of this *hikayat* based on a manuscript held in the National Museum in Kuala Lumpur. It is highly likely that this is a copy of the same manuscript Winstedt used for his study in 1920. Below is a summary of the *hikayat* (Jamilah Haji Ahmad, 1980).

Once upon a time, a god called Dewa Laksana Dewa lived in heaven with his wife, Cahaya Khairani. Putri Cahaya Khairani gave birth to a very beautiful baby girl and they called her Putri Langgam Cahaya. The baby grew to be an even more beautiful young maiden.

One day, Putri Langgam Cahaya was playing in the garden and picking flowers. Suddenly, a grasshopper landed on her; her heart began to flutter and beat inexplicably quickly. Later, she came upon Mambang Segara Indra bathing in a pool near the garden. Mambang Segara Indra could not contain himself when he saw the beautiful Putri Langgam Cahaya, and he began to hug and kiss her. The princess was angry and told him that if he was serious, he should formally ask her parents for her hand in marriage. She was outraged by Mambang Segara Indra's audacity and presumptuous behaviour. Feeling both humiliated and infuriated, Mambang Segara Indra resolved to use magic to revenge himself on the princess. He took a magnolia flower and recited a spell over it. A few days later, while the princess was playing in the garden, he threw the flower at her. The flower hit the princess on her chest. Soon after, the princess became pregnant. When her father found out that the girl was pregnant, he was furious and cursed her by turning her into an ugly woman, shunned by all. She was banished to the earth.

Putri Langgam Cahaya gave birth to very handsome baby boy deep in the forest. She found a dilapidated hut and made it her home. Every day she would go out to look for odd jobs in order to eke out a living for herself and her son. Fortunately, she met an old man who was kind to her. Despite her dire circumstances, she managed to raise her son. One day, while she was out working, a man came to her hut to show her son a baby snake. Putri Langgam Cahaya's son wanted the snake and paid the man a bowl of rice. When Putri Langgam Cahaya came home and found out what her son had done, she lost her temper and scolded him for buying a useless snake with the rice she had worked hard to earn. Her son listened in silence, and did not say a word. Several days later, he bought an eaglet and paid for it with another bowl of rice. And then he bought a white baby mouse and gave away yet another bowl of rice in exchange for it. His mother did not say a word. The boy was very happy. Each day he would play with his three pets.

After some time, the baby snake grew larger. Horns started to sprout from its snout and it turned into a fine, powerful and impressive-looking dragon. All day long, the boy would ride on the back of the dragon parading with it around the village, with his pet eagle flying close overhead, and the mouse scampering to the left of the dragon trying to keep pace with them. The village boys all wanted to play with him. They gave him rice and all kinds of fruit. The harbour master also asked him to play in his village and showered him with presents of rice and clothes. Everyone who saw the boy gave him gifts. Soon, even the king heard about the boy and his amazing pets. He asked the boy to come to the capital to play and rewarded him with rich gifts, huge amounts of rice, and an assortment of new clothes.

As time went by, the dragon grew larger and larger. Soon it became too big to fit in the river where the boy kept him. One night, the creature secretly slunk away to return to Green Lake, the home of his ancestors. The princess's son—thereafter referred to in the *hikayat* as the "poor boy" (*"budak miskin"*)—followed it, and received a ring from the dragon king, his pet dragon's grandfather. The ring had great magical powers and could feed a thousand people. On his journey home, the poor boy stole a magic wand from a dragon chief who had been assigned to take the magic ring back from him. The poor boy then gave the ring to an old man in exchange for a machete (*parang punting*) that could protect its master and slay his enemies of its own volition. By the time he reached home, his mother had begun to worry about him.

The *hikayat* continues with the tale of King Indra Maha Dewa. The king went to the island of Cahaya Purnama to practice asceticism so that the gods might grant him a child. On his way home, he was confronted by an enormous dragon king who refused to let him pass. Before he was allowed to continue on his way, Indra Maha Dewa had to promise that if the child were a girl, she would marry the dragon king. Not long after, King Indra Maha Dewa's wife gave birth to a very beautiful baby girl; her face was as radiant as the full moon. The daughter was named Princess Mengindra Sehari Bulan. As the princess grew older, she became even more beautiful. When the princess was old enough to marry, the dragon king, Naga Gangga Indra, sent his envoy to demand that the king fulfil his promise. King Indra Maha Dewa was terrified and pleaded for three months in which to prepare a feast for the wedding. King Indra Maha Dewa dispatched messengers to appeal to other kings for help. The king promised his daughter's hand to anyone who could defeat the dragon king. Kings came from everywhere, accompanied by their armies. A raft was built and a cabin constructed for the princess. The princess was then asked to sit in a large metal strongbox placed inside the cabin. Escorted by the kings and their men who followed behind in boats, the raft floated down to the river mouth. When they reached the estuary, the dragon king breathed a huge plume of fire in the direction of the kings and their men. Their boats began to bob and rock violently, making everyone seasick—all except for the poor boy who had managed to sneak on board one of the boats. The kings did not dare follow the princess's raft any further.

The poor boy introduced himself to the princess and they began to exchange verses. He also told the princess that he would fight the dragon king if she promised to be his wife. The dragon king then ordered his legion of dragons to attack the princess' s raft. In response, the poor boy ordered his magic weapon to attack the dragons. The machete cut off the heads of large numbers of dragons. A flock of eagles carried her raft to shore, while also pecking at the eyes of the dragons. The chief of the dragon army reported these events to the dragon king who then summoned his brother, who was even bigger than he was. His brother, who was the size of an island, soon came and swallowed the princess's raft and the poor boy as well.

The eagle told the mouse about the calamity that had befallen their master, and it reported this to Mambang Segara Indra, the poor boy's father in heaven. Mambang Segara Indra immediately assembled an army of demons and descended to earth to fight the dragons. The attacks and counter-attacks continued for a long time and showed no signs of abating. Both sides suffered massive casualties. The dragon that had swallowed the raft eventually succumbed to its wounds after having its heart pierced and its innards slashed by the poor boy trapped inside its stomach. The poor boy managed to free himself from the dragon's body and was subsequently reunited with his father who gave him the new name of Mambang Segara Beranta Indra. When Naga Gentala attacked him, Mambang Segara Beranta Indra asked Rakna Gempita, the dragon of the Green Lake, to come and help him. Rakna Gempita also eventually killed Naga Gangga Indra, the dragon king. Thereafter, Rakna Gempita became king of all the dragons in the sea.

Before Mambang Segara Indra returned to his celestial abode, he gave a magic gemstone to his son, now known as Mambang Dewa Keindraan. (The stone could create a whole city in the blink of an eye.) Mambang Dewa Keindraan ordered Rakna Gempita to take the princess's raft ashore. Then he said farewell to the princess and returned home to his mother. As soon as the kings saw that the princess was safe, they rowdily jostled with one another to reach the raft. All of them claimed to have fought and defeated the dragons. Only one dared tell the princess's father the truth and he suggested that the king hold a contest in which the princess would choose her husband by showering golden flower petals over the man she preferred.

Everyone attended the contest. However, the princess did not choose any of them. When she saw Mambang Dewa Keindraan disguised as a poor boy, she immediately threw the golden flower petals over him as he walked in front of her. The princess having made her choice, preparations soon began for the wedding. Using the magic gemstone he had been given by his father, Mambang Dewa Keindraan created a whole new kingdom, complete with a moated city, for his bride and himself. The white mouse, who was actually Dewa Indra Bayu, the god of the wind, was sent to invite Mambang Segara Indra, the bridegroom's father, to the wedding. The king of the eagles, the poor boy's other pet, was none other than the deity Dewa Darkasila; he was sent to heaven to invite Mambang Dewa Keindraan's grandfather, Dewa Laksana Dewa, to come down to earth and to remove the curse that he had cast on Mambang Dewa Keindraan's mother. Finally, when the moment designated as an auspicious time for their wedding arrived, Mambang Dewa Segara and Princess Mengindra Sehari Bulan were married in a joyful ceremony. On his journey home after the wedding, Mambang Dewa Keindraan had to fight ninety-nine princes who had laid in wait to snatch the princess away from him. With the aid of his friends, the king of eagles and the dragon king Rakna Gempita, Mambang Dewa Keindraan was able to defeat the ninety-nine princes. Many of them were killed, the others surrendered. Mambang Dewa Keindraan became king of the land of Indra Maha Dewa and lived happily ever after with his wife, Princess Mengindra Sehari Bulan.

4.3 *Hikayat Langlang Buana*

This is probably a very old *hikayat*. The number of Arabic words found in this *hikayat* is far fewer than in Roorda van Eysinga's version of the *Hikayat Sri Rama*. According to H. C. Klinkert, "This hikayat was written in pure Malay, probably at a time when the Malays were not yet acquainted with the Arabic *syair* form." There are many short *pantun* and *seloka* verses in this *hikayat* but no lengthy *syair* at all (Ronkel, 1909: 75-76). Below is a summary of the *Hikayat Langlang Buana*, based on the manuscript published by Balai Pustaka in Jakarta (Commissie Voor de Volkslectuur, 1913).

Once upon a time, there was an emperor named Maharaja Puspa Indra who lived in the heavenly realm. His daughter's beauty was unmatched. Her complexion was so lustrous that she glowed like gold, bedazzling all who set eyes on her. Maharaja Puspa Indra built a castle in the meadows of Pelanta Cairani for his beautiful daughter, Putri Kesuma Dewi. She was bethrothed to the son of Raja Indra Dewa, Raja Indra Syah Peri.

The story tells that a king ruled over a kingdom in the mortal world called Lela Gembara. His name was Puspa Indra Kuci. One night, this king dreamed that an old man told him to pick a bunch of jasmine. According to the old man, the jasmine would turn into a brave and handsome prince. When the king woke up, he did exactly what the old man had told him. After some time, the queen gave birth to a handsome baby boy who was as resplendent as an emerald. Accordingly, he was named Indra Bumaya.

Indra Bumaya grew to be an even more handsome young man. He had excellent manners, was well-spoken and adept at performing whatever task he was set. Moreover, he was also well-skilled in the arts of war. One night, Indra Bumaya dreamt that a maiden led him to the celestial world and showed him a portrait of Putri Kesuma Dewi. As soon as he saw the portrait, Indra Bumaya fainted for seven days and seven nights. When he finally regained consciousness, he begged his father to give him permission to look for the princess he had seen in his dream.

Indra Bumaya then set out towards the land of the setting sun, crossing vast treks of land and dense forests. All the wild beasts bowed their heads as he passed, as if bowing to a king. He finally reached a very tall and large mountain. There he met a woman who instructed him to become the disciple of Sri Maharaja Sakti so that he could further hone his skills in the arts of warfare. To reach Sri Maharaja Sakti, Indra Bumaya had first to meet Maharesi Antakusa. Before they parted, the woman presented Indra Bumaya with a magic stone that could conjure up different varieties of birds and bunches of jasmine.

Maharesi Antakusa greeted Indra Bumaya with great respect. The seer said that if he wished to marry Putri Kesuma Dewi, he had to go to Maharesi Kesna Cendra. He cautioned Indra Bumaya not to fall in love with a beautiful maiden who lived in a particular house he would pass during his journey. Before they separated, Maharesi Antakusa gave Indra Bumaya a magic stone which could summon the wind, the rain, thunder and lightning, as well as make thousands of people magically appear.

Indra Bumaya then continued on his journey and eventually reached the beautiful fields of Antah Berantah. In the middle of the plains, he found a bunch of jasmines and a talking parakeet. While playing in the field, he saw a green beetle magically transform itself into a house, and in that house he saw a very beautiful woman. Indra Bumaya remembered Maharesi Antakusa's warning and began to leave but found that the field had somehow turned into a sea. Indra Bumaya threatened to kill her. The woman was afraid and told him that her name was Candra Lela Nur Lela. Indra Bumaya decided to regard her as his sister. Putri Candra Lela also gave Indra Bumaya a magic stone that could release four *jinns*.

When Putri Candra Lela's fiancé, Raja Johan Syah Peri, heard about his fiancée's newfound relationship with Indra Bumaya, he was angry and attacked Indra Bumaya. The battle lasted seven days and seven nights, both men proving unbeatable. Maharesi Antakusa heard of the conflict and came to make peace between the two men. Raja Johan promised to help Indra Bumaya find the princess of whom he had dreamed, while Indra Bumaya persuaded Putri Candra Lela Nur Lela to marry Johan Syah Peri. The couples were soon married amidst much gaiety and merriment in a lavish ceremony attended by many in Johan Syah Peri's palace.

After some time, Indra Bumaya left Putri Candra Lela Nur Lela and Johan Syah Peri to seek out Sri Maharaja Sakti. He received a magic stone and an arrow from Johan Syah Peri. The stone could restore a dead person to life, while the arrow could transport a person in the blink of an eye to any destination, even one that might otherwise take seven hundred years to reach. Not long after, Indra Bumaya reached a vast plain where he found a huge lake the size of the sea. A fairy king lived in the lake, ruling over a vast empire. The king had a beautiful daughter called Putri Mandu Ratna. She was fourteen years old, "her body shone like a mirror, her hair was curly, her lips were the colour of a ripe pomegranate, her forehead was shaped like a new moon, her cheeks were smooth like the skin of a mango, her nose elegant like a jasmine, her chin was like a ship's figurehead, and her disposition genteel and refined."

Putri Mandu Ratna came to the lake to bathe. Indra Bumaya watched as she powdered, shampooed and scrubbed herself. Turning himself into a beautiful parakeet, Indra Bumaya allowed himself to be caught by the princess and taken back to the palace. At the palace, the parakeet regaled the princess with *pantun* verses and told her stories about his country of origin and his wonderful master, Indra Bumaya, who would soon arrive at the palace. He then turned himself into a canary, and next into a beautiful floral bouquet. After that, he changed himself back to his original human form and sat on her right. Putri Mandu Ratna was delighted with his presence and the pair exchanged more *pantun* verses.

His Highness Raja Baharum Dewa, the princess's father, however, was displeased and ordered his guards to capture Indra Bumaya. Using his magic stone, Indra Bumaya summoned an army of *jinns* to fight the king's guards, while at the same time reassuring the frightened princess. Johan Syah Peri heard of Indra Bumaya's predicament and also came to his assistance. When Raja Baharum Dewa learned that Indra Bumaya was the son of Raja Lela Gambara, he was overjoyed. The battle stopped and Indra Bumaya and Princess Mandu Ratna were soon married.

After some time had passed, Indra Bumaya remembered Putri Kesuma Dewi and asked for permission to resume his quest. With the help of Maharesi Kesna Cendra and Langlang Buana, as well as the magic arrow given to him by Johan Syah Peri, Indra Bumaya reached Mount Indra Nagar, the abode of Sri Maharaja Sakti. For seven months Indra Bumaya learned all kinds of magic skills from Sri Maharaja Sakti. After that, he called for Raja Johan Syah Peri who came at once. Together they ascended to the celestial world.

There, they were told by a celestial nymph, Seludang Mayang, that it would be betrothed for them to meet Princess Kesuma Dewi: the princess had already been bethrothed to another, and her father had confined her in a glass palanquin seven layers thick. When they learnt this, Johan Syah Peri transformed himself into a bent old man, while Indra Bumaya changed himself into a baby just learning to crawl. The old man then took the baby from village to village, beating a drum as he sung and danced. News of this soon reached Putri Kesuma Dewi. She secretly took the pair into the forbidden part of the palace where she was confined. As soon as he saw her, the baby fainted. The princess picked him up and put in her lap. She then begged her parents to allow the baby to stay with her in the palace. In the middle of the night however, Indra Bumaya changed himself back to his true form. The princess woke in shock to find a handsome man hugging and kissing her. Although she tried to escape, Indra Bumaya managed to persuade her to stay. For seven days and seven nights Indra Bumaya remained in the princess's chamber. The *hikayat* does not end there. It continues with a story of Langlang Buana ordering a golden peacock to fly the princess to a cave. Only after rescuing the princess from the *jinn* who guarded the cave, and defeating her fiancé, Indra Syah Peri, was Indra Bumaya able to live happily ever after with the princess of his dreams.

4.4 *Hikayat Si Miskin* or *Hikayat Marakarma*

There are various manuscripts of this *hikayat*—five in the National Museum of Jakarta, two in Leiden, and one in London. This very popular *hikayat* has been published several times: (a). J. S. A. Van Dissel: *Hikajat Si Miskin*, J. E. Brill, Leiden 1897; (b) Ch. van Ophuijsen: *Hikajat Si Miskin*, P. W. M. Trap Leiden 1916; and (c) Datoek Madjoindo: *Hikajat Si Miskin,* Djambatan & Gunung Agung, Djakarta. Although the present hikayat contains a *pantun* that mentions both Christians and the Dutch, it is still considered a *hikayat* of the early transitional era. It contains few Arabic words. Three Hindu motifs can be found in this *hikayat*, as follows:

1. A deceitful astrologer;
2. A brother and sister are separated, and the sister is married to a prince;
3. A greedy sea captain who covets other men's wives and property.

Below is a summary of the story.

A king who lived in the celestial world was once cursed by the god Batara Indra. The king and his wife were expelled from their celestial abode and sent down to earth to live a life of poverty in the kingdom of Antah Berantah which was ruled by Maharaja Indra Dewa. The king became known as *si Miskin,* the Pauper. Every day Si Miskin would tramp from place to place in order to eke out a living. But everywhere he went, people would pelt him with stones and pieces of wood. As a result, he and his wife were forced to survive on scraps of rubbish. After some time, Si Miskin's wife became pregnant and wanted to eat some mangoes growing in the king's palace. Although he was afraid, Si Miskin eventually asked the king for a mango. Raja Antah Berantah kindly gave him some. Not long after that, Si Miskin's wife wanted to have a jackfruit from the king's orchard. Again the king gave him one. Si Miskin was amazed.

One auspicious day, Si Miskin's wife gave birth to a fine, handsome baby boy. The boy was named Marakarma, which means "child of hardship". Si Miskin's life changed after the birth of his son. He found himself suddenly in possession of a huge amount of gold. Furthermore, by praying to the gods, a kingdom miraculously appeared. He called the kingdom Puspa Sari, and took the title of Maharaja Indra Angkasa, giving his wife the title Ratna Dewi. Not long after, a princess was born into the world and named Nila Kesuma. Puspa Sari became a thriving kingdom. Many traders came to the kingdom. The news of Si Miskin's good fortune disturbed Maharaja

Indra Dewa, the king of Antah Berantah. Before long, he came to know that Si Miskin was looking for an astrologer. Maharaja Indra Dewa sent his astrologer to convince Si Miskin that his children would bring him bad luck. Si Miskin swallowed the astrologer's lie and banished his children. Puspa Sari was subsequently consumed by fire and Si Miskin became a pauper once more.

Marakarma gained many magical skills from the various *jinn*s, *raksasa*s and serpents he met while in exile. One day he caught a bird. As his sister wanted to eat the creature, he set off to find some firewood. His search took him to a village where he was accused of being a thief and beaten black and blue. While he lay unconscious on the ground, the villagers bound Marakarma and threw him into the sea.

The tale then tells of Raja Puspa Indra of Pelinggam Cahaya whose son, Mengindra Sari, refused to marry. One day, while he was out hunting, Mengindra Sari found Nila Kesuma crying under a banyan tree. He took Nila Kesuma back to the palace and married her. She henceforth became known as Mayang Mengurai.

Marakarma was washed ashore on a beach inhabited by a *raksasa*. He was found by Princess Cahaya Kairani, the daughter of Raja Malai Kisna, who had been captured by the monster. However, as the princess was still too small to eat, the giant spared her. The princess hid Marakarma. Later they both escaped on board a ship which happened to sail close to the coastline. The *raksasa* finally died after he fell into a pit of spikes built by Marakarma.

The ship's captain wanted to steal the princess and take Marakarma's belongings for himself, so he pushed Marakarma into the sea. A fish took pity on Marakarma and brought him to Pelinggam Cahaya, the ship's next port of call. There, Marakarma was nursed back to health by a sorceress, who later told him about Princess Mayang Mengurai, his sister. By chanting magical incantations over a floral arrangement that he used as a medium, Marakarma was able to communicate with his wife, Princess Cahaya Kairani. She went to the palace and told the king everything. The ship's captain was subsequently arrested and executed. The people rejoiced.

Not long after this, Marakarma returned to Puspa Sari. The kingdom had been turned into a thick, unruly jungle. His mother made her living collecting firewood. Marakarma revealed his true identity to her and prayed that Puspa Sari be restored to its former glory. His wish was granted by the divine Dewata Raya. Soon after, his sister and his wife both arrived in Puspa Sari. The kingdom regained its former prosperity. Maharaja Indra Dewa of Antah Berantah was jealous and attacked Puspa Sari. After heavy fighting, Maharaja Indra Dewa was finally defeated and his daughter married to Princess Cahaya Kairani's brother. Marakarma visited his father-in-law, Maharaja Malai Kisna, in Mercu Negara. Before long, he became Sultan of Mercu Negara.

4.5 *Hikayat Berma Syahdan*

The *Hikayat Berma Syahdan* is a special hikayat in that it bears the name of its author (most texts do not). One manuscript in Jakarta, Koleksi C. St. 11, describes Syaikh Abu Bakar Ibn Omar as its writer. He is said to have been 128 years old and lived, it is claimed, since the time of Nuh, the prophet Noah. The manuscript is dated 28 April 1858.

A Leiden manuscript, however, names Syaikh Ibn Abu Bakar as its author. This is corroborated by another Jakarta manuscript, Bat. Gen. 216, from Bengkulu (West Sumatra), which also mentions

Syaikh Ibn Abu Bakar. Winstedt is of the opinion that the hikayat can be traced back to the fifteenth century, the time of the Malaka Sultanate.

Below is a summary of the Leiden Manuscript (following Juynboll, 1899). The manuscript is 928 pages long and is divided into three parts.

Part 1

The *hikayat* begins with Berma Syahdan chasing after a green beetle which is a manifestation of Princess Nur ul-'ain. The princess's friend, Mandu Hirani, was also passionately in love with the ravishingly handsome Berma Syahdan, and had ordered her lady-in-waiting to bring Berma Syahdan to her palace. Mandu Hirani's father, Maharaja Syah Gerak Gempa, was furious and had the palace surrounded. Raja Berkianah then sent his son, Ardan, to help Berma Syahdan. Maharaja Gerak Gempa asked Princess Nur ul-'ain's father, Maharaja Darjanus, for assistance. To help Berma Syahdan, Princess Nur ul-'ain taught him various magical skills with which to fight her father. But that was futile. A genie kidnapped Berma Syahdan and threw into the divine ocean (*Bahr* Allah).

The King of Spirits, Mengantara, rescued Berma Syahdan. After Berma Syahdan's disappearance, Ardan attacked the enemy forces. Maharaja Gerak Gempa was worried because his daughter was also missing. He later discovered that Princess Mandu Hirani had been taken away by Berma Syahdan in a magical overlaid perfume box.

The story then tells that Ardan married a princess from a kingdom that had been conquered by Maharaja Datya Bujangga. Raja Burandan Syah came to help Ardan kill Datya Bujangga. Ardan then met his elder brother, Masradan. A letter of invitation was sent to his father.

Meanwhile, Mengantara took Berma Syahdan to a mountain where he acquired a host of magical powers after successfully slaying some serpents that attacked him. Berma Syahdan then came to a palace where he killed a *raksasa* monster who was the incarnation of a mighty king cursed by Batara Indra. Finally, Berma Syahdan acquired a magical iron horse.

Part II

Berma Syahdan caught a fairy. To earn its freedom, the fairy had to teach Berma Syahdan how to walk under the earth and on top of the water. Using his new powers, Berma Syahdan made his way to the edge of the sea where he fought a mighty king, Nila Pertiwi Rangga Samanda. The foes were equally matched, so they eventually agreed to make peace with each other. As a token of friendship, Nila Pertiwi Rangga Samanda released one thousand and forty of his old enemies and presented Princess Komala Dewi Ratna Jamjam to Berma Syahdan to be his wife. Berma Syahdan then returned to the kingdom of his friend, Mengantara.

Raksa Dewa Indra Berma, the son of a god, asked for the hand in marriage of Princess Indra Komala, daughter of Raja Dahar Syah. But as Mengantara was also in love with the princess, Berma Syahdan abducted her for him. A war broke out. Berma Syahdan emerged victorious. Dahar Syah surrendered and handed over his daughter to Mengantara.

Berma Syahdan heard from a Brahmin that Princess Indra Kusuma Dewi, the daughter of Raja Burandan Syah, was exquisitely beautiful. Berma Syahdan asked for her hand in marriage but was rudely refused. Insulted, Berma Syahdan attacked the kingdom of Raja Burandan Syah.

Burandan Syah appealed to Maharaja Asmara Gangga and his vassals for help. Meanwhile, Berma Syahdan's sons, Indra Syah Peri and Indra Dewa Syah, also came to his aid. The battle between the two sides continued for a long time. Hoping to end the war, Burandan Syah then summoned Maharesi Raja Bayu. After a terrible battle in which Berma Syahdan and Maharesi Raja Bayu both used every piece of magic they had, Maharesi Raja Bayu eventually admitted defeat and retreated to his hermitage.

The battle continued. Numberless soldiers fell as Burandan Syah rained his arrows upon them. Finally, Burandan Syah called upon Kanhu Barnasib. Berma Syahdan sent his son, Indra Syah Peri, to fight Kanhu Barnasib. The son, however, was unable to defeat their foe and was himself captured. Fortunately, Maharaja Syah Gerak Gempa came to his rescue by sending his *jinn* to free Indra Syah Peri by carrying him to Qaf hill. The manuscript ends rather abruptly with this confrontation between Kanhu Barnasib and Indra Dewa Syah Peri.

Part III

Indra Dewa Syah Peri eventually defeated and captured Maharaja Kandu Barnasib, who surrendered his daughter to Indra Syah Peri to be his wife.

Raja Indra Syah Peri returned to his father accompanied by a *jinn*. Berma Syahdan was blessed with two granddaughters whom he named Nur l-'ain and Putri Mandu Hirani. Berma Syahdan finally defeated his enemy Syah Burandan. Batara Indra descended to earth and made peace between the warring parties. Berma Syahdan then revived all the kings who had been killed in battle.

4.6 *Hikayat Indraputra*

The *Hikayat Indraputra* is an old hikayat. It was mentioned by Valentijn (1726) and parts of it were quoted in Werndly's *Maleische Spraakkust* (1736). The *hikayat* can also be found in the Makassarese, Buginese and Achehnese languages, as well as in the Cam language of Indo-China, though the Cam tale does not bear any trace of Islamic influence. This suggests that the tale spread to Indo-China before the coming of Islam to the Malay Archipelago (Winstedt, 1920b: 145-146).

According to S. W. R. Mulyadi in her dissertation on the *Hikayat Indraputra* undertaken at the University of London, this *hikayat* is mentioned in three other works (Mulyadi 1983: 21-8). Nuruddin ar-Raniri wrote in his book *Sirat al-Mustakim* (1634) that we "should use books that have no value in Islamic law, such as the *Hikayat Sri Rama*, the *Hikayat Indraputra* and suchlike, as toilet paper, as long as they do not contain Allah's name." Another work, the *Bustanus Salatin* (1637), exhorts its readers not to allow their sons and daughters to read "useless" tales such as the *Hikayat Indraputra,* as it only contains lies. A similar exhortation can also be found in the *Taj as-Salatin*. Strangely enough, in the Philippines, this *hikayat* is considered an Islamic epic and is sung in the mosques of Maranu as a way of propagating the Islamic faith. Below is a summary of the *hikayat* based on a manuscript published in Kuala Lumpur (Ali Ahmad, 1968). A summary of the *Hikayat Indraputra* can also be found in R. O. Winstedt (1922b: 46-53).

Indraputra, the son of Maharaja Bikrama Puspa, was a wise and intelligent prince; he was also strong and well-versed in the magic arts. But luck was not on his side in the beginning. When he was young, he was taken by a golden peacock. He fell into a garden and was raised by a kindly fairy godmother. Later, he was adopted by the prime minister.

The story continues. Raja Syahsian had no heir. One day, he went hunting and saw a fawn crying over the body of its dead mother who had been shot with an arrow. The king was so moved by what he saw that he wanted a son even more. He had heard that there was a powerful *maharesi* named Berma Sakti who lived in a hermitage on a distant mountain. The *maharesi* was reputed to be able to help those who desired a child. But as the mountain was so remote and surrounded by a dense jungle full of dangerous wild animals, no one dared travel there. Indraputra offered to undertake the journey.

Indraputra set off and experienced many strange occurrences on the way. He encountered a skull that could talk, killed a giant *raksasa,* and slew a man-eating monster. He also came upon a realm populated by Muslim *jinns*, who took the form of monkeys by night but became human beings by day. He befriended the sons of mighty kings, both human and *jinn*. He also acquired various magical powers during his quest, such as the power to conjure up a whole city, as well as the power to bring the dead back to life. He married three beautiful princesses before finally reaching Berma Sakti's abode on the mountain. There, Berma Sakti gave him the remedy for which he had come and taught him various magical skills. "My son," Berma Sakti said to Indraputra, "just close your eyes and make a wish, and you can be assured that whatever you wish for will come true." Indraputra closed his eyes. When he opened his eyes, he found that he had somehow been magically transported back to the garden of the fairy godmother where he grown up.

Raja Syahsian and the prime minister were overjoyed. After the queen took the magic potion—a bullet-wood flower (*bunga tanjung*)—she became pregnant. She gave birth to a beautiful baby girl named Princess Mengindra Sri Bulan. In the meantime, having been accused of dalliance with several ladies-in-waiting in the king's palace, Indraputra was cast into the ocean. He was washed ashore on the beach of a country whose capital was made of black stone. The king received Indraputra with great honour and presented him with a magic piece of cloth that could cure all types of ailments.

Princess Mengindra Sri Bulan, in the meantime, grew to maturity. Many princes came from far and wide to win the favour of Raja Syahsian in the hope of marrying his daughter. One day, the princess fell ill. There was not a healer in the land who could cure her. The gong was sounded and the announcement made that whoever could cure the princess, no matter how lowly he might be, would become the king's son-in-law. Indraputra cured the princess of her affliction. His marriage to the princess, however, was not without its difficulties. Many vindictive ministers and disgruntled princes who had coveted the princess for themselves tried to harm Indraputra. Others were spiteful and did all they could to discredit him. These treacherous princes and ministers killed Indraputra three times. And he was revived by each of his three wives in turn. Eventually, the rival princes and ministers submitted themselves to Indraputra. Shortly after after his marriage to Princess Mengindra Sri Bulan, Indraputra began to miss his parents. Indraputra set out to visit them, taking his four wives with him. His parents were delighted to see them all and held a grand festival. In this atmosphere, Indraputra was crowned king and given the title Paduka Sultan Mengindra. The celebrations continued for forty days and forty nights.

The *Hikayat Putra Jaya Pati* is a shorter version of *Hikayat Indraputra.* The relationship between the two works is not clear. What is clear, though, is that the longer version contains the specific motif of the search for a remedy to cure the king, while the short version has no such goal. The story is as follows (R. O. Winstedt, 1922c).

Prince Jaya Pati was the son of Raja Kalwandu of Langkam Jaya. A horse ran away with Prince Jaya Pati when he was young, taking him to a mountain. The horse told the prince that he would one day fight against gods, demons, *jinn*s and all kinds of spirits. The divine sage, Begawan Narada, would teach him a range of magic skills. Then the horse vanished.

After some time in Begawan Narada's hermitage, Prince Jaya Pati decided to return home. He had proven himself to be Begawan Narada's most valiant and best loved pupil. Before he left, Begawan Narada gave him a flying mat that could manifest four warriors and their armies.

After passing through thick forests, Prince Jaya Pati reached Samandra Lake. A mysterious voice advised him of a nearby danger. The prince advanced carefully and killed a demon who wanted to kill him. He took the demon's sword. Not long after, Prince Jaya Pati reached a vast field. The field contained the playground of Princess Cindra Lela. With the help of Malik Indra, the caretaker of the garden, Prince Jaya Pati was able to spy on the princess. A close friendship soon developed, based on the joyful exchange of poems. Her father, Raja Gangga Wijaya, tried unsuccessfully to separate his daughter from Prince Jaya Pati. The princess' fiance, Raja Indra Warna, attacked Prince Jaya Pati but was killed in the fight.

The princes who had studied with Prince Jaya Pati under Begawan Narada offered their assistance. They made peace between Prince Jaya Pati and Princess Cindra Lela's father. A very grand wedding was held. All the women were awed by the prince's gallant appearance. After the wedding, the prince returned to his own country where he ascended the throne. During his reign, his titles were Maharaja Bikrama Indra Dewa and Paduka Seri Sultan Putra Jaya Pati Alauddin Syah.

4.7 *Hikayat Syah Kobat*

Hikayat Syah Kobat, or *Syah al-Kamar,* is mentioned by Werndly in his grammar book (1736). There are only a few manuscripts of this *hikayat* in existence. If we examine the contents of the manuscript published by Dewan Bahasa dan Pustaka, Kuala Lumpur, it appears that this hikayat has been freely adapted from *Hikayat Indraputra.* Perhaps it even came from the same source. Below is a summary of the tale (based on the Dewan Bahasa dan Pustaka manuscript).

Syah Kobat Lela Indra was the son of Syah Perasyat Indra Laksana of Athrap, a vassal state of the monkey king, Maharaja Belia Indra. Each year, Athrap had to pay tribute to the monkey king. Syah Kobat was profoundly saddened by the condition of his kingdom.

One day, Syah Kobat was kidnapped by his own great-grandfather, Brama Indra Sakti. The old man wanted to teach him various kinds of magic. At Brama Indra Sakti's place, Syah Kobat increased in maturity and prowess in all kinds of magic. One day, the king of *jinns* kidnapped Syah Kobat. Using the magical skills he had acquired, Syah Kobat rescued Princess Camti Ratna Dewi. Because she was already betrothed, he had to fight with all her other suitors. Syah Kobat defeated all of them and married the princess. The other princes became his friends. Syah Kobat received the title of Syah Kobat Johan Arifin from his great-grandfather, Brama Indra Sakti.

The story next tells that Syah Kobat decided to return to his father's kingdom. On the way, he came across an island surrounded by a sea of fire. Syah Kobat met Tuan Putri Sekanda on this island and married her. Her brothers were angry and attacked him. With the help of his friends and Brama Indra Sakti, Syah Kobat won the battle.

Then Syah Kobat reached a vast field called Padang Tawil. Here Syah Kobat fought the king of monkeys, Maharaja Belia Indra, who had conquered his father's kingdom. The battle was intense.

The story of Princess Cahaya Khairani follows. She was not only beautiful but brave as well, and had fought against many powerful princes in order to test her own magical abilities. Princess Cahaya Khairani was attracted by Syah Kobat's good looks and his magical prowess. Disguising herself as a man called Johan Ali Perkasa, she challenged Syah Kobat to a fight. Syah Kobat, however, glimpsed the face of a beautiful princess and swooned. Johan Ali Perkasa was captured by the *jinns* who were helping Syah Kobat. Only after Syah Kobat released Johan Ali Perkasa did he discover that his adversary was actually a woman. Sultan Ahmad, the princess' father, was delighted and married Syah Kobat to his daughter.

Enraged, the princess's fiance, Dewa Cahaya Indra, unsuccessfully attacked Syah Kobat and was taken prisoner. Dewa Cahaya Indra escaped to the palace of his father, Syah Alam Dewa. Both sides prepared for war. Thousands of soldiers joined Syah Alam Dewa's army. Thousands too pledged their support for Syah Kobat. The battle began, and many men lost their lives on the battlefield including Syah Alam Dewa and Dewa Cahaya Indra. Syah Kobat was victorious and took Princess Kemala Di Raja as his fourth wife.

Syah Kobat continued his journey to his father's kingdom. He reached a vast field. There he built a state complete with highways, a capital and a drainage system. He called this land Warkah Indra.

Finally Syah Kobat reached his father's kingdom. The king was delighted. Syah Kobat then invited his parents to visit the state he had built. Lavish celebrations were held in his honour. Syah Kobat's younger brother also married a beautiful princess. The end of the story tells that Syah Kobat was a great king while Warkah Indra became the biggest country in the whole world.

4.8 *Hikayat Koraisy Mengindra*

According to R. O. Winstedt, there is only one known manuscript of this *hikayat*. This manuscript was printed in Singapore. Winstedt apparently did not know of the *Hikayat Koraisy* (v.d.Wall Collection 146) held in the National Museum of Indonesia, Jakarta. At first I was not sure whether the *Hikayat Koraisy* was an alternate title for *Hikayat Koraisy Mengindra*. But after seeing the name "Sultan Di Padang Saujana Halam" (in which "halam" is used for "alam"), I accepted that the two manuscripts are the same work. There are actually two manuscripts of *Hikayat Koraisy* in the Jakarta Museum. The story in brief, based on the v.d.Wall Collection 146, is as follows:

There were once four kings who were brothers. The only ones who played an active role in the story were Sultan Indra Maharaja (later called Merdu Sakti) and Sultan Gempita Gunung. Koraisy (Koraisy Mengindra Raja Alam) was the son of Sultan Indra Maharaja. Koraisy was betrothed to Sri Udara, the daughter of Sultan Gempita Gunung. Because of the interference of another woman, Hatifah Maya Dewi, the engagement was cancelled. Sri Udara was subsequently married to Agas Paduka Alam, but she did not love him and despised him to the end of of his life.

Disappointed, Koraisy left the kingdom to study magic. Once he had obtained various powerful weapons, Koraisy then continued his travels.

The further stories are about war and love. Koraisy came to the land of Mangarma Indra and married Princess Seraja Sri Danta. And it was to be expected that after helping the king defeat an invading army, Koraisy married yet another princess.

Koraisy then continued his journey and arrived at a kingdom where its king and two other people were being held prisoner by a *jinn*. Koraisy killed the *jinn*. But due to his carelessness, the *jinn* blew Koraisy away to a distant place, where he had to fight another *jinn* called Jumala Indra. A war ensued. And as expected, Koraisy won and received another wife. In the concluding part of the tale, Koraisy went back to his native country and ascended the throne in place of his father.[1]

4.9 *Hikayat Indra Bangsawan*

The *Hikayat Indra Bangsawan* is a good example of a *hikayat* belonging to the transitional era. Hindu motifs are found in this *hikayat*, such as the search for a magic bamboo flute, the rescue of a princess whose kingdom had been destroyed by a *garuda* bird, the search for the milk of a tigress to cure a princess blighted by a malady, or the killing of a *raksasa* who covets the princess. But Indra Bangsawan's wedding ceremony was conducted by a Muslim judge (*qadi*), in the presence of eunuchs who were devout Muslims. And after Indra Bangsawan was crowned, his title was "Sultan". There are six manuscripts of this hikayat in the library of the National Museum, Jakarta, including one published by Balai Pustaka. The contents of these manuscripts are similar. But as it turns out, only one manuscript in the v.d. Wall Collection 162 actually contains a longer story than the Balai Pustaka manuscript. It tells how all nine princes defeated by Indra Bangsawan returned to their respective kingdoms in disappointment. The next year they sent tribute to him. The further story is that Raja Mangkubumi (Syah Peri) had a son called Indra Berahi, while Indra Bangsawan had son named Indra Pramana.

This *hikayat* was lithographed in Singapore in 1310 and 1323 Hijrah. There is also an adaptation of this *hikayat* in Achehnese. Below is a summary of the 1927 text of the *Hikayat Indera Bangsawan*.

---

1 The version of the *Hikayat Koraisy Mengindra* published by Dewan Bahasa dan Pustaka has a slightly different plot.

The story tells that there was once a king named Indra Bungsu. After a long time, he still had no heir. So one day, he ordered that recital of the Quranic verse, Doa Qunut, be held and alms distributed to ascetics and the poor. Eventually, his wife, Princess Sitti Kendi gave birth to two sons. The elder son was born carrying an arrow, while the younger one was born with a sword. The delighted king named his elder son Syah Peri, the younger one was given the name Indra Bangsawan.

When the two princes reached the age of seven, it was decreed that they should take lessons in Qur'an recital with Mualim Sufian. After they learned this, they studied the fundamentals of Islam, from jurisprudence to linguistics and hermeneutics, and became proficient in all these areas. After some time, they studied weaponry, magic and military strategy. Then the king faced a dilemma–which son should be enthroned as the next king? They were both heroic. If one became king, the other one would surely feel slighted. The king devised a cunning solution. He told his sons that he had met a young man in a dream. The youth had said that whoever could find the magic bamboo flute he possessed would be fit to be king.

On hearing these words, Syah Peri and Indra Bangsawan asked permission to look for the magic flute. They passed through many dense forests, crossed many mountains, and traversed thick wildernesses, as they travelled east. Then one day a fierce storm raged and a typhoon descended; it was so dark and turbulent that they could not see a single thing. The two brothers became separated. After the storm subsided, they started to look for each other.

Syah Peri put his fate in the hands of Allah the Almighty once he was separated from his brother and walked with all his might. After some time, he saw a palace surrounded by a beautiful garden. He went up to the palace and saw a drum hanging there. He beat on the drum. Suddenly he heard a voice telling him to stop his beating. He took a knife and cut the drum open. Princess Ratna Sari emerged. She explained that her kingdom had been conquered by a *garuda*. Her parents had hidden her in the drum, together with a jar containing her belongings and ladies-in-waiting. Syah Peri promptly released the ladies-in-waiting. When the *garuda* appeared, Syah Peri killed it. Syah Peri and the princess became husband and wife, and were waited on by her attendants and chief nursemaid.

Meanwhile, Indra Bangsawan was looking for his brother. He reached an immense field and entered a cave where he encountered a *raksasa*. The giant became his foster grandparent and informed Indra Bangsawan that he was in the kingdom of Antah Berantah that was ruled by Raja Kabir. Raja Kabir had been conquered by Buraksa and made to promise that he would surrender his first-born child, son or daughter, to Buraksa as tribute. If he did not, his kingdom would be destroyed. The *raksasa* added that Raja Kabir had proclaimed that whoever killed Buraksa would marry his lovely daughter. Nine princes had already come in response to the challenge. The giant suggested that Indra Bangsawan help Raja Kabir. He gave him a magical sarong and taught him a secret gesture. The magic sarong could turn Indra Bangsawan into a child. The gesture could transport him to faraway places in the blink of an eye.

Indra Bangsawan made the gesture and immediately arrived in Antah Berantah. He turned himself into a curly-headed boy. Raja Kabir was so enchanted that he adopted the boy as a playmate for Princess Kemala Sari. The princess was delighted and named him the Jungle Boy, Si Hutan. She also gave him the task of looking after her two pet goats, one male, one female.

One day, Princess Kemala Sari told Si Hutan about her cousin Princess Ratna Sari whose country had been destroyed by a *garuda*. She also told him that the monster bird would be killed by Syah Peri, adding that Syah Peri had a twin, Indra Bangsawan, who would destroy Buraksa. "When would this Indra Bangsawan appear?" she wondered. Princess Kemala Sari was desolate. Si Hutan tried to cheer her up by singing some sweet pantuns. This made her laugh and her affection for Si Hutan increased.

One day, Princess Kemala Sari's eye was extremely sore. The palace astrologers said that the princess could only be cured with milk from a tigress that was still nursing its cub. The king decreed that whoever obtained this milk would marry the princess. On hearing this, Si Hutan filled a bamboo tube with goat's milk and hung it on a tree. He took out his magic sarong and, changing back to his original form, waited under a tree. Before long, the nine princes came to ask for the goat's milk, thinking it was tiger's milk. Indra Bangsawan told them that he would not sell the milk but would willingly give it to anyone who allowed him to insert a hot iron rod into their thigh. The nine princes lifted up their sarongs so Indra Bangsawan could pierce their thighs. They joyfully presented the goat's milk to the king, but the royal physician determined that the milk was not from a tiger. Meanwhile, Indra Bangsawan had obtained genuine tiger's milk from his *raksasa* grandfather and shown it to the king. The royal physician confirmed that this was indeed tiger's milk. After he squeezed the milk into the princess' eye three times, she was cured.

The time came for the princess to be given to Buraksa. The king designed a pavilion where the princess could wait for Buraksa. An urn filled with water was placed under the pavilion for Buraksa to drink. The nine princes hid behind the urn. Whoever killed Buraksa by cutting off his seven noses and seven eyes, would marry the princess.

And so the king left the princess at the pavilion in the middle of the field. Later Si Hutan arrived. The princess was so touched by his loyalty that she named him Si Kembar, The Twin. Si Kembar asked the princess's permission to leave her side for a short time and went to meet his *raksasa* grandfather. The giant gave Si Kembar a green horse and showed him how to kill Buraksa. After that, Si Kembar mounted his horse and rode to the princess' pavilion. He introduced himself as a nameless forest-dweller who had come to watch the nine princes kill Buraksa. The princess invited him into the pavilion. After securing a trap at the mouth of the urn and tying the trap's rope to his horse's neck, Si Kembar instructed his horse to pull the rope when Buraksa came to drink from the urn. He then entered the pavilion. Soon after, Buraksa arrived amidst thunderous din. Si Kembar comforted the terrified princess on his lap.

When the Buraksa saw there was water in the urn, he took a drink, putting his head in the mouth of the urn. Si Kembar's green horse pulled the rope tight, trapping Buraksa around the neck. Si Kembar quickly stabbed Buraksa and cut off its seven noses and seven eyes. Then Si Kembar bid the princess goodbye and vanished. Surprised, the princess wondered if the young man might indeed be Indra Bangsawan. Then the princes emerged. They saw that while Buraksa was dead, his eyes and noses were gone, so they cut off his ears, scalp, fingers, hands and legs. The king did not believe that they had killed Buraksa as they had not brought the items he had specified. After a while, Si Kembar arrived with Buraksa's eyes and noses and so the king offered him the princess. But Si Kembar refused, as he felt his social status was too low. For her part, the princess was delighted to accept him.

The nine princes were furious and attacked Antah Berantah. Si Kembar feared that the king would not be able to repel the attack and went to his *raksasa* grandfather's abode to borrow a sword and a horse. The next day, the two large armies met in battle, with the soldiers slashing, shooting, stabbing, punching, slapping and beating each other. Many men died. The king's forces could not withstand the attack and began to retreat. Indra Bangsawan attacked the nine princes' armies, slashing to the left and right. He scattered the princes' men and then vanished. The same thing happened the next day: when Indra Bangsawan saw that the king's army was on the verge of losing, he emerged and then vanished again. No one knew who he was. But the king was sure that the young man was Si Kembar, as he was nowhere to be seen in the palace while the battle was in progress.

The nine princes also asked themselves who the young man was. But they decided to attack Antah Berantah once more. Another terrible battle began. Much blood was shed and enormous numbers of soldiers killed. The king's troops retreated to the protection of the fortified city. Only the king remained on the battlefield. Seeing this, Indra Bangsawan once again attacked the enemy, slashing right and left, and scattering the foe. Indra Bangsawan escorted the king back to the palace and went back out to chase the princes. Unable to defend themselves, they surrendered. Indra Bangsawan forgave them and revealed his true identity. The nine princes pledged to be his brothers.

The king also wanted to know Si Kembar's identity. One day, he called the princess and Si Kembar and asked them why they had yet to be married as he had commanded. The king refused to hear their explanation and confined them to the central part of the palace. One night, Si Kembar felt warm, so took off his sarong and bathed in the princess' bathroom. The next day, the princess found that the bathwater had been used up and complained to the king. The king told the princess to pretend to be asleep and if Si Kembar took off his sarong, she was to hide it. Night fell. Indra Bangsawan felt itchy. So he took off his sarong and went to bathe. The princess hid his sarong and Indra Bangsawan could no longer disguise himself. He confessed that he was indeed Indra Bangsawan from Kobat Syahrial.

The king was overcome with joy. He wanted to seat Indra Bangsawan next to the princess immediately, but Indra Bangsawan asked for a postponement of three days. He used the time to visit his *raksasa* grandfather. The giant gave him a magical gemstone that could make his every wish come true; he could even create a whole country complete with loyal subjects. And inside the stone were two people to administer these subjects, Dekar Sari dan Dekar Dewa. After three days, Indra Bangsawan returned to Antah Berantah. He built a complete city on the edge of the kingdom. He also built a golden bridge from his kingdom to the princess' palace. The forthcoming wedding was celebrated for forty days and forty nights. Indra Bangsawan and the Princess Dewi Kemala Sari were married by the *qadi*; his payment of the dowry was witnessed by two eunuchs who were staunch Muslims.

The next day, on the pretext of attending to the pet goats, Indra Bangsawan visited his *raksasa* grandparent to claim the magic bamboo flute that had been promised to him. After another ten days, Indra Bangsawan asked the king's permission to go and fetch his parents. As preparations were being made for the journey, Indra Bangsawan and his wife were suddenly stricken with a serious illness, which might even have been fatal. No physician could cure them. The royal astrologer discerned that the illness had been caused by Buraksa's sister but the couple would recover.

The story next tells that Syah Peri dreamt of meeting his brother Indra Bangsawan on top of an extremely high mountain. The next morning, he bid goodbye to his wife and went in search of Indra Bangsawan, taking a magic gemstone with him that could cure any type of illness. After a long journey, he reached Antah Berantah. Disguising himself as a Sheikh, he presented himself to the Sultan. He placed his magic gemstone in a container of water and wiped Indra Bangsawan's face and body with the water. He did the same with the princess. They both recovered immediately. The whole country was jubilant. Syah Peri told them about his journey to Antah Berantah. The king kept a vigil for forty days and forty nights to fulfil the vow he had made when his daughter and son-in-law fell ill. As an expression of his gratitude, Indra Bangsawan gave his own magic gemstone to Syah Peri. The brothers and their wives then returned to Kobat Syahrial. Indra Bangsawan gave his father the bamboo flute and was later crowned king. Sultan Indra Bangsawan proved himself to be a generous monarch, who was especially sympathetic towards mendicants and the poorest and most destitute of his subjects.

4.10 *Hikayat Jaya Langkara*

This *hikayat* is mentioned by Werndly in his 1736 grammar. Few manuscripts of this *hikayat* exist, except for the *Hikayat Makdam dan Makdim* (SOAS London), which is a version of this *hikayat*, and a fragment kept in Jakarta (Bat. Gen. 53). The best known text is the manuscript held by the National Library of Singapore. The Singapore manuscript was copied on 15 Rabiul-awal 1237 H. (1863). Its owner was a resident of Kampung Malaka called Muhaidin. Winstedt has written a summary of this hikayat. A copy in romanised script can be found in the RAS Library in London. Below is a summary of the Singapore manuscript.

There was once a king called Saiful Muluk who ruled over the vast kingdom of Ajam Saukat. He was married to Princess Sukanda Rum. However, as she had not borne him any children, the king also married Princess Sukanda Bayang-bayang. After some time, Princess Sukanda Bayang-bayang gave birth to twins, Makdam and Makdim. Princess Sukanda Rum, afraid of losing the king's love, prayed for a child. Her prayers were answered. She gave birth to a handsome baby boy named Jaya Langkara. He was born during a time of prosperity in the kingdom, when food was cheap and abundant, and business was booming. The court astrologers, warrior chiefs and all the people gave thanks to God for this blessed situation.

The king sent his Makdam and Makdim to a *qadi* to enquire about Jaya Langkara's future. The scholar predicted that Jaya Langkara would one day be a mighty king with such powerful magical skills that no other king would be able to defeat him, and every wild animal would bow before him. When they heard this, Makdam and Makdim were filled with resentment. They lied to their father, saying that if Jaya Langkara was to be allowed to stay, the whole kingdom would perish and rice would become extremely expensive. The king believed them, and banished Jaya Lengkara and his mother.

Jaya Langkara and his mother took shelter in a cave inhabited by giants, tigers, snakes and scorpions. One day when he was hungry, his mother discovered that her breastmilk had dried up as she had not eaten for forty days. Jaya Langkara threw himself onto the ground in a tantrum. By the grace of God, water flowed from Jaya Langkara's finger, like water from a river. His mother sipped the water and found her breastmilk had returned. She suckled Jaya Langkara and bathed him. As time passed, Jaya Langkara grew to maturity. The forest became his playground and the place where he hunted animals for food.

One day, Raja Saiful Muluk fell gravely ill. No physician could cure him. An astrologer said that the only remedy was the white saffron flower which grew on a mountain in Egypt. As no one else was willing to undertake the journey, Makdam and Makdim departed for Egypt.

Meanwhile, the king of Madinah was also seriously ill. Even the best physicians could not cure him. His daughter, Princess Ratna Kasina, dreamt that the saffron flower on a mountaintop in Egypt could restore her father to health. Accompanied by the Prime Minister and many of her subjects, Princess Ratna Kasina set out to find the flower. They struggled through thick forests and trecked up and down mountains. A large number of the princess' retinue died. The Prime Minister and remaining attendants decided to return to Madinah. Princess Ratna Kasina continued the journey on her own. After some time, she met Jaya Langkara. Makdam and Makdim also arrived at that place at the same time. They decided to continue the journey together. When they reached the mouth of a cave, Jaya Langkara entered first and emerged with a princess who was:

> very beautiful, she was as radiant as the full moon, her forehead glowed like the eastern star, her nose was like a jasmine flower, her cheeks curved and smooth like mango, her ears as intricate as gold-stamped cloth, her hair wavy like palm flowers in bloom, her eyebrows like curved spurs, her teeth like red saga seeds, her chin as smooth as a quail's egg, her waist as small as an ant's waist, her legs as slim as a donkey's, her heels like engraved mangoes, her arms pleasantly plump, and her calves like ripe ears of rice.

The princess was Princess Ratna Kasina. The dragon guardian of the cave, Naga Guna, had provided a cat to protect her. The dragon welcomed them warmly and took them to the summit of the mountain. He explained that, as the mountain was in the centre of the ocean, the saffron flower would appear at high tide. In the meantime, the dragon wished to sleep, which it did for the next forty days. Impatiently, Makdam and Makdim demanded that Jaya Langkara urge Princess Ratna Kasina to fetch the flower. As soon as she touched it, the flower took root in the palm of her hand. Makdam and Makdim tried to remove it but could not. Jaya Langkara was able to take only a single leaf. As soon as he did, Makdam and Makdim pushed him into the sea. Jaya Langkara managed to survive by holding on to the leaf. When the dragon woke, he quickly sent two of his cats to find Jaya Langkara.

Princess Ratna Gemala, daughter of the king of Egypt, also dreamed of the saffron flower. She vowed to neither eat nor drink until she had it. Princess Ratna Dewi, the daughter of the king of Portugal, also had the same dream and wanted the flower as well. Her father sent two ministers to find it. One of them set out to trick the king of Egypt while the other one climbed to the top of the mountain, where he met Makdam, Makdim and Princess Ratna Kasina. He captured them and put Makdam and Makdim in prison.

Naga Guna rescued Jaya Langkara and they traveled to Portugal. Jaya Langkara defeated a priest in argument and forced him to convert to Islam. With the help of a Muslim king of *jinns,* Jaya Langkara freed Makdam and Makdim. Ratna Kasina and Ratna Dewi discovered Jaya Langkara's true identity. A feast was held. Jaya Langkara suggested that Ratna Dewi and Makdam should be married. The happiest outcome of all was that they had found the white saffron flower.

The Prime Minister (*Mangkubumi*) of Egypt tried to steal the flower from Jaya Langkara but could not. Jaya Langkara forgave him when he heard why he wanted the saffron. Jaya Langkara traveled to Egypt to propose that Princess Ratna Dewi be married to Makdam. The king of Egypt agreed. Then Jaya Langkara departed for Ajam Saukat, accompanied by Ratna Kasina. In Ajam Saukat, he cured the king, his father. After a while, Jaya Langkara returned to the forest to look for his mother. Ratna Kasina soon followed him, as she was no longer able to tolerate Makdam and Makdim's advances. Due to their desire to have the princess, the evil twins tried to kill Jaya Langkara. Naga Guna saved Jaya Langkara and took him and Princess Ratna Kasina to Madinah. The king of Madinah was happy to see them. Jaya Langkara married Princess Ratna Kasina. The king of Madinah married Jaya Langkara's mother. Soon afterwards, Jaya Langkara was crowned king of Madinah. During his rule, the kingdom flourished and expanded. The most powerful kings sent tribute to Madinah every year.

That is the gist of the National Library of Singapore manuscript of the *Hikayat Jaya Langkara*. The *Hikayat Raja Takbir* (Collection C. St. 142), held by the National Museum of Indonesia library in Jakarta, is another version of the *Hikayat Jaya Langkara*. It contains a similar plot and subplots. The only difference lies in the names of the characters. Jaya Langkara is called Panji Mas Mirang (later Panji Pandi Semirang); his two brothers, from different mothers, are called Jongkat and Jongkir; their father is King Takbir Mukif from the kingdom of Hamasfati. The princess of Madinah is called Firi Manggeri.

Hikayat Raja Takbir adds the tale of Panji Mas Mirang's adopted brother, Abdul Rahman. Abdul Rahman was a poor but very devout young man. He was married to a beautiful girl, Salamah. Every day he begged for alms. Even though he was poor, he was also well-mannered and generous. On three occasions, he gave up the money he received to different animals: a toad, a mouse and a snake. The king heard about Salamah's beauty and sent his mangkubumi to ask for her. Abdul Rahman had no choice but to give up his wife. Salamah suffered because of the separation and died of grief. The mouse, snake and toad came to help Abdul Rahman. The snake helped him win the heart of the king's daughter, while the toad took Abdul Rahman to heaven to be reunited with his wife.

4.11 *Hikayat Nakhoda Muda*

The *Hikayat Nakhoda Muda,* also known as *Hikayat Sitti Sara* or *Hikayat Raja Ajnawi,* has great interest for European readers because the plot was used by Shakespeare in his play *All's Well That Ends Well.* Shakespeare's plot was borrowed from Boccaccio and may have originated in India.

This story was also found in the eleventh century *Katha Sarit Sagara,* an Indian compilation of legends and folktales. This story is also told in folktales from Kashmir and Sri Lanka.

There are two manuscripts of this *hikayat*. The Leiden manuscript (Cod. Or. 1763 [i]) was copied in Batavia in 1825. The Jakarta manuscript (Bat. Gen. 77) is a copy by W. M. Donseleer and bears the date 29 November 1860; it is based on an 1814 manuscript from Makasar. Balai Pustaka published the Jakarta manuscript in 1934 but changed the names of the characters to correspond with the Leiden work. This is the story as told by the Balai Pustaka text.

There once was a king named Raja Gaznawi who ruled a vast kingdom. Raja Gaznawi was a just and benevolent ruler. One night, he dreamed of a beautiful girl dressed in red, who served him a delicious meal of roast lamb's liver and kidneys. The king fell passionately in love with the girl. The prime minister's two sons, named Husain Mandari and Husain Mandi, were willing to search for the girl.

And so the Husain brothers set out. They enquired at the homes of kings, military officers and high dignitaries, but could not find the girl. The young men then ventured further and soon reached the border of Batavia. There they met a woodcutter and told him they were looking for a house without a kitchen. Their strange actions aroused the old man's suspicions. They opened their umbrellas in the forest, wore socks and leg coverings when crossing rivers, and called bridges with no handrails "monkey bridges". Finally, they advised the old man that he should always cough before entering his house. The old man ignored their advice. When he reached home, he found his daughter Sitti Sara bathing and saw her breasts.

The old man told Sitti Sara about the two young men. Sitti Sara replied that the brothers surely had good reasons for their odd behaviour. For example, had her father coughed to signal his return, she would have been able to cover herself and he would not have been embarrassed by the sight of her naked body.

After a few days, Sitti Sara sent her servant, Si Delima, to take food to the two young men. The food consisted of thirty sweet buns, seven curries, and a gourd filled with water. Sitti Sara asked Si Delima give them the following message: "A month has exactly thirty days, a week has seven days, and sometimes the tide is high." The two men gratefully accepted the food and gave Si Delima one and a half ounces of gold. The next day, Sitti Sara sent the same amount of food and the same message. This time, Si Dilema met her lover on the way and gave him a bun, a bowl of curry, and some water. Seeing that there was less food than before, the two young men replied: "The month consists of thirty days less one, the week of just six days, and the tide is low." In this way, Sitti Sara learned of Si Delima's dishonesty.

One day, Sitti Sara invited the two young men to her home. She served them roast sheep livers and kidneys. Husain Mandari and Husain Mandi were astonished. In their minds, there could be no doubt that Sitti Sara was the girl of whom the king had dreamed. They drew her portrait and sent it to the king. His Majesty was overjoyed to see that the girl in the picture was the girl he had seen in his dream. An envoy was then sent from Gaznawi to ask for Sitti Sara's hand in marriage. When her parents accepted the proposal, Sitti Sara was led in a procession to be married to the king. Once they were married, the king treated her with the utmost care, as if he were "carrying a bowl filled to the top with oil", to quote an old proverb.

After some time, the king went hunting in the forest. He shot a deer in the head, killing it. The deer's fawn came and wept over its mother. The king remembered that he had no child of his own and decided to sail to Langkawi Island. He told his wife that he would return only when she bore him a child, his ring had been transferred onto his wife's hand, his mare was with foal, and all his seven barns were fully stocked. Sitti Sara was silent; she did not utter a single word.

Once the king left, Sitti Sara summoned Husain Mandari and Husain Mandi to discuss her situation. She instructed them to prepare a boat equipped with all the necessities, including timber and water. She also asked for a mare, a set of goldsmith's tools, and a chessboard. Disguising herself as a ship's captain, Sitti Sara sailed for Pulau Langkawi. She introduced herself to the king as a skipper from Dangsekan and challenged him to a game of chess.

And so, Sitti Sara (who now called herself Nakhoda Muda) proceeded to pit her wits against the king in a game of chess. She wagered all the contents of her ship in the game. The king lost the first three games and had to give up his horse, his ring and all his worldly goods to Nakhoda Muda. Sitti Sara introduced the king's stallion to the mare she brought with her. She also instructed a goldsmith to make a counterfeit of the king's ring. In the fourth game, Nakhoda Muda wagered his concubine. This time she deliberately lost and presented herself to the king, disguised as Nakhoda Muda's concubine. She spent seven days with the king before he eventually sent her back to Nakhoda Muda. When she returned to her ship, Sitti Sara set sail for Gaznawi, having achieved all that she wanted.

After several months, Sitti Sara's pregnancy became obvious. On an auspicious day, she gave birth to a handsome boy who resembled his father, the king. At about the same time, her mare too delivered a male foal. When the king eventually returned to the kingdom, he found that Sitti Sara had a son. Thinking that she had betrayed him during his absence, the king flew into a rage and wanted to kill her. Sitti Sara immediately revealed all she had done, explaining to her husband how she had disguised herself as a man and tricked him into playing a game of chess. The king was so pleased with her explanation that he loved her even more after having heard it. And so Sitti Sara spent the rest of her life as the queen of Gaznawi. Husain Mandari and Husain Mandi were appointed ministers. And that is how the story of Nakhoda Muda ends.

Although there are only a few extant copies of the *Hikayat Nakhoda Muda*, the tale itself is quite popular. A manuscript of the *Hikayat Bayan Budiman* (v.d. Wall Collection 173), kept in the library of the National Museum in Jakarta, contains this story. This *hikayat* was also published in *Maleisch Leesboek,* No. 52, edited by Ophuijsen. Finally, we should also mention that there is also a *hikayat* whose contents bear some resemblance to the *Hikayat Nakhoda Muda* in the library of the National Museum in Jakarta, the *Hikayat Maharaja Bikrama Sakti*. There are probably six copies of this *hikayat* and it was lithographed in Singapore around 1900 (R. O. Winstedt, 1921b: 104-109). The story is as follows.

Maharaja Bikrama Sakti and his queen ruled over the kingdom of Mihran Langkawi. When they passed away, they were survived by their two children, a prince and a princess. The prince was named Maharaja Johan Syah, the princess Ratna Kemala. One day, Maharaja Johan Syah set out on a voyage, calling himself Nakhoda Lela Genta. He found a seed on an island which could instantly grow into a tree. He then anchored at Branta Indra and gambled with Maharaja Dekar Alam, using his magic seed as a wager. But he lost and had to work in the palace as a singer.

After some time had passed and her brother, Maharaja Johan Syah, had still not returned, Princess Ratna Kemala disguised herself as Nakhoda Muda and set sail in search of him. She also stopped at the place where he had taken a handful of magical seeds. But unlike her brother, she took some of the soil too. In the kingdom of Branta Indra, she also wagered the magic seeds in a game with the king. She won, as she had first covered the area with the soil she had brought earlier from the island. The princess and her brother visited Langgadura, which was ruled by Sultan Mengindra Sakti. Her intention was to propose on behalf of her brother to Princess Indra Madani. The Crown Prince, Bikrama, tried to detain her, as he suspected that she was really a woman.

Sultan Mengindra Sakti taught Bikrama various ways to ascertain Nakhoda Muda's real gender. A parrot overheard the sultan and warned Ratna Kemala. Bikrama Indra invited Ratna Kemala to eat with him and join him in gambling, cockfighting, tree-climbing, dancing and jumping. In all these activities, Ratna Kemala proved to be his equal. But when she found herself forced to spend the night in Bikrama Indra's bedroom, she told him two long tales to pass the long night. The next morning, she returned to her ship. The parrot then told her that her next test would involve a bath together with Bikrama Indra. Ratna Kemala was also able to extricate herself from this difficult situation.

In the end, Bikrama Indra married Princess Ratna Kemala, after he proved his prowess in archery in a contest in which ninety-nine other princes also took part. When the other princes tried to take Princess Ratna Kemala by force, they were defeated. The princess' brother married Princess Mandani.

Finally, it should be mentioned that the *Hikayat Nakhoda Muda* is the title of a rather well-known biography (G. W. J. Drewes, 1961). This biography was written by Laudin in 1788; it gives biographies of the author's father and grandfather, as well as details of the activities of the English and Dutch in the Malay Archipelago. Its realistic content is a far cry from the fantastical *hikayats* that are featured in this chapter.

4.12 *Hikayat Ahmad Muhammad*

The *Hikayat Ahmad Muhammad*, also known as *Hikayat Serangga Bayu* or *Hikayat Sukarna dan Sukarni,* was once a popular *hikayat.* There are many different manuscripts. As the basis of my discussion, I present below the contents of the *Hikajat Soekarna dan Soekarni,* published by A. F. von de Wall (1908).

The tale tells that a minister of the kingdom of Indra Pura, named Maha Jaya, once bought a child and called him Ratna Kasihan. As Ratna Kasihan was a boy of good character, Minister Maha Jaya entrusted him with looking after his possessions. After some time, Maha Jaya adopted Ratna Kasihan and gave him a wife. Then he was appointed as the captain of a ship and told to trade with different countries. When Ratna Kasihan returned home, he found that his adopted father had passed away, leaving him all his wealth. Ratna Kasihan did not need to travel overseas anymore but could do all his business in Indra Pura. His wealth grew and he then moved to Gendara Giri, where his business was even more successful.

One night, Ratna Kasihan dreamed that the moon and sun appeared and shone their light over him. Later, his wife gave birth to twin boys, Sukarna and Sukarni. When the boys reached the age of seven, they began to learn how to recite the Quran. They were given a bird as a reward for their efforts. Every day, they played with their pet after class. When they completed their recitation studies, they received lessons in swordfighting and archery.

One day, a merchant was exploring a market near Ratna Kasihan's town when he saw the boys' pet bird and wished to buy it. He became even more eager after an astrologer predicted that the person who ate the bird's head would become a mighty king and whoever ate its liver would become a powerful and wise minister. The merchant sent a friend to offer a very high sum for the bird. But Ratna Kasihan was unwilling to part with it. And so, the merchant decided to befriend Ratna Kasihan and his wife, in the hope that one day his wish to own the bird would come true.

And so a friendship developed between the merchant and Ratna Kasihan and his wife. One day, Ratna Kasihan left to attend to his business matters overseas. While he was away, the merchant began to implement his plan to persuade Ratna Kasihan's wife to part with the pet bird. Overcome by his persuasive manners and sweet words, Ratna Kasihan's wife gave him the parrot. He quickly passed it to his cook. By chance, Sukarna and Sukarni arrived home from their archery and swordfighting class and asked for some rice. Since there was nothing available to serve with the rice, the cook let them have the bird. Sukarna ate its head while Sukarni ate the liver. According to the story, the twins were unaware that they were eating their beloved pet bird. Had they known, they would surely have refused, because they had always loved animals. They would not even hurt a fly. "Remember, all creatures, whether big or small, are all God's creations," the writer reminds his readers.

The merchant was disappointed to learn that Ratna Kasihan's sons had eaten the bird's head and liver. He looked for the astrologer to explain what had happened. The astrologer told him: "It is a most wonderful bird. When it is eaten, it returns to its original form: body, head and liver. It will not disappear like other food." Without hearing what else the astrologer had to say, the merchant looked for a way to gain the bird's head and liver. He decided to kill the twins and ordered four of his slaves to do so. One of the slaves felt sorry and told the twins' governess of the evil plan. She quickly warned Sukarna and Sukarni, urging them to run away to any place that their fate would take them. Upon realising that he now had no way of getting what he wanted, the merchant became despondent. For seven days and seven nights, he refused to eat or sleep. His body grew emaciated and his eyesight deteriorated. He then died.

This is what happened to Sukarna and Sukarni when they fled from home. Despite walking a long distance, they did not feel ill, hungry or thirsty, because of the head and liver of the bird they had eaten. They reached a large, tall mountain and, resting under a shady tree, soon fell asleep. When Sukarni awoke, he found that Sukarna was no longer by his side. He searched for his brother by following the tracks of an elephant. A trail of torn pieces of cloth reassured Sukarni that his brother was still alive. After some time, he reached the home of a fairy godmother, who told him that a young man had been chosen by a magic elephant to be king, as the former king had passed away without leaving an heir. Sukarni was convinced that the young man in the story was his brother, Sukarna. He hesitated to meet Sukarna, afraid that as his brother was now great and powerful, he would no longer want to recognize him. So he asked the old woman to adopt him as her grandson. He hid his true identity, telling her that his name was Serangga Bayu.

After some time, Serangga Bayu wished to take a wife and asked the old woman if she knew a girl of good character who would make a good wife. The old woman replied that there were only two such girls in the whole kingdom, the daughters of the Prime Minister, and that they were as beautiful as they were intelligent. Putri Sulung, the elder princess, was already married to the young man who had just been crowned king. The younger princess, Putri Bungsu, did not want to marry. On hearing the old woman's words, Serangga Bayu made an exquisite flower arrangement for Putri Bungsu. The princess was so impressed that she sent two of her ladies-in-waiting, Dang Lela Seganda and Dang Lela Mangurna, to the old woman to ask for more bouquets. Serangga Bayu not only made more bouquets, he even sent her the ring from his finger. Putri Bungsu praised Serangga Bayu even more and guessed that he might possibly be the young man of whom she had dreamed. Nevertheless, she did not show the picture of the man in her dream to the two ladies-in-waiting. Imagine their surprise when they saw Serangga Bayu's picture in Putri Bungsu's bedroom. The princess became even more eager to meet the young man from her dream.

Serangga Bayu was also keen to meet the princess. But what could he do? The old woman suggested that Serangga Bayu learn magic from an ascetic. On the way, Serangga Bayu met two men arguing over three magic weapons: an arrow, a begging bowl and a carpet. The arrow could release swarms of bees and hornets; the bowl could provide all sorts of food; while the carpet was a flying carpet. Serangga Bayu took all these items and flew back to his fairy godmother. He then asked her to help him meet the princess.

Serangga Bayu and Putri Bungsu met in a garden. She was convinced that he was the man she had seen in her dream. They shared betel leaf and talked. Later Serangga Bayu flew the princess to an island where they could enjoy themselves. Putri Bungsu began to worry that he might fly her to some unknown destination and never bring her back to her kingdom again. So she took the magic carpet while Serangga Bayu was asleep and flew home by herself. When Serangga Bayu woke, he found that the princess had gone. With a heavy heart, he wandered around the island. Soon he saw a ship sailing close to shore. He asked if he could come aboard. On the ship, he met an official who had been sent by Raja Derma to ask for Putri Bungsu's hand in marriage. Serangga Bayu showed the envoy his magic arrow that could release swarms of bees and hornets. The envoy showed Serangga Bayu his magic sword; the sword could chop, strike and slash without any human assistance. Serangga Bayu took the magic sword from its owner. Once the ship reached Putri Bungsu's kingdom, Serangga Bayu ordered the envoy to turn back and return home to Raja Derma. The envoy could only obey the command because he was terrified of Serangga Bayu's two magic weapons.

Serangga Bayu decided to ask for Putri Bungsu's hand in marriage. He entered the princess' chambers and spoke with her. A jealous governess reported this to the Prime Minister who quickly arrived with guards. Serangga Bayu released bees and hornets from his magic arrow to sting them. He then flew over their heads on his magic carpet to frighten them. The guards fled and reported the situation to Sultan Sukarna. When the sultan arrived, Serangga Bayu came out of the princess' pavillion and began to explain about his background. Before he could finish, the sultan reached out and held him tightly, kissing his long-lost brother and crying with joy. Sultan Sukarna then celebrated the marriage of Serangga Bayu and Putri Bungsu. Serangga Bayu replaced his father-in-law as the Prime Minister. He became famous as a wise Prime Minister, who treated one and all with courtesy and consideration. After some time, Sultan Sukarna sent two of his ministers to fetch his parents so they could all live together. He had well-appointed palace built for them. He also conferred a high status on the old woman as a reward for her services in raising Sukarni. Sultan Sukarna continued the kingdom and Sukarni as his just Prime Minister.

The contents of this manuscript are rather different from those of the *Hikayat Ahmad Muhammad* lithographed in Singapore in 1889 (29 Rabiul-akhir, A. H. 1307). R. O. Winstedt has written a summary of this hikayat in his well-known work, *A History of Classical Malay Literature* (1958: 203-204). According to *Hikayat Ahmad Muhammad*, the sons of Ratna Kasihan were called Ahmad and Muhammad. The princesses they married were called Sitti Baghdad and Sitti Saadad. Ratna Kasihan's wife only handed over the pet bird to the merchant's son after he bewitched her. In this *hikayat*, Serangga Bayu is said to have been asked to pay seven gatekeepers a thousand dinar each before being allowed into the palace of Sitti Saadad. At their first meeting, he drank wine and vomitted up the pet bird's liver. Sitti Saadad then washed the liver and ate it again.

There are two further *hikayat* that claim to be translations from Javanese. A version held in Jakarta (Koleksi Br. 435) includes a character called Betaljemur, who is Betalkemur from Menak, or Buzurjmihr, from the *Hikayat Amir Hamzah*. Raden Sadan Sapal, Dewi Asmai and Princess Kurajsyin from the *Hikayat Amir Hamzah* also appear in *Hikayat Ahmad Muhammad*. Below is a summary of the Jakarta manuscript (Koleksi Br. 435), which consists of several parts or episodes.

The first part tells of Ahmad and Muhammad. The conflict between the various characters is very interesting. Muhammad becomes the King of Egypt, not Ahmad. Sitti Baghdad deceives Ahmad again and again, and for this, Ahmad persists in trying to kill her, but is never successful. Another difference is that Ahmad and Muhammad are the sons of a priestly king and students in the magic arts of a sage called Syaikh Jagung.

The second part describes Ahmad's voyage to an island and his meeting with Dewi Soja, daughter of Prophet Muhammad. Due to a misunderstanding, a fight arose between Ahmad and Dewi Soja. The Prophet's companion, Omar, had to come and make peace between them. In the end, Ahmad and Dewi Soja are married in a lavish celebration. Not long after this, Ahmad sets out to find his brother, leaving behind his pregnant wife.

The third part tells how the king of Abyssinia proposed to Sitti Baghdad. Because the proposal was rejected, the king then sent his ministers Wiramaya and Wira Santika to kidnap Sitti Baghdad. Ahmad rescued the princess and forced Wiramaya and Wira Santika to become Muslims.

Sitti Baghdad was kidnapped again, this time together with Ratna Komala. And once again, Ahmad rescued them, defeating the ghost (*buto*) who had kidnapped them. The manuscript ends at this point.

The Leiden manuscript (Cod. 3249) is also said to be an adaptation of a Javanese poem; it was summarised by Prof. Vreede in his *Katalogus*. On examining Vreede's summary, however, I found that the Javanese poem is closer to the Jakarta manuscript (Koleksi Br. 435) than it is to the Leiden one. This manuscript is comprised of several episodes.

The first episode relates how Ahmad rescued Sitti Baghdad from a ghost and married her. Raja Habesi (in the Jakarta manuscript: Abyssinia) proposed to Sitti Baghdad but was rejected. He declared war. Dewi Soja gave birth to a son, Air Maya, who rescued Ahmad. Raja Habesi was defeated and forced to retreat.

A continuation of the manuscript, Cod. 3314, tells that Raja Syam sent Air Maya (or Er Maya) to find Raden Mantri. Raden Mantri accompanied Princess Puspa Ratna Komala back to her kingdom and married her. Finally, Raden Mantri returned to Egypt.

4.13 *Hikayat Syah Mardan*

The *Hikayat Syah Mardan,* also known as *Hikayat Indra Jaya* and *Hikayat Bagermadantaraja,* is a popular tale; it has been translated into several regional languages including Javanese, Makasarese, Buginese and Sasak. In 1736, Werndly wrote: "this hikayat is a fairytale written for children who love to read." And perhaps due to Werndly's influence, Hollander (1845) included a very long extract from this *hikayat* in his anthology.

G. W. J. Drewes has studied this *hikayat* and its Javanese version (the *Angling Darma*). He argues that this *hikayat* is not an Islamic story, and does not originate from the Middle East. There are no Arabic elements in the *Angling Darma* at all. The stories meant to convey a religious message are almost certainly later additions. For example: Syah Mardan is a very devout man; even in the worst situations, he never neglects his prayers. And he always teaches the major principles of Islam to each woman he marries. Syah Mardan also debates religious issues in his conversations with angels and clergy too (Drewes, 1975: 15).

Here is a summary of the *Hikayat Syah Mardan,* based on the *Hikajat Raja Moeda Sjah Mardan* (1916).

Raja Bagerma-Dantajaya of Dahrulhastan had a very handsome son, Raja Muda Syah Mardan. The prince was quick and nimble in his actions, sweet in his words, and wise in his ways. At an early age he undertook classes in religion and philosophy taught by a Brahmin.

After some time, the Brahmin asked permission to return home. Syah Mardan and his retinue escorted him there. On the return trip, Syah Mardan did some hunting. While pursuing his prey, Syah Mardan became separated from his retinue and lost his way in the forest. Many of his subjects died of hunger and thirst during their long search for him.

Some time later, Syah Mardan saw a palace. The palace contained Princess Kemala Ratna Dewi, the daughter of Raja Dahrul Merjun, who was being held captive by a giant. As he was afraid to take her home with him, the princess turned Syah Mardan into a canary. Syah Mardan flew on to the palace of Princess Siti Dewi, the daughter of Raja Dahrul Hayam. The princess was delighted by the canary and kept it in a golden birdcage. Because of the bird, she neglected her daily tasks; she no longer wove, sewed or embroidered. She even forgot about her parents. Every day she was busy playing with her pet. When she did visit her parents, she was pale and listless. The king ordered his ministers to investigate the matter. The princess' governess admitted that the princess' behaviour had changed since she had come into possession of the bird. The cage and the canary were taken before the king. The king was so angry he wanted to kill the bird. A Brahmin suggested that further investigations be undertaken before killing the creature. He suspected that the canary was not really a bird. He then stroked the back of the canary and a man emerged from inside the bird. This was reported to the king. This time His Majesty was not angry; in fact, he allowed Syah Mardan to marry Princess Sitti Dewi. Lavish celebrations were held on a vast scale. After some time, Syah Mardan asked his wife's permission to resume his travels. He made one request of her: If she gave birth to a boy, he was to be named Panji Lelana; if the child was a girl, her name should be Ratna Dewi.

Syah Mardan, now called Indra Jaya, eventually came to a high mountain where he met a holy man, Syah Salamuddin, who explained to him the importance of worship and charity. Syah Mardan stayed with the holy man for forty days and learned various sacred arts. Finally, he took his leave and resumed his travels once more.

After some time, Indra Jaya met Lukman al-Hakim, an extremely devout preacher, and his son Jin Katob. Lukman al-Hakim questioned Indra Jaya on the difference between traditional ways of prayer and the Muslim way of worship, as well as why the dusk prayers were shorter than the night prayers. Lukman al-Hakim praised Indra Jaya's knowledge and explained to him the the four stages of spiritual growth—*syariat, tarikat, hakikat* and *makrifat*—in which the disciple progressed from keeping the law and affirming his bonds with his fellow seekers, to an understanding of the essence of reality, and, finally, spiritual union with the divine.

After another seven days and seven nights, Indra Jaya saw an enormous mosque on a hill near the sea. But there was no one inside the mosque. Suddenly a thousand riders on winged horses came to pray, martyrs who had died in holy wars. They dwelt before the throne of God and came to earth each day to perform their prayers together. One of them explained the meanings of submission (*taslim*) and belief in an Omniscient God (*murakabah*). Their leader also asked Indra Jaya about prayer and the things one should do before performing ritual prayer. Indra Jaya answered each question in detail. Then the thousand martyrs vanished. Indra Jaya remained in the mosque until midnight. Then an angel appeared and presented him with four *jinns,* named Yakiba, Yanuh, Yaidaka and Yautad. These *jinns* could carry Indra Jaya to distant lands and fulfil his every wish. The angel and Indra Jaya then discussed the Five Principles of the Muslim faith.

Indra Jaya continued his journey. He followed the coast and, forty days later, came to an enormous, tall city. He saw a large mother-of-pearl shell and commanded Yautad to open it. Inside the shell were two people. They were so weak they could hardly move. Indra Jaya revived them by feeding them porridge and water. The two people were the king and queen; their kingdom had been destroyed by a *garuda*. Indra Jaya found the beautiful Princess Candra Sari hiding inside another shell. He summoned his four *jinns* to kill the *garuda*. Through Indra Jaya's fervent prayers, the whole population were revived. Everyone was very happy, and in the midst of this rejoicing, Indra Jaya and Princess Candra Sari were married.

After a while, Indra Jaya asked to be allowed to resume his journey. While he was resting under a tree, the brother of the *garuda* he had killed swooped down and took him to feed to its offspring. However, the baby birds refused to eat Indra Jaya and, instead, appealed to their father to take Indra Jaya to Dahrulkiam Hill.

The king of Dahrulkiam ruled over an exceedingly vast realm. He had a very intellligent daughter named Jalusilasikin. She was so charming that everyone was captivated by her. Unfortunately, she had been silent since birth and refused to talk. The king announced that anyone who could make his daughter talk would marry her. However, should he fail, he would be thrown into prison and executed. So far, thirty-nine princes had been imprisoned.

One day, Indra Jaya presented himself before the king, accompanied by a Brahmin he had met along the way. Indra Jaya was taken to meet Jalusilasikin. Indra Jaya and the princess looked at each other and immediately fell in love. He encourage her to speak by using a most extraordinary method. He transferred his soul into a curtain, a candle, a betelnut container, and then, the scarf in the princess' hand. Each of these objects asked a riddle. Indra Jaya deliberately gave the wrong answer to the various riddles. And each time, Jalusilasikin corrected him. The king was overcome with joy on hearing the princess speak with such wisdom. And so preparations were made for the wedding of Indra Jaya and Jalusilasikin.

Indra Jaya spent the next three months happily with his bride. One day, his wife asked him a number of questions related to the daily prayers, the creation of the heavens and the earth, the creation of the vault of heaven, the throne of God, His Pen, and the Seven Grades of Being. Indra Jaya answered her questions in great detail. Jalusilasikin was pleased and her love for her husband increased even more.

After some time, Indra Jaya remembered his parents and asked to be allowed to return home in order to see them. During the journey, his way was blocked by the thirty-nine princes who had failed to make Princess Jalusilasikin speak. Indra Jaya sent one of his palanquin-bearers to warn the princes. But his warning was rejected. And so a war began. When one of his palanquin-bearers was killed, Indra Jaya transferred his soul into the bodies of the other bearers. Thus fortified, his men inflicted heavy losses on their enemies. The princes were terrified and begged Indra Jaya to forgive their treachery.

After the battle ended, Indra Jaya continued his journey. On the way, Jalusilasikin saw an Indian plum tree and asked for its fruit. Indra Jaya killed a monkey and transferred his own soul into the primate's body so he could climb the tall tree and pluck its fruit for his wife. At that moment, a Brahmin, acting on an evil impulse, transferred his soul into Indra Jaya's body. But Jalusilasikin knew that her husband's soul still resided in the monkey's body.

When the journey was resumed, the monkey followed along behind. They soon reached Indra Jaya's country of origin. Raja Bagerma Dantajaya warmly welcomed his "son". Jalusilasikin had to decide how to kill the Brahmin. One day, she went to the Prime Minister's home and told him about her problem. The Prime Minister promised to help. He told the Brahmin that Jalusilasikin wanted to stage an animal fight. If the Brahmin's ram won, the princess would willingly marry him. The Brahmin quickly searched for a strong and aggressive ram and tended the beast very carefully. The princess' animal, on the other hand, was scrawny and almost too weak to move, as it had been deprived of food and water. The day of the fight arrived and the two rams were pitted against each other. With just one blow, the princess' ram collapsed and died. The princess cried and threatened to commit suicide if her ram was not brought back to life. Upon hearing her plea, the Brahmin unwittingly transferred his soul into her dead sheep. And so the ram was resuscitated. Instantly, Indra Jaya released his soul from the monkey and entered his rightful body once more.

His wife bowed at his feet. Raja Bagerma Datajaya also embraced his son and kissed him. The king proposed that Indra Jaya replace him on the throne. Indra Jaya became the new king, taking the name of Raja Syah Mardan, and became famous throughout the realm. Raja Syah Mardan also adored his other wife, Sitti Dewi, whom he had left in Darul Hayam. He conjured up Darul Hayam and made it sail through the air, to take a position beside Darul Hastan. Then he invited his other wife, Princess Candra Sari, whom he had saved from the *garuda, to* be reunited with him as well. From then on, Syah Mardan lived happily with his three wives in Darul Hastan.

The story returns to Princess Komala Ratna Dewi. After being held captive by a giant and turning Syah Mardan into a bird, she later gave birth to a handsome baby boy. An eagle flew the princess and her son to the kingdom of Darul Merjun. Her father, the king, was delighted to be reunited with his daughter. The baby, Raden Panji Lelana, was raised with great love. When Raden Panji Lelana grew up, he set out to find his father, accompanied by a foolish servant, Surapenggi. Along the way, they encountered his three stepmothers. Raden Wira Lelana had defeated Syah Mardan and forced the women to flee from the kingdom. Raden Panji Lelana took his stepmothers back to their palaces and freed his father. The usurper was forced to hand over his daughter, Indra Cahaya, to be Raden Panji Lelana's wife. At the same time, King Nusantara arrived from Hindustan to propose to Princess Indra Cahaya. While battle raged between Raden Wira Lelana and King Nusantara, Raden Panji Lelana (now known as Raja Dilila) flew to Hindustan to make love to Raja Nusantara's concubines, who numbered one less than two thousand. Turning them all into jasmine flowers, he placed the women in a gold container and took them back to Darul Merjun. When he reached the kingdom, the battle was still in progress. Raja Dilila ran onto the battlefield and shot his magic arrow, killing Raja Nusantara. Everyone shouted for joy. Raja Dilila showed the concubines to his wives. Kings came from every land came and offered him tribute. The kingdom of Dahrul Merjun expanded and prospered under his rule.

4.14 *Hikayat Isma Yatim*

This *hikayat* is at least two hundred years old. It was first mentioned by Valentijn in 1726 and is discussed by Werndly in 1736. Roorda van Eysinga published this work in Jakarta in 1825. Later, Part One was published in Singapore "for children studying in Malay schools". The exact date of original publication is unknown but a fifth printing was undertaken in 1912.

R. O. Winstedt disagreed with Werndly's opinion that the language of this *hikayat* is beautiful, quoting a section which he found to be rife with non-Malay expressions. Winstedt explained that this *hikayat* is a good example of a *hikayat* from the transitional age: the Hindu and Javanese influences have worn thin while Malay literature in general had fallen into the hands of translators and editors who imitated the literary style of Persia and Arabia. One proof of this imitation lies in the division of the work into chapters and the provision of summaries as part of the introduction to each chapter.

There are many manuscripts of this *hikayat*. The stories are basically the same, although there are also some variations here and there. For example, Cod. Or. 1747 begins with the story of Dewa Putra, the king of Samandar Pura Negara, and the birth of his son, Indra Mengindra. Indra Mengindra married Indra Dewi, the daughter of Raja Lila Mengindra of Masulipatana. During her exile, Princess Ratna Kendi gave birth to Princess Puspa Ratna Komala. Once, Princess Ratna

LITERATURE BELONGING TO THE PERIOD OF TRANSITION FROM HINDUISM TO ISLAM

Komala attacked a prince who had proposed to her but whom she had rejected. She was defeated and taken prisoner. Below is a summary based on Roorda van Eysinga's Singapore manuscript and a handwritten manuscript held in the National Library of Singapore.

Once upon a time, a minister from the India, Megat Nira, played a game of chess against an army chief in the presence of the royal council. Megat Nira lost and decided to go abroad to Masulipatana. Some time later, in the middle of the night, a fierce typhoon raged, thunder roared, lightning flashed, and tall trees crashed to the ground. Based on these signs, Megat Nira knew that he was about to be blessed with an extremely wise child. Time passed and soon Megat Nira's wife gave birth to a very handsome son. They named the boy Isma Yatim and raised him with love.

Isma Yatim soon grew and took lessons in Quranic recitation from a holy man called Sufian. Isma Yatim very quickly mastered the sacred art and was appointed to supervise the other students. He composed a book filled with analogies and parables, which delighted all who read it. And due to the popularity of the book, Isma Yatim earned a good amount of money. He became well-known and many young people came to study under him.

Some time later, Isma Yatim wrote another book, containing advice on the proper conduct of kings. The king was delighted and rewarded him with a set of beautiful clothes. He was also invited to become a courtier. At court, he composed various other outstanding works. The king was even more delighted and showered still more gifts on Isma Yatim. He was also asked to supervise the laying of a golden carpet in the palace. His meticulous work earned him a promotion to the post of valet.

One day, a ship arrived, laden with all sorts of woolen goods. The king sent Isma Yatim to meet the ship's captain, with orders to select the finest woolen garments. Isma Yatim carried out his task with great diligence. He explained to the captain the conditions of trade and the two men quickly became friends. The ship's captain gave Isma Yatim a chest for the king. The magical chest contained a glass box. The box contained a turquoise-studded betelnut holder. The betelnut holder contained two sapphires. When placed in a tray, one of the stones displayed two peacocks that were well-versed in the art of pantun recitation. The other stone, when placed on a throne, displayed a beautiful and radiant princess. However, the captain warned Isma Yatim not to mention the princess to anyone.

The king was delighted with the chest of drawers. He gave gifts of gold, silver and beautiful clothes to the ship's captain. He also gave the captain a parcel of land large enough to house a whole village. Each night the king played with the precious stones. He was highly amused by the pantuns which the peacocks recited. One night, Princess Ratna Kendi emerged and played tricks on the king's concubines and the young ladies of the palace. She changed their clothes and jewellery about, and untied their hair. Then she washed herself in the king's bathroom. After that, she went to the king's bedroom. When the king awoke, she vanished. She repeated these pranks over the next few nights. Upset, the king threatened to kill the ladies-in-waiting and security guards. From what the king told him, Isma Yatim was certain that the mischief-maker was the princess of the sapphire. He offered to keep guard.

During the night, he related a number of amazing stories. These stories told how kings should behave, how they should sleep, and certain matters pertaining to the likes and dislikes of men and women. When Isma Yatim described the preferences of men, the occupants of the palace gathered on the other side of the wall to listen. Late in the night, Princess Ratna Kendi emerged to bathe in the royal bathroom. Isma Yatim quickly roused the king who hurried to see Princess Ratna Kendi. The princess cried as he hugged and kissed her. The king was overjoyed. A lavish feast was held and Isma Yatim was promoted to Treasurer. While he held that position, once-poor merchants prospered and needy orphans became rich. Then Isma Yatim was promoted again, this time to military commander and given a beautiful bride.

The King of Constantinople, Raja Rum Safedan, heard that Raja Mengindra had a beautiful princess who lived in a sapphire and wanted her for himself. He sent his army to attack Raja Indra Mengindra. Isma Yatim was appointed to ward off the attack. He did not fight, but instead, secretly entered Raja Rum's palace. Raja Rum was terrified; he ordered his army to retreat and swore allegiance to Raja Indra Mengindra. For his services, Isma Yatim was promoted yet again, this time to Prime Minister. During his Prime Ministership, Samandar continued to expand; its people prospered, no one wept because they did not have enough money for their needs. Isma Yatim also provided for orphans. When a minister passed away, Isma Yatim divided his inheritance according to the rules of Islamic law and would care for his child until he was able to be employed in the palace. If a military commander died, the child would be encouraged to learn how to use weapons and the art of warcraft.

After some time, Princess Ratna Kendi became pregnant. The queen was worried that the king would love Princess Ratna Kendi more than herself after the child was born, so she looked for a way to have the princess banished from the palace. One day, the queen put some poison in the rice flour cakes that Princess Ratna Kendi sent to the king, and then accused her of trying to poison him. Furious, the king ordered Isma Yatim to kill Princess Ratna Kendi. But Isma Yatim not only spared her life, he also built her a beautiful palace. After some time, the princess gave birth to a beautiful baby girl who glowed with the radiance of the full moon. The baby was named Dewi Rum. The king, however, was miserable, as he believed that he still had no child of his own. The queen regretted her actions. Seeing their condition, Isma Yatim then told the king that Princess Ratna Kendi was still alive. He pointed out that "according to God's law, a pregnant woman should not be killed", and revealed that Princess Ratna Kendi was with child at the time of her sentencing. The king was overcome with joy and was grateful to Isma Yatim for his wisdom. Everyone in the kingdom, even the most humble subjects, was treated to a lavish feast that lasted for forty days and forty nights.

A short time after, His Majesty fell ill and passed away. Before his death, he had entrusted Isma Yatim with the care of his daughter and everything in the palace. Isma Yatim carried out the king's instructions perfectly. Dewi Rum became the new sovereign with the title Mengindera Sri Bulan (thereafter referred to as Tuan Putri, the Sovereign Princess). Many princes came to ask for her hand. In response, Isma Yatim asked the suitors to be patient, as Tuan Putri was still too young to marry.

Isma Yatim educated Mengindera Sri Bulan in a most unusual way. He found a talking lantern to teach Tuan Putri the ways of a married woman, as well as how to make her husband love her forever. As Tuan Putri grew, she became even wiser and more beautiful. Princes continued to come to ask for her hand in marriage. Among the suitors was Raja Indra Mempelai, the son of Raja Syahdan Mengindra, who was not only handsome, but was also very capable in the performance of his duties and extremely pleasantly mannered. Tuan Putri accepted Raja Indra Mempelai's proposal. And so, a royal wedding was held. The festivities continued for forty days and forty nights. After some time, Raja Indra Mempelai expressed a wish to visit his parents. He was accompanied on the journey by Tuan Putri's mother and the queen. And thus the kingdom of Raja Indra Mempelai continued to enjoy peace and tranquility.

REFERENCES

Ali Ahmad, (ed.)
1968.   *Hikayat Indraputra,* DBP, Kuala Lumpur.

Balai Pustaka
1934.   *Nachoda Moeda, (Sitti Sara and Radja Gaznawi),* Djakarta.

Blagden, C. O.
1929.   "Hikayat Maharaja Ali," *JMBRAS,* 7 (3), pp. 415-436.

Brandes, J.
1894.   "Dwerghertverhalen uit den Archipel-Javaansche," *TBG, XXXVII.*

Brakel, L.
1979.   "On the Origins of the Malay Hikayat," *RIMA,* 13, No. 2.

Chambert-Loir, H. (ed.)
1982.   *Hikayat Dewa Mandu,* Jakarta.

Datoek Madjoindo.
1959.   *Hikayat Si Miskin,* Djakarta.

Dissel, J. S. A. (ed.)
1897.   *Hikayat Si Miskin,* Leiden.

Drewes, G. W. J.
1961.   "De Biografie Van een Minangkabause Peperhandelaar in de Lampongs," *VKI,* Vol. 36.
1975   *The Romance of King Angling Darma,* (Bibliothec Indonesia no. 11), The Hague.

Eysinga, Roorda van
1825.   *Hikajat Isma Yatim,* Jakarta.

Fraissinet, J. C.
1849.   *Geschiedenis van Vorst Bispoe Redja,* Leiden.

Hikayat.
1913.   *Hikajat Langlang Boeana,* Weltevreden.
1916.   *Hikajat Radja Moeda Sjah Mardan,* Weltevreden.
1927.   *Hikajat Indera Bangsawan,* Weltevreden.

Hollander, J. J. de
1845.   *Geschiedenis van Djohor Manikam,* Breda.

Iskandar, T.
1965.   "Hikayat Nakhoda Muda," *DB,* IX, 8.

Jamilah Hj. Ahmad (ed.)
1980.   *Hikayat Parang Punting,* Kuala Lumpur.

Juynboll, H.H.
1899   *Catalogus van de Maleische en Soendaneesche Handschriften der Leidsche Universiteits-Bibliotheek,* Leiden Brill.

Mulyadi, S. W. R.
1983.   *Hikayat Indraputra,* (Bibliotheca Indonesia 23), Holland.

Ophuijsen, Ch. A. Van (ed.)
1916.   *Hikayat Si Miskin,* P. W. M. Trap, Leiden.
            "Hikayat Bayan Budiman," *Maleisch Leesboek,* no. 52.

Ronkel, Ph. S. Van
1909.   "Catalogus de Maleische Handschriften," *VGB,* Deel LVII pp. 75-76.

Roorda van Eysinga, P. P.
1825.   *Hikayat Isma Yatim,* Batavia.

Valentijn, F.
1724-1726. *Oud en Niew Oost Indien,* Vol. 1-5, Van Braam Oder de Linden, Amsterdam.

Wall, A. F. von de
1908.   *Hikajat Soekarna & Soekarni,* G. Kolff & Co.

Werndly, G.H.
1736.   *Maleische Spraakklunst, uit de Enige Schriften der Maleiers Opgemakt,* Amsterdam.

Winstedt, R. O.
1920a.   "Hikayat Jaya Langkara," *JSBRAS,* 82, pp. 147-150.
1920b.   "The Date of Hikayat Indraputra," *JSBRAS,* 82, pp. 145-146; 85, pp. 46-53.
1921a.   "Hikayat Puspa Wiraja," *JSBRAS,* 83, pp. 96-103.
1921b.   "Hikayat Nakhoda Muda," *JSBRAS,* 83, pp. 104-109.
1922a.   "Hikayat Si-Miskin or Marakarma," *JSBRAS,* 85, pp. 41-45.
1922b.   "Hikayat Indraputera," *JSBRAS,* 85, pp. 46-53.
1922c.   "Hikayat Putra Jaya Pati," *JSBRAS,* 85, pp. 54-57.
1922d.   "Hikayat Indra Bangsawan," *JSBRAS,* 85, pp. 58-61.
1922e.   "Hikayat Parang Puting," *JSBRAS,* 85, pp. 62-66.
1958.   "A History of Classical Malay Literature," *JMBRAS,* 31 (3), pp. 203-204.

5 Literature of the Islamic Age

We do not know for certain when Islam arrived in the Archipelago or from where it came. In general, scholars believe that a tombstone belonging to a Muslim woman found in Leran (Gresik) and dated 1082 is the oldest remaining Muslim relic. Scholars also agree that a Muslim village must have existed there at that time. According to these scholars, Muslim traders very seldom brought their families with them on long journeys. When they stayed in a place for a considerable time, they would marry the local women after converting them to Islam. However, the woman whose grave was found in Leran was certainly not a convert. Her father's and grandfather's names were also appended to hers on the gravestone: "Fatimah binti Maimun ibn Hibatullah" (S. Q. Fatimi, 1963: 39).

After this discovery, there are no other findings that attest to the presence of Islam in the Archipelago for the next 200 years. However, further indications of the presence of Islam surfaced in the 13th century. In 1292, Marco Polo reported that a large number of people in Perlak (in Acheh) had already embraced Islam. In 1297, Al Malikus-Saleh, the first Muslim king of Samudra Pasai, passed away.[1] At about the same time, Pasai sent an envoy to China. The envoys were Muslims and were called Hasan and Sulaiman. This meant that at that time, Pasai had a sufficient number of Muslims among its populace for some of them to be selected as important state officials.

The rapid growth of Islam in the Archipelago is connected with the spread of Islam across the world during that time. In 1196, Gujarat was conquered by Muslims. This meant that the Gujaratis, who came to trade in this region in great numbers, were now made up of not just Hindus but included Muslims as well, possibly of other ethnicities. In 1258, Baghdad fell into the hands of the Mongols and as a result, inland trade came to a halt. Muslims started venturing out to sea to explore distant lands in the East. These two factors helped Islam to spread quickly in the Archipelago after the thirteenth century.

The oldest Islamic artefact in Malaysia is an inscription written on stone, found in Terengganu and dated either 1303 (H. 702) or 1386. Scholars believe that a Muslim village certainly already existed there at that time. Even so, Islam only gained a definite foothold in the Malay Peninsula with the establishment of the Malaka Sultanate. Malaka was originally a small fishing village.

---

1 On the islamicisation of Samudra Pasai, see the *Sejarah Melayu* (ed. A. Teeuw), 1952, pp. 58-61.

But due to its strategic location, it became a favoured stopover for ships that plied between India and China—and it soon prospered to become a busy trading centre. A large number of traders stopped here, including many Muslims. Around 1400, the sultan, founder of the Malaka sultanate, Prameswara, embraced Islam and took the name Megat Iskandar Syah. He then married the princess of Pasai, which at that time was considered a busy trading centre. After this, Malaka became even more well-known.

Malaka became a reputed centre for Islamic learning. It had such a good reputation that two Muslim *walis* (saints) from Java, Sunan Bonang and Sunan Giri, went to study there. Due to the king's conversion to Islam and the high volume of trade conducted by Muslims in Malaka, its population subsequently embraced Islam en masse. Moreover, the religion had many attractive features from an ideological perspective. It taught the brotherhood of all races and does not recognise any caste division or ethnic discrimination. When someone becomes a Muslim, he or she is embraced as a member of a larger community. This was true not only for the common subject, but for the tributary kings who were still under the tutelage of Majapahit as well. So it is not surprising that by the end of the 15th century, nearly all the kings in the coastal areas of Java had been converted to Islam. Long before then, however, the Chinese had already recorded that the population of Sumatra in Aru, Samudra, Pidir and Lambri had already embraced Islam as far back as 1416.

The fall of Malaka to the Portuguese is an important turning point in the spread of Islam in the Archipelago. The fall of the sultanate led to an exodus of Muslim traders from Malaka to other areas, such as Acheh and the coastal areas of Java. Gradually, Acheh replaced Malaka as the centre of Muslim trade. The Javanese coastal cities also sprang back to life. The Achehnese disseminated Islam to the Minangkabau and to other areas in Sumatra. Javanese traders who were new converts brought Islam together with their goods to Maluku, then Makasar and Bugis. This way, Islam spread to the whole of the Archipelago.

The question of the origin of Islam in the Archipelago is still a matter of considerable debate. The general consensus is that Islam came from India; which part of India, however, is still the subject of contention among scholars. Some suggest Gujarat, others say Malabar, Coromandel or elsewhere in South India. Indonesian scholars, however, dispute this view, maintaining that Islam came directly to Indonesia from Arabia (Risalah: 265). S. Q. Fatimi, who undertook a study of Islam in Malaysia (i.e., the Malay Archipelago), was of the opinion that the Muslim communities of Arabia, Bengal, Persia and China all contributed to the spread of Islam in Malaysia (S. Q. Fatimi, 1963). Slametmuljana, on the other hand, propounded a different theory: Islam came to Java from China (Slametmuljana, 1968). A new book based on a dissertation submitted at the University of Indonesia supports this theory (Tan Ta Sen 2010).

Many theories have been proposed about the way in which Islam was disseminated in the Archipelago. The more significant ones are as follow:

(a) The trade theory, which contends that Islam was disseminated by Muslim traders who came to conduct business in the Archipelago.

(b) The missionary theory, which asserts that Islam was spread by Indian missionaries.

(c) The Sufi theory, which argues that Islam came to the Archipelago via the Sufis—a view put forward by A. H. Johns (1961a).[2]

(d) The political theory, which maintains that the kings of that era embraced Islam to win the support of Muslim traders. Thereafter, the general population followed their rulers and also converted to Islam.

(e) The anti-Christian theory, which proposes that Islam gained popularity in reaction to the arrival of the Portuguese in the Archipelago.

(f) The theory of Islam's innate appeal, which suggests that the Islamic doctrine of equality and brotherhood proved to be more attractive to new converts than Hinduism's divisive caste system.

All these theories have been discussed by a Filipino professor in a lengthy paper (Majul, 1962: 339-397).

Islamic Literature

What do we mean by the term "Islamic literature"? Some believe that Islamic literature must "bear Islamic values"; others maintain that Islamic literature has to be "based on incidents related in the Quran and Hadith and teach *tauhid* (the oneness of God)". If we used such a yardstick to evaluate classical Malay literary works, we would probably have to reject a substantial part of this literary heritage. A major portion of classical Malay literary works, including those which include stories from the Quran, contain many values that are in conflict with Islamic teachings. This can be better understood if we examine the history of Islamic expansion throughout the world. Islam as a religion gains a foothold in a particular region by converting its populace but is, at the same time, also influenced by the local culture. That is why when we talk about Islam, we usually talk about it as it pertains to a particular context, for example Islam in India, in Pakistan, in China, in the Malay world and so on. J. D Pearson in his *Index Islamicus*, a catalogue of Islamic writings published between 1906 and 1955, did not give an explanation as to what it is he meant by "Islamic", save only to say that the ambit of his index/catalogue covers those territories which have come under the dominion of, or were influenced by, Islam. Franz Rosenthal, in an article on "Literature" published in *The Legacy of Islam,* also did not elaborate on what he meant by 'Islamic' literature. However, one can gather from his discussion on the subject that what he meant by Islamic literature is simply literature written by Muslims (Schact, 1974). R. O. Winstedt in his famous book too did not attempt to define Islamic literature. Rather, he considered all works imported into the Malay world by Muslims as Islamic literature (or "Muslim legends") (Winstedt, 1969: 89).

From the above discussion, we can probably draw the conclusion that Islamic literature is a literature about Muslims and their pious deeds. Muslim Malay literature is the literature written in Malay by Muslims in this region.

---

2 See Tan Ta Sen, "'Chen Ho' penyebar Islam dari China ke Nusantara," *Kompas*, Jakarta, 2010.

Malay literature of the Islamic era has several distinctive features:

Firstly, it was written after the emergence of Islam and the creation of the Jawi script. Malay was the lingua franca of the region even before the arrival of Islam but developed rapidly after the advent of Islam. From being a spoken or colloquial language used for everyday interaction, it became a language of civilization, specifically Islamic civilization. It was through the Malay language that Islam, and concomitantly, literature with an Islamic bent, spread across the Archipelago. It is not an overstatement to say that the Malay language is veritably an Islamic language.

Secondly, a major part of the literary corpus belonging to this era consists of translations or adaptations of works written originally in Arabic or Persian. These translations or adaptations were carried out by two groups of people. The first group was made up of Malays who had gone to Arabia to study and subsequently stayed there. The second group were the merchants from South India who flocked to various ports all over the Archipelago during this period. The work produced by the first group consisted mainly of religious books, while the second produced predominantly narratives (*hikayat*) meant for entertainment. It is probably due to this reason that a German scholar once described Malay literature as a literature of trade, a literature that was conceived and was born in the company of merchants and traders. Local literary creations at the time were few and far between.

Thirdly, the identity of the authors of this period and the dates in which their works were originally written remain largely unknown. Nevertheless, there is evidence that these works were created after the arrival of Islam and the development of the Jawi script. In other words, Malay literature of the Islamic period can be deemed as being some of the earliest works of literature in the Malay language. These works were then translated into the myriad languages of the Archipelago.

As the authors and dates of these literary works are generally unknown, it is difficult to construct a historical timeline to delineate the development of this literature from beginning to end. Thus for this reason, R. Roolvink proposed that tentatively the best method to examine Malay literature of the Islamic age is to classify it into different genres or categories. Below are the five categories of Malay literature of the Islamic period discussed by Roolvink (*EI*, III, 1960: 1230-1235):

1. Stories from the Quran
2. Stories about the Prophet Muhammad
3. Stories about the Prophet's Companions
4. Stories about Defenders of the Islamic faith
5. *Kitab* Literature (scholarly books)

5.1 Stories from the Quran

These consist of stories about prophets or persons mentioned in the Quran. In the first century *hijrah* (the beginning of the Muslim calendar, marked by Prophet Muhammad's migration from Mecca to Medina in 622 AD), frequent reference was made to the existence of a group of people called *qass* (Arabic, plural: *qussas*), storytellers. Their task was to recite the Quran, and to study and interpret its meaning, in mosques throughout the Muslim empire. This practice continued for many centuries. It was only in the fourth century Hijrah that the stories of the Muslim prophets were compiled into a single *kitab*. The person who made this compilation was the famous translator Al-Thalabi, i.e., Abu Ishaq Ahmad ibn Muhammad al-Thalabi (died 1036). Not long after the publication of the book *Al-Thalabi,* stories about the prophets emerged in Persian and in other languages of Central Asia (Thackston, 1978: xiv-xvi).

However, the best-known book of stories about the prophets was the *Qisas-al-anbiya* which was compiled before the 13th century by al-Kisa'i, whose identity is still debated by scholars. Some believe al-Kisa'i was Muhammad b. Abd. Allah al-Kisa'i who lived during the caliphate of Harun Al-Rashid. This is denied, however, by the author of the entry on "al-Kisa'i" in the *Encyclopaedia of Islam*, who claimed that al-Kisa'i was unknown (*EI*, Vol. V, 1980: 176). Regardless of his true identity, al-Kisa'i is widely recognised as a storyteller *par excellence.* He certainly knew how to capture the attention of his readers and listeners. His sources were not limited solely to the Quran or its interpretations. He also drew inspiration from local stories and tales of fantasy such as those found in the *One Thousand and One Nights.* It is this compilation of stories about the prophets by al-Kisa'i that really popularised the genre.

Quranic stories are didactic in nature, that is, they are meant to teach moral lessons. These are "lessons for those with a discerning mind" and "guidance and blessing for the faithful" (Surat 12: 111). From these stories the followers of Islam learn what deeds will please Allah and earn His reward, and what deeds will incur His wrath and punishment. It is not an overstatement to say that the Quranic stories are the quintessential missionary literature. Characters mentioned in the Quran are all looked upon as champions of Islam who defended the concept of the oneness of God. Muslims frequently turn to these stories in the Quran as a source of guidance from which they can derive lessons. The prophet Joseph (Yusuf), known for his unshakeable faith and forgiving nature (he bore no grudges against his brothers, even though they tried to harm him), as well as the prophet Job (Ayub), who displayed fortitude in the face of Allah's gruelling tests of his faith, for example, are held in high esteem and regarded as exemplars.

The most famous Collection of Quranic stories in Malay is the *Kisah Al-anbiya.* Many manuscripts of this *kitab* are held in the Leiden, London and Jakarta libraries. Six manuscripts of the *Kisah Al-anbiya* can be found in the Central Museum Library of Jakarta (now the National Library). Four of them – the *Kitab Ahlu Tafsir* (v.d.Wall 66), the *Kisasul Anbiya* (v.d.Wall 67), the *Hikayat Fir'aun* (v.d.Wall 68) and the *Anbiya* (Cohen Stuart 122) – have been studied by the Dutch scholar, D. Gerth Van Wijk (Wijk, 1893: 239-345). However, it is not known who the authors were or when the manuscripts were written. All we know is that the *Kisasul Anbiya* was transcribed by an Encik Husain, a Bugis who lived in Kalang, Singapore; and that the *Hikayat Fir'aun* was transcribed by a Mr Mohammad Syam from Lingga. As for the *Suratul Anbiya,* the manuscript belonged originally to a certain Baharuddin, who lived in Gang Trunci, Kampung Norbek. There is a note on the first page stating that the manuscript took eight months to transcribe, accompanied by a gentle reminder to borrowers of the book not to stain the book and to return it to its rightful owner as soon as they have finished reading it. The fee for borrowing the book was ten cents a day. The book itself cost f.15.

Like the various stories known as *Hadis* (Traditions of the Prophet), the *Kisah Al-anbiya* is also prefaced with an *Isnad',* a list of names of the people who were responsible for transmitting the story from one person to the next. Among the names frequently mentioned in this list are

Abdullah ibn Abbas (died 687), Muhammad al-Qalbi, Ka'ab al-Ahbar (died 652) and Wahab ibn Malik and Sa'abi (died 1059).

Haji Azhari Khalid's translation of the *Kisah Al-Anbiya* from Arabic to Malay resembles the *Suratul Anbiya* (Cohen Stuart 122). It is highly likely that both of these works came from the same source. Unfortunately, the dates of translation and publication are not stated. What is mentioned is that the book was corrected by Muhammad Tahir al-Indonesia, a Malay scholar who lived in Egypt. Regardless, what is certain is that Haji Azhari Khalid's *Kisah Al-Anbiya* was very popular. It was repeatedly issued by many renowned publishers, such as Sulaiman Mari'i in Singapore, Darul Ma'arif in Penang, and Menara Kudus in Jakarta. According to Hamdan Hassan, Egyptian publishers of religious books, such as Mustafa al-Babi al-Habi wa Awladihidi Misra, also published an edition of the *Kisah Al-Anbiya* in 1348H or 1929AD (Hamdan Hassan, 1982: 72). Below is a summary of the manuscript published by Sulaiman Mari'i. In the summary, further references are made to another summary, written by D. Gerth van Wijk, of the Jakarta manuscript.

The story begins with the creation of the sky and the earth. According to the story, Allah formed the sky and earth from a white pearl he had already created. Firstly, he created water from the pearl. Then he created fire; the fire evaporated the water, turning it into steam and foam. From this cauldron of steaming foam, Allah created the sky and the earth. He next created hills to hold the earth in place. Through his divine will, the water too stayed in its place. He then created an enormous fish; a gigantic bull with vast horns sat on the back of the fish. And Allah placed the seven layers of the world on top of the bull's horns.

Next, Allah created animals to inhabit the Earth; he also created the sun, the moon and the stars to decorate the sky. He then created his throne, heaven and hell. He next created a bird and a handful of mustard seeds. When the bird finished eating the mustard seeds, it died. Then Allah created seventy men who lived in different eras on earth with the life of each one spanning 70,000 years. Thereafter Allah created a race of *jinns* to populate the earth; they were later wiped out from the face of the earth by Allah for having disobeyed his laws. This is followed by the story of the angel of death, Izrail (Azrael), who entreated Allah to allow him to go to earth to serve God there.

5.1.1 Adam

God wanted to create a human being to live on earth, so he commanded the angel Jibrail (Gabriel) to descend and take a handful of clay. Jibrail however was unable to carry out God's order, as were the angels Mikail (Michael) and Israil. Finally, Izrail agreed to perform the task. For this reason he was also given the task of taking the lives of Adam's progeny at the time of death. And so Adam's physical form was created. God breathed life into Adam's body and Adam began to live. God then created a horse that took Adam to the seven tiers of Heaven. All the angels prostrated themselves before Adam. Only the Devil (Iblis) refused, and he was subsequently banished from heaven.

Adam had no companion in heaven as there was no one like him. Feeling sad, he lay on his right side one day and fell asleep. Allah then created Siti Hawa (Eve), the mother of all mankind, from one of Adam's left ribs. When Adam woke, he saw a beautiful woman sitting by his side. Allah married them to each other and told them they could enjoy all the bounty of heaven, except for one thing—they were not to go near the *khuldi* tree. So Adam and Siti Hawa lived happily in heaven.

The story continues. Iblis was always looking for a way to deceive Adam. One day, Iblis managed to persuade the snake that guarded the gateway to heaven to take him to the khuldi tree. Iblis then sat on the tree and began to weep. This caused great consternation amongst the heavenly nymphs, who came to find out what was the matter. Siti Hawa came too. Iblis told them that he was crying because Siti Hawa would soon have to leave heaven. Iblis told her that if she wanted to stay, she would have to eat the fruit of the *khuldi* tree. Deceived by Iblis's words, Siti Hawa not only ate the fruit but persuaded Adam to do the same. As soon as they ate the fruit, all the finery and adornments covering their bodies suddenly vanished, leaving them exposed and naked. Scabs too suddenly appeared on Adam's body. They desperately tried to cover their modesty with leaves but to no avail. They ran around heaven like madmen. Consequently God then commanded Jibrail to cast them down to Earth. Adam landed in Serendib (Sri Lanka), while Siti Hawa arrived in Jeddah. Both Adam and Siti Hawa wept pitifully over the fate that had befallen them. Adam cried so much that his tears formed a river; Siti Hawa's tears became mascara and henna, and the tears that reached the ocean became pearls, which is why these accessories became customary adornments for women. One day, Jibrail came to ask Adam to perform the pilgrimage to Mecca. Adam and Siti Hawa were reunited at Mount Arafat. The couple wept tears of joy. All the angels in heaven wept too. Then Allah opened the curtains around heaven and Adam saw that the words "*La ilaha illah 'Ilah, Muhammad Rasul Allah*" (There is no God but Allah and Muhammad is His Messenger) were inscribed on each pillar of the divine throne. Then Adam entered the holy *Kaaba* and completed the pilgrimage. Next Jibrail took Adam to the Namer River, where Adam saw the souls of all his future descendants lined up in never-ending rows from east to west. Among them were prophets, saints and the God-fearing, as well as hypocrites, heretics and idolators. Allah then commanded the angel Hajarul Aswad to write down every agreement He had made with Adam. This covenant was then put inside the mouth of the angel Hajarul Aswad who was turned to stone. On Judgement Day, Hajarul Aswad would be turned back into an angel again and he would reveal who among mankind would go to heaven and who to hell.

The Prophet Adam returned to Serendib with Siti Hawa. One day, Jibrail brought Adam seven pieces of metal. He taught Adam how to make fire, forge metal, and sow wheat and cotton. Jibrail also brought an oxe to help Adam carry water. Then Adam made bread and, once it was baked, ate it with Hawa. Hawa set the leftover bread to one side. That is why to this very day, women save half of everything they have, and use the other half as they see fit. One day, a black mark appeared on Adam's forehead. The mark became bigger and bigger every day, until the whole of his body, except for his face, was black. Jibrail taught Adam how to fast. After three days, the black mark disappeared. Adam and Hawa's descendants were born in Serendib. The sons who were born first were married to daughters who came later.

Adam had a son called Kabil (Cain). Kabil was always arguing with Habil (Abel), as his pretty sister had been given to Habil, while he himself had to marry Habil's sister and she was not as pretty as his own sister. Their quarrel was overheard by Adam who ordered the two young men to each bring a sacrifice to a hilltop. "The person whose sacrifice is accepted by God is the one who is right," said Adam. God accepted Habil's sacrifice but Kabil was still not satisfied. He looked for a way to kill Habil. One day, while Habil was sleeping under a tree, Kabil struck him on the head, smashing his skull. He then surreptitiously buried Habil's body and went to look for Habil's wife, intending to take her for himself. Suddenly, the earth opened and swallowed Kabil up to his chest.

At Allah's command, angels descended and beat him to death. News of Habil's death reached Adam and Hawa. They went in search for his grave and, upon finding it, wept for two hundred years before returning to Serendib. Some time later, Adam's offspring asked him for money to begin trading. Jibrail brought a handful of gold and silver pieces from heaven and buried them on a hill. Those who had asked for money were told to go to the hill. "The one who reaps the most will profit the most," Adam told them.

5.1.2 Sis

One day, Adam wanted to taste the fruits of heaven. So he sent his son, Sis (Seth), to heaven to bring back the fruits. Not only was Sis granted the fruits of heaven that his father requested, he also received a heavenly nymph as his wife. Not long after this, Adam fell gravely ill and passed away, leaving this mortal world for the world to come. Sis was anointed to replace his father, Adam, as *caliph*, God's representative on earth. Sis's son, Arfus, succeeded him in due course. Arfus had a very beautiful daughter named Mahlila. She was so beautiful that people came from every land to admire her. When Mahlila passed away, her son, influenced by Iblis, made a likeness of her and showed the statue to anyone who wished to see it. People were so awestruck by the beauty of the image that they started to worship it. It became known throughout the world that people had begun worshipping idols.

5.1.3 Idris

Idris was originally known as Kharuj but because he was such an avid student of Allah's holy book, he became known by the name, Idris, derived from the Arabic word, *daras,* "to study". Idris was a pious servant of Allah. One day, the angel Izrail came to test his faith. Firstly, Izrail assumed human form and dared Idris to slaughter a goat they found grazing nearby. Then Izrail urged him to eat a bunch of grapes hanging on a vine. Despite his hunger, both times Idris refused to take what belonged to others. Idris then ate what Allah bestowed upon him. When it was revealed to him that he had been talking with the angel of death, Idris fainted, although only for a few minutes. He announced that he would like to experience death but did not want to remain dead; he wanted his soul to be brought back to his body, as it was not yet time for him to die, and moreover he still wanted to devote the rest of his life in the service of Allah. Allah then commanded Izrail to grant Idris's wish. Izrail took Idris's soul, leaving his body limp and lifeless only for a second. By the will of Allah, Idris was then immediately restored to life. When he revived, Idris asked to see heaven and hell. In hell, he saw hell-fire burning like a raging inferno, its huge conflagration of black and red flames creating an all-consuming, terrifying, thunderous roar. Idris fainted. When he regained consciousness, he was taken to heaven. There he saw two swift rivers; they were whiter than milk and sweeter than honey. On their banks stood trees with trunks of gold, branches of precious stones, and pearls for fruits. Idris prostrated in prayer and praise of Allah, Almighty and Exalted. Not long after this, the angel of death appeared and told Idris that it was time for him to leave heaven. Heaven, said the angel of death, is only for those who have died and passed through the travails of hell. Idris replied that he had already fulfilled this injunction and insisted on staying in heaven. Only God had the power to remove him from heaven, Idris maintained. So Allah decreed that it is "forbidden for any prophet to enter heaven before the last prophet, Muhammad, His messenger." Idris was thereafter taken to the seventh tier of heaven where he spent his days offering prayers and supplication to God. For his piety and devotion, Idris was held in the highest of esteem by all his descendants. Then Iblis urged them to build an idol in Idris's likeness so that they could pay homage and worship him every day. Thus Adam's descendants were led further astray from the true path, until God created Nuh (Noah) to teach mankind not to worship idols.

5.1.4 Nuh

The Prophet Nuh's real name was Syakrin. Because of his sorrow at his people's sinful idol worship, he was given the name Nuh (Noah). The story tells that although Nuh was chosen by God to preach Islam, he was relentlessly persecuted by his own people for the first forty years of his life. After years of missionary work, he had managed to convert only fifty people. One day, he publicly implored an assembly of his people to embrace the faith, but they violently rejected his message. They beat him so badly that he suffered injuries to his head and bruises to his thighs. Not long after, he attended a gathering of his tribe, only to have them hurl rocks at him. Even his wife thought him insane.

Despairing, Nuh appealed to Allah. Jibrail was sent to bring Nuh a seed from heaven. Nuh sowed the seed. For forty years he lived as a recluse in his own home, with little contact with the outside world. During this time, the seed grew into a massive tree. God then commanded Nuh to build an ark. He found four workmen who agreed to help him build the ark on the condition that Nuh find them a wife each. Nuh agreed to their request, though he wondered how he would fulfil his promise to them, considering that he had only one daughter. However, when he reached home, he found four beautiful young maidens waiting for him, all of whom looked exactly like his daughter. He also found that his horse, donkey and cat were missing. So, he had the four maidens married to the four workmen. After they had been married for a while, Nuh asked his sons-in-law about their new wives. One told him that his wife behaved like a donkey; another said his wife was fond of slapping and biting, just like a cat; another complained that when angered, his wife was prone to kicking and biting like a horse; his fourth son-in-law said that his wife possessed a maturity of mind, patience, and a flawless character. From their various accounts, the Prophet Nuh was able to discern which of the four girls was his own daughter.

Eventually, the ark was completed. All of Nuh's tribesmen came to see it and made fun of him. The non-believers even boarded the ark and defecated in it. One day, a man suffering from leprosy went up the ark to relieve himself. As he was climbing into the ark, he accidentally fell into the huge mound of human excrement and was cured at once. On hearing this, everyone who suffered some form of affliction came to the ark and took the filth home as a cure. Before long, the ark was clean again.

Soon after, Jibrail told Nuh to gather every plant seed and animal species—both wild and domesticated—and to load them onto the ark, together with all the household provisions he required. Nuh and his followers were also told to board the ark. His wife and wicked children refused to join him. Soon, rain fell from the sky and water gushed from holes in the earth. Before long, the flood waters covered the entire land; the hills were entirely submerged. The Prophet Nuh hoisted his sails, and by the grace of God, the ark began to float. Well into the journey however, the amount of human waste in the ark began to be overwhelming. Nuh went to the elephant and stroked its forehead; a pig emerged from its back and ate up all the excrement. Iblis, who had managed to stow away on the ark, imitated the Prophet Nuh. He rubbed the back of the pig; a mouse crawled out of the pig's snout. The mouse began to gnaw at the wood of the ark and destroy all the goods on board. To stop this, the prophet stroked the back of a tiger; a cat emerged and ate all the mice. That is why cats and mice are sworn enemies to this very day.

For seven months, rain poured from the sky and water gushed from the earth. Then, at the Prophet Nuh's command, the rain suddenly stopped and the floodwaters began to recede. When the waters subsided, the ark rested on top of Mount Judi. Nuh sent a duck out to find out if the flood had completely receded. The duck was so happy that it flew here and there, forgetting about the task it had been set. That is why the duck can no longer fly very far. So Nuh sent a dove instead. The dove performed its task perfectly. And that is why the dove has remained man's beloved friend to this day.

The Prophet Nuh disembarked from the ark and sowed all the plant and fruit seeds he had brought with him. All the seeds were accounted for, except one—the grape seed which Iblis had stolen. Iblis agreed to return the seed on the condition that he be allowed to water the grapevine with his own urine. The Prophet Nuh had no choice but to agree to this proposal. According to Muslim clerics, Iblis also sprayed the mature grapevine with the blood of pigs and dogs. That is why Muslims are forbidden by God from drinking wine and rice wine.

The Prophet Nuh then used the wood of the ark to build a mosque. Nuh subsequently had children, grandchildren and great-grandchildren, and repopulated the world with his descendants. When he was 1700 years old, he gathered his descendants and told them: "The world is like a house. We come in through one door and leave by another. But we must always keep our covenant with Allah." With these final words, the Prophet Nuh returned to the mercy of God.

5.1.5 Hud

The descendants of Prophet Nuh spread to every corner of the world. Soon mankind once again filled the whole earth. For seven hundred years, humanity was spared the pains of disease and death. They forgot about death and began to worship idols. God then sent the Prophet Hud to guide mankind back to the true path but his exhortations and warnings were ignored. Consequently, the crops began to fail and famine spread across the land. God instructed Prophet Hud to leave the country with his family, before He unleashed a violent tempest. The heathen laughed at Hud. By the will of God, violent winds blew through the country and destroyed the non-believers. Only the Prophet Hud and his descendants were spared. At the age of 460, the prophet passed away.

About one hundred years after the ferocious typhoon, Iblis emerged to once more lead mankind astray. He taught people to make idols and worship them. This incurred God's wrath and He sent a mosquito to destroy the idols. In addition, He also sent Prophet Saleh to the world.

5.1.6 Saleh

The Prophet Saleh came into the world to bring his people back to the right path by not worshipping any god but Allah. His people, however, demanded that he perform a miracle as a sign that he was indeed a prophet.

One day, he assembled all his people on a field. In the middle of the field stood a huge rock. As Prophet Saleh prayed, the rock began to scream, like a woman giving birth. After some time, a camel emerged from the rock. The moment it was born, the camel struggled to its feet, stood on the rock, and steadily grew bigger and bigger. By God's will, the camel became pregnant and gave birth to a baby camel. Suddenly, a well sprung up next to the rock. The camel came down from the rock to drink from the well and started to graze on the grassy field. Witnessing this miracle unfolding before their very eyes, Saleh's tribe was convinced and embraced the faith. The prophet warned them not to kill the camel lest they incur God's wrath. They were however allowed to drink the camel's milk which it seemed to produce in abundant supply. The excess milk that was not consumed was made into oil and sold. Proceeds from the sale of the camel's milk fats made Prophet Saleh's tribe very prosperous indeed.

Not long after, however, avarice crept into the heart of one of the members of the Prophet Saleh's flock. With the help of nine others, the traitor killed the camel. The baby camel managed to escape and vanished into the forest. Prophet Saleh then prophesied to his people that God would unleash his scourge upon them for their sin. Some defied his warning by stuffing their ears with cotton; others dug holes to hide in, all in the hope that they would not hear Jibrail's blood-curdling cry when he came for them. Their foolish attempts to save themselves came to nought. When the dreaded day arrived, Jibrail descended upon them with a thunderous roar and felled them all. The Prophet Saleh thereafter moved to another country. After some time, he passed away.

5.1.7 Ibrahim

The story of Prophet Ibrahim (Abraham) is preceded by an account of the birth of Namrud (Nimrod). This prelude is not found in the Singapore manuscript. While out hunting one day, the king of Canaan met a beautiful maiden, Saliha. The king killed Saliha's husband and took Saliha back to his castle, where he made her his wife. Some time later, Saliha gave birth to a horrible baby: its body was black, it was cross-eyed, and a poisonous viper protruded from its nose. The baby was given to a shepherdess to raise. The poor shepherdess however was so afraid of the child that she left him by the side of a river. A wolf took care of the baby until the shepherdess returned. As the baby was raised by a wolf, he was named Namrud. The boy grew rapidly. When he reached adulthood, Namrud killed his father and proclaimed himself king.

Time passed and Namrud became a mighty king. Many kingdoms and realms fell at his feet. One day, his soothsayers divined that a baby boy who was about to be born would destroy his kingdom. They also informed Namrud that this child had not yet been conceived. So King Namrud promptly issued a decree forbidding women throughout his kingdom from sleeping with their husbands. One night, Azir—Namrud's most trusted palace guard—was visited by his wife while he was on duty guarding Namrud. It was thus that the baby whose birth was much feared by Namrud, was conceived. The next day, the soothsayers announced to Namrud that the baby they had warned him about had already been conceived and was now in its mother's womb. Namrud then ordered that all pregnant women be forced to abort their babies.

Fearing that her as-yet-unborn son would be killed by King Namrud, Ibrahim's mother went and hid in a deserted cave. In due course, she gave birth to a very handsome baby boy; his face was so radiant it shone. Ibrahim's mother wrapped him in a cloth and, leaving him in the cave, returned home. After her departure, Jibrail came and placed Ibrahim's fist in his mouth. By God's Will, milk flowed from one of Ibrahim's fingers and honey from another. Three days later, Ibrahim's mother returned to the cave and was amazed to find that her baby was still alive. She bathed and cleaned the baby. Thereafter, she visited the cave every seven days.

Ibrahim soon grew and was taken home by his mother. One day, while the people were out in the town square celebrating a religious festival, Ibrahim entered their temple and destroyed all the idols he found there. When he was finished, he hung the axe he used around the shoulders of the largest idol which he had spared. Ibrahim was arrested and brought before Namrud. The crowd clamoured for Ibrahim to be burned alive. An area in the centre of the town square was fenced with rocks and filled with firewood. But through divine intervention, the raging fire cooled, while the firewood sprouted roots and leaves grew thickly around Ibrahim. Ibrahim sat on a throne brought from heaven by Jibrail and a spring gushed in front of him. Furious, Namrud ordered his soldiers to push the stone walls onto Ibrahim. The stones did not fall but remained suspended above his head like clouds. Rain began to shower from these clouds and extinguished the fire. Ibrahim returned to his mother.

God then commanded Ibrahim to travel to the kingdom of Syam. On the way, he stopped at Khazan, where Princess Sara chose him to be her husband. Sara was the prettiest princess in the kingdom and her beauty was unrivalled throughout the whole world. Before long, Ibrahim resumed his journey, accompanied by his wife. They reached a country called Ukhmus which was ruled by an evil king who had no compassion for any of God's creatures. The tyrannical ruler moreover could not lay his eyes on another person's beautiful daughter or wife without coveting her for himself. When Ibrahim learnt of this, he asked Princess Sara to hide inside a chest. His attempt to conceal his wife failed. Ibrahim was imprisoned and Princess Sara taken before the king. The king was delighted to see the beautiful Princess Sara. He stepped forward to approach her. But by the will of God, the king's feet were rooted to the ground and his hands turned into stumps. Three times he reached out to touch her but each time he tried, his hands became stumps. The king repented. Ibrahim was promptly released from prison and Princess Sara received an array of noble clothes together with a 12-year-old slave girl whom they named Hajar (Hagar). Ibrahim then left Ukhmus and soon arrived at an oasis in the Palestine desert. People started to gather there in large numbers and a settlement soon grew. Ibrahim preached the true religion to them. Subsequently Jibrail brought a rock from heaven and built a mosque from this rock. To this day, that mosque is known as the Baitul Maqdis, the mosque of Jerusalem.

Ibrahim was sent by God to Babil (Babylon) to command Namrud to embrace the Faith. Not only did Namrud refuse to accept Islam, he declared war against God. He built a flying chariot so that he could shoot an arrow at God. Jibrail deflected the arrow and it hit the whale that was carrying the earth. The arrow was then returned to Namrud. Thinking that he had defeated God, Namrud was elated. Once again Ibrahim came to the Namrud's palace to try to convince him to submit to the Faith. Enraged, Namrud assembled a vast army to fight Ibrahim. God sent an army of mosquitoes to attack Namrud's army. The mosquitoes entered the brains of Namrud's men and sucked their blood dry. Many of Namrud's men died. Namrud escaped and sought refuge in his palace. The chief of the mosquitoes pursued Namrud, entered his brain through a nostril, and sucked all his blood. And so Namrud too died. His people subsequently converted to Islam. Ibrahim then returned to the Baitul Maqdis.

Princess Sara was very happy to see Ibrahim again. She gave him Hajar. Ibrahim and Hajar enjoyed themselves together. It was God's will that the glow on Ibrahim's face should be transferred to Hajar's face. Princess Sara's jealousy made her very angry. She summoned Hajar, pierced her earlobes, and placed gold ear-rings on her as a mark that she was a slave, but this only served to make Hajar look even more attractive. This incensed Princess Sara even more. She asked Ibrahim to banish Hajar to a desolate place where no one could live or any vegetation grow. Ibrahim was forced to comply with his wife's wish. Hajar was heartbroken and wept. Nine months later, Hajar gave birth to a handsome baby boy, Ishmael (Ismail). After giving birth, Hajar went to look for water but there was not a drop to be found. Unable to find any water, she returned to check on her baby, only to leave his side again to resume her fruitless search. Seven times she walked back and forth from where her baby was, looking for water, but without any success. (This is the reason why it is obligatory for pilgrims on the Hajj to walk back and forth seven times between the hills of Safa and Marwa, to remind them of the ordeal that Hajar endured.) Hajar then saw a spring bubbling from the heel of her son's footprint in the sands. As soon as she removed a rock that was blocking the mouth of the spring, water began to gush out from the ground. Hajar called the spring "*zam-zam*", which means "overflowing". Soon afterwards, a shepherd came and asked Hajar for permission to set up camp near the spring. In exchange for water from the spring, the shepherd promised to give Hajar ten bushels of whatever vegetables, crops and livestock he had. Before long, other shepherds arrived. Then more and more people came and settled there. One day, Ibrahim felt a great longing to see Hajar and his son, Ismail. So he went to that barren and desolate place in the desert and saw that it had become a thriving and prosperous settlement. Hajar recognized him at once and washed his hair. Ibrahim then picked up his son, and hugged and kissed him. Hajar told him everything that had happened to her. Shortly after, Ibrahim went back home to his wife, Princess Sara.

One day, Prophet Ibrahim had a dream over four consecutive nights. On the first three nights, he dreamed that God instructed him to sacrifice two hundred camels. On the fourth night, God commanded him to sacrifice his son, Ismail. With a heavy heart, Ibrahim felt compelled to carry out God's order. He told Hajar that he was going to take Ismail out to a feast. After Ibrahim left, Iblis came to tell Hajar that Ismail was about to be killed by his father. Hajar did not believe that a father would kill his own son. Iblis persisted by disclosing to her that Ibrahim was carrying out God's commandment. To this, Hajar replied, "If it truly is Allah's commandment, then no one should disobey it." Iblis then told the same thing to Ismail. Instead of instilling fear in the boy, Ismail was unperturbed; in fact he even urged his father not to hesitate and to carry out God's order at once so that Iblis could not lead them astray. When they arrived at Mina hill, Ibrahim asked his son to throw stones at Iblis each time he tried to lead them astray. Three times Iblis tried to persuade them not to obey God's commandment, and three times they hurled stones at him. That is why to this day, Hajj pilgrims throw stones at three pillars on the hill in Mina, each pillar marking a spot where Ibrahim and his son defied Iblis. Ibrahim gazed at his son's face. He was moved to see his son's handsome and radiant face and was distraught that the boy had to die at thirteen. However, Ibrahim steeled himself to carry out what God had ordered and made preparations to sacrifice the child. He tied his son's legs and hands together, as one would a cow that was about to be slaughtered. Jibrail suddenly appeared and brushed his wings against Ibrahim's knife, rendering it so blunt that it could not hurt Ismail. Jibrail also brought a sheep from heaven to be sacrificed in place of Ismail, as God was satisfied with the piety and devotion Ibrahim had shown.

Soon afterwards, God commanded Ibrahim to travel to Mecca to establish the direction that Muslims should face when they prayer, and to build a house of worship beside the zam-zam well. After some time, the house of worship, named the Ka'abah, was completed. The Prophet Ibrahim then prayed that God would bless all who visited the Ka'abah.

As time passed, the Prophet Ibrahim and Princess Sara grew old and were past child-bearing age. They spent their days in pious devotion worshipping Allah. Once, Ibrahim fasted for seven days and seven nights. At the end of the seventh day, two handsome youths visited them. Princess Sara had a calf slaughtered for the visitors. But their guests did not partake of the food; instead each sat with his arms tightly folded across his chest. Ibrahim and Sara then learned that their guests were angels, on their way to punish the debauched and heretical people of the Prophet Luth (Lot). They had stopped at Prophet Ibrahim's house to tell him that he and Princess Sara would soon be blessed with a child.

The Prophet Ibrahim wanted to see Allah's punishment of the apostates and asked if he could go with them. Jibrail granted his wish and together they set out on their journey. Before long, they arrived in Sodom[3], their journey having been greatly shortened, as the angel responsible for holding the earth in place had shrunken the land at Jibrail's request, so that they could arrive there more quickly. They then made their way to Prophet Luth's home. Within a short time, news had spread all over the country of the arrival of the Prophet Ibrahim and the two young men. The licentious inhabitants of Sodom surrounded Luth's home and, in their lust, tried to take the handsome young men away. The Prophet Luth refused to hand over his guests. Jibrail came to Luth's aid, and brushed the hands and faces of the baying crowd with his wings. In an instant, their hands were turned into stumps and their faces became featureless, devoid of noses and eyes. This completely terrified the crowd, and they asked Prophet Luth for forgiveness.

Prophet Luth then prayed for them, and their hands and faces became normal again. Even so, they were far from repentant. Instead, they wanted to kill the Prophet Luth. They surrounded his house and closed the city gates to prevent him from escaping. However, by clinging onto Jibrail's wing, Prophet Luth and his family—except for his unfortunate wife—managed to escape. Allah then punished the people of Sodom. His angels rained fire and brimstone upon them; Jibrail split the earth open and threw them into the abyss, sending the Sodomites to an agonizing death. The Prophets Ibrahim and Luth fainted when they saw this. Jibrail revived them with a gentle stroke of his wings, and said: "Had there been even one among them who was righteous, the Lord God Almighty, Creator of the Universe, would have spared that person."

Subsequently, Prophet Ibrahim returned to his homeland. He became even more devout in his worship of Allah. Princess Sara conceived and nine months later, she gave birth to a beautiful baby boy. Ibrahim named him Ishak (Isaac).

---

3   The denizens of Sodom were sexual deviants—its men were homosexuals, the women were lesbians.

One day, Prophet Ibrahim was walking in an oasis which was as flat as it was empty. He thought, "If only there was some water so I could cleanse myself before I pray." By the will of God, a spring bubbled forth. The Prophet Ibrahim then said to himself, "There is no one as noble and yet as poor as I am." Then Jibrail appeared and said that Prophet Muhammad was nobler than him; and that a man who lived on a hill in Canaan was poorer than him. And so Prophet Ibrahim went up the hill in Canaan, where he met a very tall man sitting on a rock, singing praises of Allah. The man was the Prophet Hud. When he learned the purpose of Ibrahim's visit, Hud took him to his home on an island in the middle of the sea. When they met a tiger that lived in a cave on the island, it bowed its head in respect to the Prophet Ibrahim. Eventually, they arrived at Prophet Hud's dwelling: his only possessions were a chipped bowl, a tattered mat, and a stick made of dried wood. The Prophet Hud explained that he used the chipped bowl to take water for his ablutions before prayers; the old mat was his bed; and the stick was the implement he used to grow the fruits he ate. Then the Prophet Ibrahim was taken to a cave where he found a man lying down on a golden bell. The man appeared to be asleep but was actually already dead. Over his head was a golden sign on which was written, "I am a mighty king who once ruled over a vast empire. A thousand kingdoms have I vanquished and a thousand princesses have I taken as my wives; but after enjoying all the pleasures that life has to offer, in the end, death awaited me. Oh all ye kings and powerful men, let not yourselves be deceived by this ephemeral world." Ibrahim wept contritely when he read these words. Hud told Ibrahim to take as many precious stones as he wished from the cave. Ibrahim declined, however, saying that even if he did, he would have to leave them behind on this earth one day. Ibrahim then asked the Prophet Hud to pray for him and ask Allah to forgive him his sins. The Prophet Hud declined, saying that he had been praying for forty years but his prayers had not yet been answered. Ibrahim asked him what he had been praying for. Hud replied that he had prayed that he might meet the Prophet Ibrahim. Ibrahim then introduced himself and the two prophets shook hands. Hud was overjoyed to learn that his prayers had finally been answered and he became Ibrahim's disciple. After some time, Prophet Ibrahim returned to Syam and continued to devote himself to Allah.

Meanwhile, Ismail had a son, Kidan, who had grown to be a young man and later became the king of Arabia. During this same time, Ibrahim's other son, Ishak, also grew, married and had two sons, Esau and Yakub (Jacob). Esau became king of Byzantium while Yakub stayed with his father, Ishak. Prophet Ibrahim continued to live to a ripe old age. One day, he called his sons and all his descendants around him and told them to observe three basic precepts: firstly, do not become too engrossed in thinking about what you will eat tomorrow; secondly, do not fail to observe the fasting month; and thirdly, give priority to the tasks of the afterlife over those of this world. Not long after this, the Prophet Ibrahim fell ill and passed away. He was buried in the mosque at Baitul Maqdis in Jerusalem.

5.1.8 Ishak

After the death of the Prophet Ibrahim, the Prophet Ismail asked that he be bequeathed a small portion of the inheritance left by his father. The Prophet Ishak (Isaac) refused to share his inheritance with his half-brother, saying that he was the son of a concubine, whereas he, Ishak, was the legitimate son and, moreover, of royal blood. The angel Jibrail came and predicted that the last prophet, Muhammad, the greatest prophet of all, would be born of Ismail's line, while Ishak's descendents would become Jews and Christians. He also added that Ishak's line would become slaves.

The Prophet Ishak wept as he contemplated the fate of his descendants. He cried for twelve years until he became blind. He then beseeched God for forgiveness. His sins were forgiven. Jibrail came to the Prophet Ishak and said that among his descendants would be the Prophet Musa (Moses) and his people would be blessed with the Torah, a divine book which would contain God's teachings. Thereafter, the Prophet Ishak's vision was restored and he was able to see again.

5.1.9 Yakub and Yusuf

The story tells that the Prophet Ishak loved his son, the Prophet Yakub (Jacob), very much. One day, the Prophet Yakub prepared a lamb dish for his father, and for this he was rewarded with a blessing. His younger brother was hurt that his father did not give a blessing to him as well and harboured a grudge against the Prophet Yakub, even planning to kill him. On his mother's advice, Yakub sought refuge at the house of his mother's brother, Liyan. Liyan had two daughters. The Prophet Yakub fell in love with the younger daughter. As a dowry, Liyan asked Yakub to perform the Hajj. After completing his pilgrimage to Mecca, Prophet Yakub was married to Liyan's elder daughter. Then he went on the Hajj again, after which he married Liyan's younger daughter, Rahil, whom he had first loved. He also took his wives' two female servants as his wives too. The Prophet Yakub had twelve children from his four wives. Yahuda, his son from his first wife, and Yusuf, from his second, are the most best-known of these twelve children.

Yusuf was an extremely handsome young man. His radiant good looks were like the rising sun and unrivalled throughout the world. A white glow emanated from a spot between his eyebrows, while a shimmering black glow sparkled from a spot on his right cheek. He had a fair complexion, lustrous wavy hair, a slender neck, a broad manly chest, a slim waist, strong, muscular calves and a sharp prominent nose. And when he laughed, the sparkle from his teeth lit up his whole face so that he was bedazzling to behold.

Yusuf was his father's favourite. One day, Yusuf dreamt that while he was playing with his friends, the wind blew his playmates' staves into the sky, whereas his own staff remained rooted to the ground, but grew longer and longer until it reached the sky. Later on, he had another dream in which the sun, the moon and eleven stars prostrated themselves before him. The dream was interpreted as a sign that Yusuf's parents and his eleven brothers would, in the future, bow down before him. When Yusuf's brothers heard about his dreams, they wanted to kill him.

One day, Yusuf's brothers invited him to play with them in a field known to be inhabited by dangerous wild animals. In the middle of the field, they found a well and pushed Yusuf into it. They then told their father that Yusuf had been eaten by a tiger. The Prophet Yakub did not believe them; he ordered his sons to catch the tiger and to bring it to him. Yusuf's brothers captured a tiger that happened to be prowling in the field at that time and immediately took it to the Prophet Yakub. To their amazement, the tiger began to speak and denied having eaten Yusuf. The tiger said that it had actually come from Egypt to visit its family. The Prophet Yakub was utterly dejected when he heard this. Even a tiger loves its own family, but his own children had dared to kill their own innocent brother. The Prophet Yakub wept so hard he became blind.

One day, a merchant, named Malik Ibn Dair, rescued Yusuf from the well. Yusuf's brothers, who happened to be there at the time, told the merchant that Yusuf was a servant of theirs who had tried to escape. The merchant bought Yusuf from his brothers for 18 *dirhams*. When they reached Egypt, the merchant took Yusuf to a market to be sold. All the traders at the market stood with their mouths agape when they saw how handsome Yusuf was and wanted to buy him at once. In the end, Yusuf was sold to the highest bidder, an Egyptian vizier named Kitfir (Pitifar, Potiphar, in other manuscripts), for a very high price. Kitfir had no children and treated Yusuf as if he were his own son. He also asked his wife Zulaikha to treat Yusuf with great respect. And so Zulaikha tenderly looked after Yusuf. However, as time went by, her love for him became physical. Zulaikha tried to seduce Yusuf many times, but to no avail. One day, Zulaikha called Yusuf to come to her newly-built chamber in the palace. When he arrived, Zulaikha was already waiting for him, dressed in her most beautiful clothes. She beckoned Yusuf to sit next to her and asked him to make love to her. In return, she promised to reward him with gold and silver. Zulaikha's behaviour shocked Yusuf. Finally, she pulled Yusuf onto her bed and flung off her clothes. Upon seeing her loveliness, Yusuf was overcome with desire. At that very moment, fortunately, he saw a sign from God and was thus saved from temptation. Yusuf immediately rose from the bed and tried to flee. Zulaikha chased him and grabbed his clothes, ripping them in the process. At that very moment, Kitfir appeared. Zulaikha lied, saying that Yusuf had tried to assault her. Enraged, Kitfir wanted to kill Yusuf. An infant who had witnessed what had truly happened miraculously spoke up from its cradle and testified that Yusuf was innocent, as his clothes had been ripped from the back. Kitfir forgave both his wife and Yusuf and asked them not to tell anyone else what had happened. Not long after, however, the ladies of the royal court and the nobles' wives somehow learned of the scandal and began to treat Zulaikha with contempt. Zulaikha wanted revenge. One day, all the ladies were invited to a party and each given an orange and a small knife. As the courtiers began to peel the oranges, Zulaikha called Yusuf into the room. Immediately the women forgot what they were doing. They were so busy staring at Yusuf that they did not realise that they were cutting their own fingers! Zulaikha's husband learned of her deed and had Yusuf thrown into jail.

While Yusuf was in prison, Jibrail came to him to give him solace. The angel taught him to interpret dreams and administer the law. One day, two young men, Saki and Khabaz, were brought to Yusuf's prison cell, accused of trying to poison the king. Both of them confided to Yusuf about a strange dream which Yusuf helped to interpret. The dream signified that Saki would eventually be released from prison by the king, whereas Khabaz who would be impaled. Yusuf's interpretation was proven to be true. Before Saki was freed from prison, Yusuf made him promise that he would tell the king that Yusuf had been falsely accused by Kitfir. Once he had been released, however, Saki forgot his promise. For seven long years, Yusuf remained in prison. One night, Malik Rian, the king of Egypt, dreamed he saw seven fat cows being eaten by seven lean cows, and seven green stalks of wheat split open by seven withered stalks of wheat. No one could tell the king the meaning of his dream. Saki suddenly remembered Yusuf and his ability to interpret dreams. Yusuf agreed to interpret the king's dream, on the condition that the king agreed to investigate why he had been imprisoned. Zulaikha and all the ladies of the court were summoned. Zulaikha admitted her guilt and told the court how she had lusted after Yusuf despite her marriage to Kitfir. Yusuf was then released. He explained the dream to the king: Egypt would enjoy seven years of prosperity, followed by seven years of famine. Yusuf was appointed as the king's vizier, in the place of Kitfir who had died two years earlier. Yusuf then prepared the kingdom for the seven years of hardship it would have to endure. The story tells that Zulaikha approached Yusuf for help during the famine. Although she had wronged him, Yusuf gave her all the help that she needed. One day, Jibrail appeared before Yusuf and asked him to accept Zulaikha, as they had already been married in heaven. Zulaikha however declined the match, insisting that she was too old and sickly to be married to him. At that very moment, Jibrail appeared and stroked her face with a *syajarah* leaf; she was immediately transformed into her beautiful younger self and cured of all her illnesses. Despite her having been Kitfir's wife for many years, she was still a maiden as their marriage had never been consummated.

Many people fled to Egypt in search of food during the famine, including Yusuf's brothers. The first time they sought help from him, Yusuf gave them enough food to tide them over in their time of need. The second time, Yusuf detained Benjamin (his blood-brother) in an attempt to force an apology from his brothers for what they had previously done to him. Yusuf showed them a letter bearing the seal of Yahuda, his half-brother; this left them with no choice but to admit that they had indeed sold their brother Yusuf into slavery. Yusuf prayed to Allah to forgive his siblings for their sins and, to show that he had made his peace with them, he embraced and kissed them. Yusuf invited the Prophet Yakub, their father, to come to Egypt and be reunited with all of his sons. Yakub had lost his eyesight as a result of crying for so long over his beloved son Yusuf, but his vision was fully restored. Not long after this, the Prophet Yakub finally died. Time passed and Yusuf too reached the end of his life. Before he died, he reminded his people not to worship any other God but Allah. He also prophesied that one day his people would be oppressed by a cruel ruler, but that they would be saved by Prophet Musa (Moses). Prophet Yusuf then breathed his last. His brothers quarrelled among themselves over where he should be buried as they each wanted him to be laid to rest in their own village in order to obtain God's blessings. In the end, they all agreed to throw Yusuf's body into the river Nile, in the hope that the Prophet Musa would one day find his remains.

In one tale, it is recounted that the Prophet Musa searched everywhere for the body of Prophet Yusuf while leading the Israelites out of Egypt, but could not find it. A blind hunchbacked woman told the Prophet Musa that she would reveal where Yusuf's body could be found, if the Prophet Musa promised to restore her eyesight and stay with her. Prophet Musa was at first hesitant to meet the woman's conditions until a commandment came from God, telling him to fulfil the woman's wishes. Finally, Prophet Yusuf's body was found and brought to Baitul Maqdis, to be laid to rest near the grave of his father, the Prophet Yakub.

5.1.10 Musa

One night, Pharoah dreamed that he saw a tree rising up into the sky. Suddenly, the tree fell to earth and settled in the middle of a field, where it began to sprout thick foliage, providing shelter for many creatures. Pharoah was shaken by this dream and asked his astrologer to interpret its meaning. His astrologer foretold that a boy from the tribe of Israel would soon be born, who would one day destroy Pharoah's kingdom. On hearing this, Pharoah issued a decree forbidding the men of the Israel tribe from approaching their wives. But one night Hail, the wife of Pharoah's favourite court minstrel Amran, longed for her husband and went looking for him in Pharoah's palace. By God's will, all the palace guards had fallen asleep and all the lights were extinguished. Thus Musa was conceived. While Musa was still in his mother's womb, the court astrologer again warned Pharoah about his existence. Pharoah then ordered that all pregnant women in his realm be forced to abort their babies and all their husbands be imprisoned.

Nine months later, Hail gave birth to a fine baby boy. One day, one of the king's servants, who had been charged to spy on pregnant women and those who had just given birth, paid her a visit. Fearing that her newborn son would be discovered, Hail hid him in a pot of boiling water and closed the lid. She decided it was better to kill the baby herself, rather than have him forcibly taken away and killed by Pharoah. As soon as the king's spy left, she lifted the lid, to find the baby sitting up in the pot and not hurt in the least. She prostrated herself and gave thanks to Allah. Suddenly, she heard a voice telling her to put her baby in a box and cast him into the waters of the Nile. By divine will, the box was found by Asyiah, Pharoah's wife. Asyiah's daughter held the baby on her lap. As soon as she did, the disease on her hand was suddenly cured. Pharoah too liked him and named the child Musa. He then called for a wet nurse to breastfeed Musa. However, the baby refused milk from all the women who came to feed him. It was only when Hail arrived that he began to suckle. She was paid 300 dinars a month to look after Musa.

One day, the infant Musa was brought before Pharoah. Musa slapped Pharoah's face and pulled his beard. The searing pain travelled to Pharoah's brain; he was so enraged that he wanted to kill Musa. His wife, Asyiah, placated him by saying that Musa was only a child and did not know what he was doing. She suggested that if gold and burning embers were to be placed in front of Musa, he would in all likelihood reach out to touch the embers. Pharoah then ordered that some gold and hot embers be placed in front of Musa. Musa reached out to grab the embers. When he felt the heat of the burning embers, he stuffed his hand into his mouth. Though Musa's tongue was burned, his hand was unscathed. According to the story, Musa's tongue was burned because he had once called Pharoah "father"; his hand, however, was unharmed because it had slapped Pharoah and pulled his beard.

Musa turned eight. One day, he punched a Copt, killing him. Pharoah wanted to arrest him, but Musa fled from Egypt. When he reached a well, he saw many people drawing water. Musa helped two young girls and their father, the Prophet Syuaib, asked them to invite Musa to their home. Syuaib offered Musa one of his daughters in marriage if he would work for him for the next eight years. Musa gladly accepted the offer and married Safur. As a wedding gift, the prophet gave Musa a staff he had received from heaven. After the wedding, Musa became a shepherd; his job was to tend and feed the sheep. One day, while Musa was watching over his father-in-law's sheep near a riverbank, he fell asleep. As he slept, a group of serpents attacked his sheep. Musa's staff immediately changed into an enormous serpent and devoured the other serpents.

The Prophet Musa tended Syuaib's sheep for ten years. One day, Musa asked his father-in-law for permission to take his wife and their flock on a journey. Syuaib agreed and, as a reward for giving Musa his blessing, his vision and physical strength were restored. So the Prophet Musa set out with his wife and his flock. Their journey took them in and out of forests and across all sorts of terrain. Soon, Safur began to give birth in the midst of a terrible thunderstorm. Darkness quickly surrounded them. The Prophet Musa ran to find firewood. He saw a light in the distance. Thinking that it was a fire, he walked towards the light. When he reached the top of a hill, he saw that the light actually came from a brightly burning bush. The Prophet Musa suddenly heard a voice declaring: "I am your God and the God of the entire universe." The voice ordered him to take off his sandals as he was standing on sacred ground. As soon as he had removed his sandals, they turned into a scorpion. Musa was then told to drop his staff; it immediately turned into a snake. He was terrified. The voice told him to pick up his staff again and commanded Musa to go to Egypt to oppose Pharoah. Musa was also told that his newborn son would be raised by a heavenly nymph and his sheep tended by a tiger. Musa was also allowed to take his brother Harun (Aaron) with him as his minister.

One day, Musa and Harun presented themselves before Pharoah. They asked the king to recite the Muslim profesion of faith in Allah and his prophet Muhammad, and promised him that God would grant him untold earthly rewards if he did. Musa performed a miracle, but Pharoah still refused to embrace Islam. Pharoah then summoned his sorcerers to pit their skills against Musa. The king's sorcerers conjured up many snakes but when Musa cast his staff down, it turned into a huge serpent and swallowed all of the sorcerers' snakes. The sorcerers immediately prostrated themselves before Musa. Then, Musa hit a tower which was being constructed on Pharoah's orders; the tower collapsed, killing all the labourers. Pharoah refused to change his mind. He brutally murdered Asyiah, his faithful wife, who had become a Muslim. Pharoah ordered the arrest of Musa and the slaughter of the Israelites.

God sent a series of calamities. First, a famine destroyed much of the population, then a deluge swept over Egypt, followed by swarms of locusts, weevils and all sorts of pestilence which blighted all the fruits and crops in the land. Egypt was beset by an plague of frogs and finally, every morsel of food turned into blood. Pharoah's people could not endure any more suffering and begged him to accept Islam. Pharoah was still unmoved. One day, Musa asked his tribe, the Israelites, to borrow gold, silver and beautiful clothes from Pharoah's people and the Copts. That night, angels descended from heaven and killed the Copts. With the Copts gone, Musa then led the Israelites out of Egypt towards the Red Sea. As soon as Pharoah heard of their flight, he commanded his army to pursue them. When Musa and the Israelites reached the Red Sea, Pharoah and his army were close behind them. Musa struck the sea with his staff; the waters parted, creating a path by which the Israelites could safely cross to the other side. When Pharoah's soldiers arrived, they attempted to cross the sea by the same path that the Israelites had used. But while they were in the middle of the sea, the waters suddenly closed around them and drowned them, and Pharoah as well, who was at the head of the army. Musa and the Israelites returned to Egypt. He confiscated Pharoah's wealth and distributed it among the Israelites, making them all very rich from the spoils. Musa continued to remain true and steadfast in his devotion to Allah. One day, Jibrail instructed him to bring Safur and his two daughters to Egypt.

He was then told to wear clothes that Jibrail had brought for him from heaven, and taken to Mount Tursina (Sinai). As soon as he set foot on the mountain, the mountain suddenly soared into the heavens. When he reached the top of the mountain, Musa prayed that God would manifest himself. A multitude of angels appeared in terrifying forms, shouting loudly. Musa was commanded to look at the mountain. He fell to the ground and his body disintegrated. Mount Tursina also broke apart. The whole world shook. The sky seemed to be collapsing. Jibrail held on to Mount Tursina to prevent it from completely crumbling away. Musa finally regained consciousness. He begged Allah's forgiveness for asking to see Him. "Verily no creature can see His glorious being." God then bestowed the Torah upon Musa. When he returned to Egypt, Musa was shocked to find his people worshipping a golden calf. Enraged, he threw down the stone tablets on which the Torah was inscribed and they broke into pieces. Samiri, who had influenced the Israelites to build the idol, was expelled from Egypt. Many of the Israelites fell ill. Many more died under an avalanche of rocks. The golden calf was cast into the river. Whoever drank water from the river swelled up, their livers cracked and they died. The Israelites returned to the true path.

There was once a man named Karun, who was a skillful and talented goldsmith. He became very wealthy. However, the richer he became, the greedier and more arrogant he was. When asked to give charity in the service of God, he responded by saying that he had amassed his wealth not because of God's blessing but due to his own skills and enterprise. No dervishes were invited to attend his wedding. The guests consisted of only the very wealthy. One day, God commanded Musa to demand Karun to pay his tithe to the poor. Again and again Karun tried to postpone his debt. Finally, in a bid to stop Musa pestering him, Karun paid a pregnant woman to slander Musa. Fortunately the woman did not dare lie in the presence of Musa. Musa was angry with Karun and prayed that Allah would destroy Karun and his kinsfolk. In answer to his prayers, the earth opened up and swallowed Karun and his followers.

One part of the story also tells of the meeting between the Prophets Musa and Khidir. On three occasions, Khidir tested Prophet Musa's patience with his strange behaviour. The first time the Prophet Khidir broke the wooden boat in which they were travelling. Next, he abducted and killed a child. On the third occasion, he helped mend the fence belonging to two orphans that had fallen into disrepair. On each of these occasions Musa rebuked Khidir and each time he was told to be patient. Finally Prophet Khidir explained the reason behind each of his strange deeds. The boat belonged to ten poor people and was their sole means of livelihood. Had the boat remained in good condition, it would certainly have been confiscated by the cruel and avaricious king of the country they were visiting. Now that their boat had been damaged, the men would be left in peace. The child had been killed for the good of his parents. Allah would bestow upon them someone more innocent and filial than he was. Perhaps they would be blessed with a daughter; she might marry a prophet, who would lead his people on the right path. Underneath the fence belonging to the two orphans lay gold and silver, left by the orphans' father. Had the fence fallen into disrepair, the treasure would surely have been stolen by others. That was why he had repaired it. Thus did the Prophet Khidir explain his seemingly strange and inexplicable actions.

5.1.11 Ayub[4]

The Prophet Ayub (Job) was a devout and wealthy man. He always helped the poor and those in need. One day Iblis came to Allah and said that the only reason why Prophet Ayub gave thanks to Allah was because God had given him enormous wealth. If his wealth were taken away, he would surely stop praising Allah. Iblis then sought God's permission to test Ayub's faith.

First Iblis destroyed all of Ayub's livestock, then he ruined his orchards. Finally, Ayub's beloved children lost their lives. The Prophet still thanked Allah for His blessings. Iblis then

---

4 This story is not found in the *Kisasul Anbia*. However, Mrs A. Ibrahim has written a summary of a manuscript kept at the National Museum of Indonesia Jakarta entitled "Hikayat Nabi Ayub Dimurkai Allah" (The Tale of Prophet Ayub Who Incurred the Wrath of Allah). See Edwar Djamaris 1973, *Singkatan Naskah Sastra Indonesia Lama Pengaruh Islam* (A Summary List of Manuscripts of Classical Indonesian Literature With An Islamic Influence), pp. 16-20.

asked permission to test Prophet Ayub's faith by subjecting him to physical suffering. Again Allah granted Iblis permission but warned him not to damage Ayub's liver or his tongue. Iblis then proceeded to torture Prophet Ayub. Iblis breathed into Prophet Ayub's body and made him itch all over. The more he scratched, the more he itched. Eventually, the whole of his body became infected. He was covered in blood and pus, and his wounds were filled with crawling maggots. The stench was revolting. He was driven out from his village, accompanied only by his faithful wife, Rahmah.

According to the story, while the Prophet Ayub was suffering from this serious affliction, Iblis approached Rahmah and told her that the meat from a goat slaughtered without invoking Allah's name, cooked in pig-fat and palm-wine, would cure the Prophet Ayub's condition. Rahmah believed Iblis but the Prophet Ayub realized the deception and scolded her. On one occasion, Rahmah cut off her hair to buy food for herself and her husband, as no one was willing to employ her anymore. Iblis whispered in the Prophet Ayub's ear that Rahmah had lost her hair as a punishment for her unfaithfulness to him. Inflamed with jealousy, the Prophet Ayub vowed that he would lash his wife a hundred times if he ever recovered from his illness. For seven years the Prophet Ayub suffered from the vile disease. Finally, he prayed Allah to punish him if he had sinned; if he had not, he asked God to pour out His grace and blessings upon him. As soon as he uttered this prayer, a group of clouds suddenly descended and he heard a voice saying that he had been forgiven his sins and his wealth would be restored once more. The voice also told him to touch the ground with his foot and to bathe in the spring that would emerge from his footprint. The Prophet Ayub did as the voice commanded. By the will of God, his affliction was cured. Rahmah was overjoyed. They hugged each other and praised Allah's greatness. Suddenly the Prophet Ayub remembered the oath he had made—that he would whip his wife a hundred times if he recovered from his disease. Without hesitation, he reached for his whip and began to beat her. Allah, in His omnipotence and compassion, softened his blows and Rahmah felt no pain at all. Both husband and wife thereafter led a happy life together. Although they were as wealthy as before, they were even more devout and more willing to help those in need.

5.1.12 Yunus[5]

The Prophet Yunus (Jonah) was inspired by Allah to tell his people to worship Him. They did not listen to him. Eventually, Yunus warned his tribe that as Allah was about to punish them, they should leave their homes at once. This warning too went unheeded. The day soon arrived. A group of dark clouds covered the city and the children's skins turned black. Yunus's people looked for him everywhere but could not find him. They regretted not having listened to his warning, and decided to repent, asking for Allah's forgiveness. Allah had mercy on them and forgave them.

Meanwhile, the Prophet Yunus returned to the city, only to find that none of the city-dwellers' skins were black, as the revelation had predicted. Yunus began to fear for his life, as according to the law of that country lying was a crime punishable by death. The Prophet Yunus fled and took refuge on board a ship. The ship was becalmed in the middle of the ocean. The Prophet Yunus announced that the ship had run into trouble because there was a sinner on board. But who could

---

5   The tale of Prophet Yunus is the last story in the *Kisasul-Anbiyah*; its storyline also differs from the one here. See D. Gerth van Wijk, op. cit. p. 575.

it be? No one knew. They decided to put the matter to the ballot: the person whose name was drawn would be cast into the sea. Yunus's name was drawn three times and he was consequently thrown overboard. A large fish came and swallowed him, eventually leaving him on dry land. Jibrail then appeared and explained that his people had been spared Allah's punishment for they had repented and had agreed to worship Him. The prophet continued on his journey and met a boy who told him that he hailed from Yunus's own tribe. The Prophet told the boy he was Yunus. The boy later related his meeting with the prophet to the king. The king did not believe the boy and wanted to kill him for lying, but the earth and the trees testified that the boy had told the truth. The boy's life was spared and in time he became king.

5.1.13 Elias[6]

Ajab, King of Baalbal, was an idolator. His wife, Isabil, was cruel and had no qualms about killing anyone she disliked. On one occasion she even had a friend of her husband, Masdaki, killed and his beautiful garden seized.

The Prophet Elias (Elijah), grandson of Prophet Harun, denounced Isabil for her wicked ways in the presence of the king. The king was so enraged, Elias had to flee for his life. He hid in a remote, inaccessible mountain. The king's son contracted a mysterious illness that could not be cured by any of the idols the king worshipped. The king's wise men suggested that their prayers to their idols were ineffective because Elias was still alive. King Ajab then summoned his guards to look for the Prophet Elias. The Prophet Elias told them that the king's son had not long to live and urged them to embrace Islam. The king's men returned to the palace in great fear. The second time, King Ajab sent fifty soldiers to capture Elias, but all of them were consumed by a fire. Finally, on his third attempt, King Ajab sent a group of believers to find him; only then did Elias agree to return to the kingdom. When he arrived, the king's son had already died. King Ajab was overcome with grief. The Prophet Elias escaped once more to his hiding place in the mountain.

Eventually the Prophet Elias became bored living in the mountain and returned to his own country. Upon his return, he stayed in the home of Prophet Yunus's mother. Yunus was still a baby. One day, Yunus fell ill and died; the Prophet Elias brought him back to life. On another occasion, the Prophet Elias prayed to Allah for power over the rain. Allah answered his prayers. For three long years no rain fell; the crops withered and died and many people perished from hunger. Elias himself barely managed to survive; he lived off food brought to him by birds. On still another occasion, the Prophet Elias cured his namesake, Elias, a widow's son. From then on, Elias became a faithful companion of Prophet Elias.

After three years, Prophet Elias went to the people of Israel and called on them to worship the One God. The king of the Israelites agreed to do so only if Prophet Elias would make rain fall from the sky. The Prophet Elias prayed and a heavy shower of rain suddenly fell from the sky. The Israelites soon turned back to worshipping idols. On seeing this, the Prophet Elias prayed that Allah would take him to heaven. Soon afterwards, the Israelites were attacked by their enemies. King Ajab and his wife Isabil were killed in the garden they had taken from Masdaki. Their bodies were left there to rot and no one buried them.

---

6   This story is not found in the *Kisasul-Anbiyah*.

5.1.14 Daud

In time the Israelites became more and more self-destructive; they committed adultery and drank alcohol. They also resumed their war against the Amalik. This time they were defeated. The Amalik confiscated the Israelite symbol of their sovereignty—the Ark of the Covenant. The Amalik tried to destroy the Ark but could not, neither fire nor axe could harm it. When they took the Ark into their temple, the temple collapsed and the idols inside fell to the ground. Finally the Amalik decided to get rid of the Ark by tying it to the back of a wild buffalo and releasing the creature into the forest.

Not long after this, a new king, named Talut, was chosen to be ruler of Israel. He was the only one who could hold the sword of heaven in his hands. He also brought back the Ark of the Covenant. The Israelites did not heed Talut's advice and drank water from the river which Allah had forbidden; as a consequence, their stomachs became as big as the belly of a pregnant woman. Only three hundred and three people remained faithful to their covenant with Talut.

Among the enemy was an indomitable commander called Jalut (Goliath). King Talut promised half his kingdom and his daughter to whomever could defeat Jalut. The Prophet Daud (David) killed Jalut, with three stones he picked up in the middle of the road. However, King Talut broke his promise. He did not hand over half his kingdom. He refused to marry his daughter to Daud, because Daud was dark-skinned and ugly, with eyes like those of a cat. In the end, he relented and allowed Daud to marry his daughter. Even so, the king tried to kill Daud several times, but he himself died during one of these attempts. So Daud was crowned king in his place. According to the story, Daud's voice was most melodious. When he recited the Torah, water would stop flowing and wild beasts would cease what they were doing in order to listen to him. Daud was granted the Book of Psalms and also became an excellent ironsmith.

Daud asked Allah to test him as He had tested the prophets before him. One day, while Daud was sitting at home, a bird entered his house. He chased the bird and eventually found himself in a garden where a beautiful maiden was washing her hair. Her name was Batseba. He knew that she already had a husband but that their marriage had not formally been solemnised. Iblis persuaded Daud to send Batseba's husband, Uria, to fight in a holy war; Uria died a martyr. After his death, Daud took Batseba to be his wife. The marriage produced a son, the Prophet Sulaiman (Solomon).

One day, two men came to Daud and asked him to help settle a dispute. One of them asserted that his only sheep had been taken by the other man, who already had ninety-nine sheep. Daud then said that if this was indeed true, then the first man had truly been betrayed. The moment Daud said those words, he realised his own mistake. He already had ninety-nine wives and yet he had still taken Batseba. Uria was indeed an unfortunate man and Daud had betrayed him. Daud wept. He then went to Mount Tursina and, weeping, prostrated himself before Allah. His body was covered by his tears. For forty days and forty nights he neither ate nor drank. Jibrail sent him to Uria's grave, to beg for his forgiveness. At first, Uria refused to forgive Daud. But later, on Jibrail's advice, Uria forgave him. Daud returned home. Every day he prayed the set prayers, promising to fulfil Allah's laws so that no one would want to follow their base desires or cause injury to others. When it came to the observance of the law, his son Sulaiman, was wiser than the father.

5.1.15 Sulaiman

The Prophet Daud returned to the eternal world from this impermanent world. So Prophet Sulaiman became king of a vast kingdom. All creatures, including mankind, *jinn*s and wild animals, came and bowed before him. He could understand the languages of the birds and animals. Even the wind served him, by carrying his carpet wherever he wanted to go.

One day, the hoopoe bird told Prophet Sulaiman about Queen Balkis who ruled the vast kingdom of Saba. Her palace was massive. Twice a day, she would worship the sun. Prophet Sulaiman sent an envoy to ask her to embrace Islam. The princess discusssed this with her ministers and decided that she would put Prophet Sulaiman's wisdom to the test. And so, she sent her envoy to Prophet Sulaiman with many gifts of gold and silver. The prophet was asked to differentiate between the boys and girls in a group of children who were all dressed in the same way, as well as determine which of a pair of horses was male and and which was female. The Prophet Sulaiman was able to solve these problems at once. Princess Balkis then visited the prophet herself. Before she arrived, *jinn*s carried her palace to Prophet Sulaiman's palace. The princess was awestruck by the Prophet Sulaiman's greatness. The prophet then married her and she became a Muslim.

One day, the wind carried the Prophet Sulaiman to an island. He met a king in the middle of the island and killed him, taking the king's daughter as a wife. But the woman could not stop thinking of her father; even sweet words, cuddles, or being carried around by her maids, failed to comfort her. Because he loved his wife so much, the Prophet Sulaiman allowed her to make a statue of her father and to worship him. One day, when the Prophet Sulaiman had to undertake a particular task, he gave his ring to a woman to mind. He did not know that the woman was a *jinn*, Astar Khi. After receiving the ring, Jin Astar Kih assumed the prophet's throne. The prophet was not allowed to return to his kingdom. He walked to the Baitul Maqdis mosque in Jerusalem, and prayed there for three days and three nights. Then he continued his journey until he reached a fishing village. He stayed with a fisherman and worked for him. His payment was two fish a day. The fisherman's daughter was attracted to Prophet Sulaiman. And so, the girl and Prophet Ibrahim were married.

After some time, a *jinn* loyal to Prophet Sulaiman began to wonder if the person on the throne was really the prophet, as his behavior had changed so much. The "king" hid all the holy books and he imposed forms of punishment that were contrary to Islamic law. The *jinn* knew that a non-Muslim *jinn* could not tolerate hearing the holy book being recited. One day, the loyal *jinn* deliberately read the holy book in front of Astar Khi. Shocked, Astar Khi leapt into the air and threw the Prophet Sulaiman's ring into the sea. A fish swallowed the ring and the prophet eventually received that fish as his wages. Thus the Prophet Sulaiman recovered his lost ring and resumed his throne.

The prophet continued buiding the mosque his father, the Prophet Daud, had left unfinished. When it was almost time for him to die, Sulaiman sat on his throne, holding his staff. Jibrail came and took his soul but no one knew. A year later, the staff disintegrated due to the action of termites; only then did people realize that the Prophet Sulaiman had passed away.

5.1.16 Armia and Aziz

The Prophet Sulaiman's son, Prophet Armia, diligently reminded his people to avoid evil but they ignored him. One day, the King of Hindustan led his army against the Israelites. The terrified Israelites gathered in the mosque in Jerusalem. Armia asked them to recite the Torah. As they did so, a strong wind came and blew away the Hindustani soldiers and their elephants. But the people of Israel soon returned to their wicked ways.

One day, the King Raham met a beautiful woman and they began to live together. She soon became pregnant and gave birth to a child. However, she did not want to look after the baby and left him in a temple. A dog found the baby and took care of him. One day, the baby's mother came to the temple and discovered that her baby was still alive. She took the boy home and named him Bakht Nasar, "the idol's good fortune". Bakht Nasar grew up to be very strong, although he was also extremely ugly. The other children were afraid of him. One day, the Prophet Armia visited Bakht Nasar and made him promise that, he would look after Prophet Armia and his descendants. Bakht Nasar took a job as the chief warden of a prison. One day, he led a prison revolt, which toppled the king. Bakht Nasar assumed the throne and made himself the new king. Other countries soon fell under his rule. One day, Bakht Nasar attacked the Baitul Maqdis in Jerusalem. The terrified Israelites asked Prophet Armia for help. The prophet advised them to pray and read the Torah in the mosque. By the grace of God, Bakht Nasar's soldiers ran away and he himself retreated to his own country.

After a while, Bakht Nasar made another attempt to invade the Baitul Maqdis. The Prophet Armia and his family were absent from Jerusalem at the time. The prophet produced the letter of agreement made between himself and Bakht Nasar. Bakht Nasar had great respect for the prophet. According to some interpretations of the story, had the Prophet Armia been in the city during the attack, Bakht Nasar would never have won. However, because he was not there, Bakht Nasar defeated Baitul Maqdis quite easily; his army killed seventy thousand Israelites, burned all the copies of the Torah, and pillaged the city's great wealth.

The next story tells of Aziz. One day, God asked him to leave the desert and go to the Baitul Maqdis, as not even a single person there could recite the Torah. On the way to the city, Aziz ate a piece of fruit he had found and fell asleep. When he awoke, he found that his donkey, which he had tethered to the tree, had become a pile of bones. Aziz was told that he had slept for a hundred years. By the grace of God, the donkey revived and carried Aziz to Jerusalem. Aziz called on the Israelites to return to the true faith and worship God; he also taught them to read the Torah. Before long, the Israelites who had been imprisoned by Bakht Nasar returned to Jerusalem. Bakht Nasar was killed by one of his own guards.

5.1.17 Zakaria and Yahya

After the death of the Prophet Aziz, the Israelites returned to their sinful ways until Allah sent the Prophets Zakaria and Yahya (John) into the world.

The Prophet Zakaria was very old but had no children. He constantly prayed to Allah that he might be blessed with a virtuous son who could to take his place and lead a life of devotion to Allah. The prophet's wife became pregnant and gave birth to a son they named Yahya. Until he was three, Yahya constantly wept; he was never happy and never played with other children. When asked why he behaved like that, he replied that Allah had created him as he was and never told him to play or enjoy himself.

Despite his advanced years, the Prophet Zakaria constantly warned the Israelites against committing sin. Angered, they conspired to kill him. One day, the Israelites followed Zakaria. He stopped at a tree and suddenly vanished. Iblis told the men that the prophet had entered the tree and asked them to cut it down. The prophet died, leaving this transitory world for a better one. When Prophet Yahya heard of his father's death, he refused to leave his room. Day and night, he wept and worshipped God.

One day, a woman came to the Prophet Yahya, and asked to be allowed to marry her brother-in-law. The Prophet Yahya told her that such a marriage was forbidden by the law of God. The woman returned home and invited a large group of people to eat and drink at her house. When they were drunk, she asked them to kill the Prophet. But even after he had been beheaded, the prophet kept repeating "It is forbidden. Forbidden". The woman disregarded the judgement; a wind blew her into the middle of a field and she was eaten by two tigers.

5.1.18 Maryam and the Prophet Isa

Although Amran and his wife, Janah, were old, they had never had any children. Each day, Janah prayed for a child who would worship God. She became pregnant and promised to give the child to the temple so he could completely devote himself to God. "But what if the child is a girl?" her husband asked. Amran died shortly afterwards and Janah gave birth to a beautiful baby girl whom she named Maryam. Allah promised that Maryam and her offspring would be protected from Iblis' temptations and evil schemes. One day, Janah took Maryam to the temple and asked the elders to take care of her, so that she could devote her life to the worship of God. The elders quarreled because each of them wanted to be her guardian. They finally agreed to settle the matter by throwing their pens into the river. The person whose pen floated would have the right to raise Maryam. All the pens sank, except for the one that belonged to the Prophet Zakaria. And so Maryam was raised by the Prophet Zakaria. He taught her both secular and religious knowledge. When she turned twelve, the Prophet Zakaria built her a mosque. She stayed there, fasting during the day and praying at night. Each day the Prophet Zakaria brought her two cakes to eat. One day, he forgot to bring her food. Angels visited her from Heaven, bearing fruit. She grew and began to menstruate. This made her sad. The Prophet Zakaria told her she should stop fasting and praying for seven days. After that, he asked her to bathe in the river. Seventy angels came to bathe her. Jibrail appeared before Maryam in the form of a young man. He told her that she would become pregnant, then took a handful of earth and blew it into her mouth. Maryam became pregnant and the community sent a trustworthy woman to investigate the circumstances. The baby popped his head out of her belly and announced that he was the Prophet Isa, the spirit of Allah.

After nine months, nine days and nine hours, Maryam was ready to give birth. She was sent to an arid place which had not seen water for a thousand years. But when Prophet Isa came into the world, a spring gushed forth and a date palm, which had been dead for one and a half years, sprouted leaves and bore fruit. However, the Israelites were angry and wanted to kill Maryam as she had given birth to a child out of wedlock. When the Prophet Isa saw the Israelites arrive with the intention of killing his mother, he stood up and coughed. His cough could be heard for a vast distance. Everyone was shocked. The Prophet Isa explained that he had been created to pray, pay the tithe, and do good in Allah's name. The Israelites then recited prayers in God's honour.

When the Prophet Isa grew, his mother sent him to study with a holy man. One day, his teacher taught him how to recite the alphabet. The Prophet Isa asked his teacher to interpret the alphabet. The holy man became angry and wanted to beat him. Isa calmed the man and explained the meaning of the alphabet to him. Next the Prophet Isa was sent by his mother to learn how to dye cloth from a dyer. One day, when the dyer was not at home, the Prophet Isa put all the fabrics into a vat full of black water. When the dyer returned and saw what had happened, he rolled on the ground and wept, as he was sure that all the fabrics had been ruined. But when the owners came to collect their fabrics, Isa was able to give them exactly what they wanted. A Jewish woman said she wanted cloth dyed green, then later changed her mind and wanted white. The Prophet Isa became angry and called the old woman a monkey. She immediately turned into a monkey.

When the Prophet Isa reached puberty, Allah taught him various kinds of knowledge. One day, God commanded him to go to the land of Jil Kaf. He was accompanied by his former teacher. As he walked, hills bowed down before him, and river banks closed so that they could pass across. The king of Jil Kaf was willing to accept Islam, if the prophet would show him a miracle. And so Isa cured lepers and restored sight to the blind. The king wanted his dead parents brought back to life. The Prophet Isa was able to fulfil this request too. As a consequence, the king and his ministers all entered the faith.

One day, the Prophet Isa told his mother that the world was transient and only the world to come was eternal. He invited her to worship with him on a hill. Another time, the Angel of Death came to take his mother's life. The Prophet Isa was very sad and asked God that he be allowed to speak to his mother in her grave. She told him that they would meet again in heaven.

Later, God commanded him to visit a saint on an island. The saint was dying and Isa was to bathe his body, pray for him and bury him when that moment came. The prophet performed all of these duties perfectly. Then Jibrail sent him to another island, a larger island. Here, he met a woman whose son was blind, mute and deaf. The Prophet Isa cured the young man and he was able to see, speak and hear. Isa asked the young man to present himself before the king and tell the king to recite the words: "*La ilaha illa Allah, wa Isa ruh Allah*". (There is no God but Allah, and Isa is the Spirit of God.) The king was furious and killed the young man; Isa immediately restored him to life. The young man was again asked to present himself to the king, and once more he was killed, his body burned, and his ashes scattered in the wind. The Prophet Isa prayed and the young man's ashes were reunited. His life was immediately restored and he looked even more handsome than before. He appealed to the king a third time. The king and his ministers finally accepted the Prophet Isa's teachings. The king also married his daughter to the young man. Before long, the young man became king.

One day, Iblis visited the Prophet Isa. Isa asked him what things could destroy a man. Iblis replied that miserliness, negligence and alcohol were all dangerous. Iblis also revealed that he had once given Isa some fruits and the prophet had subsequently forgotten to perform his prayers. Prophet Isa then gave his solemn promise to Allah that he would not think of food in the future.

A Jewish priest visited the Prophet Isa, wanting to see him perform a miracle. The priest challenged the prophet to make a clay bird come alive. The prophet did and the priest was converted. On another occasion, members of the Hawarion tribe asked for food from heaven. The Prophet Isa brought food down from the sky but insisted that it only be served to the poor. The rich abused the prophet and insulted him. He warned them of Allah's retribution, but they were not afraid. Finally, the prophet prayed that they be punished; the men and their wives were turned to swine and ran wild.

The Jews plotted to kill the Prophet Isa. They followed him wherever he went. One day, when the prophet entered a certain house, Jibrail came and took him to heaven. It was God's will that a Jewish man in the house was made to resemble the Prophet Isa and the Jews killed him instead. The moment he died, his face was restored to its original appearance. The murderers were filled with regret because they had killed one of their own people.

This completes my description of the contents of the *Kisasul Anbiya*. The text contains many additions not found in the original Arabic source, Al-Kisa'i's *Qisas Al-anbiya* (Ismail Hamid, 1983: 94-98). According to Hamdan Hassan, who has studied many of the manuscripts, the Royal Asiatic Society's copy of the *Kisasul Anbiya* is the best available text. The manuscript contains a number of other interesting additional stories and insertions. Firstly, it begins with the "*Hikayat Nur Muhammad*" (Tale of the Light of Muhammad), which is then followed by the story of the creation of the universe. And before the manuscript ends with the story of the Prophet Yusuf, there is a story of the King of Tabang who was so touched by the remarkable character of Prophet Muhammad that he wrote a will that was to be taken to the prophet after his death (Hamdan Hassan, 1990: xxvii-xxviii). These various additions to the manuscript point to the possibility that other stories of the prophets also existed in the Archipelago, in particular the *Sejarah Nabi-nabi* (History of the Prophets), by Al-Thalabi (Hamdan Hassan, 1990: xxxiv).

Nevertheless, there can be no doubt that Azhari Khalid's translation of the *Kisasul Anbiya* was the most popular source for tales about the various prophets in the Archipelago, and the major influence on similar works that were written in the region. The *Kisasul Anbiya* was also used as a form of missionary literature and played an important role in the spread of Islam in the Archipelago. It was translated into several other local languages. Its Javanese version, the *Serat Anbiya* or *Tapel Adam,* was a popular text in religious schools and was considered to be of great intellectual benefit.

Apart from the *Kisasul Al-anbiya,* which tells the stories of all the prophets, there are also chronicles which recount the lives of individual prophets, such as the *Hikayat Nabi Yusuf, Hikayat Zakaria* and the *Hikayat Nabi Musa,* to name a few. Judging from their summaries, the *Hikayat Nabi Yusuf* (v.d. Wall 100) and *Hikayat Zakaria* (v.d. Wall 104), which are held by the Central Museum in Jakarta, are similar in content to the stories of the prophets Yusuf and Zakaria summarised above (Edwar Djamaris, *Singkatan Naskah Islam).* The only tale with a slight difference is the *Hikayat Nabi Musa*. The *Hikayat Nabi Musa* does not portray Musa's struggles against Pharoah. Instead it tells of the death of the prophet at a relatively young age, as he grieved his wife's passing. His son, Abdul Maya, later became a gallant and fearless warrior (Ismail Hamid, 1983: 54).The one text which is very different, however, is the *Hikayat Raja Jumjumah,* which tells of the Prophet Isa.

5.1.19 *Hikayat Raja Jumjumah*

The *Hikayat Raja Jumjumah* (Tale of the King of Jumjumah) is never mentioned prior to the 19th century, according to Winstedt, although adaptations of this hikayat have been found in the Sundanese, Achehnese, Persian and Hindi languages and may possibly be earlier. In 1823, an English translation of this hikayat was published in the *Asiatic Journal* (294-296).

A large number of manuscripts of this hikayat are held in various libraries in Jakarta, Leiden and London. There are three versions of this hikayat in Malay. One is called the *Hikayat Maharaja Ali* and is said to have a similar plot to the *Hikayat Bispu Raja*. (Ricklefs, 1977: 142). Another is held in Singapore and is a lithographed manuscript, entitled the *Hikayat Raja Jumjumah*. Below is a summary of that last text.

One day, the Prophet Isa was walking through a desert in Syam when he stumbled upon a skull that had been bleached by the sun. He prayed that the skull might be able to speak so that they could have a conversation. His prayer was granted. The skull said that that he was King Jumjumah, a powerful and wealthy king who had once ruled over Syam. Many other great kings were his vassals and sent him tribute. With his untold wealth he built refuges for the poor and provided them with food and amenities. For four hundred years he ruled over his realm. Then one day, he suddenly fell ill.

Even the most skilled physicians in the land could not cure him. After several days, the angel of death came to take his life. Other angels assisted the angel of death to pin down the king's neck, legs and hands, so that he could neither move nor speak. His mouth was filled with molten copper. He was then soundly beaten about the face. The soul left his body. After his burial, he was plunged into the thick black flames of hell. Next, he found himself standing alone in a vast empty field. The two recording angels, Munkar and Nakir, appeared and asked him to recount all his earthly deeds. The two angels were so terrifying that they looked like ferocious tigers ready to pounce on their quivering victim. When they spoke, tongues of fire came from their mouths. "Never mind about the pain they might inflict; just the sight of these angels is enough to send everything in the seven layers of heaven and earth trembling." The king was then asked: "Who is your Lord? Who is your Prophet? What is your religion? And where is your grave?" He could not give a satisfactory answer to any of these questions. As a result, the angels crushed him until every bone and sinew in his body was broken. Then he was taken to witness the terrible punishments that await those who disobey Allah. He also saw the four thrones to the right and left of Allah's own throne that await those who have earned God's favour. Then he was thrown into hell. His swollen and bloated body became bigger than any mountain in Syam. He was so large that if someone were to ride a winged horse around him for three days and three nights, that person's journey would still not be finished. He was dressed in clothes made from a type of hide that attracted all sorts of snakes, scorpions and centipedes; the reptiles crawled over his body, biting and stinging him, as he screamed in pain. Then he was hung upside down. Finally he was released by the angel Zabaniah but not before the angel had disfigured his face with fire. He was fed a type of fruit that was full of thorns and shaped like a pig. He was given molten copper to drink; the liquid burned his mouth and incinerated his innards. Then the angel Zabaniah hurled him into a pit full of snakes, scorpions and centipedes, and a river filled with crocodiles.

Nothing and no one could save him from the scourge of hellfire or the ravages of the snakes and crocodiles except the deeds of charity he had committed in his lifetime. In hell he saw the punishments that would be meted out to sinners who neglect their daily prayers, who do not pay the tithe, who drink alcohol, break their promises, play forbidden musical instruments, and engage in excessive profitmaking. Among the wrongdoers were women who had been unfaithful to their husbands, or disobedient, had asked for a divorce or aborted their babies. Seeing the horrors of Allah's punishments, King Jumjumah then begged for Allah's forgiveness and acknowledged the Greatness of God. The Almighty then forgave him his sins and commanded the angel Zabaniah to release the king from Hell. This is the story of the bleached skull. The skull subsequently asked Prophet the Isa to pray to Allah that he might be brought back to to life so that he could spend his days worshiping God. The prophet agreed; he covered the skull with a piece of white cloth and, by God's grace, King Jumjumah was restored to his former humanity. The king returned to his kingdom and recounted his amazing story to his ministers. He also announced that he no longer wished to be king. Instead he lived in an ordinary house and spent the rest of his days fasting and praying, begging Allah to forgive him for all his sins. Some people say King Jumjumah lived for eighty years; others say forty. Still others say he lived only forty days.

The above is a summary of the lithographed manuscript held in Singapore. The story in the final part of the Jakarta Museum manuscript (Bat. Gen. 228) is somewhat different again. In this version King Jumjumah spent a further twelve months in his mother's womb before being reborn, not as a king but as a commoner. In this new life, he was pious and devoted to the service of Allah, as he sought forgiveness for all the sins he had committed in his previous life. He regularly visited the Prophet Isa. One day, at the prophet's request, he recounted to a congregation of fellow believers his experiences in hell so that they would know the terrible punishments that await sinners in the afterlife. Sixty years later the angel of death came and claimed his life. This time he was taken to heaven and rewarded with all the blessings and gifts that heaven has to offer, and given the most beautiful clothes. The manuscript ends with a call to all Muslims to fulfil their religious obligations as prescribed by Allah.[7]

5.2 Stories of Prophet Muhammad

One of the Pillars of Islam is the belief in Allah's Messengers. As the *khatam al-anbiya*, the Seal of the Prophets or the Last Messenger, the Prophet Muhammad is the chosen prophet who is held in the highest of esteem by Muslims. He is regarded as a paragon of virtue; his life and deeds are considered exemplary. It is therefore not surprising that the stories of Prophet Muhammad have always been very popular.

These stories can be divided into three categories. The first category consists of biographical accounts of his life from the time he was born until the time of his death. These stories have probably originated from the biographical *Sirah* literature written and compiled after his death, although Sirah literature is not the only source of the Prophet Muhammad story. The stories of the Prophet Muhammad are regularly intermingled with legends and myths that glorify the much-

---

7 A Romanised Malay transliteration of the Jakarta Museum manuscript by Jumsari Jusuf was published in *Manusia Indonesia*, Vol. 5, Nos. 4, 5 & 6, pp. 389-415.

loved and highly venerated prophet. There are only two *hikayats* in the Malay language that tell the whole life story of the prophet, namely the *Hikayat Nabi* and the first part of the *Hikayat Muhammad Hanafiah*. Other *hikayats* give accounts of a single incident or period in the prophet's life; for example, the *Hikayat Nur Muhammad* narrates the story of his birth, and the *Hikayat Nabi Wafat* recounts the circumstances leading to his demise.

The second type of stories depicts the miracles performed by the Prophet Muhammad. These stories also originated from the *Sirah* as well as from the better known *hadis* (utterances, deeds and teachings ascribed to the Prophet). These stories too aim to glorify the exalted status held by Prophet Muhammad as the Last Messenger of God. Among these *hikayats* is the *Hikayat Mikraj* which relates the story of Prophet Muhammad's night journey from the Masjid Al-Haram, The Sacred Mosque, in Mecca to Al-Aqsa Mosque in Jerusalem and his ascension to Heaven. Other examples of stories of this kind are the *Hikayat Bulan Berbelah* and the *Hikayat Nabi Bercukur*.

The third category is known as "the *maghazi* story", a genre that chronicles the Prophet Muhammad's military feats and conquests in his quest to spread Islam. These stories emerged soon after the prophet's death and quickly gained popularity. They are often memorised and recited for the moral lessons that can be derived from them.

The dates of the Prophet's battles can usually be determined, except for those he fought at Badar and Khandak. The *Hikayat Raja Khandak (Tale of King Khandak)*, written in Malay, tells the story of a king named Khandak who had a son named Badar; it was probably written as a result of the uncertainty and confusion over the dates of these two wars. Another battle, the Battle of Uhud, was the source of inspiration for the *Hikayat Raja Lahad (The Story of King Lahad)*. Most of these battle stories, however, are fictitious or hail from the Malay world itself.

Besides the above three categories, mention should also be made of tales that tell stories of the Prophet and his family, such as the *Hikayat Nabi Mengajar Anaknya Fatimah (Tale of Prophet Muhammad Teaching His Daughter Fatimah)*. In this *hikayat*, the Prophet reminds his daughter not to disobey her parents and her husband, as disobedience to one's parents and husband is equal to disobedience to Almighty God. The *Hikayat Nabi Mengajar Ali (Tale of Prophet Muhammad Teaching Ali)* also contains the Prophet's teachings on *syariat* (law), *tarikat* (spirituality), *hakikat* (truth) and *ma'rifat* (knowledge). We shall proceed with a discussion of the following five *hikayats* or tales of Prophet Muhammad:

(i) *Hikayat Nur Muhammad* (Tale of the Light of Muhammad)

(ii) *Hikayat Bulan Berbelah* (Tale of the Split Moon)

(iii) *Hikayat Nabi Bercukur* (Tale of the Shaving of the Prophet)

(iv) *Hikayat Nabi Wafat* (Tale of Prophet Muhammad's Death)

(v) *Hikayat Muhammad Hanafiah* (Tale of Muhammad Hanafiah), Part 1.

5.2.1 *Hikayat Nur Muhammad*

The *Hikayat Nur Muhammad* (Tale of the Light of Muhammad), also known as the *Hikayat Kejadian Muhammad* (Tale of Muhammad's Coming into Being), is a popular *hikayat* among Muslims inclined to mysticism. From the ninth century onwards, the Sufis spoke of "*Nur*

Muhammad", the "Light of Muhammad". They believed that the Light of Muhammad is the spirit that was created by Allah and passed down through the line of prophets from Adam to Muhammad (Ismail Hamid, 1983b: 29-30).

There are numerous manuscripts of this *hikayat*. Seven of them can be found in the library of the Central Museum in Jakarta, although their contents vary. Two of them, MI 378C and MI 388F, have the same contents as a manuscript lithographed in Bombay. MI 406B contains the tale of the Prophet shaving his beard, while MI 96 and MI 642 include some other stories such as the *Hikayat Nabi Mengajar Anaknya Fatimah* and a tale entitled *Patana Islam*. The tales in MI 643A and MI 644, on the other hand, show strong differences from the lithographed manuscript. Below is a summary of the Bombay manucript.

Before Allah the Almighty created the universe, He first created the *Nur*. For fifty years the Light prostrated itself in worship of God. Thereafter the Muslim *ummah* (nation) was required to observe the Five Pillars of Islam, namely:

(i) to make the Profession of Faith (*kalimah syahadat)*,

(ii) to perform the five daily prayers,

(iii) to fast during the month of Ramadhan,

(iv) to give alms, and

(v) undertake the Hajj in Mecca.

Then Allah created a beautiful and noble bird. From the body of the bird, He created Ali (the Prophet Muhammad's son-in-law), Hasan and Husain (the Prophet's grandsons), Fatimah (his daughter), Abu Bakar and Umar (his Companions), Amir Hamzah and Abbas (his uncles), and Khadijah (the Prophet's wife).

The Light of Muhammad was then granted the seven seas—the seas of knowledge, kindness, patience, reason, thought, blessing and light—and was asked to swim in them for a thousand years. When the Light was told to expand, at that very instant, by God's command, 24,000 prophets were created. From the drops of water that fell from the eyes, ears, shoulders, nose and hands of the Light, were created the thirteen *mursal* prophets (apostles or messengers who were sent to their respective peoples to preach God's message), four angels, the divine *kalam* (the word of God), the *loh mahfuz* (tablet of destiny), the holy *kursi* (God's throne), the seven heavens, the sun and moon, the wind, water, fire, the *syajara,* the tree of Tooba in paradise, the ring that bears the Prophet Sulaiman's seal and the Prophet Musa's staff. Thereafter the Holy Spirit was passed down from the Prophet Adam to Syesy, and from Prophet Ayub to Prophet Musa.

Then Allah created the four elements: first, water; second, earth; third, wind; and fourth, fire. The Light was asked to manifest itself to these elements. Wind, fire and water were all very proud of their own strength. They declared that they had the power to do anything they wanted. But the Light convinced them that the wind was nothing more than a servant to the seafarer who sails; fire nothing more than a slave to the cook; and water was but a servant to the cleaner of filth and dirt. Only Allah, the most exalted and glorified God, Nur Muhammad reminded them, is infallible and free of imperfections. Upon hearing this, the three elements believed in Islam and were converted. The earth, on the other hand, showed the Light due courtesy, humility and deference, as well as its awe of God. Moved by earth's show of respect, the Light embraced and kissed the earth. It observed that man's character too is ruled by the four elements. A person governed by wind is intransigent and unyielding; one governed by fire is hot-tempered; another influenced by water is placid and cool-headed; while a person who exhibits earthly characteristics tends to blow hot and cold but is usually generous.

The *hikayat* ends by describing the many benefits and rewards a person will receive from reading or listening to this tale. "Whoever keeps or reads this *hikayat* will receive the same benefit or reward as one who reads the Torah, the Gospel, the Psalms and the Quran. The angels Jibrail, Mikail and Israfil will protect that person and his reward will be equivalent to that bestowed upon those who perform the Haj or those who go around the Kaabah seven times." Further, "Whoever reads this *hikayat* every night or day will be blessed with the same reward lavished upon a martyr, with seventy treasure troves open to him."

The MI 643A (v.d. Wall 76A) is another manuscript of this *hikayat*. Its contents are wide-ranging. Besides its account of the genesis of the Light of Muhammad and its transmission down the prophetic line, it also briefly tells the stories of the Prophets Adam, Nuh, Ibrahim and Ismail. These are followed by tales of the Hashimite clan to which Prophet Muhammad belonged, the birth of Prophet Muhammad and the story of his life, and tales of his family members and companions, Abu Bakar and Umar Ibn Khatab. Umar and Ali Ibn Abi Talib were among the first four caliphs. It is perhaps for this reason that the *hikayat* is entitled *Keturunan Nabi Muhammad* (The Prophet Muhammad's Lineage).

This *hikayat* is also called the *Tarikh Mukhtasar* and is a translation of a Persian book entitled *Rudatul Ajab,* itself translated into Arabic under the title *Umdatul Ansab (The Tree of the Prophet's Genealogy)*. This particular manuscript was finally transcribed on Saturday, 10 Rabiul Akhir in the Hijrah Year 1253 by Haji Shamsuddin from Bintan.

Besides its version of the The Light of Muhammad tale which differs from the summary given above, MI 644 (Cohen Stuart 119) also gives accounts of angels and demons, depicts the harrowing experience of a person in the throes of death, the punishment that awaits him in the grave, gives advice on how to avoid such a punishment, explains what happens to the soul once it departs from the body, describes the signs of the end of the world, and so on.

Muhammad Fanani from the *Pusat Pembinaan dan Pengembangan Bahasa* (The Centre of Language Learning and Research) in Jakarta has conducted a fuller study of all the manuscripts of the *Hikayat Nur Muhammad* in the collection of the Central Museum's library.[8]

Hikayat Bulan Berbelah

The *Hikayat Bulan Berbelah* (Tale of How the Moon Split) is also known by the title *Hikayat Mukjizat Nabi* (Tale of the Prophet's Miracles). Besides the Malay text, this *hikayat* can also be found in the Buginese and Makassarese, although, oddly enough, not in Achehnese.

---

8   Muhammad Fanani, *Hikayat Nur Muhammad dalam Kesusasteraan Lama* (The Tale of the Light of Muhammad in Classical Literature), Jakarta, 1979/1980 (mimeograph).

Manuscripts of this *hikayat* can be found in London, Leiden and the Jakarta Museum. Their contents are the roughly the same. Below is a summary of the lithographed manuscript of Bombay.

One day, the tale tells, the Prophet Muhammad gathered his family members and friends to teach them about the faith and to lead them to recite the Profession of Faith. The Prophet also proclaimed that he was the last messenger of God, the Seal, head and leader of all the prophets. When Abu Jalil heard this, he quickly informed King Habib and demanded that the Prophet Muhammad prove himself by showing them a sign of his prophethood. He pointed out that all the prophets before Muhammad had signs that attested to their prophethood: Nuh had an ark that could fly in the air; Ibrahim emerged unscathed from Pharoah's furnace; Musa's staff could turn into a snake, his sandals into scorpions; Sulaiman had a magic ring and crown; when Daud prayed, all the trees prostrated themselves in prayer with him; and Isa could bring the dead back to life and could speak with the skull of a dead man.

The next day, King Habib gathered all his troops and subjects on the Field of Abtah. The only persons missing were the members of the Hashimite clan. Abu Jahil suggested that the Prophet be forced to attend the assembly, and even be dragged there if necessary. On hearing that the Prophet was to be "dragged" to the assembly, Ali, his son-in-law, was outraged and was ready to defend the Prophet's honour. King Habib then decided to send one of his commanders to demand the Prophet's presence. Before the commander arrived, Jibrail came to the Prophet with seven thousand angels and told him about the commander's impending visit. The Prophet set out for Abtah Field. Although he walked there alone, it felt to the onlookers as though he were being accompanied by thousands of followers. Claps of thunder crashed in the sky and the earth trembled. When he arrived the king demanded to be shown a miracle: the moon must come down from the sky, circle the Kaabah seven times, and then recite the *kalimat syahadat* aloud so that everyone present could hear it. Muhammad was next commanded to make the moon enter the right sleeve of his gown and leave through his left sleeve. After that, he was to split the moon into two, so that one half would go to the west and the other half to the east, and then make the moon whole again as if it had never been split. If the Prophet could perform this miracle, King Habib promised that he and all his subjects would do whatever the Prophet said and would embrace Islam.

King Habib and his subjects followed the Prophet Muhammad to Mount Kulis. The Prophet prayed to Almighty God and called upon the moon to do as King Habib had asked. By the will of God, the moon came down to earth and fulfilled King Habib's commands. Astounded, King Habib and his subjects accepted Islam. Only Abu Jahil and his tribesmen refused to embrace the faith. Upon returning to his palace, King Habib remembered his daughter who had no arms and legs. He sent her to Prophet Muhammad. The Prophet covered her with a blanket and prayed. Before he could finish his prayers, the girl was already sitting up by herself and had grown both arms and legs. King Habib was overjoyed and rewarded the Prophet with an array of gifts, and bowed before him. In the manuscript v.d. Wall 96, kept in the Jakarta Museum, the daughter born without any arms or legs is not the king's real daughter as portrayed in the other manuscripts. The king does not immediately convert to Islam after witnessing the miracles performed by the Prophet. Instead, he sends his soldiers to capture the Prophet Muhammad and Abu Bakar. With Ali's help, the Prophet and Abu Bakar manage to escape. During their escape they meet Amir Mahmud who has been sent by the King of Rome to investigate reports of the Prophet's miracles. By the will of God, water gushes out from between the Prophet's fingers like a spring, enough for all the Roman soldiers to drink. Amir Mahmud is convinced by the Prophet's miracle. He returns to Rome to tell the king about the miracle he has witnessed. The king then sends him back again to help the Prophet in his battle against the King of Mecca. The battle is intense. King Habib loses and is converted to Islam.[9]

The lithographed *hikayat* ends with a warning that whosoever doubts the miracles described will be hurled into the deepest recesses of hell and suffer the various tortures and punishments that await there. Whoever follows in Abu Jahil's footsteps, the *hikayat* cautions, will not be safe as long as he lives and will not be blessed in this life or the hereafter. It also reminds readers to recite the "Al-Fatihah", the opening chapter of the Quran, before they commence reading the *hikayat*.

5.2.2 *Hikayat Nabi Bercukur*

Although this *hikayat*, The Story of How the Prophet Shaved His Beard, was not mentioned by Werndly, it has been translated into Javanese, Sundanese, Achehnese as well as Buginese and Makasar langugages. There are many manuscripts of this *hikayat*. A note written as marginalia in a Leiden manuscript (Cod. Or. 1953 (v)) reads: "This *hikayat* was copied by Rafidzi but is not to be believed." Apparently this *hikayat* was considered by devout Muslims of the time to contain deviant religious teachings. Below is a summary of the story according to the lithographed manuscript from Bombay.

The *hikayat* begins with a claim that whoever reads it from beginning to end will have their sins forgiven by Allah the Almighty for all time. One day, according to the tale, a companion of Prophet Muhammad asked Abu Bakar what special significance there was behind the Prophet having shaved himself; before whom he shaved; and what skullcap did he wear at the time? To these questions Abu Bakar replied: "Verily Allah's prophet shaved upon his return from his battle with the King of Lahad on the nineteenth day of Ramadhan, which was a Monday." Once, when the prophet was reading the Quran, Jibrail appeared before him, to convey God's command that Muhammad should shave. The prophet asked the angel before whom he should shave. And who would shave him and what skullcap should he wear? And so Jibrail entered the presence of Almighty God. God told Jibrail that His apostle should shave before the Light and that Jibrail himself would shave him. His skullcap would be from the greenest leaf that could be found in heaven. With these instructions, Jibrail searched heaven to find the leaf and made a cap for the apostle, just as God had commanded.

On the nineteenth day of Ramadhan, a Monday, the Prophet shaved his beard. Allah instructed His heavenly nymphs to go down to earth to collect the shaved hair of his apostle, each taking a strand to make into an amulet. Altogether a hundred and twenty six thousand, six hundred and sixty-six strands of the prophet's hair were cut that day, and not a single one of them ever touched the ground. That was exactly how many celestial nymphs were sent from heaven.

The *hikayat* concludes with Allah's word promising a reward to those who read this tale. "Whoever owns this *hikayat* will be saved from the perils of this mortal life and the hereafter, will not suffer the pains of death, and will be spared the terrifying questions of Munkar and Nakir."

---

9   S. W. Roedjiati, Singkatan *Hikajat Bulan Berbelah* (Summary of the *Hikajat Bulan Berbelah*), kept in the Institute for Language and Literature (now the Language Centre), Jakarta, (unpublished).

The Prophet Muhammad is also purported to have said that whoever rejected the *hikayat* was not his follower. The book should not fall into the hands of heathens and infidels. "Whoever has faith in this *hikayat* will be protected from calamity and danger; wicked people will not slander him and thieves shall not enter his house; he will be safe and secure wherever he goes; he will triumph in battle; and no weapon will harm him as a result of the blessings of this *hikayat*."

5.2.3 *Hikayat Nabi Wafat*

According to Van Ronkel, the *Hikayat Nabi Wafat* (The Death of the Prophet) or *Hikayat Tatkala Nabi Pulang Ke Rahmahtullah* (Tale of the Prophet Passing on to the Afterlife) belongs to the genre of *Wafat Nameh* which abounds in Persian folklore. This *hikayat* is not mentioned by Werndly but translations of it already existed in the Makasarese and Buginese languages. The tale can also be found in the *Hikayat Muhammad Hanafiah*, edited by L. F. Brakel (1975). Below is the tale according to the lithographed manuscript from Bombay.

One day, as Allah's apostle was returning from his prayers at the mosque, Jibrail and the Angel of Death appeared before him. The apostle wept when he heard that the Angel of Death would soon take his life. He did not cry because he loved the world or was reluctant to leave his family. He cried because he was afraid that his flock would leave the faith and abandon Islam after his departure. The angel Mikail appeared before him and asked him to recite the verse: "*inna li llahi wa Inna ilaihi rajiun*", Surely we belong to Allah and to Him shall we return. Thereafter, Jibrail, Mikail and the Angel of Death returned to God in heaven.

The prophet told his family about the angels' visit. When they heard the news they began to weep. Fatimah, the prophet's daughter, pulled her hair and beat her breast as she wailed. The prophet told her that such actions are forbidden by Allah. Grief should be hidden discreetly in one's heart. Fatimah asked him when and where they would meet again. The Prophet Muhammad replied that they would meet each other again on the day of judgement, at the bridge of Siratulmustakim (the bridge over hell that everyone must attempt to cross at judgement day), or the Kalkausar river (a stream in Heaven), or at the field of Mahsyar (the gathering place on Judgement Day), or in heaven itself. The prophet then walked to the mosque with slow, heavy steps, followed by his family. After his prayers, the prophet announced to the congregation that as he was about to meet his maker, and that he wanted to settle any debt he had contracted and make amends to anyone he had unwittingly hurt during his lifetime, so that he would not have anything to answer for on the day of reckoning. The congregation bowed their heads and wept, except for one man, Akasah. He stood up and claimed that, during the recent holy war, the prophet had struck him with a horsewhip. The prophet then asked the *bilal* (a functionary of the mosque) to fetch a whip for Akasah to settle the score. The prophet's companion Abu Bakar, his daughter Fatimah and his son-in-law Ali, each offered to take the prophet's place. Akasah refused, saying he would only strike the person who had struck him. He added that he was naked when he was whipped. On hearing this, the prophet took off his gown. When Akasah saw the prophet's navel, he became hysterical and kissed the prophet's navel. He said, "Oh venerated one, I have already had my wish fulfilled."[10] The moment Akasah kissed the prophet's navel, his face shone like the full moon and his voice sounded as sweet as

---

10 Akasah had once heard the prophet say, "Whoever sees my navel, that is a good omen that he will be a denizen of heaven."

that of a bird in heaven. The prophet then proclaimed to the congregation, "If you want to know what a person in heaven looks like, then look at Akasah's face." He reminded his people that they should be dutiful in performing the five daily prayers and always be kind to orphans.

The prophet walked home holding onto Ali's shoulder. Not long after, the Angel of Death arrived in the form of a young man. The prophet realised immediately who the man was and why he had come. He told Fatimah to open the door to let the young man in. The angel of death told Muhammad that the gates to the skies and heaven were open, and that the celestial nymphs are waiting for him to arrive in heaven. The Angel of Death then returned to the presence of Almighty God to invite Jibrail to come down to Earth. Before he departed this life, the prophet advised his daughter Fatimah to take good care of her husband, cherish and obey him. The prophet instructed his companions that they should be mindful of their duty to God and avoid evil. The prophet then passed away.

5.2.4 *Hikayat Muhammad Hanafiah*, Part 1

The *Hikayat Muhammad Hanafiah* consists of three parts.

The first part is the story of Prophet Muhammad; the second, the story of Hassan and Hussain; and the third, the story of Muhammad Hanafiah. A fuller discussion of this *hikayat* will be given in Section Three on the *Tales of the Prophet's Companions,* below. Meanwhile here is a summary of the first part of this *hikayat* as found in a manuscript lithographed in Singapore. This part was omitted from the *Hikayat Muhammad Hanafiah* text published by L. F. Brakel.

The tale begins with the story of the creation of the *Nur* of Prophet Muhammad. After its creation, the Light lay prostrate before God for five thousand years. Then, God created the prophets Adam, Nuh, Ibrahim and Isa. God next commanded Jibrail to take the essence of the earth, from which He created the embodiment of the Last Messenger. This essence was passed down until it reached Amir Abdullah. The story then shifts to Fatimah Syam, a woman well versed in the Torah, who learnt from the holy book that the Last Prophet would be born as the son of a man from whose forehead a light radiated as bright as the planet Venus. That man was Amir Abdullah. And so Fatimah Syam went to see him. Amir Abdullah was willing to take Fatimah Syam as his wife, but first he had to ask permission from her father. On his way home Amir Abdullah saw that his wife Aminah was as beautiful as a heavenly maiden. When they reached home, they consummated their marriage. By the will of God, the light from Amir Abdullah's forehead was transferred into his wife's womb. When Fatimah Syam saw that the light had gone from Amir Abdullah's forehead, she cried and rolled on the ground.

Six months later Amir Abdullah died. Fatimah gave birth to a baby boy—the Last Messenger of God. On the day he was born, all the idols shattered, the fire that perpetually burned in front of them was extinguished, the oceans dried up and Nursyirwan's palace crumbled and fell to the ground. White clouds appeared and sheltered the prophet. According to one *hikayat*, many miraculous things were observed about his birth: the prophet is said to have been born already circumcised and his navel already healed. No dirt could cling to his body nor could any mosquito bite him. He was named Muhammad, 'he who is praised by the entire universe'.

When he was an infant, the prophet refused to be breastfed by his mother. A search was made to find a wet nurse. Seventy women were approached to breastfeed him but all of them refused, as Muhammad came from a poor family and had no father.[11] Eventually a Syrian woman, Halimah, agreed to nurse Muhammad as she could not find work with a rich family. Halimah received God's blessings for nusing Muhammad—the arid land on which she lived became green and fertile, her crops flourished, and her scrawny goats soon became fat. In time the prophet turned twelve. He was playing with Halimah's children in a field one day when he was taken captive by two men in white. They laid him on the ground, cut open his body and then stitched him up again. When Halimah heard from her children what had happened, she consulted a fortuneteller. The fortune teller wanted to kill Muhammad. Halimah feared for the apostle's life and took Muhammad back to his grandfather, Abdul Mutalib.

Time passed and soon Abdul Mutalib fell ill and passed away. Abu Talib, Muhammad's uncle, was appointed Muhammad's guardian. One day, when Muhammad was eighteen years old, Abu Talib was paid a visit by Siti Atikah who told him to find a wife for his nephew. Unfortunately however, Abu Talib was not a man of means and could not afford to pay for the prophet's wedding expenses. So Siti Atikah went to ask for help from Khadijah, a rich and beautiful businesswoman. Khadijah agreed to let Muhammad accompany her caravan on its annual trading mission to Syria but first she wanted to see what the prophet looked like. When he arrived, Khadijah glanced through a thin curtain and saw that "the face of Allah's Messenger shone like the full moon, his forehead was as radiant as the sun, while his hair was wavy and lustrously black like the sheen of a beetle's carapace... when he stood he was head and shoulders above others, no one was taller than him; when he walked white clouds sheltered him; and when he stopped somewhere, the scent of his body lingered there for three days." Khadijah was so fascinated by Muhammad's good looks that she wanted to marry him straight away. And so the Messenger worked in Khadijah's caravan trade, reaping great profits for her. Allah's Prophet twice displayed miracles. One day, during the Jewish New Year, the Jews' lanterns were extinguished and refused to light again while Muhammad was still in the city. On another occasion, the prophet was able to complete a long journey that would have normally taken many days within an amazingly short time. Even so Khadijah did not pay the prophet his wages until Atikah came and asked for the money to use as payment for Muhammad's wedding expenses. Khadijah then confided her love for Muhammad to Atikah. Having been granted blessings from both their families, Khadijah and Muhammad were married. After the wedding, Khadijah presented Muhammad with all of her wealth and everything she owned, apart from the clothes she was wearing. The couple was blessed with four daughters, Zainab, Ruqayyah, Kulthum and Fatimah.

Muhammad constantly retreated to Mount Judi to pray. When he turned forty, Jibrail came to him with God's revelation and taught him to recite:

Asyhadu an la ilaha illa 'Ilah

Wa asyhadu anna Muhammad Rasulullah

(There is no God but Allah

And Muhammad is his Messenger)

---

11 According to Brakel's text and a summary he provided (pg. 81), it was Prophet Muhammad who refused to be breastfed by these women.

As soon as he reached home, Muhammad taught Khadijah to recite that verse. Thus, Khadijah was the first to embrace Islam. "Surely, anyone who does not maintain the faith, will dwell in Hell." After some time, Khadijah fell ill. On her deathbed, she asked Muhammad where they would meet again in the hereafter. (In *Hikayat Nabi Wafat,* Fatimah posed this same question.)

One day Muhammad was downcast to see that his daughter Fatimah was still unmarried. A young man named Amiru Mukminin Ali wished to marry her but he felt himself unworthy to be the Prophet's son-in-law and could not pluck up the necessary courage to ask for her hand in marriage. Day and night, he asked Allah to grant him Fatimah as his wife. His prayer was finally answered and he was married to Fatimah in heaven. According to one tale, Ali had previously gone to find work in order to earn some money to pay for his wedding. He managed to earn three dinars but he gave all his money away to a man in need. He then borrowed money and bought a camel, from which he made a large profit. Later Muhammad revealed to Ali that the man who approached him for help was in actual fact an angel who had been sent to test his piety. Ali and Fatimah were married for the second time. For her dowry Fatimah asked that all women who had sinned against their husbands to be forgiven. From this marriage, Fatimah and Ali were blessed with two sons: one named Hasan, the other Husain.

The story goes that Abu Lahab was Muhammad's most bitter enemy. One day, he threw a stone at Muhammad and injured the prophet's leg. Abu Bakar was so enraged that he wanted to kill Abu Lahab. Muhammad was able to stop him and said that the blood that flowed from his injured leg would make it easier for his followers to cross the Siratal Mustakim, the Bridge over Hell. Crestfallen, Muhammad went to Atikah's home to spend the night. Fearing that the prophet's enemies would come to attack him, Atikah stood guard with a sword in her hands. An angel made her sleep while Jibrail carried Muhammad into the sky.

In another version, it is said that the ascension of Prophet Muhammad to Heaven (the *mikraj*) was the consequence of an argument between the sky and the earth as to which one of them was the more powerful. The earth claimed that it was nobler because the Prophet Muhammad had walked on its surface. The sky wept and prayed that it too might be blessed with the Prophet's footprints. Allah then instructed Jibrail to take the Prophet Muhammad to Jerusalem on a celestial winged steed, the *burung burak,* and then up to Heaven.

On yet another occasion, the Prophet Muhammad asked Jibrail which one of them was older. Jibrail said that according to the Tablet of Destiny (*Loh Mahfuz*), the Prophet Muhammad was only sixty years, six months and six days old. Muhammad then showed Jibrail the star on his head. Jibrail admitted that Muhammad was older than he was. When Muhammad was exactly sixty-six years, six months and six days old, he fell ill and passed away. This story of his passing is the same as that told in the *Hikayat Nabi Wafat.*

5.3 Tales of the Prophet Muhammad's Companions

According to Ismail Hamid, "Sahabat" (*al-Shahabat*) is an Islamic term for those people who were closest to Prophet Muhammad. The expanded meaning of this term encompasses everyone who had ever met or spoke to the Prophet Muhammad (Ismail Hamid, 1983:108). The closest companions were the first four caliphs: Abu Bakar Al-Sidik, Umar ibn al-Khattab, Uthman ibn

Affan and Ali ibn Abu Talib. Of these four, the stories about Ali ibn Talib are the most popular. Ali is depicted as a strong and brave warrior, who fought alongside Prophet Muhammad in all his battles. The popularity of Ali may have been due to his position in Islam. The Shias revere him as the first Imam. His sons, Hasan and Hussain, the grandsons of the prophet, are also held in high esteem. The same could also be said about Muhammad b. al-Hanafiah, Ali's son from his second wife. Their stories can be found in the *Hikayat Muhammad Hanafiah*.

The second caliph, Umar ibn al-Khattab, was very strict about following the syariah law. His story is told in the *Hikayat Abu Syahmah*. The *Hikayat Abu Bakar,* despite its name, deals more with Umar al-Khattab than Abu Bakar. Moreover, the stories of the prophet's companions also include the stories of early converts such as Tamim Al-dari: as well as some episodes from the prophet's life, such as his marriage to Mariah, a girl sent to him by an Egyptian ruler.

Below are the five *hikayats* which belong ot the category of tales of the Prophet's Companions:

(i) *Hikayat Muhammad Hanafiah*

(ii) *Hikayat Tamim Al-dari*

(iii) *Hikayat Abu Syahmah*

(iv) *Hikayat Sama'un*

(v) *Hikayat Raja Khandak*

5.3.1 *Hikayat Muhammad Hanafiah*

The *Hikayat Muhammad Hanafiah* and *Hikayat Amir Hamzah* are both very old. According to the *Sejarah Melayu*, one night in 1511, just before the Portuguese launched their attack on Malaka, the two *hikayats* were recited to the soldiers who were about to defend the country. The fact that the *Hikayat Muhammad Hanafiah* is an old *hikayat* can also be proven by the existence of a fragment of it (about 60 pages long) in the library of Cambridge University in England. This fragment was first owned by a scholar of Arabic at Leiden University, Professor Erpenis; he obtained it from Captain Pieter Willemsz Floris, who visited Acheh in 1604. R. O. Winstedt has also pointed out that the fragment contains archaic forms of certain words, specifically *kutaha* and *tambang,* which were rarely used at that time.

Scholars originally believed that the *Hikayat Muhammad Hanafiah* had an Arabic source. After examining the fragment kept in Cambridge University, Van Ronkel argued that the *Hikayat Muhammad Hanafiah* is a translation from Persian. The reasons given by Van Ronkel for this conclusion include: the profuse praise of Hasan and Husain; the use of the term *"peygambar"* for the Prophet Muhammad, which means 'prophet' in Persian; most importantly, the existence of two Persian manuscripts in the library of the British Museum entitled:

(1) *Kisah al-mukminin Hasan Wa Husain* (The Tale of Hasan and Husain, Devout Believers); and

(2) *Hikayat Muhammad Hanafiah* (Tale of Muhammad Hanafiah).

The contents of these two manuscripts are similar to the contents of the second and third parts of the *Hikayat Muhammad Hanafiah* (Brakel, 1975:12). L. F. Brakel who edited the *Hikayat Muhammad*

Hanafiah for his doctorate at the Leiden University provided further proof for the Persian origin of the chronicle. Firstly, the division of chapters in the Persian and Malay manuscripts is similar. Secondly, the name Muhammad b. al-Hanafiah when translated into Malay becomes Muhammad, son of (bin) Al-Hanafiah. In Persian, the relationship of Muhammad and the woman al-Hanafiah is expressed by what is termed *ezafat*, denoted by the letter 'e'; this was omitted in the text. The Malay translator ignored this *ezafat* and erroneously translated the hero's name as Muhammad Hanafiah. Thirdly, many Persian names can be found in the text, such as Ummi Kulsum and Immi Salamah. Lastly, there is a Persian manuscript which can explain the anomalies found in the Malay text (Brakel, 1975: 13-15). Nevertheless, Brakel does not dismiss the possibility that the *Hikayat Muhammad Hanafiah* could have been derived from the Arabic historical text compiled by Abu Mikhnaf (perhaps transmitted through a Persian translation) (Brakel, 1975: 28). Abu Mikhnaf's book is entitled *(Akhbar) Maqtal al-Husain* and recounts the events that led to the death of Husain, as well as the Al-Muktar rebellion against the Bani Ummayah (Brakel, 1975: 5).

The first part of the *Hikayat Muhammad Hanafiah* has been dealt with above. Below are stories from the second and third parts.

The second part of consists of the *Hikayat Maktal Husain.* When Husain was young he found an angel with burned wings. Husain stroked the angel's wings. By the will of God, the angel's wings were restored and it flew back to Heaven. Jibrail foretold that the angel would not visit Earth again except on the day of Husain's death at the hands of infidels. When Hasan and Husain were still young, Jibrail often came down to Earth to play with them. On one occasion, on the eve of Eid-ul Fitri, Jibrail brought clothes for the prophet's two grandsons. Hasan chose a green coloured tunic and it was prophesied that he would one day be poisoned. Husain, on the other hand, chose a red tunic and it was foretold that he would be killed in battle on the plains of Karbala. Muawiyah had been told that his son would take the life of the prophet's grandson and vowed to himself that he would never marry. One night while he was cleaning himself after answering nature's call, a scorpion stung him on his penis. The pain was excruciating. According to the physician, the only way to remove the pain was for him to marry. Desperate to relieve his agony, Muawiyah married a woman who was too old to bear children. But by the will of God, his old wife gave birth to a son they named Yazid.

Eventually, Fatimah, the Prophet Muhammad's daughter, passed away, as did Abu Bakar, one of the prophet's companions. Umar became the caliph. War was declared against all infidel nations. Ali defeated the King of Kisri and the descendants of Nusyirwan Adil and captured them. The King of Kisri and his son refused to embrace Islam and were killed. His two daughters, Syahrbanun and Nurnas, were persuaded by Ummi Salamah to accept Islam and spared. They were then persuaded to marry. Syahrbanun was prepared to take a husband, on the condition that all her assets were returned to her and she was allowed to marry a man of her own choosing. One day, the Prophet's companions, together with various princes and noblemen, gathered in front of her. Syahrbanun watched them from her dais as they paraded before her. Umar, Usman, Ali, Saad Wakkas, Amar Madi Karib and Khalid Walid, all failed to win her heart. She finally chose Husain and they were married. Her sister, Nurnas, married Muhammad, Abu Bakar's son. Yazid, who was standing behind Husain, felt humiliated; he said nothing but vowed to avenge himself.

Umar ruled as caliph for nine years. One night, Umar was stabbed on his way to pray by a disgruntled slave who felt he had been unfairly punished by Umar. Umar died before he could appoint his successor. Not long after, the Umayyah clan managed to have Usman chosen as the new caliph through a subterfuge. As soon as he was appointed, Usman gave high-ranking leadership positions to his family members, such as Muawiyah and Abu Sufian. Marwan Hakim, who had been banished from Madinah, was also allowed to return to the city.

Because Usman was always occupied with religious activities, most of his duties as caliph were delegated to Marwan Hakim, who was experienced in carrying out such work. One day, a delegation from Syam and Egypt arrived with a proposal that Muhammad, Abu Bakar's son, be installed as their caliph. Usman accepted the proposal. And so Muhammad prepared to leave for Egypt. When Marwan Hakim found out, he wrote a letter to the caliph of Egypt, urging him to kill Muhammad as soon as he arrived in Egypt. The letter bore the seal of the caliph's ring. Somehow Muhammad discovered the contents of the message. He was furious and showed the letter to his family members; they too were angered when they read it. Together they went to Usman's home and killed him. When they arrived, Usman was reciting the Quran. They threw his body onto a rubbish dump and it remained there for seven days and seven nights. Wild animals stood guard over his corpse so that it would not be defiled. His body was eventually discovered by Ali who gave him a proper burial.

Ali was chosen to be the next caliph by the other surviving companions of the Prophet, such as Abdurrahman Auf and Zubair Awam. Aisyah, the Prophet Muhammad's wife, however objected to Ali's appointment as he had refused to investigate Usman's murder. With a massive army at his command, Muawiyah attacked Ali. The attack was was unsuccessful. Ali's army comprised only seventy soldiers but they were sufficient to defeat Muawiyah's forces. Aisyah regretted her actions. And so Ali remained in Madinah. His family members were made kings, including Muhammad Hanafiah, who was crowned ruler of Buniara.

Muawiyah, though defeated in battle, had not yet lost hope. He went to an old woman and paid her to kill Ali. The old woman found a young beautiful maiden whom she promised to give to one of Ali's slaves, Muljam, if Muljam was prepared to kill Ali. Blinded by his desire for the young woman, Muljam agreed and assassinated Ali as he stepped out of the mosque.

After Ali's death, Muawiyah became king of Madinah. One day, Muawiyah sent an envoy to ask for the hand of Zainab, the daughter of Jafar Taiyar, on behalf of his son, Yazid. Zainab refused Yazid's proposal but instead accepted that of Amir Hasan, the prophet's grandson. Yazid vowed to kill Hasan and Husain when he came to power in Madinah. Yazid later wanted to marry Abdullah Zubair's beautiful wife. Muawiyah succeeded in tricking Abdullah Zubair into divorcing his wife. His wife, however, refused to marry Yazid. Instead, she married Husain. Yazid's resentment toward the brothers grew even deeper. "When I become king, I will revenge myself by killing Hasan and Husain," he swore to himself.

After some time, Muawiyah passed away and the throne fell into Yazid's hands. He soon began his plan to kill Hasan and Husain. He successfully persuaded the wife of a military commander in Madinah to poison Hasan. (According to another account, one of Hasan's wives was persuaded to poison her own husband.) After Hasan died, Yazid became obsessed with killing Husain. He sent a letter to Utbah, a military commander in Madinah, promising to reward him with wealth and a high title if he killed Husain. When Utbah refused, Yazid threatened to hire another commander, Umar Saad Malsum, to kill Utbah himself. Utbah was still afraid to kill Husain. He said that as long as Husain was in Madinah they would not be able to kill him. So they asked the King of Kufah, Ubaidullah Ziyad, to trick Husain into going to Kufah. The King of Kufah invited Husain to visit his kingdom. Ummi Salamah cautioned Husain about the danger awaiting him. That night Husain dreamed that he met with all the prophets and angels. In the dream, the Prophet Muhammad told him that heaven was being prepared for his arrival. Despite the warning and Ummi Salamah's premonition, Husain departed for Kufah with a small group of followers.

After a while, their camels and horses were so exhausted they lay down and refused to get up again. The men decided to establish their camp. When they cut the trees around them for firewood, the trees began to bleed and they realized that they were standing in the plains of Karbala, the place where Prophet Muhammad had predicted Hussain would die. They soon ran short of water, as Yazid's army had dammed the river. Their animal-skin water bags had all been gnawed by mice. They had no choice but to endure their extreme thirst. The battle began. One after another, Husain's men died as martyrs. Eventually, even his sons, Kasim and Ali Akbar, lost their lives. Only then did Husain think of appealing for help from his relative, Muhammad Hanafiah, who was now king of Buniara. Buoyed by this prospect, he leapt into the battle field and killed many of his enemies. As the battle waged on he found himself near a river. But remembering how many of his friends had died from not being able to drink, he did not give in to his thirst. Exhausted, Husain fell to the ground. None of his enemies dared approach him. Finally the swarthy Simir Laain, a man with nipples like a dog's, came forward and beheaded Husain. Husain died a martyr on Friday, the tenth of Muharram. When he died, the Throne and the Vault of Heaven trembled, the moon and sun grew dim, and for seven days and seven nights the Earth was in tumult.

After the martyrdom of Husain, Yazid's army sacked the house of the Prophet Muhammad. No one dared to go near Ummi Salamah. A soldier who took hold of Ummi Salamah's daughter was blinded, by God's Will. Yazid offered compensation for Husain's death, if Ummi Salamah would submit to him. When she refused, Yazid was furious. When Fatimah, Ummi Salamah's daughter, asked him for some water to drink, he gave her the head of Husain.

Yazid ordered that all sermons in the country be read in his name. A minister, Marwan Hakim, pointed out that the sermons were not valid if not read by Zainal Abidin. At first, Zainal Abidin refused to read the sermons in Yazid's name. Triumphantly Yazid ordered that the drums be beaten throughout the land in celebration. Eventually sermons given in all the lands he vanquished were read in his name. Zainal Abidin and all the members of the house of the Prophet Muhammad became his prisoners.

The third part of the chronicle is the actual Story of Muhammad Hanafiah. The story tells that Muhammad (Hanafiah) was in the midst of his daugher's marriage celebrations when he received news of the deaths of Hasan and Husain. He immediately dispatched letters to all his family members holding positions of leadership in the neighbouring countries, and then lead his army against Yazid's forces. Yazid was at that time digging a pit to kill all the members of the Prophet's household. On hearing the news of Muhammad Hanafiah's impending attack, he prepared himself for battle. Muhammad Hanafiah's tribesmen came from everywhere with their armies to help him. An intense battle ensued. Both sides suffered heavy casualties. In the end Yazid's army could not withstand the onslaught and he appealed for help to the kings of Portugal, China, Abyssinia and Ethiopia.

After scoring a decisive victory and amassing considerable riches, Muhammad Hanafiah stopped the battle for two days. During that time he went to Madinah to visit the grave of the Prophet Muhammad and prayed in the mosque there. That night the Prophet Muhammad appeared in a dream and told him to avenge the deaths of Hasan and Husain. The next day Muhammad Hanafiah marched upon Damascus with his army. The armies of Yazid's foreign allies had already arrived and the ensuing battle was fierce. During the fighting, Muhammad Hanafiah fell into his enemy's trap and lost one of his arms. Yazid wanted to burn him alive but fortunately Muhammad Hanafiah was rescued by one of his friends. His severed arm was found and re-attached to his sholder. By God's Will, the arm functioned again as normal.

The next day Muhammad Hanafiah arrived in Damascus with his army. They crossed the moat surrounding the city, broke through the city walls and entered the city. Terrified, Yazid tried to escape. A mass of clouds, formed by Husain's spirit, followed him everywhere he went. Yazid was afraid and fell into the pit he had dug, breaking all his bones. Meanwhile Muhammad Hanafiah was able to free Zainal Abidin and members of the Prophet's family from prison. He then sat Zainal Abidin on the jewel-studded throne. The coronation drums played. Muhammad Hanafiah and all his family and army formed rows and paid homage to Zainal Abidin. Then a sermon was read out in the name of Zainal Abidin for every inhabitant of the city to hear. After some time, all of Muhammad Hanafiah's family and friends returned to their homeland, leaving Muhammad Hanafiah alone to look after Zainal Abidin.

One day, Muhammad Hanafiah heard that Yazid's tribe had gathered in a cave. Muhammad Hanafiah went to ambush them. Many of Yazid's tribesmen died at the sword of Muhammad Hanafiah. In the cave, blood flowed like a swollen river. Suddenly a voice cried out, telling Muhammad Hanafiah to stop the carnage. Ignoring the voice, Muhammad Hanafiah continued to harass his enemies. The voice thundered once again, this time even louder than before. Startled, Muhammad Hanafiah threw his sword away and fell to his knees. By the will of God, the mouth of the cave closed. Allah had fulfilled His Will for His servants.

That is a brief outline of the story of the *Hikayat Muhammad Hanafiah*. For Shiites, this *hikayat* serves as a highly revered sacred story. Muhammad Hanafiah is considered a messiah, Allah's Guided One. He did not die and will one day return to lead his followers again. The Sunnis, however, have certain reservations about the contents of this *hikayat*. Perhaps this explains why there is a prefatory note on the first page of the Singapore lithographed manuscript that, in part, reads:

> May no one who reads this *hikayat* or hears about the wars waged by Yazid, Muawiyah and others, cast any aspersion on Yazid, Muawiyah and others, and do not call them unbelievers, for they are just like us.

The Shiites must have had a great deal of influence in Indonesia in the past. To this day, their influence can still be clearly seen. In Padang, Sumatra, for example, the death of Husain is still commemorated in a play known as "*tabut*". During the day of mourning, the martyrdom of Husain and his funeral is re-enacted. The actors wail and make an extravagent display of their grief throughout their performance. The story in the play goes something like this:

One day, Jibrail visited Prophet Muhammad and gave him a handful of earth. The angel foretold that if the earth turned red, the prophet's grandson, Husain, would die a bloody death. The prediction became reality. After Husain's death, his friend, Nustul, tried to take a precious stone from Husain's bowl. Suddenly, Husain's corpse came to life and slapped Nustul till his face was all blue and black. The corpse then took hold of Nustul and would not let him go. Nustul was only able to escape by cutting off Husain's hands but he fainted soon afterwards. While he was unconscious, he saw angels, the Prophet Muhammad and celestial nymphs accompanying Husain's coffin at his funeral procession. When he regained consciousness, Nustul regretted his actions. He went to the Kaabah to ask for Allah's forgiveness. Jaafar ibn Muhammad, who was circumambulating the Kaabah at the time, heard Nustul's prayers and advised him to do as he had been told in his vision during his fainting spell. He would hopefully be forgiven by Husain for doing so. That is the reason for the observance of the *tabut* in remembrance of the martyrdom of the Prophet's grandsons (S. W. Roedjiati, 1961: 83-90).

Perhaps it is due to this festival that the Minangkabau call the month of Muharram (the first month of the Islamic calendar) the Tabuik Month. The Achehnese call it Asan-Usen Month, after Hasan and Husain. In Java, people partake of a porridge called *bubur* Suro (Asyura in Arabic), and Muharram is also called the month of Suro.

5.3.2 *Hikayat Tamim al-Dari*

Tamim al-Dari was a real historical figure. A Christian, he converted to Islam seven years after the Hijrah Era began. It s said that he advised Prophet Muhammad on the use of oil lamps in the mosque. There was already a story about Tamim al-Dari in the oldest collection of Hadis, and it was this story that gave birth to a *hikayat* in Arabic that was later translated into various regional languages such as Sundanese, Malay, Buginese, Makassarese and Achehnese. Translations of this story are also available in Spanish, Urdu and Afghan.

There are many manuscripts of this *hikayat*. One that is well-known is the Raffles No. 50 manuscript, held in the collection of the Royal Asiatic Society in London. According to this manuscript, the *Hikayat Tamim al-Dari* was adapted from an Arabic book entitled *Tarikh al-Hijrat*. R. O. Winstedt, however, disagrees with the notion that the *Hikayat Tamim al-Dari* was adapted directly from Arabic. Instead, he believes it was more likely to have been adapted from an adaptation in an Indian language. This is proven by the use of Persian and Sanskrit, and the account of the sinking of the King of Hind's ship which can be found in this *hikayat*. Even so, Winstedt concedes that this *hikayat* was copied from an older *hikayat*. The orthographic forms used in this *hikayat* are similar to those in the manuscript of *Hikayat Bayan Budiman* (in the Bodleian library) from circa 1600.

Below is a summary of the story based on the manuscript in the National Library, Singapore.

One day, a companion of Prophet Muhammad named Tamim al-Dari asked his wife, Khaulah, to accompany him to bathe at a well. He was afraid to go there by himself as he had once heard the prophet say "every well is an abode of *jinn*s." Tamim's wife refused to go with her husband but mocked him instead, "Hey *jinn*, come and take this cowardly man." Tamim plucked up his courage and went to the well. While he was there, a *Jinn Afrit* (a race of clever, cunning *jinn*s) spirited him to a land populated by infidel *jinn*s. Despondent Tamim had no choice but to remain there.

Four years after Tamim's disappearance, his wife went to see Amirul Mukminin (leader of the believers) Umar, another companion of the Prophet, and told him of her predicament. She asked him for permission to re-marry as she had no means to fend for herself. Umar advised her to be patient and gave her some money to support herself. This continued for seven years, four months and ten days. Then Khaulah came to see Umar again and repeated her request. Umar granted her wish and Hadrat, a man from Khaulah's tribe, agreed to marry her and look after her children. All that remained was for Khaulah to wait out her *iddah* time (a widow's waiting period after her husband's death before remarriage) until the marriage could be finalised.

This is what happened to Tamim during his captivity in the land of the infidel *jinn*s. One day, an army of Muslim *jinn*s attacked the infidel *jinn*s. Tamim helped the Muslim *jinn*s and they granted him his freedom. He then went to live in the country of the Muslim *jinn*s and taught the king's children to recite the Quran. Tamim dreamed of his family and realised how much he missed his own wife and children. The king of *jinn*s then instructed one of his capable subjects to take Tamim back to Madinah. As he was being flown across the sky, Tamim was so engrossed listening to the voices of angels reciting the *syahadat* (declaration of faith), *tahlil* (acknowledgement of God's Oneness) and *tahmid* (praises of Allah), that he forgot to say his own prayers. An angel hit the *jinn* carrying Tamim with an arrow and it turned to ash. Tamim fell into the sea and swam to an island in the middle of the green ocean. Feeling desolate, Tamim began to cry but he heard a voice which soon cheered him. Then Tamim started to walk until he reached a land inhabited by demons. He met a demon who was blind in one eye and had an elephant's trunk for a mouth. When the demon heard that Tamim was separated from his wife, she was overjoyed. Not long after leaving the land of the demons, Tamim met another *jinn Afrit* who took him to a cave. When the entrance of the cave opened, Tamim saw a majestic house inside which turned out to be the palace of the Prophet Sulaiman. When the *jinn Afrit* attempted to steal the Prophet Sulaiman's ring, a snake bit him and he died.

Tamim continued his journey and met an enormous animal that asked him to enter its stomach. Inside the monster, Tamim met Dajal, the anti-Christ. Dajal is so tall that his head touches the sky and his body is huge. He was blind in one eye. Tamim engaged him in a question-and-answer session. When Tamim recited the Profession of Faith, Dajal diminished in size and could hardly be seen. When Tamim told him stories of Muslims committing sins, Dajal grew larger. An angel appeared and struck Dajal with its staff. Dajal's body became small again. Leaving the monster's stomach, Tamim boarded an Indian ship. One night, violent winds and a typhoon whipped the waters into massive waves. The ship shattered, killing everyone except Tamim. He managed to save himself and swam to an island that was inhabited exclusively by women.

Once again Tamim resumed his travels, entering and leaving various countries and feeling extremely hungry and thirsty the whole time. He then met a third *jinn Afrit* who gave him food. The *jinn* also changed himself into a beautiful bird. When he recited the Profession of Faith, *la ilahaillallah, Muhammad Rasul Allah (There is no God but Allah, Muhammad is his Messenger)*, a doorway opened. He saw many people inside who were leaning against swords covered by their own blood, their fragrance sweeter than limes. Around him were rivers filled with various delights. Tamim walked hither and thither, helping himself to the delights. He felt that he could stay there forever. Then the angels Jibrail and Mikail came on their white steeds and chased Tamim away. They told him that he was in Paradise, which was only intended for those who had died. Tamim pointed out that the Prophet Idris had once visited Paradise, even though he had not died. Allah replied that Idris had actually experienced death. Then Tamim asked how he could return to Madinah and was told to just keep walking. He saw a glow in the distance and made his way towards it. The light came from the fire lit by hermits to cook their food. Nearby, Tamim found a green cave filled with precious stones. He tried to take the precious stones but a snake told him to throw them away. Then a young man appeared. He told Tamim to recite the verse *Ayat Kursi* (The Throne verses), in order to protect himself from a great danger. Tamim resumed his journey, still feeling very thirsty and hungry. He wept as he thought of his wife and children. Then a beautifully dressed, handsome man appeared. The man took Tamim to a hill to see the strange things that exist in Allah's world. Tamim saw a pregnant bitch barking at the litter that was still in its belly. He saw an old woman trying to hide her true age behind her beautiful clothes, bangles and rings. A man collected water from the well and poured it into a leaking pot. Another man carried a huge pile of firewood and walked hither and thither without ever stopping. Then Tamim met the Prophet Khidir, who told him the names of the places he had visited and the stories of the people he had just seen. The prophet felt so sorry for Tamim that he asked the clouds to take Tamim back to Madinah.

Tamim reached home just before his wife's wedding. He forbade the wedding and quarreled with Hadrat, Khaulah's intended husband. Umar could not resolve the dispute and consulted Ali, Prophet Muhammad's son-in-law. Ali remembered that Prophet Muhammad had once described a couple of coin-sized birthmarks on Tamim's back and thigh. Tamim's identity was thus confirmed. The wedding was cancelled. Tamim shaved, cut his fingernails, bathed, and changed his clothes. Ali said, "Behold this man. He has just returned from Paradise."

There are actually two versions of *Hikayat Tamim al-Dari*. The text summarised above and the Raffles 50 manuscript are both long versions. The Cod. Or. 1719 manuscript in the library of the University of Leiden is an abridged version. The most significant differences between the abridged and long versions are as follows,

(1) in the abridged version, a *jinn* swooped down and made off with Tamim not because he was bathing at the well, but because his wife cursed him for forgetting to say his prayers;

(2) Tamim did not meet the Dajal in the abridged version. He only met Dabbat al-Ardl;

(3) the abridged version also does not mention the two angels on white steeds, Jibrail and Mikail;

(4) the abridged version recounts how Tamim returned to Madinah by reciting a prayer taught by Prophet Khidir (H. H. Juynboll, 1899: 209).

The University of Cambridge manuscript has been recently published in Kuala Lumpur (Walyunah Hj. Abd. Gam., 1989).

5.3.3 *Hikayat Abu Syahmah*

Abu Syahmah was the son of the second caliph, Umar Ibn Khatab. It is said that Abu Syahmah was whipped by the ruler of Egypt for drinking alcohol. When he returned to Madinah, he was again whipped by his father and died. From this incident, there emerged a story that has been told in various regional languages, such as Malay, Javanese, Sundanese and Achehnese. There is also a text in Hindi called *Qisaa-i Abu Syahma* (The Story of Abu Syahma).

There are many manuscripts of this *hikayat* in the library collections in Jakarta, Leiden and London. In the National Library of Singapore, there is a similar manuscript, copied in 1837 by Mohamet Arif, a teacher at the Raffles Institution. Only one Leiden manuscript (Cod. or. 1720 (1)) and one Singapore manuscript do not mention Abu Syahmah's participation in the holy wars. Below is a summary of the story according to the lithographed Singapore manuscript.

Abu Syahmah was the second son of Caliph Umar. He was outstandingly handsome. One day, he fought alongside his father Umar in the religious war in the country of Kalwan. Due to Umar's royal majesty, the enemy broke their ranks and ran. Umar returned to Madinah after scoring a decisive victory. After some time, Abu Syahmah fell ill with fever. Umar was dejected at the sight of his son's illness. All of Prophet Muhammad's Companions as well as family members made the same vow that Ali made on behalf of his sons, Hasan and Husain. Umar also swore an oath. By the will of God, Abu Syahmah recovered.

One day, the Prophet's Companions and family members asked Abu Syahmah to recite the Quran. He recited the holy book in a clear, loud voice. All who heard him were filled with joy and praised his skill. Abu Syahmah became arrogant because of the sweetness of his own voice. God disapproved of his arrogance and decided to punish Abu Syahmah.

One day, Abu Syahmah went to play in a field. He met a Jew who told him that his face was as pale, and his body as thin, as a chronic invalid. When he heard of Abu Syahmah's recent illness, the Jew revealed that he had just the right kind of medicine to cure him completely. Deceived by the words of the Jew, Abu Syahmah drank the medicine. Shortly after, his head throbbed. He completely lost his mind and the ability to speak. He tried to go home but no longer knew the way. The Jew took Abu Syahmah to his house and asked his daughter to give him whatever he desired. Abu Syahmah slept with the Jewish girl and behaved in a sinful manner.

The next day, when Abu Syahmah came to his senses, he was filled with regret and fear. But he could do nothing. With an anxious heart, Abu Syahmah returned home. After some time, the Jewish girl gave birth to a baby. The baby looked exactly like Abu Syahmah. One day, when Abu Syahmah's father, Umar, was praying in the mosque, the Jewish girl came to see him, carrying the baby in her arms. She told Umar what Abu Syahmah had done. Umar was shocked. He could not say a word. Umar gave the girl forty dirhams for the baby's needs. Umar then returned home and asked Abu Syahmah what had actually happened. Abu Syahmah admitted his mistake and accepted the punishment prescribed by Allah's law. With a heavy heart, Umar took Abu Syahmah before a crowd to receive a hundred lashes. Everyone wept as Abu Syahmah was being whipped. Even the birds and animals cried. The angels in Heaven also pitied Abu Syahmah. After the hundredth lash, Abu bade farewell to those gathered there and died.

Ali and Usman were so upset by the death of Abu Syahmah that they wanted to kill all the nonbelievers in the land. Unfortunately they could not fulfil their wish, as they had to keep vigil over Abu Syahmah's body. By the will of Allah, they fell asleep and had the same dream They dreamed that Prophet Muhammad was seated at the pulpit in the mosque, while Abu Syahmah sat on his left. To the prophet's right was his Companion, Abu Bakar. The dreamers were told that Abu Syahmah had been given a noble status, as his father, Umar, had inflicted the appropriate punishment upon him. Then the Prophet advised Ali and Usman not to kill any Jews except those who deliberately refused to embrace Islam. Then Ali and Usman woke up. After this, all the Jews in the land accepted Islam.

5.3.4 *Hikayat Sama'un* (Ph. S. Van Ronkel 1909: 458)

The *Hikayat Sama'un* is based on a minor episode in the life of Prophet Muhammad. It is said that before the Prophet conquered Mecca, he had sent many letters to appeal for help and ask for acknowledgement that he was God's Apostle. The response was disappointing. Only the ruler of Egypt, Mukaukas, a Greek, sent two slave girls, one of whom was Mariah al-Kibtiyah. Mariah later married the Prophet. They were blessed with a son who unfortunately died a year later. This episode gave rise to a *hikayat* which was later translated into various languages such as Malay, Javanese, Sundanese, Achehnese as well as Arabic.

There are two versions of this *hikayat* in Malay. One of them (v.d.Wall 92, Museum Jakarta) was adapted from Javanese. This is stated on the first page and can also be seen from the use of many Javanese words. The other version (Cohen Stuart 31, Museum Jakarta) is adapted from Arabic. This is apparent from its language which has characteristics of Arabic, such as 'masuk atas' (enter above), 'berkata bagi' (say for), 'hamba dari segala hambaku' (servant of all my servants), 'hari dari segala hari' (day of days), and 'tiada diketahui dengan dia oleh seorang', or *lam yaklam bihi abad* in Arabic which means 'unrecognised not even by a soul'. Besides this, each page contains an utterance or exclamation in Arabic. Many Arabic words are used, sometimes with their meanings given in Malay. J. J. De Hollander (1893: 335), and H. H. Juynboll, in his catalogue (1899: 319), are both of the opinion that this *hikayat* originated from Arabic. Van Ronkel had also shown that the two manuscripts of the *Hikayat Sama'un* are undoubtedly translations from Arabic.

C. Snouck Hurgronje disagrees. While there are Arabic versions and Malay versions that have been influenced by the Arabic version, we cannot come to the conclusion that this *hikayat* was the work of an Arabian author or that it came from the Arabian Peninsula. The language is very poor. It is clearly the work of a non-Arab. Hurgronje expounds this view in *The Achehnese II* (173-4). Van Ronkel adds that the *hikayat*'s contents also show that its author was not an Arab. No Arab person would depict Prophet Muhammad as the King of Madinah, as this *hikayat* does. The ferocity of Muslim warriors in war would also not have been likened to that of a "tiger pouncing on a herd of goats". It should no longer be in doubt therefore that this *hikayat* was composed in the Archipelago.

If this *hikayat* was not adapted from Arabic, then from which language was it adapted? One of the Malay versions maintains that this *hikayat* was adapted from Jawi (Javanese). Van Ronkel however was not convinced by this view either. Islamic literature—especially stories of the prophets in the Javanese language—is usually translated from Malay. This time however he was faced with an Islamic *hikayat* which is said to have been adapted from Javanese. He conducted further investigations, analyzing two Javanese versions and their relationship with the Arabic, Sundanese and Malay versions. From this study he discovered that the link between the two Javanese versions is not as close as first appeared. One of them, manuscript 133, is closer to the Malay version, manuscript 92. The other Javanese version, which contains the story of Semangun (Sema'un) incorporated in the *Menak* stories, is closer to an Arabic version, to another Malay version (manuscript 31), and to a Sundanese version, than to other Javanese versions. These two

A HISTORY OF CLASSICAL MALAY LITERATURE

Javanese versions bear evidence of having been adapted from Malay. Van Ronkel thus concluded that the *Hikayat Sama'un* was initially written in Malay. Two copies of this original Malay version were then made. One was adapted into Javanese and later re-translated into Malay. The other one was translated into three languages: Javanese (in the case of the *Menak* stories), Arabic and Sundanese. The Arabic translation was then re-adapted into Malay, which gives the effect as if the original *hikayat* was written in Arabic. Van Ronkel then drew up a *stemma codicum* to show the relationship between the various versions.

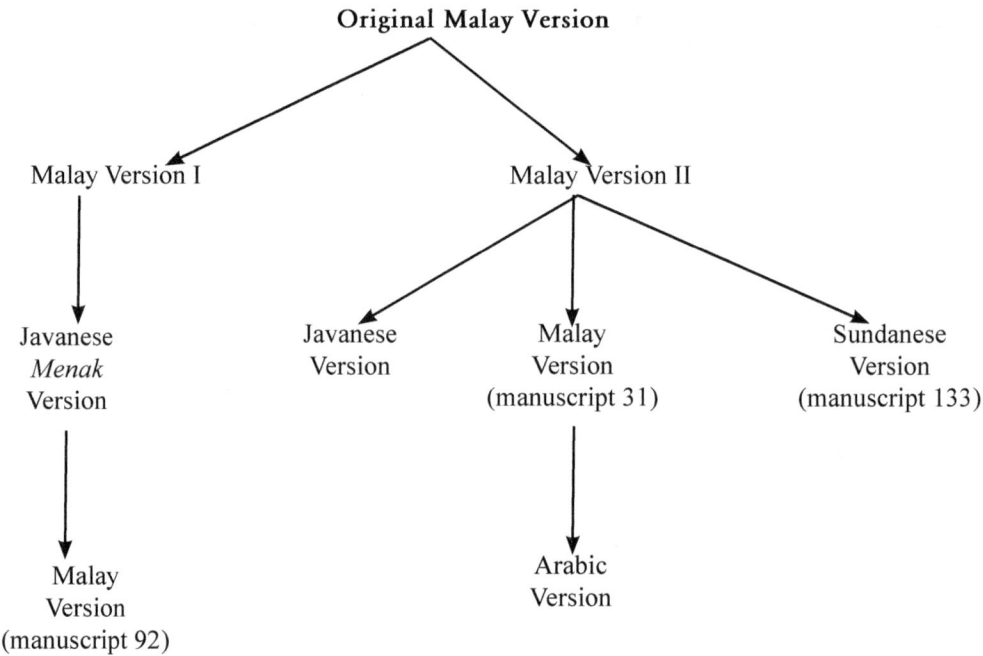

The *Hikayat Sama'un* lithographed in Singapore is similar to manuscript 92 in the Central Library, in that it begins with a statement by the Prophet Muhammad to Ali: "Whoever among my followers, man or woman, disseminates or listens to this *hikayat* will surely be forgiven his sins for forty years by Allah the Exalted and Glorified." However, the words underlined are omitted. Below is a summary of the manuscript printed in Singapore by Mr Muhammad Said bin Haji Rasyid.

There once was a powerful heathen king named Khalid who continually worshipped idols in the hope that he would be granted a son. By the will of Allah, his queen gave birth to a boy. The child was extremely handsome. After he was born, the boy prostrated himself before Allah and recited the Profession of Faith. His parents named him Sama'un. It is said that Sama'un refused to be suckled until his mother embraced Islam. So the queen converted to Islam. When he was just three days old, Sama'un was already able to talk to his parents about matters related to Islam. Once, the Prophet Muhammad and Jibrail paid him a visit, as it had been foretold that Sama'un would grow up to become a great warrior.

It is told that when Abu Jahal heard of Sama'un's reputation as a mighty and fearless fighter, he paid Sama'un a visit. Sama'un, however, said to him, "Hey Abu Jahal, you are the enemy of the Prophet Muhammad. One day I will cut off your head." When Abu Jahal heard these words he ran helter-skelter back to his home. Surakal, Abu Jahal's chief minister, suggested that he pay a warrior from Alexandria named Kinam to kill the Prophet. By the will of God, Kinam lost his way and arrived at Sama'un's home. He was immediately killed by Sama'un. Abu Jahal then sent forty warriors to the Prophet Muhammad, demanding that he punish Sama'un for killing the man from Alexandria. Jibrail intervened and explained that Sama'un had killed Kinam because he had been sent to assassinate the Prophet. The forty warriors then returned to Abu Jahal. He ordered them to kill Sama'un. Armed with many weapons and heralded by a fanfare of drums, trumpets and flutes, the forty warriors marched to Sama'un's home. Sama'un ran amuck and charged into their ranks, killing them all. Abu Jahal was far from satisfied. He then sent four thousand men to kill Sama'un. On another occasion Abu Jahal wanted to hold a wedding for his daughter, Dewi Nasiah. One night, Sama'un came to Abu Jahal's home, kidnapped Dewi Nasiah, and took her to the Prophet Muhammad. Sama'un and Dewi Nasiah were married in the presence of Allah's Apostle. Abu Jahal had no choice but to accept Sama'un as his son-in-law.

King Bakti of Sari's daughter, Dewi Mariah, was as beautiful as she was well-mannered and wise. One night, she dreamed that a shining light from Heaven fell into her lap. She was told that it was the light of Prophet Muhammad. Dewi Mariah fell passionately in love with the prophet. She yearned for him so much that she wrote to him, pleading to become his slave. The prophet received her letter in good faith and sent an emissary to King Bakti to ask for his daughter's hand in marriage. King Bakti rejected the proposal on the grounds that the Prophet was poor and not of royal birth. Meanwhile, the prophet heard that Dewi Mariah was refusing to eat, drink or sleep, because of her longing for him. The prophet's wife Aisyah suggested that they take Dewi Mariah by force. Prophet Muhammad refused to wage a war for the sake of a woman unless it was God's command. Not long after, Jibrail appeared with a command from Allah for him to do so. And so the prophet prepared to battle King Bakti. All the Prophet's companions vowed to help bring Dewi Mariah home to the Prophet, or divorce their wives if they should fail in their mission. The Prophet and his companions then set out for Sari to fight King Bakti. After some time, they ran out of water. The Prophet took a pebble from the river and held up his palms to the sky, beseeching Allah for help. By the will of God, cool, clear water gushed out of the pebble and everyone was able to quench their thirst. Soon they found themselves just outside Sari. Jibrail appeared and asked Sama'un to enter the city first.

All of the military commanders of Sari wanted to capture Sama'un. He ran amuck and killed most of them, including Kalil, a minister. King Bakti ordered two more of his commanders, Kaim and Kairul, to fight Sama'un. The battle raged on. Sama'un was badly wounded; his body was full of gashes and lacerations, "like a cucumber sliced for a fruit salad". Only the sinews holding his bones together remained intact. Jibrail appeared to the Prophet Muhammad and commanded him to leave for Sari at once in order to help Sama'un. Meanwhile, King Bakti had summoned his mighty and fearless minister, Temenggung Kuari, with orders to behead the Prophet Muhammad and Sama'un. The battle intensified.

Many of Muhammad's troops were martyred on the battle field. Sama'un fought against Temenggung Kuari. Kuari was no match for Sama'un who beheaded him. Seeing the situation,

King Bakti was too afraid to fight any longer and decided to retreat back into the city. He ordered his men to gather wood, douse the wood in oil, and to place the wood around the city. The wood was then set alight. The city's bulwark burst into flames, becoming a sea of fire. Dewi Mariah escaped from the city, accompanied by her ladies-in-waiting and nine thousand of her subjects.

Not long after this, Dewi Mariah and her subjects embraced Islam. The Prophet Muhammad ordered Ali and Sama'un to ask King Bakti to convert to Islam. King Bakti refused to renounce the religion of his ancestors for fear that he would not be able to meet his parents in the afterlife. He was killed. All of his subjects converted. Anyone who was a Muslim shared in the generous spoils of war taken from Sari. The sounds of merrymaking and joyous celebration could be heard throughout the land. Thereafter, Sama'un took his leave and returned home.

5.3.5 *Hikayat Raja Handak*

The *Hikayat Raja Handak* (also Khandak or Hunduk) is a popular *hikayat* and there are many manuscripts of it. Eleven can be found in the library of the Central Museum; one of them, MI 657 (v.d.Wall 91), was edited by Mohd. Pozi bin Haji Masurori in 1978 for his Master of Letters degree at the National University of Malaysia.

The theme of the *hikayat* is inspired by the blockade of Madinah by the Prophet's enemies. *Handak* or *Khandak* (in Arabic) or *Kandak* (in Persian) actually refers to the moat that was dug in front of Madinah to repel enemy attacks. The name of King Handak's son, Badar, was actually the name of a place where a fierce battle once took place. And the name of his daughter, Zalzadi, was the name of Ali's donkey. Clearly many misunderstandings among the Malay community lie behind this fantastic *hikayat*. In it, a month-long journey could be completed in just a day and Ali's sword extended itself as far as the eye could see. When Ali screamed, it was as if the sky had fallen and the world was coming to an end. Below is a summary of the manuscript lithographed in Singapore.

The chronicle begins by saying that whoever reads or listens to this story will receive great blessings from God. After his father's death, King Handak, the son of the Prophet Sulaiman, renounced Islam and started to worship idols instead. The king had a son, Badar, and a daughter, Zalzadi. One day, King Handak was told that many of the idols he worshipped had been destroyed by Ali, the son-in-law of the Prophet Muhammad. The king was furious and summoned a multitude of his fiercest military commanders and brave subjects to attack Madinah and Mecca. Jibrail came to the Prophet Muhammad and told him that God had said that he should not be afraid of King Handak's attack. He also told the Prophet that 70,000 angels would assist him. Any person who fought King Handak would be engaged in a holy war and would enter Paradise.

The Prophet Muhammad summoned all his companions. Ali was chosen to lead them into battle. War ensued. When Ali let out three loud shouts, three thousand of King Handak's men died. Shocked, King Handak sent a slave to find out how many military commanders were in the Prophet's army. He reported to the king that the Prophet's army contained 64,000 soldiers, led by four commanders. King Handak was encouraged to learn that he had the larger army and prepared for battle with renewed confidence. Ali charged at the infidels' army. His sword extended itself as far as the eye could see. Many of King Handak's men died; their bodies formed huge piles, and their blood flowed like a river. King Handak's troops broke ranks and ran in all directions.

The King of Handak gathered his subjects once more. He also summoned his son, Badar, and his daughter, Zalzali. He hosted an enormous feast for forty days. King Kaskin was offended because he had not been invited to the celebrations. Feeling slighted, he assembled his own subjects to attack King Handak. However, a young *jinn,* who lived on Kaf Hill, managed to persuade King Kaskin not pursue his attack; instead, he suggested that the king should accompany him to the bottom of the ocean to find King Solomon's treasure. Hostilities between the armies of the Prophet Muhammad and King Handak resumed again. Ali single-handedly killed many of King Handak's men and eventually collapsed with exhaustion. The Prophet Muhammad immediately rushed to his side. Throwing small pebbles at King Handak's men, the Prophet managed to hurt them enough for them to beg for forgiveness. Many of them embraced Islam and fought alongside Ali.

King Handak however was adamant. He sent seven of his best warriors and 70,000 soldiers to attack Madinah and Mecca. By the will of God, all seven heroes became blind and deaf. They did not dare face King Handak and most of them converted to Islam. One of the warriors, Jalal, reported his compatriots' defection to King Handak. King Kaskin and his subjects joined forces with King Handak. But, by the will of God, he killed many of his own troops. King Kaskin resumed his search for the Prophet Sulaiman's treasure. Jibrail appeared and took his life.

King Handak still refused to surrender. He gathered all the *jinn*s, sprites and fairies he could muster to fight Ali. The fighting became even fiercer. Many of the unbelievers lost their lives. Their bodies formed piles as tall as hills and their blood formed an ocean. Ali's donkey swam in the sea of blood making a deafening noise; the sound was like waves crashing at the shores of Kalzum during a typhoon over the foothills of Kaf. Allah then sent 70,000 angels to help Ali. Jibrail summoned the hills, mountains, rocks, wood, flies, mosquitoes, wasps and animals to help Ali. The battle entered its third month. Ali was exhausted and again fell unconscious. His horse flew into the air. He woke up to find himself facing King Handak and King Badar and asked them to accept Islam. When they refused, he killed them. King Handak's subjects ran helter-skelter into the jungle. Princess Zalzali ran to Kaf Hill. Ali ordered the people of Madinah and Mecca to plunder King Handak's kingdom. The pillaging continued for more than a hundred days and a hundred nights. All of the golden idols in the kingdom were destroyed.

When the king of the *Ifrit* heard that King Handak and King Badar had been killed by Ali, he assembled his military commanders and subjects. A Muslim *jinn* warned Ali of this forthcoming attack. Meanwhile a battle broke out between King Ifrit and his son, Kuru Kasfri, because of the king's refusal to give his son a magic sword. God commanded Ali to help Kuru Kasfri and they were in turn helped by a Muslim *jinn* under the orders of the Prophet Isa. King Susal and Jabal Kaf also came to support King Ifrit. So did Turngga. In the battle, King Ifrit and King Susal were killed. Princess Zalzali escaped to Kaf Hill and appealed to King Perlela for help. Parlela was later killed in battle. When the war ended, Jibrail told the Prophet Muhammad of God's word that all Muslims who had died in battle were martyrs and their sins had been forgiven by Allah.

5.4 Tales of Islamic Warriors

Stories of this category usually deal with historical figures who lived before the birth of Islam. Due to their contributions to the later spread of Islam or their amazing feats, they are regarded as warriors who helped spread Muslim teachings. Iskandar Zulkarnain (Alexander the Great) and Amir Hamzah conquered countries that refused to accept Islam; Saif Dzul-Yazan helped the Himyarite (Homerite) king to defeat the King of Abyssinia who was a Christian; while Sultan Ibrahim taught his followers that the mortal world is transient and that one should not violate the rights of others. Most of these stories came from Arabic or Persian sources. A few of the more important warrior tales are discussed below.

5.4.1 *Hikayat Iskandar Zulkarnain*

The *Hikayat Iskandar Zulkarnain* describes the life of Iskandar, Alexander the Great (365-323 BC), the son of Philip of Macedonia. In his short life, Iskandar conquered Egypt and Persia, and his army traveled as far as India. Even during his lifetime, tales of his achievements were already widespread. The English poet Chaucer has written:

The story of Alisaunder is so commune
That every wight that hath discrecioun
Hath heard somewhat or all of his fortune

The *Hikayat Iskandar,* or *The Alexander Romance,* emerged after his death in Babylon at the age of thirty-three from poisoning. This *hikayat* is partly historical and partly a legendary account of Iskandar's exploits. It was later translated into various European languages, including Medieval Latin, Greek, French and old German. Adaptations of the *hikayat* can also be found in Syrian, Arabic, Persian, Turkish, Hindi, and, in Indonesia, in Javanese, Buginese and Malay.

The Malay *Hikayat Iskandar Zulkarnain* is very old. The first tale of the *Sejarah Melayu* derived its material from "*hikayat yang termasyhur itu*" ("this famous *hikayat*"), namely the *Hikayat Iskandar Zulkarnain.* The King of Singapore who fled from the island and founded the Malaka Sultanate was also named Raja Iskandar Zulkarnain, because "when the prince was born, the midwife pressed on his head to make it symmetrical, balanced and equal from top to bottom, left to right."("Zulkarnain" can be translated "two horned".)

So what was the origin of the Malay Iskandar story? According to P. J. van Leeuwen's dissertation, the *Hikayat Iskandar* was either derived from, or adapted out of, Arabic but not necessarily from any specific Arabic version. The reason for this claim was that Al-Suri was mentioned as the supposed author of the Arabic version. There are various Malay manuscripts in which Al-Suri is referred to as the *hikayat*'s writer, according to R. O. Winstedt, but these manuscripts also insist that he took his text from a work by Abdullah ibn al-Mukaffa, who translated *Kalilah wa Dimna* into Arabic. Winstedt also disagrees with the view that Al-Suri is the author of the Wilkinson version kept in the Cambridge University. According to Winstedt (1938: 1-2), the Cambridge or Wilkinson manuscript used an Arabic-Persian source written in India. C. Hooykaas (1927: 162) is more inclined towards Van Leeuwen's view. From its contents as well as the style of its language, the *Hikayat Iskandar* is closer to the Arabic versions. Even so, C. Hooykaas could not specify which Arabic manuscript was used, as there are glaring differences, as well as similarities, with each version.

There are at least four sources for the Iskandar stories in Arabic and Malay, according to Van Leeuwen (1937: 14-18).

(i) Pseudo-Kallisthenes

Kallisthenes was a historian who accompanied Iskandar during his expeditions. However, Iskandar's biography was not written by Kallisthenes, thus the term "Pseudo-Kallisthenes". The Pseudo-Kallisthenes was written in Egypt in Greek. It tells how the Egyptian Pharaoh, Nectanebus, fled when his kingdom was attacked by enemies from Persia. He reached Macedonia, where Olympias, the queen of Macedonia, fell in love with him. Iskandar was their child. A prophecy later foretold that the Pharaoh would return to Egypt as a young man and drive the Persians out of the country. When he grew up, Iskandar and his army swept into Africa through Italy. In a temple in one of the lands he conquered, he was proclaimed to be the son of a god. His army then conquered Persia, killing Darius, its king, and all his followers. The king of India too was eventually vanquished. In India, Iskandar had the opportunity to speak with a group of wise Brahmins and he met a tribe of Amazons. After a while, Iskandar returned to Babylon, where he was subsequently poisoned (P.F.1968: 580-581).

(ii) Syah-Nama

The *Syah-Nama* is a famous Persian epic. Its author, Firdaus (940-1020), tells the history of Persia from the creation of the world and all living things, including Gayumart the first human being, right up to the defeat of the Persians by the Arabs. The story of Iskandar is contained in this epic. Dara I married a princess from Macedonia. After some time, he began to dislike her and sent her back to Macedonia. Shortly after, the princess gave birth to a son called Iskandar. The King of Macedonia, humiliated by Dara I's rejection of his daughter, announced that Iskandar was his own son, born from one of his concubines. Thus, when Iskandar defeated the King of Persia, Dara II, and ascended the throne, he was actually taking possession of what was rightfully his. In one version, Iskandar is said to be the Zulkarnain mentioned in the Quran who is purported to have lived during the time of Prophet Musa (Browne, 1977: 112-119).

(iii) The Quran

Chapter 18 of the Quran (Surat Al-Kahfi), verses 83-101, claims that Iskandar conquered the various tribes that lived in the lands where the sun set and rose. He punished sinners and rewarded the righteous. Iskandar also erected an iron wall to protect a tribe from being attacked by Ya'juj and Ma'juj (Gog and Magog). The plot of the *Hikayat Iskandar* is broadly influenced by the story found in the Quran.

(iv) Legends

Many well-known Muslim legends were also incorporated into the *Hikayat Iskandar*. These include the story of the Prophet Khidir, who was well-versed in the magic arts, astrology and various strange, foreign languages. In one of the stories, Prophet Khidir found the elixir of life for which Iskandar had been searching. Beside this, travel stories and geography may also have influenced some variations in the *Hikayat Iskandar*.

According to a story in the *Sejarah Melayu*, a descendant of Iskandar travelled to Bukit Si Guntang in Sumatra and became king of Palembang. The present day Malay kings still claim to have descended from Palembang. The kings of Perak have a keris and seal which they claim belonged to Iskandar. A lullaby sung to sleeping princes also states that the King of Perak is descended from Iskandar. These Malay rulers are not the only ones to claim Iskandar as their ancestor. Sultan Bayazid, a sultan of Turkey in the fourteenth century, also claimed descent from Iskandar. Apparently, Afghan fighters have a predilection for carrying red flags, the flag of Iskandar.

There are two versions of the *Hikayat Iskandar*, namely a Sumatran and a Malayan version. The oldest Sumatran version is the Leiden manuscript Cod. Or. 1970 (Juynboll, 1899: 191-194). This manuscript dates to 1713 and was once owned by an Arab, Omar ibn Sakhr Ba'abuj, who lived in the Malay Archipelago. Another manuscript, Codex 1696, was published by Khalid Hussain (1967). The oldest Malay version is the manuscript donated by R. J. Wilkinson to Cambridge University. The Wilkinson manuscript was transcribed in Sungai Ujung in 1902.

There are some differences between the two versions. The Sumatran version opens with praises to Allah, the Lord of the entire universe. It then tells of how Allah showed Adam who his descendants would be, and continues with an account of the ancestors of Bahaman, who appears in the *Pasai Chronicles*. The Malayan version begins with the tale of Bahaman and his marriage to his own daughter. This tale is also told in more detail. The Sumatran version ends with the marriage of Iskandar to Princess Nuraini. The Malayan version contains other stories, such as the marriage of Iskandar and Prophet Khidir's daughter; Iskandar's visit to the undersea world; as well as Iskandar's unsuccessful search for the elixir of life and how it was found by Prophet Khidir. The Iskandar story in its entirety can be found in the fourth manuscript described by Winstedt (1938).

Summary

Allah revealed to Adam that he would have many descendants. He told the prophet that Ibrahim would be the father of all the prophets; Muhammad the noblest and most loved of all the prophets; Solomon would have great power over *jinn*s, demons, humans and wild animals.

Upon hearing that the Prophet Daud would live for only sixty years, Adam offered to give forty years from his own lifespan of a thousand years to Daud. Adam then went down to earth. The story advances nine hundred and sixty years; the angel of death has come to take Adam's life. Adam regretted that he did not give forty years of his life to Daud as he had promised. That is why Allah commanded Adam's descendants that all promises should henceforth be made in writing and in the presence of witnesses to preclude them from being broken. Thereafter Allah created all the kings, and out of all the rulers He made after Prophet Sulaiman, none was greater than Iskandar Zulkarnain.

Next, the *hikayat* traces the genealogy of the King of Babylon, beginning with Gayopart and ending with King Bahaman. He followed the Zoroastrian religion based on the teachings of the prophet Zoroaster (or Zarathustra). In Zoroastrianism, it is not forbidden for a father to marry his own daughter. King Bahaman married his daughter Princess Humani. After some time, the princess became pregnant and soon King Bahaman had a premonition that he would not live much longer. He assembled all the noblemen and officials of his court and decreed that, after his passing, the child who was still in his wife's womb would be his heir. A few days later King Bahaman passed away and Princess Humani was installed as regent. Within just a few days of ascending to throne, Princess Humani began to relish her newfound position. She was soon reluctant to relinquish her power. When her baby was born, Humani was far from pleased. In fact, she planned to kill the baby as soon as it was born so that no one would be able to take her power away. On the advice of her lady-in-waiting, the baby was placed in a chest and sent out into the river. A washerwoman found the baby and named him Darab, which means "from water and wood", as he was found in a wooden chest on the river.

Darab soon grew up; he learned to read the Quran and to write. He also later learned to ride a horse. He soon realised however that he was not actually the son of a washerwoman but a boy who had been found in a chest by the river. Darab was saddened by the fact that he did not know the identity of his father. One day, Princess Humani gathered all her military commanders to test their skills. Darab took part in this competition and emerged the winner. Princess Humani was attracted to him and asked him about his origins. She entrusted a general, Mihran Dailami, to look after Darab as she considered him her special guest.

King Qilas of Rome ordered his army to attack and plunder all the kingdoms around its borders. Mihran Dailami was appointed to command the army against King Qilas' forces. One night a heavy rain fell and the ground began to flood. Mihran Dailami left his tent to check on his soldiers. He heard a voice from the sky say, "Take good care of that house there, all of you, for the king of all the world is sleeping inside." Mihran Dailami then went inside the house, and found Darab sleeping there. He took Darab to his tent and asked the boy to tell him the story of his life.

A few days later, they fought the Roman army. Darab killed many of Rome's fiercest fighters, including Yeryis, the chief military commander. When Yeryis fell, the troops panicked and scattered in all directions. Although Mihran Dailami's army looted the kingdom of its great wealth, Darab took just a spear for himself. Mihran Dailami sent someone to fetch the washerwoman who had found Darab when he was a baby, so that he could verify the young man's origins. It then became clear that Darab was Princess Humani's son. Princess Humani was delighted. She confirmed Darab's origins and said that he would ascend the throne as the late king had commanded. The coronation drums were beaten and musical instruments were played to celebrate the occasion. Princess Humani then surrendered the kingdom's treasury to Darab. Darab became the first to receive the title "Syah Alam" (King of the World). The army pledged its allegiance to him.

The story next tells that King Darab married Princess Safiya Arqiya, the beautiful daughter of King Qilas. Unfortunately however, her breath was unpleasant. King Darab found a physician who cured her by giving her an Alisander's leaf (horse parsley) to chew. However, as soon as she was cured, King Darab's love for her waned and he subsequently sent her back to her father. Shortly after, King Darab married Sudagin, the daughter of Mihran Dailami, and the couple were blessed with a son they named Dara.

Two months later, Princess Safiya realised that she was carrying King Darab's child. When the time came, she gave birth to a baby boy whom she named Alexander (Iskandar) after the plant that had cured her. When Iskandar grew up, he became the student of the great Aristotle, the famous sage and philosopher. With the passage of time, King Qilas passed away and Iskandar ascended to the throne. King Darab, meanwhile, was replaced by his heir, Dara. Now that King Darab had died, Iskandar decided to stop sending tribute to Babylon. King Dara was furious and brought his army to attack Rome. Iskandar prepared to go to war against King Dara. And so the two armies faced each other. By the will of God, King Dara's soldiers were defeated and scattered, with the Roman army in hot pursuit. King Dara lost many of his men and though he managed to escape, Iskandar was always close behind him. Soon after, Iskandar brought news of his victory to his mother Princess Safiya. Princess Safiya quickly revealed that King Dara was Iskandar's own brother. Iskandar was happy to learn this and was prepared to forgive King Dara. But it was too late. King Dara had already been killed by two of his soldiers. Raja Iskandar had the traitors arrested. They were taken to a hill and impaled.

The story further tells that Raja Iskandar soon became intoxicated by his own power and glory. One day, Satan tempted him to turn his back on the true faith. Aristotle wrote to Iskandar, encouraging him not to abandon his religious duties but to no avail. God sent the Prophet Khidir to him; Iskandar had the prophet arrested and imprisoned. Urged on by Satan, he even tried to kill Khidir. All his attempts failed. An angel released Prophet Khidir from prison and took him to the top of a hill. Those ordered to arrest Prophet Khidir were burned alive. Finally Iskandar himself led an army to capture the Prophet. But Khidir was not afraid of King Iskandar. A dialogue took place between the two men about faith. King Iskandar was eventually persuaded to embrace the true faith, the religion of the Prophet Ibrahim. The Prophet Khidir taught King Iskandar all aspects of religious knowledge for forty days. Then the prophet received God's commandment to be King Iskandar's spiritual mentor and guide him in all his endeavours.

King Iskandar gathered his troops together. First he marched to Constantinople to persuade his teacher, Aristotle, to join him. His teacher declined but gave him a ring which would tarnish and discolour when it came into contact with poisoned food. King Iskandar then embarked on his campaign of expansion. When he arrived in Rumaya-al-akbar, King Iskandar was presented with precious stones and rare exotic gems by its king. In Andalusia, King Nikmat, a Muslim, welcomed King Iskandar warmly. He ordered his people to help King Iskandar cross the sea to Ethiopia. The Prophet Khidir, who was fluent in Ethiopian, successfully converted the five idolatrous Habsyi kings to the true faith. But that was not all. The five also wanted to join Raja Iskandar on his campaign. They left their wives and children on an island in the middle of the Lulumut Sea.

After some time, King Iskandar's journey took him to an ant hill where he met a man standing on a horse. Both the man and his horse were made of copper and gold. The man gave directions to King Iskandar and his army. Iskandar later captured a man called Fatah, who was riding a giraffe. Fatah brought the Prophet Khidir to see his king, Raziya, a worshipper of the planet Venus. Fatah had converted to Islam and intended to kill his king. Imagine his surprise however when he found out that his king already knew what he intended to do. But his surprise turned to joy when he heard that King Raziya had already embraced Islam.

King Iskandar continued his journey and saw many wonders of the world, including an amazing palace built by King Solomon, and the Dome of the Rock, built by the *jinn* Sakhr. Iskandar and his army also came to a hill made of emeralds, and entered a tunnel guarded by five horsemen carrying swords. They then reached a vast and prosperous country called Jabalsa. Its king, Abud, was a sun-worshipper. Abud twice sent assassins to kill the Prophet Khidir but both attempts failed. Khidir was then tricked into going to an island, with the intention he would be set upon and eaten by a *jinn*. While this was happening, Raja Abud attacked King Iskandar's army. A fierce battle broke out. Jibrail came to help King Iskandar. The Prophet Khidir prayed and God unleashed a hurricane and fire from the sky which obliterated all of Raja Abud's forces. Raja Abud himself died in the conflagration and his subjects embraced the true faith.

King Iskandar then continued his journey in the direction of the setting sun until he reached a vast plain. There he met a motley crowd of weird people: a tribe whose men had only one leg each but whose women had four legs each; and a tribe that worshipped the planet Saturn. On top of a hill, Iskandar found a Muslim *jinn;* the *jinn* gave him two precious stones of unusual length and thickness. Iskandar had the precious stones fitted into a crown which he then wore. It is said that Raja Iskandar is also known by the name Zulkarnain, "two horns", because the gems on his crown were worn by no one but kings.

King Iskandar again resumed his journey and after some time reached a land that smelled like cotton and whose hot climate made it impossible for anything to grow. Iskandar was attacked by a race of *jinn*s who had intermarried with humans. These *jinn*s refused to convert to Islam, and he killed them all. Then Iskandar reached Mount Kaf, the home of the descendants of the Prophet Yusuf. Ten learned men well-versed in reciting the Torah came to visit Iskandar. They taught King Iskandar a variety of useful religious knowledge, including this aphorism: "everyone on this earth is a visitor and everything we possess is a loan. One day we will all return to whence we have come." They also showed King Iskandar the way to the land of the setting sun. King Iskandar set sail and soon reached the land of the setting sun. The next moment, the sun set with a noise like thunderclap crashing across the sky. On either side of the sun stood two enormous angels. It was their duty to guard the sun as it rose and set. On hearing the thunderous din of the setting sun, King Iskandar collapsed. The Prophet prayed and the king regained consciousness. For three days, Iskandar prayed for the sun to show its glory again.

Then Iskandar and his army marched towards the Orient. After some time, they reached a plain where two hills stood, connected by a chain of gold. The hiding place of Prophet Sulaiman's treasure lay through an opening in the hills. The descendants of *jinn* Sakhr were guarding the treasure; they told King Iskandar that the Prophet Sulaiman had bequeathed his riches to him. Iskandar divided the treasures among his generals and subjects, and continued on his journey. On the way, he met a tribe that worshipped the night, and a species of fly that was the size of a hill. Iskandar converted the tribe to Islam, and frightened the gigantic flies away. Soon, Iskandar reached a country called Qiarawan, which was ruled by Raja Hawas. The king had a daughter, Princess Syamsul Bahrain, who was betrothed to a prince named Muslim, the son of Raja Gidagah from Barbar. When Raja Hawas heard of the arrival of Raja Iskandar's army, he disguised himself as a fortune-teller and infiltrated Iskandar's army. His plan was to murder Iskandar. His evil intention was thwarted by the Prophet Khidir and he was forced to convert to Islam. When he returned to his kingdom, he gathered his army and attacked King Iskandar. The battle was so intense that nothing could be heard except the relentless and frightful clash of weapons. Raja Hawas was subsequently killed in battle and Princess Syamsul Bahrain captured. King Iskandar then disguised himself and went to meet King Gidagah. King Gidagah recognised him and tried to kill him. But the Prophet Khidir once more managed to rescue King Iskandar. Raja Gidagah and his subjects embraced Islam. His son, Muslim, also converted in order to marry Princess Syamsul Bahrain.

King Iskandar had been away from Macedonia for twenty years while travelling to the lands where the sun sets and to the country of Barqa. During that time, news arrived that Darinus, son of King Dara of Egypt, had become a follower of the Zoroastrian faith. Iskandar conquered many powerful countries, including Egypt. In Alwah, Iskandar was attacked by Raja Harza, but the attack was repelled by Muslim. Raja Harza himself was killed in battle. Harza's brother, Harab, came to lend his support, but was captured while he was sleeping and killed. The same fate befell their sister, Tubah, whose magical powers could conjure up the sea and fire. Iskandar then defeated Raja Kibta who later embraced Islam. One of Kibta's men tried to kill Iskandar but his hands, by the will of God, shook so violently that he dropped the sword he was holding and pierced his own foot, thus killing himself. Raja Bijah, a relative of Raja Kibta, also became a Muslim on the advice of Kibta. His daughter, who refused to follow his example, met her death in battle.

After some further time, Iskandar and his men reached Egypt. The king, Palang, sent five spies to kill King Iskandar but they were all captured. One was killed; the remaining four were released. The Prophet Khidir visited Raja Palang and urged him to convert to Islam. Raja Palang tried to kill the prophet by serving him a poisoned date but he accidentally ate the poisoned fruit himself. At that moment, he realised the Greatness of God and recited the Profession of Faith. Palang surrendered his wealth to the Prophet Khidir, instructing him to give some of his treasure to his three daughters and the rest to Raja Iskandar. Raja Palang finally succumbed to his own poison and all his subjects later became Muslims.

Raja Iskandar then set out for Syam. On the way, he met a band of Israelites who had been banished by their king, Raja Tibus. A messenger from Raja Tibus later arrived. Iskandar disguised himself as the messenger so that he could meet Raja Tibus. Tibus had been waiting for support from Raja Darinus before deciding whether to embrace Islam or not. Iskandar's disguise was discovered and he was captured, only to escape seven days later. The Prophet Khidir brought the army to save Iskandar. The two armies engaged in a fierce battle. Tibus was killed in the war. His widow, Nurani, pretended to surrender to Iskandar but had devised a plot to take her revenge. She sent her beautiful and cunning daughter Princess Nuran to poison King Iskandar. However, one of Iskandar's generals found out about the princess's plan. Instead of executing her, Iskandar simply asked her to accept Islam. After her conversion Princess Nuran, who was secretly in love with Iskandar, married him; he too had fallen in love with her.

The Sumatran version ends at this point. The Malayan version takes the story further. Iskandar continued to conquer the various nations. He killed Darinus and took his daughter, Ruqaiyatu Kubra, to be his wife. Khidi of Hind also gave his daughter, Badrul Qumriya, to Iskandar. (This story was repeated by the writer of *Sejarah Melayu*).

From this point on, the Iskandar stories become more fantastical and mysterious. Iskandar reached the vast ocean that spans the entire world and met Mikail and the other angels. He sank to the bottom of the ocean in a chest. A fish swallowed the chest but later spat it out so that Iskandar could be reunited with his army. Iskandar then continued his journey. He passed through Mecca and reached a pitch-black field, covered by the veil of darkness. The field was said to contain the Fountain of Life, which could give eternal life to all who drank from it. Iskandar secretly went in search of the fountain but failed to find it. On the other hand, the Prophet Khidir, who was not intending to find the magic fountain at all, discovered it almost by accident. Iskandar was disappointed.

Nearly all the Iskandar stories end here. Only the fourth Winstedt manuscript carries the tale further. Iskandar built several cities. While digging one day, he found an inscription that told of the futility and impermanence of this world. Not long after, Iskandar fell ill and died. The Winstedt manuscript ends with the Prophet Khidir's reflections on the fleeting nature of the world. He divided Iskandar's wealth among his vassals and their armies.

5.4.2 *Hikayat Amir Hamzah*

The *Hikayat Amir Hamzah* is a popular war story. The *Sejarah Melayu* (Story 34) relates that when Malaka was about to be attacked by the Portuguese, the Malay warriors asked Sultan Ahmad for a recitation of the *Hikayat Muhammad Hanafiah*. Instead the sultan gave them the *Hikayat Amir Hamzah*, telling them that he hoped that they would be as courageous as Amir Hamzah. It was only after listening to an explanation by one of the warriors that he finally gave them the *Hikayat Muhammad Hanafiah* as they had originally requested.

This is proof of the possible age of this *hikayat*. Winstedt has argued that the *hikayat* must have already been written by 1536, perhaps in the 15th century or the early part of the 16th century (Winstedt, 1958). Hooykaas, on the other hand, offers two other posibilties (Hooykaas, 1947). The *Hikayat Amir Hamzah* may be a later work because it is mentioned in the *Hikayat Hang Tuah* that Hang Jebat read the *Hikayat Amir Hamzah* to the king, and we know that the *Hikayat Hang Tuah* is a comparatively later work.The reference to the *Hikayat Amir Hamzah* in the *Sejarah Melayu* may then either be an anachronism or a later insertion. However, there is other evidence to suggest how old this *hikayat* really is. There are a number of Amir Hamzah tales written in Middle Javanese, a language which began to develop after the 14th century. As Islamic literature was usually first written in Malay and then translated into other regional languages, the *Hikayat Amir Hamzah,* must certainly be very early. Moreover, the *Hikayat Amir Hamzah* contains many adventure stories and tales set in countries in mainland Asia. A familiarity with these countries was only possible prior to the 17th century; after the Western monopoly over trade in the region was enforced, contact with the mainland of Asia was no longer possible. The third piece of evidence for the early date of the *Hikayat Amir Hamzah* is its predominantly Syi'ah milieu.

The *Hikayat Amir Hamzah* covers over a thousand pages. The two Leiden manuscripts studied by Ph. S. Van Ronkel – Manuscript A (1697) and Manuscript B (1698) – consist of 91 tales, spread across 1225 and 1843 pages respectively. The plot in both manuscripts is almost the same. One difference is that the introduction in Manuscript A is written in broken Persian, whereas that of Manuscript B is in fluent and grammatical Persian. The most distinctive difference of all, however, lies in the names of characters.

1 Sources

Ph. S. Van Ronkel concluded that the *Hikayat Amir Hamzah* was derived directly from the Persian, and not from the Arabic language as several other scholars had previously asserted. Ronkel pointed out that, firstly, in both the Persian and the Malay versions, Abdul Muttalib is described as being Hamzah's father (while in the Arabic version, Hamzah is the son of Kinana). Secondly, the division of chapters in the Malay version is similar to that in the Persian text. Thirdly, part of the introduction in the Malay version is written in Persian. Fourthly, there are many Persian words and verses throughout the Malay version. Fifthly, the plots of the Persian and Malay versions are very similar. Sixthly, if a typically Arabic word is found in the Persian version, the same word is repeated in the Malay version. The similarities are so great that one manuscript can be used to correct the reading of the other manuscript and vice versa.

A comparison of the Persian and Malay versions also clarifies the relationship between the two Malay manuscripts. Manuscript A offers a more accurate adaptation of the narrative of the Persian text, while Manuscript B can be relied on for a more correct spelling of names. The tale in Manuscript A furthermore is more factual, whereas Manuscript B is full of Persian verses and proverbs.

Amir Hamzah was, in fact, a historical figure. He was the uncle of Prophet Muhammad. Although a relative of the prophet and a member of the Hashemite clan (to which the prophet also belonged), Amir Hamzah initially treated Muhammad as an enemy. But he later repented and became one of Muhammad's most reknowned warriors, particularly for his role in the battles of Badr and Uhud. Amir Hamzah died after being stabbed by an Ethiopian slave at the instigation of Muawiyah's mother. The Persians so revere Amir Hamzah that legends and myths that have developed around him are not always historically accurate. Moreover, fictitious and sometimes fantastical elements were often added as embellishments. Other additions were also made to the story. Prof. Van Ronkel has shown that several incidents that were attributed to Amir Hamzah were actually the exploits of Rustam. This can be verified from the *Syah-Nama* (*Book of Kings*) compiled by Firdausi. Van Ronkel has shown that several other stories in the *hikayat* were also taken from the *Syah-Nama*, such as those about Gustehem Lohrast, Behnam and others. Other legendary sources, such as the *Hikayat Seribu Satu Malam (One Thousand and One Nights)*, have enriched the *Hikayat Amir Hamzah*. Van Ronkel concludes that the original version of the *Hikayat Amir Hamzah* was a diverse collection of various stories and legends that served to glorify Islam and its warriors (Van Ronkel, 1895: 239-242).

The *Hikayat Amir Hamzah* is a very popular tale. It has been translated into many different languages. The first translation was into Arabic and was done so long ago that Van Ronkel felt the need to prove that the original version of the *Hikayat Amir Hamzah* was actually written in Persian and not Arabic (Van Ronkel, 1895: 82-90). It should be mentioned that the Arabic version is quite different from the Persian one. In the Arabic version, Hamzah is said to be the grandson of a man called Kinana. There is no mention of his father. The reason why Buzur was sent to Mecca also differs in the Arabic version.

The *Hikayat Amir Hamzah* can be found in several Indian languages, such as Hindi and Bengali, as well as in various languages of the Malay Archipelago. Besides giving an account of the deaths of Hasan and Husain, the Bugis version also depicts Muhammad Hanafiah's quest for revenge. An important version is the Javanese version known as *Menak*, which means 'warrior'. The Javanese version is the source of the Sundanese and Balinese versions. The *Menak* is a well-known Javanese literary work. This is evident from the widespread practice of deriving Javanese names from the characters in the *Menak*. The best known *Menak* version was written by Jasadipura in the late 18th century. According to research by scholars such as Van Ronkel, the *Menak* is actually an adaptation from the Malay tale, the *Hikayat Amir Hamzah*, but the scope of its contents is much broader than the Malay version, in accordance with the generally more elaborate Javanese narrative style. For example, the Malay version might tell how Hamzah advanced against the enemy, defeated his foe's most fearsome warriors, forced them to beat a hasty retreat, and subsequently captured their city. In the Javanese version, the *Menak*, the scene would be depicted in the following way. Once Hamzah has charged to the fore, this is followed by a long and detailed descriptions of the opposing army; the traits of several of the well-known military commanders on the battlefield; the dialogues and conversations that transpired between the two sides; an exhaustive depiction of the battle itself; a meticulous picture of the besieged city; and finally an ornate paean to victory. Thus, a story that can be told in a single page of Malay requires ten pages in Javanese. With further supplementary stories and secondary plots, the *Menak* eventually became a vast tale with an enormously complicated storyline (Van Ronkel, 1895: 188; Hooykaas, 1947: 155-156). It needs to be mentioned here that the *Menak* is also a source of tales used in *wayang golek* puppet theatre.

Below is a summary of the *Hikayat Amir Hamzah* (following Van Ronkel's synopsis).

2 A Synopsis of the *Hikayat Amir Hamzah*

Kobad Syahriar was king of Medain. His prime minister was Khawajeh Alqasy, a close friend of Bekhti Jamal. One day, Khawajeh Alqasy foretold that misfortune would befall Bekhti Jamal. To prevent this happening, Bekhti Jamal was advised to stay indoors for forty days. On the thirty-ninth day, however, Khawajeh Alqasy invited his friend to go for a walk. During the outing, Bekhti Jamal stumbled upon a treasure chest. Khawajeh Alqasy killed Bekhti Jamal in order to have the treasure for himself. Before he breathed his last, Bekhti Jamal asked his friend to look after his pregnant wife and baby.

Bekthi Jamal's widow gave birth to a boy named Buzur Jamir. When the boy was nine years old, he finished his studies and became a fortune-teller. His training showed him the idenity of his father's murderer. Afraid that his crime would be known, Alqasy planned to kill Buzur. However, the person he hired to kill Buzur spared the young fortune-teller's life and hid him so that he could not be found by Alqasy. King Kobad had a dream and asked Alqasy to interpret its meaning but he could not. Buzur was summoned to the palace. He was able to interpret the king's dream and also told the king about Alqasy's treachery. Alqasy was executed and all his wealth given to Buzur. Thereafter, Buzur served as the royal astrologer. He eventually became the prime minister of Medain. He prophesied that the king would be blessed by God with the most perfect son, whom he would name Nusyirwan. He also foretold that enemies from Arabia would attack the kingdom. The king then ordered that all pregnant women in his realm to be killed.

In Mecca, a son named Amir Hamzah (hereafter referred to as Hamzah) was born to Abdul Muttalib. His servant, Omayya al-Damri, also fathered a son, named Amir ibn Omayya (hereafter referred to as Amir). Buzur, who had been given the task of killing all the pregnant women and their babies, spared the lives of the two newborns. He foretold that the two were destined for future greatness and gave their parents large sums of money. When Kobad passed away, Nusyirwan became the new ruler. Bekhtek, a son of Alqasy, became a minister. Buzur returned to Medain and was warmly received.

Time passed. Hamzah and Amir were soon seven years old. The boys were extraordinarily strong. Once they defeated a champion wrestler who had never been beaten before. At school, both boys, but most especially Amir, were mischievous pupils. They once sold their teacher's shirt. When they were hungry, they stole eggs.

Next, they learned archery from a reknowned archer. Hamzah acquired the Prophet Ishak's arrow and this further increased his powers. He then studied the martial arts with Jibrail on a mountain. In Prophet Sulaiman's garden, the two young men acquired a horse of incredible stamina and speed. They also found an array of weapons whose powers were known far and wide.

With these skills, Hamzah and Amir were able to recover the tribute sent from Mecca to Nusyirwan which had been stolen. One of the robbers, Mokbil Halabi, later became Hamzah's loyal follower. In Yemen, Hamzah defeated Princess Hamai Taif, who had vowed that she would only marry the man who could defeat her in combat. Hamzah did not marry the princess but gave her away to Tauk Tariq who loved her.

Hamzah defeated a young warrior Amir ibn Ma'di Karib who, together with forty of his relatives, quickly offered his services to Hamzah. When he heard of Hamzah's courage, Nusyirwan wanted to meet him. Hamzah was warmly welcomed on his arrival at the palace. Nusyirwan complimented Hamzah on his horse. One of Nusyirwan's warriors disagreed and Hamzah was forced to fight the man. Gustehem, another of Nusyirwan's warriors, planned to kill Hamzah but he was no match for Hamzah; he and his sons were defeated. Gustehem then turned to Alqasy and Zubin for help. Alqasy was defeated and embraced Islam.

Hamzah fell in love with Nusyirwan's daughter, Mihrnigar. Their relationship caused an uproar in the palace. Nusyirwan sent two of his sons to capture Hamzah but they themselves were captured by Hamzah. Nusyirwan was worried for his sons' safety but was reassured by Buzur that no harm would come to them. On the third day, Hamzah released both of Nusyirwan's sons.

Raja Syelpal of Serendib sent a letter to Nusyirwan, saying that he had been driven out of his kingdom by a giant called Lendehur. Bekhti suggested that Nusyirwan offer the hand of Princess Mihrnigar in marriage to whomever could bring to him Lendehur's head. The real intention behind this proposal was to get rid of Hamzah. Hamzah and Amir set out. Many strange incidents happened during their journey to the island where Lendehur lived. On one island they were attacked by a creature that strangled its victims. On another island, Amir obtained many magical objects which had been passed down from the prophets Adam, Ibrahim, Ismail and Sulaiman. Their arrival was warmly welcomed by Syelpal. The warriors wasted no time in attacking Lendehur. No one could defeat the ogre. Gustehem, Hamzah's sworn enemy, was almost killed by the monster. Finally, Hamzah stepped forward and killed Lendehur after seventeen days of fighting.

Hamzah called for a singer to entertain him. Gustehem paid a female slave to sing and then poison Hamzah. The poison rendered Hamzah unconscious for forty days. Lendehur, who had converted to Islam, chased Gustehem out of the kingdom. Gustehem returned to Medain and announced the news of Hamzah's death. When Gustehem heard that Hamzah was still alive, he fled to Zubin in Turkestan.

After Hamzah recovered, he began rebuilding the kingdom of Syelpal. When his work was done, Hamzah returned home, bringing Lendehur with him. Nusyirwan promised Mihrnigar to a nephew, Olad Merzeban, who had long been in love with her. Amir and Lenduhur captured Olad by a trick. Everyone was very happy, especially Mihrnigar.

Bekhtek reminded Nusyirwan that the condition for Hamzah's marriage to Mihrnigar was Lendehur's head. Lendehur was willing to sacrifice himself but Hamzah said nothing. When Nusyirwan ordered Lendehur's head be cut off, Hamzah intervened and instead called for the arrest of Bekhtek. Amir caught Bekhtek and gave him a sound trashing.

Later Bekhtek asked Nusyirwan to kill an old woman and to pretend that Mihrnigar had died. Everyone in the kingdom grieved over her death. Amir was suspicious and exposed the deception. When Hamzah learnt of Bekhtek's plot, he was furious. Bekhtek explained that he was only trying to put Hamzah's love for Mihrnigar to the test.

Bekhtek still wanted to kill Hamzah. He asked Nusyirwan to announce that three of his vassals had refused to pay tribute and that whoever could defeat these rulers would win Mihrnigar's hand. Once again Hamzah accepted the challenge. Bekhtek instructed Qarun, who was sent to accompany Hamzah on his journey as a guide, to poison Hamzah. The plot was uncovered; Qarun was apprehended but was spared. Hamzah succeeded in defeating the kings of Greece and Rome. Adi, the king of Greece, was killed and his nephew forced to embrace Islam. The king of Rome was prepared to let his nephews convert to Islam. In Egypt, however, Hamzah was tricked by Aziz and imprisoned on an island. When Mokbil heard the news, he rushed to the island but by the time he arrived, the ruler of the island had already taken Aziz's daughter, Zuhrah Banu, to be his wife. The prophet Ibrahim manifested himself; he ordered Zuhrah to marry Mokbil and help Hamzah escape. Zuhrah killed her husband and gave Hamzah's weapons back to him.

They returned to Egypt. Aziz fought his daughter and lost. Mokbil married Zuhrah Banu after she converted to Islam. Aziz's niece, Nasir Syah, wanted to marry but he declined her proposal.

Hamzah challenged Nusyirwan to a battle. In the battle, Hamzah killed Gustehem and his sons but was himself wounded in a clash with Zubin and carried on his horse to Mecca. When Hamzah was hungry, Mihrnigar stole some food for him. Amir was able to infiltrate the enemy camp many times. During one of his raids, he managed to abduct Nusyirwan, Bekhtek and Zubin. Nusyirwan was unharmed. Bekhtek and Zubin had to pay a ransom; they were beaten and forced to shave their beards before they were released.

There were two cities on Mount Kaf—one ruled by a Muslim fairy called Azra; the other by an infidel *jinn Ifrit*. The Ifrit had overthrew Azra and one of his ministers, Salasil, urged Azra to seek Hamzah's help. Hamzah came to Azra's aid and killed the *jinn*. Azra rewarded Hamzah with Prophet Sulaiman's magic hat. On his way home, Hamzah fell asleep and was captured by Habra

Diw, the Ifrit's son. When Hamzah woke, he killed Habra Diw. Hamzah subsequently fell in love with the king's niece, Asman, and married her.

Their marriage was blessed with a daughter named Quraisy. One day Asman overheard Hamzah praising Princess Mihrnigar. She felt jealous and disappeared. Hamzah looked everywhere for her. During his search, the Prophet Khidir appeared and warned him that his quest would be fraught with many dangers. The prophet gave him a length of rope and Hamzah entered an opening in the ground. He chased away all the *jinn*s he found there.

While he was exploring this nether world, he came across a beautiful garden where he was tricked by infidel fairy. Luckily, a bird came to his rescue. In another garden, an infidel fairy appeared and asked Hamzah for forgiveness, promising to show him the way out. Next, Hamzah released a *jinn* who had been imprisoned by Prophet Sulaiman at the request of an old woman. The ungrateful *jinn* repaid Hamzah's kindness by attacking him. Furious, Hamzah wanted to kill the *jinn* but it begged him for forgiveness and gave Hamzah a magic horse.

A severe famine gripped the land. Amir ibn Ma'di Karib approached a passing caravan to spare them some food; he helped save the caravan from a band of robbers. Amir was elected as their ruler and chose a wife. However, the queen died the next day. Amir ibn Ma'di Karib refused to be buried with his queen as custom dictated and was imprisoned. Hamzah resolved the situation and the whole city converted to Islam.

Hamzah and Amir entered the city amidst much rejoicing. The next day war broke out. The enemy forces were completely crushed and the spoils of war distributed among the victors. Bekhtek, Zubin and Nusyirwan fled to Homum in Damascus.

The lavish celebrations lasted forty days. Hamzah sent an envoy to Homum. Another battle began. Damascus fell. Meanwhile, Nasir's daughter had mysteriously become pregnant. One night she had had a dream and gone to look for Hamzah. He was not in his tent. She took one of his clothes and wrapped it around herself. As soon as she did, she became pregnant. Later, she gave birth to a son named Omar ibn Hamzah (hereafter simply referred to as Omar). Hamzah was delighted to meet his son.

Hamzah formally proposed to Mihrnigar and Nusyirwan warmly accepted his proposal. Bekhtek encouraged Hamzah to sack Zubin's palace. Hamzah did so. He captured Zubin's niece, Gul-rukh, and gave her to Omar to be his wife. He also captured Zubin's wife and his mother and married them to Amir ibn Ma'di Karib and Amir. The whole city was decorated to celebrate the weddings. Not long after, Gul-rukh gave birth to a son named Kobad. Nusyirwan was elated at the birth of his grandson. The child grew very quickly.

Zubin encouraged Nusyirwan and Bekhtek to flee to Behman in Turkestan. Hamzah's army pursued them and a further battle ensued. Behman and Bekhtek were defeated. The news arrived that Syaddad Abu Omar Habsyi had surrounded Mecca. Hamzah returned at once and repelled the enemy. Syaddad converted to Islam. He was still displeased with Nusyirwan and marched to Medain. Nusyirwan and Bekhtek were captured. Believing that that Hamzah had been killed by Syaddad, Nusyirwan sent Zubin and Behman to attack Hamzah's army. Behman was promised Mihrnigar if he succeeded. Behman surrounded Hamzah's men but he was killed by Omar during the battle.

Hurmuz planned to free his father Nusyirwan from Syaddad. His mother appealed to Hamzah to help. Once again Syaddad tasted defeat at Hamzah's hands and he decided to join forces with Zubin. Kobad, Hamzah's son, was killed by one of Zubin's slaves. The battle raged on. Lendehur killed Syaddad. Zubin quietly approached Mihrnigar and wounded her. She died from her injuries. Hamzah was devastated. That night the Prophet Ibrahim appeared and tried to console Hamzah by telling him that he would soon find an even prettier wife.

Qaren, the son of the king of Akko, wanted revenge for his father's death at Hamzah's hands. He kidnapped Hamzah and Mokbil and imprisoned them. Qaren's sister received a revelation from God to set Hamzah free and marry him. After Hamzah was freed, Qaren was captured and executed for refusing to convert to Islam. A huge festival was held to celebrate the wedding of Hamzah and Qaren's sister.

Alju-Syeh Gezi, Qimas and Keyus launched a series of attacks against Hamzah's army. They lost the battles and were forced to convert to Islam. Meanwhile, Hamzah had fallen in love with Princess Gil-Sowar and married her. Hamzah had spurned a Chinese princess, Urnekir, in the past, and she was inflamed with jealousy when she heard of his new marriage. She wanted to kill Hamzah and his new bride. However, her plot failed and instead she was killed by Gil-Sowar. Nusyirwan was distressed, as he loved Princess Urnekir. Disguising himself as as merchant, he set out for China. On the way, he was robbed by a bandit, Behram. None of the kings Nusyirwan visited believed him when he told them who he really was. Finally, he had no choice but to work with some charcoal-burners, in order to feed himself. Even then, he did not dare reveal his true identity. The queen sent a letter to Hamzah asking him to look for Nusyirwan. Nusyirwan was surprised when he later discovered that Hamzah had come to rescue him. He was nonetheless grateful. Hamzah eventually married Nusyirwan's daughter. Bekhtek was unhappy with these events and devised various schemes to kill Hamzah.

Bekhtek slyly convinced King Erdebil, Cup Gurden, and Raja Malek to send their armies against Hamzah.They were defeated and made to convert to Islam.

In the meantime, Princess Gil-Sowar had given birth. Refusing to accept the child, Hamzah placed him in a cot and pushed him out to sea. Princess Asman found the baby and raised him on Mount Qaf. The baby was named Badi ul-Zaman. When Badi ul-Zaman grew up, he went in search of his father and was finally acknowledged by Hamzah.

Semendun-hezar-dest, who was said to be invincible, kidnapped one of Hamzah's children; for this, he was put to death. Raja Herum from Bardada who had never lost to anyone else was also defeated by Hamzah. Hamzah took Herum's sister as his wife.

Amir was furious with Bekhtek who had been the cause of so much bloodshed. He disguised himself as a cook and cut Bekhtek into tiny pieces. He cooked the remains and served the dish to Nusyirwan. Nusyirwan was furious that Buzur had failed to predict this. Hurmuz, Nusyirwan's son, ascended the throne in his father's place. Buzur's son, Siyawekhasy, and Bekhtek's son, Bakhtiar, were chosen as viziers. Bakhtiar convinced Hurmuz to seek help from a number of other kings to wage war against Hamzah.

Gawilingi sent Zerduhsht to lead an army of tigers against Hamzah. The tigers were destroyed by Herum and Amir. Hurmuz then sought help from Sersal, the cannibal prince of Dal. Every day, Hurmuz had to provide human flesh for Sersal. Hurmuz regretted asking Sersal for help.

Siyawekhsy, Buzur's son, suggested that Hurmuz ask Hamzah for help instead. Hamzah was willing to help on the condition that Hurmuz sincerely embraced Islam. After an intense battle, Hamzah defeated Sersal and bound him. Sersal became a Muslim.

Next, two other kings were defeated and subsequently converted to Islam. Finally, Gawilingi too was defeated by Hamzah and he too repented. Zerduhsht was set alight and died in his vault. Amir also killed two of Zerduhsht's daughters who wanted to avenge their father's death.

Hamzah decided to meet the Prophet Muhammad and was warmly welcomed by the apostle. Hamzah deepened his understanding of Islam and dutifully carried out all its commandments.

Muhammad heard that the infidels had come together to attack him. Before long, an intense battle took place. Gawilingi was killed by Pur Hindi. Hamzah was furious and killed Pur Hindi. Hindi's mother gathered the armies of Rome, Syria, Ethiopia and Abyssinia, and surrounded Hamzah's army. Hurmuz had also been persuaded to join forces with them. He marched with thousands of his soldiers to Mecca and reached Mount Ubud. When Muhammad was told of this, he said, "Why should I be afraid of this army? My uncle will crush them in no time at all." These words angered Allah. The next day, Muhammad's troops were soundly beaten. The Muslim warriors fell one after another —first Lendehur, next Sa'd ibn Omar, and then Amir ibn Ma'di Karib. Ali was hit in the leg by an arrow, and Muhammad himself lost two teeth. When Hamzah received news of these events, he was enraged. He charged into the thick of battle and killed many of the enemy. He chased Hurmuz, captured him, and cut him into two pieces. Hamzah pursued the remaining infidel army. He finally made his way home, carrying a large haul of the spoils of war.

Hamzah however was beginning to feel uneasy. One of his horse's shoes had dropped. He remembered Buzur's prophecy that he would soon meet his death when his horse lost a shoe. Hamzah thought to himself, "I have defeated all the infidels, so who can kill me?" At that very moment, Pur Hindi's mother, who had been watching Hamzah's every move, seized her opportunity and hacked the leg of Hamzah's horse. Hamzah fell and was killed. Pur Hindi's mother was aware that Hamzah had a daughter who would no doubt try to avenge her father. To avoid the daughter's wrath, Pur Hindi's mother went to see Prophet Muhamamd to seek his forgiveness. The prophet forgave her.

A few days after, Asman and Quraisy arrived in Mecca with an army of a thousand *jinns*. They demanded that Pur Hindi's mother be handed over to them. It is said that it was at this time that the *Surat al-Jin* (The Chapter on the *Jinn*) was revealed by Allah. Prophet Muhammad explained to Hamzah's daughter, "Had your father not died, he would not have been assured of a place in heaven. Now look up to heaven." They looked up and saw Hamzah sitting in an honoured place by God's side. On seeing this, Hamzah's wife, Asman, and daughter, Quraisy, praised God.

Another story of the loss of Prophet Muhammad's teeth is as follows:

One night while Aisyah was sewing she dropped her needle on her bed. She looked for the needle could not find it. The Prophet Muhammad entered the room, and his teeth were so white that they shone a light on the missing needle, revealing where it had fallen. Muhammad thought, "What excellent teeth I have!" Immediately, two of his teeth broke.

The last story tells about Ali's great courage. When he was hit in the leg by an arrow, his friends tried to pull it out. Ali appeared to feel no pain.

5.4.2.1 *Hikayat Badi ul-Zaman*

The *Hikayat Amir Hamzah* continues the story of Badi ul-Zaman, Hamzah's son who was set adrift at sea. This tale is not found in the Persian version. The story is as follows.

Badi ul-Zaman lost his way in the forest. After some time, he reached the country of Zemin Turan, which was ruled by Raja Sadr-Alam. The king had a daughter, Julus ul-Asyikin. When Badi was brought before the princess, he fell in love with her. The princess refused to be separated from Badi and they ran away to a secret place in Turan. Her father was furious when he heard that they had eloped. He sent an army to capture Badi but he beat them off. When the king discovered that Badi was Hamzah's son, he accepted him as his son-in-law. The ruler celebrated a lavish celebration in their honour.

Saif-Alam and his three brothers attacked Raja Sadr-Alam. They were no match for Badi and were forced to embrace Islam. Meanwhile, Hamzah and Amir went in search of Badi but could not find him anywhere. Amir continued his search alone. He came to a land ruled by the arrogant Syahsyah Alam Rabbul-samawati Wal-ardi. Disguising himself as a singer, Amir attended a festival at the palace. When the king and other dignitaries were all drunk, Amir shaved off the king's beard and ran away with a considerable amount of treasure. Amir soon arrived in Turan and found Badi at last. Everyone rejoiced. Hamzah wanted to go to Turan to be reunited with his son but he first had to fight against the kingdom of Ambar.

Hurmuz allied himself with Syahsyah Alam's army and advanced on Ambar. The two sides were soon engaged in an intense battle. Both armies suffered many casualties. Hamzah defeated many rulers and most of them converted to Islam, the most famous being Separdar. After forty days, Hamzah killed Syahsyah Alam. The people of Ambar embraced Islam. Separdar became the new king of Ambar.

Hamzah then set off for Turan to meet Badi. The festivity held to celebrate this joyous occasion lasted forty days. Not long after, Hamzah missed his parents and wished to return home. With a heavy heart, he bade his friends farewell. Many of them were sad to see him go and bade him a tearful goodbye.

5.4.2.2 *Hikayat Lahad*

Jibrail appeared to the Prophet Muhammad, warning him that the king of Lahad had ordered his army to surround Mecca. Mecca prepared for war. Not long after, an intense battle took place. At first, many of the enemy were killed on the battle field and there were no Muslim casualties. As the war continued, however, the Muslims found themselves outnumbered and were on the verge of surrendering. Hamzah rode his horse into the enemy line. Although he killed many enemy soldiers, he himself was fatally wounded. His enemies tore out his liver and ate it, believing that they would become as courageous as he had been.

Abu Bakar and Muhammad hid in a well. One of Muhammad's teeth broke after it was hit by a stone thrown at him by an enemy. Jibrail reported to Allah about the indignity Muhammad was suffering. Allah sent Jibrail to Madinah to rescue Muhammad.

Jibrail visited Ali and his wife, Fatimah, and said, "Allah is all-knowing." Ali sighed ruefully, wishing his leg was fully healed. Jibrail immediately healed Ali's wounded leg. Ali straightaway returned to the battle field. He captured Lahad and took him to Muhammad. Lahad accepted Islam and was pardoned. They then went to look for Hamzah's body and gave him a proper burial. Hamzah's daughter, Quraisy, came to the battlefield to see her father for the last time. The Prophet Muhammad asked her to look up to the heavens and when she did, she saw Hamzah dressed in white, surrounded by angels and looking very happy. She also saw all the warriors who had perished in battle smiling beatifically. Everyone on earth rejoiced at the sight. Thereafter, Prophet Muhammad returned to Mecca.

5.4.2.3 *Hikayat Amir Ibn Omayya*

One day Amir ibn Omayya asked the Prophet Muhammad about the time of his death. The prophet replied that Amir could die anytime he chose, after he saw the angel of death. Amir was elated as he thought he would never have to die.

One day in Ramadan, a young man visited Amir, claiming that he was the angel of death. Amir fled. Wherever he went, he saw people digging graves. Each time he asked for whom the grave was being dug, the answer was always the same: "For Amir ibn Omayya." Accepting that he could not escape death, Amir purified himself, bathed, and lay down in one of the graves. Angels then came to the grave and covered him with earth.

5.4.3 *Hikayat Saif Dzul-Yazan*

The *Hikayat Saif Dzul-Yazan* is an adaptation of an Arabic book entitled *Sirat Saif Dzul Yazan (The Life of Saif Dzul Yazan)*. The story describes a battle between the king of Himyar (in ancient Yemen) and the king of Abyssinia. Raja Saif Rad lost and was forced to flee in search of help, first to Istanbul and then to Medain. He passed away in Medain. After his death, the king of Abyssinia was defeated in battle and was banished from his kingdom. An Arab writer, Abul Ma'ali, later wrote the book *Sirat Saif Dzul-Yazan*.

The *hikayat* was probably popular because of its resemblance to a Malay *hikayat*. Manuscripts can be found in the Jakarta Museum, as well as in Leiden and London. A manuscript in the Jakarta Museum (v.d. Wall Collection 117), copied in Malaka in 1285 (hijrah year 1834), identifies a Tamil man, Hasan ibn Farsab, as the manuscript's owner. Another manuscript exists and is also known by the title *Hikayat Siti Kamariah*.

This text has been published in Singapore several times, including a manuscript belonging to Haji Muhammad Amin which was lithographed in 1894. In 1958, the Malayan Branch of the Royal Asiatic Society published the manuscript belonging to Hassan bin Hussin Malaka, dated H. 1280 (1829 A.D). More recently the manuscript was republished in a romanised version by the Malayan Publishing House, edited by Rosmera.

According to Ph. Van Ronkel (1942), it is difficult to ascertain the identity of the original author. Several manuscripts suggest that this *hikayat* was adapted by a mixed-race Arab who knew Arabic and who was also proficient in the Malay language. However, the Leiden manuscript and the Singapore lithographed text contradict this assertion. These two manuscripts are littered with broken Arabic phrases and often spell the names of characters in the story incorrectly.

Summary of the Story

There was once a king in Yemen named Dzul-Yazan. His vizier was Yathrib. Dzul-Yazan built a city named Madinat al-Ahmar in a state he had conquered. Fearing for his kingdom, Saif al-Rad of Abyssinia sent a beautiful female slave, Kamariah, to poison Dzul-Yazan. The plot was discovered. Kamariah confessed but was pardoned by Dzul-Yazan and taken as his wife. When he died, Kamariah ascended to the throne.

She gave birth to a son who was held in high esteem by all her viziers. Kamariah became jealous of her newborn son and decided to dispose of him. The abandoned baby was suckled by a doe. He was later found by a hunter who took him to Raja Malik Afrah who had just become the father of a baby girl. Malik Afrah adopted the boy and named him Wahsy al-Fallah; he named his daughter Syamah. A vizier, Sekardium, predicted that the two infants would bring calamity to the kingdom and advised the king to kill them both. The king refused. Instead he sent Wahsy al-Fallah to be trained in the use of weapons. Sekardium had hired a *jinn* to kidnap Syamah. But Wahsy al-Fallah came and freed her. He then asked for her hand in marriage.

Wahsy al-Fallah's proposal was accepted on the condition that he kill a giant named Sa'don and bring its head to the king. He overcame various obstacles, with the support of Syamah, and finally met the giant. Sa'don was no match for Wahsy al-Fallah and conceded defeat. Together they all made their way back to the kingdom. Sa'don offered his head to the king, but the ruler spared him. The king and the monster became good friends.

Sekardium, the evil vizier, still wanted to kill Wahsy al-Fallah. He persuaded the king to order the young man to search for a magic book called the *Tarikh Nil*.

After surviving many dangerous events, with the help of others—first Tamah and his mother Akilah, and later the Muslim *jinn* Aksah—Wahsy al-Fallah eventually obtained two magic weapons that would help him gain possession of the magic book. The first was a magic cap which could make him invisible; the second was a ring with which he could kill his enemy simply by pointing at him.

The treacherous vizier Sekardium wrote to the king of Abyssinia, Saif al-Raden, urging him to ask for Syamah's hand in marriage. Sa'don was furious and killed the king's envoy. Saif Dzul-Yazan arrived while Sa'don was fighting Raja Malik Afrah, and stopped the war.

The cunning Sekardium was still not satisfied. He tried to trick Saif al-Rad into attacking Raja Malik Afrah. Fortunately Raja Saif al-Rad was not deceived and instead formed an alliance with Raja Malik Afrah. Together with Dzul-Yazan and Sa'don, Malik Afrah visited Said al-Rad. Saif al-Rad told them about a queen who was about to attack his kingdom. Saif Dzul-Yazan was sent to investigate the matter. The queen was Dzul-Yazan's mother, Kamariah. Kamariah recognised her son and told him that she was prepared to hand the throne over to him. However, when Saif Dzul-Yazan fell sleep, she stabbed him. Saif Dzul-Yazan however did not die; he was saved by two magical birds. He continued on his journey and met a saint, Syeikh Akhmim, who wanted to give him his daughter, Jidah. Saif Dzul-Yazan declined the offer and returned home.

Kamariah persuaded Saif ar-Rad to marry Syamah by telling him that Saif Dzul-Yazan had died. But before the wedding could take place, Saif Dzul-Yazan returned. Saif Dzul-Yazan and

Saif ar-Rad's armies fought each other. Saif Dzul-Yazan prevailed and many of Saif ar-Rad's men perished at his hands. Thereafter Saif Dzul-Yazan married Syamah. Kamariah asked him for forgiveness; he freely gave her his pardon. However when the two love birds were distracted, Kamariah stole the magic golden tablet and commanded its *jinn* guardian to cast the husband and wife out of the kingdom.

Saif Dzul-Yazan was exiled far away from Syamah. Syamah was sent to a land whose inhabitants worshipped goats. She was held captive and during her imprisonment gave birth to a baby boy named Damir. Saif Dzul-Yazan journeyed through the land of people with long, sharp fangs and finally arrived in the country of goat-worshippers. He too was captured and was about to be sacrificed together with Syamah. Aksah, a Muslim *jinn* who had promised Saif Dzul-Yazan that he would always help him whenever he was in trouble, appeared and carried them away to a safe place.

In another episode, Saif Dzul-Yazan killed a tiger. This earned him the gratitude of the kingdom's ruler, Abutat. Abutat lusted after Syamah; this led to a war with Saif Dzul-Yazan. Raja Abutat was captured but before Said Dzul-Yazan could harm him, Saif Dzul-Yazan was taken to a volcano by a *jinn* sent by Kamariah. Saif Dzul-Yazan was captured at the volcano by a sorcerer who wanted to burn him alive. Fortunately, another sorcerer, Bernoh, received a divine revelation telling him to free Saif Dzul-Yazan. Aksah then took Saif Dzul-Yazan and Bernoh to Abutat's kingdom, where Abutat was engaged in a war against his subjects. The cause of the civil war was this: after failing to win Syamah, Abutat realised the greatness of Allah and converted to Islam; his subjects on the other hand did not yet want to do so. Saif's arrival soon put an end to the war.

Aksah took Syamah back to her father's kingdom. Bernoh went to Kamariah's kingdom, followed by Saif Dzul-Yazan and Abutat. During the journey, they were kidnapped under Kamariah's orders by another *jinn* and taken to an island. Saif Dzul-Yazan managed to free himself and escaped to China, where he restored the eyesight of the blind Chinese princess, Nahidah, and later married her. They were both later taken by a *jinn* to Kamariah's kingdom. Once again, Kamariah begged for forgiveness and was forgiven. When Saif Dzul-Yazan was asleep, Kamariah again stole his magic gold tablet and ordered its guardian *jinn* to fly Saif Dzul-Yazan high into the skies then hurl him down to earth. Aksah appeared and again rescued Saif Dzul-Yazan. On his way home, Saif Dzul-Yazan stole Princess Muhiy an-Nufus's flying suit and thus forced her to marry him.

As a result of Bernoh's magic, Kamariah fell sick. She sent news to Saif ar-Rad, who then dispatched one of his military commanders, Raja Maimun, to attack Bernoh and Sa'don. Forty sorcerers, former friends of Bernoh, came to support Maimun. Fortunately, Saif Dzul-Yazan and Abutat arrived in time to help Bernoh. Maimun was defeated and embraced Islam. Bernoh however was captured by the forty sorcerers. Saif Dzul-Yazan and his army would have been destroyed by them, had not Akilah come to save them all. Akilah gave Saif Dzul-Yazan a special costume that could protect him from being abducted by *jinns* and human beings. Kamariah once again begged her son's forgiveness. When Saif Dzul-Yazan fell asleep, Kamariah stole the magic costume with the assistance of princess Nahidah. Tamah found out and killed Nahidah. Kamariah fled to China where she was finally killed by Tamah. Saif Dzul-Yazan was angry when he learnt about his mother's death, but not for long. Soon afterwards, he married Jidah, the daughter of a saint, whose proposal he had earlier rejected.

Princess Muhiy an-Nufus recovered the flying suit and returned to her homeland pursued, by Saif Dzul-Yazan. With the help of Aksah, they were reconciled. Saif Dzul-Yazan and Princess Muhiy an-Nufus then returned to Madinat al-Madinat, where Saif Dzul-Yazan ruled fairly and justly for many years.

5.4.4 *Hikayat Sultan Ibrahim Ibn Adham*

Ibrahim Ibn Adham was born in Balk (present-day Afghanistan) in 730 A.D. In 748 A.D., he moved to Syria and lived there as a Sufi for more than a quarter of a century. He was killed in battle against the Byzantine Christians. He was 47 years old at the time of his death.

There are many legends about Ibrahim Ibn Adham. Some—such as the time he swore he would never hunt again— appear to have a Buddhist influence. One day, when Sultan Ibrahim was out hunting, he heard a voice telling him to stop hunting. He dismounted and changed his clothes. Disguised as a shepherd, the sultan traveled far and wide.

Like many Sufis, Ibrahim ibn Adham was careful to only eat *halal* food. He was always prepared to work for a living, unlike some mystics who pretended to rely completely on the generosity of others. He worked as a farm laborer and maintained a simple diet.

The story of Ibrahim Ibn Adham is very well known in the Islamic world. It exists in the Arabic, Persian, Turkish and Hindi languages, as well as in Malay, Javanese, Buginese and Achehnese. The tale of Ibrahim Ibn Adham in Malay however is not an adaptation from a foreign source but an original creation, even though many elements found in the Malay version were undoubtedly taken from foreign sources. This is the conclusion of Russel Jones, who undertook a study of a Malay manuscript of the *Hikayat Sultan Ibrahim* for his PhD at London University in 1969 (Jones, 1985).

According to Jones, there are at least three Malay versions of the *Hikayat Sultan Ibrahim* (Jones, 1968: 8-9).

[a] Chapter IV, Section 1 of the *Bustanus Salatin*, compiled by Nur al-Din al-Raniri in Acheh in 1640. This version was edited by Russel Jones and published by Dewan Bahasa dan Pustaka in 1974.

[b] The unabridged version of about 125 pages long, which has not yet been published.

[c] The abridged version published by Roorda van Eysinga in 1822 which has been reprinted many times. This version is also entitled *Hikayat Sultan Ibrahim*.

The *Bustanus Salatin*, Chapter IV, Section 1, contains 25 well-known tales about Ibrahim Ibn Adham. These stories depict the rewards of meditation, repentance, charity and belief in God. About three-quarters of the stories are taken from the *Raudal-Rayahin* compiled by al-Yafi'i.

The unabridged version shares the same plot as the abridged text, with one exception: the reason for Ibrahim Ibn Adham's decision to leave his kingdom. It is told that Sultan Ibrahim established a grand and well-fortified city. He then assembled all his subjects and asked them if there was any thing lacking in the city. A mendicant replied that while the city was beautiful, it was also transient. Only heaven and hell are eternal. Sultan Ibrahim realised the folly of his grandiose dreams. He abdicated and vowed to devote himself to Allah.

The unabridged version also contains many more ethical teachings than the abridged text. The unabridged version explains, for example, the circumstances under which a person's prayers will not be answered by Allah. Also, Sultan Ibrahim pointed out when he was captured by the Badul tribe during his journey to Mecca that the only supplies he had with him were patience, gratitude, complete faith in Allah, and acceptance of His will.

The four unabridged versions studied by Russel Jones were produced at different times between 1775 and 1880, but the original must have been much older than this. All the manuscripts identified Syaikh Abu Bakar from the Hadramaut (a former state in Yemen) as their narrator.

Below is a summary of the abridged version printed in Singapore by Kelly & Walsh Limited in 1911.

Sultan Ibrahim Ibn Adham was a famous king of Iraq and a just ruler. One day he thought, "This world is like a beautiful dream; but when you finally wake, you will have nothing." This realization led him to pass over the administration of his kingdom to his vizier. He departed from the palace alone, equipped with only a walking staff, a knife, a begging bowl and a ring. He left his palace at a time when "no animal had yet roused from sleep to look for food, the stars were still bright in the sky, and all the birds were still in their nests."

After some time, the king felt hungry and thirsty. He saw a clear, sparkling river, and bathed and drank. He also ate a pomegranate he found floating in the river. As soon as he had eaten half the fruit, he realised that he had eaten something without the permission of its owner. He regretted his action and went to search for the owner of the piece of fruit.

The orchard belonged to Syarif Hasan and was extremely productive. It was tended by two of his friends, Syaikh Ismail and Muftihi 'l-Ariffin. One day Syarif Hasan felt that the hour of his death was near and called for his daughter. His daughter, Siti Saleha, was beautiful, kind and intelligent. Syarif Hasan's dying wish was that she should marry a man called Sultan Ibrahim and be faithful to him. He asked his friends to watch over his daughter. Having said these words, Syarif Hasan then passed away. Muftihi 'l-Arifin comforted Siti Saleha and told her to be strong. He related the story of Prophet Muhammad's daughter, Fatimah, who had only one set of clothes because her father had spent all that he owned to honour a visitor.

Sultan Ibrahim arrived to ask forgiveness for not having sought the owner's permission before eating the fruit. Siti Saleha replied, "Whoever wants to be absolved from the sin of eating a pomegranate must marry the one to whom it belongs. If he does not, the fruit will not be *halal*." On the advice of Muftihi 'l-Arifin, Sultan Ibrahim married Siti Saleha. She was a good wife to him.

One day Sultan Ibrahim told his wife that wanted to continue his journey. He asked her not to be sad, as they would be reunited in heaven. He also said: "This world is like a woman dressed in beautiful clothes, who seduces anyone who lays eyes on her. The moment you come closer, you will realise how old and decrepit she truly is." With that, Sultan Ibrahim left on his travels. Soon after, he reached Mecca and entered the The Sacred Mosque to pray. Each day, he circled the Kaabah seventy times.

The story continues that not long after her husband's departure, Siti Saleha gave birth to a pleasant, handsome baby boy. She named him Muhammad Tahir and raised him carefully. When

Muhammad Tahir grew, however, none of the other children wanted to play with him. They taunted him, saying that he was illegitimate. Ashamed, Muhammad Tahir ran home to ask Siti Saleha about his father and asked for her permission to find him.

Before long, Muhammad Tahir arrived in Mecca. Sultan Ibrahim was overjoyed to meet his son. He hugged and kissed the lad and couldn't bear to be separated from him. Distracted by his reunion with his son, Sultan Ibrahim forgot to circle the Kaabah. Filled with regret, he chased his son away, threatening to cut off his head if the boy refused to go. So Muhammad Tahir left his father. He went to Iraq, taking with him the ring his father had given him.

The Vizier of Iraq was happy to see Muhammad Tahir and wanted the youth to be crowned king in place of his father. But Muhammad Tahir declined, as he had no interest in worldly power. He nevertheless shared with the vizier some of his ideas on kingship. A king should treat all of his subjects fairly; he should appoint four ministers who are wise and noble to manage his kingdom's affairs; and he should also appoint a brave warrior well versed in warfare to command his army.

Taking with him a few precious stones, Muhammad Tahir then went back to his mother in Kufah and told her all that he had experienced during his travels. Siti Saleha for her part never forgot to ask God to bless her husband each time she prayed. And each year the vizier of Iraq sent eight camels laden with food and riches to Muhammad Tahir for as long as he lived.

REFERENCES

Alatas, Syed Hussain
1963. "On the need for an historical study of Malaysian Islamization," *JSEAH,* 4, 1, pp. 62-74.

Al-Attas, Syed Naguib
1970. *Preliminary statement of a general theory of the Islamization of the Malay-Indonesia Archipelago,* Kuala Lumpur.
1972. *Islam dalam sejarah dan kebudayaan Melayu,* Kuala Lumpur.

Aliman bin Mahmud
1936. *Hikayat Amir Hamzah,* Singapore.

Arif Abdullah
1983. *Nabi-nabi dalam Al-Quran,* Semarang.

Asiatic Journal
1823. "Hikajat Raja Jumjumah atau Tengkorak Kering."

Asdi S. Dipodjojo
1981. *Kesusasteraan Indonesia pada Zaman Pengaruh Islam,* Yogyakarta.

Bey Arifin
1972. *Rangkaian Cerita dalam Al-Quran,* Singapore.

Bladen, C. O.
1924. "A Note on the Trengganu Inscription," *JMBRAS,* 2 (2), pp. 258-263.

Brakel, L. F.
1975. *The Hikayat Muhammad Hanafiah,* Bibliotheca Indonesia 12, The Hague.

Browne, E. G.
1977. *A Literacy History of Persia,* Cambridge.

De Josselin de Jong, P. B.
1965. *Agama-agama di Gugusan Pulau-pulau Melayu,* Kuala Lumpur.

Douglas, F. W.
1955. "The Manuscripts of *Hikayat* Iskandar," *JMBRAS,* 28 (1), pp. 161-162.

Drewes, G. W. J.
1968. "New Light on the coming of Islam to Indonesia," *BKI,* 124 (4).

Edwar Djamaris, et al.
1973. "Singkatan naskah sastra Indonesia lama pengaruh Islam." *Bahasa dan Kesusastraan,* special edition no. 18.

ENCYCLOPAEDIA
1953. *Encyclopaedia of Islam,* shorter edition, Leiden.
1960. *Encyclopaedia of Islam,* new edition, Leiden.

E. Pf.
1966. "Alexander Romances" in *Encyclopaedia of Britannica,* I, pp. 580-581.

Fatimi, S. Q.
1963. *Islam Comes to Malaysia,* Singapore.

GAPENA
1984.   *Kesusasteraan Melayu dan Islam,* Kuala Lumpur.

Gibb, H. A. R & J. H. Kramers.
1953.   *Shorter Encyclopaedia of Islam,* Leiden.

Hafis Ghulam Sarwar
1937.   *The History of Islam,* I. I, Lahore.

Hamdan Hassan
1982.   "Kisah al-Anbiya dalam sastra Melayu," *Majalah Dewan Sastra,* pp. 72.
1990.   *Surat al-Anbiya,* Kuala Lumpur, DBP.

Hamka
1960.   "Permulaan Islam di Indonesia," *PustakaBudaja,* 2, 8, pp. 35-42.

Hill, A. H.
1963.   "The coming of Islam to North Sumatra," *JSEAH,* 4 (1), pp. 6-21.

Hollander, J. J. de.
1893.   *Handleiding bij de Beoefening der Maleische Taal en Letterkunde.* Breda: Koninklijk Militaire Academie.

Hooykaas, C.
1947.   *Over Maleische Literatuur,* Leiden.

Hurgronje, Ch. Snouck.
1906.   *The Achehnese II.* Translated by A. W. S. O'Sullivan. Vol. 2. Leiden.

Ismail Hamid
1983a.   *Kesusasteraan Melayu dari Warisan Peradaban Islam,* Kuala Lumpur.
1983b.   *The Malay Islamic Hikayat,* Kuala Lumpur.

Jassin, H. B.
1991.   *Bacaan Mulia,* Jakarta, Djambatan.

Johns, A. H.
1961a.   "Sufism as a category in Indonesia literature and history," *JSEAH,* 2.
1961b.   "The role of sufism in the spread of Islam to Malaya and Indonesia," *Journal of Pakistan Historical Society,* 9, pp. 145-161.
1966.   "From Buddhism to Islam," *Comparative Studies in Society and History,* IX, 1, The Hague.

Jones, Russel
1974.   *Bustanus Salatin,* Bab IV, Fasal 1, DBP, Kuala Lumpur.
1983.   "Ibrahim Ibn Adham. A summary of the Malay version", *Studies in Islam,* 5, pp. 7-21.
1985.   *Hikayat Sultan Ibrahim ibn Adham. An edition of an anonymous Malay text with translation and notes,* Berkeley.

Jumsari, Jusuf
1969.   "Iskandar Zulkarnain dalam sedjarah dan dongeng," *Buletin Museum,* No. 1, March, pp. 6-17.
1970.   "*Hikayat Radja Handak,*" *Manusia Indonesia,* (4 & 5 & 6).
1971.   "*Hikayat Radja Djumdjumah,*" *Manusia Indonesia* 5, 4 & 5 & 6 & 6, pp. 389-415.
1978.   *Hikayat Nabi Yusuf,* Jakarta.

Khalid Hussein.
1967.	*Hikayat Iskandar Zulkarnain,* Kuala Lumpur.

Knappert, Jan
1937.	*De Maleise Alexander Roman,* Meppel.
1985.	*Islamic Legends* I & II, Leiden.

Mahmoed Yunus
1960.	*Tafsir Qur'an Karim,* Djakarta.

Mahjul, C. A.
1962.	"Theories of the introduction and expansion of Islam in Malaysia," International Association of Historians of Asia, Biennial Conference Proceedings, Taiwan.

Majumdar, B. K.
1966/1967."The role of Indian religion in Southeast Asia," *Quarterly Review of Historical Studies,* 6(3), pp. 132-139.

Muhammad Fanani
1979/1980.*Hikayat Nur Muhammad dalam Kesusasteraan Lama,* Jakarta.

Nieuwenhuijze, C. A. O. van
1969.	"The legacy of Islam in Indonesia," *The Muslim World,* 59 (3 & 4), pp. 210-219.

Paterson, H. S.
1924.	"An early Malay inscription from Trengganu," *JMBRAS,* 2 (3), pp. 252-258.

Ricklefs, M. C. & P. Voorhoeve
1977.	*Indonesian Manuscripts in Great Britain,* London.

Ronkel, Ph. S. van
1895.	*De Roman van Amir Hamza,* Leiden.
1896.	"Het Cambridge Handschrift Ll. 6.5 en het Leidsche handschrift der Hikajat Mohammed Hanafiyya," *BKI,* 46, pp. 54-56.
1899.	"Over invloed der Arabische syntaxis op de Maleische," *TBG,* 41, pp.498-528.
1909.	"Het verhaal van den held Sama'un en van Maria de Koptische," *TBG,* 43, pp. 444-481.
1942.	"De Maleische versie van den Arabischen populairen roman van den held Saif Ibn Dzi'l-Jazan," *BKI,* 101, alf. 1, pp. 117-132.

Rosmera
1965.	*Hikayat Malik Saiful-Lizan,* Singapore.

Roolvink, R.
1960.	"Literature", in *The Encyclopedia of Islam,* New edition, Vol III, pp. 1230-1235.

Roedjiati, S. W.
1961.	"Tjerita Tabut," *Bahasa dan Budaya,* Th. IX, No. 3/4, pp. 83-90.
1969.	"Hikayat Raja Jumjumah," *Bahasa dan Kesusasteraan,* 2 (3), pp. 14-18.
1969.	Singkatan *Hikayat Bulan Berbelah,* Jakarta.

Samad Ahmad, A.
1987.	*Hikayat Amir Hamzah,* Kuala Lumpur.
1988.	*Hikayat Umar Umayah,* Kuala Lumpur.

Schact, Joseph
1974.   *The Legacy of Islam* (edition II), Oxford.

Siti Chamamah Soeratno
1991.   *Hikajat Iskandar Zulkarnain: Analisis Resepsi,* Jakarta.

Skinner, C.
1965.   "The influence of Arabic upon modern Malay," *Intisari,* 2 (2), pp. 34-47.

Slamet Mulyana
1968.   *Runtuhnya Keradjaan Hindu-Djawa dan Timbulnya Negara-negara Islam di Nusantara,* Bharata, Djakarta.

Soewita Santoso
1971.   "The Islamization of Indonesian Malay literature in its earlier period," *Journal of the Oriental Society of Australia,* 8 (1 & 2), pp. 9-27.

Tan Ta Sen
2010.   "Cheng Ho" penyebar Islam dari China ke Nusantara," *Kompas,* Jakarta.

Teeuw, A. & T. D. Situmorang
1952.   *Sedjarah Melayu,* Djakarta.

Thackston, W. M.
1978.   *The Tales of the Prophets of al-Kisa'i,* Boston.

Wahjunah Hj. Abd. Gani
1989.   *Hikayat Tamin al-Dari,* Kuala Lumpur.

Wijk, D. Gerth van.
1893.   "De Koranische Verhalen in het Maleisch," *TBG,* 35 (3-4), pp. 239-245.

Winstedt, R. O.
1923.   "Hikayat Sultan Ibrahim," *JMBRAS,* 1 (1), pp. 251-253.
1938.   "The date, authorship, contents and some new MSS of the Malay romance of Alexander the Great," *JMBRAS,* 16 (2), pp. 1-23.

Zuber Usman
1960.   "Sedikit tentang permulaan Islam di Indonesia," *Pustaka Budaja,* 2 (7), pp. 10-12

6 Framed narratives

There are various famous framed narratives (*cerita berbingkai*)[1] in Malay literature, including the *Hikayat Bayan Budiman*, the *Hikayat Kalilah dan Dimnah* and the *Hikayat Bakhtiar*. The framed narrative is said to have originated from India and traveled to the Archipelago along a number of different paths. Such works often contain several stories within the main story itself. Usually one or more characters in the story narrates the tale and then a character in that inner tale will take over the further narration, as a way of substantiating or corroborating the previous story. The inner or smaller story will, in turn, contain further sub-stories that will add to the further length and breadth of the story as a whole. For example:

> To illustrate the danger of trusting one's enemies, a teacher told the story of an owl and a crow. A crow once had its feathers plucked by its king; it fled, seeking refuge with the king of owls. A minister in the owl's court advised the king to kill the crow since one cannot, the minister argued, change the nature of the crow, just as one cannot change the nature of the mouse according to the tale of the mouse who became a human being. He then proceeded to tell the tale of the mouse who, in her human form, was asked to choose a husband; she chose a mouse. Another minister related another story, designed to convince the owl king to take advantage of the quarrel between the crow and its king. This story described a hermit who, because his enemies were busy fighting among themselves, took the opportunity to escape from their clutches and save himself.

Another characteristic of the framed narrative is that its animal characters are often given human qualities. These animals are not only expert story-tellers, they are also adept at giving advice to their masters on various human problems.

In India, the framed narrative is often referred to as *akhyayika*, which means 'story', and *katha,* which means 'pleasing'. Based on their different aims, the Indian framed narrative can be divided into three categories:

1. Stories compiled to convey religious teachings. These include tales from the *Jataka* as well as other stories from the Buddhist and Jain traditions.

---

[1] According to Prof. Tjan Tjoe Siem, the *cerita berbingkai* is not what R.O. Winstedt called the 'Cycles of Tales', but in fact the 'Cycles of Tales with a Frame' or 'The Frame-story' (*raamverhaal*).

2. Stories that are intended to impart political doctrines and secular knowledge. Among such stories are the *Pancatantra* and other stories derived from this collection of animal fables.
3. Stories that are intended merely to entertain. They are not meant to be didactic nor do they make moral teachings their main emphasis. Among the stories in this category are the *Vetalapancavimsati* and *Sukasaptati* (Winternitz, 1959: 304).

The framed narrative is very old. Through various means, the genre spread widely and we would be hard put to find a folktale in Asia or Europe whose origin cannot be traced to India. In fact it is so ubiquitous that it has attained the status of world literature. This is probably the reason why at one time scholars held the view that India was the source of all stories. This theory is, of course, no longer accepted. What is clear is that many stories did come from India.

Below is a discussion of three major framed narratives that have become part of Malay literature: the *Pancatantra*, the *Hikayat Seribu Satu Malam* (Tales of a Thousand and One Nights), and the *Sukasaptati*. This will be followed by a discussion of the *Hikayat Bakhtiar*.

6.1 *Pancatantra*

The Sanskrit literary work, the *Pancatantra*, is known throughout the world. In Malay, it is called the *Hikayat Kalilah dan Dimnah*. Much research has been done on the origins of the *Pancatantra*. According to a German scholar, the original version of the *Pancatantra* has been lost. A similar work, the *Tantrakhyayika*, dates back to about the third century B.C. Other versions can be found in northwest and south India. Sometime prior to 570 A.D., the northwest Indian version was translated into Pahlavi (Middle Persian) on the order of King Khosrau Anusyirwan (531-579). This Pahlavi version, entitled *Kerataka wa Mamanaka*, was the work of Arzt Burzoe, who also added other Indian stories as well as an introduction. Unfortunately this Pahlavi version too has been lost. However before it disappeared, a well-known Syrian sage, Bud, translated it into Syrian, calling it *Kalilaq wa Damanaq*. In 750, Abdullah al-Muqaffa translated the Syrian text into Arabic as *Kalilah wa Dimnah*. It was this Arabic version that really popularized the *Pancatantra*. Most European and Asian translations and adaptations of this tale derive from this Arabic translation. In the tenth century, the Arabic text was translated back into Syrian again. This Syrian translation was then translated into English under the title, *The Fables of Bidpai*. (Bidpai is the corrupted form of the Sanskrit word *Vidyapati*, which means "The Knowledgeable One".) Later, translations into Greek, Hebrew, Latin and German began to emerge. The best known of these is the Latin translation by Johannes von Capua, a Jew. From Latin, the tale was translated into Spanish and then into Italian and eventually into French. The Italian translation was rendered into English by Thomas North and was known by the title *The Moral Philosophy of Doni* (London, 1570 and 1601) (Winternitz, 1959: 336).

One of the many translations of this tale is the significant Persian translation by Nasrullah in 1142. Nasrullah's translation was later improved upon, and its language refined, by Husain Ibn Aliah-Wa'iz (1470-1505), who then gave it the title *Anwari Suhaili*, or *The Light of Suhaili*. This is a very important piece of translation and it too has been translated and adapted into various languages in the West and East.

Another well-known translation is the Turkish *Humayun Nameh,* or *The Book of Kings*, translated by Ali bin Saleh and presented to Sultan Sulaiman (1512-1520). Galland and Cardonne later translated this Turkish translation into French. The German translation was based on this French translation. Before we move to a discussion of the various versions that are to be found in Malay and the other languages of the Malay Archipelago, it is best that we also describe the content of this collection of stories.

Contents

The *Pancatantra* is not a romance. Rather, the stories are intended to be didactic and to impart moral teachings in a pleasant manner. Two special terms exist in Sanskrit for this kind of stories: *nitisastra* (moral knowledge) and *arthasastra* (worldly knowledge). Originally such stories were used to teach royal princes about worldly matters. This is explicitly stated in the introduction *(kathamukha)* of all extant versions found today. Over time however, the *Pancatantra* became a guide book for all levels of society, its use no longer confined exclusively to the instruction of princes. The origins of the story are as follows:

There was once a wise king in the city of Mahilaropya in South India; his name was Amarasakti, who was well-versed in all fields of knowledge. He had three sons but they were not interested in study. This filled the king with despair. A Brahmin, Visnusarman, promised the king that he could teach the princes all they needed to know in just six months. The Brahmin then began to teach the three princes using the extraordinary method of telling them five animal stories, each containing many other stories.

The first tale was about a wolf, Damanaka, who caused a rift between two best friends, a lion and a cow. The conversations between Damanaka and his friend, Karataka, contain a series of astute political strategems. For example, Damanaka told this story to illustrate how to dispose of one's foe: in order to get rid of its enemy, the snake, a crow stole a gold chain and then dropped it into the hole where the snake lived. The owner killed the snake.

The second tale tells how the weak can save themselves from the threat of a powerful enemy if they work together. To illustrate this, he told the story of a flock of birds who were caught in a net. Using their combined strength, the birds managed to fly away, carrying the net with them. A mouse gnawed a hole in the net to free them.

The third story elucidates the politics of war and peace. The lesson is that one should not trust one's enemy too easily. This is shown through the story of a crow who pretended to submit to the owl and allowed its feathers to be plucked. The crow's plan was to find out where the owl lived. The owl was unaware of the crow's plan and it was this naivety that eventually led to its death. This framed narrative serves to instruct its listeners on how to overcome an imposing and formidable enemy by creating strife and discord within the enemy's ranks, using subterfuge and cunning ploys, pretending subservience in order to deceive one's enemy, and so forth.

The fourth story illustrates how easily a gullible person can be deceived by flattery. An example of this is the tale of the crocodile and the monkey: the monkey tricked the crocodile into believing that the monkey had left its liver hanging on a tree. The story embedded within this story in turn is of a donkey with no liver or ears, and imparts a similar moral lesson: do not readily trust false praises and sweet words.

The fifth story illustrates the perils of acting hastily without deliberation and forethought. The example given here is the story of a mongoose that was killed by its owner; the owner rashly concluded that the mongoose had killed his baby when, in actual fact, the mongoose had saved the child from a cobra. The story serves as a companion piece to another story, about a Brahmin who is prone to reverie and daydream like the Mat Jenin of Malay folklore.

Differences between the Sanskrit and Arabic Texts

To understand the origins of the story of the *Pancatantra* in Malay as found in the *Hikayat Kalilah dan Dimnah,* we need to know how the original story in Sanskrit differs from the translated version in Arabic, as well as from the other languages into which it was translated. As has already been mentioned, the Sanskrit version begins with the story of King Amarasakti (Sudarsana in the Southern version; Sugadarma in the Tamil version) of Mahilaropya (Pataliputra in the Southern version; Padlipurvam in the Tamil version), who was worried about the ignorance of his children. A Brahmin offered to educate the princes in six months. This story however is not found in the Arabic version or its successors. In its place instead is the story of a sage named Bidpai (or Baibaba) who, perturbed by the autocratic rule of King Dabshelim, decided to offer the monarch his counsel. At first Dabshelim took this as an affront but later realized his shortcomings and instructed Bidpai to write a book. When the book was completed, King Dabshelim listened to the advice it contained.

Another difference lies in the story of Damina. In the Sanskrit version, the story tells how Damina tried to cheer a lion up after the death of a cow. In the Arabic version, Damina himself received the death sentence. A further difference is that the Sanskrit version contains only five chapters, while the Arabic version and its successors consist of thirteen or more chapters each (Brandes, 1891: 7-9).

The Arabic version contains four forewords. The first is a foreword by Ibnul Muqaffa to the Arabic translation. This is followed by a foreword by Bahnud bin Sahwan to explain why the *hikayat* was written. The third recounts the story of Barzoe's mission to India. The fourth contains Barzoe's biography, written by Buzurjmihr bin Bakhtekan. The Arabic version has been translated into Malay twice, by Ismail Djamil and Haji Khairuddin respectively.

Malay Version

There are four versions in Malay, namely:

1. The *Hikayat Kalila dan Damina* mentioned by Werndly in his book on Malay grammar in 1736. This *hikayat* was later published by J. R. P. F. Gonggrijp in 1876 under the same title, and reprinted in 1892.
2. The *Hikayat Panjatanderan* translated from Tamil in 1835 by Abdullah Munsyi with the help of his friend Tambi Matu Berapa Patar. This *hikayat* has been printed several times. It was later adapted by Van Ophuijsen as a reader for students from a book of the same title printed

in Singapore in 1887, which was meant for school pupils in Malay language schools in Singapore, Penang and Malaka on the instruction of the Inspector of Government Schools.

3. The *Dalang atawa segala cerita dan dongeng yang telah dikarangkan oleh Hakim Lokhman dan Bidpai* (Storyteller or every legend and fairytale ever written by Magistrate Lokhman and Bidpai) translated into Malay by J. R. P. F. Gonggrijp in Batavia in 1886, based on Stoopendaal's Dutch translation from the French in 1781.

4. The *Hikayat Kalila dan Damina* translated from the Arabic (by Ibnul Muqaffa) into Malay by Haji Khairuddin in 1962 and by Ismail Djamil in 1964.

The version mentioned by Werndly and published by Gonggrijp is the best known of the four versions. It is somewhat different from the Tamil version translated by Abdullah. According to R. O. Winstedt, the Tamil version is the oldest to be found in South India. It is this version that later reemerged in the *Katha Sarit Sagara* and it is from this same South Indian version that the origins of other versions of this tale can be traced.

Origins

According to the scholar, J. Brandes, who has made an in-depth study of this particular framed narrative, the Malay version bears some similarities to the Nasrullah version in the Persian language (Brandes, 1891: 11-13). Firstly, the foreword by Bahnud to the Arabic version is missing. Secondly, the Malay version, like the Nasrullah version, comprises sixteen chapters. It states: *"To begin: it is told by the person whose tale this is, that this story was translated into Persian from an Indian language: this book is thus made up of sixteen chapters—ten of which are from the Indian langage, and six from the Persian language."* Thirdly, the sequence of stories in the Malay version follows that of Nasrullah's text. Fourthly, a particular bird is called *pujani* in the Sanskrit version and *punzah* in the Arabic, but *gubarrah* in the Persian and *gebrah* in the Malay versions. There are therefore some significant similarities between the Malay and Persian versions.

The Nasrullah version however is not the only source for the Malay version, as the latter contains several additional stories: for example, the story of the cat and the dove, the story of the Sultan of Kashmir, and the tale of the Elixir of Life. These three stories are found only in the *Anwari Suhaili* compiled by Hussain Wa'iz. Besides these three stories, the Malay version also contains other stories not found in any other version at all, whether by Ibnul Muqaffa, Nasrullah or Hussain Wa'iz. For example: the tale of the Arab and his wife, and the tale of the hermit and the mouse. Finally, the *Hikayat Kalilah dan Dimnah* also contains stories found only in the *Hikayat Golam*, a separate work originally written in Arabic (see 6.5 below).

This concludes our discussion on the origins of this *hikayat*.

Summary of the *Hikayat Kalilah dan Dimnah*

The Malay version described by Werndly and published by Gonggrijp begins with the story of King Horman Shah, the son of Nusyirwan (and thus, not with Nusyirwan himself). The king heard about a Hindu sage named Said who possessed a very precious book. Barzuyeh was promptly sent to Hindustan to make a copy of this book. He did such an excellent job that, as a reward, he was allowed to take anything he wanted from Said's library. Barzuyeh declined but asked instead that his name be included in a story being compiled by Khoja Buzur Jamahir. Khoja Buzur Jamahir then set himself in earnest to complete the task before him.

The story begins with the advice that all mankind should pursue learning, even if it means having to travel as far as China. One should carefully evaluate whatever one learns. The knowledge that one has obtained must be evaluated objectively, otherwise one's fate will be no better than that of the thief who was cheated by a merchant. A further story is then told about Taif who was willing to slaughter his own son for the sake of prolonging the life of the king. After that the story of Kalila and Damina begins.

There was once a king named Raja Iskandar Shah who was troubled by the foolishness of his children. He went to a wise Brahmin, Suma Sanma, and asked him to teach his children. Suma Sanma told them five beautiful stories about:

(1) The person who spread slander in order to separate two lovers.
(2) The man who helped a sick friend.
(3) The warning against believing in the sweet words and flattery of one's enemy.
(4) The avaricious person who lost the wealth he had worked hard to earn because he coveted another man's riches.
(5) The lesson that one ought to think through one's actions and not act on impulse.

In order to further elaborate on these five stories, the Brahmin told other tales. To teach the king's children the moral that a person who slandered others would eventually be punished, the Brahmin narrated the Tale of an ox named Satarubuh and the King of the Lions.

An ox named Satarubuh was once abandoned by its owner in the forest. One day the ox let out a loud moo. The King of the Lions was afraid and sad when he heard the ox's mournful cry. Damina, a wolf, wanted to know why the King was so sad. Another wolf, Kalila, advised Damina not to interfere in the affairs of others, or he might suffer the same fate as the Monkey whose inquisitiveness caused its tail to be caught in a trap. Ignoring Kalila's advice, Damina bravely went to the Lion King and told him the story of the Fox who owned a drum that made a noise each time the wind blew. With Damina acting as their intermediary, a close friendship developed between Satarubuh and the Lion King that far exceeded the bond the King of the Lions had with any other animal. This made Damina jealous. Kalila pointed out that Damina had only himself to blame and told the following tales to illustrate his point:

(a) The hermit who lost his fortune to his student, a thief.
(b) The Fox who died because he drank the blood of a hunter.
(c) The pimp who died after swallowing poison.
(d) The story of a woman with a broken nose.

Kalila advised Damina not to resort to calumny or slander. Damina ignored Kalila's words and instead recounted the following stories to show that even the weak can defeat the strong:

(a) The Cormorant who killed a snake.//
(b) The Egret who tried to trick a crab but lost his life instead.//
(c) The Mousedeer who killed a Tiger.

Damina went to see the King and urged him to take swift action against any potential act of treachery lest he suffer the same fate as the three fishes in a pond. After that Damina went to see Satarubuh and told him that the Lion King was planning to kill him. Satarubuh wondered what he had done wrong to have incurred the anger of the King and began to relate the tale of the tilawi bird who tried to fight the waves (with a further accompanying story of the bird and the monitor lizard).

Satarubuh then went to the King. The two creatures fought. The King was slightly wounded but Satarubuh was killed in the fight. Kalila condemned Damina for what he had done and recounted the following tales:

(a) The scribe who beat his own son for a misdeed he did not commit but who spared the real culprit, his servant.
(b) The charlatan who claimed to be a doctor but who did not know the right medicine to prescribe to his patient, thus causing the death of a princess.
(c) The eagle-handler and the slave who betrayed his master's wife.

At his trial, Damina was unable to defend himself. Following the testimonies of the leopard and the fowl, Damina was found guilty and thrown into prison. Deprived of food and drink, Damina eventually died in prison.

To elaborate on the second story that the wise man associates with people of noble character, the Brahmin proposed the tale of the pigeon who befriended the crow, the mouse, the deer and the tortoise. One day the mouse told how he became friends with the pigeon. Once upon a time, the mouse lived in a hermitage and ate the scraps a kind hermit set aside for it. One night, the hermit had a visitor who told him the story of a woman who had put some hulled sesame seeds in the sun to dry but these later turned into unhulled sesame seeds. (This framed narrative then leads into another story about the tale of a greedy hunter). The guest suspected that the mouse was the culprit and suggested that they search for the mouse's hole. When they found it, they dug and discovered that not only had the mouse hidden a lot of sesame seeds but that he had also stolen a lot of gold. They took the gold. In his poverty, the mouse had only the pigeon to comfort him. The tortoise tried to lift the mouse's spirits by telling him the story of a cat who ate a baby dove and who was subsequently killed by the bird's owner. The tortoise ended his story with a word of advice about the five things in a man's life which will not last forever: first, shadows; second, association with people of ill-repute; third, sexual desire; fourth, good looks and the esteem of others; and fifth, material wealth and fortune.

As soon as the tortoise had finished telling his story, the deer came running with news that a hunter was approaching the village to befriend the mouse and his friends. When the deer found himself caught in the hunter's net, the mouse gnawed a hole in the net for him to escape. When the tortoise found himself trapped, the deer stood in front of the hunter pretending to be too exhausted to run. When the hunter tried to catch him, the deer sprinted away to safety, distracting the hunter long enough for the tortoise to escape.

A further tale about the crow and the king of owls was narrated to elaborate on the moral of the third story that one should not trust one's enemies. One night, an owl attacked a crow. The next day, the king of the crows held a meeting with all his ministers. A wise crow by the name of Karkenas pointed out that war is not something to be taken lightly and that if they did decide to wage war on their arch-enemy, this decision should be kept a closely guarded secret. To illustrate his point, he told the story of the Sultan of Kashmir who was murdered after his plan to kill his concubine's lover, a singer, was revealed. Karkenas also told how the owls and the crows first became enemies. According to this story, a crow once advised a stork not to choose the owl to be king and told the stork the following stories:

1   A mousedeer tricked a herd of elephants into thinking that he was an emissary of the Moon King to keep them from drinking at the same watering hole as himself.
2   The sembul bird who complained to a hermit cat about his quarrel with a deer only to be eaten by the cat.

Following the advice of the crow, the stork decided not to choose the owl as king. Unfortunately, the owl overheard what the crow had said to the stork and from that day onwards the king regarded the crow as his enemy. With the permission of his own king, Karkenas the wise crow flew to the owls and told them that he had been banished by the king of the crows. This raised the suspicion of the owl's ministers; they cautioned their king to beware of enemies who tried to influence him with flattery, and in turn told him the following stories:

(a) The artisan who was betrayed by his treacherous wife;
(b) The mouse who became a woman and who, when asked to choose a husband, preferred a mouse over a man as her spouse.

Karkenas the wise crow argued that there is merit in forgiving one's enemies and used the story of an ascetic and an emir's wife to drive home his point. The owl ministers however remained unconvinced and continued to regard him with suspicion. Karkenas then told them another story—this time about a tale of the hermit who turned the mouse into a human being and the mouse's wife into a dog, and then changing them back again into mice. Against his ministers' better judgement, the Owl King granted Karkenas refuge in his kingdom. After some time, Karkenas flew back to his king with a scheme to destroy the owls. Once the plan was carried out successfully and the owls vanquished, Karkenas drew an analogy between his actions and those of the snake who betrayed and killed the frog he served.

To elaborate on the fourth story about working hard to gain something only then to relinquish it, the following stories were narrated:

(a) The tortoise and the monkey who left his liver at home;
(b) The donkey with no liver and no ears who was killed by the Tiger.

The following tales were told regarding the fifth story which teaches its listeners not to embark on an endeavour without due preparation:

(i) The ascetic who killed an innocent mongoose (this contained another story about a man who spent his days fantasizing).

(ii) The tiger who refused to kill a wolf accused of treachery.

(iii) How King Bahzada's eyes were pierced by the lady-in-waiting of a princess he was about to marry.

(iv) The king who killed an innocent merchant and lived to regret his action.

(v) The king who executed one of his ministers only to discover later that the minister was innocent and had been maligned by another minister. When the king realised his mistake, he had the offending minister put to death too. (This story contains another story: the tale of the hornbill king who proposed to the sparrow.)

(vi) King Kabasi who ordered the execution of his stepson. Fortunately, a minister rescued the boy and thus saved the king from regretting his rash action and his wife, Her Highness the Princess, from dying of a broken heart.

Besides stories exhorting listeners not to act rashly, other tales contain the following moral lessons:

1. No enmity or love lasts forever. Exemplified by:
   (a) The cat and the mouse.
   (b) The prince and the gebrah bird.
2. Do not ignore your own duties in order to perform the tasks of others. Exemplified by:
   (a) The hermit and his novice who studied Hebrew.
   (b) The four friends who carried out their own duties.
3. Be patient and forgive those who wrong you unintentionally. Exemplified by:
   (a) The patient man, Abu Sabar, who was chosen king.
   (b) The King of Yemen who pardoned the slave who later saved his life.
4. He who does evil begets evil. This moral is exemplified in the tale of the goldsmith and the hunter.

The king's sons enjoyed the Brahmin's stories and became more receptive to his teachings and advice. Brahmana Suma Sanma was handsomely rewarded by the king.

On the whole, the Gonggrijp manuscript is similar to the *Hikayat Kalilah dan Dimnah* translated by Ismail Djamil and Haji Khairuddin. However, many of the framed stories are quite different. There are several risqué tales pertaining to relationships between men and women, which have either been replaced by more decent stories or omitted completely. The greatest differences are with the *Pantja Tanderan* translated by Abdullah Munshi. Below is a summary of that text for the purposes of comparison:

Once upon a time there was a king in the country of Padali Parum called Raja Saudagarma who was sad because his four sons were so ignorant. So he sought the help of a Brahmin, Sumasanma, to teach his sons. The Brahmin was an extraordinary teacher who taught his young charges by using an unusual method—he told them stories. There were five stories:

(1) The two lovers;
(2) The two friends who assiduously kept their promise to each other;
(3) The man who ruined the life of another and then saved him again.
(4) The man who gave someone a gift but who later lived to regret it;
(5) The man who acted on impulse and later regretted his action.

The first tale tells of the king of lions cringed when he heard the loud cry of an ox. The wolf Galilah was curious to know what had frightened the Lion King. Damina, a fellow wolf, advised Galilah not to interfere in the affairs of others by telling him the tale of the monkey who ended up with his tail in a trap after meddling in matters about which he knew nothing. Galilah insisted that a minister's duty was to help his troubled king and set out to visit the monarch. Galilah assured the king that he had nothing to fear and admonished him by saying that a king who is easily intimidated does so to his own detriment. To illustrate this, he recounted the tale of the war drum which was hit by a stick and inadvertently made a noise. Thanks to Galilah's efforts, the Lion King soon became firm friends with the ox. Daminah became envious and lamented that both he and Galilah had only themselves to blame for the King's friendship with the ox. He drew an analogy between what they had done and the story of the boy who betrayed a Brahmin's trust.

Galilah wanted to break the close bond between the Lion King and the ox, so Damina told him the following tales about how to dispose of one's enemies through the use of cunning:

(i) A crow, who was enemies with a snake, once stole the queen's precious necklace and dropped it into the snake's lair. When the necklace was found, people thought the snake was to blame and killed it.

(ii) Once, a mousedeer who was about to be eaten by a lion, brought the lion to a well and showed him his own reflection. Thinking that he was looking at another lion who was about to snatch his prey from him, the lion pounced on his own reflection and drowned.

(iii) An old egret, no longer able to fish, once promised to take a school of fish to a lake with clear waters. Instead, the egret flew one fish a day to a rock where he ate them. He told the same lie to a crab, but when he tried to eat it, the crab clamped its pincers around his neck and cut the egret's throat. In the end, they both died.

Galilah tried to start a quarrel between the Lion King and the ox. He told the King that oxen are untrustworthy beasts and warned that one day the ox would attack him when he least expected it. Galilah then told the king the tale of the mite and the bedbug to show that he who keeps company with scoundrels will himself meet an ignoble end. Galilah went to see the ox and insinuated to him that being on such close terms with the king was akin to being friends with a venomous snake. He then told the ox the tale of a crow who was friends with a camel. According to the story, the crow and the wolf offered themselves as food to the Lion King. The lion however rejected them as they were too small to satisfy his appetite. Following his companions' example, the camel then offered himself to the lion. The moment he did, the King pounced and ate him. Galilah then asked the ox: "The depths of the ocean can be plumbed, but can anyone fathom the human heart?"

Galilah urged the ox to fight the Lion King rather than wait to be killed. He then recounted the story of the plover who fought the sea, which tells of a female plover who refused to lay her eggs on the beach and insisted on building a nest elsewhere. Her mate, the male plover, was equally adamant about staying, and tried to convince her by telling her the story of someone who refused to listen to their partner's advice. Once upon a time there was a tortoise who befriended a pair of birds. They promised to take him flying by holding a stick in their beaks for the tortoise to grasp in his mouth. The birds advised the tortoise not to open his mouth while they were in the air, but the tortoise ignored the warning and fell to his death. After listening to this story, the female plover was still unconvinced: she argued that it is prudent to foresee danger and take precautions before danger arrives.

She then proceeded to tell him the tale of the three fishes. Once upon a time there were three fishes—a strong fish, a clever fish and a stupid fish. The clever fish heard that a fisherman was coming to set a trap in their pond and suggested that they swim away to safety before danger arrived. The strong fish however disagreed and said that they could rely on their wits to escape danger. He recounted the tale of the robber who was tricked by a wily merchant. The smart fish however did not want to wait and quickly leapt into another pond. When the fisherman arrived, the strong fish and the stupid fish were both caught. The strong fish pretended to be dead and was thrown onto dry land. As for the stupid fish, he was first scaled and then thrown onto dry land. Only after the fisherman had allowed the pond water he had dammed to flow again, and only after the two fishes had spent an agonizing time on dry land, were they able to leap into another pond and make their escape. Despite this story, the male plover continued to ignore his wife's advice and insisted on building their nest by the sea. When the moon was full, the tide rose and swept the plover eggs into the sea. Before finishing his story, Galilah told the ox that the best time to attack the Lion King was on a rainy day, when the lion's eyes would become red, his hair stand on end and his tail held high in the air. The ox was deceived by Galilah's words and prepared to attack the Lion King.

Daminah scolded Galilah for his wickedness and related a story to show that he who betrays others would eventually be betrayed himself. In the story, two merchants' sons went off to trade. One made a profit of 500 dirhams, the other made nothing. The shrewd one who made a profit gave half of his earnings to the fool who had failed to make any profit. Not happy with this, the scoundrel schemed to steal the rest of the money from his friend. He suggested that all the money be buried under a tree for safekeeping. That night, he took all the money and accused the other man of stealing it. The matter came before a magistrate. The scoundrel told the magistrate that the tree would bear witness to what happened and asked his father to hide in the tree so that when the magistrate asked the tree to testify, his father could lie on his behalf. His father however refused to do this and told his son that his actions were no better than that of the egret in the tale of the egret who lost her eggs. In this tale, an egret discovered that her eggs had been eaten by a snake and decided to teach the snake a lesson. She took some fish from a mongoose's burrow and placed them outside the snake's den. When the mongoose found the fish in the snake's den, he thought the snake had stolen them and killed the snake. Despite his father's protests, the scoundrel forced him to hide in the tree. When the magistrate heard the tree 'talk', he became suspicious and set it on fire. As a result, the scoundrel's father died in the fire. The scoundrel was arrested and executed.

Next, Daminah told the tale of a crooked merchant. A merchant entrusted a thousand *pikul* of iron (about 60,000 kg) to a fellow merchant. The second merchant sold the iron and kept the money. He told his friend that the iron had been eaten by mice. The first merchant then kidnapped the crooked merchant's daughter, telling him that an eagle had swooped down and taken his daughter. The crooked merchant refused to believe this and brought the matter before a magistrate. The magistrate asked: "Can an eagle really fly off with a young girl?", to which the owner of the iron replied: "Can mice really eat a thousand *pikul* of iron?" With this, the dishonest deed of the crooked merchant was revealed to the court. He was forced to pay the rightful owner the price of the thousand *pikul* of iron. And his daughter was eventually returned to him. Daminah concluded his story with the saying, "Whoever digs a well for others to fall into, will fall into the well himself." Galilah realised that what he had done was wrong and rushed to the Lion King. But it was too late. When he arrived, he found the ox dead at the feet of a morose Lion King who mourned the death of his friend. Galilah tried to comfort the Lion King by saying that "We must kill those who try to kill us, even if they are our brothers or our own children." The Lion King found comfort in these words and was eventually cured of his misery.

Tantri

Tantri is the name given to the stories of the *Pancatantra* that are popular in Java and Bali. These stories are so popular that the term "*tantri*" itself is sometimes taken to mean "*animal tales*". C. Hooykaas wrote a dissertation on the origins of the *tantri* stories in 1929. According to this Dutch scholar, a version of the *Pancatantra* entitled *Tantra Carita* (better known today by the title *Tantri Kamandaka*) was translated into Middle Javanese, using the Kadiri and Demung metres. The verse adaptation was then translated into Balinese.

The major difference between the *Tantri* and the *Pancatantra* is that the introduction to the *Pancatantra* is not found in the *Tantri*. In its place is an introduction taken from the *Tales of One Thousand and One Nights*, which tells of a king, who having been cheated by his queen, was bent on taking revenge on all women. Every night he would marry a maiden and in the morning she would be killed. Almost all of the women in the kingdom died. Only one survived—Dyah Tantri, the daughter of a minister. She was not only beautiful but also intelligent. By telling the king stories she was able to soothe the king and lived happily ever after with him.

There are four framed stories contained in the *Tantri* as opposed to five in the *Pancatantra*. The first is the tale about the buffalo and the lion. A wolf managed to create a rift between the buffalo and the lion, and they both killed each other. In the end the wolf suffered the same fate as his victims. The stories within the story too are quite different. The stories of the *Tantri* can also be found in the languages of Laos and Thailand.

6.2 *Hikayat Seribu Satu Malam*

The *Hikayat Seribu Satu Malam (Tales of A Thousand and One Nights)*, or *Alf Laila Wa Laila*, is perhaps the most famous work of Arabic literature as far as the non-Arab world is concerned. Children all over the world have almost certainly heard the stories of Ali Baba and the Forty

Thieves, Aladdin and the Magic Lamp, and The Adventures of Sindbad. The stories from the *Thousand and One Nights* began to spread in Europe in the twelfth century and its literary techniques were imitated by Boccaccio in the *Decameron* (1353) and Chaucer in *The Canterbury Tales* (1387). In the eighteenth century, A. Galland (1701-1717) translated the work into French, and from the French it was then translated into the other languages of Europe.

The *Hikayat Seribu Satu Malam* is not the product of a single author. The stories originated from the *Hazar Afsana*, a work in Pahlavi (the old Persian dialect), which was later translated into Sanskrit. *Hazar Afsana* means "a thousand stories", although there are in actual fact only 200 tales in the book. The main narrative tells of a king who married a different woman each night, only to have them executed the next morning. In the end a shrewd princess, Sh'ah Razad, managed to captivate the king by telling him a different tale each night, with the help of her lady-in-waiting, Dinazad. In the second half of the eighth century, these tales were translated into Arabic and given the title *Alf Khurafa* (A Thousand Tales), which later became *Alf Laila* (A Thousand Nights). As there were fewer than a thousand stories, further efforts were made to add more stories to the collection. Most of the additional stories are set in tenth and eleventh century Baghdad; some tell of epic voyages to distant lands. The caliph Harun Ar-Rasyid is mentioned in a number of these stories, as is his vizier Ja'far.

The stories began to gain popularity in Egypt during the eleventh century. Although the framed stories remained the same, Shah Razad became the vizier's daughter and Dinazad, her sister. During the reign of Sultan Mamluk (1250-1317), many tales set in Egypt were also added to the book. Its title, *Alf Laila,* was later changed to *Alf Laila Wa Laila* (*One Thousand and One Nights),* following the Turkish title, *Binbir Gece Masalları*. The phrase "bin bir" does not imply the exact number of a thousand and one but simply a very large amount; nevertheless it was loosely translated to mean that number. It is clear from the explanation above that the *Hikayat Seribu Satu Malam* began to take its present form in the mid-sixteenth century.

Although the *One Thousand and One Nights* contains many tales which remain popular in the Malay world, such as 'Ali Baba,' 'Aladdin and the Magic Lamp,' 'The Voyage of Sindbad,' 'Abu Nawas' and 'Tajul Muluk', it was not until the 1960s that a complete translation of the original work was published in Malaysia. An earlier lithographed translation appeared in Singapore in five parts, printed between 1878 and 1879. The tale begins with the story of a king by the name of Shah Rizar who ruled over a kingdom located near the border of India and China. The king loved his queen very much. One day, however, he found the queen with one of the palace slaves and had them both killed. His heart broken, the king paid a visit to his brother, Shah Zaman, the king of Samarkand. Coincidentally, he also came to know that his brother's queen was having an affair with a black Ethiopian slave. Each lady-in-waiting in his brother's palace also had lovers who disguised themselves as ladies-in-waiting. Shah Rizar told his brother what he had found out. Disappointed, the two brothers left their kingdoms and traveled to foreign lands. During their travels, they met a woman who was kept in a glass case by a *Jinn Ifrit.* Despite her imprisonment, the woman had somehow managed to have sexual relations with men. By the time they met her, she had already ravaged a hundred men.

She arrogantly told the two royal brothers, "If a woman intends to commit an evil deed, no man will be able to stop her." She also advised Shah Rizar and his brother not to put too much faith in womankind. The woman's words made a deep impression on Shah Rizar. Thereafter he ordered his prime minister to bring him a different maiden each day. He would marry her, then have the girl killed the next day. Vast numbers of women disappeared. People throughout the land cursed the king day and night. Under these terrible circumstances, Siti Shah Rizad, the beautiful and intelligent daughter of the prime minister, asked to be presented to the king. Her father tried to dissuade her by telling her a tale about the donkey and the buffalo, to warn her of the dangerous consequences of her intended actions. Siti Shah Rizad was adamant and told her father that if she died, she would become a martyr; but if she succeeded, then every woman in the kingdom would be saved.

And so, accompanied by her sister, Dinazad, Siti Shah Rizad was presented to the king. That night, Dinazad asked her sister to tell a story. Siti Shah Rizad politely declined, saying that she would tell a story only if the king agreed. The king was happy to agree. And so Siti Shah Rizad began to tell them a story. When the story reached its climax, dawn broke. The king was eager to find out how the story ended and deferred Siti Shah Rizad's execution. The next night, with the king's permission, she continued the story, stopping again at daybreak. This continued for one thousand and one nights. By this time Siti Shah Rizad had given the king three sons and he had been cured of his hatred of women.

The complete Singapore lithograph of the *Hikayat Seribu Satu Malam* is 500 pages long but contains only eight principal stories, namely:

(i) The merchant and the *jinn* (p. 64)

(ii) The fisherman and the *jinn* (p. 101)

(iii) The tricking of the prince of Black island (p. 162)

(iv) The knave betrayed by his friend (p. 272)

(v) The third story of Siti Baghdad, told by a fairy (p. 362)

(vi) Siti Aminah's tale (p. 401)

(vii) The three mangoes (p. 416)

(viii) Nuruddin Ali and Badruddin Hasan (p. 437)

The Singapore lithograph must have been intended to have a sequel, since the words "to be continued" are written at the end of page 500. This sequel has never been found.

The *Thousand and One Nights* has also been translated by Onn bin Jaafar, following the English translation of Richard Burton, 1850 to 1885. Although Burton's translation consists of 16 volumes, Onn bin Jaafar's Malay translation contains only eight tales. Three of these are not to be found in the Singapore lithograph, namely:

(i) The hunchback;

(ii) The enchanting Ghanam bin Ayub; and

(iii) Raja Omar Ibni Al-Mulman and his princes.

Onn bin Jaafar's translation was originally published in Jawi script in Singapore in 1930, and later re-published in romanised form in Kuala Lumpur in 1978.

There is also a thirteen volume edition published by the Dewan Bahasa dan Pustaka in Kuala Lumpur; this translation was based on the Arabic and compiled by Hassan Jauhar, Muhammad Ahmad Baranik and Amin Ahmad Al-Atar.

6.3 *Sukasaptati* and *Hikayat Bayan Budiman*

The *Sukasaptati,* or Seventy Tales Told by a Parrot (Malay, *bayan*) is a collection of well-known framed stories. There are many manuscripts of this book, often with different contents. However its main framed narrative remains the same, and can be retold as follows:

Once upon a time there was a merchant named Haradatta, who had a son, Madanasena. There is nothing Madanasena liked better than spending time making love with his wife, Prabhawati. He totally neglected his responsibility to earn a living *(artha)* and his moral duties *(dharma)*. This saddened Haradatta. A Brahmin, named Triwikrama, offered to help the merchant. Triwikrama bought two birds, a crow and a parrot, and gave them to Madanasena. The birds were clever and were wonderful storytellers. They told Madanasena and his wife many tales containing valuable moral lessons. Madanasena finally realised that he had neglected his responsibilities and made plans to go away to trade. He entrusted his wife to the care of the two birds.

During her husband's absence, Prabhawati felt unhappy. Her friends encouraged her to take a lover. As she was dressing to meet her lover, the crow reproached her for what she was about to do. Prabhawati took offence and tried to strangle the crow. Fortunately the bird managed to escape. The parrot meanwhile pretended to support Prabhawati, telling her that she had every right to follow her desires, as long as she was as discreet as Gunasalini. Not knowing the story of Gunasalini, Prabhawati's curiosity was aroused and she asked the parrot to tell her the story. And so the parrot told her the story of the adulterous Gunasalini, who managed to escape the consequences of her actions through her cunning and trickery. When the story reached its climax, the parrot turned to Prabhawati and asked: "What should Gunasalini do now?" Prabhawati pondered this question throughout the night and forgot to meet her lover. Night after night the parrot would tell tales culminating with a question. Altogether the parrot told Prabhawati a total of sixty-nine tales before Madanasena final return. In this way the wily parrot was able to prevent Prabhawati from committing an indiscretion during her husband's absence (Winternitz, 1959: 378-379).

Tales such as these are meant as mere entertainment. More than half are tales of adultery, featuring adulterous women who successfully manage the consequences of their illicit affairs through the use of cunning and deception. The rest are stories of devious scoundrels, wise judges, and clever and wily characters who can solve difficult riddles.

Unfortunately the original *Sukasaptati* manuscript has been lost. The German scholar, Richard Schmidt, published two versions he considered to be the *textus simplicior* and *textus ornatior* of the original. He was unable to say when the two versions were written.

The *Sukasaptati* has been translated into various languages, the most significant of which is the Persian *Tutinameh*, based on a badly written earlier version. The translator, Nakhshabi, omitted several stories he deemed inappropriate, replacing them with others from the *Vetalapancavimsati* (Twenty-five Ghost Tales). The *Tutinameh* was translated in 1330, and a hundred years later was translated into Turkish. The *Tutinameh* was also the source of several translations into the languages of Western Asia and Europe. At the end of the eighteenth century (*circa* 1793), the *Tutinameh* was rewritten in a more modern form of Persian by Mohd Qadiri. This framed narrative arrived in the Malay world along with the spread of Islam and was rendered into the Malay as well as the Buginese and Makasarese languages. There are also two versions of the parrot stories in Javanese: one is called *Cantri,* and the other *Cerita Bayan Budiman* (The Story of the Wise Parrot). Both contain forewords taken from *Tales of A Thousand and One Nights.* However, the stories they contain are very different from each other and the contents of the Javanese *Cantri* also differ from those of *Hikayat Bayan Budiman.* Only one story in the *Cantri* is to be found in the Malay version—the tale of the man who gave half his life to his wife. Besides this, both Javanese versions contain more animal tales than the Malay version. Perhaps that is why the *Cantri* is sometimes considered to be a Javanese language version of the *Pancatantra*.

6.2.1 The *Hikayat Bayan Budiman*

The *Sukasaptati* is best known in Malay as the *Hikayat Bayan Budiman* (The Story of the Virtuous Parrot). It is also known by other titles, such as the *Hikayat Khojah Maimun* (The Story of Khojah Maimun), *Hikayat Khojah Mubarak* (The Story of Khojah Mubarak) and *Cerita Taifah* (The Tale of Taifah). A comparison between the *Hikayat Bayan Budiman* and Nakhsyabi's Persian translation of the *Sukasaptati* shows that twelve of the 52 stories found in the former derive from the latter work. On the other hand, a comparison with Mohd. Qadiri's more recent Persian translation shows that only eight stories from this text can be found in the *Hikayat Bayan Budiman*. This fact could perhaps help us in our search for the source of the *Hikayat Bayan Budiman*. According to Winstedt, the *Hikayat Bayan Budiman* was barely known in the Malay Peninsula before 1800. It nevertheless became a very popular *hikayat,* as can be seen from the large number of manuscripts that are available. In 1920, Winstedt published two manuscripts of this *hikayat* from the Raffles collection.

It is not known who originally compiled this Malay work. Both the manuscripts of Van der Wijk (Jakarta no. LXVII) and Van der Tuuk (Leiden Cod. 3208) state that it was translated and compiled by Kali Hasan. The date of translation was given as 773 AH, 1371 AD. I quote from the relevant sections of these manuscripts:

o The beginning of the thirteenth story: "This hikayat was translated from Persian to Javanese (i.e., Malay in Jawi script) by Kali Hasan."

o Prior to the twenty-first story: "This parrot tale was retold by Kali Hasan in the year 773 of the calendar of the Prophet Muhammad (peace be upon Him), which was a Dal year".[2]

o Prior to the twenty-fourth story: "This is the story of Sultan Adam recounted by Kali Hasan from the *Bayan Budiman* (Tales of the Parrot) which he used to instruct his descendants."

o And finally: "This is the story of the *Hikayat Bayan Budiman* as told by Kali Hasan. It is as I heard it being imparted to his descendants. Thus concludes the *Hikayat Bayan Budiman*."

---

2   J. Brandes disagrees with this calculation. See J. Brandes, 1899, p. 443.

According to Winstedt, the parrot tales were first translated into Malay around 1600. The Bodleian Library in Oxford holds a fourteen-page manuscript that was bought from a sailor, Edward Pococke (1604-1691). Another manuscript, 2606 [327], in the India Office Library, claims to have been copied in 1808 but first narrated in the Wau year, on Sunday, the 18th day of Saaban, 1008 AH, or 1599 AD. Winstedt observes that both the fine language and orthography, which are older than the *Hikayat Sri Rama*, show that this *hikayat* was already part of Malay literature at the time of the Malaka Sultanate, in the mid-16th century (Winstedt, 1958: 96).

The following is a gist of the manuscript published by Winstedt:

There was once a wealthy merchant in the land of Ajam called Khoja Mubarak. He vowed that he would feed the poor and the ascetics if God would grant him a son. Finally his wife gave birth to a beautiful baby boy. They named him Khoja Maimun and they raised him with great love. When Khoja Maimun had completed his studies of the Quran, his parents married him to Bibi Zainab, the beautiful daughter of a merchant. Khoja Maimum and his new bride were very devoted to each other.

One day, Khoja Maimun bought a parrot for 1000 dinars. The parrot was not like other birds, it was very special: it had come from heaven and was able to predict events ten days before they happened. On the parrot's advice, Khoja Maimum bought all the goods a caravan from Babel would need, and he made a huge profit. Not long after this, Khoja Maimun bought another bird—this time a female mynah.

The two birds helped Khoja Maimun and his wife to live contentedly together. Each day the two birds told them wonderful stories. One day, Khoja Maimun decided to set sail in order to participate in the trade at sea. Before he departed, he told his wife that should she need to make a decision during his absence, she should first consult with the two birds. Khoja Maimun then set sail, leaving his wife in the care of the two birds—Bayan Budiman, the Wise Parrot, and Tiung Rencana, the Resourceful Mynah Bird.

After a long time away without her husband, Bibi Zainab began to miss him very much. One day, as she sat at the window of her palace looking at the street outside, the prince of Ajam passed by.

By the will of Allah, both the prince and Bibi Zainab were strongly attracted to each other. Engaging an old woman as his go-between, the prince sent a message to Bibi Zainab expressing his desire to meet her. When Bibi Zainab heard the prince's sweet words, she agreed to meet him that very evening.

Night fell and Bibi Zainab dressed to meet the prince. Before setting out, she remembered her husband's words and went to consult the mynah bird. The mynah told her that what she was planning to do was forbidden by Allah and His Messenger. Angrily, Bibi Zainab grabbed the mynah from its cage and threw it to the ground, killing it. On seeing Bibi Zainab's cruel treatment of the mynah, the parrot pretended to be asleep. Bibi Zainab then went to him for his opinion. The parrot knew that if he did not agree with Bibi Zainab, he too would be killed.

He therefore had to think of a way of distracting Bibi Zainab. He pretended to agree with what Bibi Zainab wanted to do and assured her that he would keep her secret. After all, he said, his situation was exactly the same as that of another parrot whose feathers were plucked out by a merchant's wife. Not knowing what the parrot meant, Bibi Zainab was curious to hear the tale about the other parrot. By the time the parrot had finished telling his tale, it was already daylight and Bibi Zainab had not been able to meet the prince. Every night the parrot would tell her a story and she would be so captivated that she would forget to keep her appointment with the prince. This continued for twenty-four nights until Khoja Maimun finally returned home. In this way, Bibi Zainab was saved from moral danger. The twenty-four tales told by the parrot are as follows:

1. The parrot whose feathers were plucked out by a merchant's wife

There once was a merchant's wife who committed adultery with a holy man while her husband was away at sea. Not long after, the merchant returned and discovered that his wife had betrayed him. The merchant vented his fury on his wife each day. His wife secretly blamed their pet parrot, suspecting that the parrot must have told her husband about her affair. So she plucked out all the parrot's feathers and threw the bird into a drain that carried waste water from washing rice. When her husband came home, she told him that the parrot had been eaten by a cat. Her husband did not believe her and drove her out of their home. The woman took refuge at the shrine of a saint (*sheikh*). Everyday she swept the shrine and prayed that she and her husband would be reconciled one day.

The parrot remained hidden in the drain. After his feathers grew back, he flew to the sheikh's shrine and hid behind the tombstone. When the merchant's wife came to pray that her husband would take her back, the parrot told her that she would first have to shave her head and eyebrows. When the woman did so, the parrot emerged from his hiding place and laughed at her. But when he saw that she was truly remorseful, the parrot promised to help her win back her husband.

So one day, the parrot flew back to his master and told him that he had indeed been eaten by a cat but had been brought back from the dead in order to convince the merchant that his wife had not lied. The merchant regretted chasing his wife out of the house and took her back again. From that day on, he and his wife lived happily together.

2. The story of Taifah

There was once an Iraqi warrior named Taifah who served the King of Tabristan. One day, Taifah arrogantly boasted that no one among all the king's soldiers was more devoted than he was. His words made the king angry.

One night, the King of Tabristan was awakened by a noise. He went to his balcony, and peering out through the lattice-screen of the balcony, saw Taifah standing guard. The king ordered Taifah to find the source of the disturbance.

Taifah was surprised to discover that the sound came from a beautiful woman. The woman told Taifah that the King of Tabristan had lost the mandate of heaven and he would soon be dead. She added that if Taifah wished to restore the king's sovereignty and ensure that he lived a long life, then Taifah should kill one of his own beloved sons. Because of his uncompromising sense of devotion to his king, Taifah agreed to do as the woman had told him. However, just as he was about to take the life of his son, the beautiful maiden stopped him. She told him that because he had proven that he was truly and selflessly devoted to his king, the king's power would increase and Almighty God (may He be glorified and exalted) would bless His Majesty with a long life. Their conversation was overheard by the king. The king was so touched by Taifah's devotion that he rewarded the warrior with a province of his own and great wealth.

3. The jealous husband

This is a story about an extremely jealous husband. After he married, he refused to work for fear that his wife might engage in some improper act. When his income had finally run out, his wife encouraged him to continue with his trading by telling him a tale about a husband who had faith in his wife. The husband still remained at home. She finally gave him a flower to take with him, saying that the flower would wither should she be unfaithful to him during his absence.

The husband set sail and eventually reached a country that was suffering a severe drought. The leaves on the trees were scorched and withered but the flower his wife had given him remained as fresh as ever. The king was puzzled and asked the merchant to explain how the flower remained fresh. The king did not believe the merchant's explanation. He ordered several of his servants to go to the merchant's house and try to test the man's wife. She tricked them one after another, and they were all trapped in a hole in the ground. When the king arrived, the merchant's wife asked the three servants to come out and wait on the king. She told them that if they wished, they could also lure the king into the hole. When the king heard this, he regretted not believing the merchant and he gave a large amount of gold to the merchant's wife. The king also told the merchant of the unwavering fidelity and shrewdness of his wife. From that day on, the merchant and his wife lived in mutual trust and affection.

4. The woodcarver and the goldsmith

Once there were two good friends—a woodcarver and a goldsmith—who traveled together to a foreign land to seek their fortunes. The two found employment looking after an idol at a temple. One day, they informed the worshippers that the idol wanted to move to another location. That night, they took the golden idol and buried it. The next morning, they announced that the idol had left. Under the pretext of searching for the idol, they returned home. They buried the statue in a deserted spot near where they lived.

Time passed and the goldsmith, overcome by greed, stole the statue. The woodcarver knew what had happened; he bought two birds and trained them to feed on a statue he had carved in the goldsmith's likeness. One day, he kidnapped the goldsmith's two young children and hid them. He told his friend that the children had turned into birds. The case was brought before a judge. The judge ordered that the birds be set free. The moment they were released, the birds flew to the goldsmith's lap; and they kept flying back to him despite his efforts to chase them away. The judge declared: "It is clear that the goldsmith's children have indeed turned into birds." He went on to say that this was probably a punishment for some sin the goldsmith had committed. The goldsmith realised his fault and asked the woodcarver to forgive him. The woodcarver returned his two children to him.

5. The parrots who refused to listen to their father

A parrot warned his three chicks not to make friends with the young of the mongoose. To reinforce his advice, he told them the tale of the baby monkey who was killed because of his friendship with a merchant's son. The chicks did not want to listen to their father's advice. One day, a boy caught the young mongooses. The father mongoose felt very sad and angry beause the boy had taken his children and not the young parrots. On the advice of a wolf, the mongoose led the boy to the parrots' nest. When the parrots saw the boy, they pretended to be dead. The boy took the parrots and threw them to the ground. They all flew away. The father however was not so lucky. The boy caught him and sold him to the king. The father parrot was only reunited with his wife and children after he cured the king of an illness.

6. The hermit, the woodcarver, the goldsmith and the weaver

One day, a hermit, a woodcarver, a goldsmith and a weaver met on a journey. Night fell and they found a place to camp for the night. Because there were many bandits in the area, the travelers decided to take turns to keep watch. During their respective vigils, they practised their individual trades. The woodcarver carved a statue of a beautiful maiden. The weaver wove a beautiful piece of cloth and draped it over the statue, while the goldsmith created a piece of jewellery. The hermit in his turn prayed that the statue would have life. When morning came, the four travelers found the statue had turned into an extremely beautiful woman. They argued over who should own her. As they could not resolve their dispute, they decided to bring the matter to a judge. Along the way, they met two men who also tried to lay claim to the living statue. When the matter reached the judge, he claimed that she was his concubine who had disappeared some time ago. A loud argument broke out because each man wanted the woman. By the will of God, a young man arrived and suggested that they take the woman to a large tree in the middle of a field. Again by the will of God, when they reached the tree, it miraculously split into two halves. The woman stepped into the tree and her voice rang out: "I have now returned to whence I came."

7. The King of Hindustan who used the words of a goat

There was once a King of Hindustan who loved his wife very much. One day when he was out hunting, he chanced upon a female snake being unfaithful to her husband. The king cut off the snake's tail with his machete. The snake's husband was grateful and taught the king how to understand the language spoken by the animals. The snake warned the king not to teach his newfound knowledge to anyone else. If he did, he would die.

One night, when the King of Hindustan was in bed, he overheard two cockroaches sharing a joke and he burst out laughing. The queen realized that her husband could understand what the animals were saying and she begged him to teach her. The king asked her to wait seven days. On the seventh day, while the king was walking alone in the garden, he heard a male goat scolding his wife: "I am not going to get you grass from the bottom of the pond! If I drown, you will marry someone younger; and if you die, so would I." The female goat was stung by her husband's rebuke and said nothing.

The goat's words reminded the king of his wife's excessive demand. When the queen complained that she would die if he did not teach her the language of the animals, the king replied with the same words as the goat had used. When the queen heard the king, she too said nothing.

8. The prince who befriended a sheikh, a snake and a frog

Once a prince went into exile because his brother had just ascended to the throne and wanted to kill him. On the way, he met a *sheikh* (a pious and learned man), dancing in the middle of the road and gave the *sheikh* a *kati* of gold. The *sheikh* thanked him and then transformed himself into a young lady to accompany him. Later, while bathing in a river, the prince rescued a frog by offering his thigh to the snake who was eating him. Their wives urged the frog and the snake to show their gratitude to the prince; the two creatures transformed themselves into humans and also became the prince's travel companions.

Soon, the prince entered the service of a king. One day, when the king accidentally dropped his ring, which was an heirloom, into a pond, the frog retrieved it. Later, when the king's daughter was bitten by a venomous snake, the prince's snake cured her. The king was very grateful. He gave his daughter to the prince and made him king of the realm.

9. Seri and Ferhad

There was once a king in India who had a concubine and a slave, both of whom he was very fond. The concubine, Seri, was very beautiful and she was also skilled in embroidery. The slave, Ferhad, was very handsome and a gifted calligrapher. The king would often asked Ferhad to create designs for Seri to embroider. Because they often work closely together, the two soon fell in love. It was impossible, of course, for the lovers to express their desire for each other and the anguish they felt soon took its toll on them. Before long, the king realised what was happening and looked for a way to kill Ferhad. At first, he ordered him to catch a tiger and then to fight a rampaging elephant. Ferhad succeeded at both of these tasks, thanks to a special mantra seeking Allah's blessings which he learnt from an old man. The king then had him put in chains and thrown into a well, but he still managed to escape, again with the help of the power of the magic mantra. Finally, the king ordered Ferhad to make water flow from the top of a hill. Again he succeeded. Frustrated, the king then sent an old woman to kill Ferhad. The old woman told Ferhad that Seri had died. Ferhad was so shocked that he fainted. He never regained consciousness, and eventually died. When Seri heard of Ferhad's death, she too fainted and died. On seeing his beloved Seri dead, the king stabbed himself and died beside her.

10. The princess who killed all her husbands

Once there was a princess who killed each of her husbands as they slept beside her. In all, she murdered forty princes less one. When the prince of Turkistan heard about her, he decided to marry her, despite his parents' strong objections.

After sailing a great distance, he finally reached the princess's kingdom and they were subsequently married. Each night, the prince forced himself not to sleep. One night he could no longer keep his eyes open and fell asleep. As soon as he did so, the princess immediately tied his hands and feet, intending to cut his throat. The prince woke and seeing what his wife was about to do, smiled and told his wife that it was a pity she did not appreciate the benefit of having a husband. He then went on to tell her a story about the doe, who greatly loved her husband. By the grace of God, the princess realized her mistake and untied her husband. She bowed before him, saying: "Now I realise what it means to have a husband. I used to think that all men were animals."

11. King Nur Shah's marriage to the princess of his dreams

Once upon a time, King Nur Shah of Tur dreamed that he was enjoying himself with a beautiful princess whose name and location were unknown to him. Somehow, his prime minister was able to draw a picture of the princess from the king's description. Armed with this picture, the prime minister then went in search for the woman. When he reached a certain island, he met a ship's captain who told him that the woman in the picture looked very much like the princess of Rum. He added however that the princess had decided not to marry, because she had once seen a peacock abandon a peahen and their chick which subsequently died in a fire. The prime minister immediately returned to his own land and told the king the news.

On the king's orders, the prime minister rented a warehouse in Rum. He spent his time trading and writing. One day, he sketched a doe galloping up a hill, leaving behind a buck and their fawn to drown. When the princess heard the prime minister explanation, she remarked: "If that is the case, then your king is the right husband for me." Not long after, King Nur Shah married the princess; her name was Putri Indera Kemala, and they were very happy together.

12. The Prophet Sulaiman and the porcupine

Once upon a time, the King of Jinns presented the Prophet Sulaiman with a vial containing the elixir of life. Unsure of whether he should drink the elixir, the prophet sought the advice of his ministers. They all urged him to drink the potion and become immortal. Only the porcupine disagreed. He said that there was no point in living forever once your loved ones—your wife, descendants and friends—were dead. When he heard the porcupine's words, the prophet smashed the vial against the ground.

13. The story of Sabur

There was once a man named Sabur who left his wife and children in order to seek his fortune in Damascus. As he was a fine letter-writer and an excellent calligrapher, he soon found a good job. First he was employed by the prime minister, then by the king. As he was an honest man, the king soon appointed him as the royal treasurer.

One day while the king was starting out on his travels abroad, he realised he had forgotten his prayerbeads and sent Sabur to fetch them. While Sabur was at the palace, the queen made improper suggestions to him. Sabur rejected her advances. Angered, the queen accused Sabur of behaving indecently towards her while he was retrieving the king's prayerbeads. The king was furious and wanted to kill Sabur. He gave Sabur an orange and told him to take it to a camphor collector; the collector had previously been told to kill anyone who brought him an orange. However one of the king's slaves who had been sent to investigate the matter unwittingly took Sabur's orange. He was captured by the camphor collector and burned alive. The King of Damascus realized that Sabur was innocent.

Sabur asked the king's permission to be allowed to return to his village. The king agreed but warned him not to stay the night at the home of an old man with a young wife, or to act without due consideration. Sabur forgot the king's advice. During his journey, he stopped for the night at the home of a relative of his cousin, Jibur, a 190-year-old man whose wife was only 18 years of age. Because he recklessly disregarded the advice given to him, Sabur nearly met with misfortune. He realised later that there was truth in the King's words. After some further time, Sabur finally reached his village. He arrived at his house at night and found a young man there. Sabur wanted to kill him. However, he again recalled what the king had said to him. He shone an oil lamp on the young man. The young man was his son.

14. Raja Kilan Shah and his son

Raja Kilan Shah, the king of Istanbul, had a very handsome son called Raja Johan Rashid. After many years on the throne, King Kilan Shah fell seriously ill. On his deathbed, he instructed his prime minister and senior officials to serve his son faithfully. He advised Raja Johan Rashid to rule fairly and justly. He then passed away and Raja Johan Rashid became king.

Raja Johan Rashid proved to be a cruel ruler. He ignored the advice of his prime minister and other senior court officials. His kingdom was soon in the grip of a severe drought and many of his subjects died of hunger. The prime minister and other senior members of the palace decided to kill the king. The kingdom's senior cleric proposed that they first try to persuade the king to mend his ways. Only if he refused should they then proceed with their plan. Raja Johan Rashid refused to repent and decided to flee. During his flight, he was attacked by a band of Bedouins; they took everything he owned, leaving him with only a few scraps of clothing. Raja Johan Rashid realised the error of his ways and became a holy ascetic.

15. Raja Harman Shah

There was once a king, Raja Harman Shah, who was married to Princess Kamarul'ain, the beautiful daughter of Raja Sain. Raja Harman Shah's brother, Raja Ahmad was married to the beautiful Princess Safiah. One day, while playing a game of checkers with Princess Kamarul'ain at her palace, Princess Safiah set eyes on Raja Harman Shah for the first time and was immediately overcome with desire for her brother-in-law. So consumed was she by her forbidden desire that she soon became gaunt and pallid. Before long, she could no longer contain her feelings for Raja Harman Shah and wrote him a love poem to express the depth of her passion. He rejected her love but nevertheless sent her his scarf as a token. Princess Safiah became obsessed with the scarf and smothered it with kisses as if it were her lover. Two days later, she became so overwrought that she fell ill. After another twenty days, she died. Raja Ahmad loved his wife very much. To console him,

Raja Harman Shah revealed the cause of Princess Safiah's illness and subsequent death. When he learned that his wife had died pining for another man, he ceased grieving for her. Not long after, he remarried and found happiness with his new wife, Princess Rabiah, the daughter of the King of Kisar.

16. Raja Gementar Shah whose soul could leave his body

There once was a king of Babylon called Gementar Shah. One day while he was out hunting, the king caught a young deer but its mother escaped. Raja Gementar Shah ordered his prime minister to chase the mother deer. After some time, the prime minister returned. He had not been able to find the deer; however, he had met a sheikh who knew how to make his soul leave his body. He had also met a princess who had decided to never marry for fear of sinning against her husband. The prime minister's report aroused the king's interest and he prepared to set out in search of the princess.

First he went to see the sheikh to learn how to make his soul leave his body. Then he travelled to the palace of Princess Kamariah. Raja Gementar Shah promised to forgive her for any sin she might commit against him in the future. The princess and Raja Gementar Shah were married.

Shortly afterwards, the king took his new bride back to Babylon. On the way, the princess craved some tamarind, but his servants could not find any. Eventually Raja Gementar Shah was forced to find the tamarind for his wife himself. He transferred his soul into the body of a monkey, so that he could climb up a tamarind tree, leaving his body on the ground. Not long after, the prime minister came looking for him and found the king's lifeless body. An evil thought entered his mind. He transferred his soul into the king's body and buried his own. Having found some tamarind, Raja Gementar Shah returned to the spot where he had left his body, only to find that it was gone. He realised that he had been betrayed by his own prime minister. Trapped in the monkey's body, he followed Princess Kamariah and gave her the tamarind. The princess was happy and became very fond of the monkey.

Meanwhile, the prime minister, who now inhabited the king's body, spent all his time on ram fights. He arranged fights each day and bet a thousand dinars each time. One day, he wagered five thousand dinars. By the will of God, the prime minister's ram collapsed and lay motionless on the ground. The prime minister quickly transferred his soul into the body of the ram. In an instant the ram rose up and continued fighting. When the king, who was still trapped in the monkey's body, saw that the prime minister's soul had left his kingly body, he quickly transferred his soul back to his rightful place, finally reuniting his soul with his own body and leaving the monkey lifeless once more. Knowing that the prime minister's soul was in the ram, the king then ordered the ram be killed. The prime minister quickly transferred his soul into the body of the monkey. The monkey was killed too. When the king returned to the palace, his wife asked him about the monkey. The king told her about the prime minister's evil deeds. The princess was shocked and said to the king, "If that is so, then I have done you wrong." The king replied, "I forgive you. You did not know what was happening and meant me no harm."

17. The man who gave half of his life to his wife

There was once a man who loved his wife very much. When she died, he offered half of his life so that that she should live again. His wife recovered. Not long after, his wife left him for a wealthy ship's captain. She swore before a judge that she had never married her husband. The man implored God to give him back the half of his life he had given her. By the will of God, the woman died there and then.

18. Khoja Astor and the young Abyssinian slave

A rich merchant lived in Tabaristan. His name was Khoja Astor. Khoja Astor owned a young Abyssinian slave of whom he was very fond. He thoroughly spoiled the slave and ignored all his misdemeanours. Even when the slave squandered all his wealth, Khoja Astor did nothing. When Khoja Astor eventually fell ill and died, his grandsons captured the slave and killed him.

19. Raja Mansur Shah and Her Highness Princess Ratna Gemala

There once was a king named Raja Mansur Shah who loved his wife, Princess Ratna Gemala, very much. But although he loved his wife, Mansur Shah loved his concubine, Nila Wati, even more. In her jealousy, Princess Ratna Gemala did all she could to win back her husband's affections. Eventually Raja Mansur Shah loved her more than his concubine. He gave her his throne and the kingdom.

20. Siti Hasanah

Siti Hasanah was a devoted wife. One day, her husband left on a sea voyage to trade and entrusted Siti Hasanah to his brother's care. During his absence, his brother fell in love with Siti Hasanah. When his sister-in-law rejected his advances, he accused her of having committed adultery. He produced four false witnesses and she was sentenced to be stoned to death. As she was being punished, Siti Hasanah fainted and her body was thrown into a deserted spot. A Bedouin found her on his way to commit a robbery and took her home. The Bedouin's wife felt sorry for the woman and nursed her so that her wounds slowly healed. To repay their kindness, Siti Hasanah became their maid and helped them look after their child. The Bedouin husband and wife soon grew very fond of Siti Hasanah. Misfortune struck her again. An Abyssinian slave belonging to the Bedouin couple became infatuated with Siti Hasanah. She did not return his feelings and the slave killed the Bedouin child. Although the couple knew that Siti Hasanah had not killed their child, they could no longer bear for her to live with them. They gave her four hundred gold dirhams and told her to leave.

During her journey, she met a thief who was about to be impaled for stealing four hundred dirhams from the king. Siti Hasanah used her four hundred dirhams to pay back the money the thief had stolen so that he could be set free. Once he was freed, the thief proved to be ungrateful. He demanded Siti Hasanah satisfy his lust. When she refused, he sold her to a ship's captain. A merchant on the ship bought her from the captain and led her to his cabin. When she refused to follow him, he tried to force her. Siti Hasanah felt helpless. She prayed earnestly to Almighty God for help. In an instant a typhoon sprang up; it battered the ship and blew everyone overboard. After the storm had finally abated, Siti Hasanah found herself alone on the ship. She disguised herself as a man and sailed to the nearest port. Once ashore, she gave all the riches in the ship's hold to the ruler of the country where the ship had docked. Overjoyed, the king presented her with a set of beautiful clothes and gave her a whole village to administer. In time, he gave Siti Hasanah control of the kingdom. When he died, she became the new ruler. Siti Hasanah was a just and generous monarch. She found favour in the eyes of Allah; her prayers were effective and He always granted everything she requested. Sick people from all over the country came ask her for medicine. She soon became renowned throughout many lands.

In the meantime, her husband returned home. He discovered that his wife was not there and that disaster had befallen his brother, who was now blind. He brought his brother to Siti Hasanah's kingdom to seek a cure. They were accompanied by the four false witnesses, who had also been stricken with various diseases. Raja Hasanah agreed to cure them, on the condition that they confessed to their wicked deeds. She asked her husband if he was willing to forgive them. "Yes," he replied. As soon as he said this, Raja Hasanah cured her accusers. She then revealed her true identity to her husband, who was overjoyed to be reunited with his wife. Later, she went to prepare to say her prayers. As Allah had destined it, she died while she was prostrate in prayer.

21. A man and his two friends

There was once a rich merchant who lived in the land of Madi Negara. The man's son was very handsome. While he was still very young, the boy learned to recite the Quran from a religious teacher. He was also taught all the skills and knowledge a young man should know, as well as weaponry and how to deal with other merchants and traders. When the boy reached maturity, the merchant gave his son a large amount of gold and sent him to find some friends. The young man quickly had forty friends. The merchant was surprised as his son had previously never possessed more than two friends. He then asked his son to put his forty friends to the test.

One day, the merchant's son invited his friends to a banquet. He told them that his life was in danger, as the king wanted to kill him for flirting with one of the queen's ladies-in-waiting. When his friends heard this, only one of them was willing to do anything to save him. The merchant then called the son's original two friends and told them of his son's predicament. One of them said that he was willing to give all that he owned if it would help save the merchant's son from the punishment of the king. The other said he would not only give up all his wealth but also his life to save the young man. The merchant then turned to his son and told him that of all his friends, only one deserved to be considered a true friend and advised his son to remain loyal to that one young man.

22. King Adar Shah

There was once a king who treated his subjects very cruelly. One day, he decreed that: "Whoever mills paddy must produce equal amounts of rice and chaff. If you mill eight gallons of paddy, there should be eight gallons of rice and eight of chaff." Not long after that, the prime minister came to the king and told him that his subjects were finding it very difficult to comply with his order. The king refused to cancel his decree. He said that his command was like an elephant's tusk: once raised, it cannot be withdrawn.

Eventually the king passed away and was succeeded by his son, Raja Adar Shah. After ascending to the throne, Raja Adar Shah often disguised himself and mingled with his people. He heard nothing but complaints about his late father's harshness. To silence criticism of his father's evil reign, Raja Adar Shah behaved even more cruelly than his father had. To avoid further suffering, the unhappy citizens fled the kingdom and sought refuge in neighbouring lands. This provided an opportunity for his enemies to attack the kingdom. The whole royal family was taken prisoner by the invaders.

23. Sultan Adam

Sultan Adam of Baghdad once ruled a vast empire. Kings from all over sent him rich tributes and exotic gifts. Sultan Adam had a son called Nasruddin Alim Shah.

One day, a Malabari craftsman came to see the king and presented him with a set of bird figurines made of gold, silver, diamonds and emeralds. These figurines could speak, thanks to the wizardry of the craftsman. One day, the king went to the Malabari craftsman and asked him to create a toy, the likes of which had never been seen before by any other king. When the bird figurines learnt of his request, they exchanged verses with each other, mocking man's desire for the excessive and the unreasonable. The king heard the birds and reflected on his request. Suddenly he heard a voice speaking from inside his own body: "I am Passion and the request came from me." Sultan Adam was terrified but wanted to see Passion. By the will of God, Sultan Adam began to cough and a lizard fell out of his ear. It was Passion. The king fed Passion all sorts of delicious food. As a result, the lizard, who was also Eve, grew too large to fit back into the king's ear, and because she could not return to where she had come, the king slew her.

Not long after this, Sultan Adam disappeared, and his son Nasruddin assumed the throne. Sultan Nasruddin sent out a search party to look for his father but they could not find him. One night, Sultan Nasruddin dreamed that his father was in Istanbul, so he quickly sent his emissaries to look for him there. Sure enough, Sultan Adam was in Istanbul. He had become an ascetic, called himself Nuruddin, and was living with a humble brother barber. The old king, who now wanted to be known as brother Nuruddin, returned to his kingdom but could not be persuaded to resume his throne. After some time, he announced that he wanted to go to Mecca to live with a community of Islamic scholars. He spent the rest of his days in Mecca, reciting the Quran and living a devout life.

24. Raja Ghair Malik

There once was a king of Hindustan named Ghair Malik. The king decided not to remarry after his wife died. One night, the king had a dream in which a very beautiful woman emerged from the sea and entered the palace. The king fell in love with the woman. He asked his two sons, Sahil and Naim, to find her. After some time, Sahil returned and told his father that they had been separated in a storm.

After Naim became separated from Sahil, he was washed ashore on a beach where he later met a sheikh with magic powers. The sheikh told Naim that the woman in his father's dream was the daughter of a pagan *jinn* who was locked away in an iron chest. The sheikh urged Naim to help the Muslim *jinn*s in their war against the pagan *jinn*. He taught Naim a magical spell that would help him in the battlefield. Naim left and joined the Muslim *jinn*'s army. The pagan *jinn* was defeated and forced to convert to Islam. Naim subsequently returned to Hindustan with the princess from his father's dream and the king eventually married her.

***

This completes the twenty-four stories the parrot told Bibi Zainab. The work ends by saying that she wanted to feed the parrot sweets and bathe it in a golden bowl. Upon hearing her intentions, the parrot predicted that her husband, Khoja Maimun, would return the following day. The bird asked her to put on her most beautiful clothes and most fragrant perfume in order to receive him. Bibi Zainab did as she was told. The next day, Khoja Maimun arrived and was overjoyed to see his wife again. He hugged and kissed her, and they behaved like newlyweds. Not long after, Bibi Zainab encouraged her husband to release the parrot so that it could return to its wife and children. The parrot was very grateful. About a week later, it returned, bearing beautiful flowers from the forest where it lived.

6.4 *Hikayat Bakhtiar*

Hikayat Bakhtiar is the Malay name for a Persian book that originated from India, the *Bakhtiar Nama*. It should be noted that sixteen of the 24 stories in the *Hikayat Bayan Budiman* described above can be found in the *Hikayat Bakhtiar;* namely stories 2, 3 (only the inserted stories), 4, 8, 9, 10, 11, 12, 13, 15, 16, 17, 18, 19, 20 and 22. It is also interesting that the sixteenth story is told as a series of continuous tales encapsulating stories 15 to 28.

The overall plot is a very old one. At the beginning of the tenth century, the historian al-Mas'udi wrote a book, *Sindbad Nama* (The Book of Sindbad, or "the tale of the seven viziers"), which tells the following story:

Once upon a time, a king placed his son in the care of a religious scholar called Sindbad so that he could learn various types of knowledge and practical skills. Sindbad knew that the prince's life was in danger and instructed him to observe a vow of silence for seven days. During this time, the prince was slandered by the king's favourite concubine, who accused him of impropriety. Seven viziers tried to save the prince's life by telling stories to the king in order to delay the prince's execution. After seven days, the prince finally told the king the truth.

In *Sindbad Nama,* there were seven viziers who tried to save the prince's life through telling stories; in *Bakhtiar Nama,* on the other hand, ten viziers tried not to save Bakhtiar's life but to incriminate him instead. The story goes like this:

Once upon a time, King Azadbakht and his wife were forced to flee their kingdom. They abandoned their newborn son in order to save his life. A bandit found the prince and raised him as his own son. Not long after, the prince and his adopted father were arrested by the king. The king felt sorry for the young man and decided to take him into his service. He called him Bakhtiar.

Bakhtiar proved to be an intelligent and clever young man and quickly achieved a high rank. This made the king's ministers jealous. Together they conspired to accuse him of impropriety with the queen. To protect her own reputation, the queen claimed that Bakhtiar had tried to seduce her. For ten days, each of the king's ten ministers told stories to convince the king of Bakhtiar's guilt and have him executed. To counter their allegations, Bakhtiar also told a story. However, he was found guilty. On the eleventh day, the day of his execution, the bandit who had raised Bakhtiar came forward and revealed the true circumstances behind his origin. The king realised that Bakhtiar was his own long-lost son. He sentenced his ten ministers to death. Bakhtiar was crowned king, replacing his father on the throne (Arberry, 1958: 165, 170-171).

There are two versions of the *Hikayat Bakhtiar*, a shorter version and a longer one. The shorter version has been published several times. It was first published by A. F. von de Wall in 1880 as a "reader for indigenous students." This version was reprinted in 1889. The longer version is discussed by J. Brandes in two important papers (Brandes, 1895; 1899). Here is a summary of the shorter version:

A king learned that his brother was plotting to overthrow him. In order to prevent a civil war, the king fled into exile, taking his queen with him. During their exile, the queen gave birth to a baby boy. They were forced to abandon the child in the forest. He was found by a wealthy merchant named Idris, who was out hunting one day. The merchant took the child home and placed him in the care of his wife, Siti Sara. They raised the boy as if he were their own son.

Bakhtiar, as they called him, soon grew up to be a clever young man; he was not only able to read the Quran well, but was also good at reciting literary texts and writing letters. One day, Idris presented Bakhtiar before the king. His Majesty was so impressed by the intelligence of the young man that he asked Bakhtiar to live in the palace. From that time on, the king consulted less and less with his ministers. He left everything to Bakhtiar to decide. The king's ministers resented this and one of them, Tahkim, devised a plot to have him killed. Tahkim asked his wife to steal a shawl belonging to one of the king's favourite ladies-in-waiting, and to place it on Bakhtiar's pillow. He then accused Bakhtiar of impropriety. Bakhtiar was arrested and imprisoned. The ministers urged the king to execute him without delay. To delay his execution, Bakhtiar told the king five stories. These were as follows:

i. One day, a trapper presented the king with a bird of exquisite beauty. The king was so delighted that he appointed the trapper as a minister. One of the other ministers, Muhammad Julus, was so jealous that he wanted to kill the trapper. First, he provoked the king to ask the bird-trapper to determine the sex of a bird. The trapper was able to accomplish this with the help of a holy man. Next, Muhammad Julus provoked the king to command the trapper to bring him princess Mengindra Sari of Rum. The trapper did this too but he had to provide a ship made of gold for the princess to sail from Rum. When the princess finally arrived, the trapper then asked the king to order Muhammad Julus to produce twelve black buffalos with white eyelids to be slaughtered for each step she had to climb up to the palace. Muhammad Julus was only able to produce eleven buffalos and was executed.

ii. One day a fisherman visited the king of China, bringing a gift of fish eyes. In return he asked for a single-edged knife. The fish eyes were made of diamonds and precious stones. The king presented a knife to the fisherman and he even gave him a monkey named Burun. Burun could not only dance but could also talk. He persuaded a princess to marry his master, the fisherman. After the wedding or, more precisely, after a failed attack by his enemies, the fisherman changed his ways and later became the king.

iii. One day, the king declared a curfew in his kingdom: "Nobody is allowed out in the streets tonight. Anyone found wandering outside at night will be arrested, and anyone who resists arrest will be killed." A merchant named Hassan went out that night to see what was going on, following the advice of his wife Siti Dinar, a clever and astute woman. The king went out to check that his men were carrying out his orders and was arrested by Hassan for breaking his own curfew. The king was so pleased with Hassan for having shown his wise discretion that he made Hassan his chief minister. One of the king's ministers, Abu Fadl, however, was jealous and plotted to bring about Hassan's downfall. Abu Fadl made a public confession that he had had an adulterous affair with Hassan's wife. According to the law of the land, a man whose wife was guilty of adultery was himself liable to the death sentence. Consequently, Hassan was arrested and imprisoned. Siti Dinar thought of a way to save her husband. She publicly accused Abu Fadl of not only committing adultery with her but also of stealing her golden shoes. Abu Fadl vehemently denied her accusations, saying: "I have never seen this woman before, let alone had an affair with her." And so by his own admission, it was proven that Abu Fadl's earlier allegation against Siti Dinar was false and he was subsequently impaled.

iv. There once were two royal brothers. The elder brother was a king; the younger was a rebel, bent on overthrowing his brother. To prevent bloodshed, the elder brother abandoned his throne and went into exile with with his queen and their two children. They travelled far and soon reached a river near the sea. The king wanted to cross the river but there was no boat to take them to the other side. So the king had first to help the queen across the river. When he returned for his two sons, they had vanished, taken by a fisherman who had found them alone by the riverbank. The king then swam back to the other side of the river, only to find that his wife was gone too. The queen had been kidnapped by a sailor who took her back to his ship's captain. When the captain heard her story, he took her on board and treated her kindly.

The king roamed wherever Allah, Lord of the entire universe, led him. He eventually came to a place where a sacred elephant chose him as the new king. One day, the fisherman arrived in the kingdom with his two adopted sons. The king was impressed by the boys and appointed them as his pages.

Not long after this, a ship sailed into the port, wanting to trade and establish good relations with the king. The king invited the ship's captain to a banquet. The captain declined at first because he had no one he could trust to look after his ship. The king ordered his two pages to guard the captain's ship. Eventually, the two boys became weary. To prevent his younger brother falling asleep, the older page began to tell him stories about their childhood. The queen overheard him. She came out to greet the two boys, with tears streaming down her face, and hugged and kissed the lads. The members of the ship's crew were shocked, thinking that the captain's wife was behaving improperly. They captured the boys and handed them over to the king. Furious, the king ordered that the boys be executed.

The executioner led the boys to the outskirts of the city. When they reached the edge of the city, the city's gatekeepers refused to open the gates for them. Instead, they warned the executioner against acting rashly. The first gatekeeper told them the tale of a father, his son, and their cat. A farmer went to work on his rice-field, leaving his infant son in the care of his cat. When he returned, he found his cat with blood around its mouth. The farmer immediately assumed that the cat had killed his son. He killed the cat. Later he discovered the head of a snake on the ground near the child's cradle. He realized what had happened and was filled with remorse.

The second gatekeeper told them the tale of a man and his dog. One day, a man returned home to find his trusty dog sitting in the front yard with its mouth covered in blood, and his wife lying dead next to it. The man struck the dog with his machete. He then went inside his house and found the dead body of a man lying on his bed. He finally understood what had actually happened and was overcome with regret.

The third gatekeeper told them a tale about the king who wanted to build a palace. One day, a king consulted his astrologer about an auspicious time to build a new palace. "Oh sire, master of the universe," the astrologer very respectfully replied, "there is indeed a moment so propitious that if your majesty were to build your palace at that time, all the furnishings will turn to gold. When I strike this gong, it will be the moment to begin building." When the astrologer sounded the gong, the king's ministers hurried to build the palace. But they were not quite quick enough. An old man dropped a bunch of bananas when he heard the gong, and decided to plant them where they lay. The palace was completed but none of its furnishings turned to gold. The king had the astrologer killed. However, when the king heard that the old man's tree had begun to bear golden bananas, he was filled with regret.

When day finally broke, the gatekeepers went to see the king. Bowing before him, they humbly said, "Oh sire, ruler of the world, we beseech you to investigate this matter thoroughly, lest your majesty live to regret your actions." The king summoned the two pages. He discovered that they were his sons and that the woman was his wife.

v. The fifth tale is the story of a fish that was ordered to swim about and perform tricks to entertain a spoilt princess. This story is not found in the version published by Von de Wall but can be found in the manuscript (v.d. Wall 179, MI 554 H) published by the Language Centre, Jakarta (Edwar Djamaris, 1978).

We now return to the original story of Bakhtiar. After seventeen days, the merchant Idris was summoned by the king. Idris revealed that Bakhtiar was not his real son and that he had found him in the forest while he was hunting. The king realized that Bakhtiar was his own son and was greatly relieved to have found him alive. Not long after, Bakhtiar was crowned king.

The longer version contains more stories than the shorter version—67 in all. Of these, 16 are taken from *Hikayat Bayan Budiman*. There are others taken from *Tajus Salatin* (*Crown of kings*), *Bustanus Salatin* and *Serat Nawawi* in Javanese. According to Winstedt, one can also find tales from the Abu Nawas collection, the Quran and Hadith, in the longer version. This is probably why Winstedt refers to the longer version of the *Hikayat Bakhtiar* as an anthology of Persian and Arabic stories.

The version of the *Hikayat Bakhtiar* that was edited by Baharuddin bin Zainal and published by Dewan Bahasa dan Pustaka, Kuala Lumpur, is similar to the longer version of this hikayat. It also mentions that Bakhtiar was adopted by Rusdus (or Rasdas). The king who sentenced Bakhtiar was King Adil, the king of Turkestan (Turkisna). Stories 7 to 13 are also found in this longer version. The Dewan Bahasa text also includes tales that are not found in either the short or longer versions, for example, story 14, a tale about a wicked friend. This tale reminds me of the fantastic chronicles of the transition age, in which characters can change into animals or objects in order to fight their enemies. Such stories do not fit with the overall tenor of the *Hikayat Bakhtiar*. Perhaps the Dewan Bahasa version—based on a manuscript belonging to Tengku Ibrahim bin Tengku Muhammad of Kelantan—is also intended to be an anthology of various tales taken from different sources.

6.5 *Hikayat Golam*

The *Hikayat Golam* is also known as *Hikayat Raja Azbakht* and *Hikayat Zadab Bokhtin*. The chronicle was first mentioned by Werndly in 1736. According to one Leiden manuscript, the *Hikayat Golam* was translated from the Arabic by Abdul Wahab of Siantan.

The main story of the *Hikayat Golam* closely resembles that of the *Bakhtiar Nama*. In this narrative, Raja Azbakht is said to have ruled a kingdom called Adan in Ajam (Persia), and Bakhtiar is called Golam. As in *Bakhtiar Nama*, Golam was adopted by a bandit. Raja Azbakht was forced to flee his kingdom for secretly marrying Mahrut, the daughter of his prime minister.

There is one major difference between the *Hikayat Golam* and the *Hikayat Bakhtiar*: in order to save himself, Golam tells only nine tales. Of the nine framed stories, seven that are found in the *Hikayat Kalilah dan Dimnah* appear as the fifth story in *Hikayat Bakhtiar* and illustrate the folly of acting hastily without first fully investigating the situation. It should also be noted that all nine framed stories can also be found in one of the versions of the *Hikayat Seribu Satu Malam*.

A summary of the story according to a manuscript in the Museum Pusat (MI 555/v.d. Wall 132) published by Pusat Bahasa (Nikmah A. Soenardjo 1978) is given below.

There once was a king named Raja Zad Bukhtin of Ajam, who ruled over a large kingdom. One day, while walking outside the city with his ministers, he saw a very beautiful woman:

> ... her eyelids were as dark as kohl. Her fingers were as slender and tapered as porcupine quills, her eyebrows were beautifully curved like graceful arcs, her cheeks were as round and as golden as the skin of a mango. Her forehead was like a sliver of the moon, her hair fell in gentle waves, her lips were full and as red as ripe saga seeds. Her breasts were round, her waist was slender, her calves were firm like ripe ears of rice, her heels were shaped like the eggs of a quail.

The king took the beautiful maiden back to his palace and made her his wife, unaware that she was the daughter of his own prime minister, Ashbahanda.

Prime Minister Ashbahanda was angry that the king had slighted him. He gathered a large army of soldiers and attacked the kingdom. The king and his queen fled and sought refuge in the forest. One night, the queen gave birth to a baby boy; she left the child beside a river. Harami, a robber, raised the child as if he were his own son. Eventually, the exiled King, Zat Bukhtin, returned to his palace, following the death of his father-in-law, Prime Minister Ashbahanda.

One day, the leader of a train of caravans captured Harami and his adopted son, Golam. He gave the boy to the king. King Bukhtin grew fond of Golam and adopted him as his son. Both the king and queen loved Golam very much. This made the palace ministers jealous. One night, while carrying out his duty guarding the palace, Golam stumbled and fell unconscious at the foot of the king's bed. The ministers seized this opportunity and accused him of dishonourable conduct. Golam was sentenced to death. In an attempt to save himself, Golam began to tell stories to the king. He told the king nine tales, as follows:

i. The tale of the unlucky merchant. There was once a merchant who faced a series of misfortunes. He sold wheat and lost money. He set sail to seek his fortune abroad and his ship sank. He then worked on a farm for a greedy sheikh, but was not paid his wages. Next, ten pearl-divers gave him some pearls; he was arrested and accused of stealing the pearls. He then became the keeper of the royal treasures but he was then accused of spying on the king's daughter. He eventually died in prison.

ii. A merchant beat his two sons and threw them into the sea, after he failed to find a purse containing his money. Not long after, the merchant bought a young slave at the marketplace. He later discovered that the slave was one of his sons. Some time after that, a king from a neighbouring kingdom wanted to kill his own son whom he had sent out on a trading mission. The merchant pleaded for the prince's life to be spared, and told the king his own story about how he had once been impatient with his two sons and lived to regret his impetuous actions. After hearing the merchant's story, it was revealed that the king was the merchant's other long-lost son.

iii. Abu Sabar eventually became king and was reunited with his wife and children.

iv. Raja Bazad's eyes were plucked out because he was impatient to look at his fiancée, the princess of Egypt.

v. Raja Dadanini killed his minister so that he could marry the minister's virtuous daughter. Once they were married, the king heard slanderous remarks about his wife's chastity and wanted to kill her. In the end, his wife was saved by Raja Khasruwan, who killed Raja Dadanini.

vi. Raja Bukhta lost his kingdom because of his own arrogance. After hearing the story of Raja Khadayadanin, Raja Bukhta repented and surrendered his fate to God. In the end his kingdom was restored.

vii. Raja Bakirad pardoned a boy for shooting an arrow that accidentally cut off his ear. He was later saved by the same boy. It turned out that the boy was the son of Raja Humayun.

viii. Raja Ilan Shah hastily executed his loyal slave, Abu Taman, without first ascertaining the truth of the matter. When he later realized the truth, he regretted his action but it was too late. At their wedding, his queen, Princess Nila Utama, the daughter of the King of Turkey, told stories of Abu Taman's long years of loyal service and how much she respected him; he was like a father to her. Not long after, the princess died of grief. Raja Ilan Shah lived the rest of his life alone and in misery.

ix. A queen ordered the death of a son from her previous marriage for fear the king would think of her as a loose woman. She later regretted her action. Fortunately, the minister assigned to kill the boy had spared his life and placed him in hiding. The king forgave his wife. The whole kingdom rejoiced.

When he had finished telling the king these tales, the ministers again urged the king to kill Golam. Everyone gathered to watch the execution so that they could see for themselves the punishment awaiting those who dishonor the king. Among the spectators was Harami the bandit. He revealed that Golam was the king's own son, whom he had found by the riverside. Raja Zat Bukhtin was first shocked, and then delighted. In time, Golam subsequently succeeded to the throne.

This edition of *Hikayat Golam* is replete with advice and moral teachings, very often citing God's commandments as found in the Quran. Various Arabic and Malay verse forms, interspersed with *gurindam* (couplets) and *pantun* (quartrains), can also be found in the hikayat.

6.5 *Hikayat Maharaja Ali*

The *Hikayat Maharaja Ali* (The Tale of Emperor Ali) is very different from the *Hikayat Bakhtiar*. It begins with Maharaja Ali being driven out of his kingdom by his eldest son, Baharum Shah. While crossing a river, Maharaja Ali was swallowed by a crocodile. His two children escaped unhurt and were adopted by a boatman. The maharaja's wife, Queen Haynah, was abducted by Raja Serdala. When Raja Serdala tried to embrace her, Queen Haynah prayed to God for protection. Raja Serdala's arms suddenly became very short.

This is followed by an episode taken from the *Hikayat Jumjumah* (see 5.1.19, above). A skull begged the Prophet Isa (Jesus) to be allowed to live again. The prophet granted this wish. The skull belonged to Maharaja Ali and as soon as he was brought back to life, the maharaja returned to his kingdom and reclaimed his throne.

From this point on, the narrative is similar to that of the *Hikayat Nakhoda Muda* (see 4.11, above). Raja Serdala arrived at Maharaja Ali's kingdom in search of a cure for the curse placed on him that had resulted in his arms becoming short. Two of Maharaja Ali's pages—his long-lost sons—were assigned to guard Raja Serdala's ship while he was ashore. Queen Haynah heard the pages telling each other stories about their childhood and, realising that they were her sons, came out to embrace them. All three of them were imprisoned. Their jailkeeper turned out to be Baharum Shah, Maharaja Ali's eldest son. Maharaja Ali's family was finally reunited once again.

This concludes our discussion of the framed narrative.

REFERENCES

Abdullah bin Abdul Kadir Munshi
1887. *Hikayat Pancha Tanderan,* Singapore.

Amin Maulani
1972. "Ikhtisar Isi Naskah Hikayat Washiyyat Luqman 'I-Hakim (W. 125)," *Manusia Indonesia,* 6, 3 & 4, pp. 131-145.

Anon
n.d. *Hikayat Alf Laila Wa Laila, yakni Hikajat Seribu Satu. Malam yang terlalu indah-indah ceritanya.* Parts 1-5, lithographed, Singapore.

Arberry, A.J.
1958. *Classical Persian Literature,* London.

Baharuddin Zainal
1963. *Hikayat Bakhtiar,* Kuala Lumpur.

Blagden, C. O.
1929. "Hikayat Maharaja Ali," *JMBRAS,* 7 (3), pp. 415-436.

Brandes, J.
1891. "Het Onderzoek naar de oorsprong van de Maleische Hikajat Kalila dan Damina," in *Feestbundel - De Goeje,* pp. 79-106.
1893. "Een paar bijzonderheden uit een handschrift van Hikajat Kalila dan Damina," *TBG,* 36 (4), pp. 394-416.
1895. "Nadere opmerkingen over de Maleische bewerkingen van de geschiedenis der tien vezieren. Hikajat Golam, Hikajat Kalila dan Damina (laatste gedeelte) en de daarom te onderscheiden, bij de Maleische voorhanden uiteenlopende Hikajat Bakhtijar," *TBG,* 38 (3) pp. 101-273.
1899. "De inhoud van de groote Hikajat Bakhtijar, volgens een aanteekening van Dr. H.N. van der Tuuk," *TBG,* 41, pp. 292-299.
1899. "Iets over het Papegaai-boek, zoals het bij de Maleiers voorkomt," *TBG,* 41 (5-6), pp. 431-497.
1931. "Het probleem van de Maleische Hikajat Kalila dan Damina," *TBG,* LXXX, pp. 172-185.

Browne, E. G.
1956-1959. *A Literary History of Persia* 1-4, Cambridge.

Edwar Djamaris
1978. *Hikayat Bakhtijar,* Jakarta.

Gerhardt, Mia I.
1963. *The Art of Story-Telling,* Leiden.

Gongrijp, J. R. P. F.
1892. *Hikajat Kalila dan Damina,* Leiden.

Haniah
1978. *Hikayat Kalilah dan Daminah,* Jakarta.

Hooykaas, C.
1929. *Tantri, de Middel-Javaansche Panchatantra-bewerking,* Leiden.

Ismail Djamil
1950. *Hikajat Kalila dan Damina,* Jakarta.

Jumsari Jusuf
1970. "Tjerita-tjerita Berbingkai," *Manusia Indonesia,* 4 (1 & 2), pp. 47-57.

Keith Falconer, I. G. N.
1885. *Kalila and Dimna or the Fables of Bidpai,* Cambridge.

Khairuddin bin Hj. Muhammad (tr.)
1962. *Hikayat Kalila dan Damina,* Kuala Lumpur.

Muhammed A. Sumsar
1978. *Tuti Nama/Tales of a Parrot,* The Cleveland Museum of Art.

Nikmah A. Soenardjo
1978. *Hikayat Gulam,* Jakarta.

Onn bin Jaafar
1978. *Hikayat Seribu Satu Malam,* Kuala Lumpur.

Ophuijsen, C. A. van
1972. *Hikayat Galila dan Damina,* Zalt-Bommel.

Panchatantra
1967. *Panchatantra* (translated by Arthur W. Ryder), Chicago & London, 1967.

Panzer, N. M.
1968. *The Ocean of Story being C. H. Tawney's translation of Somadera's Khata Sarit Sagara,* I-X, Delhi.

Ryder, A. (tr.)
1967. *Panchatantra,* Chicago & London.

Voorhoeve, P.
1933. "Het Boek der tien vizieren in het Maleisch," *TBG,* 73, pp. 427-435.

Wall, A.F. von de
1880. *Hikajat Bachtijar,* Batavia.

Winstedt, R. O.
1958. *Hikayat Bayan Budiman,* Singapore.

Winternitz, M.
1959. *A History of Indian Literature* (translated into English by Subhadra Jha), vol. 1, Delhi.

7 The Literature of Islamic Theology[1]

The literature of Islamic theology ("*Sastra Kitab*", a *kitab* is a book or a scholarly tome) is potentially enormous. On the one hand, R. Roolvink (1971) suggests that Islamic theological literature includes studies of the Quran, *tafsir* (the interpretation of the Quran), *tajwid* (Quranic recitation), *arkan ul-Islam* (the pillars of Islam), *usuluddin* (theology), *fikih* (jurisprudence), *ilmu sufi* (Sufism), *ilmu tasawuf* (mysticism), *tarikat* (the different religious orders), *zikir* (chanting the names of God), *rawatib* (non-obligatory prayers), *doa* (supplications), *jimat* (talisman), *risalah* (tracts), *wasiat* (wills) and *kitab tib* (folk medicine and spells). In a narrow sense, however, Siti Baroroh Baried limits *sastra kitab* to the mystical literature (*sastra tasawuf*) that developed in Acheh during the 17th century (Sulastin Sutrisno et al. 1985: 291).

Mystical literature is certainly a very important part of Islamic theological literature in Malay. According to A. H. Johns, mystical literature played an important role in the spread of Islam in the Archipelago. Firstly, the Sufi mystics were adept at imparting the doctrines of Islam in terms that the local populace could understand. Secondly, mysticism itself had its own attraction, as joining a religious order (*tarikat*) meant that one became part of a large and supportive family. Furthermore, many *tarikat* members were well-travelled merchants, who had studied in Islamic centres all over the world. During the first half of the 17th century, four main Sufi brotherhoods—the Qadiriyah, Naksyabandiyah, Syatariah and Suhrawardi—all flourished in Acheh (Hall, 1962: 37-47).

We can glean a little bit about the activities of the Sufis from the *Sejarah Melayu* (Malay Annals), which tells us that many *maulana* (religious scholars), *syaikh* (leaders) and *makhdum* (Sufi masters) arrived in Malaka to teach and spread Islam. The scholar Abu Ishak sent his book, *Daru'l-Mazlum (House of the Oppressed)*, to Sultan Mansur Syah. Maulana Yusuf taught metaphysics to Sultan Mahmud. These servants of Allah were regarded as holy men who possessed extraordinary supernatural powers. One of the holy men was reputed to have pointed his arrow at Thailand and, as a result, the prince of Siam collapsed and died. On another occasion, a ship's captain found his perfectly seaworthy vessel mysteriously shattered after he disputed the words of one of these holy servants of Allah. It is not surprising then that mysticism and the Sufi orders had an enthusiastic following in the Archipelago. Malaka soon became known as the "gateway to Mecca".

---

[1] I wish to thank Prof. Baroroh Baried for her advice which has proven to be invaluable in the writing of this chapter.

After the fall of Malaka to the Portuguese in 1511, the Muslim merchants and scholars who had once congregated at its port dispersed to other parts of the Archipelago. Gradually Acheh replaced Malaka as the centre of Islamic scholarship in the region. Muslim traders and scholars began to flock to Acheh. It is related in *Bustanus Salatin* II/13 that, during the reign of Sultan Ali Ri'ayat Syah (1568-1575), an Islamic scholar from Egypt, Muhammad Azhari (who was also called Syaikh Nuruddin), came to Acheh in order to teach metaphysics. In 1582, two other scholars arrived from Mecca. One of them, Syaikh Abdul-Kadir ibn Syaikh ibn Hajar, taught Sufi doctrines from the book *Saifu'l-Qati* (*The Sharp Sword*), a treatise that discusses *a'yan thabitah* (the divine fixed prototypes). The other, Syaikh Muhammad Yamani, was an expert on *syariah* (law). Sometime between 1580 and 1583, Syaikh Muhammad Jailani Hamid, an uncle of Nuruddin Ar-Raniri, arrived to teach logic and jurisprudence. When a great number of his students showed an interest in pursuing studies in mysticism, Syaikh Muhammad Jailani traveled to Mecca to deepen his knowledge of Sufism. He returned to Acheh a few years later and proved to be an extremely popular teacher. Fifty years later, on 31 May 1637, Nuruddin Ar-Raniri himself arrived in Acheh (Siti Chamamah 1982: 19-21).

As a centre of Islamic scholarship, Acheh was not spared the turbulent developments that arose elsewhere in the Islamic world. It was at this time that the controversy over the concept of *wahdaniyah* or *wujudiyah* (panentheism) and its doctrine of *wahdat al-wujud* (existential monism) shook the Arab world. The teachings also had a profound impact on Acheh. Many Achehnese became followers of Ibn Arabi (died 1240 AD/ 678 H), who argued: *Wujud al-makhluqat 'ain wujud al-khalik*, "The being of created beings manifests the being of their creator." Both Hamzah Fansuri and, later, Syamsuddin al-Sumatrani espoused this doctrine. Nuruddin Ar-Raniri, however, was fervently opposed to the teachings of *wujudiah*. A violent polemic erupted between the two schools of thought. Victory did not depend on which side was the more skilful in presenting its arguments but on the patronage of the ruling sultan. When Nuruddin Ar-Raniri obtained the support of Sultan Iskandar Thani (1637-1641) and was appointed mufti, or the royal *syaikh*, he denounced the adherents of *wujudiyah* as infidels and apostates, and ordered the burning of all books that contained *wujudiyah* doctrine. These developments disturbed the people of Acheh and eventually forced Nuruddin Ar-Raniri to leave the country suddenly in 1644. When Abdur Rauf returned to Acheh in 1661, he earned the favour of Sultanah Tajul-'alam Safiatuddin Syah (1641-1675) and her successor, Sultanah 'Inayat Syah Zakiyatuddin Syah (1678-1688), and he tried to restore calm among the local Muslim community by writing several books that purported to teach true doctrine.

In this chapter we will discuss the works of the four theologians mentioned above. We will also consider several other books that can also be considered important theological literature, namely *Kitab Seribu Masa'il (Book of a Thousand Questions), Tajus Salatin* and *Wasiat Lukman al-Hakim (Testament of Judge Lukman)*. Finally, we will briefly talk about the works of several *ulama* (theologians), who wrote in Palembang in the eighteenth century and in Patani in the nineteenth century.

7.1 Hamzah Fansuri

Hamzah Fansuri is a famous Sufi proponent and poet. Even so, little is known about his life. Scholars disagree, for example, on the actual period during which he lived. Kraemer, Doorenbos and Winstedt maintain that Hamzah Fansuri lived in the first half of the seventeenth century. This is, however, disputed by Voorhoeve and Drewes, who argue that Hamzah Fansuri lived in the second half of the sixteenth century. Hamzah Fansuri, they argue, was a follower of Ibn Al-Arabi, and taught Arabi's doctrine of the Five Spiritual Stations. His teachings did not reflect any knowledge of the tenets of the Seven Spiritual Stations that later characterised Syamsuddin's teachings. Syamsuddin learnt about the Seven Spiritual Stations from a book by Muhammad b. Fadlullah al-Burhan Puri entitled *At-tuhfa al-mursala ila ruh al-nabi* (A Tract in honour of the Prophet's Spirit), written in 1590. A copy of the book was sent to Acheh at the request of a student who had studied under him. The book was well received in Acheh due to the efforts and support of Syamsuddin. By this time, Hamzah Fansuri was remembered with respect by the people of Acheh but only as someone belonging to a bygone era (Drewes and Brakel, 1986: 2-3).

Hamzah Fansuri's birthplace is also the subject of contention. Scholars generally agree that Hamzah Fansuri was born in Barus, a town on the west coast of North Sumatra between Singkel and Sibolga. The name "Fansuri" had long been used to refer to seamen or traders who were associated with that town. According to Syed Naguib al-Attas (1967: 46), however, Hamzah Fansuri was born in Syahri-Nawi, or Ayuthia, the capital of Siam, built in 1350. Syed Naguib al-Attas based his conclusion on the following lines by Hamzah:

Hamzah nin asalnya Fansuri
Mendapat wujud di tanah Syahr Nawi.

(Hamzah who came from Fansuri
Attained his being in Syahr Nawi)

Drewes disagrees with this interpretation. He asserts that the words "*mendapat wujud*" mean "received teachings on *wujudiyah*". In the second half of the sixteenth century, Syahri Nawi was a popular hub for Muslim traders from India, Persia, Turkey and Arabia. Certainly a great number of Muslim scholars would have lived there as well. According to Drewes, Hamzah Fansuri became acquainted with the teachings of *wujudiyah* in Syahri Nawi, then later taught them himself in Acheh (Drewes & Brakel, 1986: 5-6). Drewes also refutes the idea that Hamzah Fansuri travelled from Barus to Kudus (either Jerusalem or a town in Java):

Hamzah Fansuri di dalam Mekah
Mencari Tuhan di bait al-Kabah.
Di Barus ke Kudus terlalu payah
Akhirnya dapat di dalam rumah.

(Hamzah Fansuri in Mecca
Searched for God in the Holy Ka'bah
From Barus to Kudus
is a very difficult journey
Finally I found Him in my own house)

According to Drewes, the preposition "*di*" in Achehnese means "from". "*Terlalu payah*" means "too difficult" or "need not have been undertaken". Based on this interpretation, Drewes argues that Hamzah Fansuri did not actually make the journey from Barus to Kudus, only that he said such a trip would have been too arduous and, more importantly, wholly unnecessary in his search for God (Drewes & Brakel, 1986: 8-9).

Most of Hamzah Fansuri's works were written in *syair* verse forms. In fact, his *syairs* were among those first written in Malay. The *syair* will be discussed in a separate chapter, so we will only consider Hamzah Fansuri's prose works here. Thanks largely to the work of Doorenbos (1933) and Syed Naguib al-Attas (1978), three of Hamzah Fansuri's works in prose have been edited and published. The three are as follows:

i. *Asrar al-'Arifin* (The Secret of the Gnostics)
ii. *Syarab al-'Asyikin* (The Lover's Drink)
iii. *Al-Muntahi* (The Adept)

7.1.1 *Asrar al-'Arifin* (The Secret of the Gnostics)

Asrar al-'Arifin, or to give the work its complete title *Asrar al-'arifin fi bayan 'ilm al-suluk wal-tawhid,* (Treatise of the Gnostics on the Mystical Journey and the Oneness of God), contains the gist of *wujudiyah* teaching as propounded by Hamzah Fansuri. In the introduction of this book, Hamzah wrote that man is created by Allah from nonbeing and given perfect form, complete with ears, heart, soul and intellect. It is therefore incumbent upon us to search for God in order to attain knowledge (*ma'rifat,* spiritual enlightenment). To help the Muslim community learn about the nature, attributes and the names of Allah, Hamzah Fansuri then composed a 15-stanza *syair,* complete with explanatory notes. In this *syair* he explains that God's divine nature is inseparable from His Attributes. Among His Attributes are life, knowledge, will, power, speech, hearing *(sami')* and sight *(basir).* He also explains that Allah's divine attributes can be found in *haqiqah Muhammad* (the reality of Muhammad) or the Light of Muhammad. Once one attains spiritual truth about God and gains knowledge of Him, one still has to carry out one's religious obligations as laid down by *syariah* (religious law). Hamzah continues:

> *Hubaya-hubaya jangan keluar dari kandungan syariat, karena syariat itu umpama kulit, haqiqat itu umpama otak. Jika tiada kulit binasa otak. Misal kelambir sebuah dengan kulitnya, dengan tempurungnya, dengan isinya, dengan minyaknya... Dengan empat itu, maka sempurnalah hukumnya.*

> (You must absolutely never leave the duties of the *syariah,* because the syariah is like the skin, *haqiqat* is like the brain. Without the skin, the brain perishes. Like a coconut and its skin, its shell,

its flesh and its oil... With all four, it becomes complete.)

7.1.2 *Syarab al-'Asyikin* (The Lover's Drink)

Syarab al-'Asyikin, also known by the title *Zinat al-Muwahidin* (Ornament of those who believe in the Oneness of God), outlines the path that leads to Allah and spiritual enlightenment. Hamzah Fansuri claimed to have written the book in "Jawi" (Malay in Arabic script) for the benefit of those who did not speak Arabic or Persian. He also insisted that mystical knowledge was so esoteric that only the brightest of students guided by the most capable of teachers could master it.

The book consists of seven chapters.

Chapter 1	outlines the various religious obligations imposed by the *syariah*, namely: the profession of faith (*syahadat*), prayer, giving alms, fasting during the month of Ramadan, and undertaking the pilgrimage to Mecca.
Chapter 2	states that the *tarikat* (the path of the Sufi brotherhood) is none other than *hakikat* (knowledge that comes from communion with God), because *tarikat* is the beginning of *hakikat*. And the beginning of *hakikat* is repentance, that is, detachment from worldly goods and affairs in order to strive for the next world.
Chapter 3	states that *hakikat* is also the end of the journey. One who has reached this station will not know sorrow or joy, humility or pride, riches or poverty, pain or comfort, as everything will be the same for him. He is able to look beyond his physical existence and see Almighty Allah in everything; for the mystic, the existence of everything in the universe is proof of the existence of Allah.
Chapter 4	states that a person who has achieved mystical knowledge through his oneness with God knows the secret of the Prophet Muhammad and all of God's Attributes. The Almighty is One, without equal; eternal, atemporal; the creator, uncreated; without form, without color; everlasting, immortal; indivisible, not made of separate parts; unbroken, unblemished; incomparable, without peer or companion and none is like Him; not bound by space or time, without an end...
Chapter 5	states that God's essence is impossible to understand and beyond human comprehension. Sufis refer to this Divine Essence as *la ta'ayun* (the Unseen). That which can be seen or perceived is *ta'ayun* and includes knowledge, existence, *syuhud* (witnessing Allah in everything), and the physical creation.

THE LITERATURE OF ISLAMIC THEOLOGY

Chapter 6   elaborates on the attributes of God, the Exalted and Glorious one, mentioned in Chapter 4 above. In addition, this chapter also includes a question-and-answer section on religious topics, such as the difference between Muslims and *kafirs* (unbelievers), when both are created by God.

Chapter 7   explains the concept of ecstasy (*berahi*) and devotion (*syukur*). Ecstasy is the highest state to which a person can attain. It is higher than any other state, as true ecstasy is a gift; nothing that one can do produces it, because it comes from Allah. A person in a state of ecstasy is not afraid of death; death is a bridge that will bring the lover to his beloved. This does not mean one should take one's own life. Death here means to surrender to Allah in *tajrid* (seclusion) and in *tafrid* (submission). The enemy of ecstasy is *budi* (the mind), which leads to an attachment to life, the desire for wealth and power, and makes men long to be kings and ministers.

There are only a few remaining manuscripts of this book. The one held in the library of the University of Leiden, Cod. Or. 2016 (1), includes many very archaic spelling features, although it was transcribed fairly late, in 1738 or 9 Rejab 1116 H (Juynboll, 1899: 272-273).

7.1.3 *Al-Muntahi* (The Adept)

Al-Muntahi is a guidebook for those who are already well versed in *wujudiah* teachings. Hamzah Fansuri does not present his views in a systematic way, but simply gathers verses from the Quran, the *hadith* (traditions about the Prophet Muhammad), and the sayings of Sufi mystics and poets, in order to explain the axiom "*Man 'arafa nafsahu fa qad 'arafa rabbahu*" (He who knows himself, knows God). Some of the Sufi sayings quoted were considered "dangerous": for example, the words of Mansur al-Hallaj, "*Ana 'l-Haqq*" ("I am the Truth"), and the pronouncement of Sayid Nasim, "*Inni ana 'l-llah*" ("I am Allah") (Syed Naguib Al-Attas, 1970: 334). When Nuruddin Ar-Raniri attacked the teachings of *wujudiah* as pioneered by Hamzah Fansuri, the bulk of his criticism was centred on this book.

There are only a few remaining manuscripts of this book. Syed Naguib has published a facsimile of the Leiden manuscript Cod. Or. 7291 (III), together with an English translation. According to Drewes, the manuscript is incomplete. Syed Naguib, however, believes that while this manuscript does contain several lacunae and discrepancies, it is possible to bridge these gaps by referring to its Javanese translation (Syed Naguib al-Attas, 1970: 224).

7.2 Syamsuddin Al-Sumatrani

We do not know much about the life of Syamsuddin Al-Sumatrani. However, the *Bustanus Salatin* (The Garden of Kings) and *Hikayat Acheh* (The Chronicle of Acheh), and the travel narratives of a number of Europeans who visited Acheh at the end of the sixteenth and early seventeenth centuries, all tell us that Syamsuddin was a very important figure in the Achehnese royal court. The *Hikayat Acheh* notes that when Sultan Alauddin Ri'ayat Syah (1589-1604) held a ceremony to mark the completion of his grandson Sultan Iskandar Muda's training as a warrior, Syamsuddin was one of the Achehnese dignitaries present. Frederick de Houtman, who wrote the first Malay-Dutch word list, mentioned that he met a *syaikh* who acted as the king's chief royal adviser during his visit to Acheh in 1599. In 1602, Sir James Lancaster, an envoy of Queen Elizabeth I, signed a trade agreement with *qadi* Malik al-Adil, whom he referred to as a "bishop". According to C. A. O. van Nieuwenhuijze, who studied Syamsuddin's works for his doctorate at Leiden University (1945), the "bishop" or "*qadi*" was Syamsuddin al-Sumatrani. He further adds that Syamsuddin's role in Acheh was similar to that of Faidi and Abdul Fadi, advisers to the Mogul Emperor Akbar in India. What we can deduce from this is that Syamsuddin was a very influential ulama during the reign of Sultan Iskandar Muda Mahkota Alam (1606-1636). He also had a great number of students. However, when Sultan Iskandar Thani (1636-1641) ascended the throne and transferred his patronage to Nuruddin Ar-Raniri, Syamsuddin's influence diminished. His books were considered to contain deviationist teachings and were burned. Syamsuddin died in 1630, soon after the Achehnese forces were defeated by Malaka.

As a result of the sultan's command, very few of Syamsuddin's books have survived to this day; those that remain are no more than incomplete fragments. One of these is the *Mir'at al-Mu'min* (Mirror of the Faithful). This manuscript presents a series of questions-and-answers about Islamic beliefs; according to Werndly, there are 211 questions in all. The Leiden manuscript (Cod. Or. 1700), however, contains only 95 questions. It discusses the nature and attributes of Allah, the *syahadah* (profession of faith), *tauhid* (the unity of God), *makrifat* (mystical knowledge), *iman* (faith) and Islam. The discussion on faith is the longest section, and covers issues such as belief in angels, apostles and prophets, God's holy books, the day of resurrection and judgement, and so on.

Another of Syamsuddin's works to have survived is *Mir'at al-Muhaqqiqin* (Mirror of those who seek the truth). According to the Leiden manuscript, Cod. Or. 1332, this book was commissioned by Marhum Mahkota Alam (Sultan Iskandar Muda). The beginning and end of this manuscript are missing. The manuscript is a compilation of tracts, including *Kitab al-Haraka* (Book of Movement), *Mir'at al-Qulub* (Mirror for the Heart of the Devout), *Nur al-Daqa'ik* (Light of the Subtleties of Mystical Knowledge) and *Usul Tahqik* (Principles of Realisation). The contents deal with mystical knowledge, the nexus between God's Attributes and His Essence, types of *zikir* (chants), and *martabat* (spiritual stations), the Seven Stations of the Soul being expounded at considerable length. Besides writing in Malay, Syamsuddin also wrote in Arabic.

According to van Nieuwenhuijze, Syamsuddin's teachings can be summarized as follows:

1 Allah

(a) Allah. Allah is the God who has revealed Himself through His apostles and His holy books. He should be worshipped by all Mankind. God is the primary being, the source of all being and the only reality.

(b) God's Essence. The nature (*zat*) of Allah is beyond human comprehension. It exists above everything else and is not available to our understanding. "The being of Almighty God is Eternal *(baka)* and beyond time *(kadim)*. He is never new, has neither breadth *(ard)* nor body *(jism)*, has no abode and cannot be seen with our eyes. Verily, he is One." His divine essence exists and is the source of all that exists. Therefore, everything that exists is inseparable from the existence of Allah. The existence of Allah encompasses everything that is seen as well as everything that is unseen.

(c) Relationship between God's Essence and His Attributes. God's attributes are identical with His Essence. Although we speak of these two terms, they do not refer to two different things. God's essence is to His attributes as the ocean is to its waves. As such, His attributes are His essence; His essence is His attributes, to wit, His twenty attributes. And these twenty divine attributes contain all the other relative *(idafi)* attributes.

(d) The Divine Attributes. The twenty divine attributes can be divided into three groups, namely:

 i Transcendental *(Salabiya)* or Existential *(nafsiya)* attributes;
 ii Immanent *(ma'ani)* attributes; and
 iii Spiritual *(ma'nawiya)* attributes

Both God and his servants possess these twenty attributes. The only difference is that God's attributes are hidden within those of His servants. Moreover, Allah's attributes are timeless *(baka)*; His servants' attributes are impermanent *(fana)*. Allah has no origin; His servants come into being from non-being, just as a person looks into a mirror and sees a reflection there. The one who looks into the mirror has been, and will be, for all time *(kadim)*; the reflection is *muhdath* (newly created) and transient.

(e) The Names of God. The Names of God are important in Sufism. At the level of *ahadiya* (apophatic oneness, in which all words are inadequate), God's absolute names are hidden within His Essence. At the level of *wahda* (kataphatic oneness), God has shown Himself through the signs of His divine revelation *(su'un)*, His attributes and His names. Subsequently, His names manifest His unity in plurality *(wahidiya)*.

(f) Afal. This means having faith that Allah created all creatures, bringing them into existence from non-existence.

2 Muhammad

There are two different schools of thought in Sufism regarding the position of Prophet Muhammad. He plays a central role in the teachings about the Seven Stations. *Ahadiya* is the initial station of the manifestation of God's essence; *wahda* is filled with the real being of the Prophet; in *wahidiya*, he is the prototype of all worldly phenomena including that of humanity. In Sufi doctrine, the creation of the world included three levels: God, The Word, and The World.

3 *Wujudiyya* Doctrine: The Seven Stations of Being

There are Seven Stations, or degrees of being, namely: *ahadiya* (apophatic oneness), *wahda* (kataphatic oneness), *wahidiya* (oneness in plurality), *alam al-arwah* (the world of spirits), *alam al-amsal* (the world of material forms), *alam al-ajsam* (the world of bodies) and *alam al-insan* (the world of mankind). The first three stations are eternal and timeless or, in other words, immanent and perpetual. The other four stations are *muhdath*, newly created; they are veritable shadows.

According to Syamsuddin, the shadows and the one to whom the shadows belong are One. Put simply, God and His creatures are one. God's creation, including mankind, is God. The Seven Stations are a path to God. Syamsuddin explained this issue in one of his books:

> *Maka sekalian martabat itu karam kepada martabat insan. Barang-kali kita ingat dan tahu kepada benar-benar manusia Allah; itulah* wahidiya *kepada kita. Maka barangkali kita ketahui bahwa sesungguhnya sifat kita tidak lain daripada sifat Allah: maka itulah* wahda *kepada kita. Maka barangkali luputlah kita daripada nama dan sifat, maka itulah ahadiya kepada kita. Tetapi sekalian kata ini jangan ia dikata, maka tiada ketempatan di sana adanya: ia itulah dinamai titian sirat al-mustakim. Wa'llah bi'llah, jangan lagi syak. Wa'llahu a'lam bil-sawab. Tamat.*

(All other stations are merged at the station of the Perfect Man. Perhaps we truly know and are well aware that mankind is God; that is *wahidiya*. Perhaps we know that our attributes are none other than Allah's attributes; that is *wahda*. Perhaps too we are devoid of names and attributes; that is *ahadiya*. But all of these things should not be discussed; they have no place at the bridge called *Sirat al-mustakim*, 'the straight path'. *Wa'llah bi'llah,* by God I swear that you must never doubt this. *Wa'llahu a'lam bil-sawab* [Only God knows the truth]. The end.)

4 The Oneness of Existence

The followers of *wujudiyah,* including Syamsuddin, held a different interpretation of the *kalimah syahadat* (the profession of of faith) from the conventional understanding. The profession states: *la ilaha illallah*, There is no God but Allah. They explained the actual meaning of the creed as: "I do not exist, only God exists". Syamsuddin wrote:

> *Adapun artinya tiada wujudku ini hanya wujud Allah: artinya tiada wujudku ini, esa sendirinya hanya dengan kuasa Allah, karena wujudku ini hanya wujud* wahmi *jua, artinya: wujud menjadi tiada kuasa sendirinya, hanya menerima segala gelar-gelaran juga: tiada nyawa dan tiada tubuh kepada tilik segala arif, hanya dengan kuasa Allah juga. Adapun tubuh kita yang zahir ini, hanya seperti ombak; adapun tubuh kita yang batin ini, artinya nyawa kita, hanya seperti haluan. Adapun wujud Allah, artinya Allah Subhanahu wa Ta'ala itu, seperti laut yang maha dalam. Adapun ombak dan haluan itu hanya hukumnya laut juga...*

(Indeed "I do not exist, only God exists" means that I do not exist independently; I exist only by Allah's power, for my existence is only *wahmi* (illusory), meaning that I do not exist by my own power. Every gift that I have has been given to me. I have no life, no body, not a single iota of intelligence, but for the power of Allah. Indeed our physical body is like a wave; our spiritual body (the soul) is its movement on the sea. Allah's existence, that is to say Allah the glorified and exalted one, is like the deep ocean. And the wave and the direction that it takes are part of that ocean...)

At other times, Syamsuddin stressed that the concept of the oneness of existence is a difficult doctrine to understand and that the student of Sufism needs to be guided by a wise teacher. It is, he cautions, a teaching that should not be discussed in public:

I'lam, ketahui olehmu hai Talib, bahwa sesungguhnya rahasia Allah Ta'ala maka sifat Ia adanya: sifat itu tiada lain daripada zat Allah Ta'ala. Itulah ada dalam keadaan insan. Oleh karena itulah maka dikatakan bahwa insan itulah Allah dan Allah itulah insan dan insan itu pun mengaku Allah dan Allah itulah aku. Tetapi rahasia itu terlalu sukar, jikalau tiada dengan isyarat guru yang kamil dan jika tiada murid yang bijaksana, niscaya tiada akan diperoleh, karena (tetapi) dengan hawa nafsu sahaja menjadi mazhab kafir zindik ia; itulah ia. Demi Allah, jangan tuan keluarkan rahasia ini kepada bukan tempatnya. Wa'llah bi 'llah wa kalam Allah, karena Allah, jangan ditunjukkan kepada bukan orang-orangnya, karena rahasia ini terlalu sukar. Tamat.

(Know, O Student, that the secret of Almighty God's attributes is this: His attributes are none other than His Essence. And His Essence exists in Mankind. And that is why it is said that Mankind is Allah and Allah is Mankind, and Mankind then declares himself to be God and God to be me. But that secret is very difficult to understand; without a perfect teacher by his side, and if the student is not astute enough, he will never learn the secret. With just his own ego to guide him, he will become a heathen and a heretic. By God, you must never reveal this secret in the wrong place. By the Word of Allah, do not reveal this secret to the wrong people, for this secret is extremely complicated. The end.)

Syamsuddin and Hamzah Fansuri were both eminent members of the *wujudiyah* movement. But they also represented two different Sufi schools of thought. Hamzah Fansuri was a mystic, spurred on by the spiritual yearning for a closer relationship with God. Syamsuddin was a philosopher who felt the need to uncover the reality of all that exists and its ontological union through the "oneness of being". However, both Syamsuddin and Hamzah Fansuri recognized and agreed on the reality of God. The major difference lay in Syamsuddin's belief that one needs a perfect teacher to follow the right path in one's efforts to know God and to draw closer to Him. The Sufi's ultimate goal is gnosis *(makrifat)*, the spiritual knowledge of everything around one. Only at the level of gnosis can mankind be delivered from the constraints of earthly existence and through this insight become one with God.

7.3 Nuruddin Ar-Raniri

Nuruddin Ar-Raniri b. Ali b. Hasanji b. Muhammad Hamid ar-Raniri al-Quraisyi al-Syafi'i was a prolific writer and Muslim scholar. He wrote 29 books on a wide range of fields, including jurisprudence, *hadith*, theology, mysticism and world history. Even so, little is known of his life. Scholars commonly agree that Nuruddin was born in Ranir (now Rander), a thriving port city near Surat in Gujerat. Nuruddin began his theological studies there, then later studied in the city of Tarim, in the Hadramaut. One of his teachers was Syaikh Said Abu Hafs Umar bin Abdullah Ba Syaiban, who later became the spiritual leader of the Sufi brotherhood, Rifa'iyah. Syaikh Said Abu Hafs Umar helped Nuruddin join a mystical order and he became known as Syaikh Nuruddin. In 1030H (1621), Nuruddin undertook the pilgrimage to Mecca and he also visited the Prophet's tomb in Madinah. We do not know how long Nuruddin stayed in Mecca and Madinah. We can be sure that he made full use of his time in Arabia to interact with the Malay community and to deepen his knowledge of the Malay language, which he had already begun studying in Rander.

From Mecca, Nuruddin returned to Rander. The city was in decline as a result of competition from the Portuguese who were beginning to have a stranglehold over its trade. In 1630, Rander fell into Portuguese hands. Nuruddin left to seek his fortune in the Malay Archipelago. He arrived in Pahang and began to write in Malay. The kingdom had been ruled by Acheh since 1618 and it is likely that while he was there, he met the Sultan of Acheh, later known as Sultan Iskandar Thani.

In 1047H (1637), Nuruddin travelled to Acheh and was warmly received by Sultan Iskandar Thani. It is said that Nuruddin had previously visited Acheh, but received no support from Sultan Iskandar Muda, the sultan of Acheh. Now, with Sultan Iskandar Thani's backing, Nuruddin was given the opportunity to propagate his teachings. Nuruddin engaged in fierce debates and declared that the followers of *wujudiyah* were infidels; if they did not repent of their blasphemous beliefs, they should be killed. The books of Hamzah Fansuri and Syamsuddin were put to the torch. As a consequence of his extreme actions, Nuruddin was forced to leave Acheh in 1054H (1644). Apparently, Sultanah Safiatuddin, Sultan Iskandar Thani's widow, did not approve of Nuruddin's brutal measures and was responsible for his departure. Nuruddin died in Rander in 1069H (1658).

The following is a discussion of some of Nuruddin's most important works.

7.3.1 *Sirat al-Mustakim* (The Straight Path)

This book is considered to be the oldest book on jurisprudence in Malay and was sent to Kedah when the kingdom first converted to Islam. It is still studied in Muslim institutes of higher learning and is regarded as an invaluable source of religious guidance. However, the *Sirat al-Mustakim* is difficult for the non-Achehnese reader to understand, as it contains many Achehnese terms and idiomatic expressions. This may have inspired the well-known scholar Muhammad Arsyad al-Banjari to write a similar work entitled *Sabil al-Muhtadin (The Path of the Guided)*. The two works are often published together (Ahmad Daudy, 1981: 66).

The *Sirat al-Mustakim* consists of seven books, which deal with the following subjects: ritual purification (*taharah*), prayer, almsgiving, fasting, the pilgrimage, laws on hunting and slaughter of animals, and the rules governing permitted (*halal*) and forbidden (*haram*) foods. It also denounces traditional narratives, such as *Hikayat Sri Rama* and *Hikayat Indra Putra,* describing them as only fit to be used as toilet paper:

> *Bermula bersuci itu wajib, sebab keluar sesuatu yang basah pada salah satu daripada dua jalan. Jikalau darah sekalipun melainkan mani jua. Maka istinjak itu dengan air atau batu atau barang benda yang suci lagi kasap yang dapat menghilangkan najis itu; dan tiada harus bersuci dengan sesuatu benda yang dihormati pada syarak, seperti tulang dan kulit yang belum disamak atau barang sebagainya, tetapi harus beristinjak dengan Kitab Taurat dan Injil yang sudah berubah daripada asalnya dan demikian lagi harus beristinjak dengan kitab yang tiada berguna pada syarak seperti Hikayat Sri Rama dan Indra Putra dan barang sebagainya, jika tiada dalamnya nama Allah* (Siti Chamamah, 1982: 132).

> (First and foremost, cleansing is obligatory after the emission of bodily fluids from either one of the two orifices, including blood and semen. Cleansing should be done with water or stone, or something pure and having a rough texture which can remove the impurity. One must not purify oneself with something that is forbidden by religious law, such as bone or unprocessed animal

skin or such like. One may instead cleanse oneself from impurities using the Torah or Bible, for these have been corrupted from their original form. One may also use books of no religious value such as *Hikayat Sri Rama* and *Indra Putra* or other similar works, as long as they do not contain Allah's name in them.)

The book on ritual purification consists of five chapters: they explain the different types of impurity and how to purify oneself from them; how to perform the ablutions required before prayer; the circumstances in which one must purify oneself; how to cleanse oneself with earth when water is not available (*tayamum*); and how women should purify themselves after menstruation or giving birth.

The book on prayer deals with times of prayer and the relevant conditions that must be observed; prayer while traveling; congregational prayers; how to pray when one is afraid; prayers to be recited during solar and lunar eclipses; prayers for rain; and funeral prayers.

The book on almsgiving explains the various forms of tithe relating to livestock, crops, gold and silver.

The book on fasting lays down the rules to be observed during the obligatory fasting month; the penalties for not fasting; the prohibition on sexual relations during the fasting month; how one can repay for a missed day of fasting; and how to perform *iktikaf* (a period of spiritual isolation at a mosque) during Ramadan.

The book on the pilgrimage explains the rules and regulations relating to the major and minor pilgrimages (*umrah*); the prescribed attire to be worn; circumambulation of the Kaabah; walking between the hills of Safa and Marwah (*sai*); standing at Mount Arafah (*wukuf*); recitation of the prayer "There is no God but Allah" (*tahlil*); and so on. This book also discusses various dogmas (*akidah*).

The books on hunting and food are both relatively short (Siti Chamamah, 1982: 402-407).

7.3.2 *Bustanus Salatin*

The *Bustanus Salatin,* or its full title *Bustan al-Salatin fi Dhikr al-Awwalin wa 'l-Akhirin* (The Garden of Kings and the Beginning and End of All Things), is the longest work ever written in the Malay and covers more than 1250 pages. The seven chapters encompass a diverse range of topics, including an explanation of natural phenomena; the history of the world and the Malay Archipelago; and the rule of various devout and ascetic kings. There are numerous manuscripts of this book, although many contain only or two chapters. The most complete manuscript is held in the library of the University of Malaya. The manuscript, measuring 20cm by 15cm, consists of five chapters totaling 787 pages, with 19 lines per page.

The *Bustanus Salatin* has played an influential role in the development of traditional Malay literature. The foreword to the *Sejarah Melayu* (Shellabear edition) is drawn from this book. Significantly, Chapter 2, Part 12, names Bendahara Paduka Raja as the author of *Sejarah Melayu*. The writer of *Hikayat Hang Tuah* based his description of the palace and gardens of the Sultan of Rum on an account of Sultan Iskandar's garden that is to be found in this book (T. Iskandar, 1966: 5-6).

The following summary of *Bustanus Salatin* is based on the manuscript held at the University of Malaya, with some further reference to Siti Chamamah's commentary (1982) and to Grinter's dissertation at the University of London (1979).

The first of the *Bustanus Salatin*'s seven chapters tells of the creation of the heavens and the earth. It describes the creation of the Light of Muhammad, Sacred Scripture (*luh mahfuz*), God's Word (*kalam*), the vault of heaven (*arasy*), God's Throne (*kursi*), the banner of glory Muhammad will carry on Judgement Day (*liwa al-hamd*), the angels, the heavenly tree (*sidratul muntaha*), the *jinn*s (*jan*), the seven levels of the sky, Heaven, the celestial nymphs, the angelic Kaabah (*baitulmakmur*), the sun, the moon and the stars, comets (regarded as satanic manifestations), clouds, cold water, ice, dew, lightning, thunderbolts, thunder, the major celestial bodies, the cow that supports the seven layers of Earth, the Kaabah, earthquakes, tremors, as well as the myriad oceans and rivers, and the various planets, their climates and contents. A later book describes the different tribes and ethnicities to be found throughout the world.

Chapter II is consists of 13 sections.

Section One describes the lives of the prophets who received divine revelation and were commanded by Allah to preach their message to others (*mursal*), as well as those who received divine revelation but were not required to spread God's words;

Section Two describes the lives of the kings who ruled after the Prophet Adam;

Section Three discusses the reigns of the kings who ruled Yunan (Ionia, an ancient region of central coastal Anatolia in present-day Turkey) and Syam (Syria);

Section Four discusses the kings of Egypt;

Section Five discusses the kings of Arabia;

Section Six discusses the kings who ruled Kundah in the land of Najd;

Section Seven discusses the kings of Hijaz near Mecca;

Section Eight discusses the birth of Prophet Muhammad, and describes his descendants;

Section Nine discusses the rule of the house of Umayyah over the land of Syam;

Section Ten discusses the Abbasid Caliphate;

Section Eleven discusses the kings who have ruled the Hindustani kingdom of Delhi;

Section Twelve discusses the kings of Malaka and Pahang;

Section Thirteen discusses the kings of Acheh.

The University of Malaya manuscript and that of R. J. Wilkinson (Wilkinson, 1900) do not contain Section 11 on the Muslim kings of Delhi. Section 12, on the kings of Malaka and Pahang, is also missing. Instead, Section 13 on the history of Acheh becomes Section 11 and ends with this sentence: "It is said that he who humbles himself before Almighty God will be rewarded by Him with great prestige" (T. Iskandar, 1966: 45).

Chapter III is divided into the following six sections:

Section One describes the attributes a king must possess before he can ascend to the throne: he must be a Muslim, a free man (i.e. not a slave), male, from the Quraisy tribe, brave, fair-minded and uphold all of the religious laws set out by Islam.

Section Two discusses the conduct of the ancient caliphs and kings. Caliph Umar bin Khatab is singled out and praised as an exemplary leader, who ruled with such humility and impartiality that he did not even spare his own son when the latter was in the wrong. The section also delineates the attributes of a just king, which include: piety, a sound mind, a sound education, good intentions, and being able to rule according to the religious law.

Section Three stipulates the prerequisites for appointment as a a judge (*kadi*). A kadi must be a Muslim, of sound mind, a free person, male, impartial, of good eyesight, and well versed in the Quran and Hadiths.

Section Four deals with the essential attributes of a vizier (*wazir*) and a military leader (*hulubalang*). It is said that a king requires the following if he is to rule properly:

i. a wise vizier;
ii. a trusted treasurer (*bendahara*);
iii. servants who are loyal and supportive, and
iv. religious scholars (*ulama*s) who can give good advice on religious matters.

It is further explained that a vizier must possess the following qualities: he must be God-fearing, diligent in the performance of his religious obligations, loyal to his king, brave, trustworthy, deserving of the respect of the military and the kingdom's subjects, and sympathetic to trade.

Section Five describes the necessary attributes of a royal envoy: a God-fearing nature, piety, knowledge, trustworthiness, intelligence, good conduct, and smoothness of speech.

Section Six discusses the qualities and duties of a preacher (*khatib*). Above all, a *khatib* must be well versed in religion, for he needs to be able to follow the example set by the ulamas before him so that he will be blessed in this life and the hereafter.

Chapter III was initially thought to be lost. However, Roolvink pointed out that this chapter is included in the University of Malaya manuscript (see J. Bastin & R. Roolvink, 1964: 242). It is now known that a manuscript of the *Bustanus Salatin* held in a library in France also contains this chapter (Cabaton, 1912: 217).

Chapter IV consists of two sections.

The first section describes the conduct of a number of ascetic kings and pious saints, such as Sultan Ibrahim Ibn Adham. On seeing the power and the glory of Allah, Ibrahim Ibn Adham left his kingdom to devote himself to the service of God. He renounced the material world and led a simple life as a goatherd, a carpenter, and a gardener. His noble conduct and piety are depicted in many ways in this section.

Following the tale of Sultan Ibrahim Ibn Adham, this section then tells the story of other kings who gave up their privileged lives in order to worship the divine, in the belief that the kingdoms they had built were impermanent and would eventually decay. The only lasting realm, they were convinced, was Heaven. Therefore, a man must do as many good deeds as he can in this world, believe in the world to come, and always think of his own mortality. At no time should he allow himself to become enamoured with worldly possessions. Two stories are also told about Iskandar Zulkarnain to show that the mortal world is merely ephemeral, and that we should not be overly concerned with it.

The second section depicts the lives and conduct of Allah's saints. Among those depicted are the Prophets Khidir, Musa and Isa. The story told of Isa reminds us of the miracles narrated in *Kisah Anbya,* such as his creating a bird out of earth; and his bringing to life an unborn child from a clump of meat, then asking the child to preach Islam to a king.

The longest story deals with Husna, who attained sainthood because she remained steadfastly faithful to her husband despite the trials and tribulations she had to endure. Husna was left in the care of her husband's brother while her husband was away trading. As it turned out, the brother secretly lusted after her. When she rejected his advances, her brother-in-law paid four men to falsely accuse her of adultery. As a result, Husna was stoned for a crime she had not committed and her body dumped in the grounds of a cemetery. By the grace of Allah, she was protected from wild animals. A Bedouin subsequently found her and took her home. Unfortunately, however, one of the Bedouin's slaves also became infatuated with her. When his feelings were not returned, he took his revenge by killing one of the Bedouin's children and blaming Husna for the murder. As a result, she was driven out of the Bedouin's house. Roaming the countryside in poverty, she came to a certain village and saved a young man from being impaled. Far from showing his gratitude, he sold her as a slave to a passing merchant. When the merchant tried to force himself on Husna, his arms suddenly became paralysed.

When another merchant also tried to force himself on her, Husna prayed to God for help. All of a sudden, a fierce storm broke out and blew everyone on the ship overboard. Disguised as a man, Husna sailed the ship to a distant land. When she came ashore, she presented the cargo to the king. Husna and the king soon became close friends and he appointed her as his vizier and then *khatib*. When he died, she became king.

God always answered King Husna's prayers. She cured all manner of illnesses and afflictions. Her fame soon spread far and wide. By this time, her husband's brother had become blind, while the four false witnesses and the Bedouin's wicked slave had all been cursed with some form of affliction. They came to the palace to seek a cure. Husna agreed to help them but only if they confessed what they had done to deserve their sufferings. The men acknowledged their sins. On hearing their accounts, Husna's husband finally realised what had happened. However, Husna demurred when he tried to hold her, saying that she wanted to pray first. After she had prayed, Husna asked God to take her life before her husband could have close physical contact with her. Her wish was granted and she immediately passed away. According to another version of the story, her husband then died of a broken heart as he lamented by the side of her grave.

Apart from the earlier part on Sultan Ibrahim Ibn Adham, edited by Russel Jones in 1974, this chapter has been translated into Romanised Malay by Catherine Anne Grinter in her doctoral dissertation at the University of London (Grinter, 1979).

Chapter V consists of two sections. The first tells stories about the tyranny of kings; the second describes the conduct of wicked viziers. A despotic king wanted to buy the house of a woman who lived near his palace. When the woman refused, he had the house demolished. For his tyranny, Allah punished the king by having his palace and everything in it swallowed up by the earth. This story is a warning to all kings not to be arrogant or listen to the evil instigations of their viziers, and to treat their subjects justly. Viziers and members of the royal family who oppress the poor and the weak should be punished. Viziers are also advised to guard closely the king's secrets in accordance with the oath they have undertaken. There is a series of stories warning against telling secrets to women or placing your trust in an unfaithful woman.

Chapter VI consists of two parts.

The first deals with the conduct of persons who are noble, compassionate, mighty and valiant. The second talks about the importance of holy wars waged in the name of Allah by the Prophet Muhammad and his companions, as well as those waged by kings in ancient days.

Chapter VII consists of four parts.

Part one discusses knowledge and reason, and the high value of both. It also considers man's propensity for both benevolence and wickedness. Part two of the chapter is missing. According to the manuscript studied by Tudjimah (1961), Chapter VII states: "The seventh chapter deals with reason, knowledge, intuition, medical science, and the characteristics of women as described in various strange and amazing chronicles".

Part three talks about human anatomy (*ilmu tasyrih*), medicine (*ilmu tabib*), and related matters, drawing on several chronicles for relevant material.

Part four discusses the sanctity of marriage and the conduct of various women, drawing on various strange and amazing chronicles.

7.3.3 *Asrar Al-Insan Fi Ma'rifa Al-Ruh Wa 'l-Rahman*

Nuruddin's work, *The Secrets of Man in Knowing the Soul and God the Merciful,* is divided into two chapters.

Chapter one consists of six parts.

The first part deals with the Oversoul (*Ruh al-azam*) and the many names that are used with reference to it.

The second deals with the attributes and the reality of the Oversoul.

The third part deals with the heart (*kalbu*), its various names, and the reason why it is called the heart.

The fourth part deals with physical desires (*nafsu*) and their tendencies.

The fifth part deals with the mind—its nature, location, and its dispositions.

The sixth part deals with the secrets of the soul, the heart, the subconscious, mind, superconsciousness (*sirr* or *khafi*), mystical insight (*waridat*), will (*khatarat*), and with divine inspiration (*ilham*) and *wahyu* (revelation).

Chapter Two contains five parts.

Part one deals with the human body and its creation.

Part two describes God's instructions to the soul.

Part three presents a conversation between God and the soul as He extracted it from one of Adam's ribs.

Part four is a further consideration on the nature of the soul from the moment it was taken from the body of Adam and placed into the womb of Siti Hawa (Eve); the soul's command to Adam's semen (*nutfa*); as well as the various secrets Allah has placed in man's physical body.

Part five deals with the greatness of the soul, its location, and where it goes after it leaves the physical body (Tudjimah, 1961: 210-211).

This book was commissioned by Sultan Iskandar Thani and was completed during the reign of Sultanah Safiatuddin. It draws extensively on the writings of leading Sufi authorities such as Ibn Arabi, Imam Ghazali, Al-Hallaj and Abd al-Razak al-Kashani, and includes many quotations from the Quran and the hadis traditions. This book has been published in Arabic script by Tudjimah as part of her doctoral thesis, with annotations of the sources used by Nuruddin and a lengthy commentary (1960: 211-244).

7.3.4 *Hujjatu'l-Siddik li daf i 'l-Zindik*

In the *Argument of the Learned against Apostasy,* Nuruddin discusses the different views about existence held by four disparate schools of thought *(taifa)*: namely the theological scholars *(mutakallimin)*, the Sufis, the ancient philosophers *(hukama falasifah)* and the followers of *wujudiah*.

(i) The theological scholars believe that there are two types of existence: the existence of Allah and the existence of the world. The existence of Allah is real *(hakiki)*, but the existence of the universe is unreal *(majasi)*. Nuruddin agrees with the theological scholars on this point, although he also argues that all existence is ultimately one, because it is part of the essence of Almighty God. The metaphorical belongs to the real in the same way that a person's reflection belongs to the one who looks at the mirror or a shadow belongs to the person casting it. Whoever believes that The True and Exalted God (*Haqq Ta'ala*) and His creation are one and the same is an infidel.

(ii) The Sufis believe in the unity of existence, that is, the Divine Essence, and that the universe has no existence but is only a manifestation *(mazhar)* or a (shadow *(zill)* of the True and Exalted God.

(iii) The ancient philosophers believed that the existence of Allah and that of the universe are both eternal *(kadim)*; as such the universe arises naturally from Allah's essence in the same way that heat is produced from the essence of the sun. As long as the sun exists, so too will heat. Likewise, as long as the essence of Allah exists, so too will the universe. Allah's essence and the universe are inextricably linked from the very beginning and will exist together forever. Nuruddin considers this doctrine to be heretical.

(iv) Nuruddin divides the proponents of *wujudiyah* into two groups: those who believe in the oneness of God *(muwahid)* and those who are apostates *(mulhid)*. The description *wujudiyah* is used for both as they both use the term *"wujud"* to talk about the existence of God. The *mulhid* believe that all existence is one and stems from Allah's existence. Thus they insist that Allah's existence is man's existence and man's existence is Allah's existence. In other words, the universe is Allah and Allah is the universe. The Islamic creed "*la ilaha illa 'llah*", which the Sufis interpret as "I am non-existent, only Allah exists", is given a new meaning by the *mulhid*: "I do not exist as anything other than as Allah's existence". Therefore, to the *mulhid*, both man and Allah are of one and the same kind and being *(sebangsa dan sewujud)*. Nuruddin denounces such an interpretation as a blatant example of apostasy and presents the arguments of several Sufi authorities, who reject the doctrine and assertions of the *mulhid wujudiyah*.

The *muwahid wujudiah* on the other hand state that "the existence of Allah is one; without plurality, without limit, without sum or parts, without constitution or constituents, without seed or physical body..." Therefore the universe does not contain an endless variety of objects, even if that is how it seems to our eyes. In short, the statement that *Haqq Ta'ala* (God the True and Exalted) and the universe are one means that "*Haqq Ta'ala* and the universe are neither separate nor unified, as their separation or unity is predicated upon two existences." Nuruddin agreed with this doctrine, and quoted the views of several Sufi authorities, who espoused the same belief as that of the *muwahid* school.

Hujjatu'l-Sidik has been the subject of much debate. It was published in facsimile form by P. Voorhoeve in 1955 and re-published in 1966 with an English translation by Syed Muhammad Naguib Al-Attas. The translation drew such severe criticism from G. W. J. Drewes (1974) that Al-Attas found it necessary to defend himself at considerable length (Al-Attas, 1975). Both Drewes' criticism and Al-Attas' deserve our serious attention. At the very least, this polemic proved that the Malay language—and in particular, the Malay lexicon related to theology—is not as simple as people might have thought. More recently, the book has been the subject of a thesis written by Kun Zachrun Istani towards the degree of Master of Arts at Gadjah Mada University in 1981.

7.3.5 *Tibyan fi Ma'rifati 'l-Adyan*

The start of this book, *Discourse on the Knowledge of Religion,* states that Nuruddin confronted the *mulhid* followers of *wujudiyah* and heretics in a head-to-head debate, during the reign of Sultan Iskandar Thani. Following this debate, Nuruddin issued a fatwa that anyone who believed in *wujudiyah* should be killed. After the death of Sultan Iskandar Thani, his successor, Sultanah Safiatuddin, ordered Nuruddin to write this book to put an end to deviationist ideas and to defend the syariah. This book consists of two chapters.

Chapter one describes the different religions practised from the time of Prophet Adam to the time of Prophet Isa. Allah created Adam as the ideal embodiment of humanity. Some of Adam's progeny professed the true faith, others worshipped idols and statues. Then Allah sent the Prophet Nuh to bring Mankind back to the right path. The Prophet Idris too was assigned the same task. By the time of Prophet Ismail, every idol and pagan symbol had been buried. Iblis the devil, however, dug up these statues and men made even more idols. This incurred Allah's wrath, and He rent the seven skies and reduced the hills to rubble. The Jews and the Christians became infidels *(kafir)*, although they were not polytheists *(musyrik)*.

Nuruddin then writes about the following groups:

(1) The *taba'iyah,* those who worship idols;
(2) The *hukama munajjim* or *falakiyah,* who worship the moon, the sun and the stars;

(3) The *majusi*, who worship fire and are divided into three sects: Zamzamiyah, Syamaniyah and Samaniyah;

(4) The *dariyah* or *mulhid*, who do not worship phyisical objects but believe in occasional manifestations of the divine;

(5) The *tanasukhiyah*, who are divided into four sects: first, the Brahmins of India; second, the sect that Hamzah Fansuri and Syamsuddin Sumatrani followed, which is deviationist, and the Munawiyah who live in China and Tibet; third, those who believe in reincarnation. (The fourth sect is not named.)

(6) The *Ahlu Kitab*, Followers of revealed scriptures, are made up of ten groups, but only three of these are named:
   (i) The Brahmins;
   (ii) The Jews; and
   (iii) The Christians.

The second chapter describes the various sects to be found among the followers of Prophet Muhammad. According to Sunni Islam, these 72 sects are derived from six major groups: the Rafidiyah Kharijiyah, Haruriyah, Jabriyah, Khadariyah, Jahmiyah and Murji'ah. The chapter then discusses *mulhid* Sufis, whom Nuruddin condemns as infidels and heretics. Among the influential Sufi figures mentioned are Mansur Al-Hallaj and Syaikh Abu Yazid, as well as Hamzah Fansuri and Syamsuddin Al-Sumatrani. Hamzah Fansuri's declaration: *"Man' arafa nafsahufa qad 'arafa rabbahu" (He who knows himself indeed knows God)*, is vehemently attacked, as is Syamsuddin Al-Sumatrani's assertion that God and creation are identical. In his conclusion, Nuruddin calls for the destruction of all *wujudiah* books and those that advocate a revisionist form of Islam.

The book gives a brief summary of, and commentary on, the *wujudiyah* teachings that Nuruddin considered heretical. It also mentions that Nuruddin had written a book called *Nubza fi da'wa 'l-ziil ma'a Sahibihi* (A brief explanation on the shadow's demands to its owner), and another entitled *Durrat al-Fara'id bi syarh al-aka'id (A pearl of wisdom on religious faith)*. This reference is important for any research on seventeenth century Achehnese literary activity. So too are the references to Hamzah Fansuri's *Asraru'l-Arifin* and *Al-Muntahi*, and Syamsuddin Al-Sumatrani's *Mir'atu'l Muhaqqiqin* (Mirror of the Seeker of Truth) and *Khirkah (The Sufi Robe)* or *Haraka (Blessing)*. Without his references to the authorship of these works, their authorship would not have been known.

7.3.6 *Hill al-Zill*

A Treatise on the Metaphor of the Shadow is an adaptation of an Arabic work entitled *Da'wa 'l-Zill ma'a Sahibihi (The Shadow and its Owner)*. In it, Nuruddin states that the universe is the shadow of Allah. Although the universe and Allah are the same, they are also very different. Allah is *hakiki* (real); the universe is *khayali* (illusory). Allah exists; man and the universe only appear to exist. This work was written by Nuruddin at the request of his friends to refute the claim made by the followers of *wujudiah* about the common identity of Allah and the universe.

7.3.7 *Shifa al-Kulub*

This book, *Balm for the Heart*, was written to dispel the doubts of those who do not believe in God. The *wujudiyah* have given an erroneous interpretation of the profession of faith; Nuruddin seeks to explain its true meaning and the right way of chanting the *kalimah syhadat* as a repetitive prayer.

7.3.8 *Jawahir al-Ulum fi Kasyf al-Ma'lum*

A Gem of Knowledge for Knowing the Universe consists of five chapters. The introduction describes the virtue of knowing the real. The first chapter deals with existence; the second, Allah's attributes; the third, the names of Allah; the fourth, the *a'yan thabita* (divine fixed prototypes); and the fifth, the *a'yan kharijiyah* (the external modes of the Divine Essence). Nuruddin again mentions several books written by Hamzah Fansuri and Syamsuddin. Once he completed this book, Nuruddin returned to Ranir. The epilogue *(khatimah)* was written by one of his students (Ahmad Daudy, 1981: 73).

7.3.9 *Fath Al-Mubin 'ala Al-Makhidin*

A Clear Victory Over All Heresies was written in 1675 (1068H), after Nuruddin had returned to India. Upon its completion, Nuruddin sent a copy to every ulama in the Malay Archipelago. The manuscript of this book was long thought to have been lost but was later recovered from a private library in Banda Acheh. Its contents, according to Ahmad Daudy, are as follows.

The book opens with the history of the opposition to the teachings of *wujudiyah* in Acheh, which followed Nuruddin's arrival in Acheh and the debate he initiated. Many of the *wujudiyah* sect's books were burnt as a result of this debate. During the reign of Sultanah Safiatuddin, a *wujudiyah* figure, Saifurrijal, returned from India and revived the movement once more. This resurgence so angered a particular member of the Sunni community that he reacted by killing a large majority of *wujudiyah* followers.

The book continues with a detailed commentary by Nuruddin of the arguments put forward by members of the *wujudiah* group. Among the arguments he attacks are: their understanding of the concept of *wahdatul wujud* (pantheism); their interpretation of the phrase, *Inna lillahi wa inna ilaihi raji'un* (verily we belong to Allah and to Him we return); and what they take to be the meaning of the profession of faith. Nuruddin also rejects the notion that a mystic can be free from religious duties. At the end of the book, Nuruddin warns Muslims not to read books by the followers of *wujudiyah,* as they use many terms that are difficult to understand, especially by those with a weak grasp of the obligations of religious law (Ahmad Rifa'i Hassan, 1987: 1-35).

7.3.10 *Akhbar al-Akhira fi Ahwal al-Kiyama*

The above are Nuruddin's main works in Malay. He also wrote in Arabic. One of his well-known Arabic works is *Akhbar al-Akhira fi Ahwal al-Kiyama* (News from the Afterlife on Matters

Pertaining to Judgement Day). This book has been translated into Malay, Achehnese and various other regional languages.

There are over ten manuscripts of this book still in existence. One of these, Jakarta, ML 804 (Br. 275), was published by Edwar Djamaris in 1983. Its contents are as follows.

The book consists of seven chapters.

Chapter one describes the creation of the Light of Muhammad and is very similar to the *Hikayat Nur Muhammad.*

Chapter two is on death and experiences undergone at the portal of death *(sakratul maut).* The angel of death has an enormous body; those who have Allah's name always on their lips will not feel any pain when he takes their soul. At the moment of death, one will hear voices from the sky, the earth and the grave. Once the body has been buried, angels will enter the grave to ask the dead to list all the good deeds they have done in this world. The angels will be followed by Mungkar and Nakir, whose voices boom like thunder and whose eyes flash like lightning. Thereafter, the soul descends once more to the body and weeps upon seeing the body's decay. A year later, the soul will be transported to a place where the souls of the dead gather as they await the day of judgment.

Chapter three is missing.

Chapter four describes the signs that herald the day of judgment. These signs are divided into two categories: spiritual and physical. There are many spiritual signs: most especially, mosques will be lavishly equipped and furnished but fewer people will come to perform congregational prayers. The physical signs include the emergence of a huge cloud of smoke that will cover the entire world, and the coming of the Imam Mahdi (the Messiah), who will rule the world. This will then be followed by the appearance of Dajjal, the Antichrist; Yakjuj and Makjuj (Gog and Magog); and *Dabbatu'l-ard* (the Beast), who will all try to destroy the world. The Imam Mahdi will defeat Qustantinah but will not be able to vanquish Dajjal, who will be full of slander and temptation. Jesus will destroy Dajjal and his legions. Next, Yakjuj and Makjuj will attempt to annihilate the world and all that is in it, but Allah will fill their ears with worms. After they die, the world will reek with the stench of their rotting bodies until the rain sent by Allah washes their bodies into the sea.

An army from Ethiopia will arise to destroy the Kaaba and the Beast will emerge from the bowels of the earth to separate the Muslims from the heathens. The Beast has the appearance of a cow, the eyes of a pig, ears like an elephant, horns like a deer, a neck like a camel, and a waist like a cat. The souls of Muslims killed by him will rise to heaven and return to God their creator. Only the most evil of men will be left behind on earth. In the midst of these events, the day of judgment will come.

Chapter five relates that on the day of judgment, Allah will command the angel Israfil to blow his trumpet to signal the cessation of time and the end of all life in the seven layers of heaven and the earth. All of creation, including the seas, the mountains, the sky, the sun, stars and moon, will perish and be no more. The Angel of Death will also take the lives of the angels Jibrail, Israfil, Mikail and finally, even his own. The chapter then tells of the gathering of all creation on the plains of Mahsyar. The first to be resurrected by Almighty God will be the angels Israfil, Jibrail, Mikail and Israil. At His command, they will be sent to the angel Ridwan with instructions to decorate heaven and to invite the Prophet Muhammad to enter it, riding his steed, the *burak*, and carrying the Banner of Glory (*Liwa'u-Muhammad*) in his hand.

When Israfil blows his trumpet the third time, all of mankind will rise from their graves and take on different forms. Those who have slandered other people will look like swines; those who have sinned will look like monkeys; those who have pretended to be pious but did not practice what they preach will have pus all over their mouths; those who lied under oath will be burned by the fires of hell; those who succumbed to their sinful desires will reek of foul odours; those who did not give alms will behave like drunken men; those who have profited from charging high interest will look like cows. But those who regularly prayed and fasted, and those who died as martyrs, will emerge from their graves with a radiant glow emanating from their forehead. Those who performed the pilgrimage to Mecca will joyfully shake hands with the angels.

Having been raised from the dead by Allah, men will stand on the plain of Mahsyar in a state of thirst and hunger, except for the prophets and their families, and those who fasted while they were alive. The Prophet Muhammad will pray to Allah to cease the suffering of those gathered in that place. Thereafter, Allah will throw the heathens and the hypocrites *(munafiqun)*, who claimed to believe in Islam but denounced it in their hearts, into hell and will usher the true believers of Islam *(mu'min)* into paradise.

Chapter six describes the different levels of hell and the various punishments that await the damned. The Prophet Muhammad on hearing about the horrors of hell, will break down and weep, beseeching Allah to spare his followers from its torments.

Chapter seven tells of the one hundred levels of paradise. It also describes the pleasures of paradise: its rivers are whiter than milk, sweeter than honey, and more fragrant than musk. Its trees perpetually bear fruit and their branches so heavy that one can pick the fruit by simply stretching out a hand, whether one is standing, sitting or recumbent beneath them. Of all the trees in paradise, the one that has the most delectable fruit is the *syajaratu'l-tubi,* the *sidratu'l-muntaha* tree. The face of each heavenly nymph created by Allah has four colours: white, green, yellow and red; her body is made of saffron; her hands of musk, and her neck from chalk. Whenever a heavenly nymph descends to earth, one can smell the scent of musk. This chapter ends with praises and benedictions to Allah the exalted.

This book was compiled on the orders of a sultan, who is not named—possibly Sultanah Safiatuddin (Ahmad Daudy, 1981: 72).

7.4 Abdur Rauf Singkel

Abdur Rauf Singkel was a famous and reasonably prolific Achehnese mystical writer. Although little is known about his life, it seems likely that he was born in 1615 or 1620 in Singkil, a regency in southern Acheh. His father was an Arab named Syaikh Ali and his mother was a woman from the prosperous town of Fansur Barus. For this reason, Abdul Rauf also wrote his name as Abd ar-Rauf Ibn Ali al-Fansuri. In 1642, Abdur Rauf left Acheh to further his studies in the Middle East. His sojourn abroad lasted nineteen years. In 1661, he returned to Acheh.

At the end of his book, *Umdat al-Muhtajin,* Abdur Rauf provides further details about his education. He studied under various well-known scholars and mystics in Mecca, Medina and Yemen, and he lists their names in the epilogue. He also gives the names of those scholars and mystics whose books he had read or browsed while composing his own book. Among his teachers was Ahmad Al-Qusyasyi, the head (*khalifa*) of the Syatariyah Sufi order. After the death of Ahmad Al-Qusyasyi in 1661, Abdur Rauf received the blessings of the new leader of the Syatariyah order, Mulla Ibrahim, to establish a school in Acheh. Thus began his career as a teacher and an author. Abdur Rauf's fame as a scholar soon spread and he began to attract students from far and wide. Acheh was an important stopover for pilgrims from Java and other parts of Indonesia on their way to Mecca, and many visitors also took the opportunity to study religion and Sufism under Abdur Rauf during their short stay there. Perhaps for this reason, the Syatariyah order is popular in Java and the name Abdur Rauf appears in the genealogy of many masters of this order. One of Abdur Rauf's works, *Daka'ik al-Huruf,* is quoted in a Javanese translation of *al-Tuhfa al-mursala ila ruh al-nabi,* The Gift Addressed to the Spirit of the Prophet, an important treatise on mysticism (Johns, 1965: 11).

Abdur Rauf wrote many works on a wide array of subjects, including religious law *(fikih)*, spirituality and religious practices *(tasawuf)*, the Oneness of God *(tauhid)* as well as Quranic interpretation *(tafsir)* and prophetic traditions (*hadith*). Unfortunately, most of his works, with the exception of his commentary on the Quran, are now kept mainly as relics in museums and libraries. We will discuss a few of his major works below.

7.4.1 *Umdat al-Muhtajin ila Sulukl Maslak 'l-Mufridin*

An Enchiridion for those who seek to take the path of the Ascetics consists of seven chapters. Chapter one explains the meaning of the phrase "*la ilaha ila 'llah*", there is no god but God, and discusses the attributes of Allah and His Messenger. Chapter two explains the rules for *zikir* (devotional chanting). The word *"zikir"* comes from the Arabic *"dzakara"*, "to remember". The fire of *zikir* can burn away all sins and every evil impulse; a person who has just finished *zikir* should not immediately drink water, for the water would extinguish the fire of *zikir*. Chapter three contains the tradition (*hadith*) about the Messenger of Allah which explains the virtues of the profession of faith. Chapter four describes the characteristics of a person deep in *zikir*, "totally immersed in the profession of faith".

Chapter five describes the origins of mysticism and the rituals for initiation into a Sufi order. The story is told that Ali once asked the Messenger of Allah the shortest way to the presence of God. The Messenger replied that one will be rewarded if one remembers God in solitude: "*alaika bimudawamati dzikri 'llahi fi 'l-khalawati.*" So Ali said the *kalimah syahadah* three times in a loud voice with his eyes closed. Another story says that a person who wants to draw closer to Allah must join a Sufi order and be guided by a syeikh. He must pass through certain rituals before he can be initiated. Chapter six is on *ratib,* the practice of chanting *la ilaha illa 'llah*. Chapter seven reiterates the processes of devotional chanting. The book concludes with a list of teachers and the books Abdur Rauf had read (Rinkes, 1909: 59-91).

7.4.2 *Kifayat Muhtajin*

This book was commissioned by Sultanah Tajul Alam Safiatuddin. It begins with a discussion of the doctrine of *a'yan thabita,* the divine fixed prototypes, a topic of great concern to the religious scholars of Acheh at that time. Abdur Rauf presents his views in a simple way. Before the universe was created, Allah was completely absorbed in Himself. He then created the universe from the Light of Muhammad, in order to manifest Himself. The universe was like a body without a soul or an unpolished mirror. He then created Adam to be His representative and rule the world. *A'yan thabita* refers to a universe that is yet to come into being. *A'yan kharijah,* the outward modes of divine existence, is a shadow of the *a'yan thabita* in the same way that the universe is a shadow of Allah. The shadow is not the same as the object that casts it; but, at the same time, it is also not different from it. The shadow exists because the thing exists. This, according to Abdur Rauf, is the nature of the relationship between creation and the creator: the existence of creation depends on the existence of Allah (Rinkes, 1909: 39-41).

The title of this book is perhaps a misnomer. According to *The Achehnese II* (Snouck Hurgronje, 1906: 17, no. 6), this book is only a summary of *Umdat al-muhtajin.* According to Ph. S. van Ronkel's catalogue (1921: 138-139), this book is the *Umdat at-muhtajin,* but with a shorter title. D. A. Rinkes has said that the text is similar to that of two manuscripts, *Syatariyah I* (Bat. Gen. 336) and *Syatariyah II* (Bat. Gen. 349), which can be found in the library of the National Museum in Jakarta (Rinkes, 1909: 41).

7.4.3 *Mir'at at-Tullab*

The *Mir'at at-Tullab fi Tashil al-Ma'rifat al-ahkam al-Syar'iyah li 'l-Malik al-Wahhab* (Mirror for all those who seek to study Allah's laws so that they can better understand them) was written at the request of Sultanah Tajul Alam Safiatuddin. In his preface, Abdur Rauf expresses his initial reservations at accepting the task: he considered his "Jawi" (Malay) inadequate, because he "had been away at sea trading and living in Yemen, Mecca and Medinah for too long." However, with the help of two of his brothers, he wrote this book for those who aspire to hold the post of *kadi.* He also mentions that the main source of his book is *Fath-al-Wahhab,* a commentary *(syarah)* on a book entitled *Minhaj at-Tullab* by Abu Yahya Zakariyah 'l-Ansari. *Minhaj at-Tullab* is a summary of *Minhaj al-Talibin,* by Imam Nawawi (died 676 H), which is an abstract of another book, *al-Muharrar,* written by Imam al-Rafi'I (died 623 H). Imam al-Rafi'I's book in turn is based on two books by Imam al-Ghazali (died 505 H), entitled *Al-Wasit fi al-Mathab* (A Legal Digest) and *Al-Basit* (The Spread) (P. Daly, 1982: 38-39).

There are numerous manuscripts of *Mir'at at-Tullab.* One that has received considerable scholarly attention is Cod. Or. 1633, in the library of the University of Leiden. This was a gift from the ruler of Gorontalo to Prof. Reinward, a frequent visitor to Indonesia between 1816 and 1822. It consists of three volumes: the first deals with matrimonial law; the second with commercial law; and the third with criminal law. S. Keyser has written a paper on volume one. A. Meursingle included a large portion of *Mir'at at-Tullab* in his guide to Islamic law, *Handboek van 't Mohammedaansche recht* (Amsterdam, 1844). The *Mir'at at-Tullab* is 724 pages long. It deals with the topics commonly found in many books on Islamic law, such as those pertaining to buying and selling *(hukum bai'),* civil law *(muamalah),* inheritance law *(hukum faraid),* matrimonial law, criminal law, *hudud* law (the punishment of various crimes) and so on. It omits topics covered in Nuruddin's *Sirat al-Mustakim,* such as purification *(tahara),* prayers, alms, fasting and the pilgrimage. In 1982, Peunoh Daly completed a doctoral thesis on marriage law, based on the first volume of this book, for the Faculty of Islamic Law, Syarif Hidayatullah University, Jakarta in 1982.

7.4.4 *Daka'ik al-Huruf*

In *The Subtleties of Letters,* Abdur Rauf explains several key terms for the benefit of those who choose to take the path of Allah. A sound grasp of these concepts is crucial, for "taking their meaning at the surface or exoteric level as they are popularly understood by the layman would make one a kafir." Once one understands the true meaning of these terms, one can learn much more about them.

He then expounds on the meaning of the following two stanzas by Syaikh Muhy al-Din ibn Arabi, drawing on the understanding he has received from his own teachers:

> *Kunna hurufan aliyatin lam nukal*
> *Muta'alikatin fi dhura a la-kulal*
>
> *Ana anta fihi wa nahnu anta wa anta hu*
> *Wa'l-kullu fi hu hu, fasal amman wasal.*
>
> (We were lofty letters, (yet) unuttered,
> held latent in the highest peaks of the hills;
>
> I am you in Him and we are you, and you are He;
> and all is He in Him, ask those who have attained.)
>
> (Trans. Johns 1955, 69.)

God created through the word "*kun*" (Let there be) and we are latent in everything and in each other, as well as in God.

Next, the book explains that God or the creator is not the same as the creatures or created things: "It is clear that the servant is a servant, and God is God; the servant cannot be God, and God cannot be the servant." In other words, the universe can never be the same as Almighty God.

Further it is explained that there are four levels of Islamic monotheism *(tauhid uluhiyat, tauhid af'al, tauhid sifat* and *tauhid zat).* These levels are epitomized in the phrase "*la ilaha illa 'llah*". As such, Muslims are urged to become intimate with "*la ilaha illa 'llah*" and to chant it regularly. There are many benefits to be derived from the zikir.

The conclusion states that the person closest to Allah is one who yields all his mortal attributes to God's attributes and submits his essence to God's essence. In other words, the closest person to Allah is one who dies before death comes for him.

The *Daka'ik Al-Huruf* was edited and translated by A.H. Johns, based on two Leiden manuscripts, Cod. Or. 7243 (Sn H. 15) and Cod. Or. 7643 (Sn H. 21), with the omission of a number of sections of Cod. Or. 7243 (Sn H. 15) that enumerate the different types of *zikir*, as well as different methods of *zikir* and their benefits (A. H. Johns, 1955 a & b).

7.4.5 *Tarjuman al-Mustafid*

The *Rendition for the one who derives benefit* is a commentary on the Quran. As a work of exegesis, it has been widely used in the Malay Archipelago for over three centuries and is still popular. It is easily obtainable as many manuscripts exist and it has been printed numerous times, in Istanbul, Singapore, Penang and Jakarta.

In general, this work is regarded as a translation of a commentary by Al-Baidawi (died 685 H/1286): the title page of the Singapore edition states: "*huwa al-tarjamah al-jawiyah li 'l-tafsir al-musamma Anwar al-tanzil wa asrar al-ta'wil li'l-imam al-kadi ... al-Baidawi.*" The page prior to the list of contents provides the names of three Malay ulamas who edited the translation: Syaikh Ahmad Patani, Syaikh Idris Kelantani, and Syaikh Daud Patani. They state that the text was translated by al-Syaikh Abdur Rauf al-Fansuri; it is accurate and faithful to the original, being without any addition or modification. However, P. G. Riddel, who studied this book for his doctorate at the Australian National University, is of the opinion that *Tarjuman al-Mustafid* was translated word-for-word from another work, *Tafsir Al-Jalalayn* (The commentary of the two Jalals). The *Tafsir al-Baidawi* was only one of many sources of reference used (Riddel, 1984: 74-75). Further, Riddel also suggests that one of Abdur Rauf's favourite students, Daud Rumi, contributed to the writing of this book. One of the sources of reference used by Daud Rumi for this enterprise was *Lubab al-Ta'ujil fi Ma'ani al-Tanzil* (Riddel, 1984: 53). The names of the three ulamas were added much later. Perhaps Snouck Hurgronje's assertion that Abdur Rauf translated *Tafsir al-Baidawi* confirmed Riddel in this erroneous conclusion. It is important to note that Riddel based his surmise only on the interpretation of section 16 of the Quran, which contains the three chapters: *Surah al-Kahfi* (The Cave), *Surah Maryam* (Mary) and *Surah Taha* (Ta-Ha). Hopefully, one day other scholars will compare the *Tarjuman al-Mustafid*'s commentary on other sections of the Quran with those of *Tafsir Al-Jalalayn* and *Tafsir al-Baidawi*. Until then, the true authorship of the various interpretations in *Tarjuman al-Mustafid* will remain a subject of contention.

7.4.6 Other Works by Abdur Rauf

According to Voorhoeve (1952: 108-116), Abdur Rauf wrote at least 21 books in his lifetime, although there are considerable doubts about whether he really wrote some of the works that have been attributed to him, such as *Bayan Tajalli* and *Mau'izat al-Badi* (or *Mawa'ith al-Badiah*). Wan Mohd Shanghir Abdullah, for example, has argued that the *Bayan Tajalli*, which elaborates on a *zikir* to be recited at the threshold of death, is the work of a different Abdur Rauf, because it bears the date 1200H/1874. He also claims that *Al-mawa'izul Badiah*, a book of moral advice for Muslim men and women, is the work of Syaikh Abdurrauf Mansuri and not Abdur Rauf al-Fansuri (see Mohammad Daud Mohammad, 1987: 63-71).

Abdur Rauf wrote one book in Arabic: the *Tanbih al-mashi al-mansub ila tariq al-Kushashi* (Directions for those who follow the path of al-Qushashi). It was translated into Indonesian by Mohammad Badri as part of his studies for the Master of Arts degree from FS UI, Jakarta. *Tanbih al-mashi* was written to serve as a guide to those who want to be close to Allah. The way to do this is to strengthen one's belief in the Unity of Allah, perform one's religious obligations, and carry out other practices such as chanting *zikir*, reciting the *salawat* (blessings on the Prophet Muhammad), remembering God's divine essence, leading an ascetic life, and so on. These instructions were compiled by Abdur Rauf based on the teachings imparted by his teacher, Syaikh Safiya'l-din Ahmad bin Muhammad al-Madani al-Ansari al-Kusyasyi (Mohammad Badri, 1975: 100).

Abdur Rauf taught and wrote in Acheh for nearly thirty years. His many students hailed from all corners of the Archipelago and he was a highly respected ulama, famed for his open-mindedness and the prudence he showed before passing judgment on those accused of sin. His devoutness and piety were widely renowned, and this legendary status probably gave rise to the myth that Abdur Rauf brought Islam to Acheh. Certainly, he did play a significant role in spreading knowledge about Islam. Abdur Rauf died in 1693 and was buried near the mouth of the river Acheh. After his death, he was commonly known as *'Syaikh Kuala'* (the Syeikh at the River Mouth) and his grave became a popular pilgrimage site. His name is also immortalised in the name of the Syiah Kuala University in Banda Acheh.

7.5 *Hikayat Seribu Masalah*

Hikayat Seribu Masalah or *Masa'il Seribu,* Tale of a Thousand Problems, was very popular during the middle ages. The book was written in Arabic but when it was written is not known. It was first mentioned in a summary of *Al-Tabari,* written in Persian by Abu Ali Muhammad al-Bal'ami, which makes reference to another book entitled *Mesa'il.* The *Mesa'il* tells of a Jewish scholar, Abdullah Ibn Salam, who posed a series of difficult questions to the Prophet Muhammad. When all his questions were answered satisfactorily, Abdullah Ibn Salam realised that he was in the presence of a true prophet and immediately embraced Islam. One of the questions he posed, for example, was: which part of the earth will not be touched by the sun's rays until the end of the world? The Prophet Muhammad answered: the bottom of the sea parted by Prophet Musa with his staff when he was being pursued by the Pharaoh during the exodus from Egypt.

The *Mesa'il* is, without question, the source of the *Thousand Problems.* The two books serve the same purpose and pose the same questions. Al-Bal'ami finished his summary in 963 A.D. and the *Thousand Problems* must therefore have existed before this date. It was translated into Latin in 1143.

According to Pijper, who studied this book for his Doctoral degree from Leiden University, the Malay *Hikayat Seribu Masalah* was adapted from a Persian manuscript edited in India. (Among the examples of Indian influence are the statement that the Prophet Adam, came down to earth "in India near Silan hill"). The vast number of manuscripts is suggested by the existence of different versions of some tales. For example, in one version, Allah created the earth and the sky from an emerald. The gem disintegrated as Allah shaped it; the resulting smoke rose to form the seven layers of the sky, the rest became the earth. In the second version, Allah created earth from a pearl and water from a jewel. When the wind blew, the water became a fruit and was subsequently transformed into the seven layers of the world. There are also two different versions of the story about Judgement Day and how Israfil will blow his trumpet at that time.

There are 15 manuscripts of the *Hikayat Seribu Masalah* in Malay. Pijper published Bat. Gen. 19 (Van Ronkel Nr. CCC), held by the Central Museum, which was transcribed by Ki Agus Muhammad Mizan in 1237H (1865) in Palembang. The work of the scribe is evident in the influence of Palembang Malay in this manuscript, as well as in the liberties he has taken to 'improve' the manuscript. Winstedt's *History of Classical Malay Literature* mentions a 1757 Palembang manuscript, also written in Palembang Malay. According to Pijper, this is the Central Museum's manuscript Bat. Gen. 200 (Van Ronkel Nr. CCCII), and it shows a strong Minangkabau influence. Further research is needed to confirm this claim. Below is a summary of the manuscript edited by Pijper in 1924.

The *hikayat* begins with the story of Abdullah ibn Salam, who lived in Khaybar, some 150 kilometres to the north of Medina. He received a letter from the Last Messenger, the Prophet Muhammad, inviting him and his people to embrace Islam. Abdullah and his tribesmen agreed to accept Islam if the prophet answered one thousand questions. They both participated in a subsequent discussion.

In regard to matters of Islamic belief, Muhammad stated that he was both a prophet and an apostle. There are many religions and each differs from the others depending on the beliefs of its followers. Islam is the religion of Allah. Only those who profess the Muslim declaration of faith will enter heaven. Asked to describe the angel Jibrail, the prophet said that Jibrail is "neither male nor female, his face is like the full moon, and he shines very brightly." He further described Jibrail as having many wings, each one of them enormous. When asked about numbers, he explained that one cannot become two: Allah is the one and only God and has no peer or partner. Two cannot become three as Prophet Adam and Hawa were two. The same can be said of the divine essence and Allah, the moon and the sun, morning and night, tall and short, far and near, all are two. He was also able to explain why three cannot become four, and four cannot become five, and so on till thirty.

This was followed by a series of questions and answers on the creation of Adam, the sky, the sun, the moon and the stars. Next, the prophet described the nature of hell. After that, he told how the sky and the earth were created, how Judgement Day will come about, and the torment that awaits those in Hell. In reply to Abdullah ibn Salam's questions posed in the form of riddles, the prophet's answered:

(1) Iron born of rock is a child stronger than its father.
(2) The wind is stronger than fire.
(3) The Betara bird always flies into the sky while still clinging to its perch.
(4) Mary is the only woman to have given birth to a child without knowing a man.
(5) Eve was the only woman to be born from the body of a man.
(6) The prophet Jonah continued to live while still in his grave.
(7) A child will resemble the mother if she is more passionate than the father at the moment of conception. If the father is more passionate at that moment, then the child will take after him.

Next comes the story of the creation of the Prophet Adam, his exile from paradise and banishment to earth, and his sons, Kabil (Cain) and Habil (Abel). This is followed by an account of the Prophet Musa (Moses) dividing the sea with his staff, and the story of Prophet Nuh (Noah) and the ark. The Prophet Muhammad then answered questions about the creation of the earth; about Mount Saud, from where unbelievers will enter hell; the nature of heaven; the creation of the Nur (Light); the nature of hell; and the Day of Judgment. The book ends with the Prophet stating Adam's age when he died.

After listening to Prophet Muhammad's answers, Abdullah Ibn Salam accepted that: "Allah is one, He has no equal, begets not and is not begotten, and is beyond form and comparison." He and his people embraced Islam and became Muslims. Allah's Last Messenger shared a feast with Abdullah and his kinsfolk, giving thanks to God the exalted.

The *Hikayat Seribu Masalah* is mentioned as early as 1726 by Valentijn in his well-known book. The *hikayat* has been translated into Javanese from an unknown manuscript in Malay. To this day, it can still be bought at bookshops in Singapore and Malaysia.

7.6 Tajus Salatin

Tajus Salatin, The Crown of Kings, was written to serve as a guide for kings and princes. There are many such books and they can be found all over the world. In Europe, Machiavelli's *Il Principe* (The Prince), written during the fourteenth century, outlined the strategies a king should employ to rule his kingdom. In India, the *Kautilya-Arth-Sastra* (The Book of Wisdom) deals with similar subjects. Originally, the *Pancatantra* too was intended as a political guidebook for princes.

The *Tajus Salatin* belongs to this tradition but with one significant difference. In India, the king was considered to be a god, or the reincarnation of a god, and it was almost impossible for a commoner to assume this position. In Europe, the king was considered to be an ordinary man, even though he occupied an exalted position. In the Islamic world, the king was considered a mortal, subordinate to Allah's laws just as his subjects were, but he was also seen as having been entrusted with particular duties and obligations because he was the representative of Allah on earth (*khalifatu 'llah fil-ard*). A book like the *Tajus Salatin* served as a reminder to rulers in the Islamic world of their sacred duties.

The *Tajus Salatin* was either written, or translated, by a man called Bukhari Al-Jauhari (Bukhari the jewel merchant) or Bukhari of Johor. According to Ph. S. van Ronkel, the book was translated from a Persian text which is now lost. To support this contention, van Ronkel identifies various sources and influences of Persian origin that can be found in the *Tajus Salatin,* including *Siyar al-Muluk*, by Wazir Nizam al-Muluk (born in 1017 or 1018), as well as a number of popular Persian tales, such as *Mahmud and Ayaz; Khusrayu and Syirin* and *Yusuf and Zulaika*. As further proof of Persian influence, van Ronkel points to the many sentence structures which follow the syntax of Persian; the many Persian phrases that are quoted; and the verses which follow the popular forms of *mathnawi, ruba'i* and *ghazal*. Moreover, the names of princes and court ministers are also characteristically Persian (Ph. S. van Ronkel, 1899). Winstedt agreed with van Ronkel, in a paper he wrote in 1920 and in his literary history (1958). However, C. Hooykaas disagreeed; he suggested that although the *Tajus Salatin* has an Arabic title and its content is Persian-Muslim in nature, the book was written in Acheh in Malay (1947: 166). T. Iskandar also disagreed with Ph. S. van Ronkel and attempted to refute him point by point (see Iskandar's essay in Mohammad Daud Mohammad, 1987: 104-105).

Both Werndly and Valentijn mention the *Tajus Salatin*. Werndly, in particular, praises its admirable language and elegant style, asserting that it is the finest book in Malay. R. O. Winstedt was less impressed and believed that there were many errors in the language used in the book.

In 1827, the book was published in Batavia, together with a Dutch translation by Roorda van Eysinga. Since then, various parts of it have often been included in numerous anthologies, such as the *Bunga Rampai* edited by De Hollander. The *Tajus Salatin* was extremely popular during the nineteenth century. Abdullah Munsyi used the book's principles of physiognomy *(ilmu firasat)* in order to try to understand Raffles. When Raffles urged the Sultan of Singapore to trade with him, the Sultan declined, using the very arguments he had read in the *Tajus Salatin*.

This book was further republished in 1966 and again in 1979. Khalid Hussain's edition, 1966, was based on the Leiden manuscript, Cod. Or. 3053. The language of this manuscript is poor and, as a result, the text is almost incomprehensible. Jumsari Jusuf's shorter 1979 text utilises the Central Museum's manuscript, No. Br. 394, and is easier to understand. The following summary draws on these three published texts.

The *Tajus Salatin* consists of 24 chapters. It opens with praises to Allah the Almighty, then prays for blessings on the Prophet Muhammad and his righteous companions—Abu Bakar al-Sidik the truthful, Umar the just, Usman the honest and faithful, and Ali the warrior. Bukhari then states that his intention in writing this book is to make known the duties of kings and ministers, military commanders and subjects alike, and all matters related to them, as well as to provide worthy and abiding examples for them to follow. "Therefore," he writes, "this book is named *Tajus Salatin*, which means *The Crown of Kings*."

The first part of the book states that man needs to know himself in order to know his origin and the source of his existence. The Prophet Muhammad has said "He who knows himself, knows his God" (*"Arafanafsahufa 'qad 'arafa rabbahu"*). Man was created by Allah from nothing, and "is kept by Him from evil so that he may be aware of who he is, and he has been given the gifts of character, speech, hearing and sight, smell, taste and all manner of pleasures." Indeed, a man should be thankful for all the blessings bestowed on him by Allah, who is munificent beyond compare.

The life of a man is divided into three parts or stages—the beginning, middle and end. Before he was created by Allah, the universe already existed. Long after he has died, the universe will continue to exist. In the beginning, a man is a base and lowly creature; but in the middle stage of his existence he is the recipient of innumerable blessings and pleasures. God protects a man from destruction and helps him control his desires *(nafsu)*.

Man is made up of four elements—earth, water, wind and fire. His character varies according to the degree of the different elements in his body. If the mixture of elements is balanced or moderate, he will be healthy and lead a peaceful life. If there is an excess or a deficiency in any of the four elements in his body, a man may easily fall ill. "O thou who art righteous, remember the power of Allah, who has created the seven layers of earth, making them vast and deep."

This section ends with a description of the final stage of human life when God takes back all the blessings he has given man. At this time, he will be separated from kith and kin. His corpse will be buried in the graveyard. He will then be visited by an angel, who has been commanded by Allah to gather all the bodies that have fallen as far as the eye can see, from east to west. The dead will be resurrected on the field of *Mahsyar* and shown the deeds that they have done during their time on earth. Those who have done evil or wrong will be tortured by hellfire and no one will come to their aid. Those who have done good deeds, on the other hand, will find the doors of paradise opening to them.

The second part of the book talks of God and His creation of the universe and everything in it, including the deeds of his servants. Because of this, a man should learn about the divine essence, attributes and gnosis (*ma'rifat*). God's first attribute is His oneness; nothing is like unto Him. His other attributes include hearing, seeing and His eternal existence. All men must believe in God's commands as transmitted by His Messenger, for example the teachings about the torment that awaits the dead in their graves.

The third section compares our life on earth with a wayfarer's journey to his final destination. A man's first stop is in his father's loins; then he reaches his mother's womb; his third stop is the world; his fourth, the grave; his fifth, the field of Mahsyar; and thereafter to heaven or hell, where he will remain forever. In other words, life on earth is a bridge to the hereafter.

The fourth section states that the world is transient and, as a consequence, man should have death always on his lips and constantly remember the grave.

The fifth section tells that the Prophet Adam was made God's representive on earth (caliph), but was then exiled to earth for his transgressions. Adam constantly reminded his followers of his wrongdoing. Next come stories of the simple lives of prophets and kings: Musa, who chose to live in poverty; Yusuf, who fasted to the point of exhaustion; and Daud, who became an ironmonger. This is followed by the story of the Prophet Muhammad and his daughter Fatimah, both of whom also knew extreme hunger. The first four caliphs—Abu Bakar As-Sidik, Umar, Usman and Ali— lived humble and devout lives while they were in power. The remuneration they received from the public coffers was returned to the treasury after they died.

Next, the book describes the ten conditions required of a good king. First, he must be of a mature and discerning mind, able to tell right from wrong; second, he must be knowledgeable; third, he must choose persons of an astute and discerning mind to be his ministers; fourth, he must be able to inspire loyalty and admiration in others; fifth, he must be generous; sixth, he must always remember those who have served him well; seventh, he must be courageous; eighth, he must be modest as regards the amount of food, drink and sleep that he requires; ninth, he should spend only a minimum amount of time in the company of women; and tenth, he must be a man. Nevertheless, if a king dies without a male heir and is survived only by the female members of his family, then a female heir can assume the throne. This condition is interesting, as a number of further female rulers reigned in succession in Acheh, following after the reign of Sultanah Safiatuddin, the first female ruler of Acheh. The last female ruler, Kamalat Syah, ascended to the throne in 1688 but was forced to abdicate in 1699 after an edict (*fatwa*) of the Syarif of Mecca forbade women becoming monarchs (Riddel, 1984: 23). Section six of the book describes a just king as one who governs fairly, and shows benevolence and mercy to those who are oppressed.

Section seven describes the conduct of a just king. He should surround himself with wise and righteous advisers. He should watch over his subjects to ensure that no one is oppressed or persecuted. He should keep his word and ensure that whatever he commands is carried out. In ancient times, just kings divided their days into four parts: one part was devoted to the service of Allah the Exalted; one part was used to conduct the affairs of state, scrutinizing his subjects, both oppressors and oppressed alike, deliberating over administrative matters, and conferring with the learned and wise; another part was used to practice weaponry, archery and so on; and the fourth part was for eating and sleeping.

Section eight tells of the just king, Nusyirwan Adil, who was a pagan. It is said that when his tomb was opened, Nusyirwan Adil's body showed no signs of decay and he looked as though he was merely sleeping. Three rings were found on his fingers. The words "never do something without first consulting those who are righteous" were engraved on the first ring. The words "never be neglectful of your subjects" were engraved on the second ring. And on the third ring were the words, "do not be perturbed by the misdeeds of others, whether they be your loved ones or your enemies." Another tale is told of a Chinese king, who cared for his people and always wanted to hear what they had to say. When he became old and deaf, he asked them to write to him about their problems, and to come dressed in red when they needed to see him. A good person's name lives twice: once while he is alive, a second time after his death, when his good name lives in the memory of those who survive him.

Section nine tells of evil rulers who mistreated their subjects. Two kings, one in Basra, another in Isfahan, had their kingdoms destroyed because they tyrannized a woman subject.

Section ten states that a king can only perform his duties well if he has able ministers. A kingdom is like a palace that rests on four pillars; if one of the pillars is missing, the palace will collapse. The four pillars are: firstly, a wise, patient, caring and noble senior minister; secondly, a brave, noble and compassionate military commander, who will protect the king and his subjects; thirdly, an honest, truthful and trustworthy treasurer (*khazin*), who can look after the king's wealth; and fourthly, a shrewd and inquisitive agent (*mukhbar*), who can advise the king about what is happening in the kingdom.

This section also describes the relationship between the king and his ministers, as well as the proper behaviour of a minister. A minister must fulfill all of twenty-seven conditions. The most important of these are that he must:

(i)   devote himself to the service of Almighty God;

(ii) be grateful to the king for the grace and favour bestowed upon him;

(iii) counsel the king, so that his actions do not transgress the religious law;

(iv) produce wealth, as well as raise a well equipped army;

(v)   protect visitors to the realm and the poor from persecution and oppression;

(v)   be benevolent and broadminded in all things;

(vi) behave honorably, undertake good deeds, and follow a strict moral code;

(vii) safeguard the interests of his king in both temporal and spiritual matters;

(viii) possess useful allies and friends, who can help him to serve the king;

(ix) choose competent retainers to whom he can delegate the king's work.

Section eleven states that the word *(kalam)* is the greatest of all the things created by Allah the Exalted; the entire universe was created through the word and without it, nothing existed. Everything created by God was created through His word.

Section twelve states that a messenger must be honest in word and deed; he must not lie and he must convey accurately the message that has been entrusted to him.

Section thirteen describes the twenty-five conditions required of all officials appointed by the king. These conditions say little about personal character; instead, they are mainly concerned with how those officials should speak and carry out the king's work. Significantly, an official is advised to give precedence to Allah's work before his service of the king.

Section fourteen describes the care of a child. When a child is seven days old, an *akikah* ceremony should be held: the child's hair is to be shaven and a feast served to guests of the family. When the child is six years old, he should be circumcised, taught proper manners and given a suitable name. When he is seven years old, he should begin to sleep separately from his parents and learn how to perform his prayers. When he reaches sixteen or seventeen years old, his parents should find him a wife. This will end his parents' duties and they will no longer be responsible for him.

Section fifteen states that a man should have a proper regard for himself. A man who respects himself will live a noble life, doing what is right according to his sense of moral obligation, and saying the right words at the appropriate time and place.

Section sixteen states that there are seven signs of a virtuous man, including: good deeds, humility, having Allah's name always upon his lips and beseeching His help in times of difficulty. Hakim Lukman once said that whatever knowledge a man possesses is wasted if he is not a virtuous person.

Section seventeen deals with the proper qualities of a king. Among the ten qualities are these:

(1) a king should regard himself as if he were one of his own subjects;
(2) a king should always open his doors to his subjects, so that they can bring all their issues to his attention;
(3) a king should follow in the footsteps of other righteous, noble and just kings, and emulate their example;
(4) a king should be compassionate when he is required to punish offenders;
(5) a king should never transgress the laws of Allah and the *syaria,* and should always consult with ulamas and sages.

Section eighteen states that there are four fields of knowledge that are of use in reading human character, namely: *ilmu nubuat* (insight); *ilmu wilayat* (genetics); *ilmu hikmat* (divination); *ilmu kifayah* (a knowledge of bodily marks) and *ilmu firasat* (the meaning of those marks).

Section nineteen elaborates on the sciences of *kifayah* and *firasat.* The ability to assess a person's character or personality from his physical appearance is a useful way to distinguish between a good and a bad person. A person with a large head, for example, is usually intelligent, whereas one with a small head is uncultured or a boor. The hair, eyes, ears, nose, mouth and neck all reflect an individual's character.

Section twenty talks about the duty of a king to his Muslim subjects. A king should protect his subjects and not usurp their property. If a subject breaks the law, his transgression should, wherever possible, be pardoned. If a punishment needs to be meted out, it must be done in a compassionate manner. Apart from that, a king should also build a mosque for his people, instruct his subjects to do good deeds, and isolate the delinquent.

Section twenty-one prescribes twenty conditions for non-believers who live under the rule of a Muslim king. Among these are:

(1) they must not build new shrines for worship or restore old ones when their shrines fall into disrepair;
(2) they must not wear the same attire as Muslims;
(3) they must not keep spears, swords or *keris* (daggers) in their homes;
(4) they must not wear rings set with jewels;
(5) they must not sell wine, *tuak* (fermented coconut or rice wine), or other alcoholic beverages;
(6) they must observe their traditional customs and practices, in order to distinguish themselves from Muslims and other non-Muslims;
(7) they must not give their descendants Muslim names; and
(8) they must not own Muslim slaves.

Section twenty-two speaks of generosity *(sakhwat)* and compassion. It tells of Hatim Thai, a very generous man who gave whatever was asked of him, even his own life. Because of his magnanimity, he lived in peace and had many loyal friends.

Section twenty-three talks about the importance of keeping one's promises (*wafa'uhud*). The Prophet Ismail once waited three days for a friend who had promised to meet him. A certain king once spent everything he had in his treasury on the poor in order to fulfill his promise to God, even though he was advised by his ministers not to do so.

Section twenty-four contains Bukhari's final message to his different readers. He hopes that his book will serve as a principled companion for righteous Muslim kings, and encourage them to rule justly and with forethought. He hopes that it will help ministers and military commanders to fulfill their duties to the king. He further hopes that it will teach rational subjects, who have a profound faith in God, to love their king. Finally, he requests scribes to copy his book faithfully and accurately. This section ends with a *mathnawi* verse.

7.7 *Hikayat Wasiat Lukman Hakim*

This work presents *The Last Will and Testament of Judge Lukman*, a well-known figure in the Islamic world, who was also famous in pre-Islamic times as a warrior and a sage. In Chapter 31 of the Quran, Lukman is portrayed as a wise man and the source of numerous proverbs. In Arabic, the word *"amsal"*, "proverbs" (plural of "*misal*"), also refers to tales and fables. Lukman was as renowned for his fables as Aesop was in Europe. On one occasion, when he was expected to serve his guests the best food he had, Lukman confounded everyone by offering them offal. He then explained that there was no better food than a kind tongue and a good heart. On another occasion, when he was asked to serve the worst food, he again served his guests offal, arguing that there is nothing worse than an unkind tongue and a black heart.

Lukman's name occurs at many places in Malay literature. There are stories about him in the *Hikayat Syah Mardan*. The *Tajus Salatin* quotes his proverbs, while the *Bustanus Salatin* mentions his name together with the names of Aisyah, the Prophet's wife, and the Muslim scholar, Syafi'i. Most importantly, there is a whole *hikayat* about him called *Hikayat Lukman Hakim*. This manuscript is rare. The only known manuscript is held in the Central Museum (v.d. Wall Collection, 125), Jakarta. It has been transliterated by Edwar Djamaris et al. (1985). Below is a summary of the manuscript.

The *hikayat* begins by saying that some religious figures regarded Lukman Hakim as a prophet. Others considered him a saint or holy man. Then follows Lukman's instructions to his son as contained in the section called *"Nasihat Lukman"* (Lukman's Advice). Lukman taught his son not to neglect his duty to Allah and never to worship any other god. The young man should also reduce the amount of time he spent sleeping and eating, in order to have more time to devote to Allah.

Wisdom can be acquired in three ways:
(1) **through** righteous speech and action;
(2) **through** silence accompanied by righteous thoughts; and
(3) **by** avoiding those who are evil.

Four traits distinguish the noble, the wise, the wretched and those who are intoxicated by alcohol. Four things are detrimental to man, namely: intemperate rage, frivolity, indolence and intemperate haste. There are four types of vile behaviour: miserliness, indifference towards one's friends and relatives, perjury, and a lack of shame.

The book ends by describing four offences that will destine their perpetrators for hell. These are: firstly, when a king appropriates his subject's possession and cruelly punishes his people; secondly, when a king is derelict in his duty to his kingdom and neglects the welfare of his subjects; thirdly, when a person slanders another person; and fourthly, when a person has no self-regard for his own salvation and is oblivious to death.

7.8 Abd Al-Samad Al-Palimbini

During the eighteenth century, Palembang replaced Acheh as the centre of theology and literature written in Malay. The names of twelve writers are still known to us and no doubt there were many others as well. The best known of these writers are Abd Al-Samad Al-Palambini, Shihabuddin b. Abdallah Muhammad, Kemas Fakhruddin, Kemas Muhammad b. Ahmad, and Sultan Mahmud Badruddin, the author of the *Syair Sinyor Kosta*.

Abd Al-Samad was a famous ulama, although little is known of his life. We do know that he lived for a long time in Mecca and that he studied and taught there. One of his teachers was Muhammad Al-Saman (died in 1776 A.D./1190 H), founder of the Samaniya Sufi order. His students included Syaikh Daud bin Abdullah al-Fatani, another ulama who wrote many books.

Abd Al-Samad maintained a close relationship from Mecca with ulamas in the Malay Archipelago through his correspondence. In 1772, Abd Al-Samad wrote two letters to the authorities in Central Java at the request of two of his students returning to Java (see Drewes, 1977: 222). Moreover, he wrote many books in "Jawi" (Malay) for the use of his students studying in Mecca, including the following:

7.8.1 *Zuhrat al-Murid fi Bayan Kalimat al-Tawhid*

This book is based on a lecture given in 1178 H (1764 A.D.) in Mecca by Ahmad al-Damanhuri, an Egyptian ulama who later became a professor at Al-Azhar University. It deals with logic (*mantik*) and theology (*usuluddin*).

7.8.2 *Hidayat al-Saliki fi Suluk Maslak al-Muttakin*

This book is adapted from a series of works by Al-Ghazali entitled *Bidaya al-Hidaya* and was completed in 1192 H. Its aim, as stated in the book's title, is to describe the spiritual journey of the God-fearing man. The book consists of a preamble and seven chapters. The preamble speaks of knowledge that is beneficial to man, and the excellence of those who seek knowledge.

Chapter I	outlines the main tenets of Sunni Islam (*ahli sunnah wal-jamaah*).
Chapter II	describes the proper way to pray and the different types of prayer; the proper way to fast; and the benefits of reciting the *Surah Al-Kahfi* (The Cave), *Surah Ikhlas* (Sincerity) and *Surah Yasin* (Ya-Sin).
Chapter III	preaches against outward vices, such as gossip and controversy. This chapter also explains the concepts of *halal* (what is permissible) and *haram* (what is forbidden).
Chapter IV	preaches against inner vices, such as gluttony, verbosity, anger, spitefulness, stinginess and over-attachment to material wealth and worldly matters.
Chapter V	discusses inner piety, including penitence, patience, grace, sincerity, faith and the fear of Allah.
Chapter VI	talks about the rewards and quality of chanting *zikir*, and how to chant in the proper way.
Chapter VII	explains the relationships that should hold between men, and between mankind and God the creator. This chapter also elaborates on the proper conduct that should be observed by a pious man, a student, a child, a father, and a friend.

7.8.3 *Siyar al-Salikin ila 'Ibadat Rabb al-'Alamin*

The Path of the Wayfarer in His Devotion to the Lord of the Entire Universe is a translation of Imam Al-Ghazali's *Lubab Ihya 'ulum al-Din* (Essence of the Revitalisation of the Religious

Sciences), which is a summary of his *Ihya 'ulum al-Din* (Revitalisation of the Religious Sciences). Abd. Al-Samad began work on this translation in 1193 H (1779 A.D.) and completed it in Taif during 1203 H (1788 A.D.). The *Siyar al-Salikin* is a rather loose translation of Al-Ghazali's work; some parts of it have been expanded by the inclusion of various supplementary notes.

The Path of the Wayfarer is still widely used in Islamic boarding schools throughout Indonesia and has been reprinted many times. The most recent reprint, by Pustaka Nasional, Singapore, does not include the year of publication. The spine gives another title, "*Al-Jawhar al-Mawhub* (A Beautiful Gift of Jewels)" and the details "composed by Ali b. Abd Rahman al-Kelantani in 1888 (1306 H)".

The book consists of a preamble and four sections. The preamble describes the rewards of knowledge and the benefit it brings to those who acquire it. The first section discusses the theological tenets of Sunni Islam, and the overt forms of religious observance. The second section describes proper conduct related to eating, drinking, marriage, and the performance of worldly duties, as well as the difference between *halal* and *haram*. The third section discusses the acts that may negate a person's good deeds, namely outward and inward vices. The fourth section describes the power of supplication *(munajat)* to help a person avoid those things that can nullify his pious deeds. The book concludes by giving a list of books that the student of Sufism would find useful.

7.8.4 *Tuhfat al-rahibin fi bayan haqikat Iman al-mukminin*

According to Drewes (1976), the Central Museum manuscript v.d. Wall collection 37, *Tuhfat al-rahibin fi bayan haqikat Iman al-mukminin* (A Gift of Insight into the Faith of the Pious), is also the work of Abd Al-Samad. After studying manuscript MS4024 held in Leningrad, Drewes concluded that the *Tuhfat* is an anthology of fragments from other works. This manuscript can be summarised as follows:

The book is composed of three chapters and a conclusion (*khatimah*). In Chapter 1 Abd Al-Samad discusses the differences between the Sunnis and the Mu'tazilite philosophers concerning faith (*iman*), Islam, and the relationship between faith and Islam. Chapter 2 discusses the existence of Satan (*iblis*), demons and *jinn*s, and the differences between them. Chapter 3 deals with apostasy (*ridda* or *murtad*), based on existing works of Islamic jurisprudence. To conclude, Abd Samad answers the questions: What is sin? How many sins are there? And what is repentance? Among the fragments taken from other works is the explanation in Chapter 2 of the *"kaum mulhid yang bersufi-sufi dirinya"* (the heretics who pretend to be Sufis) and the *bidah* (deviationists), taken from *Tibyan fi ma'rifat,* by Nuruddin Ar-Raniri. The conclusion is followed by a treatise by Abdur Rauf on the torments of death, the contents of which are taken from Al-Qurtubi's *Tadhkira* (Drewes, 1976: 273-290).

7.9. Shihabuddin b. Abdallah Muhammad

Shihabuddin b. Abdallah Muhammad translated *Sharah yang Latif atas Mukhtasar Jawharat al-Tawhid* (A Beautiful Exegesis on a Summary of the Gem of Islamic Theology) (Raf. Mal. 48), written by Ibrahim al-Laqani (died 1631). In addition, he composed two short treatises: one on the meaning of the profession of faith; the other on Allah's twenty attributes.

7.10 Kemas Fakhruddin

Kemas Fakhruddin lived in Palembang during the second half of the 18th century. Little is known of his life, except that he spent four years in India. A well-known translator from Arabic, he enjoyed the patronage of Sultan Ahmad Najmuddin and his son, Pangeran Ratu, who later became Sultan Muhammad Baharuddin (1774-1804).

Among his translations is the *Futuh al-*Sya'am, a history of the earliest Islamic conquests. He also adapted Zakariyya al-Ansari's *sharh* (exegesis) of *Risala fi 'l-tawhid* (Treatise on the Affirmation of Divine Oneness), by Syaikh Raslan al-Dimshiqi (died 540 H/ 1146 A.D.). This treatise was written to refute the teachings on the Seven Stations of Being that were popular in Palembang at that time. However, in Drewes' catalogue of manuscripts, this adaptation is listed as *Kitab Mukhtasar* (Drewes, 1976: 274). Both *Kitab Mukhtasar* (Short Commentary or Summary) and Zakariya al-Ansari's exegesis of *Risala fi 'l-tawhid* have been republished by Drewes (1977), with an English translation.

7.11 Kemas Muhammad b. Ahmad

Muhammad Ibn Ahmad wrote the *Hikayat Syaikh Muhammad Saman*. Snouck Hurgronje noted that chronicles describing the lives of pious men, like Saman, were popular in the Archipelago and considered to be sacred as they offered their readers many rewards (*pahala*). Often, the sick would vow to read such books in the hope that they might be cured (Snouck Hurgronje II, 1906: 218). At the request of the Sultan of Palembang, Muhammad Ahmad also translated the *Bahr al-ajaib* (The Magic Sea) from Arabic into Malay.

7.12 Daud ibn Abdullah ibn Idris Al-Fatani

We now turn to the theologians of Patani. The first of these was Daud ibn Abdullah. Syaikh Daud, as he was often called, was a very productive ulama who lived during the 19th century. According to H. W. Mohd. Shaghir Abdullah, Syaikh Daud produced at least 59 works in both Malay and Arabic (Shaghir Abdullah, 1990c, 55-56); these deal with a variety of subjects, including jurisprudence, mysticism, theology, worship and faith. Not much is known of his life, except that he lived and taught for a long period in Mecca and students came to him from all over the Archipelago. Among his students were Syaikh Muhammad Zain bin Faqih Jalaluddin Acheh, who wrote *Bidaya al-Hidaya* (The Beginning of Guidance); Syaikh Zainuddin bin Muhammad Al-Badawi as-Sambawi, who wrote *Sirajul Huda* (The Guiding Light); and the Sultan of Sambas himself, Muhammad Syafiuddin. Below are several of Syaikh Daud's most important works.

7.12.1 *Idah al-Bab li Murid al-nikah bi '1-sawab*

*A Treatise on the Ideal Marriage (*v.d. Wall Collection 14*)* is a short treatise on marriage and divorce. Written by Syaikh Daud in 1809, its contents were taken from prominent books on Islamic jurisprudence, such as the commentary on *Minhaj al-Talibin* (A Manual of Islamic Law) by An-Nawawi, the *Fathal-Wahhab* by Zakariya al-Ansari, the *Tuhfah* by Ibn Hajar al-Haitami, and the *Nihaya* by Ramli.

Syaikh Daud used these same sources to compile his *Bughyat al-Tuttab li Murid Ma'rifat al-ahkam bi 'l-sawab*, another early work. Its contents examine the topics of cleansing and purification, prayer, funeral rites, almsgiving, the distribution of alms, fasting, spiritual retreats, as well as the greater and the lesser pilgrimages. The manuscript of this text held by the Central Museum in Jakarta is called *Ghayat al-Tullab* (v.d. Wall Collection 1).

7.12.2 *Al-Durr al-Thamin*

Syaikh Daud completed his translation of this short treatise, *A Pearl of Great Value,* in Mecca in 1816-1817. It discusses issues of faith, such as the belief in destiny (*takdir*) and free will (*iktisab*).

7.12.3 *Minhaj al-'Abidin ila Jannan rabb al-'Alamin*

Completed in Mecca in 1824, *The Path of Believers to the Paradise of the Lord of the Universe* deals with mysticism. It draws on three works by Al-Ghazali: *Ihya' 'Ulum Ad-din, Kitab al-Asrar,* and *Kitab al-Kurban ila Allah.*

7.12.4 *Furu' al-Masa'il wa Usul al-Masa'il*

Syaikh Daud's greatest and most important work, *The Branches and Trunks of Questions,* was written between 1838 and 1841. The book is based on Ramli's *Fatawa* and Husain b. Muhammad al-Mahalli's *Kash al-anom as'ilah al-anam.*

The book has remained popular among Muslims in the Archipelago as a source of religious teachings. It discusses everyday issues, such as purification, prayer, alms, fasting, the greater and the lesser pilgrimage, and *halal* and *haram.* The book also debates issues of Islamic law relating to buying and selling (*bai'*), inheritance (*fara'id*), marriage, crime, religious wars, and other matters such as the emancipation of slaves.

This concludes our discussion of a few of Syaikh Daud's important works. Readers who would like to find out more about his other works are referred to the essay by Matheson and Hooker published in *JMBRAS,* Issue 61 (1988).

Besides Syaikh Daud, there were many other ulamas from Patani who wrote theological works. Matheson and Hooker (1988) list sixteen other scholars whose works are still widely read. Three of them, like Syaikh Daud, wrote their major works in Mecca in the 19th century. They are as follows.

7.13 Syaikh Ahmad b. Muhammad Zain Patani

Syaikh Ahmad (1856-1906) not only taught, he also worked as an editor of Malay books for the Turkish government in Mecca. It was due to his tireless efforts that many of the works of Syaikh Daud and other ulamas were published. Among his own works were the *Faridat al-Fara'id fi'ilm al-'aqaid,* a treatise on monotheism and Islamic theology; and *Al-Fatawa al-Fataniyyah,* which answers questions posed to him by students from the Archipelago.

7.14 Muhammad b. Ismail Daud al-Fatani

Although little is known about this ulama, he was the author of a book that is still widely used in religious schools. The book is called *Matla' al-Badrayn wa Majma' al-Bahrayn* (Rise of the Two Full Moons). It discusses the pillars of Islam and faith, as well as the common legal subjects of buying and selling, representation (*wakil*), the division of inheritances, and crimes such as murder or adultery. Another book, *Wishah Al-Afrah wa asbah al-Falah,* also deals with the pillars of Islam and *iman,* but focuses more specifically on the subjects of purification and prayer.

7.15 Zain al-Abidin b. Muhammad Al-Fatani

Two of his books are still used today: *Kashf al-Litham,* a treatise on Man and inheritance law; and *'Aqidat al-Najin,* a translation of al-Sanusi's book on the creed, *Umm al Barahin.*

7.16 Other Indonesian Theologians

There were other prominent theologians from other parts of the Archipelago who wrote in Malay. Banjarmassin produced Muhammad Arsyad b. Abdullah al-Banjari, the author of the *Sabil al-Muhtadin*; Muhammad Nafis b. Idris al-Banjari, author of the *al-Durr al-Nafi;* and Muhammad Tayib b. Mas'ud al-Banjari, author of *Miftah al-Jannah.* Ahmad Khatib b. Abd. Al-Ghafar Sambas, from Sambas, wrote *Fath al-'Arifin.* Sumbawa too had her own theologians: Muhammad Zainuddin b. Muhammad al-Badawi As-Sambawi, a pupil of Syaikh Daud, wrote *Siraj al-Huda*; Muhammad Ali b. Abd Al-Rasyid al-Sambawi wrote *Al-Yawaqit wa 'l-Jawahir.* Acheh's neighbour, the Minangkabau region, has produced writers such as Syaikh Ismail b. Abdillah Al-Khalidi Minangkabawi, the author of *Kifayat al-Ghulam fi Bayan Arkani Islam*; and Ahmad Khatib b. Abd al-Latiff Minangkabawi, who wrote *Al-Shumus al-Lami'ah.*

7.17 Conclusion

This concludes our chapter on theological literature (*kitab jawi* as it is known in Malaysia and Singapore). Many of the books discussed here are adaptations or translations of Arabic works; only now and then do we find the authors expressing their own opinions. Nevertheless, these texts served as a basic form of religious fare for the people of the Malay Archipelago, prior to the arrival of Europeans and the establishment of modern schools. Today, theological literature is still read in religious schools, prayer houses (*surau*), and residential colleges (*madrasah* and *pesantren*) all over the Malay Archipelago and further afield, including southern Thailand and Mindanao in the Philippines. Patani is now part of Thailand but the *kitab Jawi* are an important part of their Malay cultural identity (Matheson & Hooker, 1988: 4). In Malaysian schools, it is compulsory to study the Jawi script, even though Romanised script is now the official orthography. Here too Jawi is considered an integral part of Malay culture.

We began this chapter by quoting Roolvink's entry in the *Encyclopaedia of Islam,* in order to show the vast range of theological literature in Malay. Roolvink based his conclusion on the manuscripts he found in public libraries, especially that of Leiden University. There are still many more manuscripts held in private libraries all over the Malay Archipelago. Although Syaikh Daud Patani, for example, produced at least fifty-nine works, Matheson and Hooker were able to find only twelve of them, while noting that nine others were held in various libraries (1988: 21). The discovery of new manuscripts continues. This chapter provides merely an initial introduction to the intellectual history of theology throughout the Malay Archipelago. Much more in-depth study is required.

REFERENCES

Al-Attas, Syed Naguib
1963.   *Some Aspects of Sufism as it is understood and practiced among the Malays,* Singapore.
1966.   *Raniri and the Wujudiyyah of 17th century Acheh,* Singapore.
1967.   "New Light on the Life of Hamzah Fansuri," *JMBRAS,* 40 (1).
1970.   *The Mysticism of Hamzah Fansuri,* Kuala Lumpur.

Abdullah Asghir, H. W. N
1990.   *Syeikh Daud bin Abdullah al-Fatani,* Shah Alam.

Ahmad Daudy
1978.   *Syeikh Nuruddin Ar-Raniri,* Jakarta.
1981.   *Allah dan Manusia dalam Konsep Syeikh Nuruddin Ar-Raniri,* Dissertation, IAIN, Jakarta.

Ahmad Rifa'i Hasan
1987.   *Warisan Intelektual Islam Indonesia,* Jakarta.

Arberry, A. J.
1956.   *Sufism,* London.

Bastin, J. & R. Roolvink
1964.   *Malayan and Indonesian Studies,* Oxford.

Chaidar
1978.   *Syech Nawawi Albantani Indonesia,* Jakarta.

Chatib Quzwain, M.
1985.   *Mengenal Allah, Suatu Studi Mengenai Ajaran Tasawuf Syaikh Abdus Samad al-Palimbani,* Jakarta.

Doorenbos, J.
1933.   *De Geschriften van Hamzah Fansoeri,* Dissertation, Leiden.

Drewes, G. W. J.
1954.   *Een Javaansche Primbon uit de zestiende eeuw,* Leiden.
1955.   "De herkomst van Nuruddin Ar-Raniri," *BKI,* 111, 2, 1955.
1976.   "Further data concerning Abd al-Samad Palimbani," *BKI,* 132 (2 & 3), pp. 267-269.
1977.   "Direction for Travellers on the Mystic Path," *VKI,* No. 81.

Drewes, G. W. J. and L. F. Brakel.
1986.   *The Poems of Hamzah Fansuri,* Dordrecht.

Edwar Djamaris (ed.)
1983.   *Khabar Akhirat Dalam Hal Kiamat,* Jakarta.

Grinter, Catherine Anne
1979.   *Book IV of the Bustanus-Salatin: A Study from the Manuscripts of a 17th Century Malay Work Written in North Sumatra,* Dissertation Ph.D., London University.

Hadiwijono, H.
1967.   *Man in the Present Javanese Mysticism,* Dissertation, Amsterdam.

Hall, D. G. E.
1962.   *Historians of South East Asia,* London.

Hidding, K. A. H.
1947-48   "Indonesische Mystiek." *Indonesie*, I.

Hurgronje, Ch. Snouck
1906.   *The Achehnese* (Translated by A.W.S. O'Sullivan), vol. 2, Leiden.

Israeli, R. & A. H. Johns.
1984.   *Islam In Asia*, Vol. II, Colorado.

Iskandar, T.
1964.   "Nuruddin ar-Raniri," *DB*, 8 (10), pp. 436-441.
1965a.   "Hamzah Fansuri," *DB*, 9, (2), pp. 53-56.
1965b.   "Bokhari al-Jauhari dan Tajus-Salatin," *DB*, 9, (3), pp. 107-133.
1965c.   "Shamsuddin as-Sumatrani", *DB*, 9, (4), pp. 148-455.
1965d.   "Abdurrauf Singkel," *DB*, 9, (5), pp. 195-200.
1966.   *Bustanus Salatin,* Chapter II, Article 13, Kuala Lumpur.

Johns, A. H.
1953.   "Nur al-Daka'ik: edition of a Malay text by a 17th century Sumatran Mystic," *JRAS*, pp. 137-151.
1955 a & b "Daka'ik al-Huruf by Abd. Rauf of Singkel," *JRAS*, April, pp. 55-73; October, pp. 139-158.
1955c.   "Aspects of Sufi thought in India and Indonesia in the first half of the 17th century," *JMBRAS*, 27 (1), pp. 70-77.
1957.   "Malay Sufism as illustrated in an anonymous collection of 17th century tracts," *JMBRAS*, 32 (2), pp. 1-111.
1965.   *The Gift Addressed to the Spirit of the Prophet,* Canberra.

Jones, R.
1974.   *Nuruddin's Bustanus Salatin, Bab IV, Pasal 1,* Kuala Lumpur.

Jumsari Jusuf
1978.   *Tajus Salatin*, Jakarta.

Juynboll, H. H.
1899.   *Catalogus of Malay, Minangkabau, and South Sumatran Manuscripts in the Netherlands,* Two Volumes, Leiden.

Khalid Hussain (ed.)
1966.   *Taj-Us-Salatin,* Kuala Lumpur.

Kun Zachrun Istanti
1981.   *Pembahasan Naskah Hujjat Al-Siddik Li Daf al-Zindik,* Master's thesis, Gadjah Mada University, Yogyakarta.

Meursingle, A.
1844.   *Handboek van't Mohammedaansche,* Amsterdam.

Mohammad Badri
1975. *Tanbih Al-Moshi,* Master's thesis, FSUI, Jakarta.

Mohammad Daud Mohammad
1987.   *Tokoh-tokoh Sastera Melayu Klasik,* Kuala Lumpur.

Mohd. Nor bin Ngah
1982.   *Kitab Jawi Islamic Thought of the Malay Muslim Scholars, ISEAS,* Singapore.

Mohd. Shaghir Abdullah, H. W.
1990a. *Syaikh Daud bin Abdullah al-Fatani, Ulama dan Pengarang Terulung Asia Tenggara*, Kuala Lumpur.
1990b. *Wasiat Abrar Peringat Akhyar*, Kuala Lumpur.
1990c. *Syaikh Muhammad Arsyad Al-Banjari, Pengarang Sabilah Muhtadin,* Kuala Lumpur.
1990d. *Faridatul Faraid, Syaikh Ahmad Al-Fatani,* Kuala Lumpur.
1991. *Khazanah Karya Pusaka Asia Tenggara,* vols. I & II, Kuala Lumpur.

Muhayudin Hj. Yahya
1986-1988 *Ensiklopedia Sejarah Islam,* 6 vols, Bangi, Malaysia.

Nicholson, R. A.
1967. *Studies in Islamic Mysticism*, Cambridge.

Nieuwenhuijze, C. A. O. van
1945. *Sjamsu 'l-din van Pasai*, Dissertation, Leiden University.
1948. "Nur al-Din al-Raniri als bestrijder der Wudjudijah," *BKI*, 104, pp. 337-414.

Peunoh Daly
1982. *Hukum Nikah, Talak, Rujuk, Hadanah dan Nafkah Kerabat dalam Naskah Karya Abd Al Rauf Singkel*, Dissertation, IAIN Syarif Hidayatullah, Jakarta.

Pijper. G. F.
1924. *Het boek der duizend vragen,* Leiden.

Riddel, P. G.
1984. '*Abd Al-Rauf of Al-Singkel's Tarjuman Al-Mustafid.* Ph.D. dissertation, ANU, Australia.

Rinkes, D. A.
1909. *Abdoerraoef van Singkel,* Dissertation, Leiden University.

Ronkel, Ph. S. van
1899. "De Kroon der Koningen" (Tajul Mahkota), *TBG,* 41, pp. 55-69. 1921.
1943. *Supplement-Catalogus der Maleische en Minangkabausche handschriften in de Leidsche Universiteits*, Leiden.
"Raniri's Maleisch Geschrift: expose der religies," *BKI,* 102.

Roolvink, R.
1971. "Indonesia-Literature," *The Encyclopaedia of Islam*, Revised edn., vol. III, pp. 1230-1235.

Roorda, Van Eysinga, P. P.
1827. *De Kroon aller Koningen van Bocharie Djohor naar een oud Maleisch handschrift vertaald,* Batavia.

Siti Chamamah Soeratno
1982. *Memahami Karya-karya Nuruddin Ar-raniri*, Yogyakarta.

Steenbrink, K. A.
1984. *Beberapa Aspek Tentang Islam di Indonesia Abad ke-19*, Jakarta.
1988. *Mencari Tuhan dengan Kacamata Arab*, Yogyakarta.

Sulastin Sutrisno, Darusuprapta & Sudaryanto
1985. *Bahasa-Sastra-Budaya, Ratna Manikam Untaian Persembahan Kepada Prof. Dr. P. J. Zoetmulder,* Yogyakarta.

Tudjimah
1961.   *Asrar al-insan fi ma'rifa al-ruh wa'l-Rahman*, Jakarta.

Valentijn, F.
1724-1726. *Oud en Nieuw Oost Indien*, Vol. 1-5, Amsterdam.

Matheson, Virginia. & M. B. Hooker.
1988.   "Jawi Literature in Patani: The Maintenance of an Islamic Tradition," *JMBRAS,* 61, pt. 1, pp. 1-86.

Voorhoeve, P.
1951.   "Van en over Nuruddin al-Raniri," *BKI,* 107, pp. 353-368.
1952.   "Bayan Tajalli," *TBG,* No. 85, pp. 87-117.
1955.   *Twee Maleise geschriften van Nuruddin ar-Raniri,* Leiden.

Winstedt, R. O.
1920.   "Taju's-salatin," *JSBRAS,* 81, pp. 37-38.
1920.   "Bustanu's-Salatin, its date and author," *JSBRAS,* 82, pp. 151-152.
1923.   "Some Malay mystics, heretical and orthodox," *JMBRAS,* 1, 2, pp. 312-318.

Sample of a Malay Manuscript: *Hikayat Hang Tuah*

8 Historical Literature

Historical literature is the richest, and probably the most important, branch of Malay literature. Almost every kingdom in the Archipelago had its own history. This told of events that had happened in the palace and focused on the fortunes of the kingdom over several generations. The idea behind the writing of such a history usually came from within palace circles and its audience too was commonly restricted to members of the nobility. This explains why historical literature was seldom produced outside the palace (C. Hooykaas, 1947: 89).

The word *sejarah* comes from the Arabic word *syajarah,* which means 'a tree'. *Syajarahal-nasab,* for example, means a genealogical tree. Another term often used to refer to history is *salasilah* (or *silsilah*), which means 'a chain'. From the use of these terms, we can conclude that *silsilah* or lineage lies at the heart of Malay historical literature. R. Roolvink has shown that the *Sejarah Melayu* only gradually grew to become the *Sejarah Melayu* we know today. The Malay view of History is different from that of the West. The English word 'history' comes from the Latin, *historia,* which means a study or systematic account of real past events, narrated in a chronological fashion. The German term *Geschichte* (or *geschiedenis* in Dutch) is derived from the verb, *geschehen,* which means 'to happen' or 'to occur'. Thus history is something that have actually happened and historians define history as a set of facts about the development of human society.

Historical literature has attracted much attention from scholars and various in-depth studies have been undertaken. However, scholars are still divided over the value of historical literature. There are some who argue that historical literature makes no distinction between myth and history. R. A. Kern, for example, argued that historical literature should not be taken seriously because, although it contains elements of history, it is deeply mired in fairytales and fantasy (J. J. Ras, 1968: 12-15). Even J. C. Bottoms, who espoused the study of historical literature as a possible source of Malay history, claimed that the Malays regarded their own historical literature as being nothing more than a form of entertainment: "Accuracy, completeness, organised exposition were not the vital principles; what best pleased were legend, fantasy, and a pleasant hotchpotch of court and port gossip" (J. C. Bottoms, 1962: 180).

On the other hand, some scholars have recognized the value of Malay historical literature. Writing on the *Salasilah Kutai* in 1888, Snouck Hurgronje commented that historical writings are a particularly interesting branch of literature. An awareness of such writings provides an insight into the Malay character, as well as into Malay laws and customs.

Hoesein Djajadiningrat too has paid tribute to the value of historical writings. He considers historical literature, which he refers to as "local traditions", to be a valuable source of historical data. He argues that without the *Hikayat Raja-Raja Pasai,* for example, it would not have been possible to ascertain the identity of a historical figure like Malikul Saleh, whose gravestone can be found in Samudera (H. Djajadiningrat, 1965: 75-76).

R. O. Winstedt too has given due recognition to historical literature. While speaking of the *Hikayat Merong Mahawangsa,* a work based more on fantasy than historical truth, he nevertheless argued that the more contemporaneous an account is with the life and times of its writer, the more relevant and reliable it will be as history. Furthermore, Winstedt widely refers to works of historical literature in his many studies of the history of the Malay states. This is perhaps the highest tribute ever paid to Malay historical literature.

Let us now examine the structure of Malay historical literature or historiography. Historical literature usually consists of two strands. The first is mythical or legendary in nature. Its contents tell of ancient times, the origins of kings and the beginning of their reigns, as well as how and why a certain custom or tradition came into being, and so on.

In the *Sejarah Melayu* (Malay Annals), for example, it is said that the Malay kings were the descendants of Raja Iskandar (Alexander the Great), who came down from Bukit Si Guntang. In the *Hikayat Raja-Raja Pasai* (The Pasai Chronicles), the King of Pasai is said to be descended from a boy raised by an elephant and a girl found in a clump of bamboo (Putri Betung, Bamboo Princess). In *Hikayat Aceh,* the kings of Acheh are also said to have been the descendants of a man who married a princess who emerged from a clump of bamboo (Putri Buluh, Bamboo Princess). Almost all Malay historical literature begins with a similar story, in which the ruling monarch is said to be descended from a mighty king such as Raja Iskandar or the Prophet Adam (as in *Sejarah Tambusi*). At the very least, these kings claimed an extraordinary royal ancestor, possibly a legendary female ancestor such as Putri Betung, Putri Buih (Bubble Princess), Putri Kayangan (Celestial Princess), a prince or princess who was the product of ascetic practices.

The second strand is more historical, especially when the author is talking about events which happened in his lifetime. Even then, tales which discredit the king are usually minimized or sometimes excluded altogether. A good example is the revised version of the *Sejarah Melayu,* composed in 1612. This version deliberately highlights the relationship between the sultan and the *Bendahara* (treasurer), who later became the last Sultan of Malaka. Sultan Alauddin Syah is said to be the son of Sultan Mansur Syah and the Bendahara's daughter. According to the original version of *Sejarah Melayu,* however, Sultan Alauddin Syah was Raja Radin, the son of Sultan Mansur Syah and a Javanese woman. Both the original and the 1612 version fail to mention the sultan's brother, Sulaiman Syah, although his name is mentioned in the Portuguese records and his gravestone has been found in Sayong, Johor. Stories that are considered historical therefore still need to be verified against Portuguese, Dutch or English records before they can be considered to be accurate historical sources.

In some respects, Malay historical literature is similar to Javanese literature. Both aim to explain the divine nature of the king and his actions. Both trace the genealogy of the ruler to divine kings descended from heavenly beings. The similarity between the two, however, ends here. The Javanese believed that the king is more than a worldly sovereign. He is a living god on earth, who possesses supernatural powers. By deifying and venerating these former kings, it was believed that these spiritual forces could be revived and the powers of the current king enhanced. For this reason, Javanese historical literature was often loose with facts and aimed instead to construct narratives tracing the king's ancestry to supernatural forces in order to legitimize his power and right to rule (Hall, 1962: 4). We need to recognize this background if we are to make proper use of historical literature.

Another type of historical literature is that of the Buginese and Makasarese. Buginese historical literature is usually more credible than either the Malay or the Javanese. The Buginese were in the habit of keeping diaries, saving treaty documents and recording the genealogies of their kings. They then used these documents to compile their historical records. As a result, whenever we read Malay historical literature that is influenced by Buginese tradition, we often find the narrative to be rather disjointed. An episode in one chapter sometimes seems to have no relation at all to other episodes within the same chapter. This tendency can be seen in the *Silsilah Melayu dan Bugis*, *Tuhfat Al-Nafis* and, to some extent, in the *Sejarah Raja-Raja Riau* and *Hikayat Johor*.

Buginese historical literature can also be divided into two parts. The first presents myths and legends about divine kings who have come from the celestial realm. However, in this case the author frequently uses words such as *"konon"* ("it is said that"), *"menurut setengah kaul"* ("according to some accounts"), and so on. The second is the historical part. The narrative here is often Buginese-centric and intended to glorify the Buginese themselves (J. Noorduyn, 1965: 138).

The following is a discussion of some of the more important works of Malay historical literature.

8.1 *Hikayat Raja-Raja Pasai*

The *Pasai Chronicles* is the oldest surviving work of historical literature in Malay. It tells of events that took place from 1250 to 1350, from the reign of Malikul Saleh to the Majapahit conquest of Pasai. Winstedt contends that this hikayat, or at least part of it, has been quoted, at times verbatim, in Chapters 7 and 9 of the *Sejarah Melayu,* and therefore a large part of this hikayat had certainly been written before 1511 when the first part of *Sejarah Melayu* was still being written. He also suggests that the hikayat was unlikely to have been written after 1524, when Acheh drove out the Portuguese and conquered Pasai. It is highly doubtful that a writer of the time—who customarily wrote with the primary intention of pleasing the court—would dare write anything about Pasai after it had become a part of the Achehnese kingdom. Winstedt therefore concluded that the *Hikayat Raja-Raja Pasai* was written in the 14th century (Winstedt, 1938: 129).

Winstedt further adds that the influence of the *Hikayat Raja-Raja Pasai* on the *Sejarah Melayu* was not only confined to its adaptation and incorporation in Chapters 7 and 9 of the latter. Its writing style and the way it was written too were followed in the *Sejarah Melayu*. For example, the etiological myths which explain the origin of place names, the tale of Hang Tuah's travels, and the story of how the King of Malaka embraced Islam, are all taken from the *Hikayat Raja-Raja Pasai*.

The language used in the hikayat is good Malay with very few archaisms, with the exception of the use of the interrogative particle *"kutaha"*.

A. H. Hill, who edited the *Hikayat Raja-Raja Pasai* and translated it into English, believes that this hikayat is the oldest Malay literary work in Malakan Malay. He points out that in the *Hikayat Raja-Raja Pasai* one can find early traces of *"bahasa dalam"* (court language). Although many archaisms, including *"kutaha"*, had begun to disappear from Malay literature, a few of them can still be found in the hikayat, for example, *"nentiosa"* (for *"senantiasa"* [always]), *"penah"* (for *"pernah"* [used to, has/have]), *"kendiri"* (for *"sendiri"* [alone, by oneself]) and *"mangkin"* (for *"makin"* [more]*)* (Hill, 1960: 29-31).

R. Roolvink suggests that the writer of the *Sejarah Melayu* must have read a manuscript of the *Hikayat Raja-Raja Pasai* which is now no longer available. Much that later appeared in the *Sejarah Melayu* was definitely not taken from the *Hikayat Raja-Raja Pasai* as we know now it; the names of several characters and other many small details are very different from the tale of Pasai found in the *Sejarah Melayu* (Roolvink, 1954: 3). The present manuscript of *Hikayat Raja-Raja Pasai* was transcribed by Raffles' scribe in Batavia in 1814 (or 1819, according to Roolvink).

However, A. Teeuw disagrees with Winstedt. According to Teeuw's in-depth study of the text of the *Hikayat Raja-Raja Pasai,* the hikayat could not possibly have been written before the *Sejarah Melayu.* The tales in the *Sejarah Melayu,* he maintains, make more sense, they are not exaggerated and they are told in a humorous way, whereas the text of the *Hikayat Raja-Raja Pasai* was clearly written to exalt Pasai. If it is indeed true that the *Sejarah Melayu* borrowed from the *Hikayat Raja-Raja Pasai,* then those chapters would certainly have been written in such a way as to denigrate Pasai, because when this section of the *Sejarah Melayu* was written, Malaka was at the peak of its glory and Pasai was already in decline. Teeuw points out four different instances where the *Hikayat Raja-Raja Pasai* made errors in its narrative, while maintaining that the stories in the *Sejarah Melayu* appear to be, in contrast, closer to historical truth. Teeuw concludes that it is impossible that the *Hikayat Raja-Raja Pasai* could have been written before the *Sejarah Melayu* (Teeuw, 1964: 222-234).

Another scholar, Amin Sweeney, however, disputes Teeuw's theory. Sweeney is convinced that the *Hikayat Raja-Raja Pasai* was written well before the *Sejarah Melayu*. The reason he offers, however, differs from those of Winstedt and Hill. Based on the use of the words *"ia"* (he), *"sabda"* (declared), and *"ujar"* (said), Sweeney argues that the writer of the *Sejarah Melayu* was indeed influenced by the *Hikayat Raja-Raja Pasai* (Sweeney, 1967b: 94-105).

We have already suggested that the *Hikayat Raja-Raja Pasai* is a work of historical literature. To what extent can this hikayat be seen as a source of history?

Malikul Saleh was the first king of Pasai to embrace Islam. He was indeed a historical figure. His gravestone had been found—it was imported from Cambay (Khambhat in Gujarat). It is also plausible that a court intrigue led to the murder of this valiant and mighty prince. The same can be said about the story of Majapahit's conquest of Pasai. We need to be mindful however that although the hikayat is based on history, the stories it tells are more fictional than they are historical. Below is a summary of the hikayat, based on Hill's 1960 text.

1.1.1 Summary

Pasai was the first kingdom to embrace Islam. Two kings once lived in Pasai, Raja Ahmad and Raja Muhammad: they were brothers. One day, Raja Muhammad went on an expedition to clear the forest to build his kingdom. While clearing the forest, he found a young girl in a clump of bamboos. He named her Putri Betung (Bamboo Princess). Not long after, when Raja Ahmad was out hunting, he found a boy riding on top of an elephant. He adopted the boy and named him Merah Gajah. When the boy grew up, Raja Muhammad married him to Putri Betung. The couple had two boys named Merah Silu and Merah Hasum.

One day, Merah Gajah playfully plucked a strand of hair from the head of his wife Putri Betung. She began to bleed profusely and shortly afterwards died. Enraged, Raja Muhammad killed Merah Gajah. The death of Merah Gajah angered Raja Ahmad. The two brothers declared war on each other and both of them lost their lives in the ensuing battle. Merah Silu and Merah Hasum left the kingdom to look for a better place to start their lives afresh.

Merah Silu came to a river where he made himself a net to catch fish. Instead of fish, he caught worms; the worms turned to gold and he became very rich. The brothers quarrelled and Merah Silu decided to go his separate way.

He travelled upstream and met Megat Iskandar, who became very fond of him. Not long after, Merah Silu was crowned as the new king. Megat Iskandar's brother, Sultan Malikul Nasar, felt that he been bypassed and became very angry. He ordered his army to attack Merah Silu. The attack failed, however, and Sultan Malikul Nasar was forced to flee for his life.

Meanwhile, Merah Silu built a new city in a place where he encountered a giant ant (*semut besar*). The fame of the city, which he named Samudra, soon reached Mecca. In fulfillment of a command made by the Prophet Muhammad, the Governor of Mecca dispatched a ship's captain named Syaikh Ismail to bring Raja Muhammad from Mengiri to Samudra. That very night, Merah Silu dreamed that Prophet Muhammad came and taught him how to recite the Profession of Faith. The prophet also told Merah Silu that he would be crowned king and known as Malikul Saleh, the Pious King. The next day, Syaikh Ismail and Raja Muhammad, who was now a holy man, arrived. Without their having to teach him, Merah Silu already knew how to recite the Creed and the Quran. They crowned him and named him Malikul Saleh. His subjects willingly embraced Islam. Samudra was henceforth called Darul Islam, the Abode of Islam. Its two senior officials were Sayid Ali Ghiatul-din and Sayid Asmayuddin.

Sultan Malikul Saleh enjoyed a long reign. He married Putri Ganggang, the princess of Perlak. Not long after, Putri Ganggang became pregnant and gave birth to a son named Sultan Malikul Zahir.

Sultan Malikul Saleh founded the kingdom of Pasai. When he was old enough, his son, Sultan Malikul Zahir, was the next to assume the throne. Sultan Malikul Zahir had two sons, Sultan Malikul Mahmud and Sultan Malikul Mansur. When he came of age, Sultan Malikul Mahmud ascended the throne of Pasai and appointed Sayid Ghiatul-din as his prime minister. His brother, Sultan Malikul Mansur, became the ruler of Samudra, with Sayid Asmayuddin as his minister.

Samudra and Pasai soon flourished; they prospered and their population rapidly increased. Upon hearing of Pasai's rise, the Ruler of Siam became jealous and sent his army against the kingdom. Thanks to the courage of the forces of Pasai, the attack was successfully repelled. Pasai's fame continued to spread far and wide.

Sultan Malikul Mahmud had two daughters and a son, named Sultan Ahmad Perumudal Perumal.

One day during an expedition to Pasai, Sultan Malikul Mansur passed his brother's palace. Sultan Malikul Mahmud was away at that time. Sultan Malikul Mansur saw a very beautiful woman came out of the palace. He took her back to his own palace. When Sultan Malikul Mahmud heard about this, he was furious and hatched a plan to take revenge.

One day, Sultan Malikul Mahmud invited Sultan Malikul Mansur and his minister Asmayuddin to attend a celebration. Upon his arrival, Sultan Malikul Mansur was immediately arrested and thrown into prison. His minister, Asmayuddin, was beheaded. Not long after however, Sultan Malikul Mahmud regretted his harsh actions and decided to free his brother. After his release, Sultan Malikul Mansur visited Asmayuddin's grave and died while at the cemetery. Soon after this, Sultan Malikul Mahmud too died and was succeeded by his son, Sultan Ahmad.

Sultan Ahmad had thirty children, five of them from the same mother. The eldest, Tun Beraim Bapa, was known for his bravery. The second, Tun Abdul Jalil, was renowned for his handsomeness; and the third, Tun Abdul Fazil, was famed for his piety. His fourth and fifth children were daughters; their beauty was celebrated throughout the land.

Unfortunately however, Sultan Ahmad lusted after one of his own daughters. One of his ministers warned Sultan Ahmad against his incestuous intentions, but his counsel fell on deaf ears. When Tun Beraim Bapa was told about his father's unnatural lust for one of his sisters, he took his younger siblings and gave them refuge in his abode in Tukas.

8.2 *Sejarah Melayu*

The *Sejarah Melayu* or *Sulalatus Salatin* ("line of royal succession", Arabic) is considered the most important Malay historical work. The *Sejarah Melayu* has long captured the attention of scholars because of its refined language and depiction of medieval Malay society. It was published in 1831 by Munsyi Abdullah for the use of those who wished to learn the correct form of Malay language. Over the following 150 years, the *Sejarah Melayu* had been published many times and translated into various languages, including English, French and Chinese. The book has been the subject of many studies. These have particularly focused on the original form of the text, why it was written, its themes, and who its author (or editor) was.

8.2.1 The Original Text

According to R. Roolvink (1967: 301-324), the *Sejarah Melayu* was originally composed as a Malay royal genealogical record. Roolvink based his conclusion on comments by Francois Valentijn and Petrus van der Vorm at the beginning of the eighteenth century, and his own study of a manuscript held in the library of Leiden University, the *Ceritera asal raja-raja Melayu punya keturunan* (An account of the genealogical origins of the Malay kings). In the foreword to his Malay dictionary, *Collectanea Malaica Vocabularia* (1707-1708), Petrus van der Vorm gave a brief account of the history of the Malays, drawn from a genealogical list of Malay kings, which contained the years of their accession to the throne and the length of their reigns. He also provided a list of Malay manuscripts in his possession, which included the *Sulalatus Salatin*. Commenting on this book, Van der Vorm remarked: "Anyone interested in the Malay language ought to study the work entitled *Sulalatus Salatin*, or the lineage of all kings, not only on account of the language but also because of the contents which inform us about the descent of the Malay kings and the fortunes of the Malay kingdom till the coming of the Portuguese." Twenty years later, Valentijn mentioned in his *Oud en Nieuw Oost-Indien* (1726) that he possessed a book called *Soelalet Essalatina* written in the Roman script. He too gave an account of the history of the Malays and a genealogical list of their kings, with dates based on the Gregorian calendar.

From the accounts of Valentijn and Van der Vorm, it is clear that the texts of the *Sejarah Melayu* at their disposal were very different from any version that we know of today, be it the text of the highly-esteemed Raffles 18 version or any other version. The manuscript to which they referred was definitely a genealogical record of the Malay kings, a true *Sulalatus Salatin*. It is difficult however to determine the manuscript to which they actually referred. Nevertheless, Roolvink claimed that he had found a manuscript in the Leiden University library which bears strong similarities with the manuscript used by Valentijn and Van der Vorm: Cod. Or. 3199 (3), part 4. The title, *"Cerita Asal raja-raja Melayu punya keturunan"*, is an accurate translation of *Sulalatus Salatin*. Like the manuscript used by Valentijn dan Van der Vorm, this manuscript also provides the length of each king's reign as well as the dates of their coronation and death. This information is unique to this manuscript. The Raffles 18 manuscript provides information on how long each king ruled but does not give the dates for the beginning and ends of reigns; whereas the Shellabear and the Abdullah texts provide no data for either event.

Did the *Sejarah Melayu* develop from a genealogical king list? Roolvink does not think that it is possible to provide the definitive answer to this question. He quotes W. Linehan, who speaks of: "the first written material (pedigrees etc.) [which] formed a basis for the chronicle that ultimately emerged as the Malay Annals." Roolvink also mentions that E. Netscher's history of Riau, 1854, drew on three manuscripts of the *Sulalatu'l-Salatin*, information provided by the Raja Muda and his brother, as well as "an accurate and thorough comparison of dates found in some Malay manuscripts". His most convincing evidence comes from the Maxwell 105 manuscript in the library of the Royal Asiatic Society, London. On the fly-leaf of this manuscript is a note written by Winstedt that reads: "This MS. starts off as an abbreviated *Sejarah Melayu* and ends with the history of Johor and especially of Perak." This is a significant discovery. The Maxwell 105 manuscript provides no dates but does mention the length of time that each Malay king ruled. Its contents had become much more expanded than a king list but at the same time are much shorter than the text of Raffles 18. Is this manuscript an abridged *Sejarah Melayu*, or is the Raffles 18 an enlarged version of Maxwell 105? The second possibility, Roolvink suggests, cannot be dismissed offhand. What is clear is that there is a close connection between the Maxwell 105 and Raffles 18 versions. The entire first section of Maxwell 105 can be found scattered throughout Raffles 18. The opening lines of Maxwell 105 can be found on p. 51 of the printed text of Raffles 18 and the closing passage of the first part on p. 216.

To summarise: it is clear that Roolvink believes that the *Sejarah Melayu* as we know it today has possibly passed through several stages of development. It began as a king list, which stated the duration of each king's reign and gave the relevant dates. This list was then expanded with various stories to become a manuscript like the Maxwell 105; and was further enlarged with other tales and anecdotes, resulting in a manuscript similar to the Raffles 18. At the same time as the text was being enlarged, its dates were omitted.

The expansion of the *Sejarah Melayu* however did not stop there. After the fall of Malaka in 1511, a manuscript akin to the Raffles 18 was taken to Goa and it was not until the eighteenth century that the manuscript was brought back to the Riau archipelago to be further augmented. This manuscript is referred to as the "*Hikayat yang dibawa orang dari Goa*"(The chronicle that came from Goa).Where is Goa? G. A. Gibson-Hill believed that Goa referred to the Portuguese colony in India. Linehan, on the other hand, argued that Goa referred to Gua Sai, Sai Cave, on the bank of River Jelai in northern Kuala Lipis, Ulu Pahang. Meanwhile, Roolvink argued that Goa was in Sulawesi. In the eighteenth century, the Buginese brought a manuscript similar to Raffles 18 to the Riau Archipelago. This manuscript was further revised within the royal circle of the Yamtuan Muda of Riau, resulting in two different versions of the *Sejarah Melayu*, a shorter and a longer version. The main differences between the two are as follows:

(i) the longer version contains a more detailed and extensive history of the Minangkabau;

(ii) in the longer version, Hang Tuah was a prince who was given to the King of Malaka by the King of Makasar;

(iii) the shorter version ends with the death of Tuan Ali Hati, whereas the longer version continues on with other stories;

(iv) in the shorter version, the rebellion of Hang Jebat is ascribed to Hang Kasturi.

Besides these texts, there is another version of the *Sejarah Melayu* written from the point of view of the Kingdom of Siak, called the *Hikayat Siak* (Muhammad Yusoff Hashim, 1988).

That concludes our summary of Roolvink's views concerning the original form and the development of the *Sejarah Melayu*. Besides the reasons already put forward, perhaps it should also be mentioned that almost all the known versions of the *Sejarah Melayu* (Abdullah, Shellabear, Raffles 18) bear the title, *Sulalatus Salatin*, which is usually translated in Malay as *"peraturan segala raja-raja"* ("the regulation of all kings"). Roolvink argues that *"peraturan segala raja-raja"* is an error; the original words *"pertuturan segala raja-raja"* are still to be found in several manuscripts. The word *"pertuturan"* is also written in the Raffles 18 text but as Winstedt did not recognise the meaning of *tutur,* he romanised it as *"peraturan"*. The archaic sense of the word *"tutur"* in Malay was "a relative" or "family relation", as it still is in Toba Batak; it carried the same meaning as *"keturunan"*, "ancestry".

8.2.2 Purposes and Main Themes

The *Sejarah Melayu* was written to emphasise the sovereignty and the greatness of the Malay rulers. It was hoped that in this way the king's sovereign power would lead his subjects to fear him and give him their undivided loyalty, and inspire lesser kings to offer him their obeisance. Loyalty and the profound discouragement of treason are paramount concepts in Hindu culture; the *Sejarah Melayu* presents these within an Islamic framework. Loyalty is accorded to the king not because he is a god or the manifestation of a divine being, but as a result of a compact between Sri Tri Buana, the first Malay king, and the subordinate Demang Lebar Daun. According to their covenant, Tri Buana swore not to shame his Malay subjects, and in return, Demang Lebar Daun promised that the Malays would never commit treason or betray their king, no matter how vile and despicable he was. This close nexus between the king and his subjects is so vital that it is repeatedly emphasised by various kings in their dying words. The king and his subjects are like a tree and its roots: "Without its roots, a tree cannot stand." As such, a king must treat his subjects justly and offer them his protection. The *Sejarah Melayu* provides many cautionary tales about wayward rulers whose actions brought about the downfall of their kingdoms, including Singapore and Malaka.

Although the *Sejarah Melayu* was written with the intention of promoting the greatness of the Malay kings, its author did not take this to extremes. For example, Sultan Muhammad Syah (1422-1444) was described only as *"terlalu adil baginda pada memeliharakan segala rakyat"* ("very just in his treatment of all his subjects"). Sultan Muzaffar Syah (1445-1458) was said to be *"terlalu adil, murah, saksama pada memeriksai segala rakyat"* ("very just, generous and fair in his dealings with his people"). And Sultan Alauddin Ri'ayat Syah (1477-1488) was said to be *"terlalu perkasa pada zaman itu"* ("a very courageous king in his time"). The story is also told of how Sultan Alauddin often patrolled his kingdom at night and once caught a robber who was out prowling. Sultan Mahmud Syah (1488-1528) is simply described as *"terlalu baik sikapnya, tiada berbagai"* ("kind beyond compare"). On the other hand, the flaws of the Malay kings did not escape the writer's attention. The most severe criticism is reserved for Sultan Mahmud. He is portrayed as a man who could not resist the sight of a beautiful woman. Sultan Mahmud kidnapped Tun Teja, the fiancée of the king of Pahang; he dallied with Tun Biajit's wife; and in a fit of jealous rage, he killed Tun Ali when the latter was found at the home of his favourite mistress. He also had Raja Zainal Abidin killed simply because he was so handsome that the mere sight of him deeply disturbed the women in the country. Sri Bija Diraja too was killed for having the audacity to make the king wait for him to make an appearance at court. But the king's most heinous crime was killing the Bendahara and his entire family simply because the Bendahara refused to "show" his daughter, Tun Fatimah, to him.

Regardless of this, the Malays are still portrayed as being superior to other people, often in a semi-humorous manner. One episode in the *Sejarah Melayu* tells of a ruse used by Tun Perpatih Puteh, who led a delegation of Malays from Malaka to China. It was forbidden to look at the Emperor's face. The Malays introduced the emperor to *kangkung* (a type of water spinach), which they said was a special Malakan delicacy. While the emperor sat on a dais, the delegation threw their heads back and raised the uncut *kangkung*, while keeping their eyes open. They told the emperor's court officials this was the traditional Malakan way of eating *kangkung*. In this manner, the Malays were able to catch a glimpse of the Chinese emperor's face, something which no Chinese had ever done before them. The cleverness of the Malays is also highlighted in the stories told in connection with the Sultan of Malaka's visit to Majapahit. Try as they might, even the best fighters could not deprive the Malay princes of their kerises, even though they managed to divest other princes of their weapons. The Malays were also bold enough to enter the *balai larangan*, the forbidden section of the court that was used by the Majapahit princesses. They broke royal protocol when they sat with their legs outstretched in front of the Queen of Majapahit, in the pretext of playing a children's game, *sapu-sapu ringin*. So clever were they, that the Malays were able to outwit the Siamese who had never been defeated by any other people. Once, the King of Siam decided to attack Malaka. But before they could, the Siamese forces turned back and fled. The Bendahara Paduka Raja had sent the extremely courageous Tun Umar to ram the Siamese prows and ordered his men to tie a firebrand to every tree along the Malakan coast to frighten the Siamese away. Malay wit and ingenuity are again celebrated when the *Sejarah Melayu* makes fun of Maulana Sadar Johan, an avaricious ulama from the holy city of Mecca, who, because of his poor mastery of the Malay language, lost a verbal duel with a Malay nobleman. Such is the *Sejarah Melayu*'s opinion of the cleverness of the Malay race.

8.2.3 Author and Date of Composition

Before we can proceed to discuss this topic, we must decide to which text we are referring, as the *Sejarah Melayu* was written by different authors at different times. According to Roolvink (1967), there are at least seven versions of this text: a genealogical king list which details the ancestry of Malay rulers, a version represented by Maxwell 105, the Raffles 18 version, a shorter version, a longer version, a Siak version and a Palembang version. Most of these versions have not been fully studied and it is difficult to ascertain who their respective authors are or when they were written. Only the Raffles 18, the shorter, and the longer versions, state the identity of their authors and the dates of composition. Even so, scholars have not reached a consensus on these matters. According to Roolvink, the Raffles 18 text was composed in 1612 (1021 Hijrah); the shorter and longer versions were composed after 1720, possibly during the second half of the eighteenth century. Roolvink does not mention any author. According to Winstedt, on the other hand, the Raffles 18, the "*Hikayat Melayu yang dibawa orang dari Goa*", was definitely written before 1532. It was subsequently edited and improved in 1612, and the shorter and longer versions of the *Sejarah Melayu* followed. Winstedt describes the author as possibly "a half-caste Tamil" but certainly a man of "cosmopolitan culture", familiar with life in the palace, well-versed in Sanskrit, Persian, Tamil and Arab, and knowing a little Chinese and Thai. He also had an extensive knowledge of Islamic, Javanese and Indian literature, and was also most probably a Sufi (Winstedt, 1958: 129-131). Further, Winstedt is convinced that the editor of the shorter and longer versions was Tun Bambang—also known by his title, Sri Nara Wangsa—the son of Sri Akar Raja. His father was Raja Abdullah's brother.

The more commonly accepted view, however, is that Tun Sri Lanang, the Bendahara Paduka Raja, wrote—or at least definitively edited—the *Sejarah Melayu*. This claim is based on the following factors:

(1) Tun Sri Lanang's name is mentioned in the foreword of both the shorter and the longer versions.

(2) Section 12, Chapter 12 of the *Bustanus Salatin* also states that the *Sulalatus Salatin* was written by a Bendahara Paduka Raja named Tun Sri Lanang.

The foreword tells that, during the celebration of Prophet Muhammad's birthday on Sunday, 13 May 1612, which was attended by many distinguished guests, a high dignitary, Raja Abdullah, the younger brother of Sultan Alauddin Ri'ayat Syah, ordered the *Bendahara* to improve upon "a hikayat from Goa, containing various customs and traditions", so that "later generations would know what it had to say and benefit from its contents". The Bendahara was overwhelmed by the request, as he considered himself "*fakir alladzi huwa murakkabun ala jahilin*" (a humble servant, cognizant of his own deficiencies and ignorance). Bearing in mind, however, that he was a man of noble upbringing (he then proceeds to describe his lineage and its origin from Batu Sawah at the source of the Johor river), he accepted the task.

The task obviously took some time. A year later, in 1613, the King of Acheh and his armada attacked Johor. Sultan Alauddin, Raja Abdullah and all the members of the nobility, including the Bendahara, were captured and taken to Acheh. Sultan Alauddin died shortly thereafter. Raja Abdullah married the younger sister of Sultan Iskandar Muda, the King of Acheh, and was subsequently pardoned. Sultan Iskandar Muda sent Raja Abdullah back home to Johor and installed him there as king. As the newly crowned ruler of Johor, Raja Abdullah ordered the Bendahara to complete his task of improving the chronicle from Goa. The Bendahara worked assiduously on the task and eventually completed the *Sejarah Melayu* as far as the thirty-fourth chapter. In 1615, an armada from Acheh again attacked Johor. This time, however, Raja Abdullah managed to escape capture and continually moved from one hiding place to another. The tale of his adventures during this tumultuous time is told in chapters 35 to 38, which were added to subsequent editions of the *Sejarah Melayu*. There are still another eight more stories which have not been included in any published edition of the *Sejarah Melayu* to date (Hooykaas, 1947: 97).

Although Hooykaas and T. Iskandar (1964) agree that Tun Sri Lanang was the author of the *Sejarah Melayu,* Winstedt and Wilkinson did not accept this claim. Winstedt notes that the preface to the Raffles 18 text does not mention Tun Sri Lanang's name at all. Secondly, the Raffles 18 manuscript gives the correct place and day the text was compiled, that is: in Pasir Raja on Sunday; and not in Pasai on Thursday (Winstedt, 1938: 40). Wilkinson, in turn, points out that it was traditionally very unusual for a Malay to identify himself as the author of a piece of work. Even when a Malay author did refer to himself in the text, he did so with the greatest humility, often employing such self-deprecating epithets as "*fakir yang jahil murakkab*" (I am but a benighted fool) to describe himself. The author of the *Sejarah Melayu* apparently however proved to be an exception to this norm. After declaring himself an ignorant fool, Tun Sru Lanang then suddenly deigned to reveal his own name as the author of the text as well as who his forefathers were. Moreover, the Bendahara's genealogy given in the *Sejarah Melayu* is also incorrect (Wilkinson, 1933: 148).

8.2.4 The *Sejarah Melayu* as an Historical Work

If we were to assess the *Sejarah Melayu* in terms of the definition given by British historian, R. G. Collingwood, that history should be scientific, humanistic, rational and self-revelatory (Collingwood, 1961: 18), then the *Sejarah Melayu* is definitely not an historical work. But how many historical works produced by the other nations of the world can fulfill this criteria? The answer is very few, if at all. Each nation has its own tradition of writing history (historiography).

The Arab historian Al-Mas'udi (died in 956) for example, defined history as a retelling of events that revolved around kings, dynasties and particular momentous occasions. The Javanese conceived history as a narrative that augments and legitimizes the authority and power of the king, sanctioning his right to rule the world and his subjects. To the Chinese, history should be held up as a "mirror" to kings, and the role of the historian is to apportion praise or blame in assessing a king's reign, condemning tyranny and extolling justice. The fact remains that even though the *Sejarah Melayu* cannot be considered a historical work in terms of the modern conception of history, it is still the greatest piece of historical writing in Malay. It provides us with a clear picture of the development of Malay society over several centuries and teaches us how the Malays saw the world in which they lived. The *Sejarah Melayu* is undoubtedly a rich and valuable source of history. Roolvink partially admitted this when he wrote: "The Malay Annals or *Sejarah Melayu* as we know it today is primarily a book of tales and anecdotes of the past and not so much a historical work, although it contains a wealth of historical material" (Roolvink 1967: 306).

8.2.5 The *Sejarah Melayu* as a Literary Work

History has a close connection with literature. History must be well written if it is to bring the situation it describes to life. In turn, literature can use historical events to serve as its material. In ancient Greece and China, history was considered to belong to the domain of literature. *The History of the Decline and Fall of the Roman Empire*, by the English historian Edward Gibbon, is also regarded as a classic work of literature. Can the *Sejarah Melayu* be considered a work of literature? The answer is "yes". The *Sejarah Melayu* is a great literary work. It gives such a vivid picture of past events, such as the kidnapping of Tun Teja, the competition among traders in Malaka, the arrival of the Portuguese and the fall of the Malakan Sultanate, that we can almost see them happening in front of us. The narrative techniques employed in the *Sejarah Melayu* are also the equal to any used today. For example, the author does not need an abundance of adjectives to depict Hang Tuah's good looks. He simply states that wherever Hang Tuah went, women left their husbands' embraces in order to catch a glimpse of him. To describe beauty without using beautiful words is a difficult art, especially in poetry.

Below is a summary of the Raffles 18 version of *Sejarah Melayu*.

8.2.6 Summary

1. The hikayat opens by offering praises to Allah, the Prophet Muhammad and his companions. This is followed by an account telling that, in 1021 H (1612 AD), during the reign of Sultan Alauddin Ri'ayat Syah, whose capital was in Pasir Raja, Tun Bambang conveyed the request of the Yang Dipertuan Dihilir (the Regent of Johor) to the Bendahara, asking him to compose a genealogy showing the lineage of the Malay kings. So the Bendahara wrote a hikayat based on what he had heard from his ancestors and the wise men of old.

    The story begins with an attack by Raja Iskandar Dzulkarnain (Alexander the Great) on Hind (the Persian name for India). The vanquished Hindi king, Raja Kida, gave his daughter, Princess Syahrul Bariah, in marriage to Raja Iskandar. Princess Syahrul Bariah bore Alexander a son. This first chapter gives an account of Raja Iskandar's descendants down to Raja Suran Padshah.

2. Raja Sulan, the ruler of Nagapatam in India, set out to conquer other kingdoms. He conquered every state he came across, including Gangga Nagara and Lenggui. He took the princess of Lenggui to be his wife, then returned to India, where he established a vast empire named Bija Nagara.

After Raja Sulan passed away, his grandson Raja Chulan became the new ruler. Every other country submitted to him, except China. So Raja Chulan set out with his army to conquer China. On their way there, they camped at Temasik (present day Singapore). Upon learning that Raja Chulan intended to invade his country, the Emperor of China sent a boat to Temasik, loaded with rusty needles, flowering fruit trees and old men, to deceive Raja Chulan. Raja Chulan fell for the trick, believing that China must indeed be a very long way away, and returned to India.

Raja Chulan was taken by Raja Aftabul Ardl to his kingdom under the ocean and married his daughter, Princess Mahtabul Bahri. Three sons were born from this marriage. Raja Chulan later returned to India and married the daughter of the Raja of Hindustan. The rulers of Bija Nagara are descended from this union, to the present day.

3. One night, two women who owned a rice field, Wan Empuk and Wan Malini, saw a bright light shining like a fire at the top of Mount Si Guntang. When they investigated the next day, they found that the summit of the hill had turned to gold. Three young men were standing there: Bicitram, Paladutani and Nilatanam. They were the grandsons of Raja Iskandar from the line of Raja Nusyirwan, and were descended from Raja Sulaiman (King Solomon). Wan Empuk and Wan Malini immediately became very rich.

The ruler of Palembang, Demang Lebar Daun, heard of the three princes and took them back to his kingdom. Many monarchs came to pay homage to the three princes. Soon after, the eldest prince was invited to become the ruler of Minangkabau region in Andalas, with the title Sang Sapurba. The second was made king of Tanjung Pura, with the title Sang Maniaka. The youngest was crowned Raja of Palembang by Demang Lebar Daun, who became his *mangkubumi* (regent).

One day, foam came from the mouth of a cow belonging to Wan Empuk and Wan Malini. A man emerged from the foam. The man, whose name was Bat, read a decree, granting Sang Utama the title of Sri Tri Buana, Lord of the Three Worlds. Soon, Sri Tri Buana decided to marry and was presented with a number of princesses. Each woman contracted leprosy after sleeping with him, some thirty-nine in all. Sri Tri Buana then asked Demang Lebar Daun for his daughter, Wan Sendari. Demang Lebar Daun agreed, on the condition Sri Tri Buana would never humiliate his Malay subjects. Sri Tri Buana asked in return that Demang Lebar Daun swear that the Malay subjects shall never be disloyal to their rulers, even if their rulers behaved in a tyrannical or unjust manner. This is why no Malay king has ever shamed his subjects, and no Malay subject has ever rebelled against his king or disobeyed him.

After Sri Tri Buana and Demang Lebar Daun had made this covenant, Wan Sendari and Sri Tri Buana were married. When day broke, the king found that his bride had not been stricken by leprosy. He was overjoyed. The wedding festivities began. Kings, military chiefs and subjects ate and drank for forty days and forty nights.

Not long after, Sri Tri Buana set out to seek a suitable location for a new settlement. Accompanied by Demang Lebar Daun, his warrior-chiefs and ministers, Sri Tri Buana sailed across the seas. In Bintan, the king and his entourage were welcomed by the Queen, Wan Sri Beni. She installed Sri Tri Buana as raja of Bintan. Soon after, Sri Tri Buana took his leave again to explore the surrounding oceans. In Tanjung Bemban, he saw an island with sands as white as cotton; he was informed this was Temasik. He set out to sail to the island. During the crossing a severe storm began to blow. The voyagers were compelled to throw their treasures overboard but the boat continued to sink. Finally, Sri Tri Buana threw his crown into the ocean. The storm ceased. Sri Tri Buana and his crew safely reached Temasik. There they saw an animal. The creature was extremely fast and majestic. It was a lion (*singa*). Tri Buana named the island Singapore, City of the Lion, and requested Queen Wan Sri Beni to send him vast numbers of people, elephants and horses. He settled in Singapore. The island prospered. Traders and merchants came from every quarter. Its fame spread throughout the world.

4. The Batara of Majapahit soon heard of the prosperous kingdom of Singapore. Its king had not paid him homage and this made him angry. The Batara sent a letter to Singapore, made of a long shaving of wood as fine as paper and rolled like a woman's ear-stud. Sri Tri Buana immediately understood the meaning of the message and ordered a carpenter to shaved the hair of a little boy by using only an adze. The ambassador was then dismissed and told to take the adze back to the Batara of Majapahit. Enraged, the Batara ordered his warriors to attack Singapore. Singapore was victorious and the Javanese returned to Majapahit.

5. The princess of Bija Nagara, Talai Pacudi, was very beautiful. Word of her beauty soon reached Singapore. The raja of Singapore, Paduka Sri Pikrama, sent an envoy to ask her hand in marriage to his son. The proposal was accepted and Princess Talai Pacudi married the king's son. The Crown Prince subsequently ascended to the throne and took the title of Sri Raja Wikrama. He had the services of a warrior named Badang whose extraordinary strength was unmatched, not even by the champion of Perak.

When the king passed away, he was succeeded by his son, Dam Raja, who took the title of Paduka Sri Maharaja. The new king's wife became pregnant and produced a son, whose skull was inadvertently flattened by the midwife during the birth, and who was named Raja Iskandar the Two-horned.

6. Two brothers, Merah Caga and Merah Silu, once lived near Pasangan. One day, the younger brother, Merah Silu, found that the fish trap he had set was full of galley-worms. Disappointed, he threw the worms away and reset his trap. Again he found it filled with galley-worms. This happened several times. He boiled the worms. The galley-worms turned to gold, while the froth turned to silver. His elder brother, Merah Caga, became angry when he heard that his brother was eating sea slugs and wanted to kill him. Merah Silu fled to the Jerun forest. Before long, the inhabitants of the forest accepted Merah Silu as their leader. One day while he was out hunting, Merah Silu found an ant the size of a cat. He decided to establish a new settlement and named the place Samudera, which means "great ant" ("*semut besar*").

One night, Merah Silu dreamed that he met the Prophet Muhammad. The Prophet ordered him to open his mouth and spat into it. When Merah Silu woke from his sleep, his body smelled like musk. The next day, a ship arrived from Mecca. The captain, Syaikh Ismail, installed Merah Silu as ruler and gave him the title Sultan Malikul Saleh, the Pious King.

Not long after, Sultan Malikul Saleh sent an envoy to Perlak to ask for the hand of Princess Ganggang in marriage. The couple had two sons, Sultan Malikul Tahir and Sultan Malikul Mansur. Sultan Malikul Saleh founded a new kingdom, Pasai. He made his elder son, Sultan Malikul Tahir, the raja of Pasai and his younger son, Sultan Malikul Mansur, the *mangkubumi,* dividing his subjects, elephants, horses and royal ornaments equally between them.

The king of Syahrun Nuwi, ruler of a vast kingdom, commanded an enormous army. One day, hearing of the greatness of Samudera, he ordered one of his champions to capture the raja of Samudera. The ruler of Samudera was made to look after the royal chickens. The minister Sayid Ali Ghiyatul-din disguised himself as an Arab trader and helped the raja of Samudera escape. Meanwhile, Sultan Malikul Mansur, while on a visit to his brother's palace, carried off one of the ladies-in-waiting. Enraged, Sultan Malikul Tahir had his brother arrested and exiled to Manjung; his brother's minister, Sayid Asmayuddin, was beheaded. In time, Sultan Malikul Tahir regretted his actions and freed Sultan Malikul Mansur. His brother died beside the tomb of Sayid Asmayuddin, the minister whom Sultan Malikul Tahir had put to death.

The story then turns to Singapore. A servant of Allah, Tun Jana Khatib, was executed by the raja of Singapore for showing off his knowledge at court. Soon after, a school of swordfish attacked the coast of Singapore. A village boy suggested using a fence made of banana-tree trunks to protect the kingdom; he was cruelly sentenced to death by the ruler of Singapore for his ingenuity. Time passed and Sultan Iskandar Syah ascended the throne of Singapore. On one occasion, the sultan's mistresses became jealous of his favourite concubine and accused her of infidelity. Without further investigation, the furious sultan ordered that she be impaled in the market square. Her father, Sang Rajuna Tapa, the king's treasurer, was so shamed by the humiliation the Sultan had brought upon his daughter that he wrote to the Batara of Majapahit, inviting him to attack Singapore. When the Javanese arrived, Sang Rajuna Tapa opened the fortress gates to the invading Majapahit army. The Singapore forces broke and ran. Sultan Iskandar Syah fled to Seletar and then to Muar. By the power of Allah, Sang Rajuna Tapa's house was turned to stone.

Sultan Iskandar Syah built a new kingdom in Malaka. After 25 years on the throne, he died and was succeeded by his son, Sultan Megat. Sultan Megat ruled for only two years and was succeeded by his son, Raja Tengah. One night, Raja Tengah dreamed that he met Prophet Muhammad, who ordered him to recite the Profession of Faith. The next day, a ship arrived from Jeddah, just as the prophet had foretold in his dream. The chiefs of Malaka embraced Islam. Raja Tengah too accepted Islam and took the Muslim name of Sultan Muhammad Syah. He organised his kingdom properly and was extremely just in his dealings with his subjects, whom he rigorously protected. Malaka became a great kingdom, being visited by large numbers of merchants who settled there for long periods.

7. Mani Purindam was prince of Pahili in the Indian subcontinent. He fled to Malaka after a quarrel with his brother who succeeded to the throne of Pahili. Eventually arriving in Malaka, Mani Purindam married Sri Nara Diraja's daughter.

After fifty-seven years on the throne, Sultan Muhammad Syah died and was succeeded by his son, Raja Ibrahim, who assumed the name Sultan Abu Syahid. The raja of Rekan was made Sultan Abu Syahid's regent and ruled the country on his behalf. Raja Kassim, Sultan Abu Syahid's brother, managed to overthrow the sultan with the help of Maulana Jalaludin, and brought Malaka under his rule. During the uprising, both Sultan Abu Syahid and the raja of Rekan were killed. Raja Kassim ascended the throne, taking the title of Sultan Muzaffar Syah. He proved to be a just, compassionate and meticulous ruler. Sultan Muzaffar Syah ordered the compilation of a code of law in order that his ministers should administer justice in a uniform manner.

One day Bendahara Sri Wak Raja, mistakenly thought that the raja was angry with him. Feeling humiliated, he went home and committed suicide by taking poison. Sri Nara Diraja succeeded him as *Bendahara*.

8. The king of Siam demanded a letter of obeisance from Malaka. When the Sultan refused, the Siamese king sent an army to attack Malaka, led by his general, Awi Cakara. The attack failed and the Siamese army returned home. Next, it is related how Tun Perak sagely refuted various accusations made against him. Sultan Muzaffar Syah urged him to stay in Malaka and appointed him prime minister, with the title Paduka Raja. However, a great rivalry soon arose between Paduka Raja and Sri Nara Diraja, and the two advisers could often be found in serious disagreement. Sultan Muzaffar put an end to their hostility by giving one of his concubines, Tun Kudu, who was Paduka Raja's sister, to Sri Nara Diraja.

The King of Siam ordered another attack on Malaka, under the command of general Awi Dicu. Paduka Raja sent Tun Umar to carry a burning brand and attack the enemy fleet on his own. The Siamese were astounded. That night, Paduka Raja ordered his men to tie a firebrand to every tree along the coast. On seeing them, the Siamese decided that Malaka's forces far outnumbered their own. Greatly afraid, they fled back to Siam. Cau Pandan, the son of the Siamese king, asked his father to send him to attack Malaka. But before he could set out, Cau Pandan was struck by a magic arrow, shot by an Arab holy man in Malaka, and died.

Sultan Muzaffar Syah decided to send a mission to Siam to arrange a peace treaty and chose Tun Telanai, the Bendahara's extremely tactful son, to lead this delegation. The Siamese were impressed by the valour and wily diplomacy shown by the envoys. Tun Telanai safely returned home to Malaka. After forty years on the throne, Sultan Muzaffar Syah died. He was succeeded by his son, Sultan Abdul, who assumed the name of Sultan Mansur Syah. Sultan Mansur Syah was a just and humane ruler.

9. The Batara of Majapahit died without a male heir, and so his daughter, Raden Galuh Nai Kesuma, succeeded him. To prevent any slanders arising, her prime minister, Patih Aria Gajah Mada, advised Raden Galuh to choose a husband. She chose the son of a toddy-maker, who, it turned out, was the prince of Tanjung Pura. Together, they had a very beautiful daughter named Raden Galuh Cendera Kirana.

News of the girl's beauty reached Malaka. Sultan Mansur Syah fell in love with her. Accompanied by a retinue of brave and clever nobles, the sultan went to Majapahit to ask for her hand. When the Malays had an audience with the king, a dog tied in front of the hall took fright, broke its golden chain, and fled into the forest. The champions of Malaka even entered into the forbidden pavilion and sat with their legs stretched out before the sovereign. The Javanese warriors tried to disarm them but failed. Hang Tuah and his friends were the cleverest and most capable of all the delegates. Wherever he went, married women tore themselves away from the embrace of their husbands so that they could come out and see him. After some time, Sultan Mansur returned to Malaka, taking his wife, Princess Galuh Cendera Kirana, with him.

On one occasion, Hang Tuah had an affair with a lady-in-waiting from the sultan's palace. Sultan Mansur Syah was enraged and ordered Sri Nara Diraja to kill Hang Tuah. Sri Nara Diraja decided not to kill the young man but hid him instead. Soon after, Hang Kasturi also had sexual relations with one of the sultan's ladies-in-waiting. Hang Kasturi then took control of the palace. No one dared attack him. Hang Tuah came out of hiding and fought Hang Kasturi, his friend. Hang Kasturi was no match for Hang Tuah and was stabbed to death. Hang Kasturi's wife and children were put to death, and the pillars of his house dug up and thrown into the sea. Sultan Mansur Syah conferred the title of "Laksamana", Admiral, on Hang Tuah.

News of the greatness of the sultan of Malaka soon reached China. As a token of friendship, the Emperor of China sent his ambassador to Malaka to present the sultan with a royal barge, laden with needles. The Chinese ambassador explained to the sultan that each needle represented a house in China. The raja of Malaka received the gift graciously and in return sent Tun Perpatih Putih to China with a prow laden to the brim with beads of sago. The Emperor then sent his daughter, Princess Hang Liu, to marry the sultan. Ever since that time, the sultan of Malaka has offered tribute to the emperor of China.

Sultan Mansur Syah ordered Paduka Raja to attack Pahang. During the war, the King of Pahang, Maharaja Sura, was captured and imprisoned. Maharaja Sura was renowned for his knowledge of elephants. The Sultan ordered him to teach the children of the local nobility how to handle these animals.

10. One day the emperor of China contracted leprosy. He was cured by drinking the water that was used to wash the feet of the sultan of Malaka. After that, the emperor of China refused to accept tribute from the sultan of Malaka.

11. The King of Malaka ordered an attack on Siak, after Siak refused to pay obeisance to him. The King of Siak was killed and his children taken to Malaka.

One day, Raja Muhammad, the son of Sultan Mansur Syah, was out riding. A rattan ball belonging to Tun Besar, Bendahara Paduka Raja's son, accidentally hit him, knocking his head cloth to the ground. The prince's betel-bowl carrier killed Tun Besar. The Bendahara's followers wanted to avenge Tun Besar's death. Bendahara Paduka Raja was furious and banished his son to Pahang, where he was subsequently crowned king. Sultan Mansur Syah's reputation as a just ruler further increased. Malaka became such an important port that Arabic traders called it "Malakat", the market place.

12. The King of Semerluki was determined to conquer the various kingdoms throughout the archipelago. He destroyed numerous provinces in Java, but could not conquer Malaka and Pasai. Raja Semerluki then returned to Makasar.

    A learned man, Maulana Abu Bakar, came to Malaka, bringing a book he had written called *Dar al-Mazlum* (The Refuge of the Oppressed). Sultan Mansur Syah sent the book to Pasai to be studied there. Not long after, the sultan dispatched another envoy to Pasai; this time to propose a theological question: "Do the inhabitants of Heaven and Hell remain in those realms forever?" Even Kadi Yusuf who had converted many people to Islam later became a scholar under the tutelage of Maulana Abu Bakar.

    Sultan Mansur Syah wanted to marry the fairy Princess of Mount Ledang. He sent Laksamana and Sang Setia to ask for her hand. The princess issued a list of impossible demands, one of which was a gift of a bowl of blood from his own son. The Sultan replied that he could fulfill all of her demands but he would not hurt his son.

13. Sultan Zainul Abidin, King of Pasai, was deposed by his younger brother and fled to Malaka. The sultan of Malaka dispatched an army under his Bendahara, Sri Paduka Raja, to help Sultan Zainul Abidin resume his position. Afterwards, Zainal Abidin refused to pay homage to the Sultan of Malaka, saying that he had left his salutation in Malaka and had no intention of sending any other. The Bendahara and his men returned to Malaka. Sultan Zainul Abidin was soon faced with another rebellion. This time the Bendahara refused to help him.

14. The King of Champa found a small boy in the flower of a betel-nut tree. He adopted the boy and eventually married him to his daughter. Not long after, the King of Champa died in battle against the kingdom of Kujai. Two of his sons escaped; one went to Malaka the other to Acheh.

    After ruling for seventy-five years, Sultan Mansur Syah died. He was succeeded by his son, Raja Radin, who took the name Sultan Alauddin Ri'ayat Syah. Sultan Alauddin was known as a mighty ruler.

    When Sultan Alauddin fell gravely ill, he was cared for by Paduka Raja and the Laksamana. His grandmother, Raja Tua, was eager for Sultan Alauddin to die so that her favourite grandson, Raja Muhammad of Pahang, could become king of Malaka. Because of this, she was not allowed by the Bendahara and Laksamanato approach Sultan Alauddin during his illness. When Sultan Alauddin eventually recovered, he was grateful to both the Bendahara and Laksamana for their loyalty and service, and rewarded them each with their own palanquin. The Bendahara chose not use his palanquin, whereas the Laksamana never once missed an opportunity to do so.

    Once thieves were rampant in Malaka and this became a source of concern to the king. One night, Sultan Alauddin disguised himself and patrolled the city. He soon came across a thief carrying a treasure chest and killed him. From that day onwards, the city was better secured and peace was once again restored. Malaka became even more prosperous. Any country that put a man to death without first informing the sultan of Malaka was punished. Among the countries that were punished for violating this decree were Pahang and Siak.

15. The raja of Haru went to war with the raja of Pasai after an envoy sent by the kingdom of Haru was killed during a visit to Pasai. In retaliation, the raja of Haru sent his army to lay to

waste the territories held by Malaka. The attack was defeated by the valour of the Malakans, especially that of Sri Bija Diraja.

Next, the Sultan of Malaka attacked Kampar and installed his son, Raja Menawar, as ruler there. In time, Sultan Alauddin passed away and was succeeded by his son, Raja Mamat, who took the name Sultan Mahmud Syah.

Sultan Mahmud had both good and bad qualities. His crimes included the murder of Sri Bija Diraja, who was put to death for the trivial reason of dalliance with the wife of Tun Biajit, and the murder of his own brother, Raja Zainal Abidin. On the other hand, he was kind to Sri Wak Raja, who knew everything about elephants, and he willingly submitted to the spiritual teachings of Maulana Yusuf.

16. The King of Kampar, Sultan Menawar Syah, died. His son, Raja Abdullah, went to Malaka to pay his allegiance to Sultan Mahmud, who accepted him as his son-in-law and installed him as the King of Kampar.

    Bendahara Putih also passed away; he was replaced by Sri Maharaja Tun Mutahir, an extremely handsome, agreeable and sweet-tempered person. During Tun Mutahir's time as Bendahara, Malaka continued to flourish and its population further increased. On one occasion, the Pengeran of Surabaya, Patih Adam, came to Malaka for an audience with the sultan. While the Pengeran was seated in the palace hall, Sri Nara Diraja's daughter, who had just begun to walk, ran up to him. Upon seeing this, Sri Nara Diraja said to the Pengeran in jest that his daughter wanted to marry him. "So be it," replied the Pengeran. Several years later, Patih Adam returned to Malaka and carried her off by force.

17. The king of Kedah came to Malaka to request the *nobat* (drum of sovereignty). The sultan agreed and also gave him royal robes. Tun Perpatih Hitam, a minister, had an argument with a merchant, who complained to the Bendahara. A hearing was held with the Laksamana in attendance, as was the custom. Tun Perpatih Hitam was deemed to have insulted the Bendahara during the hearing and was summarily slain by the Laksamana. When Tun Husain, Tun Perpatih Hitam's son, saw his father slain, he drew his keris, and he too was killed.

18. Raja Narasinga, king of Indragiri, left Malaka and returned home, because his followers felt that they were being treated as vassals by the people of Malaka. Sultan Mahmud sent Hang Nadim to India to buy cloth for him. After completing his mission, Hang Nadim sailed home to Malaka.

    Unfortunately, a curse had been cast by a servant of Allah on Hang Nadim's ship and it sank. Hang Nadim escaped to Ceylon and eventually reached Malaka. However, when Sultan Mahmud learnt what had happened, he was furious with Hang Nadim for taking passage in a ship that had been cursed.

    About this time, Laksamana Hang Tuah died; he was succeeded in his office by his son-in-law, Khoja Hassan.

19. The Sultan of Malaka sent Sri Wak Raja to Pahang to crown Sultan Abdul Jamal as the new King of Pahang after the old king passed away. On his return, Sri Wak Raja told Sultan Mahmud of the beautiful Tun Teja, the daughter of the Bendahara of Pahang. Although she had already been betrothed to Sultan Abdul Jamal, Sultan Mahmud wanted her for himself. He promised he would comply with the wishes of any man who could bring Tun Teja to

Malaka. Hang Nadim bribed an old masseuse and eventually succeeded in bringing Tun Teja back to Malaka. Sultan Abdul Jamal was furious; he swore that he would assault Malaka with an army mounted on elephants. But before he could launch an attack, Laksamana Khoja Hassan stole his elephants. Sultan Abdul Jamal abdicated and appointed his son, Sultan Mansur, to succeed him.

20. Cau Sri Bangsa, the son of the King of Siam, attacked the country of Kota Mahligai. He vowed that he would convert to Islam if he won. As providence would have it, Kota Mahligai was vanquished. Cau Sri Bangsa founded a kingdom called Patani, named after a fisherman, Pa' Tani. After some time, Cau Sri Bangsa presented himself at the court of the Malaka Sultan to request the *nobat* be granted to him.

    A pundit named Makhdum Maulana Sadar Johan came to Malaka. Sultan Mahmud and all the nobles became his students. Makhdum Maulana Sadar Johan was called a greedy man; Sri Rama, a drunkard, once proclaimed that the scholar was only interested in money. He also found it difficult to pronounce Malay, including words such as *kunyit* (turmeric), *nyiru* (winnowing tray) and *kucing* (cat).

    Sultan Mahmud Syah sent an envoy to Pasai to enquire about a religious topic. The sultan decided against writing a letter as his missives to Pasai had often been misinterpreted. So, on the advice of his Bendahara, he first wrote his letter and then had its contents memorised by his envoy, Tun Muhammad, for the latter to convey directly to the Sultan of Pasai. Sultan Mahmud Syah was pleased with the answer he received.

21. The raja of Ligur, Maharaja Dewa Sura, attacked Pahang. Sultan Mahmud sent Sri Nara Diraja and the Laksamana to lead an army to help Pahang. The raja of Ligur was subsequently defeated and returned to his country. Malaka flourished and was a bustling meeting place for merchants. A Portuguese ship from Goa berthed in Malaka. The Franks were awed by Malaka's prosperity. Alfonso de Albuquerque, the Portuguese viceroy in Goa, ordered an invasion of Malaka. Thanks to the valour of Sri Nara Diraja however, Malaka was saved and the Franks returned to Goa.

22. Tun Fatimah, the daughter of Bendahara Sri Maharaja, was extremely beautiful. The Bendahara decided to marry her to Tun Ali, the son of Sri Nara Diraja. Before the wedding took place, Raja di Baruh, Sultan Mahmud Syah's uncle, advised the Bendahara to first show her to Sultan Mahmud Syah, as the queen consort had just died and the custom was that the ruler might wish to marry the daughter of his Bendahara. The Bendahara ignored this advice and married his daughter to Tun Ali. When the sultan saw how beautiful Tun Fatimah was, he was angry and thereafter continually plotted to bring about the Bendahara's downfall.

    Bendahara Sri Maharaja was the richest man in Malaka; he was even richer than Raja Mendeliar, an Indian who settled in Malaka and later became the Harbour Master (*syahbandar*). On one occasion, Raja Mendeliar brought a complaint against Naina Sura Dewana, the foremost merchant in Malaka. The two men asked Bendahara Sri Maharaja to adjudicate the matter. Naina Sura Dewana was afraid that Raja Mendeliar would bribe the Bendahara. He came one night and gave the Bendahara one *bahara* (approximately 170 kg) of gold. Now it happened that there was an Indian named Kitul—a relative of Naina Sura Dewana—who owed Raja Mendeliar a *tahil* (one and a half ounces) of gold. That same night, he went to the house of Raja Mendeliar and told him that Nina Sura Dewana had been with the Bendahara and given him a *bahara* of gold to have Raja Mendeliar executed. Terrified, Raja Mendeliar took a *bahara* of gold and an array of precious gems, and presented them to Laksamana Khoja Hassan. He told the Laksamana that the Bendahara planned to commit treason against the sultan and was building himself a throne, with the intention of becoming the ruler of Malaka. When the Laksamana saw the array of gifts laid before him, his better judgment deserted him. He went to the sultan and told him all that Raja Mendeliar had said. It did not take much to convince the sultan of the veracity of this report, for he already bore a grudge against the Bendahara. He ordered that the Bendahara be killed. The Bendahara's relatives and followers drew their kerises to defend him. The Bendahara ordered them not to defy the king's wishes. Subsequently, Bendahara Sri Maharaja, Sri Nara Diraja and all their relations, were killed. The only member of the Bendahara's family who survived the massacre was Tun Hamzah. After the Bendahara died, and his possessions had been confiscated, the sultan found that there was no evidence to support the slander that had been told him. He regretted putting to death the Bendahara without properly investigating the situation. Raja Mendeliar was executed for slander. Kitul was horizontally impaled and the Laksamana castrated.

The sultan appointed Paduka Tuan, the son of Paduka Bendahara, to the post of Bendahara. Bendahara Lubuk Tanah was so old, he had no teeth. He had thirty-two children, all from the same mother.

Sultan Mahmud Syah took Tun Fatimah the daughter of the former Bendahara, as his wife. Throughout the years of their marriage, she was so unhappy that she did not even so much as smile once, much less laughed. And each time she fell pregnant, she would abort her pregnancy. Only when Sultan Mahmud Syah gave her his word that he would crown a child born by her, did she cease this practice. Eventually, Sultan Mahmud Syah abdicated and retired to Kayu Ara. His only companion during this time was Sang Sura, his servant. Sultan Mahmud was succeeded by his son, Sultan Ahmad, who had no affection for the nobles and preferred to be with a few of his own friends.

23. Alfonso de Albuquerque, after stepping down from his vice-regency of Goa, led an armada against Malaka. Sultan Ahmad led his men into battle so courageously that his spirituality teacher, Makhdum Sadar Johan, who was with him, began to worry for his own safety and beseeched him to retreat to his palace. Soon night fell. All the warriors assembled in the court. To draw inspiration for the battle ahead, they listened to the *Hikayat Muhammad Hanafiah* and the *Hikayat Amir Hamzah*. The next day, the Portuguese landed. The fighting was intense. Sultan Ahmad retreated to Pagoh, to Muar, then to Pahang, and finally to Bintan. Sultan Ahmad's attitude to his courtiers remained unchanged; he continued to favour his own circle of friends. His attitude incurred the ire of Sultan Mahmud Syah who secretly ordered his own son's assassination. After the death of Sultan Ahmad, all the young men gave their allegiance to his father, except Tun Ali, who swore that his allegiance was only to Sultan Ahmad and asked to be killed. Sultan Mahmud Syah resumed the throne. Tun Pikrama was appointed Bendahara, while Hang Nadim succeeded to the office of Laksamana. Tun Fatimah bore a very handsome son, Raja Alauddin Syah. He was installed as heir to the Malakan throne and given the title Sultan Muda.

24. Sultan Abdullah, the King of Kampar, refused to acknowledge the overlordship of the dispossessed ruler of Malaka now residing in Bintan. Sultan Mahmud ordered an attack on Kampar. Unfortunately, his flotilla was defeated by the Franks and the Malays retreated to Indragiri. After the battle was over, Sultan Abdullah went aboard a Portuguese galley to see what it was like. The Portuguese immediately bound Sultan Abdullah and took him first to Malaka, then to Goa and finally to Portugal. When Sultan Mahmud heard how Sultan Abdullah had been seized, he was angry with Sultan Abdullah's ministers for not defending their king.

25. Maharaja Isak, the king of Lingga, went to Bintan to pay homage to Sultan Mahmud. When Narasinga, the King of Indragiri, came to know about this, he attacked Lingga and captured Maharaja Isak's wife and children. He then proceeded to Bintan and presented himself before Sultan Mahmud, where he was subsequently chosen by the sultan to be his son-in-law, and given the name Sultan Abdul Jalil. In retaliation for his treachery, Maharaja Isak attacked Indragiri and in turn captured the wife and children of the Indragiri king. Maharaja Isak sought help from the Portuguese, angering Sultan Mahmud Syah. He sent his army to attack Lingga but were defeated by the Franks.

Sultan Mahmud sent his army, under the command of Paduka Tuan, to attack Malaka. The attack failed. Many of the sultan's men were killed by Portuguese cannons inside the fortress. The battle was so fierce that Sultan Mahmud's elephant, which Paduka Tuan rode into battle, broke its tusk. Sultan Abdul Jalil, the King of Indragiri, took part in the battle as a spy. Sultan Mahmud scolded Paduka Tuan for not fighting hard enough but later forgave him.

26. Raja Abdul, the King of Siak, came to pay homage to Sultan Mahmud in Bintan, and was installed as the sultan's son-in-law, with the name of Sultan Khoja Ahmad. Paduka Tuan was dispatched to "the west", i.e. to Bruas and Manjong, to summon Tun Aria Bija Diraja who had not presented himself to Sultan Mahmud since the fall of Malaka. Paduka Tuan carried out his task well; he returned to Bintan with Tun Aria Diraja, who made his obeisance to the king.

27. The King of Haru, Sultan Husain, was handsome, kind and generous. He sailed to Bintan to ask for the hand of Sultan Mahmud Syah's daughter, Raja Putih. His suit was accepted and the two were married. After some time had passed, Sultan Husain returned to Haru.

28. The Sultan of Pahang presented himself to Sultan Mahmud Syah in Bintan, who married him to his daughter, Raja Hatijah.

The Portuguese attacked Bintan. Bintan fell and Sultan Mahmud Syah was forced to retreat into the jungle, before fleeing to Kampar. It was then that the sultan wanted to marry another of his daughters to the Temenggung, Tun Nara Wangsa. Conscious of the fact that he was no more than a servant of the king, Tun Nara Wangsa declined the proposal. The princess was later married to a son of the Sultan of Pahang.

Not long after this, Sultan Mahmud died and was succeeded by Raja Alauddin Ri'ayat Syah. Raja Muzaffar was deposed by the Bendahara and was taken to Perak by a merchant, where he later became king. Sultan Muzaffar appointed Tun Mahmud as Bendahara, with the title Sri Agar Raja.

29. Sultan Alauddin Ri'ayat Syah went to Pahang and married the king's sister. After his return to Hujung Tanah, he was angered to hear that Sri Agar Raja had been appointed as Bendahara of Perak. He sent Bendahara Paduka Raja to Perak to summon Sri Agar Raja. The Adipati of Kampar brought tribute to Hujung Tanah and was reminded that traditional customs still had to be observed. Thereafter, Sultan Alauddin commanded Tun Pikrama to attack Merbedang, which he successfully accomplished.

30. Sang Naya conspired with the Malays living in Malaka to attack the Portuguese while they were in church. Sang Naya collected a large number of kerises to this end but he was executed when they were discovered. The Portuguese sent an envoy to Sultan Alauddin in Pekan Tua. Sultan Alauddin killed the envoy. The Portuguese attacked Hujung Tanah. The Malays could not withstand the onslaught and retreated to Sayong, in Johor. Sultan Alauddin then sent a letter to the Portuguese commander of Malaka calling for a truce. Thereafter, peace prevailed between the Malays and the Franks.

31. Raja Jainad succeeded his elder brother, Sultan Muhammad Syah, as Sultan of Pahang and was granted the name Sultan Muzaffar Syah by Sultan Alauddin Ri'ayat Syah. On this occasion, the Sultan of Pahang sailed upriver to Sayong to present himself, together with a Singapore headman, Patih Ludang. Sang Setia ordered Patih Ludang to dismount from the barge and killed him. The Sultan of Pahang was furious. Sultan Alauddin Ri'ayat Syah had Sang Setia bound and sent to Pahang. Sang Setia was subsequently pardoned by the Sultan of Pahang.

8.3 *Hikayat Merong Mahawangsa*

Of all the works of Malay historical literature, the *Hikayat Merong Mahawangsa* deviates the most from historical truth. Winstedt remarks that had it not included a genealogy of the kings of Kedah, and borrowed parts of the foreword to the 1612 text of the *Sejarah Melayu*, this hikayat would never have been accepted as historical literature (Winstedt 1958: 133).

In one sense, this is an old hikayat. It describes the history of Kedah before the kingdom embraced Islam. It tells stories of a prince born from a bamboo stem and a princess born from the foam in a river. There is also a tale of a magic elephant choosing a king. These folktales are still told by the local people. The hikayat ends with an account of how Islam spread from Acheh to Kedah in the seventeenth century. Despite this, the form of the text as we now have it was transcribed only at the end of the eighteenth century, as there are additional stories within other stories story that have clearly been incorporated by copyists over a long period.

The text of the "Kedah Annals" has been published at three different times. It was first published by A. J. Sturrock in 1916, in *JSBRAS* No. 72. In 1968, a copy of the manuscript held in the Museum of Kedah was published by Dzulkifli bin Mohd. Salleh. This manuscript was originally transcribed by Muhammad Yusuf bin Nuruddin on 16 November 1898/2 Rajab 1316H (Dzulkifli Mohd. Salleh, 1968). This was further followed by the publication of a scholarly edition by Siti Hawa Salleh in 1970. Her edition was based on three manuscripts: the manuscript transcribed by Muhammad Yusuf for R. J. Wilkinson on 16 November 1898, the manuscript published by A. J. Sturrock, and the Maxwell 16 manuscript kept by the Royal Asiatic Society in London. Siti

Hawa Salleh's comparative study of these manuscripts reveals that the Maxwell 16 bears the most embellishments. Below is a summary of her edition.

The hikayat begins with a foreword taken from the *Sulalatus Salatin*. It is then related that a *garuda* once settled on the island of Langkawi. One day, a falcon (*rajawali*) brought news that the King of Byzantium (Rum) intended to marry his son to a princess from China. The *garuda* opposed this marriage because the two countries were so distant from each other that the young couple could never have met under normal circumstances. The *garuda* promptly sought an audience with the Prophet Sulaiman (Solomon), the greatest king in the world. The Prophet Sulaiman told him: "Oh *garuda*, if a couple is destined to meet, nothing can keep them apart – even if they were hidden in a stone or the trunk of a tree." But the *garuda* was adamant about separating the couple. "Very well then," said the prophet, "you may do as you wish."

The *garuda* then flew to China. He swooped upon the Princess of China and her ladies-in-waiting, and carried them to the island of Langkawi. There they were housed in a shelter built like a palace. Every day the *garuda* brought them food. He gave the princess and her servants everything their hearts desired. It was soon announced that the King of Byzantium had ordered Raja Merong Mahawangsa (who was married to the daughter of the king of giants, *gergasi,*) to escort the Prince of Byzantium to China. During the voyage, their ships were destroyed by the *garuda*. However, the Prince of Byzantium survived. He was washed ashore in Langkawi and met the Princess of China. They fell in love. The princess sent the *garuda* to China to fetch her some clothes and while the creature was absent the young couple were able to express their feelings for each other.

After some time had passed, the *garuda* presented himself before Prophet Sulaiman and announced that he had kept the couple apart. The prophet laughed and ordered the King of Jinns to bring the young lovers before him. The prophet then declared that there are four things in the world that are ordained but beyond man's control, namely: (1) one's economic welfare (*rezeki*); (2) death; (3) love (*jodoh pertemuan*); and (4) divorce. The *garuda* departed in shame to the Sea of Kalzum, far beyond the haunts of men, where he lived in isolation. The Princess of China and the Prince of Byzantium were sent to China by the prophet.

Raja Merong Mahawangsa had also survived the *garuda*'s attack and traveled far and wide in search of his master, the Prince of Byzantium. He stopped at an island and made friends with a race of giants. Together they built a fortified kingdom on the island and called it Langkasuka. The kingdom flourished and many people came to live there. Raja Merong Mahawangsa's fame soon spread. He sent envoys to Acheh and Kelinggi, seeking a wife for his son. In Kelinggi, the envoy met a minister from the kingdom of Byzantium. The minister ordered Raja Merong Mahawangsa to go back to Byzantium. Raja Merong Mahawangsa immediately prepared himself for the journey. Before he left, he married his son to a princess and made him king, with the title of Raja Merong Mahapudisat. He then changed the name of his kingdom to Kedah Zamin Turan, the Land of Turkestan. Raja Merong Mahawangsa then returned to Byzantium.

Raja Merong Mahapudisat ruled justly and benevolently over his ministers, guards and subjects, and the merchants who visited the kingdom. Many people came to live in Kedah Zamin Turan. After several years, the king was blessed with three handsome sons, and a daughter of exceeding beauty. Her complexion was light yellow, her body was delicately slender, and her stunning looks were unmatched at that time. He provided his sons with their own kingdoms, namely Siam, Perak and Patani, but kept the girl by his side. When Raja Merong Mahapudisat died several years later, the youngest son succeeded him on the throne and assumed the title Raja Sri Mahawangsa.

Sri Mahawangsa grew tired of living in Langkasuka because it was too far from the sea. He ordered his ministers to build another palace and called it Serokam. Not long after, his wife gave birth to a very handsome son. When he came of age, the young prince told his father that he wished to marry the granddaughter of a giant. The girl was exceedingly beautiful, fair-skinned and petite. Sri Mahawangsa tried to prevent the match, but the prince insisted on marrying the girl. Eventually, Sri Mahawangsa fell ill and died. The prince assumed the throne, taking the title Raja Sri Maha Indrawangsa. His part-giant wife gave birth to a son, Raja Ong Maha Perita Deria, who was bigger than all his peers, and as imposing in stature as he was in personality.

With the passage of time, Raja Sri Maha Indrawangsa too passed away and was succeeded by Raja Ong Perita Deria. As the new king did not like the location of the palace, he built another, calling it Kota Aur, Bamboo City, because it was surrounded by thick bamboo groves. Raja Ong Perita Deria was a wicked and cruel ruler. One day, he sprouted tusks and was then called Raja Bersiung, The Fanged King. On one occasion, the king ate a dish of vegetable curry containing a drop of blood from the tip of the cook's finger. He insisted that henceforth all his meals should be mixed with human blood. Many people were killed to satisfy his appetite. One day, a man named Kampar allowed himself to be captured by the king's men. Kampar's body was impervious to steel. The king could not kill him and began to feel very afraid. Kampar turned himself into a wild beast and attacked the king. Four of the king's ministers eventually came to his rescue. They advised the king to stop killing his subjects but he refused to listen to them. With the blessing of the queen, the four ministers led a rebellion against Raja Bersiung. Defeated, he fled into the forest.

Raja Bersiung arrived at the hut of a peasant living near Patani. He took refuge with the peasant and helped him work his land. He married the peasant's beautiful daughter and in time she presented him with a son who looked exactly like himself. When the four ministers heard that Raja Bersiung was living with the peasant's family, they sent an army to seize him. Raja Bersiung ran into a thicket of bamboo and disappeared. The ministers sent an envoy to Siam, requesting that the King help them find a suitable raja for Kedah Zamin Turan. The royal astrologers announced that the future king of Kedah would be chosen by a magic elephant. The elephant chose Raja Bersiung's son. The young man was brought to the palace and was well cared for. The queen, Raja Bersiung's former consort, instructed the youth in his duties and gave him a girl of extreme beauty to be his wife.

Kelana Hitam was the king of an island called Pulau Air Tawar. One day, he conferred with his ministers about attacking Kedah so that he could be king. The King of Siam had sent his minister, Kelahum, a general from one of the vassal states, to tell Kelana Hitam that Kedah already had a king. Kelana Hitam insisted that he would not change his mind. A battle ensued between the forces of Kelana Hitam and General Kelahum. Kelana Hitam was defeated and captured.

Raja Bersiung's son was installed as king and received the royal title, Raja Phra Ong Mahaputisat. Soon after, Minister Kelahum arrived and told him about the battle against Kelana Hitam. While he was in Kedah, Kelahum instructed Raja Phra Ong Mahaputisat on his royal duties. One day, Raja Phra Ong Mahaputisat went hunting and caught many animals. He was even more pleased by the discovery of a piece of bamboo, which he brought home with him. Some time after this, Raja Phra Ong Mahaputisat's queen gave birth to a beautiful son, Raja Phra Ong Mahawangsa. Not long after, the piece of bamboo burst open and out stepped a beautiful baby boy. The raja named him Raja Buluh Betung, the Bamboo King. Raja Mahaputisat built a new palace on a hill called Bukit Meriam. One day, there was a great flood. The queen went to the river and saw a white lump of foam floating towards her. The foam contained a beautiful baby girl, whom the queen called Putri Seluang, Princess Carp. During the reign of Raja Phra Ong Mahaputisat, Kedah continued to grow and was very prosperous. The king ruled justly over all his subjects, and there was an abundance of food.

With the passage of time, Raja Phra Ong Mahaputisat's children grew up. Raja Buluh Betung and Putri Seluang married and were encouraged to establish their own realm. A suitable bride was also found for Raja Phra Ong Mahawangsa. Not long after, Raja Phra Ong Mahaputisat fell ill and passed away; he was succeeded by Raja Phra Ong Mahawangsa. Phra Ong Mahawangsa was addicted to strong liqueur and rice wine, which he drank to keep himself healthy.

Syaikh Abdullah was a holy man from Baghdad, whose prayers were very efficacious. Among his many disciples was Syaikh Abdullah Yamani, a scholar of the Quranic recitation and interpretation. One day, Syaikh Abdullah Yamani asked his teacher's permission to meet Iblis (Satan), the chief of the devils, in order to learn about his stratagems. The teacher agreed and told him where he could find Satan.

When he met Satan, Syaikh Abdullah Yamani asked to become his student. Satan gave him a magic staff, which rendered him invisible. They went about, causing mayhem and murder. Wars also broke out as a result of the Devil's incitements. At length, they reached the palace of the alcohol-loving Raja Phra Ong Mahawangsa. When Raja Phra Ong Mahawangsa awoke and called for his usual glass of spirits, Satan handed him a glass of urine. When Syaikh Abdullah scolded the Devil, Satan became angry. He snatched his staff from the syaikh's hand and vanished. The king was shocked to see him and asked him where he had come from. Syaikh Abdullah Yamani related all that had happened and urged the king to embrace Islam. The king converted to Islam, followed by all his wives and concubines.

After his conversion, Raja Phra Ong Mahawangsa took the name Sultan Muzaffar Syah. The entire population of the country also recited the Profession of Faith. Syaikh Abdullah Yamani taught them to recite the Quran and to follow the requirements of their new faith. The news of Syaikh Abdullah's conversion of Kedah spread far and wide. When it reached Acheh, the Sultan sent Syaikh Nuruddin with two books of theology, the *Siratul-Mustakim* and the *Babul-nikah*. Sultan Muzaffar Syah had three sons: Muazzam Syah, Mahmud Syah and Sulaiman Syah.

In accordance with his father's instructions, Raja Buluh Betung departed to find a suitable place to build his own palace. While he was away, his wife, Putri Seluang, committed adultery with the son of a minister and conceived a son, Megat Zainal. The king taught Megat Zainal the tenets of Islam and how to recite the Quran. When reports of his wife's infidelity eventually reached the ears of Raja Buluh Betung, he abandoned his expedition and turned back to Kedah. During his journey, he was wounded in a fight with a group of bandits. His injuries worsened with each day until one night, he became a length of bamboo once more. The ruler of Kedah installed his sons as rulers of the two states founded by Raja Buluh Betung: Raja Sulaiman took the throne of

Langkapuri. Syaikh Abdullah Yamani returned to his teacher in Baghdad. When Sultan Muzaffar Syah died, his son, Sultan Muazzam, took the throne of Kedah.

The hikayat ends with a genealogical list that traces the lineage of the Kedah kings until Sultan Ahmad Tajuddin Syah. No dates are given and it is this list alone that justifies the work being considered as historical literature (Winstedt 1958: 133).

It should also be added that the Dutch scholar Hendrik Maier has written a study of this hikayat, *In the Center of Authority: The Malay Hikayat Merong Mahawangsa* (Maier, 1988), which makes use of modern literary theories to shed light on the text.

8.4 *Hikayat Acheh*

The *Hikayat Acheh* was written during the reign of Iskandar Muda (1606-1636). According to T. Iskandar, who edited a text for his PhD at Leiden University, this title is not accurate. The hikayat does not bear any title. The title "Hikayat Aceh" came from an opening line added by a Western scholar at the beginning of the hikayat which reads: *"Ini hikayat raja Acheh daripada asal turun-temurun"* ("This is a story of the kings of Acheh from their origins to their descendants"). A better title might be the *Hikayat Iskandar Muda*, as it was written primarily in praise of Iskandar Muda, although he is not referred to by that name in this hikayat. Instead, he is referred to by various other names such as Pancagah, Johan Alam and Perkasa Alam (T. Iskandar 1958: 17).

According to T. Iskandar, the *Hikayat Acheh* is an imitation of a Persian book called *Akbar Nama,* which was written as a paean to the greatness of the Emperor Akbar (1556-1605). There are, nevertheless, many local Indonesian influences as well, such as the *Hikayat Sri Rama, Hikayat Raja-Raja Pasai, Hikayat Iskandar Dzulkarnain, Hikayat Muhammad Hanafiah, Sejarah Melayu* and *Hikayat Malim Deman*. A. H. Johns disagrees with these suggestions. He argues that the supposed similarities between the *Hikayat Acheh* and the *Hikayat Nama* are not convincing. Rather, the *Hikayat Acheh* bears closer resemblance to the *penglipur lara* folktales, such as the *Hikayat Malim Deman* and *Hikayat Awang Sulung Merah Muda* (Johns, 1979: 47-53).

The identity of the author remains a mystery, as the first few opening pages of the text are missing. From its contents, however, we can surmise that he had a wide knowledge of foreign languages; he was proficient in Arabic, Turkish and Persian, and also knew a little Portuguese. It was thought that Syamsuddin Pasai, a Sufi scholar, may have been the author of the *Hikayat Acheh,* but there is no concrete evidence to support this view.

8.4.1 Synopsis

The first few pages of the Iskandar (1958) text of the hikayat are missing. The story begins with Raja Indra Syah, who went to China and was greatly honoured by the emperor. The Chinese emperor presented Indra Syah with the legacy of Alexander the Great and also built him a palace. Soon, Raja Indra Syah's wife, Putri Nur Kamariah, became pregnant. After exactly nine months, the thought came to her, "Wouldn't it be wonderful if my child were born in this kingdom? After all the child is the descendant of a Great King."

Raja Syah Muhammad was astonished to find a clump of bamboos. When his men cut down the bushes, an extraordinarily beautiful fairy princess, Putri Dewi Indra, emerged. Raja Syah Muhammad married her and she gave him two children, Sultan Ibrahim Syah and Putri Sapiah. One day, Raja Syah Muhammad plucked a hair that was growing from his wife's chin. Putri Dewi Indra woke up and died.

One day, Raja Syah Mahmud, the brother of Raja Syah Muhammad, saw seven celestial nymphs while he was playing near a large deep pond. He stole the magic flying raiment belonging to the youngest nymph, Putri Medini Candra, and married her. The fairy princess presented him with two children, a son named Sulaiman Syah and a daughter called Putri Arkiah. Later, when Raja Syah Mahmud scolded them over some trivial offence, calling them "children of a *jinn*" and "a fairy's offspring", Putri Medini Candra became angry. She found her wings and flew back to heaven. Raja Mahmud regretted his harsh words.

Raja Munawar Syah arranged for his grandsons, Ibrahim Syah and Sulaiman Syah, to marry their cousins, Arkiah and Sapiah. Two sons were born, Raja Muzaffar Syah and Syamsu Syah. Raja Munawar of Lamri was also descended from Alexander the Great. Similarly, Sultan Perkasa Alam Johan was descended from the great king on his father's side; on his mother's side, he was descended from Sultan Inayat Syah, the ruler of Dar al-Kamal.

Raja Muzaffar Syah, the king of Mahkota Alam, was constantly at war with Sultan Inayat Syah of Dar al-Kamal. Neither side was able to defeat the other. Muzaffar Syah devised a plan to depose his brother. He sent an envoy to ask for the hand of Raja Inayat Syah's daughter. His proposal was accepted and he sent weapons as dowry to Dar al-Kamal. Sultan Inayat Syah was overthrown. Muzaffar Syah then merged Mahkota Alam and Dar al-Kamal into one kingdom and named it Darus-Salam. He assumed suzerainty over this new consolidated realm and when he died, his son ascended to the throne and ruled under the title Sultan Ali Mughayat Syah.

Sultan Ali Mughayat Syah conquered the kingdom of Syah Deli whose ruler Sultan Ahmad was unpopular with the people. When Sultan Ali Mughayat died, his son Sultan Salahuddin ascended the throne. Sultan Salahuddin was neither compassionate nor capable. Not long after, he was overthrown and killed by his brother Sultan Alauddin Syah, the ruler of Samudera.

Sultan Alauddin Syah defeated Raja Besar, the ruler of Ujung Tanah, and took the vanquished ruler's daughter as his wife. Not long after that, he sent his army to bring Raja Besar to Acheh and presented his father-in-law with gifts of resplendent clothes. Upon the demise of Sultan Alauddin Syah, his son Sultan Ali Ri'ayat Syah ruled Acheh. Two of his brothers ruled Ghori and Mughal. Over time, the sultans grew envious of Sultan Ali Ri'ayat Syah and plotted to kill him. Their plans failed and the Mughal emperor was killed in the coup.

After the death of Sultan Ri'ayat Syah, his brother, Seri Alam, ascended the throne. Seri Alam was a very generous ruler and lavished gold, silver and clothes to his warriors and subjects. His religious officials and ministers disapproved of this and eventually deposed him. Sultan Zainal, the son of the raja of Ghori, was installed as the new ruler. Sultan Zainal was a cruel king. He spent his days watching elephant-fights. Murders were common and many people died. Even his own ministers and nobles fell victim to his intrigues. One day Raja Zainal was taken by some of his palace officials to Mahkota Alam and did not return.

The lesser kings, warriors and nobles installed Sultan Alauddin Syah as the new king. During his reign, Acheh Darus-Salam prospered and the sultan had children and grandchildren.

There was a lesser raja in Acheh named Sultan Abdul Jalil. His son, Mansur Syah, was handsome, wise and virtuous. Sultan Abdul Jalil sent an envoy to ask for the hand of Putri Raja Indra Bangsa, the daughter of Syah Alam Marhum Sayid al-Mukamil, for his son. The proposal having been accepted, a lavish celebration was prepared for the wedding of Sultan Mansur Syah and Putri Raja Indra Bangsa. Their marriage was duly solemnized and at the ceremony, Sri Raja Khatib led the congregation in praising Allah's apostle, the Prophet Muhammad, peace be upon him.

At dawn one morning, Sultan Mansur Syah dreamed that he was in a strange city when he suddenly felt the urge to urinate. He watched in amazement as his urine spread like the sea and flooded the whole of Acheh. Waking, Sultan Mansur immediately summoned his religious teacher to ask what his dream portended. The teacher explained that Mansur would have a son who will be very powerful, magnificent and majestic.

This is followed by stories of the birth, childhood, and the gallantry of Perkasa Johan Alam, Iskandar Muda. When he was conceived, the country enjoyed great prosperity. While his mother was pregnant, she had several strange and prophetic dreams. In one, she dreamed that her hairpin was the moon and her shawl a myriad of stars.

When Perkasa Johan Alam was three years old, he was given the name Raja Munawar Syah. When he turned four, his grandfather Syah Alam presented him with a gold elephant and various other playthings also made of gold. At five, Raja Munawar Syah received the nickname Pancagah (the power of five) and his grandfather gave him a pet elephant; he was already a skilled horseman. At six, he spent his time riding elephants against the other princes. At seven, he released all the elephants and recaptured them. At eight, he staged mock naval battles. When he was nine, he learned to handle all sorts of weapons. At ten, Perkasa Johan Alam beat two Portuguese envoys in a horse race. At eleven, it was prophesied that the young prince would achieve greatness and glory. At twelve, he killed a wild buffalo. When Perkasa Johan Alam was thirteen, his intelligence helped him to master the Quran and study theological works with extreme ease. On observing these prodigious talents, his grandfather Syah Alam predicted that the youth would one day conquer all the lands that had yet to come under Acheh's dominion. At fourteen, Perkasa Johan Alam learned how to capture elephants; he also displayed his courage by snaring a tiger. His fame spread: emissaries from Siam and Byzantium spoke of him to their respective monarchs. Religious circles in Madinah too were soon abuzz with talk of Perkasa Johan Alam's great courage.

After these extensive details of the heroism and accomplishments of Perkasa Johan Alam from the time he was young till he reached adulthood, the hikayat then returns to the stories of Syah Alam, his grandfather.

Syah Alam ordered Rahasia Raja, the military commander of Ghori, and Tun Bija ad-Diraja, the commander of Aru, to build a fleet of war ships. After some time, Syah Alam sent his emissaries to see if the boats were ready and to arrest the two commanders if they were not. As the boats had, in fact, not been completed, everyone feared the consequences. Tun Bija ad-Diraja killed one of the emissaries. Rahasia Raja disapproved of Tun Bija ad-Diraja's action. Afraid that Syah Alam would not forgive them, Merah Miru and Merah di Ghori allied themselves with Tun Bija ad-Diraja. Tun

Bija ad-Diraja gathered his troops. He then sent an envoy to Johor, inviting the raja of Johor to take over the throne of Ghori. The raja was initially reluctant to accept the proposal was but finally installed as their new raja.

The other emissary managed to escape from Tun Bija. He returned to Acheh and reported what had happened. Syah Alam was enraged and sent his army to attack Ghori. The attack failed. Even more infuriated, Syah Alam ordered his bravest and fiercest warriors to invade Ghori. The battle was fierce. Many men on both sides were killed. One of Syah Alam's sons, Sultan Mansur Syah, also died in the battle. Eventually the forces of Ghori were routed. The raja of Johor and his men fled and escaped.

Syah Alam was not pleased with this outcome. He ordered his men to pursue the raja of Johor. No matter where he went, the fugitive raja found the Achehnese close behind him. Finally, he built a stockade. The Achehnese surrounded the stockade. Eventually, the Johor troops had no other recourse but to negotiate a peaceful settlement. The Sultan of Acheh rejected their plea and insisted that the battle continue.

After conferring with his generals, the raja of Johor decided not to surrender and ordered his warriors to fight to the end. The Achehnese ran short of food and many men died of starvation. Finally, the Sultan of Acheh withdrew his forces and returned to Acheh. He fell ill and was unable to walk. Perkasa Johan Alam was appointed to replace him but declined, pointing out that Sultan Alauddin still had two other sons who were in the direct line of succession. These two princes were then summoned. Sultan Husain was already sovereign of Deli; while Sultan Muda was reluctant to be installed as the ruler of Acheh.

8.5 *Misa Melayu*

According to Winstedt, the *Misa Melayu* is "an attractive contemporary account" of Perak history (Winstedt 1958: 133). It outlines the genealogy of the Perak kings, from Sultan Muzaffar Syah II (1636-1653), known posthumously as al-Marhum Jalilullah, to Sultan Mahmud Syah (d. 1778), who was succeeded by Sultan Alauddin Syah. However, most of this hikayat is devoted to events that took place during the reign of Sultan Iskandar Syah who ruled from 1756 to 1770. Special emphasis is placed on activities around the palace, including such royal pastimes as fishing, riverside picnics, night celebrations, ear-piercing ceremonies, coronation rituals, and pregnancy customs. As such, this book is an important resource for the study of Malay royal customs.

It also gives a clear picture of life in eighteenth century Perak, which benefitted from its lucrative trade in tin with the Dutch. The diverse population included Javanese, Minangkabaus, Arabs, Indians and Chinese, living harmoniously together. Festival celebrations became colourful affairs and an occasion for the different races to showcase their own rich and distinct cultures.

The author of this hikayat was Raja Chulan, a blood relation of the Perak king. His father, Raja Hamid, was the brother of Sultan Muhammad Syah, the father of Sultan Iskandar Syah. He was granted the title Raja Kecil Besar by Sultan Muzaffar Syah. Raja Chulan was also actively involved in organizing the wedding ceremony of Sultan Iskandar Muda and the daughter of Sultan Muhammad Syah, Raja Budak Rasul. He was among the courtiers who accompanied Sultan Iskandar during a festival by the sea held in the sultan's honour and wrote a *syair* to commemorate the occasion. This is why the *Misa Melayu* is able to present such an interesting chronicle of the customs of the Malay kings of the time.

Many explanations have been offered for the meaning of the word *"misa"* in the hikayat's title. It was first thought that *"misa"* refers to *"misal"* (from the Arabic *"mithalan"*), meaning an "exemplar". A later explanation suggested that the term *"misa"* was used to refer to a form of chronicle that was popular in Perak, as distinct from the very popular Javanese literary forms. Yet another explanation is that *"misa"* may have been a tribute to the Panji tale, *Misa Perabu Jaya*, in which the word means "buffalo" (Winstedt 1958: 132-133). According to Buyung Adil, the buffalo is regarded in Javanese culture as a symbol of strength and courage, and the title *"kebo"* is usually appended to the name of a person who is deemed to bear these warrior-like traits. The title *Misa Melayu*, he argues, therefore means "The Malay Warrior" (Buyung Adil no date: 297). The text of the *Misa Melayu* was edited by R. O. Windstedt and published in Singapore in 1919. It appeared in the Malay Literature Series, No. 15, and was later republished by Pustaka Antara in Kuala Lumpur in 1966.

8.5.1 Synopsis

The hikayat begins with an account of the descendants of Alexander the Great. After the death of the first raja of Perak, Marhum Jalilullah, Perak was ruled by his son, the Marhum Besar or Sultan Mahmud Syah. As Sultan Mahmud Syah had no heir and his brother the Yang Dipertuan Muda predeceased him, the throne passed to the Yang Dipertuan Muda's son, Sultan Mahmud Syah (also known as Raja Raden) who ruled under the title Sultan Alauddin Ri'ayat Syah. After he died, Raja Raden was succeeded by his younger brother Raja Inu; he became known as Sultan Muzaffar Syah and ruled from Brahman Indra.

Not long thereafter, an uprising threw the kingdom into turmoil. Sultan Muzaffar Syah moved to Kuala Kangsar. His younger brother Raja Bisnu, established himself in Pulau Tiga, calling himself Sultan Muhammad Syah. Sultan Muhammad Syah had eight children. The best known of these was Raja Iskandar; he was held in high esteem by the nobility. After some time, Sultan Muhammad Syah realised the error of there being two kings in Perak and invited Sultan Muzaffar Syah to return to Brahman Indra to be reinstated as the rightful king. Muzaffar Syah returned to his palace, which had been restored to its former glory by Raja Muda Iskandar, the son of Raja Iskandar. Although Sultan Muzaffar Syah was officially the King of Perak, all power effectively rested in the hands of the Raja Muda. The officials who had followed Sultan Muzaffar to Kuala Kangsar were deprived of their posts.

Not long after this, Raja Berkabat, the son of Raja Kecil Minangkabau, attacked Perak, together with Daeng Matkah and Daeng Mencelak. The invasion was repelled by Raja Muda Iskandar. The Dutch interest in buying tin brought untold wealth to the kingdom.

Raja Alam, whose title was Raja Kecil Besar, was a favourite of Sultan Muzaffar Syah. When Sultan Muzaffar Syah returned to Brahman Indra, Raja Muda did not allow Raja Alam to accompany the sultan. Because Raja Alam resented Raja Muda, not only did he not come to the aid of Perak when Perak was attacked by Raja Berkabat but, upon learning that Raja Muda Iskandar was planning to arrest him, Raja Alam plotted with a group of Buginese to overthrow the king and Raja Muda Iskandar. With the help of the Dutch, Raja Muda captured Raja Alam and his supporters and had them banished to Malaka. Not long after this, Sultan Muhammad Syah, the father of Raja Muda Iskandar, passed away and was laid to rest in Pulau Tiga.

After the death of his father, Raja Muda Iskandar's popularity grew. He also found favour in the eyes of Sultan Muzaffar Syah who took him as his son-in-law. After the traditional rituals had been performed, the marriage of Sultan Muzaffar Syah's daughter, Raja Budak Rasul, and Raja Muda Iskandar was lavishly celebrated for forty days and forty nights.

When Sultan Muzaffar Syah passed away, he was succeeded by Raja Muda Iskandar who took the title Sultan Iskandar Dzulkarnain. To mark his coronation, the new sultan conferred honours on those who deserved them and punished those who deserved to be punished.

Before long the sultan expressed his wish to move his kingdom's capital from Brahman Indra to Cempaka Sari. A malicious Dutch interpreter seemed to suggest that Holland had dispatched a fleet to sack Perak. The sultan ordered his troops to ready themselves. When the Dutch ships arrived, they were only interested in buying tin and renewing their trading treaty with Perak. Sultan Iskandar soon resumed his plans to move his capital to Cempaka Sari, which was later named Pulau Indra Sakti.

The hikayat then gives an account of the sultan engaged in a traditional method of fishing (*menuba*). The sultan built a mosque to celebrate a major festival where performed his Idul Fitri prayers. His queen, Raja Budak Rasul, was soon with child. In the seventh month of her pregnancy, a *lenggang perut* ritual was held and there was merrymaking to celebrate the occasion as custom dictated. Guests from throughout the land came to celebrate the festivities. Not long after, the sultan decided to build a new palace. It was a magnificent piece of craftsmanship.

One day an argument over a woman broke out between a noble from Sayong and a commoner. The Sayong aristocrat seized the woman and presented her to the sultan to be his slave. The sultan suffered a mysterious illness. He was treated by traditional medicine men *(pawang)* and recovered.

Following his recovery, the Dutch again came to buy tin. As a result of a dispute over some matter, the Dutch suddenly opened fire at the port master (*syahbandar*). Furious, the sultan gathered his navy. The Dutch were afraid and negotiated a truce. They claimed that they had been shooting at a monkey, not the *syahbandar*.

After the sultan and his queen visited the tomb of his late father, the queen fell ill and passed away. The sultan spent long periods grieving her loss. After the period of mourning was over, a seaside festival was held to restore his feelings. The event is described in a long *syair* written as a paean to the sultan.

With the passage of time, the sultan also died. He was replaced by his brother Raja Muda who took the title Sultan Mahmud Syah. During the Sultan Mahmud Syah's reign, the raja of Selangor came to seek an audience with the Perak king and was honoured. Not long after, Sultan Mahmud Syah moved his court to Pasir Pulau, Sandy Island, which was renamed Pulau Besar Indra Mulia, The Large Grand and Glorious Island.

Raja Haji, a Buginese chief from Riau, came to Selangor, and with the help of the Sultan of Selangor, set out to attack Kedah. On the way, Raja Haji's army stopped at Perak, whereupon the Sultan of Selangor married the cousin of the Sultan of Perak. Raja Haji was chased out of Perak. War then broke out between Raja Haji and Kedah. Kedah was defeated. Raja Haji and the Sultan of Selangor then returned to their respective countries.

After some time, Sultan Mahmud Syah died. Raja Muda succeeded him, taking the title Sultan Alauddin Mansur Syah Iskandar Muda. He was a just and fair king.

8.6 *Hikayat Negeri Johor*

With the *History of Johor* we enter a new stage of Malay historiography. Before this hikayat, Malay historical literary works always began with folktales, legends and myths. The *Sejarah Melayu*, for example, describes Alexander the Great and the descent of his heirs from Bukit Siguntang. Both the *Hikayat Raja-Raja Pasai* and the *Hikayat Acheh* begin with the mythical tale of the bamboo princess who gave birth to the founding monarchs of these kingdoms. By way of contrast, the *Hikayat Negeri Johor* begins with a real historical event, the defeat of Johor by the south Sumatran principality of Jambi. The reason for this war is known: a conflict between the Prime Minister (*bendahara*) of Johor and the Admiral (*laksamana*) Paduka Raja. The admiral wanted to increase his influence and offered his daughter to the Sultan of Johor. As a result, the king broke off his engagement to the princess of Jambi. The King of Jambi felt insulted and attacked Johor.

The *Hikayat Negeri Johor* is also a real chronicle. The date of each event is accurately recorded. Sometimes the events are not historically significant, or there might not be any relation or causal link between antecedent events and succeeding ones, but their dates are recorded nonetheless. This characteristic of the Buginese historical writing has had a great influence on Malay historical literature. The *Tuhfat al-Nafis* (The Precious Gift), which is considered to be the most important work of Malay historical literature since the *Sejarah Melayu*, was written in this Buginese tradition. According to Ismail Hussein, who undertook a study of several manuscripts of the *History of Johor* for his master's degree, about seventy per cent of the material found in the *Hikayat Negeri Johor* can be found in the first two-thirds of the *Tuhfat al-Nafis* (Ismail Hussein, 1963b: 394).

Ismail Hussein believes that the title *Hikayat Negeri Johor* is a misnomer. The text does not describe the kings of Johor but the Buginese rajas in Riau. Only at the beginning of the hikayat is there a story about Johor, and even that serves merely to provide the background to the main events. A more accurate title would have been "A History of the Sultan in Teluk Ketapang" (*Sejarah Sultan di Teluk Ketapang*), as one of the manuscripts Ismail Hussein studied began: "This is the history of the Sultan in Teluk Ketapang" ("*Inilah sejarah Sultan di Teluk Ketapang*"). The sultan referred to is Raja Haji, and a large part of this hikayat is about him. The reign of Raja Haji marked the high point of the Buginese influence in the Malay Peninsula. With the passing of Raja Haji, their political power began to wane. Nevertheless, they retained a strong influence over Selangor and the hikayat contains many stories about events in that state (Ismail Hussein, 1963a: 347).

One of the manuscripts, considered to be the most pristine copy ever found of this hikayat, was written in Riau, perhaps by Raja Ali or someone he commissioned. The synopsis below is based on Ismail Hussein (1963b) and R. O. Winstedt (1932a: 32-45).

8.6.1 Synopsis

In 1672 (1087 H), Johor was defeated by Jambi. Laksamana Abdul Jamal built a new settlement in Riau. Sultan Abdul Jalil Syah (Marhum Besar) died and was succeeded by Sultan Ibrahim. After the death of Sultan Ibrahim, Sultan Abdul Jalil ascended the throne. During this time, a beautiful palace was built in Johor for the new sultan. Not long after, however, the palace was destroyed in a fire. Sultan Abdul Jalil then moved his throne to Riau. After being attacked by the Buginese, Minangkabau and Patanis, he returned to Johor. A second wave of attacks by the Minangkabau forced the sultan to flee to Trengganu and thereafter to Pahang. The Minangkabau, under the command of Nakhoda Sekam, launched further attacks. The sultan was killed and his sons, Raja Sulaiman and Raja Abdul Rahman, were taken by Laksamana Nakhoda Sekam to Riau to present themselves to Raja Kecil.

Six months later, the Buginese, now under the command of Kelana Jaya Putra and his brother Daeng Menepuk, attacked Riau. Raja Kecil was driven out of Riau; he fled first to Kedah and then later to Siak in East Sumatra. The Buginese installed Raja Sulaiman as sultan but in return demanded that he reward Kelana Jaya Putra and Daeng Menepuk with a high rank for helping to elevate him to the throne. Raja Kecil twice launched a military offensive against Riau but failed on both occasions.

Daeng Ali became the Yang Dipertuan of Riau and attacked Selangor. Riau was twice subject to attacks; first by Raja Kecil and subsequently by Raja Alam. Both attacks failed. In the meantime, Raja Kecil threatened to attack Trengganu. Raja Sulaiman sailed to several places including Ungaran, Pahang and Trengganu. In Pahang, Raja Sulaiman repaired his father's tomb and built a wall around it. Daeng Ali died and was posthumously known by the title Marhum Mangkat di Kota.

He was succeeded as the Yang Dipertuan Muda of Selangor by Daeng Kemboja, who afterwards returned to take up an office in Riau. Raja Haji was taken to Selangor to be married. Not long after, a quarrel broke out between Raja Sulaiman and Daeng Kemboja, because Raja Sulaiman helped Raja Buang, the son of Raja Kecil, to fight a relative of Daeng Kemboja named Raja Alam. It was rumoured that the Dutch in Malaka planned to capture Raja Haji. Daeng Kemboja came to his aid but despite his help, Linggi was defeated by the Dutch. Daeng Kemboja then fled to Rembau where he made an alliance with the raja of Rembau to attack the Dutch. Many of the Dutch-controlled areas in Malaka fell into their hands. The Dutch called for a peace treaty. Daeng Kemboja agreed and not long after arrived in Malaka to sign a treaty with the Dutch. In due course of time, Sultan Sulaiman passed away.

Daeng Kemboja built a palace in Pangkalan Rama. Raja Haji went to Linggi and then to Jambi to marry the daughter of the Sultan of Jambi. He also married the daughter of Raja Besar of Indragiri. The Tengku Raja Selangor was installed as Sultan of Selangor. His daughter married Sultan Abdullah of Kedah.

The Dutch arrived to demand the debt of the late Sultan Sulaiman to the Dutch governor in Malaka for the cost of the attack on Linggi. Daeng Kemboja settled the debt. Raja Ismail, the son of Raja Buang of Siak, attacked Riau. In Singapore, Raja Ismail was defeated by Daeng Kemboja. Sultan Ahmad, the son of Sultan Sulaiman, passed away. His brother Sultan Mahmud was still a child living in the palace of Daeng Kemboja.

Daeng Kemboja sent his sons to Selangor. Their ship was wrecked but the boys were saved by Raja Haji. Raja Haji went to Kedah where he entered into a dispute with the locals. Raja Haji won the ensuing war. Not long after, news arrived that Daeng Kemboja had died. Raja Haji succeeded Daeng Kemboja as the Yang Dipertuan Muda of Riau.

Raja Haji built two palaces for Raja Mahmud. When the raja of Selangor died, he was succeeded by his son, Raja Ibrahim. At this time, the Dutch attacked Riau. Raja Ibrahim led his subjects against Malaka. Under siege, the Dutch called for reinforcements from Batavia. The war raged on. Raja Haji was slain in the battlefield and died as a martyr. Eventually Selangor fell to the Dutch and Raja Ibrahim was forced to flee to Pekan.

Raja Ali became the Yang Dipertuan Muda of Riau, replacing his father Raja Haji. The Dutch then attacked Riau. Raja Ali fled to Sukadana, pursued by the Dutch. Wherever he went, he was unable to escape them. Finally, Raja Ali went to Siantan. Meanwhile, the Sultan of Selangor was able to return to Selangor and reclaimed his kingdom, but he could not completely drive out the Dutch. For fourteen months, Dutch vessels blockaded the river mouth at Teluk Selangor, preventing supplies from entering Selangor. This made life extremely difficult for the inhabitants. In the end, the Sultan of Selangor had to make peace with the Dutch.

The Dutch built a new warehouse in Tanjung Pinang. Sultan Mahmud went to Trengganu and asked the Yang Dipertuan Kecil to negotiate peace on his behalf with the Dutch. However, the Yang Dipertuan Kecil did nothing. The Sultan of Selangor tried to mediate between Sultan Mahmud and the Dutch but the Dutch were unwilling to accept a truce. Not long after, the English took over control of Malaka from the Dutch and returned Riau to Sultan Mahmud.

The raja of Selangor helped Raja Ali make peace with the Dutch. Raja Ali traveled to Siantan to fetch his wife and children. Not long after, a conflict arose between Perak and Selangor. Sultan Ibrahim attacked Perak but failed to subdue it. Upon his return from Perak, he stationed his brother, Raja Jaafar, in Kelang.

8.6.2 *Peringatan Sejarah Negeri Johor*

Another history of Johor is the *Peringatan Sejarah Negeri Johor,* A Remembrance of Johor's History (Kratz, 1973). It begins with a summary of Johor's history from 1672 down to the birth of Sultan Sulaiman in 1699. This is followed by a series of brief accounts describing events that took place in Johor from 1721 to 1750. As these stories are centered on Sultan Sulaiman, some scholars consider this hikayat to be a political biography of Sultan Sulaiman of Johor (Kratz, 1973: 24). The style is similar to that of the *Hikayat Negeri Johor*. The description of each event begins with a phrase such as: *"Kemudian daripada itu"* ("Thereafter"), *"pada Hijriah tahun seribu"* ("in the year one thousand Hijrah"), or *"pada Hijriah itulah"* ("in that Hijrah year"). Andaya states that the dates found in this hikayat are accurate and correspond to those found in Dutch sources (Andaya, 1978: 11). However, the hikayat makes for ponderous reading because of its dense prose and verbose style.

The name of the author of is unknown. According to Kratz, it was undoubtedly composed by someone close to Bendahara Tun Hassan, to whom a tribute is paid in a *syair* at the end of the hikayat (Kratz, 1973: 34-35).

Here is a brief summary of the *Peringatan Sejarah Negeri Johor.*

Following Johor's defeat by Jambi in 1083H, the Laksamana was ordered to build a new kingdom in Riau. There is a brief description of the reigns of Sultan Abdul Jalil Syah and Sultan Ibrahim. Sultan Mahmud, who moved to Johor with his warriors and subjects, was killed in Kota Tinggi. Sultan Abdul Jalil Syah ibni Datuk Bendahara was installed as the new ruler. "*Dan habislah silsilah raja maklum yang di negeri Malaka,*" says the text, "And so ends the genealogy of the known kings of Malaka." Sultan Abdul Jalil then moved to Pancor, where he built a palace of great beauty. Not long after however, the palace burnt down and he moved to Riau. Because many enemies from the Minangkabau, Buginese and Patani regions attacked Riau, the sultan fled to Johor. When Johor fell to the Minangkabau, the sultan moved to Trengganu and then to Pahang. While in Pahang, Laksamana Nakhoda Sekam came to take Sultan Abdul Jalil back to Riau. A letter ordered the Laksamana's men to run amok. The sultan died a martyr; his sons, Raja Sulaiman and Raja Abdul Rahman, were taken to Riau and presented before Raja Kecil.

Not long after, Kelana Jaya Putra and Daeng Menepuk attacked Riau. Raja Kecil was defeated and fled to Kedah. Many Malay rajas were taken captive. Raja Sulaiman was installed as Sultan by Kelana and Daeng Menepuk. Kelana Putra Jaya was awarded the title Raja Muda; Daeng Menepuk became the Raja Tua. At this time, many Buginese and Malays intermarried. There were frequent conflicts between Sultan Sulaiman and the Buginese living in Riau. A letter from the Raja of Pagar Ruyung reaffirmed the Malay-Minangkabau alliance, pledging that: "The sons of Minangkabau will recognise no other master except the descendants of the king of Johor."

Raja Kecil came to Riau; he made an oath in the mosque that he would surrender his claims over Johor to Sultan Sulaiman if Raja Tua and Raja Muda returned his wife to him. Despite his oath, Raja Kecil made repeated forays into Riau. On one occasion, he sent Raja Alam and Raja Emas Daeng with a large military force. Raja Alam and Raja Emas were defeated but managed to escape with their lives.

From this point on, the hikayat reads more like a diary, with no link whatsoever between one episode and the next. Among the events chronicled were the travels of Sultan Sulaiman to various places, such as Trengganu, Indragiri, Kelantan and Siantan. It also includes accounts of journeys made by other historical personages, especially that of Maharaja Denda. Births, deaths, and the appointments and installation of high-ranking court officials were also likewise chronicled. A poem was written to commemorate Orang Kaya Bungsu Tun Hassan's investiture as bendahara, and reads in part:

Bendahara Seri Maharaja
Johan bangsawan lakunya saja
Sederhana elok ditentang durja
Laksana syams berkandung teja.

Johan muhtasnya lakunya sahda
Menjadi bendahara ganti ayahanda
Johan tidak berbanyak canda
Menjadi tiang kerajaan baginda.

> The Bendaraha Seri Maharaja
> A champion amongst nobles is he
> Poised and aplomb in the face of gloom
> Illuminating and bright like the moon.
>
> August and illustrious is he
> To become a bendahara after his father
> This champion is not given to frivolity
> For a pillar of the king's government is he.

This hikayat ends in the year 1164 H. In that year, "Maharaja Denda had a headache ...", and "Encik Riau brought Nursani and his child, Encik Siti, on Saturday. And that is it, the end."

Finally, it should be noted that there is also a more recent work dealing with the reign of Sultan Abu Bakar of Johor, the *Hikayat Johor*.

8.7 *Sejarah Raja-raja Riau*

The *History of the Rajas of Riau* depicts part of the history of the Malays and Buginese in the Riau Islands. This work is also known as *Hikayat Negeri Riau*, *Silsilah Raja-raja Bugis* and *Aturan Setia Bugis dengan Melayu*. A manuscript of this hikayat kept in the National Museum in Jakarta (v.d.Wall Collection 62) mentions that Muhammad Said Muwallad Riau ibn Daeng Mempawah Bugis copied this text in Pulau Penyengat in 1274 H.

Though the identity of its author is unknown, it is generally attributed to Engku Busu, who is mentioned in the *Tuhfat al-Nafis*. It is possible that Engku Busu took some of his material from the *Hikayat Riau* (K.L. 24), composed by Raja Ali ibn Raja Jaafar, the brother of Raja Abdul Rahman.

8.7.1 Summary

Here is a summary of the K.L. 37 manuscript in Leiden, which was romanised by Jamiliah binti Juni at the Universiti Kebangsaan Malaysia.

The hikayat begins with a reminder to its readers not to engage in wrongdoing. Those who have strayed should return to the path of virtue. It then goes on to give an account of the alliance between the Malays and the Buginese.

After a battle at the Straits of Alah, the Yamtuan of Trengganu, Sultan Mansur, gave Yamtuan Raja Ismail the hand of his daughter. This angered Tengku Busu, as Raja Ismail was the grandson of Raja Kecil. Meanwhile, Sultan Mahmud ascended the throne after his own father, Sultan Sulaiman, passed away in Pahang. His uncle, Datuk Bendahara Tun Hussain, was angry that he had to pay obeisance to someone younger than himself.

Raja Kecil came to Johor to ask for the hand of Tengku Bungsu. Datuk Bendahara approved of the marriage but later insisted that Raja Kecil was only the son of a common raja and not the true son of the raja of Minangkabau. Others said that Raja Kecil was the son of Encik Pong by Sultan Mahmud, and had been raised by a Minangkabau family. Because of these rumours, Tengku Bungsu neglected her husband and was taken by Tengku Tengah to live in the sultan's palace. Raja Kecil left Johor.

Datuk Bendahara invited Raja Kecil to attack Johor, promising that he would support him. When Raja Kecil attacked Johor, the Yamtuan Muda continued his game of chess, before killing his wives and children as he did not want them to become concubines of the Minangkabau. A few of his sons survived and became Raja Kecil's servants. Raja Kecil then returned to Riau. Datuk Bendahara asked to be appointed ruler but was refused, as Raja Kecil insisted that only Raja Sulaiman had the right to be sultan.

Datuk Bendahara deeply resented Raja Kecil and invited the Buginese to attack Riau. Led by Kelana Jaya Putra, the Buginese defeated Raja Kecil and the Minangkabau. Datuk Bendahara again asked to be made raja but the Buginese too refused his request and remained in Riau. Raja Kecil, Raja Alam and Raja Buang led the Minangkabau against Riau many times, but failed each time.

Sultan Sulaiman was very fond of his Buginese allies. He made Kelana Jaya Putra the Raja Muda, and gave Daeng Menepuk the title of Raja Tua. Many Buginese also married daughters of the Riau aristocracy.

Datuk Bendahara and Yamtuan Kecik continued to resent the Buginese and resorted to all sorts of intrigues against them. Raja Muda could no longer tolerate living in Riau and sailed for Linggi, leaving only Raja Haji and his siblings behind him. The Yamtuan Kecil of Trengganu and Datuk Bendahara created further trouble in Riau. Later the Dutch arrived. Both the Yamtuan Kecil and Datuk Bendahara wanted to surrender Raja Haji to the Dutch. Raja Haji and the Buginese fled to Sungai Timun, where they built a fort and fought against Datuk Bendahara and his Trengganu allies. Unable to stop the war, Sultan Sulaiman ordered the Yamtuan of Trengganu and Raja Haji to go to Linggi in order to fetch the Raja Muda. On their way, the Yamtuan of Trengganu called at Malaka and told the Dutch that Sultan Sulaiman wanted them to attack Linggi and capture Raja Haji. One of Raja Haji's men overheard the plot and informed Raja Haji. Not long after, Dutch warships attacked Linggi. The Yamtuan of Trengganu wanted to take Sultan Sulaiman to Trengganu. But Raja di Baruh protested and news soon leaked out that Linggi had fallen to the Dutch as a result of the treachery of Datuk Bendahara and the Yamtuan of Trengganu. Sultan Sulaiman was furious when he heard this and refused to go to Trengganu. In the course of time, Sultan Sulaiman died and was initially succeeded by a close sibling. At that time, Sultan Mahmud was only forty days old.

The Dutch demanded to be reimbursed for the cost of the Linggi campaign. The debt was defrayed by Janggut, who was then the Raja Muda. When Janggut had first come to Riau from Rembau, the kingdom was in a dire state of poverty; many of its inhabitants were dying of starvation and no ships called at its harbour to trade. But due to his efforts, Riau soon flourished. Janggut kept a vigilant eye on the intrigues and plots of the various rival Malay factions. When Raja Tua was discovered to have set fire to the arsenal at Pengkalan Rama, Janggut banished him from Riau. When Raja Ismail attacked Riau, he too was defeated by Janggut. Raja Ismail fled to Trangganu, blaming the Malays for the constant enmity between the Buginese and the Minangkabau.

Marhum Janggut died and the Sultan of Teluk Ketapang succeeded him as the Yamtuan Muda. The population of Riau increased and the Buginese there lived in solidarity and harmony. Despite the blessings God bestowed on them, the Malays were still dissatisfied and intent on creating further mischief. The Yamtuan of Trengganu never ceased plotting against the Buginese. Each year the Bendahara of Pahang wrote to the English India Company, the Dutch East India Company and to Malaka, asking for help against the Buginese at Riau.

In 1141 H, Daeng Ali became Raja Muda and was later succeeded by Daeng Kemboja. In 1161 H, the oath of alliance between the Malays and Buginese was renewed. It stated that: "Whoever violates this oath will bring upon himself and all his descendants Allah's retribution." In the same year, Raja Indra Bungsu was made Datuk Bendahara. Not long after that, Datuk Bendahara and the Yamtuan Muda agreed that all Malay offenders would henceforth be tried by the Bendahara and Buginese offenders tried by the Yamtuan Muda. This was done for the betterment of the people and for the sake of the country. Not long after, the Yamtuan Muda moved to Linggi and sent a message to Riau to ask if the oath between the Buginese and Malays still prevailed. When the Yamtuan Muda died, he was succeeded his son. The Malay chiefs presented themselves before the Yamtuan Muda and implored him to cherish the descendants of Seri Paduka Marhum Besar, Sultan Sulaiman.

8.8 *Silsilah Melayu dan Bugis*

The *Genealogy of the Malays and Buginese* is another chronicle dealing with the activities of the Buginese in the Malay Archipelago up to 1737, specifically in Kalimantan, the Riau Islands and the Malay Peninsula. Scholars are generally agreed that its author was Raja Ali Haji, the grandson of Raja Haji, the powerful Buginese king who was defeated near Teluk Ketapang in 1784. His father, Raja Ahmad, was also an important political figure who went to Jakarta on a number of occasions to take part in negotiations with the Dutch.

Raja Ali Haji was born in Pulau Penyengat in Riau. When he was a boy he traveled to Mecca with his father to perform the *Hajj*. He lived and studied in Mecca for a time, and upon his return to Riau served as an advisor to his brother, the Yamtuan Muda. He spent a number of years as a teacher, writing a book on grammar, *Bustanul-Katibin* (Garden of Writers), and editing a dictionary, *Kitab Pengetahuan Bahasa* (Book of Linguistic Knowledge).

The *Silsilah Melayu dan Bugis* has a number of special features. Firstly, it is written in the historiographical tradition introduced by the Buginese to the Riau Islands, which gives the exact date for every event it describes. Secondly, there are few traces of legendary or mythical elements. Whenever the credibility of story is deemed to be dubious, the author usually indicates this by using such words as "*konon*" ("apparently" or "purportedly") or "*wa 'llahu a'lam*" ("only God knows") and so on.

Thirdly, the author makes reference to other written sources. At least eight such sources are used in this hikayat, including: *Sejarah Negeri Johor*, *Sejarah Raja-raja Riau*, *Sejarah Siak* and *Hikayat Upu Daeng Menambun* (Tale of Upu Daeng Menambun). Whenever the author includes an account from a source he deems contentious, he usually signals this with words such as "*kata kaul*" ("word has it that") or "*menurut riwayat*" ("according to the story"). Fourthly, each event narrated in the hikayat is concluded with a beautiful *syair*. Lastly, the hikayat is written from the perspective of the Buginese who were very anti-Minangkabau.

This hikayat has been published several times. It was first published in 1911 by Syed Abdullah ibn Abu Bakar al-Hadad of Al-Imam Printers in Singapore. An excerpt was then summarized in English by Hans Overbeck (Overbeck, 1926). In 1956, a reprint under the title of *Silsilah Melayu dan Bugis dan Sekalian Raja-rajanya* was commissioned by His Royal Highness the Sultan of Johor, Sultan Ibrahim. The text was transcribed by Haji Abdullah, the son of Khairuddin, a native of Juannah. In 1973, another edition was published by Pustaka Antara, Kuala Lumpur, and edited by Arena Wati. All the *syairs* in the original text were omitted and the main text itself was rearranged into 38 chapters. In 1984 a new edition was published, based on manuscript No. 209 of the National Museum Library in Kuala Lumpur. This edition is similar to the previous texts, except that it contained a foreword correcting the errors in the history of the Buginese made in earlier versions. The manuscript of this edition had been copied on 5 Rabi'ul-akhir 1282 H and belonged to Haji Abdul Ghani (Mohd. Yusof, 1980/81: 4-6).

Below is a summary based on the Arena Wati edition (1973) and Overbeck's synopsis.

After praising Allah and His prophets, the author states that he obtained a book from his devout brother, Sayid Al-Syarif Abdulrahman ibn Sayid al-Syarif Kasim, the Sultan of Pontianak, and used it as the basis of his history of the Malays and the Buginese.

According to the *silsilah,* the Buginese are descended from a queen of Luwuk, by the name of Siti Melangkai, who some say was descended from Balkis, the queen of Sheba. It then gives the genealogy of Siti Melangkai's descendants down to La Madusalat, the first Buginese raja to embrace Islam. La Madusalat begat Upu Tenriborong Daeng, who had five sons by the same mother: Daeng Parani, Daeng Menambun, Daeng Marewak, Daeng Calak and Daeng Kamase. The story then continues with the genealogy of the kings of Mempawah down to Panembahan Dikirim Kesuma, who had two sons, Duli Maulana Al-Sultan Muhammad Safiyuddin and Raden Lekar, and a daughter named Raja Surya Kesuma.

Sultan Muhammad Safiyuddin's two sons were fierce enemies. The younger son, Pangeran Agung, resented his elder brother, Sultan Muhammad Zainuddin, and led an uprising against him. Forced to flee, Sultan Muhammad Zainuddin took refuge in a mosque. His subjects secretly sent him food.

The Raja of Luwuk, La Madusalat, had three sons. The eldest was Payung, who would later succeed his father on the throne of Luwuk; the second was Upu Daeng Rilaka, who sought his fortune further west; and the youngest was Upu Daeng Biasa who went to seek his fortune in Java and Batavia.

Upu Daeng Rilaka and his five sons went to Topamana. He married the queen of Topamana and begat a daughter, Datu Ri Watu. One day while in Topamana, Daeng Rilaka was presented with a piece of iron, which he ordered to be made into a small dagger (*badik*) and an artificial cock-fighting spur (*taji*). Both the dagger and spur were revered for their supernatural powers and became the royal insignia. Some time afterwards, Upu Daeng Rilaka visited Bone. He was well received by the raja. During his stay, the raja of Bone asked Daeng Rilaka to accompany him to

Mengkasar. When the raja of Bone was about to return to his country, he ordered Daeng Rilaka to stay behind in Mengkasar. On one occasion, Upu Daeng Parani stabbed the prince of Mengkasar but was pardoned by the raja of Bone. Not long afterwards, Upu Daeng Rilaka asked leave to go to Java to see his brother, Daeng Biasa, who was now the Major of the Buginese community in Batavia. In Batavia, Upu Daeng Rilaka borrowed money from his brother to buy a boat to sail to the Malay Peninsula.

When he arrived at Siantan, he stayed with Nakhoda Alang, a Buginese whose daughter was married to Upu Daeng Parani. The news soon reached Daeng Rilaka that Raja Chulan, the son of the Minangkabau ruler, had gone to Cambodia looking for a challenger to compete against his fighting-cock and was willing to bet a large sum of money on the outcome of the fight. And so Upu Daeng Rilaka set sail for Cambodia, taking with him twelve chests filled with stones, which he pretended were pieces of silver. Daeng Rilaka's cock won and Raja Chulan gave him his ketch and all its cargo. Upu Daeng Rilaka returned to Siantan, where a son had been born to Upu Daeng Parani, named Daeng Kamboja. He later had a daughter, Daeng Tijah.

The story then provides a genealogy of the Malay kings, beginning with Alexander the Great and continuing to Sultan Mahmud who was killed in Kota Tinggi in the country of Makah Tauhid. "And so ends the line of the Malay rajas of Malaka, and the kingship passed to the line of the Bendahara Tun Habib, as it is ancient Malay custom that if a royal line dies out, the kingship is assumed by the Bendahara, who has the same origins as the king."

The story of Raja Sulaiman then follows. Datuk Bendahara encouraged Raja Kecil to attack Johor. Sultan Abdul Jalil Syah was killed by Laksamana Nakhoda Sekam. Raja Sulaiman and Raja Abdul Rahman were taken to Riau. The Minangkabau refused to install Datuk Bendahara as the raja of Riau, so he asked the Buginese to help Raja Sulaiman. This was the reason why the Buginese first came to Riau.

Sultan Muhammad Zainuddin of Matan sent a messenger to Siantan to ask the Buginese prince, Upu Daeng Parani, for assistance. Upu Daeng Parani and his four brothers sailed to Matan. Upon reaching Matan, they were able to release Sultan Muhammad Zainuddin with ease. The sons-in-law of the raja of Matan, Daeng Mateka and Haji Hafis, did not want to fight Upu Daeng Parani and his brothers, saying: *"tidak patut orang Bugis bertikam berbunuhan dengan sebab pekerjaan orang"* ("it is not right for Buginese to fight and kill one another over the machinations of others"). Thereafter, Pangeran Agung, the raja of Matan, was captured and imprisoned together with thirty female servants who became his concubines. He did not leave prison until he died.

The five Upu brothers then set sail for Riau where they defeated Raja Kecil. Raja Sulaiman asked the brothers to attack Siak and ordered them to bring back all the treasures and royal insignia of Riau that Raja Kecil had carried off with him. The brothers agreed to help but stipulated that if their assault against Siak was successful and they made Raja Sulaiman the Yamtuan and the kingdom hereditary in his family, then one of the five brothers should become the Yamtuan Muda. Furthermore, "the Yamtuan Besar's role shall be like the wife; if she is given food, only then does she eat. Whilst the Yamtuan Muda shall be the husband; his decision is to be followed in all matters." Raja Sulaiman agreed, and with the support of the Buginese in Selangor, the Upu brothers defeated Linggi. They also captured Siak after an intense battle. The Buginese princes seized the royal paraphernalia and treasures and restored them to Raja Sulaiman. Thereafter, Sultan

Sulaiman was crowned as Sultan Sulaiman Badrul Alam Syah, King of Johor, Pahang and Riau, and all their dominions. Upu Daeng Marewa was installed as Raja Muda while Daeng Parani and Daeng Gallak were married to Sultan Sulaiman's sisters, Tengku Tengah and Tengku Mandak. The coronation and wedding ceremonies were attended by a vast number of guests.

Some time after, the eldest prince of Kedah invited the Upu brothers to assist him in his quarrel over the throne with his younger brother. The Upu brothers departed for Kedah and proclaimed the elder prince as the ruler. His younger brother, the second Yamtuan, fled. Later, with the help of Raja Kecil, the ousted prince came back again to disturb the security of Kedah. Upu Daeng Parani wrote to Raja Kecil, urging him to mediate between the King of Kedah and his brother. The negotiations failed. "And so the Buginese were at war with Raja Kecil once again, creating chaos in Kedah and its vassal states." Kedah remained in a state of conflict for two years. During this time there were only brief periods of peace. At last Upu Daeng Parani wrote a letter to Raja Kecil, urging him "to fight man against man and end this matter once and for all." Raja Kecil was afraid. Instead he devised a plan to kill Upu Daeng Parani. During an attack on Raja Kecil's fort, the prince opened fire and killed Upu Daeng Parani. As a consequence, "The Buginese ran amok, killing every man of Siak and Kedah they met", and burning many villages. Raja Kecil and his followers fled to Siak. When the war ended, the Yamtuan Muda and Daeng Galak returned to Riau. The Buginese rebuilt and fortified Riau, and promoted trade. Riau flourished and its population increased. Many boats, ships, ketches, sloops, junks and merchant-vessels of all description called at its harbour to trade.

Although Raja Kecil fled to Siak after his defeat in Kedah, after a while he returned to Riau to visit his wife, Tengku Kamariah, and his son, Raja Buang. With his arrival, Riau was thrown into further chaos, as he and his followers were bent on creating trouble for the Buginese. Frequent skirmishes ensued between the people of Siak and the Buginese. "The people of Riau did not even have peace in which to earn a livelihood." Peace and trade in Riau were disrupted and the people fell into hardship. Even Raja Kecil's own followers from Siak felt that their welfare was being neglected by their leader and urged him to make peace with the Buginese. The Yamtuan Muda and Sultan Sulaiman were prepared to accept Raja Kecil's offer of peace on condition that he first swore in the mosque that he would not create any further trouble in Riau; secondly, that he demolished all his stockades, and finally, that he gave back all the people he had taken away at the conquest of Johor and returned them to Raja Sulaiman. Raja Kecil pretended to accept these conditions and returned to Siak with his wife and children. Once back in Siak, however, he thought of nothing else but of how to ruin Riau and made preparations for a new attack. When all was ready, he set sail for Riau. Again his plan failed. A few years later, he attacked Riau once more and was again defeated. With the war between the Buginese and Raja Kecil finally over, Riau was at peace and flourished. Hundreds of vessels came from Bengal, Java, the further East, China and Siam, laden with goods. "Thousands of Chinese coolies came to work for the Malays in the gambier plantations. And hundreds of Arab *sayyids* and *sheikh*s came to live in the hostels for travelers (*rumah wakaf*) near mosques and prayer halls (*surau*)."

The Sultan of Sambas, Sultan Adil, invited the five Upu brothers to visit him, and if they liked, to settle there. Upu Daeng Kamase and Upu Daeng Manambun sailed to Sambas. Daeng Kamase married the Sultan of Sambas's sister, Raden Tengah. Daeng Menambun continued his journey to Mempawah, where he was installed by Sultan Muhammad Zainuddin as the Pangeran

Emas Surya Negara. Daeng Menambun married that sultan's daughter, Putri Kesumba. He then resumed his travels and founded his own kingdom in Sebukit.

The Dutch made Upu Daeng Biyasa the Major of the Buginese community in Batavia as a reward for helping them quell a Chinese uprising in Kota Intan. He sent his son Daeng Kalola visit his other brothers and inform them that their debts with the merchants of Batavia, which the Major had guaranteed, had already been paid by him. Daeng Kalola sailed to Riau, but met with bad weather and was blown to Mempawah. There, Pangeran Emas Surya Negara asked him to take his son, Gusti Jamril, to Batavia. In Batavia, Gusti Jamril and Daeng Muda were married in a lavish ceremony attended by many guests. Gusti Jamril then asked permission to return to Mempawah. Later he traveled to Pinang Sikayuk to sell goods he had brought from Batavia. He was received with great affection by Pangeran Dipati, the Dayak chief (*penghulu*). Gusti Jamril so impressed the pangeran with his knowledge of the Quran and learning that he was offered one of the chief's daughters in marriage. Gusti Jamril replied that he would have to consult his parents. Pangeran Emas Surya Negara disapproved of the proposed marriage. Instead, he sent Damang Rilaka to present Pangeran Dipati with a list of debtors, Malays and Dayaks alike. When Damang Rilaka insisted that the debts be settled immediately, violence erupted. Pangeran Emas Surya Negara prepared to attack Pangeran Dipati and his allies. The war that ensued between the Buginese and Dayaks was intense. Eventually Pangeran Dipati and his army were defeated and he was forced to flee. After the victory, Pangeran Emas Surya Negara gathered the chiefs of the Mempawah-Dayaks in Pinang Sekayu and made them pay homage to him as the Panembahan of Mempawah.

The hikayat ends with an account of Raja Alam, the son of Raja Kecil, who was sent by his father to attack Riau in 1150 H. Mohd. Yusof Md. Nor's edition (1984) notes that Yamtuan Muda Upu Daeng Palil went to Selangor and married the daughter of Arung Palli. It also provides extensive genealogies for the various Buginese families throughout the region.

8.9 *Tuhfat al-Nafis*

Winstedt has described *The Precious Gift* as the most important work of Malay historical literature after the *Sejarah Melayu* (Winstedt, 1958: 135). He did not provide a reason for this assertion, although I suspect that he was referring to the sheer scope of the work. The book provides us with the genealogies of Malay, Buginese, Siak and Johor kings down to the founding of modern Singapore by Raffles. The events narrated are given exact dates. There are hardly any folktales or myths. The author drew on a range of historical sources and sometimes the same event is described from a number of perspectives. The work is strongly Buginese-centric and tends to glorify the Buginese, even to a point that it is at times very anti-Malay. Scholars first believed that the *Tuhfat al-Nafis* was written by Raja Ali bin Raja Ahmad. However, in 1967 an English scholar drew attention to the Maxwell 2 manuscript, held by The Royal Asiatic Society in London, which contains the following pencil notation:

> *Tuhfat al-Nafis.* Begun by Raja Haji Ahmad (also known as Ungku Haji Tua), the son of Raja Haji who died in Riau at the age of 103—continued and completed by his son Raja Haji Ali, who passed away at the age of 78. (Amin Sweeney, 1967a: 155-156).

Virginia Matheson agreed with this view in her PhD thesis on the *Tuhfat al-Nafis*. She stated that the manuscript was completed by Raja Ahmad in November 1866, then rewritten and completed by Raja Ali before his death in 1872 (Matheson, 1982: xxi).

This work has been published several times. Winstedt's edition (1932b) was based on a manuscript lent to him by Tengku Fatimah, the daughter of Sultan Abu Bakar of Johor. It was later romanised by Encik Munir bin Ali and published in Singapore in 1965. A new edition by Virginia Matheson, 1982, was based on a manuscript presented to A. L. van Hasselt in 1896 on his retirement as Resident of Riau (Matheson, 1982: xxiii). Matheson's short version contains no embellishments or revisions; Winstedt and Munir Ali's text is a longer version. Matheson has compared the language style of these two versions (Matheson, 1971). Below is a summary of *Tuhfat* based on Winstedt and Munir Ali's longer version.

After praising Allah, the author states that on 3 Syaaban 1282 H he was moved to write a history of the Malay and Buginese kings and their descendants, which he decided to name *Tuhfat al-Nafis* (The Precious Gift).

The hikayat begins by recounting the genealogy of the Malay kings from Raja Sri Tri Buana, the founder of Singapore, to the fall of Malaka at the hands of the Portuguese and the death of Sultan Mahmud (this story is similar to that in the *Sejarah Melayu*). This is followed by a genealogy of the Johor, Siak and Buginese kings, the Buginese genealogy being the longest.

Sultan Mahmud killed Megat Sri Rama's pregnant wife over a trivial matter. Megat Sri Rama, with the consent of the Bendahara and Temenggung, killed Sultan Mahmud. The Bendahara then became sultan, taking the title Sultan Jalil. Raja Kecil attacked Johor. Sultan Abdul Jalil fled to Pahang but was killed by Raja Kecil's men. Upu Daeng Parani and his brothers successfully attacked Riau. Raja Sulaiman was crowned king and received the title Sultan Sulaiman Badr Alam Syah. Raja Kecil made many attempts to take back Riau but failed to do so. He also attacked Upu Daeng Parani and his brothers in Kedah but was again defeated. When his wife Tengku Kamariah died, he went mad and used to sleep beside her grave. The stories told in the *Tuhfat al-Nafis* about the Johor, Riau and Buginese kings are not very different from those found in the *Hikayat Negeri Johor*, *Sejarah Raja-Raja Riau* or the *Silsilah Melayu dan Buginese dan Sekalian Raja-rajanya*.

Raja Alam, Raja Kecil's son, was driven out of Siak and built a new kingdom in Pulau Siantan. Sultan Sulaiman and Tun Dalam, the Sultan of Trengganu, tried to drive Raja Alam from Siantan but failed. Several months later, the Buginese arrived and defeated Raja Alam. Raja Alam then fled to Matan. Daeng Kemboja was then installed as the Yamtuan Muda.

In response to the continued scheming of Tun Dalam, the Sultan of Trengganu, Daeng Kemboja left Riau and sailed to Linggi. Tun Dalam sent for a Dutch warship to remove Raja Haji; the latter resisted and the attack was unsuccessful. Both sides then made peace. Raja Haji and Tun Dalam sailed to Malaka. Tun Dalam told the Dutch governor that Sultan Sulaiman wanted the Dutch to attack Linggi and arrest Raja Haji. The Yamtuan Muda heard of the plot and sent the Raja of Selangor to Tanjong Kling to bring Raja Haji to Linggi. Not long after, the Dutch arrived to drive the Buginese out of Linggi. The Buginese could not withstand the attack and retreated to Rembau. In the meantime, Tun Dalam had fled to Riau and, telling Sultan Sulaiman nothing about the defeat at Linggi, tried to get him and the Malays to sail to Trengganu. Sultan Sulaiman eventually learned about the defeat at Linggi and was furious with Tun Dalam who then fled to Trengganu.

Soon, the Dutch asked Sultan Sulaiman to compensate them for the cost of the Linggi campaign. After meeting with the Sultan of Trengganu, Sultan Sulaiman acceded to the Dutch request. A peace treaty was subsequently ratified with the Dutch. Raja Haji took those under his command back to Riau. Riau had been so empty and poor since the Buginese left that Sultan Sulaiman sent an envoy to Linggi to invite the Yamtuan Muda to come back. An oath of mutual allegiance was sworn between the Malays and Buginese and amity was restored.

With the passing of time, Sultan Sulaiman died, followed closely by Raja di Baruh. His eight-year-old grandson, Raja Ahmad, was proclaimed sultan. The Yamtuan Muda built a palace at Pengkalan Rama. Raja Haji became Engku Kelana. During his time as Engku Kelana, Raja Haji helped the Sultan of Indragiri repel a Minangkabau invasion. He also defeated a Minangkabau saint reputed to have supernatural powers (*keramat*) who tried to usurp the sultan, and had him executed. The Yamtuan Muda paid Riau's debt to the Dutch in Malaka from the sale of opium. Sultan Ahmad died and was succeeded by his younger brother, Raja Mahmud.

Urged on by the Malays of Riau, Raja Ismail, an unsuccessful claimant to the Siak throne, prepared to attack Riau. The Yamtuan Muda of Riau heard of the plot and moved a supply of weapons from Riau to Pulau Bayan. He also banished Raja Tua from Riau for his involvement in the conspiracy. Raja Ismail attacked Riau; although he was defeated at sea off Singapore, he managed to escape capture. He helped the Sultan of Palembang attack Mempawah. After murdering Dewa Perkasa, he then raided Siantan. He married the ruler of Trengganu's daughter. Not long after, Raja Ismail led a successful invasion of Siak and installed himself as the Yamtuan Besar. His son-in-law, a Sayid from an Arab family, was appointed as Tun Besar. The Yamtuan Besar died in Siak and was succeeded by his son, Sultan Yahya Syah.

On his way to Malaka, Raja Haji's ship ran ashore and its cargo was pillaged. When he reached Malaka, he demanded compensation from the Dutch. The Sultan of Perak appointed Sultan Salehuddin as the Raja of Selangor. Raja Haji and the Sultan of Selangor decided to demand the repayment of war expenses from the Sultan of Kedah. When he refused, they attacked Kedah and he was defeated.

Next, Raja Haji sailed for Pontianak to help Sharif Abdul Rahman in his attack on Raja of Sanggau. When he heard that Yamtuan Muda Daeng Kemboja had died, Raja Haji quickly returned to Pahang. He was subsequently made the Yamtuan Muda of Riau. Under his rule, Riau prospered. The great wealth of the Buginese made the Malays in Riau jealous and many then decided to move to Trengganu.

Sultan Salahuddin died and was succeeded by his son, Raja Ibrahim. Not long after, a quarrel arose between Raja Haji and the Dutch at Malaka over the division of certain funds. The hostilities led to war. The Dutch attacked Pulau Penyengat; the fighting lasted for almost a year, with neither side gaining an advantage. The two sides tried to negotiate a truce but talks between them failed. Sultan Ibrahim of Selangor joined forces with Raja Haji. The Dutch retreated to Malaka. Malaka was surrounded. Raja Haji built a fort at Teluk Ketapang and amused his followers by sponsoring dances (*joget*). The Dutch sent reinforcements from Batavia. They bribed Sultan Muhammad Ali of Siak to join them. Meanwhile, the Sultan of Selangor then went to Rembau to marry. The

Dutch made a surprise attack on Teluk Ketapang. Raja Haji's troops were vastly outnumbered; he died in the battle. The plan was for his body to be taken to Batavia but the ship that was to convey his remains caught fire at sea.

Assisted by Yam Tuan Muhammad Ali of Siak and Sayid Ali, the Dutch attacked Selangor. The Sultan of Selangor fled to Pahang. The Yamtuan of Siak stole all the property he could carry and sailed back to Siak, leaving Sayid Ali as Yamtuan of Selangor. Not long after, the Sultan of Selangor, with the aid of the Sultan of Pahang, regained possession of Selangor. Sayid Ali fled to Siak. The Sultan of Selangor then concluded a treaty with the Dutch.

The Buginese were forced to appoint Raja Ali as Yamtuan Muda of Riau. When the Dutch attacked Riau, the Yamtuan Muda and the Buginese fled to Sukadana. The Dutch made a treaty with the Malays in Riau, which stipulated that no Buginese was to hold public office in Riau.

Sultan Mahmud managed to drive the Dutch out of Riau, with the aid of the Raja of Tempasok. But they did not dare remain in Riau and sailed to Pahang, then to Trengganu. Sultan Mahmud asked the Sultan of Trengganu to make peace with the Dutch. The Dutch refused; their reply was so rude that it could not be read in public.

Raja Yahya became the Yamtuan Besar of Siak. Raja Muhammad Ali retired. Piracy was rife. Muhammad Ali's son-in-law, Sayid Ali, himself a notorious pirate, sacked Singgora and threatened Trengganu. The Sultan of Trengganu asked help from the English. Laughing, the English replied that they could finish Sayid Ali in three hours. In the meantime, Raja Ali had been driven by the Sultan of Pontianak. The Dutch left Sukadana and settled in Siantan. Raja Ali moved from Siantan to Langat and then to Muar.

The English took over Malaka in 1208 H (1795 A.D.). Both the English and the Dutch recognized Sultan Mahmud. The Sultan of Selangor went to Lingga and married Tengku Tengah. The Sultan of Selangor remained at Lingga for two years but could not reconcile the Buginese and Malays. He returned to his state, later defeating Perak. Upon his return from Perak, the Sultan gave Kelang to Raja Jaafar. The Yamtuan Muda Ali came to Muar and waged war on Engku Muda. Sultan Mahmud pacified them and married Raja Hamidah, the daughter of Raja Haji.

On the death of the Sultan of Siak, Sayid Ali took Siak from Raja Yahya, who fled to Trengganu, became mad and died.

Sultan Mahmud built a palace for Tengku Hamidah. Yamtuan Muda Ali died and was replaced by Raja Jaafar. During his time as the Yamtuan Muda, Raja Jaafar killed a Minangkabau holy man (Lebai Keramat). After some time, Sultan Mahmud died and was succeeded by Raja Abdul Rahman, a very pious ruler.

Major William Farquhar came from Malaka and promised to support Riau. The Yamtuan Muda signed a treaty with the Dutch instead. Farquhar was furious. Not long after, Raffles arrived in Singapore. Tengku Long, the elder brother of Sultan Abdul Rahman and the Temenggung, was installed as ruler of Singapore.

The Dutch opened a customs-station at Tanjong Pinang. A Buginese chief, Arung Bilawa, persuaded Nakhoda Medong to divorce his wife, Raja Fatimah, and then married her himself. During the wedding celebrations, cannons were discharged. This alarmed the Dutch, who summoned the bridegroom. Daeng Renggi and his men came instead. They were heavily armed and a fight broke out. Arung Bilawa fled to Singapore. After some time, he was allowed back to Riau and was given a monthly salary by the Dutch. The Yamtuan Muda Raja Jaafar returned to Riau and worked with the Dutch to make preparations for the installation of Sultan Abdul Rahman.

Sultan Abdul Rahman sailed to Pahang with his son, Tengku Besar. The Yamtuan Muda sent Raja Ahmad to lead a delegation to Batavia. They were greeted cordially by the Harbourmaster and Sayid Hassan Habsyi, the Mayor of Batavia. The Malay delegation was honoured with a dinner and later taken to watch a play (*sandiwara*). By the end of their stay, many members of the Malay delegation had died. There were not enough people left to sail the boat.

The Governor of Malaka took the Johor regalia to Malaka. Raja Ahmad was sent to Batavia to buy a ship. He then went to Pahang and later brought Sultan Abdul Rahman and his son, the Tengku Besar, back to Riau. Sultan Abdul Rahman was installed in Linggi as ruler of Johor.

Raja Ahmad, brother of Raja Jaafar the Yamtuan Muda, decided to go on the hajj with his son. On the way, they stopped over in Penang, where they were given gifts and money by their relatives. After completing the pilgrimage, Raja Ahmad went to Medinah where he bought a garden and several houses. He gave two houses to the Mufti Syafie.

The Sultan of Singapore allowed Sayid Akil to build a house and to open tin mines on Karimun Island. The Yamtuan Muda sent his men to seize control of the island. Raja Ahmad heard of this and intervened. Not long after, the Yamtuan Muda arrived and received gifts from Raja Ahmad. Raja Jaafar died; Raja Abdul Rahman became Yamtuan Muda. Tengku Besar was installed as Sultan Muhammad Syah.

Sultan Muhammad Syah went to visit the tombs of his ancestors in Johor. He then sailed to Pahang and Trengganu. When Sultan Ahmad of Trengganu died, two of his relatives, Tengku Omar and Tengku Mansur, laid claim to the throne. A civil war erupted. Tengku Omar subsequently fled to Kemaman. Sultan Muhammad Syah tried to pacify the warring parties but failed.

Although piracy continued to be rampant, it was eventually eradicated thanks to cooperation between Lingga and Riau and with the help of the Dutch. Sultan Mahmud went to Singapore and stayed there until he was sent home to Lingga by the Governor of Singapore. He was young and reckless and created a lot of trouble for the Yamtuan Muda and the Dutch.

Raja Ali Engku Kelana was appointed Yamtuan Muda. A very pious man, he forbade gambling and cock-fighting. During this time, a preacher named Syaikh Ismail came to Riau; he made a handsome profit from the teachings of the Nakshbandiah Sufi order.

A replacement had to be sought once the Yamtuan Muda Raja Ali died. The Dutch and the local chiefs chose Engku Haji Muda. Sultan Mahmud favoured Raja Muhammad Yusuf, the son of the deceased who also happened to be his son-in-law. Not long after, Sultan Mahmud was deposed by the Dutch.

Raja Abdullah was made Yamtuan Muda, and upon his death was succeeded by his son, Raja Muhammad Yusuf. Preparations were made to attack Retah. After the fall of Retah, Sultan Sulaiman installed the new Yamtuan Muda at Lingga. The deposed Sultan Mahmud travelled for a time from one country to the next—from Singapore to Pahang and thence to Trengganu and thence to Siam. Finally an English ship came for him and he fled to Besut. From there he went to Singapore and stayed in Siglap.

Tun Abu Bakar succeeded Tun Ibrahim as the Temenggung of Singapore. He was given the title Sri Maharaja Johor and often sent messengers to his relatives in Riau.

8.10 *Hikayat Banjar dan Kota Waringin*

The *History of Banjar and Kota Waringin* is a rich resource for the study of Kalimantan (Borneo) history. At the beginning of the nineteenth century, Raffles asked the Sultan of Pontianak to obtain this manuscript for him. It has been studied in detail by two Dutch scholars, A. A. Cense and J. J. Ras, as part of their doctoral work at Leiden University. Cense (1928) discussed the historical aspects of this hikayat. Ras (1968) produced an annotated critical edition, which included a comparative study of the various Malay and Javanese stories in the text (Ras, 1968). That this hikayat has twice been studied at this level certainly proves its importance.

There are at least ten manuscripts of this hikayat. The Jakarta Museum (now the National Library) has eight. Others are held in Germany and the United Kingdom. Cense and Ras have identified two versions of the text; Ras refers to them as Editions I and II. There are some similarities and some differences between them. Edition I is shorter and appears to be a summary of Edition II; its language is more succinct, while the second text is more verbose. Edition I also pays closer attention to art, court customs and government. Perhaps the most noticeable difference relates to the extent of the royal genealogy. In the shorter version, the arrival of Islam opens a new page in the history of Banjar and the story presents the further genealogy of the successors of the first raja to embrace Islam. This is in contrast with Edition II, which ends with the arrival of Islam. According to Ras, Edition I might have been a *kraton* (palace) version, while Edition II was a *wayang* version of the manuscript (Ras, 1968: 78-80).

Below is a summary of Edition I, based on the text edited by Ras.

8.10.1 Synopsis

There once was a very rich Indian merchant named Mangkubumi. He had a son, Ampu Jatmaka, and two grandsons, Ampu Mandastana and Lambu Mangkurat. In the fullness of time, Mangkubumi fell ill. He instructed his descendants that they must find a suitable place to build a city, where the soil was warm and fragrant.

After his father passed away, Ampu Jatmaka set out and, following much trial and tribulation, eventually found such a place. Ampu Jatmaka established a city there, naming it Nagara Dipa, and styled himself Maharaja Di Candi, The King in the Temple. He had a temple built, where he installed a male and female statues, and worshipped them as though they were the king and queen. He did not dare proclaim himself king, for he was a commoner and feared that he would be cursed for such impiety. Ampu Jatmaka gave orders to subdue the neighboring territories. When he received tribute, he shared it with his ministers. He organized a sound system of government. The highest official was Aria Magatsari; then the Temenggung, the four magistrates (*jaksas*), and the ministers. Each day, Ampu Jatmaka met his ministers in the royal audience hall to discuss affairs of state. Some time afterwards, Ampu Jatmaka ordered Nakhoda Lampung to fetch all the possessions and the people he had left behind in India. Nagara Dipa flourished; people were well fed and decently dressed.

After a period of time, Ampu Jatmaka decided to replace the sandalwood statues with figures of bronze. He sent an envoy to China to bring back a skilled craftsman. The country became even more prosperous. Traders of all races flocked to conduct business there.

While Ampu Jatmaka was maharaja, his children did not become involved in the affairs of government. State affairs were administered by Aria Magatsari. The palace was organized like a Javanese *kraton* and the nobles dressed in the traditional Javanese style. On one occasion, Ampu Jatmaka warned his people against foreign fashions. He also discouraged the over-production of black-pepper.

As he lay grievously ill, he advised Ampu Mandastana and Lambu Mangkurat not to become kings, because the state would be destroyed if they did. Instead they should practice asceticism *(bertapa)* and find a true monarch in that manner. He also ordered them to throw the statues of the gods into the sea. Ampu Jatmaka then died.

Ampu Mandastana and Lambu Mangkurat surrendered the administration of Nagara Dipa to Aria Magatsari, and practiced asceticism for three years. Finally, Ampu Jatmaka appeared to Lambu Mangkurat in a dream, telling him how and where he could find Nagara Dipa's future king. Lambu Mangkurat did as he was told in the dream. He met a princess called Putri Junjung Buih, Honoured Princess of Foam, who emerged from a mass of white froth. Lambu Mangkurat took the girl home and the two brothers looked after her.

After some time, Lambu Mangkurat encouraged Putri Junjung Buih to marry. She agreed but insisted that she would only marry a prince who was the product of meditation. Lambu Mangkurat's brother, Ampu Mandastana, had two handsome sons, Bambang Sukamaraga and Bambang Patmaraga. One day Putri Junjung Buih saw these two young men playing in front of her palace and gave them each a *nagasari* flower. When Lambu Mangkurat found out about this, he felt afraid that one of them would marry Putri Junjung Buih and that he would have to bow down before his own nephew. To prevent this happening, he killed them both. Upon learning of their sons' death, Ampu Mandastana and his wife committed suicide. Thereafter, Lambu Mangkurat ruled the kingdom with his officers of state: Aria Magatsari, Tumanggang Tanah Jawa, the four lords and the other ministers. Nagara Dipa continued to prosper.

Lambu Mangkurat was sad because Putri Junjung Buih was still unmarried. One night his father again appeared in a dream and told him that the man whom Putri Junjung Buih was destined to marry was a Majapahit prince named Raden Putra. The prince was the child of the sun; the king also had six other children. Lambu Mangkurat departed for Majapahit, accompanied by a large retinue. He was warmly received at the court of Majapahit and his proposal accepted. His mission in Majapahit accomplished, Lambu Mangkurat returned to Nagara Dipa. Prior to the wedding, a mysterious heavenly voice offered Raden Putra a crown, which gave him and his descendents the right to rule. Only his direct line would have Allah's blessings to wear the crown. Festivities were held to celebrate the wedding of Putri Junjung Buih and Raden Putra. His full name became Raden Suryanata, King of the Sun.

Not long after, Putri Junjung Buih conceived and bore a son whom they named Raden Suryaganggawangsa. This was soon followed by the birth of another son called Raden Suryawangsa.

Maharaja Suryanata's fame spread and rajas from far and wide bowed before him. Even the King of Majapahit, whose own empire was vast, was afraid of him. When Maharaja Suryanata's knew that his life was almost over, he called his queen and all his ministers to his deathbed. The king asked Lambu Mangkurat to take good care of his sons and again warned against following foreign customs, admonishing him about the kingdom's rules of royal succession, which he must follow. After he passed from this earth, Maharaja Suryanata was succeeded by his son, Raden Suryaganggawangsa.

Maharaja Suryaganggawangsa was as yet unmarried. After being encouraged several times by Lambu Mangkurat to marry, Maharaja Suryaganggawangsa finally said that he would only marry the daughter of Dayang Diparaja. No one knew who Dayang Diparaja was or where she lived. Lambu Mangkurat came to know of her whereabouts from a person from Singabana. Despite her parents' protest, Dayang Diparaja was forcibly taken from them and brought before Maharaja Suryaganggawangsa. He, however, refused to marry her, insisting that it was not her but her daughter that he wanted to marry. Subsequently Lambu Mangkurat did marry Dayang Diparaja.

Dayang Diparaja became pregnant. Fourteen months later, the baby was still in her womb but it could already talk. It asked to be born through an incision on her mother's left side. Lambu Mangkurat was forced to do as the baby said. The newly born child announced that her name was Putri Huripan. She refused to take milk from a woman but asked instead to be suckled by a white buffalo. Dayang Diparaja died after giving birth and her parents passed away when they heard of this.

In time Putri Huripan was presented to Maharaja Suryaganggawangsa to be his wife. She bore him two daughters. The first, Putri Kalarang, married Maharaja's brother, Pangeran Suryawangsa; the other, Putri Kalungsu, married Pangeran Suryawangsa's son, Raden Carang Lalean. Upon his death Maharaja Suryaganggawangsa was succeeded by his nephew, Raden Carang Lalean.

Carang Lalean's queen, Puteri Kalungsu, bore a son, named Raden Sakar Sungsang. When the boy was about six years old, Maharaja Carang Lalean died, ordering Lambu Mangkurat not to deviate from the kingdom's traditional customs. Carang Lalean's body too vanished from the world. Lambu Mangkurat ruled the kingdom as *mangkubumi* (regent).

About a year later, Raden Sakar Sungsang was beaten by his mother for eating uncooked cake-mixture and he was so shocked that he ran away. A trader, Juragan Balaba, found the boy and took him to Surabaya, where he raised Raden Sakar under the name of Ki Mas Lalana. When his stepfather passed away, Ki Mas Lalana himself became a trader and traveled to various foreign lands.

When Ki Mas Lalana arrived at Nagara Dipa, Lambu Mangkurat became fond of him and proposed that the young man marry the queen. Unaware that the queen was his own mother, Ki Mas Lalana accepted the proposal. When the queen discovered that she had married her own son, Putri Kalungan withdrew from public life and later vanished from the earth. Thereafter, Ki Mas Lalana ascended the throne under the name Raden Sari Kaburungan. He established a new kingdom.

Not long after this, Lambu Mangkurat vanished from the earth. Aria Taranggana became the new *mangkubumi*; he was a wise and intelligent man. He compiled a legal code, the *Kutara Masaalah Tahta Nagri* (Code for Problems of Public Law), which described the appropriate degrees of severity for the punishment of various crimes. Before he died, Maharaja Sari Kaburungan passed the care of his children to Aria Taranggana, warning him that a calamity would befall the kingdom if the old Javanese customs and traditions were not continued. He also advised against the excessive cultivation of pepper. The maharaja was succeeded by his son, Sukarama.

Maharaja Sukarama had four sons—Pangeran Mangkubumi, Pangeran Tumenggung, Pangeran Bangun and Pangeran Jayadewa—and a daughter, Raden Galung, who later married Raden Samudra, the son of Raden Bangawan. Raden Sumudra had lost his parents when he was young and was raised by Maharaja Sukarama.

One day, Maharaja Sukarama announced that Raden Samudra would be his successor. This upset the maharaja's sons, especially Pangeran Tumenggung, who declared that he and Raden Samudra would henceforth always be enemies. After Maharaja Sukarama passed away, the kingdom was thrown into chaos. Aria Taranggana remembered Maharaja Sari Kaburungan's dying words and encouraged Raden Samudra to flee, providing him with food and provisions. Pangeran Tumenggung set out to kill Raden Samudra but found that he had already escaped.

Raden Mangkubumi ascended to the throne but the heavenly crown bestowed on Maharaja Suryanata was not rightfully his. He was killed following a quarrel with his brother Pangeran Tumenggung. The brother succeeded to the throne.

Raden Samudra moved from one hiding place to another, surviving on the fish that he was able to catch. Not long afterwards, Patih Masih installed him as Raja of Banjar, with the title of Pangeran Samudra. On hearing of this, his uncle, Maharaja Tumenggong, attacked Banjar; the attack was unsuccessful. Nagara Dipa and Banjar remained enemies for a long time, but neither dared attack the other. Because Banjar lack the troops to crush Nagara Dipa, Patih Masih suggested that Pangeran Samudra seek help from Demak. The chronicle describes how the arrival of Islam in Java led to the fall of the Majapahit Empire and the rise of Demak as a new power. Patih Masih's suggestion was accepted and an envoy was sent to Demak.

The Sultan of Demak agreed to help Banjar on condition that Pangeran Samudra convert to Islam. Pangeran Samudra agreed and, following his conversion, the Sultan of Demak sent his army to help Pangeran Samudra attack Nagara Dipa. War flared between the two kingdoms. Many lives were lost but neither side was able to claim victory. Finally, Aria Taranggana suggested that Maharaja Tumenggung engage Pangeran Samudra in single combat to decide who should be king. The uncle and his nephew faced each other on the battlefield. Feeling overawed, Maharaja Tumenggung surrendered the kingdom to Pangeran Samudra. The newly converted Pangeran Samudra took the Muslim name of Sultan Suryanullah, the Sun of Allah, and sent tribute to the Sultan of Demak every year.

This is followed by the genealogy of Sultan Suryanullah down to his grandson Sultan Hidayatullah. Sultan Hidayatullah had many descendants, the best known of whom was Marhum Panembahan. When Marhum Panembahan ruled, he became very fond of one of his relatives, Rangga Kesuma. Jealous relatives slandered Rangga Kesuma and had him killed. Marhum Panembahan was saddened by this event for the rest of his days. Not long after, a new city was built.

Marhum Penembahan was succeeded by his son Pangeran Dipati Tuha; he ruled under the name Hinayatullah but was better known as Ratu Agung. One of his relatives founded a new kingdom at Kota Waringin and he was known as Ratu Kota Waringin. Ratu Agung passed away and was succeeded by his son Pangeran Kasuma Alam, who was known as Pangeran Anom. When Pangeran Anom died, his son Raden Bagus was still a child, so a relative of Ratu Agung, Pangeran Tapasana, ascended the throne instead and called himself Sultan Riayatullah (although he was better known as Pangeran Ratu). Two of Pangeran Anom's relatives later threatened him with war if Pangeran Ratu did not return the kingship to Raden Bagus. Pangeran Ratu discussed the ultimatum with his ministers. Some urged him to go to war; others advised him to make peace with the claimants. The hikayat ends with a genealogy of the rajas of Kota Waringin, from Pangeran Amas to Pangeran Ratu, Pangeran Anom's father.

8.11 *Salasilah Kutai*

A kingdom called Kutai is known to have existed in East Kalimantan from 400 AD; whether this is the same kingdom that is described in this chronicle has been the subject of fierce debate among historians. What is clear is that *The Genealogical History of Kutai* describes the reigns of the kings of Kutai Kertanegara from the kingdom's foundation in the fourteenth century to the time of Raja Pangeran Panji Mendapa in the seventeenth century.

This work follows the conventions of tradition of Malay historiography. It begins with stories of the extraordinary births of the kingdom's founders. These are followed by myths on the naming of places such as Jaitan Layar and Kutai. It also gives an account of the arrival of Islam in Kalimantan. In fact, one can find almost all the characteristics of Malay historiographical writing in this book, which is why it is such an important source for research into Kalimantan history. The book is equally important for the portrayal of the customs and rituals practiced at that time, although some historians maintain that these descriptions were largely taken from the *Tajus Salatin* and the Javanese *Wulang Reh* (Kern, 1965: 23-24).

There are three versions of the *Salasilah Kutai*. The best known is a manuscript written by Tuan Khatib Muhammad Tahir in 1265 H, which formed the subject of C. A. Mees's doctoral thesis in 1935. W. Kern published a shorter, annotated version in 1956. This version was based on a manuscript written by a resident of Kampung Panji, Awang Lambang, a descendant of Maharaja Sakti, who lived during the rule of Sultan Sulaiman (1850-1899). The contents of the two versions are basically the same, except for the story of Maharaja Sultan. According to the shorter version, Kutai converted to Islam after Maharaja Sultan returned from Majapahit. His conversion followed a wager that Tuan Tunggang Ikan Parangan could not make Maharaja Sultan's crown and shoes levitate. Not only did the crown and shoes rise; they fell to the ground as he commanded, first the crown and then the shoes on top of the crown. On another occasion, no one could find Tuan Tunggang Ikan Parangan, as he had hidden himself in the body of Maharaja Sultan. Another interesting difference between the two versions is the reference to two books presented to Maharaja Sultan and his descendants by Maharaja Pait: the *Undang-undang Braja Nanti* and the *Undang-undang Panji Salatin*.

The third text under this title is D. Adham's *Salasilah Kutai*. This is a modern work, based on various sources such as Tuan Muhammad Tahir's transcription of the *Salasilah Kutai*; Adaha's *Silsilah Raja-raja Tanjung*; a story about the Raja of Kutai from the *Sejarah Raja Bugis*; and *Raja*

Pasir by Adha Rnw. Adham's work describes the history of Kutai from the fourteenth to sixteenth centuries, when Aji Muhammad Parikesit was installed as Sultan of Kutai Kertanegara.

The following summary is based on Mees' 1935 edition.

8.11.1 Synopsis

Once, there were four states in Kutai Kertanegara that did not have kings: Jaitan Layar, Hulu Dusun, Sembaran and Binalu. The chief (Petinggi) of Jaitan Layar longed to have a son but he was too old. He undertook extreme ascetic practices to achieve his desire and one night, as he and his wife were sleeping, they heard a noise like a cannon ball hitting the ground. A voice told him to fetch the object. Petinggi Jaitan made a golden basket and in the basket he found a baby, holding an egg in one hand and a golden kris in the other. The voice told him how to look after the baby, which he did for forty days and forty nights. The baby was named Aji Batara Agung Dewa Sakti.

The Petinggi of Hulu Dusun and his wife, Babu Jaruma, also earnestly desired a child. They tried many times to find a potion to help them but could not. One dark and stormy night, as lightning flashed across the sky and claps of thunder came crashing down, Babu Jaruma and her husband suddenly felt very hungry. They looked everywhere for firewood but could not find any, so he pulled down one of the main rafters of the house and cut it up. Hidden in the recess once occupied by the rafter was a baby serpent (*naga*). He placed it in a betel nut box. The baby naga grew bigger and bigger. One night, the Petinggi and his wife had another dream telling them to build a hardwood ladder, so that the naga could go down to the river. When the naga reached the water, a storm broke out. When the storm faded, a gentle rain began to fall and the thunder receded into the distance. Babu Jaruma seemed to hear a baby crying. She went to investigate the sound and a ball of foam suddenly emerged from where the naga had disappeared into the river. Moments later, a baby emerged from the depths. Babu Jaruma heard a voice telling her to take good care of the baby and to name her Putri Karang Melenu.

When Aji Batara Agung Sakti and Putri Karang Melenu reached the age of five, they wanted to be able to walk around like other children. Both Jatian Layar and Hulu Dusun held a lavish *tijak tanah* (literally, stepping on earth) ceremony to mark this event, as the gods had commanded. In time, Aji Batara and Putri Karang Melenu became adults.

Not long after this, the Emperor of China came and challenged Aji Batara Dewa Sakti to a cockfight. If Aji Batara Dewa Sakti won, the emperor would give him his ship, together with its cargo and crew; if Aji Batara Dewa Sakti lost, he would become the emperor's slave. Their birds fought and Aji Batara's rooster won. When the time came for the Chinese emperor to hand over his ship and its contents, he asked for a delay of a day or two. During this time, he ordered his men to look for wood to build a *perahu* and for cloth to make a sail. When the boat was completed, the emperor launched his craft and tried to escape to his country under the cloak of night. The boat could not move, however, because Aji Batara had placed a curse on it, turning the water around the boat into sand. When the Chinese realised their plan to escape was doomed, they fled into the jungle. The Basap and Dayak tribes are descended from these Chinese fugitives.

One day, Aji Batara visited the mountain where the Chinese had sewn their sail and decided to call it Jaitan Layar (literally, "Sewn Sail"). He built his capital there. Then he traveled to various countries in the region cockfighting, first to Brunei, then to Sambas, Sukadana and Matan. He returned to his kingdom greatly enriched from the winnings of these cockfights.

As a result of a dream one night, Aji Batara wanted to take a wife, even though he had no one in mind. Now it happened that one day his fighting-cock escaped. Aji Batara and his servants chased it, running up and down mountains trying to catch it. Eventually the rooster came to a house and entered a coop kept under the house. The owner, Princess Karang Melenu, refused to return the bird to its owner, saying that it is customary for a cock to pursue a hen and, since Aji Batara's rooster had already "mounted its hen", he must give up his bird. Aji Batara was captivated by Putri Karang Melenu and sent his emissary to ask for her hand. His proposal was accepted and they were soon married. Before long the princess began to experience cravings. Aji Batara went hunting and, because there were no other creatures, shot a squirrel (*tupai*) with his blowpipe. The place was later named Kutai on account of its location on a barren high plateau (*kotai*). Not long after, a son was born to Aji Batara and was named Paduka Nira.

Aji Batara Dewa Sakti frequently traveled to Majapahit to take part in cockfights, get drunk and satisfy his lusts. His wife many times asked him not to go but he never listened to her. This depressed her so much that she finally threw herself off a *perahu* and drowned. When Aji Batara discovered his wife had died, he too drowned himself. The court officials cared for his son and, when the boy grew up, he took the title Aji Batara Agung Paduka Nira.

One night, Paduka Nira had a dream in which a female apparition emerged from a length of bamboo. The dream was interpreted to mean that he should find a wife. Now it happened that an old man, Maragut, and his wife lived in Bengalon and they both desperately wanted a child. One night Maragut met an old man in a dream, who told him to sleep beside the first thing at which his dog barked. The next day Maragut was out hunting, when his dog suddenly began barking at a piece of bamboo. Maragut took the bamboo home and that night both he and his wife slept with it. Early the next morning, they heard a loud noise coming from the piece of bamboo. It was like a cannon shot. They saw a baby inside the wood. A voice told them to care for the child. They named her Paduka Sori. When she grew up, Paduka Nira sent an envoy to ask for her hand in marriage. She replied that she would accept his proposal only if her clothes and ring fitted him. They fitted him perfectly. The pair were married. It was agreed that Bengalon would never again pay tribute to Kutai Kertanegara.

When the time was fulfilled, Paduka Sori gave birth to a son. Eventually Paduka Nira had five sons – Maharaja Sakti, Maharaja Surawangsa, Maharaja Indrawangsa, Maharaja Darmawangsa and Maharaja Sultan – and two daughters, Raja Putri and Dewa Putri. The kingdom of Kutai Kertanegara flourished during the reign of Aji Batara Agung Paduka Nira. Merchants flocked to her shore, and rice and food were abundant and cheap. After some time he passed away.

Maharaja Sakti conquered seven kingdoms. He then conferred with all the court officials to choose a monarch to rule over the expanded territory. Maharaja Sakti, Maharaja Suryawangsa, Maharaja Indrawangsa and Maharaja Darmawangsa all declined, so Maharaja Sultan became king and his brothers signed an agreement to serve as his ministers. Later, Maharaja Sakti and Maharaja Sultan went to Majapahit to study the royal customs and protocols. They were accompanied by Maharaja Indra Mulia from Marakaman. The Lord of Majapahit and Patih Gajah Mada taught them the ways and blessings of kingship, the duties of ministers and other high-ranking court officials, as well as the protocols to be observed in the presence of the king, and so on. After they had been there for some time, Maharaja Sakti returned to his kingdom, bringing with him a large, ornately designed gate for his new capital.

On one occasion, Puncan Karna, the Raja of Tanah Tanjung, drifted to Kutai in a boat and sought refuge there. Maharaja Sultan welcomed him, not only providing him with a house but also marrying him to his daughter, Raja Putri, who later bore him a son, Sri Gambira. Maharaja Sultan then married Paduka Suri; they named their son Mandarsah.

Sri Gambira's son was Permata Alam. Raja Putri was the daughter of Raja Mandarsah. When she was fourteen years old, she married Pangeran Temenggung Dasar Pasir, the grandson of Maharaja Sakti. When Raja Mandarsah passed away, Pangeran Temenggung Dasar Pasir succeeded him and was given the title Aji Pangeran Tumenggung Bayabaya. Raja Putri gave birth to two sons, Raja Makota and Raden Wijaya. Permata Alam was the father of two sons and a daughter.

During the reign of Raja Makota (Aji Raja Mahkota Mulia Alam), Aji Pangeran Tumenggung Bayabaya's successor, two Muslim missionaries, Tuan di Bandang and Tuan Tunggang, arrived in Kutai. Tuan di Bandang quickly returned to Makassar; Tuan Tunggang remained in Kutai. He was called "Tuan di Parangan" because he came riding on the back of a swordfish (*parangan*). He asked the king to convert to Islam. The king agreed, but only if Tuan Tunggang could prove that his magic was more powerful than the king's. The king conjured up fire. Tuan Tunggang conjured a heavy shower of rain that extinguished the king's fire. Raja Makota accepted Islam. The people kept pigs under their houses and fermented fish in pots; these were all destroyed. The missionary taught the king the Profession of Faith and the Pillars of Islam. Raja Makota became a very pious Muslim king, conquering the domains of any heathen king who refused to submit to Islam. He married and fathered many children. His first wife gave him three sons: Aji di Langgar, Aji Ratu Mangkurat and Aji di Dedung. When Aji di Langgar turned fourteen, Raja Mahkota built a beautiful mosque with ornate carvings in his honour. When Raja Mahkota died, Aji di Langgar succeeded him. Raden Wijaya, Raja Mahkota's brother, had a son named Wadu Aji.

Aji di Langgar married four wives: Tuan Rapat, Tuan Katak, Tuan Rimah and Nayai Tambun. They all presented him with children. Tuan Rimah's son, Pangeran Sinum Panji Mandapalah, later became King of Kutai and defeated Raja Marakaman and Raja Talikat in battle. The hikayat ends with a list of Aji di Langgar's descendants. The colophon states that the *silsilah* was copied by Muhammad Tahir in 1265 H, and is followed by an appendix recording a treaty between the Buginese and the Raja of Kutai.

8.12 *Hikayat Patani*

Although Patani is now a small province in the south of Thailand, it was once a prosperous Malay kingdom complete with its own busy port. The *Patani Chronicle* remains one of the earliest historical accounts of this little-known Malay-Thai border region (Teeuw and Wyatt, 1970). There are at least three manuscripts of the *Hikayat Patani*, according to Teeuw. The first (which he calls Malay Manuscript A) was copied by Munsyi Abdullah in Singapore in 1839 for the Christian missionary Alfred North, and is now held in the Library of Congress, Washington D.C. The second manuscript (Malay Manuscript B) was obtained by W. W. Skeat in 1899 while he was living in Patani and is now kept in the Institute of Social Anthropology, at Oxford University. The third manuscript (Manuscript T) is believed to have come from a Muslim court; it belonged to a retired Thai government official in Songkhla and was translated into Thai for King Rama during his visit to Patani in 1928.

The *Hikayat Patani* was first introduced to the West in 1838. In that year, T.J. Newbold published a "Note on Malayan MSS. and Books presented to the Society" in the *Madras Journal of Literature and Science*, Vol. VII, mentioning the *Hikayat Patani* and providing a brief summary of its contents. The following year, 1839, in his book, *Political and Statistical Account of the British Settlements in the Straits of Malacca,* Newbold gave a detailed account of the Malay states including Patani, based on the manuscript of the *Hikayat Patani* mentioned in his earlier publication. It is not known which manuscript Newbold used, although it was probably very close to the one copied by Munsyi Abdullah. In his book *Sejarah Kerajaan Melayu Patani* (History of the Malay Kingdom of Patani) published in 1962, Ibrahim Syukri wrote a history of Patani based on information he gathered from several Malay manuscripts, one of which is believed to be similar to the text of the *Hikayat Patani* published by Teeuw and Wyatt.

The *Hikayat Patani* covers 94 pages and, according to Teeuw, can be divided into six sections. Only the first of these (pages 1-74) can be considered to be an original part of the *Hikayat Patani*. He gives two reasons for this. Firstly, the link between the end of Section I and Section II is unclear. Secondly, Section I is written in a different style from Section II. Section I is written in the tradition of Malay historiographical writing; it glorifies the kingdom of Patani and proclaims the greatness of its kings. In contrast, Section II is packed with an often-confusing array of facts and names. Below is a summary of Section I.

8.12.1 Synopsis

Paya Tu Antara succeeded his father, Paya Tu Kerub Mahajana, to the throne of Kota Maligai, calling himself Paya Tu Naqpa. One day, Paya Tu Naqpa went hunting. His dog barked at a shining white mousedeer, which was the size of a goat. Following the sound of his dog, the king came to a house where he found an old couple, who were engrossed in catching prawns and setting nets. The old man's name was Encik Tani, Mr Farmer. Paya Tu Naqpa built his capital there and named it Patani Darussalam.

After several years, Paya Tu Naqpa fell ill. He ordered that the royal gong be sounded and an announcement made that if anyone could cure him, that man could marry his daughter. Seven days passed and no one came forward to take up the king's offer. Then a man from Pasai named Syaikh Said declared that he would cure the king but only on the condition that if the king recovered, he would convert to Islam. The king agreed but, after he was helped back to health, failed to keep his promise. The king fell ill again on two more occasions and each time he pledged to convert to Islam. Syaikh Said cured him each time. However, it was only after the third time that he finally recited the Profession of Faith and became a Muslim. After his conversion, Paya Tu Naqpa took the name Sultan Ismail Syah. Following the king's example, all his ministers, military commanders and subjects subsequently embraced Islam. Syaikh Said gave Muslim names to the king's three children: the eldest was named Sultan Mudzaffar Syah; the middle child, a daughter, was named Sitti Aisyah; and the youngest son, Sultan Mansur Syah.

Not long after, the king died and was succeeded by Sultan Mudzaffar Syah. During his reign, Patani enjoyed peace and prosperity. Following the advice of Syaikh Safiuddin, an ulama from Pasai, a mosque was built as a place where all the people could worship Almighty God. Under the king's patronage, Islam spread throughout the kingdom, from the remotest village to the capital, Kota Maligai. Some time afterwards the king went to Ayudhya. He was well received by Raja Beracau (Thai "*phra chao*," king), who proposed that Sultan Mudzaffar take a wife in Ayudhya. Sultan Mudzaffar asked for time to return to Patani. Upon his return, he consulted with his ministers and military commanders, then returned with them to Ayudhya. Raja Beracau was delighted to receive him again and provided him with a house near the gateway to Kota Wang. Sultan Mudzaffar's wife in Patani gave birth to a son, named Sultan Patik Siam. His secondary wife in Kota Wang presented him with a son, Raja Bambang.

One night, Sultan Mudzaffar and his army attacked Ayudhya. Raja Beracau fled and went into hiding. When Sultan Mudzaffar and Sultan Mansur Syah entered the palace to look for Beracau, they noticed a huge drum hanging from the doorway of the palace. He ordered a servant named Cahaya to bore a hole in the drum. By the will of Allah, Cahaya did not puncture the drum but beat it three times. When the ministers, commanders and people of Ayudhya heard the sound, they assembled and fought against the Patani army. The forces of Sultan Mudzaffar were defeated and the Sultan was killed by a bullet. Before he passed away, the Sultan ordered Mansur Syah to return to Patani. After Sultan Mansur's departure, nothing more was heard about Sultan Mudzaffar or the people of Patani who lived with him at Kota Wang, as none of them ever came back from Ayudhya.

Sultan Mansur returned safely to Patani and was installed as king. During his reign, the Sultan of Palembang twice sent his military commanders and army against Patani, but they were defeated on both occasions. Sultan Mansur Syah continued to rule. He had five daughters, of whom Raja Hijau was the eldest; and two sons—Raja Bima (from a concubine) and Sultan Bahdur Syah.

After several years, Sultan Mansur Syah fell ill and died. He was replaced by Sultan Patik Siam, who was only nine years old. Raja Aisyah was appointed to rule on his behalf; she was known as Peracau. Thereafter Patani entered a time of upheaval. First, a court official, Sri Amrat, encouraged Raja Bambang to take the throne. Raja Bambang killed Sultan Patik Siam but was himself killed by Sri Amrat. Sultan Bahdur was then installed as ruler; he was only ten years old at the time. Another court official, Sri Amar Pahlawan, encouraged Raja Bima to kill Sultan Bahdur but he too was betrayed when Sri Amar speared him. In the absence of any remaining male heir, Raja Hijau (the Green Queen) was installed as Queen. She was the first of four female rulers in Patani and took the title Peracau, as Raja Aisyah had done.

Raja Hijau accomplished three important things during her reign. Firstly, she was able to appease her Prime Minister (*bendahara*), who wanted to overthrow her; secondly, she had Sri Amar Pahlawan arrested and executed for the murder of Raja Bima; and thirdly, she built a fresh water channel from Tambangan to Jambatan Kedi. When she died, the male subjects in the kingdom were ordered to shave their heads and the female subjects to trim the length of their hair.

Upon her death, her sister Raja Biru (the Blue Queen) was installed as queen. She in turn was succeeded by her younger sister Raja Ungu (the Purple Queen), the widow of the Raja of Pahang.

Raja Ungu refused to take the title of Peracau and styled herself Paduka Syah Alam instead. The fourth sister, Raja Kuning (the Yellow Queen), was betrothed to a young Thai prince, Apya Deca. However upon his return to Thailand, Raja Kuning accepted a proposal of marriage from the Sultan of Johor. Apya Deca was furious and sought the help of the Raja Beracau to attack Patani. Their assault failed because their food supplies were inadequate and their army was forced to return to Thailand. Soon after this, Paduka Syah Alam fell ill and died. Raja Kuning again took the title of Peracau. Three months later, her husband returned to Johor, leaving behind his mother and the Crown Prince of Johor to protect the queen.

The hikayat narrates that during the Sultan of Johor's absence, the Crown Prince seduced the Queen, knowing that his elder brother was not attracted to women. The pair enjoyed each other day after day, until his interest turned to a singer (*biduanda*), Dang Sirat. The woman had a beautiful voice but she was "vile in appearance, dark-skinned, her wide face was full of blemishes, and her body was much too big". The Crown Prince installed Dang Sirat as his consort and awarded her the title Encik Puan. At the instigation of several of his cockfighting friends from Acheh, the Prince then ordered that all the daughters and wives of the ministers and warriors in Patani had "to take turns to have a private audience with him, while their fathers and husbands waited outside in the royal hall". The news threw the kingdom into an uproar. With the blessing of the Peracau, the ministers and warriors killed the Prince's Achehnese followers. The Crown Prince himself managed to escape and fled to Johor; but before he left, he killed Dang Sirat. He also left his mother behind in Patani.

Not long after, the Peracau sent the mother back to Johor. No one mentioned his debauchery. Later, Raja Lela a respected Minangkabau trader in Patani, was sent to lead a mission to Johor and was warmly received by the Sultan of Johor. Raja Kali attempted to seduce the Peracau but Almighty God did not allow him to do so. He was arrested and executed. His followers—men and women, young and old—were massacred. No one was spared; even pregnant women had their bellies sliced open and the babies torn from their wombs. The only person to survive was Raja Hujan, the grandson of Raja Kali, who managed to find a safe haven.

After some time on the throne, the Peracau fell ill and died. Her death marks the end of the genealogy of the rulers of the kingdom of Patani. It concludes Section I of Teeuw and Wyatt's *Hikayat Patani*. Although the *Hikayat Patani* cannot be regarded as "history" in the modern sense, it nevertheless remains an invaluable historical resource.

8.13 *Cerita Asal Bangsa Jin dan Segala Dewa-dewa*

Judging by its title, *The Story of the Origin of the Demigods and Jinns*, and a cursory reading of the text, one would not immediately categorize this text as a work of historical literature. It is full of fantasy and largely adapted from other works, such as the *Hikayat Iskandar Dzulkarnain*, *Hikayat Pandawa*, Panji tales, and so on. Despite this, Henri Chambert-Loir still considers it a work of historical literature. Bima is a regency (*kabupaten*) in the province of West Nusa Tenggara. Chambert-Loir argues that the history of Bima is described in three different types of text, and that this hikayat is one of those three. I agree with Chambert-Loir that every nation has a right to write its history in its own way. The *Cerita Asal Bangsa Jin dan Segala Dewa-dewa* is Bima's interpretation of its own history and deserves to be known by those who are interested in historical literature. Below is a summary of the story.

8.13.1 Synopsis

The story is divided into five chapters. Chapter I tells of the creation of the father of the *jinn*s, Jan Manjan, from a burning ember. After this, the Prophet Adam, the first man, was created from the four elements: fire, wind, water and earth. Allah breathed life (or spirit) into Adam's body. From the spirit came reason; from reason came wisdom and faith to guide man in this world.

Chapter II narrates Jan Manjan's descendants, the different types of *jinn*s and mankind. The different types of *jinn*s included the demigods (*dewa*), the spirits of the sunset (*mambang*), moon fairies (*cendera*), and sprites (*peri*). Jan Manjan's eldest son himself had two sons. The younger son's descendants became ghosts (*hantu*) and demons (*setan*). The elder son, Batara Indra Guru, had several children, one of whom was Maharaja Indra Palasyara. The younger son, Batara Indra Ratu, became the king of *jinn*s in the East *(Masyrik)*; the kings of Luwukare descended from him. The elder son, Tunggal Pandita, succeeded him and fathered two sons as well: Begawan Basugi, who became king of the *jinn*s in the West (*Maghrib*), and Begawan Biyasa who became ruler of the celestial realm. Begawan Biyasa's daughter, Julus al-Asyikin, was extremely beautiful: "her nose was like a jasmine flower, her eyes sparkled like the north star, her teeth were like bursting pomegranates, her eyebrows like a crescent moon that has just appeared at the edge of the sky, her lips like a sliver of paper, her full breasts were like a pair of bejeweled orbs".

Chapter III tells the story of the holy war waged by Sultan Iskandar Zulkarnain and his vizier Prophet Khidir against the *jinn* kings of the East and West. Thanks to Sultan Iskandar's prayers, they were able to defeat their formidable enemy, Raja Batara Tunggal. Sultan Iskandar married Princess Julus al-Asyikin. Their sons became rulers of Byzantium and Rome, Japan and China, and Coastal and Central Sumatra.

Chapter IV continues the story of Begawan Biyasa, ruler of the celestial realm. He had two children, a son named Pandu Dewanata and a daughter named Ganti Nadzraja. Pandu Dewanata married his sister and fathered the five Pandawa brothers: Darmawangsa, Sang Bima, Sang Kula, Sang Rajuna and Sang Dewa. Sang Bima and his brothers came down to earth. They waged war in Java against Maharaja Boma. During the battle, Sang Rajuna was hit by Maharaja Boma's arrow and fell unconscious. Seeing his brother injured, Sang Bima hurried to find a cure. He met an old crone, Dewa Rimbi, who said that she would give him a potion for his brother if he promised to marry her. Agreeing to her condition, Sang Bima took the potion and left to tend to his brother. Dewa Rimbi pined for Sang Bima so much that she became pregnant and gave birth to a son, Sang Katut Kaca. Later, Katut Kaca helped his father defeat Maharaja Sang Boma.

In time, Darmawangsa too joined his brothers in the battle. After the defeat of Maharaja Boma, Darmawangsa went to Gunung Seumawe in Pasai, where he spent his time reciting the Quran and meditating. It is said that when Maulana Zainal Abidin (the grandson of the Prophet Muhammad) sent two emissaries to Pasai, they were surprised to discover that the people there already knew how to recite the Profession of Faith and chant the Quran.

Chapter V tells of Bima's establishment of a kingdom. Once Sang Bima undertook a pleasure cruise to Pulau Satonda. He saw a *naga* princess and his very glance made her pregnant. She later gave birth to daughter, Indra Tasi Naga. On his return trip, Sang Bima unwittingly married his own daughter, who then gave birth to two sons: Indra Kemala and Indra Zamrud. Because of a disagreement between the two brothers, Indra Kemala went into exile. Indra Zamrud became the King of Bima. He conquered the kings of Java, Bali, Sumbawa, Ende, Sumba and Manggarai, and they all brought him tribute. Indra Zamrud married a sprite, who bore him a daughter. Maharaja Indra married his own daughter and fathered a son and two daughters. Their incestuous marriages produced eight generations of the Bima royal family (Henri Chambert-Loir, 1985).

8.14 *Hikayat Hang Tuah*

Many studies of the *Hikayat Hang Tuah* have been undertaken, ranging from Francois Valentijn's first mention of the text in 1726 to Sulastin Sutrisno's dissertation in 1983. Despite this, there is no consensus on the genre of the work. Werndly's Malay grammar, 1736, described it merely as a tale about Malay kings. John Crawford, 1820, believed that it was a worthless work of history. Roolvink suggested that it might be seen as a work of historical literature, noting that, like other works of historical literature, it is composed of two elements—the fictional and the historical (Abdul Ghani Suratman, 1964: 350).

Valentijn (1726), J. Crawford (1811), E. Netscher (1854), H. Overbeck (1922), C. Hooykaas (1947), and A. Teeuw (1960) all suggest that the *Hikayat Hang Tuah* is a historical romance. Hooykaas also describes it as a "legend". Other writers have called it an "epic" (Abu Bakar Hamid, 1974: 152). On the other hand, Netscher describes it as a "novel" which provides an important window into the Malay world. In Teeuw's opinion, the *Hikayat Hang Tuah* can be considered the first Malay novel. A novel may be defined as "a prose narrative depicting the deeds and actions of its characters according to their individual nature and personality" (*Kamus Umum Bahasa Indonesia*, 1976). Sulastin Sutrisno argues that a novel is (1) a long prose narrative, depicting human experience, (2) presented in a clear sequential order, and (3) told from a particular point of view (1983: 26-40).

I am content to consider the *Hikayat Hang Tuah* as a historical novel. Hang Tuah was a real historical figure. We know a little bit about him from the *Sejarah Melayu*. He was a commoner. His bravery and courage led to him becoming a famous warrior throughout the Malay world. His unique and unconditional loyalty to the king made him even more famous. He was an example to the common people of how they might also rise to high office. In time, myths and legends began to form around Hang Tuah. His negative aspects (the *Sejarah Melayu*, for example, describes him as arrogant) were forgotten. His good qualities were exaggerated. The heroic deeds of other men, including those of his son who also followed him as Admiral (Laksamana), were attributed to him. These influences gave rise to a work open to various scholarly interpretations.

In a chapter on Javanese elements in classical Malay literature, Winstedt describes the *Hikayat Hang Tuah* as a "Malayo-Javanese romance...modeled upon the Panji tales" (and also "the only original romance in old Malay literature"), with "an Indian supplement" drawn in particular from the *Ramayana* and Tamil oral tradition (Winstedt, 1958: 54, 56). I disagree. The *Hikayat Hang Tuah* is a thoroughly Malay text. It is so anti-Javanese, in fact, that the edition published in Indonesia in 1960 by Abas Datoek Pamoentjak nan Sati was immediately banned because it denigrated the Javanese.

Valentijn and Overbeck claim that the *Hikayat Hang Tuah* is the most beautiful piece of Malay literature ever written. Malay society has revered Hang Tuah for over two centuries. His loyalty and unwavering service to the king have been constantly praised. "Tuah will serve no master but the King of Malaka" *("Si Tuah takkan bertuan, selain kepada raja Malaka").* He has also been seen as a symbol of the Malaka sultanate. While he was alive, Malaka was prosperous. With his death, Malaka collapsed. As time passed, he came to embody the hopes and aspirations of the Malay people. It was believed that Hang Tuah had, in fact, not died but was waiting to return should the Malays need his assistance. However, after Malaya gained its independence in 1957, the popular perception of Hang Tuah started to change. Modern writers, such as Usman Awang (Tongkat Warrant), Kassim Ahmad and Ali Aziz, began to ask whether Hang Tuah was really so admirable. Instead, they championed Hang Jebat as being the real hero in the hikayat. Hang Jebat led a revolt against the Sultan when his friend, Hang Tuah, was unjustly sentenced to death on the basis of unexamined slanders. The Dutch scholar, P. E. de Josselin de Jong has argued that the unfavorable perception of Hang Tuah was associated with the decline in influence of the sultans. Moreover, Hang Jebat was seen as opposing feudal values and promoting individual freedom, qualities that were considered attractive in the post-independence era (P. E. de Josselin de Jong, 1965: 144-153). A Malay scholar, Shaharuddin bin Maarof, has subsequently rejected both Tuah and Jebat as authentic Malay heroes (1979: 29-83).

The *Hikayat Hang Tuah* has been published several times. The best-known editions are W. G. Shellabear's 1908 edition (in both Romanised and Jawi scripts) and the Balai Pustaka 1924 edition. Abas Datoek Pamoentjak nan Sati's 1960 edition was also in Jawi. Kassim Ahmad's edition of this hikayat was based on a manuscript from Kelantan and published by Dewan Bahasa dan Pustaka, Kuala Lumpur, in 1964.

8.14.1 Synopsis

Three kings came down from heaven to Bukit Si Guntang. One of them, Sang Maniaka, became the King of Bintan. The story tells that Hang Tuah moved from Sungai Duyung to Bintan. He and his friends—Hang Jebat, Hang Kasturi, Hang Lekir and Hang Lekiu—defeated a band of pirates. On another occasion, he killed an auspicious cintamani snake. Hang Tuah and his friends entered the king's service. At that time, two noblemen, Krama Wijaya of Java and Wira Nantaja of Daha, both came to Bintan and were warmly received by the king. Wira Nantaja received the title "Ratu Melayu", Ruler of the Malays, from the king of Bintan.

The king moved from Bintan to Malaka, where a palace was built for him. His brother, Sang Jaya Nantaja, was installed as the Crown Prince and he too received a palace. Not long after this, malicious rumours spread, alleging that Sang Jaya Nantaja intended to overthrow the king. The king wanted to kill his brother, but upon Hang Tuah's intercession, pardoned him. Thereafter, Sang Jaya lived as a fisherman, until he found patronage from a rich merchant and became a raja in a state in India.

The Raja of Malaka wanted to marry Tun Teja, the daughter of the bendahara of Indrapura, but his proposal was rejected. Not long after this, he sent his envoys to Java to propose to the princess of the King of Majapahit. His request was accepted but it was stipulated that he must come to Majapahit to fetch his bride. The Raja of Malaka agreed to this condition. He went to Majapahit with a large retinue of attendants, including Hang Tuah whose duty it was to guard the king. In Java, the Emperor (Batara) of Majapahit tested the bravery and intelligence of Hang Tuah and the warriors from Malaka on a number of occasions. In one episode, Hang Tuah had to fight an invulnerable warrior named Taming Sari. Through cunning, Hang Tuah was able to disarm his opponent and kill him. The Batara of Majapahit conferred the title of "Laksamana" on Hang Tuah. During their stay in Majapahit, Hang Tuah and his friends studied with a hermit, Sang Persata Nala, who lived in seclusion in Mount Wirana Pura. Not long after, the Raja of Malaka returned home, accompanied by Hang Tuah.

On another occasion, Hang Tuah's enemies accused him of having an affair with the Sultan's favorite concubine. With the help of the bendahara, Hang Tuah fled to Indrapura. Knowing that the king was still in love with Tun Teja, he decided to kidnap Tun Teja and bring her back to Malaka. The king subsequently forgave him. Tun Teja's fiancé, Megat Panji Alam, a prince from Terengganu, vowed to attack Malaka. The prince reached no further than Indrapura, where he was killed by some of Hang Tuah's friends.

The queen, Raden Emas Ayu, craved the milk of a particular coconut tree. No one dared to climb the tree except Hang Tuah. On another occasion, a pet horse belonging to the king's two sons fell into a cesspit. Hang Tuah rescued the horse from the cesspit.

The Batara of Majapahit was angry because the Raja of Malaka had taken another wife and demanded an explanation. The raja sent Hang Tuah to take a letter to Majapahit. Hundreds of Majapahit warriors ran amok and tried to kill him. Thanks to his caution and cunning, Hang Tuah was able to avoid all danger and eventually returned to Malaka. Not long after this, Hang Tuah escorted the Raja and Queen of Malaka on a visit to Majapahit. Once again, forty Javanese ran amok; they tried to kill Hang Tuah but could not. A powerful magician, Petala Bumi, also failed to kill Hang Tuah. Hang Tuah and the Raja of Malaka quickly returned to Malaka.

The Batara of Majapahit sent bands of pirates to cause mayhem in Malaka. Hang Tuah defeated them all.

Hang Tuah was slandered by court officials and the king ordered that he be killed. The bendahara hid him instead. All of Hang Tuah's regalia, including the magic keris Taming Sari, were given to Hang Jebat. Hang Jebat was deeply upset by his friend's apparent death, knowing deep in his heart that the king had grossly wronged his friend. Jebat took control of the palace. He dallied with the king's concubines and maids, and ate and drank as he wished, never returning home. The country was in an uproar but no one dared oppose him. Finally, the bendahara reminded the king of Hang Tuah. Hang Tuah was released and fought Hang Jebat. Hang Tuah tricked Hang Jebat and stabbed his unarmed comrade. Before he died, Hang Jebat ran amok and killed many people.

Again, the Batara of Majapahit sent a powerful warrior, Kertala Sari, to kill Hang Tuah and the King of Malaka. Hang Tuah defeated the plot and killed Kertala Sari.

Hang Tuah was not only a brave and feared warrior; he was also an extremely capable diplomat. The king sent him to India and China. Wherever he went, Hang Tuah always impressed his hosts with his exceptional wit and intelligence.

When the Batara of Majapahit died, the Raja of Malaka asked Hang Tuah to escort his son to be installed as the new emperor. On the way, the Prince of Brunei, Pangeran Adipati Solok, attacked their ship. Hang Tuah captured Adipati Solok, pardoned him and sent him back to Brunei.

Hang Tuah went to Thailand to buy some elephants. In Thailand, he successfully defeated seven Japanese warriors and then safely returned to Malaka. Not long after, the queen Raden Emas Ayu gave birth to a daughter, Puteri Gunung Ledang.

Raja Culan of Ceylon came to ask for the hand of Puteri Gunung Ledang. His proposal was accepted but before the wedding ceremony could be held, Raja Culan sailed to Trengganu to compete in a cockfight. Strange things happened. He won the fight but his boat sank. Then the King of Trengganu's palace caught fire. Raja Culan returned to Ceylon. Hang Tuah was sent to conquer Trenggau. He returned bringing with him two princesses.

Schools of swordfish attacked Indrapura. Hang Jebat's son, Tun Nadim, suggested that the towns people build a barrier of banana tree trunks on the beach to trap the swordfish. Soon after this, Tun Nadim was slandered and executed. The Raja of Malaka ordered Hang Tuah to attack Indrapura.

One day, the Raja of Malaka and his wives set sail for a picnic in Singapore. On the way, the king lost his crown. Hang Tuah tried to retrieve it but could not. There was worse to follow. Hang Tuah also lost his magical keris. From that time onwards, the king and Hang Tuah were always sick and never fully recovered.

Not long after this, the Portuguese attacked Malaka. Although Hang Tuah sustained serious injuries in the battle, the attack was successfully repelled. The Raja of Malaka then sent Hang Tuah to Byzantium to purchase cannons. The Laksamana fulfilled his mission perfectly.

The Raja of Malaka appointed Puteri Gunung Ledang as his successor. The king wanted to know what happened in the grave. Hang Tuah allowed himself to be buried alive. He emerged later and told the king of his experiences. From that day on, the Raja of Malaka gave alms to the poor and lived an ascetic life. The Bendahara and the Laksamana also went into seclusion. No one ever heard of them again.

After a while, the Portuguese asked for land on which to build a warehouse. One night not long after, the Portuguese bombarded the city and pillaged it. Princess Gunung Ledang fled into the remote interior of the kingdom and became queen of the Bataks.

After more time had passed, the Dutch launched an attack against Malaka, with the help of the Malays in Johor. Nothing more was ever heard again about Tun Tuah. He is not dead. He too is king of the Bataks. And when people ask him if he would ever like to remarry, he always tells them: "No, never".

References

Abas Datoek Pamoentjak Nan Sati
1960.   *Hikayat Hang Tuah*, Kuala Lumpur.

Adham, D.
1981.   *Salasilah Kutai*, Jakarta.

Andaya, B. W. & L. Y. Andaya
1982.   *A History of Malaysia*, London.

Andaya, L. Y.
1978.   *The Kingdom of Johore*, Kuala Lumpur.

Balai Pustaka
1956.   *Hikajat Hang Tuah*, Jakarta.

Bastin J. & R. Roolvink.
1964.   *Malayan and Indonesian Studies*, Oxford.

Blagden, C. O.
1925.   "An unpublished variant version of the Malay Annals," *JMBRAS*, 3 (1), pp. 10-52.

Bottoms, J. C.
1962.   "Malay Historical Works," in *Malaysian Historical Sources* (ed. K.G. Tregonning), Singapore, pp. 36-62.

Brakel, L. F.
1980.   "Dichtung und Wahrheit. Some notes on the development of the study of Indonesian historiography," *Archipel*, 20, pp. 35-44.

Brown, C. C.
1952.   "The Malay Annals. Translated from Raffles MS 18," *JMBRAS*, 25 (2 & 3).

Buyung Adil
n.d.   "Hikayat Misa Melayu," *Medan Sastra*, 2, 6.

Cense, A. A.
1928.   *De Kroniek van Bandjarmasin*, Santpoort.

Chambert-Loir, Henri (ed.)
1985.   *Cerita asal bangsa jin dan segala dewa-dewa*, Bandung.

Collingwood, R. G.
1961.   *The Idea of History*, Oxford.

Cowan, C. D. & O. W. Wolters
1976.   *Southeast Asian History and Historiography*, London.

Dzulkifli Mohd. Salleh (ed.)
1968.   *Hikayat Merong Mahawangsa*, Kuala Lumpur.

Gibson-Hill, C. A.
1956.   "The Malay Annals: The History brought from Goa," *JMBRAS*, 29 (1), pp. 185-188.

Hall, D. G. E.
1962.   *Historians of South East Asia*, London.

Hamidy, U. U. et al.
1981. *Pengarang Melayu dalam Kerajaan Riau dan Abdullah bin Abdul Kadir Munsyi dalam Sastra Melayu,* Jakarta.

Hasrun Harun
1960. *Hikayat Hang Tuah* (in Arabic), Djakarta.
1971. "Hikayat Merung Mahawangsa sebagai hasil historiografi tradisional Melayu," *DB,* 15, no. 2, pp. 531-541.

Hill, A. H.
1960. "Hikayat Raja-raja Pasai," *JMBRAS,* 33 (2).

Hoesein Djajadiningrat
1965. "Local Traditions in Indonesia Historiography," in Soedjatmoko et al. (eds.), *An Introduction to Indonesian Historiography,* New York.

Hooykaas, C.
1947. *Over Maleische Literatuur,* Leiden.

Ibrahim Syukri
1962. *Sejarah Kerajaan Melayu Patani,* Kuala Lumpur.

Iskandar, T.
1964. "Tun Seri Lanang, pengarang Sejarah Melayu," *DB,* 8-12.
1958. "Hikayat Atjeh," *VKJ,* 26.
1970. "Some Historical sources used by the author of Hikayat Hang Tuah," *JMBRAS,* 43 (1), pp. 15-47.

Ismail Hussein
1963a. "Hikayat Negeri Johor," *DB,* 7 (8), pp. 341-351.
1963b. "Ikhtisar Hikayat Negeri Johor," *DB,* 7 (9), pp. 394-401.

Jamiliah Binti Juni
1980/81. "Hikayat Raja-raja Riau," Academic Exercise, UKM, Bangi.

Johns, A.H.
1979. "The Turning Image: Myth and Reality in Malay Perceptions of the Past," in A. Reid and D. Marr (eds.). *Perceptions of the Past in Southeast Asia.* Singapore: Heineman, pp. 43-67.

Jones, Russel (ed.)
1987. *Hikayat Pasai,* Kuala Lumpur.

Josselin de Jong, P. E. De
1961. Who's who in the Malay Annals," *JMBRAS,* 24 (2), pp. 1-89.
1965. "The rise and decline of a national hero," *JMBRAS,* 38 (2), pp. 140-155.

Kalthum Jeran
1986. *Hikayat Pahang,* Kuala Lumpur.

Kassim Ahmad
1958. "Catatan tentang beberapa naskah Hikayat Hang Tuah," *DB,* 2 (10), pp. 481-488.
1959. "Mengkaji Semula Hikayat Hang Tuah," *DB,* 3 (3), pp. 119-122.
1963. "Hikayat Hang Tuah," *DB,* 7 (1), pp. 15-21.
1964. *Hikayat Hang Tuah,* Kuala Lumpur.

1964. *Perwatakan dalam Hikayat Hang Tuah,* Kuala Lumpur.

Kratz, E. U.
1973. *Peringatan Sejarah Negeri Johor,* Wiesbaden.
1980. "Silsilah Raja-raja Sambas as a source of history," *Archipel,* 20, pp. 254-267.

Kern, W.
1956. "Commentaar op de Salasilah van Kutai," *VKI,* vol. 29.

Linehan, W.
1947. "Notes on the Texts of the Malay Annals," *JMBRAS,* 20 (2). pp. 107-116.

Maier, H. M. J.
1988. *In the Centre of Authority: The Malay Hikayat Merong Mahawangsa.* Ithaca: Cornell University Press.

Matheson, V.
1971. "The Tuhfat al-Nafis: structure and sources," *BKI,* 127, pt. 3, pp. 375-392.
1972. "Mahmud, Sultan of Riau and Lingga 1923-1964," *Indonesia,* 13, pp. 119-146.
1982. *Tuhfat Al-Nafis,* Kuala Lumpur.
1989. "Pulau Penyengat: Nineteenth Century Islamic Centre of Riau," *Archipel,* 37, pp. 153-172.

Mead, J. P.
1914. "Hikayat Raja2 Pasai," *JSBRAS,* 66, pp. 1-55.

Mees, C. A.
1935. *De Kroniek van Koetai,* Santpoort.

Mohd. Khalid Saidin
1971. "Naskah-naskah lama mengenai Sejarah Negeri Johor," *DB,* 15, no. 8, pp. 339-350.

Mohd. Taib Osman
1963. "Mythic elements in Malay Historiography," *Tenggara* 2 (2), pp. 80-89.
1971. "Ulasan buku: Sejarah Melayu or Malay Annals," *DB,* 15 (2), pp. 61-64.

Mohd. Yusof Md. Nor
1980/81. Silsilah Melayu dan Bugis, M.A, Thesis, UKM, Kuala Lumpur.
1984. *Salasilah Melayu dan Bugis,* Kuala Lumpur.

Muhammad Yusoff Hashim
1988. *Pensejarahan Melayu Nusantara,* Kuala Lumpur.
1989. *Kesultanan Melayu Malaka,* Kuala Lumpur.

Newbold, T. J.
1839. *Political and Statistical Account of the British Settlements in the Straits of Malacca,* London.

Noorduyn, J.
1966. "Tentang asal-mulanya penulisan sedjarah di Sulawesi Selatan," *Majalah Ilmu-ilmu Sastra Indonesia,* 3 (2 & 3).

Overbeck, H.
1926. "Silsilah Melayu dan Bugis dan sakalian raja2nya," *JMBRAS,* 4 (3), pp. 339-381.

Parnikel, B. B.
1960. "An attempt of interpretation of the main characters of the Malay Hikayat Hang Tuah," Papers presented at the *XXV International Congress of Orientalists,* Moscow.
1979. "An epic hero and an epic traitor in the Hikayat Hang Tuah," *BKI* 132(4), pp. 403-417.

Pitono, R.
1972. "Indonesian traditional literature as a source of history," *Manusia Indonesia,* 6, pp. 99-120.

Putri Minerva Mutiara
1979. *Sejarah Tambusyai,* Jakarta.

Ras, J. J.
1968. *Hikajat Bandjar,* Dissetation, Leiden.

Reid, A. & L. Castles
1979. *Pre-Colonial State Systems in Southeast Asia,* Kuala Lumpur.

Reid, A. & D. Marr (eds.)
1980. *Southeast Asian perceptions of the Past,* Singapore.

Rogayah A. Hamid
1980. *Hikayat Upu Daeng Menambun,* Kuala Lumpur.

Roolvink, R.
1954. "Hikajat Radja2 Pasai," *Bahasa dan Budaja,* 2 (3), pp. 3-17.
1965. "The Answer of Pasai," *JMBRAS,* 38 (2), pp. 129-139.
1967. "The variant versions of the Malay Annals," *BKI,* 123, pp. 301- 324.
1980. "Sadjarah Riouw dan daerah taaloqnya," *Archipel,* 20, pp. 225-231.

Samad Said, A.
1986. *Sulalatus Salatin,* Kuala Lumpur.

Shellabear, W. G.
1869. *Sejarah Melayu,* Singapore.

Siegel, J.
1978. *Shadow and sound: the historical thought of a Sumatra people,* Chicago.

Siti Hawa Salleh
1970. *Hikayat Merong Mahawangsa,* Kuala Lumpur.

Situmorang. T. A. & A. Teeuw.
1952. *Sedjarah Melayu,* Djakarta.

Soedjatmoko (ed.)
1965. *An Introduction to Indonesian Historiography,* New York.

Sturrock, A. J.
1916. "Hikayat Marong Maha Wangsa," *JSBRAS,* 72, pp. 37-123.

Sulastin Sutrisno
1982. "Sastra dan historiografi tradisional," *Majalah Ilmu-ilmu Sastra Indonesia,* 10 (3), pp. 207-226.
1983. *Hikayat Hang Tuah: analisa struktur dan fungsi,* Yogyakarta.

Sweeney, Amin
1967a. "Sir Richard Winstedt's Summary of Tuhfat Al-Nafis," *JMBRAS*, 40 (1), pp. 155-156.
1967b. "The connection between the Hikayat Raja2 Pasai and the Sejarah Melayu," *JMBRAS*, 40 (2), pp. 268-279.

Sweeney, P. L. A.
1968. "Silsilah Raja-raja Brunei," *JMBRAS*, 41 (2), pp. 1-82.

Teeuw, A.
1960. "De Maleise Roman," Forum *der Letteren,* 1 (2), pp. 108-120.
1961. "Hang Tuah en Hang Djebat: Nationalisme, ideologie en literatuur beschouwing," *Forum der Letteren,* pp. 37-48.
1964. "Tentang penghargaan dan penafsiran Hikayat Hang Tuah," *DB,* 8 (8), pp. 339-354.

Teeuw, A. & D. K. Wyatt
1970. *Hikayat Patani - The Story of Patani,* The Hague.

Teuku Iskandar
1958. "De Hikajat Atjeh" (Hikajat Aceh), *VKI*, 26.
1964. "Suatu kekeliruan dalam Hikayat Raja2 Pasai," *DB,* 8 (5), pp. 226-230.
1964. "Tun Sri Lanang, pengarang Sejarah Melayu," *DB,* 8 (11), pp. 484-492.
1964. "Raja Ali Haji, tokoh dari pusat kebudayaan Johor-Riau," *DB,* pp. 533-540.
1965. "Misa Melayu dan pengarangnya Raja Chulan," *DB,* 9 (6), pp. 245-251.
1967. "Three Malay historical writings in the first half of the 17th century," *JMBRAS*, 40 (2), pp. 38-53.
1968. "Some aspects concerning the work of copyists of Malay Historical writings," *Peninjau Sejarah,* 3 (2).
1970. "Some Historical sources used by the author of Hikayat Hang Tuah," *JMBRAS* 43 (1).

Wake, C.
1964. "Malacca's early kings and the reception of Islam," *JSEAH,* 5 (2), pp. 104-128.

Wang Gungwu
1968. "The First Three Rulers of Malacca," *JMBRAS,* 41 (1).

Wilkinson, R. J.
1933. "The Sri Lanang Pedigree," *JMBRAS,* 11 (2), pp. 148-150.

Winstedt, R. O.
1911. "The history of the Peninsula in folk-tales," *JSBRAS,* 57, pp. 183-188.
1919. *Misa Melayu,* Singapore, (2nd reprint, Kuala Lumpur, 1968).
1921. "Hikayat Hang Tuah," *JSBRAS,* 83, pp. 110-122.
1932a. "A History of Johore," *JMBRAS,* 10 (1), pp. 164-170.
"The Early Rulers of Perak, Pahang and Acheh," *JMBRAS,* 10(1), pp. 32-45.
1932b. "A Malay history of Riau and Johore," *JMBRAS,* 10 (2).
1938. "The Malay Annals, Raffles MS 18," *JMBRAS,* 16 (3), pp. 1-225.
1958. "A History of Classical Malay Literature", *JMBRAS,* 31, 3.
1970. *The Fall of Srivijaya in Malay History,* Kuala Lumpur/ Singapore.

Yaakub Isa
1969. "Sejarah Melayu ditinjau dari beberapa aspek," *DB,* 8, (11), pp. 500-512.

Yusuff Iskandar
1971. "Hikayat Raja2 Pasai sebagai sebuah karya sejarah," *DB*, 15 (12), pp. 542-552.

Zacharias Jozef Manusama
1977. *Hikayat Tanah Hitu,* Unpublished thesis, Leiden.

Zahrah Ibrahim
1986. *Sastra Sejarah, Interpretasi dan Penilaian,* Kuala Lumpur.

Zainal Abidin Wahid
1955/6. "Some aspects of Malay History," Journal *of the Historical Society,* 4, pp. 6-10.
1966. "Sejarah Melayu," *Asian Studies,* 4 (3), pp. 445-451.

9 Classical Malay Law Codes

Classical Malay law codes provide an important resource for the study of traditional Malay governance and administration, as well as the structure of society. That is not all. Legal codes reflect traditional ways of thought. The proverb, "pound rice in a mortar, boil it in an earthenware pot", suggests that Malays had a fine regard for order. The proverb, "Where the sky touches the earth, the earth upholds the sky; in the land where you live, you must follow local custom", suggests a willingness and an ability to adapt to current conditions and the vicissitudes of change. For this reason, elements of animism, Hinduism and Islam can exist comfortably side-by-side in Malay culture.

Sir Stamford Raffles was the first person to realize the value of studying classical Malay legal codes. While he was in Penang (1805-1810), he employed four Malay secretaries to collect legal documents. He rejected the contemporary scholarly idea that Malays had no understanding of law, firmly insisting that each kingdom had its own code. The secretaries were to transcribe these codes for his earnest attention. The result of his studies was an article he published in *Asiatic Researches* (volume 12, 1818).

Even so, there have been scholars who have doubted the relevance of traditional law codes for the actual administration of justice. In one of his articles, R. J. Wilkinson advised students of the law not to bother too much about these codes. He pointed out that Malay law codes had never had the backing of any legal body and were more like "legal digests"; as such, they might suggest what the current practices might be but the laws were not always applied and individuals were not always punished for their faults (Wilkinson 1908). R. O. Winstedt was also of the opinion that these digests were nothing more than reference works; they were often ignored and a strong sultan, or a judge who sought to be on good terms with such a sultan, could easily set their provisions aside (Winstedt 1958: 136).

Malay legal codes may have only been digests, or reference books, but they were certainly used. When we read W. E. Maxwell's studies of Malay slavery and agricultural codes (Maxwell 1884, 1890), we can find many regulations and practices that match those of the *Undang-undang Malaka,* The Laws of Malaka. In the *Adatrechtbundel,* volume 24, a collection of writings on Malay law, there are many quotations that prove that the classical law codes do not only belong to the past but are still used, at least as reference works. This is the importance of studying traditional Malay codes.

9.1 *Undang-Undang Malaka*

The *Undang-undang Malaka* is the most important Malay legal code. It has been revised a number of times and adapted for use in various kingdoms throughout the Archipelago. The proof of this lies in the number of surviving manuscripts. There are more than forty of them; some are long, some are short. Some were used in specific kingdoms, such as Kedah, Patani, Johor, or Acheh. Others may have been used in Pahang, Riau, Pontianak and Brunei.

The *Undang-undang Malaka* as we know it today comprises several layers. The first layer, the core of the work, is a series of regulations issued by Sultan Muhammad Syah (1422-1444) and enlarged by Sultan Muzaffar Syah (1445-1458). As time passed, other materials were added. The whole text was copied and recopied over four hundred years. The present text seems to be a unified text, but the layers are clearly visible:

(i) The core text of the *Undang-undang Malaka*;

(ii) Maritime Laws (part);

(iii) Matrimonial Laws;

(iv) Sales and Procedures;

(v) State Laws; and

(vi) The Laws of Johor.

   (i) The Core (Chapters 1-23.2)

      The *Undang-undang Malaka* consists of 44 chapters. Chapters 1 to chapter 23.2 represent the core of the *Undang-undang Malaka* and its most important part. Customary law (*adat*) occupies a major place but the influence of Islam is beginning to make itself felt.

  (ii) *Maritime Laws* (Chapters 23.3-23.5; 24.1-24.2; 29)

      This part deals with rescuing the destitute, hiring boats, and so on. The laws were written to help regulate Malaka's rapidly expanding sea trade. They were soon considered inadequate and replaced by the separate *Undang-undang Laut Malaka,* The Malaka Sea Code.

  (ii) *Matrimonial Laws* (Chapters 25-28)

      These laws are translated from Syafi'i Muslim laws. They are introduced by a separate text, which ends *wa 'llahu a'lam,* God alone knows. In a manuscript held in Jakarta, Bat. Gen. 152, we find the words *katibuhu Syaikh Abdul Ghoyu,* written by Syaikh Abdul Ghoyu.

  (iv) Sales and Procedures (Chapters 30-42; 43.1)

This part explains the laws relating to trade (*bai'*) and legal procedure (*syahadat*) as required by Islam. It is mainly translated from Muslim legal texts such as the *At-Taqrib,* compiled by Abu Shujak, and the exposition, *Fath al-Qarib,* by Ibn Qasim al-Ghazzi. This section is the same as chapters 24-26 of the *Undang-undang Pahang,* The Laws of Pahang, edited by R. O. Winstedt and J. E. Kempe (Kempe & Winstedt, 1948).

(v) State Laws (Chapters 43.2-43.8; 44.1-44.8)

This part derives from a legal code used in the coastal regions around Malaka, which was gradually integrated into the *Undang-undang Malaka.* Unless one recognizes this, the *Undang-undang Malaka* can seem very repetitious.

(vi) The Laws of Johor (Chapter 44.9-44.11)

The inclusion of this text in the *Undang-undang Malaka* has led to a misunderstanding. There are not two separate but similar law codes; rather the *Undang-undang Malaka* and the *Undang-undang Johor* are two parts of one and the same text.

9.1.1 Date of Compilation

Each of these separate levels was composed at a different time. The core was composed at the time of Sultan Muhammad Syah (1422-1444) and expanded at the time of Sultan Muzaffar Syah (1445-1458), during the golden age of Malaka. The section on commerce and legal procedure presumably came later, after Islam was firmly established. The state laws probably derive from the beginning of the sixteenth century, after the coming of the Portuguese; while the Laws of Johor were composed on the orders of Sultan Mahmud Syah (1761-1812), the son of Sultan Sulaiman ibn Abdul Jalil Syah (1722-1760).

R. O. Winstedt did not realize that the *Undang-undang Malaka* is a hybrid text, which was composed at various times. He dates the whole text to the reign of Sultan Muzaffar Syah, because the *Sejarah Melayu* states that he "ordered that a legal book be written, so that there should be no more mistakes in the administration of government justice" (Winstedt, 1953: 31-33). No doubt this covers the core and Sultan Muhammad Syah's officials would certainly have had other codebooks of traditional adat with which to work.

I will now provide an outline of the *Undang-undang Malaka,* based on my own doctoral studies at Leiden University (Liaw Yock Fang, 1976).

9.1.2 Outline

The *Undang-undang Malaka* opens with a list of senior officials appointed by the king: the *bendahara* (prime minister), the *temenggung* (head of the army and the police), the *syahbandar* (harbour master), and the *penghulu bendahari* (the royal secretary and treasurer), and their respective duties. It then states that this law code was compiled by Sultan Iskandar Syah, also entitled Sultan Mahmud Syah, the first Malay ruler to embrace Islam.

Chapter one sets out a number of royal prerogatives: the people cannot wear yellow clothing or thin materials at certain places. If they do, they will be killed. There are certain qualities required for members of royalty and others for lesser persons.

Chapter two deals with language. Only the king can use the words *titah, patik, murka, karunia,* and *anugerah* (command, you, angry, grant and bequeath). Anyone else who does so will be killed.

Chapter three reserves the use of the colour yellow, including yellow cushions and yellow handkerchiefs, to royalty.

Chapter four deals with criminal offences. Anyone who kills, stabs, slashes, or hits another person; who pillages or steals another person's property; who falsely accuses someone else, commits perjury; anyone who falsely claims to speak on behalf of the king or refuses to obey a royal command, will be killed.

Chapter five states that anyone who kills another person without the knowledge of the king will be executed. However, it is permitted to murder another person under certain circumstances.

Chapter six states that if a person runs amok and cannot be captured, then that person may be killed. This chapter lays down the patterns of behaviour that should be followed by a minister and describes three types of criminal offence that only the king can pardon.

Chapter seven states that anyone who kills a royal slave will be fined. A thief may be killed under certain circumstances.

Chapter eight sets out the penalties for slashing or hitting another person. The penalties are less severe for a free person than they are for a slave.

Chapter nine declares that the bendahara, the temenggung, the syahbandar, and the nakhoda (admiral) may kill another person without royal permission at certain times.

Chapter ten sets out the punishment for taking a royal page or slave on a journey. If the page or slave dies, the offender will be fined.

Chapter eleven declares that if a person enters a residential area and steals something, that person may be killed. A person who steals crops or livestock can only be fined. A thief who enters a house may have his hand cut off; the other thieves, who did not enter the house, cannot.

Chapter twelve sets out the law about seducing another man's wife or daughter. The man who seduces a girl must marry her. If he seduces another man's wife, he will be fined. A man who rapes a woman will be stoned or otherwise severely dealt with (if he is married), or beaten eighty times (if he is a bachelor). A person who accuses another person of adultery but cannot provide the proof for his accusation will be fined.

Chapter thirteen deals with the process of redeeming a runaway slave. A person who steals and hides another man's slave shall have his household sequestered. It is also stated that a man who counterfeits the royal seal will be killed; the man who gives false evidence to the *bendahara* will be publicly shamed by having his face smeared with charcoal; and a man who forges the letters of dignitaries will be fined.

Chapter fourteen states that a man who contests an accusation will be ordered to immerse his hand in boiling water or molten metal to prove his innocence.

Chapter fifteen states that if another man's slave is employed to do a certain task and the slave dies, the man must compensate the original owner. The same penalty applies to a man who borrows a buffalo. A man who borrows a female slave and rapes her can only be fined.

Chapter sixteen declares that a man can only interfere in his friend's quarrels under certain circumstances.

Chapter seventeen states a man who hires someone to kill or beat another person without the knowledge of a judge shall be fined.

Chapter eighteen states that a man who commits an act of gross impropriety, namely seducing another man's fiancée or carrying out his own desires without regard for the wellbeing of others, will be fined. The chapter also describes the circumstances under which an engagement ring may be returned.

Chapter nineteen states that a new settler of a compound must share its fruits with the previous owner. If a garden is mortgaged but does not bear fruit, the mortgagee can claim double the amount he has loaned. A man who occupies a deserted estate can be sued by the owner.

Chapter twenty states that a person may cultivate a piece of "dead land" (unclaimed and unworked land), but if he cultivates "living land" (land that shows signs of ownership and utilization), he may be sued or fined.

Chapter twenty-one states that a person can be fined if he tethers a buffalo on a public highway. This chapter also prescribes the fine for stealing a buffalo.

Chapter twenty-two states that a man prematurely burns off another man's land, he must later burn it completely. Fields must also be fenced.

Chapter twenty-three states that people given food during a famine cannot be sold to redeem the debt incurred. A slave may be ordered to earn his food. A person who recovers a boat lost at sea should be paid a ransom or a reward.

Chapter twenty-four states that a person who kidnaps a royal slave shall be killed. This chapter also prescribes the rules for representing another person in matters of trade.

Chapter twenty-five prescribes who can act as a woman's guardian in a marriage ceremony.

Chapter twenty-six describes who may be a witness to a marriage.

Chapter twenty-seven states that both the man and the woman have the right to cancel a marriage contract if a defect is discovered in the other party.

Chapter twenty-eight deals with divorce.

Chapter twenty-nine deals with weights and measures.

Chapter thirty deals with trade and forbids the taking of interest.

Chapter thirty-one deals with the sale of land and the return of defective goods.

Chapter thirty-two deals with bankruptcy, amicable settlement, suretyship and borrowing.

Chapter thirty-three deals with lending capital.

Chapter thirty-four deals with trusteeship.

Chapter thirty-five deals with the acknowledgement of fault.

Chapter thirty-six deals with apostasy.

Chapter thirty-seven deals with the testimony of witnesses.

Chapter thirty-eight deals with the procedures of accusation, defence, and the taking of oaths.

Chapter thirty-nine deals with murder.

Chapter forty deals with unlawful sexual intercourse.

Chapter forty-one deals with slander.

Chapter forty-two provides punishments for the consumption of alcohol.

Chapter forty-three describes the close bond that should hold between a king, his ministers, and his people, as well as various criminal offences.

Chapter forty-four describes some royal prerogatives, as well as various criminal offences.

These are the contents of one of the most important versions of the *Undang-undang Malaka*. There are other versions that only contain nineteen chapters, two of which are held in Jakarta (Bat. Gen. 152 and Bat. Gen. 154), while a third is held in Leiden (Klinkert 67C). There other versions which contain twenty-seven chapters; these are also available in Jakarta (v.d. Wall collection 13) and (Cod. Or. 1705). Ph. S. van Ronkel's *Risalah Hukum Kanun* also contains twenty-seven chapters. There are approximately forty manuscripts containing forty-four chapters and they are the most common. Only two manuscripts contain sixty-six chapters, and they are again to be found in Jakarta (v.d. Wall 50) and Leiden (Cod. Or. 1725). The longest version of all contains eighty-two chapters and was translated into English by T. J. Newbold during the nineteenth century (Newbold 1839: 231-313).

9. 2 *Undang-Undang Laut* (The Maritime Laws)

The *Malaka Maritime Laws* were important for the whole of the Archipelago. In 1818, Raffles published an article entitled "On the Malay Nation, with a Translation of its Maritime Institutions" (*Asiatic Researches,* Vol. 12). In 1845, Dulaurier, a French scholar, published the manuscripts of three separate maritime codes. His work is little known by Southeast Asian scholars, compared to the text published 110 years later by R. O. Winstedt and P. E. de Josselin de Jong, *"The Maritime Laws of Malacca, edited, with an outline translation"*. Winstedt and de Josselin de Jong believed that they had discovered two separate maritime codes (Winstedt and De Josselin de Jong, 1956: 26). In so doing, they ignored the very important MS 6619 held in the Royal Military Academy, Breda, the Netherlands. Further, they only examined thirteen codes, while there are over forty altogether.

Based on the prefaces, contents, arrangement and language, of the various manuscripts, we can distinguish four different types of maritime Codes, as follows.

1 The Core Maritime Code

This basic maritime code is represented by two texts: MS 6619 and Vat. Ind. IV, held in the Vatican. The code was composed while Sultan Mahmud Syah (1488-1528) was still on the throne and Datuk Bendahara Seri Maharaja was his Regent (*Mangkubumi*). The Breda manuscript once belonged to the private collection of A. Reland (1676-1718), who was originally professor of philosophy and later professor of oriental languages at Utrecht. Reland may have received it from Valentijn. Despite its importance, this text has not been given the attention it deserves.

2 The Malaka Maritime Code

This version is called the *Undang-undang Laut Malaka,* The Malaka Maritime Code, because most of it is identical to the second part of the *Undang-undang Malaka* (Liaw, 1976: 9-10). After initial praise of God, the manuscript contains the following attractive appeal:

> *Ya, Ghafur al-Rahim yang amat mengampuni lagi mengasihani dengan berkat agama kekasihnya Muhammad salla 'llahu 'alaihi wa-sallam wa rahmat Allah akan sekalian umatnya yang membawa iman dan mengerjakan syariatnya minta tolong kepada sekalian sahabatnya ke hadirat Allah Ta'ala memberi syafa'at akan segala umatnya, takut akan amarnya dan nahynya, maka memohonkan ampun. Allah Rabbi al-'arshi al-karim yang amat kuasa.*

> (Oh, Merciful Pardoner, who is most forgiving and most merciful, by the blessing of the religion taught by His beloved Muhammad, peace and blessing be upon him, for all his people who believe in his doctrines and obey his law, we ask the assistance of his companions who live in Almighty God's presence in interceding for his people, that we may do those things we are commanded to do and avoid those things we are commanded not to do, and we ask for Your forgiveness. God is Sovereign, Bountiful and All Powerful.)

Then we are told that the laws were compiled in the time of Sultan Mahmud Syah who ruled Malaka. Therefore "we" must obey these laws and respect the ships' captains who stand in the place of the king in the middle of the ocean.

3 The Achehnese Version

The Achehnese version is represented by four manuscripts and forms the second part of the Achehnese text of the *Undang-undang Malaka* (Liaw, 1976: 10-11). The preface to this text states:

> *Al-hamdu li 'llahi rabbi 'l-'alamin, segala puji-pujian bagi Allah Tuhan seru sekalian 'alam 'ala al-dawam ma damat al-laye wa 1-ayyam bi hormat al-nabi khairi 'l-anam wa alihi wa ashabihi al-tabi'in ila yaumi 'l-qiyama. Amin ya rabba 'l-'alamin ya dha 'l jalal wa 'l-ikram. Maka tahlillah nur Allah pada segala 'alam, nyatalah bulan dan matahari menerang siang dan malam, takbir ma'dun nyatalah ashya al-dunia wa 'l-akhira. Maka berbunyilah burung yang indah-indah amat nyaring suaranya dan merdu daripada makhluk, maka beredarlah segala pohon zaitun, maka terkembanglah segala bunga-bungaan amat harum pada sekalian 'alam, maka bertiuplah angin yang lemah lembut di dalam syorga jannah al-firdaus.*

> (*Al-hamdu li 'llahi rabbi 'l-'alamin,* all praise to Allah, the Lord of all the worlds, *'ala al-dawam ma damat al-laye wa 1-ayyam bi hormat al-nabi khairi 'l-anam wa alihi wa ashabihi al-tabi'in ila yaumi 'l-qiyama. Amin ya rabba 'l-'alamin ya dha 'l jalal wa 'l-ikram.* The light of God shone in prayer on all the world, the moon and the sun lit the night and the day, proclaiming your glory, manifesting *ashya al-dunia wa 'l-akhira.* The birds sang sweetly among all your creatures, the olive trees flourished, fragrant flowers covered the ground, gentle winds blew in the heavenly paradise.)

After these words of praise, the purpose of writing the law code is announced: "that all that is done on land and sea may be done in peace, that all may be safe, that there may be no difficulty between our older and younger brothers in ships large and small". This is then further followed by the recording of the date of composition: "At the time of Ali Sayyidina Maulana Paduka Seri Sultan Mahmud Syah of the sovereign state of Malaka, ruling as the representative of Almighty God, a law for all people and all times".

The concluding colophon states that the manuscript was copied in Hijriah 1202 H (= 1788), during the rule of Ali Sayyidina wa Maulana Paduka Seri Sultan Jamal al-'Alam Badr al-Munir (1703-1726), who sat on the throne of Acheh Dar al-Salam, which is famous below the equator, and asks for mercy and compassion on God's faithful servants.

4 The Patani Version

The version is called *The Laws of Patani* because it mentions Patani in several places (Liaw, 1976: 11-12). There are six manuscripts of the *Undang-undang Patani* and it represents a miscellany of various legal codes. The Maritime Laws form the first part of Cod. Or. 2160, the second part of SOAS 40506 (2), and the whole of Cod. Or. 1726. This version is possibly very old; Maxwell notes that one text states that "Encik Maulana wrote this legal code based on a manuscript from the year 1083 H (1672 AD)."

This version can also be distinguished by its different preface. Cod. Or. 2160 describes itself as being "a short law code, compiled by Seri Paduka Sultan Mahmud Syah, the Sang Purba who descended from Bukit Si Guntang and became king in Malaka by the grace of Almighty God." Or. 1726 begins: "Be it known that these words are for the peaceful protection of all God's servants who work on the ocean, so that they commit no fault or improper act, so that they may be safe in this world and the next, that there shall be no dispute or faulty words or deeds done towards their friends and colleagues."

Cod. Or. 1726, Maxwell 5 and SOAS 40506 (2) all continue by stating that the laws were promulgated while "Malaka flourished under the rule of our lord Seri Sultan Mahmud Syah" and Bendahara Seri Maharaja served as Mangkubumi.

From chapter 17.2 onwards, the text continues with a miscellany of Malay laws that deal with various topics, including runaway slaves, quarrels, optional duties, divorce, theft, debt, and such like. One chapter deals with "the costume that should be worn by the Bendahara while he is traveling around Patani." The same chapter states that "these customs, laws and regulations were composed by Kadi Surjihan." Maxwell 19 does not mention "traveling around Patani" but does "prescribe rules to do with the Bendahara," and concludes: "Kadi Sadar Johan wrote this book of laws and regulations at the gracious command of his Majesty Duli Yang Dipertuan Sultan Mahmud Syah, the ruler of Malaka. The Bendahara was Datuk Bendahara Seri Maharaja. He is our lord the Mangkubumi."

Cod. Or. 2160 is completely different again. It still contains an introductory chapter on maritime law, followed by 22 chapters: 12-22 follow the *Undang-undang Malaka* and chapter 23 deals with Chinese vessels visiting Patani (Liaw, 1976: 18).

The four versions represent a homogenous corpus: they include the same contents, in virtually the same order. By comparing these contents and the language used, we can show that the versions are closely related to each other, and derive from the one source. Here is a summary of the four Maritime Codes.

9.2.1 Summary

Prologue: Various forms.

1.1 The duties of the captain and his crew, including the senior officers, middle officers and junior officers, the helmsman, anchorman, sails man and serving passengers.

1.2 Crew members who oppose the captain and officers will be beaten.

2. Anyone who commits adultery with the wife of another crewmember will be killed. If the woman is unmarried, the person will be beaten and the couple married to each other; if she is a slave, the man will only be fined. If the woman has belonged to her master for a long time, the offender may either be fined or killed. If a slave commits adultery with another slave, they shall both be beaten.

3.1 Whoever finds treasure, be it gold, silver or foreign goods, shall surrender it to the captain, but a merchant passenger (*kiwi*) who finds goods while he is ashore of his own volition shall receive two-thirds of his discovery and surrender the remaining one-third to the captain.

3.2 Whoever finds a runaway slave must surrender the slave to the captain. The original owner may redeem the slave. If the slave is sold, half of the price must be paid to the owner (should he claim it).

4.1 A person who is rescued, whether on land or at sea, must pay a fee (reward) of half a *tahil* (one and a third ounces) of gold; if there is any property involved, the person shall pay an additional one quarter of a *tahil* (a *paha*, one third of an ounce).

4.2 A merchant passenger wishing to leave a vessel must pay half a tahil; a servant shall pay a paha (Versions 1 and 4).

5. A person who uses offensive language shall receive an appropriate punishment; if he refuses, he shall be killed. If he asks to be forgiven, he shall be forgiven but will still be punished.

6. There are four crimes that, if committed aboard a ship, shall be punished with death:

    (a) any crime against the owner of the vessel;

    (b) killing the owner of the boat, the captain, an officer, or a merchant passenger;

    (c) wearing a concealed weapon;

    (d) serious misbehaviour.

7. A debtor merchant may not leave a boat until he has fulfilled his obligations (which hold for three years, three months and three days); if he wishes to leave, he will be taxed ten times his capital.

8.1 A pilot who makes a financial payment will be given a cubicle on board. During this time, he may order the crew to guard his cargo. If anyone steals his goods, the person will be fined or beaten.

8.2 A pilot who causes serious damage to a boat will be killed; he must, therefore, be diligent throughout the voyage, so that nothing untoward happens.

8.3 A pilot may not leave a boat until he has met all his obligations. (This is not present in Version 1 but is discussed in considerable detail in Version 4.)

9.1 A merchant passenger may travel on the boat in one of four ways:
   (a) he rents a cubicle in the hold;
   (b) he presents the captain with three or four tahils of gold;
   (c) he creates seven or eight cubicles;
   (d) he does not buy a cubicle but promises to pay two-tenths or three-tenths of his earnings.

9.2 A merchant passenger who makes such a payment will not be required to pay tax to the state. There shall be a senior merchant passenger (*mulkiwi*); but he must consult with the merchants in regard to all matters.

10.1 If there is a storm and it is necessary to jettison goods into the sea, this will only be done after consultation among all those sailing on the boat, because they will be the ones affected by this deed.

10.2 If the ship collides with a vessel charged to collect taxes, everyone on board will be punished (or taken as slaves, according to one version). (This article does not occur in Version 1.)

10.3 An accident at sea or in a storm shall be considered a natural disaster.

11.1 Crew members are not allowed to sit in certain places on the boat: the cross chamber, the diagonal chamber, and the forward chamber.

11.2 A merchant passenger and the senior merchant passenger may require a vessel to wait the necessary period to take on board water and firewood.

12.1 Guards must take proper precautions against the following four situations:
   (a) A debt slave absconding;
   (b) The vessel drifting onto a bank or reef;
   (c) The vessel sinking;
   (d) Another vessel approaching from any direction.

12.2 Junior crewmembers must perform their work diligently and accompany the captain while is ashore. Versions 1 and 4 also add that they must fight the enemy when required to do so.

13.1 If a ship's galley catches fire because of the negligence of a servant, the servant's master will be fined four strings of cheap Javanese coins. If the master does not pay the fine, the servant will receive forty lashes.

13.2 If the fire is due to the negligence of the owner of the slave, such a person will be fined four strings of cheap Javanese coins. (Only in Version 1.)

14.1 If there is a fight on board during which ropes are hacked or the anchor damaged, those involved in the fray will be punished. A person who carries a dagger in certain parts of the boat may be sentenced to death.

14.2 Merchant passengers who quarrel with the captain and draw their daggers anywhere on the vessel will be sentenced to death. If they are arrested but apologize, they shall only be fined.

15.1 On reaching a port, the captain shall have three days in which to conduct his own business. The merchants may then conduct their business. (This is not found in Version 1.)

15.2 A merchant passenger may not bid against the captain for the purchase of slaves and goods offered for sale. The crew shall not redeem goods or slave women without the knowledge of the captain.

15.3 If the captain wishes to visit a bay or change to a different dock, he must first consult with the other people in the boat.

16. The facilities provided to the crew will depend on the size of the vessel. (This is not found in Version 1.)

17.1 If the monsoon season changes and the ship has not yet left port, the price of his cubicle shall be returned to the merchant passenger. If it is late in the season and the boat has not yet departed, but the merchant is still aboard the boat, the captain is permitted to depart without consulting the merchant. (This is not found in Version 1.)

17.2 A merchant passenger who leaves a boat while it is moored in a bay or an estuary shall lose his cubicle, unless he can show good cause for his action. (This is not found in Version 1.)

18 Two merchants, Patih Harun and Patih Ilias, consulted with a few senior ships' captains in order to draw up this code: the captains were Captain Zainal, Captain Dewi (also called Dewa, Buri, and Diri Dewari), and Captain Ishak. When they were finished, they respectfully presented the document to His Majesty Sultan Mahmud Syah, king of Malaka, through the Datuk Bendahara who was also the Mangkubumi at that time. Sultan Mahmud Syah graciously accepted this code and proclaimed it as the law of the sea. The three captains were granted appropriate titles of respect.

This is a summary of the common elements in the various Maritime Codes. Some texts follow a different order, but all end with 17.2. There are various insertions and additions and the concluding paragraphs provide different dates for the copying of the texts. As I have already mentioned, the texts are sufficiently close to one another in their contents and language to be able to explain occasional obscurities.

9.2.2 Deviant Manuscripts

There are three deviant versions of this manuscript tradition.

1 *Undang-undang Perahu*

The *Shipping Code* is represented by Cod. Or. 12.204 and Cod. Or. 6139, Leiden University Library. This is probably the longest Maritime Code and contains 46 chapters. Chapters 1-17 follow the previously discussed texts, in the same order; the additional chapters provide additional details on hiring vessels, dividing profits, accusations, loans, deaths at sea, etc. The language used is long and complicated, although many "difficult" words have also been simplified.

2   *Undang-undang Berlayar*

The *Sailing Code* is contained in two manuscripts at Leiden University Library, Cod. Or. 12.123 and Cod. Or. 3293, and in the *Undang-undang Pelayaran* (Ml 439, Jakarta), published by Edwar Djamaris et al. The Jakarta manuscript appears to be a composite of two manuscripts: one of 86 chapters, the other of 52 chapters (Edwar Djamaris et al., 1981: 180-234). The basic seventeen chapters are spread throughout this work. The language used is poor.

3   *Undang-undang Perahu*

The single text of the alternative *Shipping Code*, Cod. Or. 3292, Leiden University Library, contains 50 chapters. Its contents are very different from those described above. The script is very poor and almost illegible. The manuscript was copied by Khalil Ibrahim. An outline of the text is provided in Mr. L. J. J. Caron's doctoral dissertation.

In conclusion, we can see that these Maritime Codes were short manuscripts intended to serve the needs of ships' captains in the same way that the Rhodian Sea Law served commercial trade and navigation in the Byzantine Empire. They were copied and adapted from pre-existing bodies of regulations to meet the contemporary needs of their users, thus accounting for the existence of different manuscript traditions in different places and at different times. For further information on the *Undang-undang Malaka* and the *Undang-undang Laut*, please refer to Liaw Yock Fang 2003.

9.3 *Undang-undang Minangkabau*

There are many manuscripts of *The Minangkabau Laws* and more than 40 are held in libraries in Jakarta, London and Leiden. Nevertheless, it has not always been easy to find a copy. Newbold complained that he had not been able to gain access to even a single manuscript (Newbold, 1939, II: 219). As a result, scholars have had to make use of the related *Undang-undang Dua Belas*, Twelve Codes, from Perak, and the *Undang-undang Sungai Ujung*, Code of Sungai Ujung (Hooker, 1968: 158; 1972: 83). The first relatively complete text was published in 1981 by Edwar Djamaris et al. This was based on the best of the 14 manuscripts studied by the editors but it is still difficult to understand because the original was so old and had been passed down through many generations before being committed to print. We need to compare many badly preserved manuscripts before we can produce a worthwhile text.

Almost all of the manuscripts bear the same title: *Undang-undang Minangkabau* (Liaw, 1965: 1-6, 16-30). Some have other titles: *Undang-undang Tanah Datar* (Lowlands Law), *Undang-undang Adat* (Customary Law), *Undang-undang Luhak Tiga Laras* (the Law of Luhak Tiga Laras), *Tambo Adat* (Legal Annals) and *Adat Istiadat Minangkabau* (Minangkabau Customary Law and Ceremony). The Code consists of three parts: firstly *Tambo Raja-raja Minangkabau,* (Minangkabau Royal Annals); secondly *Undang-undang Adat* (Customary Law)*;* and thirdly, customary law as seen from the perspective of Islam. However many surviving manuscripts only contain two of these three parts: sometimes parts one and two, sometimes parts two and three. There are some manuscripts that consist of only one part, usually either part two or part three. The ordering of the various parts, too, is not always consistent: some manuscripts begin with part two, then go back to part one.

Part one always begins with the story of Adam and his descendants. Adam had 99 children—49 girls and 50 boys, who married each other, all except for the last one. By the will of God, an angel took this youngest child high into the sky, where he married a heavenly nymph. He was called Iskandar (Alexander) and given the title "Zulkarnain," meaning "the man with two horns". At his own request, Allah sent Adam into the world to rule over mankind. King Iskandar had three sons: Sultan Sri Maharaja Alif, Sultan Sri Maharaja Depang, and Sultan Maharaja Diraja. They all set out: one sailed to Byzantium, one to China, and the third arrived at Mount Merapi, on Perca Island, known at that time as Andalas (Sumatra, but also Andalusia). This third son, Sultan Maharaja Diraja, came ashore at low tide, followed by a wise Brahmin named Ceti Bilang Pandai and his retainers. They cleared the forests, cultivated fields and erected huts. The huts grew into villages; the villages grew into states. The land of Minangkabau became well populated and prosperous.

Next we are told the story of Datuk Ketemenggungan (the founder of Patrilineal Law) and Datuk Perpatih nan Sebatang (the founder of Matrilineal Law). They appointed leaders in every state and drew up a code of law, which they called *Undang-undang nan Empat,* The Four Codes. Datuk Ketemenggungan and Datuk Perpatih divided the country into three provinces (*luhak*) and two counties (*laras*). The provinces were called Luhak Tanah Datar, Luhak Agam and Luhak Limapuluh Kota. The two counties were called Laras Kota Piliang and Bodi Caniago. The reasons for these divisions are given in some detail.

Next we are told of how Pulau Perca changed its name to Minangkabau and of the danger posed by a ship's captain who demanded an answer to two riddles, one to do with the beginning and end of a piece of wood, the other to do with the gender of two birds.

Some manuscripts also tell about the first kings to rule Acheh, Bintan, Jambi, Palembang and Indragiri.

The second part describes customary law. Here is a summary based on the *Undang-undang Luhak Tiga Laras* (Bat. Gen. 396) and a few other Minangkabau codes.

Traditional customary law can be divided into four areas or types:

(a) Authentic customary law (*Adat nan sebenar adat*);

(b) Declared customary law (*Adat nan diadatkan,* or *Hukum adat)*

(c) Accepted customary law (*Adat nan teradat)*

(d) Custom and ceremonial (*Adat istiadat).*

Authentic customary law derives from the Prophet Muhammad. It is religious law and describes those things that are permitted, forbidden, not compulsory but encouraged, not forbidden but discouraged; accusations and defenses; witnessing and oath taking. Some manuscripts state that authentic customary law is natural law; just as it is the law of nature that the goat bleats, the buffalo bellows, the ox grunts, the rooster crows, and the magpie sings. Declared customary law covers four areas:

(a) The "Two Bowls" (*Cupak nan dua*)

(b) Four Words (*Kata nan empat*)

(c) Four Laws (*Undang-undang nan empat*)

(d) Four Regions (*Negeri nan empat*).

Accepted customary law is the law regularly used in the provinces and counties. It is described in this way: "Bowls as big as bamboo poles, custom as long as the road" ("*Cupak nan sepanjang betung, adat nan sepanjang jalan*"). An ancient proverb says:

> *Di mana batang tergulung*
> *di sana cendawan tumbuh.*
> *Di mana tanah dipijak*
> *di sana langit dijunjung.*
> *Di mana negeri ditunggu*
> *di sana adat dipakai.*
>
> Wherever you find a dead tree trunk
> there you will find mushrooms growing.
> Wherever you stand on earth
> there will be a sky above you.
> Whichever country you are in
> there will be customs to follow.

Declared customary law is the most important of these four areas and will now be described in detail.

1 The Two Bowls

The first bowl is "the original bowl"; the second is the work of human hands. The original bowl is described as follows:

> *Gantang nan pepat,*
> *bungkal nan piawai,*
> *teraju nan betul,*
> *nan bertiru berteladan,*
> *berjenjang naik bertangga turun,*
> *berlukis berlembaga,*
> *nan bertakuk bertebang.*
> *nan berbaris berpahat*
> *jauh boleh ditunjukkan, hampir boleh dikakokkan*
>
> A measure that is accurate,
> justice in the right amount,
> a balanced scale,
> modeled after the exemplary,
> ascending in stages, descending in steps,

according to set rules,
the groove is notched,
the line is etched,
the far can be shown, the near can be observed

Compensate for accident, raise the fallen, the property of husband and wife belongs to both. This is the law that will "not rot in the rain or crack in the heat" ("*tiada lapuk dek hujan, tiada lekang dek panas*").

The original law is the true law; faults should be punished, issues should be resolved, white should remain white, black be black, honesty should rule in all matters.

The bowl made by human hands is the duty of wise chieftains (*penghulu*) in the provinces, counties and regions, and is like the sacrifice of a buffalo: the blood is drained, the horns are buried, the flesh is eaten. It is covered in betel, softened by time, bound by the first chapter of the Koran, Al-Fatihah. Sometimes duty is shaped by religion; sometimes it must go in other directions.

2 The Four Words

The four words are as follows.

Firstly, heritage (*kata pusaka*), which puts everything in its right place. The house is built on rock, custom is built on tradition.

Secondly, consensus (*kata mufakat*), open and free discussion which is settled by mutual agreement.

Thirdly, precedence (*kata dahulu kata ditepati*). If a matter cannot be resolved through resort to religious law or traditional custom, a temporary resolution should be achieved. If the resolution seems satisfactory after a short while, it should be adhered to thereafter.

Fourthly, compromise (*kemudian kata dicari*). If a matter has almost been almost resolved but a disagreement is raised, or another serious matter intervenes, a temporary agreement should be reached and followed for up to a month. If the compromise is satisfactory, it should be accepted.

Following these four words, manuscripts of the *Undang-undang Minangkabau* often add:

Kata raja kata melimpahkan
kata penghulu kata menyelesaikan
kata alim kata hakikat
kata pegawai kata berhubung
kata hulubalang kata menderas
kata orang banyak kata berbaluk
kata perempuan kata merendahkan dirinya menurut suami masing-masing.

The words of the king are generous
the words of the chieftains are conclusive
the words of religious scholars are sacred
the words of officials are efficient

the words of warriors are forceful
the words of common folk are confused
the words of women are humble and obedient to their husbands.

A Malay adage is then quoted: the word of the civil servant fills the general's basket, the word of the king fills the civil servant's basket, the word of the chieftain applies the law. And if there is no king, the adage continues, in the form of a six-line *pantun* verse:

Orang Mekah membawa teraju
orang Bagdad membawa telur
telur dimakan dalam puasa.
rumah bersendi batu,
adat bersendi syarak dan halur,
itulah akan ganti raja.

Those of Mecca steer the ship,
those of Bagdad supply the eggs,
eggs are eaten in the fasting month;
the house is built on rock,
custom is built on religious law and tradition,
that is how one lives if there is no king.

3 The Four Laws

The four laws are:

(1) Provincial Law;

(2) Regional Law;

(3) Civil Law; and

(4) The Twenty Laws.

Provincial Law applies to headmen and kings:

Luhak nan berpenghulu
rantau nan beraja
kampung nan bertua
tegak tiada tersondak
melanggang tiada terpampas
terlintang patah, terbujur lalu.
salah pada raja dibunuh
salah pada penghulu berutang.

The province has its chieftain
the wide world has its king
the village has its headman
you can stand tall and not hit your head

walk and not be fined
break through barriers, fit through easily.
if you offend the king, you will be killed
if you offend the chieftain, you will be fined.

The law explains that, in times of peace, twenty people can freely enter a territory or village at any time, "stand tall and not hit their head/ walk and not be fined", that is, come and go as they wish. At times of war, only ten people may do so. They are: the religious scholar, the student, the king, the chieftain, an invited guest, an expert sportsman, a parent, a physician, a teacher, and a hireling.

The Regional Law describes the appropriate organizational arrangements for the region, and covers households, mosques, settlements, minor roads and irrigation channels. Some manuscripts explain that the laws are especially meant for the senior members of society, and quote the Malay adage:

Inggris mengerat kuku
dikerat dengan siraut
akan pengerat betung tua
tuannya akan ganti lantai
elok negeri berempat suku
suku berbuat perut
kampung nan bertua
apa cupak nan di tua
elok dipakai di negeri.
arti tua di sana orang cerdik
arti muda di sana orang bodoh.

The English trim their nails
they cut them with a small a blade
we build on firm foundations
the best region has four clans
the clans have lineages
the villages have leaders
the bowls belong to the old
they should be used in the region
the old are those who are wise
the young are those who are foolish

Civil Law deals with those who commit crimes:

Salah cencang memberi pampas
salah bunuh memberi bangun
salah makan memuntahkan
salah tarik mengembalikan
utang berbayar piutang berterima
suarang beragih
berebut berketengah

> *berbetulan berbayaran*
> *bersalahan berpatutan*
> *bersalahan berpatut*
> *gaib berkalam Allah*
>
> A man who mistakenly wounds another, should make restitution
> he who mistakenly kills another, should replace him with one of his own
> he who eats something he shouldn't, must vomit it up
> he who wrongly takes something, must return it
> he who contracts a debt, must pay it
> a husband and wife who own property must share it with each other
> quarrrels must be settled
> reconciliations should be made
> wrongs should be set right
> errors corrected
> mysteries settled under an oath

The Twenty Laws discuss crimes and the evidence needed to prove them. The Laws are divided into a group of eight and another group of twelve. The eight are:

> *Pertama tikam bunuh*
> *Kedua samun sakar*
> *Ketiga upas racun*
> *Keempat sumbang salah*
> *Kelima siar bakar*
> *Keenam maling curi*
> *Ketujuh rebut rampas*
> *Kedelapan dago dagi.*
>
> First, stabbing another person to death.
> Second, robbery with violence.
> Third, poisoning.
> Fourth, illicit sexual relations.
> Fifth, arson.
> Sixth, theft.
> Seventh, personal attack.
> Eighth, insurrection.

The eight crimes are explained in this way:

"Stabbing another person to death" means killing another person with a knife.

"Robbery with violence" means taking somebody's property and killing him.

"Poisoning" means feeding someone a substance that kills him.

"Illicit sexual relations" means having intercourse with another man's wife in a secret place.

"Arson" means burning another person's house or fields to the ground.

"Theft" means stealing another person's property, at night (*maling*) or during the day (*curi*).

"Personal attack" means taking another person's property by force and making off with it.

"Insurrection" means disobeying the ancient law and causing a riot.

I should mention that the seventh crime, personal attack (*rebut rampas*), is sometimes called *"umbuk umbai"*, deceit, either through the use of sweet words (*umbuk*) or force (*umbai*).

These crimes require certain forms of evidence: stabbing requires blood and a corpse; robbery with violence, a bloody sword; poisoning, the remains of the food; illicit sexual relations, the couple must be caught in a secret place; arson, the firebrand; theft, a hole in the wall or a ladder; personal attack, a startled scream; insurrection, an infringement of the ancient law.

There is a further discussion of evidence in *The Twelve Laws*. The laws are divided into two parts: the first six are to do with what is called *"cemo"*, the other six with accusations (*tuduh*). *"Cemo"* refers to deeds that are suspicious but not conclusive:

(1) Pursuit of a possible offender;
(2) Bodily damage (a man who is wounded, a woman's hair has been cut);
(3) The possible offender has been tied up with a rope (captured);
(4) Broken cords;
(5) Possession of stolen goods.

An accusation requires clear proof leading to a charge:

(1) Crawl like a caterpillar, footprints like a snipe (evidence that the accused has been at a certain place);
(2) Smoke from a fire;
(3) Footprints;
(4) The evidence of many eyewitnesses;
(5) Caught in a trap, stung by a horse-fly;
(6) When the hornbill flies past, the *atah* fruit falls (coincidental presence at the scene of a crime).

4 The Four Regions

The four regions are the hub (*kota*), the region itself, a collection of hamlets or states united under a chief or a ruler (*negeri*), the watchtowers (*teratak*) and the regional centre (*dusun*). A hub is a broad, open settlement, surrounded by cleared forest. Once irrigation channels have been erected, it becomes a region. A mosque should be built in the middle of the area, so that authentic customary law can be taught there. The channels should be provided with officers who can maintain a lookout (*dubalang*). The lookouts require watchtowers. Open spaces and meeting chambers complete the regional centre.

These were the traditional arrangements observed in Minangkabau.

Part three presents a legal miscellany, in which different topics are often treated in an inconsistent manner. The *Undang-undang Luhak Tiga Laras* (Liaw, 1965) includes the following topics:

(1) Minangkabau customary law from a Muslim perspective;
(2) Innate human law, customary law and God's law;
(3) The "eight laws", concerning kings, matriliny, trade, merchants, human law, customary law, God's law, and scriptural law.
(4) Murder, witnesses, valid law, and such like.

The various topics, especially (2) and (3), are dealt with in considerable detail. There are three categories of innate human law: matters which seem to be logically correct, matters which seem to be impossible, and those in between. Customary law deals with matters that are real offences, those that depend on the evidence of witnesses, and those which are uncertain. The law of God touches on the essence of legal provisions in terms of chapter and verse, processes of interpretation, the determination of meaning, and the construction of proof.

Edwar Djamaris' edition of the *Undang-undang Minangkabau* is a very broad text. There are still other discussions of charges, defenses, just retribution, fines, and such like. There is also a long discussion of different types of human beings: the foolish, the mediocre, the clever, the cunning, the wise, the skilful, the virtuous, and so on. There are also discussions of various types of people and their occupations, such as those who go on to become kings, chieftains, religious officials; as well as a discussion about men and women. A long section deals with ministers and officials, and their various duties.

9.4 *Undang-undang Sungai Ujung*

The Laws of Sungai Ujung, published by Winstedt & de Josselin de Jong in 1954, derives from a manuscript that was Romanised in Malaka in 1904. An earlier version in Arabic script was copied by Datu' Makudu Sakti in 1884 but it was not used by Winstedt and de Jong. The contents of this manuscript are similar to those of Edwar Djamaris' edition of the *Undang-undang Minangkabau*, although they are arranged in a rather confusing manner and the explanations of different types of law are disorganized. Sometimes there are no explanations at all, only the laws themselves. There are also certain additions to the beginning of the text that are not found in other manuscripts.

9.5 *Undang-undang Dua Belas*

The *Undang-undang Minangkabau* was brought to Perak by Sultan Ahmad Tajuddin Syah, the first sultan, and renamed *The Twelve Laws*. The manuscript now held by the Royal Asiatic Society (Maxwell 44) was copied in Penang in 1292 H (1875). The following details of the manuscript are taken from Winstedt's summary (1953).

The most important part of the *Twelve Laws* describes the eight crimes of murder, poisoning, arson, theft, robbery, insurrection, personal attack and illicit sexual relations. There is a discussion of various social ranks: from the king, the chieftains and generals to the youths in society. There is also a lengthy discussion of the various types of ministers and their duties.

The second part deals with laws that have been influenced by Islam such as the law of reason and those pertaining to making an accusation, bearing witness and taking the oath. There are also discussions about the different type of killings and injuries.

Part three discuses a number of topics already found in the *Undang-undang Malaka,* such as theft, debt, cruelty, errant buffalo, runaway and kidnapped slaves, stolen livestock and crops, state taxes, used and unused land, and adultery. The manuscript pays particular attention to debt and adultery.

9.6 *Undang-undang Pahang*

According to Winstedt (1948), there are two manuscripts of *The Laws of Pahang:* Maxwell 17 and Maxwell 20. Maxwell 17 was transcribed in 1296 H (1819 AD) by Naina Ahmad Lebai bin Nakhoda Muhammad Husain. Maxwell 20 was transcribed in 1300 H (1884 AD) by Luakang bin Muhammad Rashid from a manuscript belonging to Dato' Sri Adika Raja, dated 1248 H (1832 M).

The code consists of four parts. The first part, chapters 1-23, was composed at the time of Sultan Abdul Ghafur Muhaiyuddin Syah, who ruled Pahang from 1592 to 1614. Part two, chapters 24-66, have the same contents as the Muslim section of the *Undang-undang Malaka,* chapters 30-42 (Liaw, 1976: 34-35); part three, chapters 67 and 68, agrees with the *Undang-undang Negeri* in the *Undang-undang Malaka* (Liaw, 1976: 36-37). Part four, from chapter 69 to chapter 92, are additions, most of which are only found in Maxwell 17. Chapter 76 agrees with chapter 44.9 in the *Undang-undang Malaka*. Here is a summary of the contents of part one.

Part one states that the code was composed during the reign of Sultan Abdul Ghafur and applies not only to Pahang but also to Perak and Johor. A preface then states that the king should look after his subjects and appoint the leaders of the state, including the regent (*mangkubumi*), the treasurer (*penghulu bendahari*), leader of the army and the police (*temenggung*), generals (*hulubalang*), harbour master (*syahbandar*), and the ministers (*menteri*). The duties of these officials are described, one by one.

(1) Only the king the can use the colour yellow for such items as curtains and tray covers. If any one else does so, the items will confiscated.
(2) Agricultural land, which is not being used by its owner, may be used by another person. If the original owner requests the return of the land, this must be done.
(3) Farmers must build fences and ditches around their fields so that buffaloes cannot enter.
(4) If a person enters a village at night and is killed, the fault will be his own.
(5) A person who shouts at another person or abuses another person's wife may be executed if the abuse is followed by violence.
(6) A man who kills another man for abusing him or his wife will not be punished.
(7) A man who discovers that another man has committed adultery with his wife, or receives true witness of such an act, may kill that other man.

(8) A servant who abuses a free man may be beaten; if he resists, he may be killed.

(9) Redeemed slaves may be returned to their original owners if they become mad, blind, suffer dropsy, or are found to be pregnant.

(10) The security of a free person who is the guarantor for another person must be protected by that person.

(11) A person who is indebted to another person's slave does so at his own risk.

(12) A debt may be reduced under certain conditions. A person who contracts a debt must repay that debt at the appropriate time and with the appropriate interest.

(13) A person who seeks to adopt a slave's child, if the mother does not wish to keep the child, must first ask the permission of the slave's owner.

(14) A person who provides a loan or some form of remuneration to a slave, without the knowledge of the slave's owner, shall not be entitled to any recompense.

(15) Persons who shelter a runaway slave shall be punished.

(16) People who sell goods through an intermediary may be entitled to reclaim their goods.

(17) Persons who find an abandoned boat must return the vessel to its owner.

(18) Persons who find gold, silver or any valuable object should bring the object to a judge.

(19) If a slave belonging to the king is beaten and dies, the person responsible, if he is a freeman, may be forced to take the place of the slave; if the person responsible is himself a slave, he may be strangled.

(20) If a person kills one or more royal buffalo, he must repay double the number of animals he has killed.

(21) If a person sells the ornaments of the king, his servant or slave, he must repay seven times the value of that object.

(22) The fines and recompenses that may be claimed by the king, prime minister, ministers, and the head of the army.

(23) Anyone who rebels against the king shall be tortured, their property confiscated, and their family enslaved.

It is clear from the above outline that the first part of the *Undang-undang Pahang* was not influenced by Islam. A person who breaks the law can be tortured. The laws depend on who commits a crime and against whom it is committed. The influence of the *Undang-undang Malaka* is also obvious. The two codes deal with the same crimes, although they sometimes provide different punishments.

9.7 *Undang-undang Kedah*

There are three manuscripts of *The Kedah Laws*. Two are held in Jakarta: the *Undang-undang Negeri Kedah* (v.d. Wall 25) and the *Undang-undang Datuk Dahulu* (v.d. Wall 57). The third is held at the University of London, (SOAS MS 40329). Winstedt has discussed a manuscript similar to the *Undang-undang Datuk Dahulu* that was published by Edwar Djamaris (1981). Winstedt states that the *Undang-undang Kedah* consists of five parts (Winstedt 1928: 57):

(1) Harbour Regulations;
(2) The Laws of Datuk Sri Paduka Tuan;
(3) The Civil Laws of Datuk Star;
(4) The Tribute to be Paid to Thailand;
(5) Miscellaneous Laws.

1 Harbour Regulations

The Harbour Regulations were compiled by Paduka Raja in 1160 H (1650 AD) at the command of His Royal Majesty Syah Alam for the benefit of his judges. The text continues: "These are the laws proclaimed at the time of Raja Setia Bijaya, when Raja Jalil Putra was the harbour master. Consultations were held between the Admiral and Orang Kaya Maharaja Indra, Orang Kaya Sri Maharaja Khan-khan, and all of the appropriate officials. At that time the person responsible for the security of the harbour (*Panglima Bandar*) was Datuk Laksamana (Admiral) Cik Syahdin."

The manuscript largely deals with port regulations and the duties of various officials. When a ship arrives, the port master (*panglima kuala*) should ascertain from where the boat has come, what it is carrying, how large the vessel is, and who is its captain. These matters should be conveyed to the harbourmaster (*syahbandar*) to be relayed to the king. When the boat enters the harbour, the harbourmaster should examine the vessel and make a complete inventory of its cargo. The harbourmaster and the police should also patrol the markets each day and fine any person found gambling, cockfighting, drinking alcohol, and such like. There are four categories of senior harbour officials (*panglima*), and their duties are to look after the estuary (*panglima kuala*), the harbour (*panglima bandar*), the hinterland (*panglima negeri*), and public security (*panglima jaga-jaga*).

Next come regulations about captains who contract debts in the market, buying and redeeming slaves, runaway slaves and people who kidnap them. There are also discussions of the ceremonial reception of letters from the European trading companies, important merchants, the governor of Malaka, the kings of Patani and Perak and such like. This part of the manuscript ends with regulations describing how the harbourmaster and the police should built houses to be rented to visiting merchants from Patani.

2 The Laws of Datuk Sri Paduka Tuan

These laws were compiled in 1078 H (1667 AD) by Datuk Sri Paduka Tuan after discussion with the senior ministers, at the command of Syah Alam, the ruler of Kota Palas. Thereafter, they were announced to Syaikh Alauddin and the religious scholars for their use and that of the *penghulu* (*kweng*). The sixteen chapters particularly discuss the duties of the *penghulu*. The *penghulu* was required to report and punish persons who infringed the rules of religion by stealing, robbery, cockfighting and gambling. He was also required to arrest those who did not pray and those whose scales were incorrect. Persons who entered a village or roamed about at night, but who did not carry a burning brand were also to be arrested. Farmers who did not put fences around their fields and livestock could be put to death. The code ends with a discussion of the proper way to receive official visitations from Thailand.

3 The Civil Laws of Datuk Star

This part of *The Kedah Laws* consists of two sections. The first outlines the duties of the chief military and police officer (*temenggung*): to build prisons, arrest criminals, and protect the state. The second describes the duties of the king, lists the words that only he may use, and describes the crimes that only he may pardon. It also reserves the use of yellow to the king and describes the colours that may be attached to trees when he goes touring.

According to the edition of *Undang-undang Perbuatan Datuk Besar Dahulu* (v.d. Wall 57) prepared by Edwar Djamaris and his colleagues, and an edition of *The Kedah Laws* presented to me by a faculty member at the National University of Malaysia, the duties of the *temenggung* are also described at the end of *The Laws of Datuk Sri Paduka Tuan*. Following this chapter, The Harbour Regulations describe the rules covering visiting boats and small craft, abandoned vessels, ships heading upriver, and the duties of the four senior harbour officials. It is next explained that everyone should obey the king, the head of the mosque, the prayer leader, the preacher, and everyone who has been appointed to a position of authority. This is followed by rules about marriage, who may represent a woman at her wedding, and about debts contracted by women. The copy of the text in my possession ends with a colophon stating that the manuscript belonged to Datuk Bandar Jalil Pahlawan of Kuala Bahang Dar Aman in the state of Kedah. The copy was made by Ismail, of Kedah, at the request Tuan Mister Pilis. Winstedt does not mention these extra regulations; perhaps they were not part of the text he studied.

I should add that part 5, mentioned by Winstedt as belonging to the *Laws of Datuk Seri Paduka Tuan,* is not included in the edition of the text with which I am most familiar, and that part 4, The Tribute to be Paid to Thailand, is only briefly included in part 2, at the end of the duties of the *temenggung*.

9.8 *Undang-Undang Sembilan Puluh Sembilan*

Three sets of law prevailed in Perak. Two have been discussed above: *The Laws of Pahang* and the *Twelve Laws*. The third is *The Ninety-nine Laws*, which were brought to Malaya by Sayid Hassan (or Hussain) al-Faradz of the Hadramaut and continued to be used by his descendants who became hereditary ministers in Perak. If the Sultan ran into a legal problem, the answer could usually be found in this text. The major edition of *The Ninety-Nine Laws* was copied from a manuscript belonging to Datuk Sayid Jaafar, a major figure in Perak at the end of the nineteenth century (Rigby, 1929).

The Laws are presented in the form of questions and answers between Raja Nasran Adil and his minister Khoja Berza Amir Hakim. According to R. J. Wilkinson, The Laws relate to the implementation of patrilineal law, although the influence of the *Undang-undang Minangkabau* is stronger than that of the *Undang-undang Malaka*. At certain points the text is also shaped by Muslim law.

The code deals with the usual topics. Considerable emphasis is placed on the requirements for holding certain senior positions, such as: the king, police superintendent, religious judge (*kadi*), mosque officials (the prayer leader and the preacher), government officers, and lawyers (*hakim*). There are also discussions of the roles of traditional healers (*pawang*) and midwives. The text also describes how one should present oneself before royalty and the ways in which a king should be chosen.

The punishments prescribed for certain crimes tend to be rather lenient. A man caught stealing for the first time must replace the objects he has taken. If he is caught a second time, however, he will lose a finger. A man who abuses, wounds or kills another person will be required to pay blood-money. "What is the use of gold, if it cannot atone for one's sins?" asks the author. If a man has illicit sexual relations with a woman, or steals another man's fiancée, the couple will be married, if that is acceptable to them both. If the woman is already married, and the couple is caught in the act, the husband may kill the offender. There are extensive discussions of marriage and divorce, topics that receive very little attention in other law codes. Other laws deal with livestock, farming and so on.

9.9 *Adat Raja-raja Melayu*

References to royal customs occur throughout works such as the *Sejarah Melayu, Undang-undang Malaka, Hikayat Aceh* and the *Misa Melayu*. Nevertheless, there is also one text, the *Adat Raja-raja Melayu,* Malay Royal Customs, that is devoted specifically to this subject.

The *Adat Raja-raja Melayu* was composed in 1193 H (1779 AD), at the command of De Bruyn, governor of Malaka. In order to fulfil this task, Datuk Zainuddin Mahbub, the leader (*Kapitan*) of the Malay community, sought the help of Lebai Abdulmuhit. Datuk Zainuddin then helped Senyur Gerci translate the final manuscript into Dutch. It was revised and enlarged several times. In these subsequent versions, the term used for the author, "*sahaya*", your humble servant, gives way to the name of Datuk Zainuddin and then, when Datuk Sulaiman became Leader, his name was used instead (Panuti, 1983: 36-37).

The text has been published three times. In 1929, Ph. van Ronkel published an edition based on three manuscripts held in London. Then, in 1964, Tardjan Hadidjaja republished a romanised edition of van Ronkel's text, and added extensive details on royal customs taken from the *Undang-undang Malaka, Kata Adat, Pantun Adat,* and *Pantun Negeri Sembilan*. Finally, Panuti H. M. Sudjiman made an extensive study of all surviving manuscripts of the *Adat Raja-raja Melayu* for his doctoral studies at the Australian National University. Panuti's is the most complete study of this work.

The customs and ceremonies described include:

(1) Customs and ceremonies for the seventh month of a queen's pregnancy;
(2) Customs and ceremonies for when the queen gives birth;
(3) Customs and ceremonies for shaving the child's head;
(4) Customs and ceremonies for the engagement of the prince when he comes of age;
(5) Marriage customs and ceremonies;

(6) Customs for fulfilling a religious vow;

(7) Royal funeral ceremonies;

(8) Ceremonies for the erection of a royal tombstone.

According to Panuti Sudjiman, there are four other manuscripts that contain additional material (Panuti, 1983: 16). This material describes:

(1) The majesty of the king and his exalted status;

(2) The nature of good fortune, as illustrated by the story of Si Miskin who rose to become Maharaja Lela;

(3) Arrangements for the inheritance of titles, such as Raja, *Megat* (the son of a princess married to a man of lesser rank), *Biduanda* (a page, the son of a chief), *Cetera* (a warrior), *Perwira* (military officer), *Sida* (courtier), and *Hulubalang* (general);

(4) The titles of ministers;

(5) The word "*melayu*" means to bow down: a Malay is humble at court and in other places;

(6) The beauty of the Malay language resides in its use of ornamental language;

(7) Requirements and prohibitions for those in the presence of the king;

(8) Words to be used only by the king and those words which must be used by his subordinates;

(9) Correspondence between the king and his subjects; and

(10) Ways of making gold ink and bullets.

Malay Royal Customs is still a very useful book, in as far as the Sultan remains the titular head in a number of Malay states and the customs it describes are still practised. Naturally some of the customs have been adapted to meet contemporary needs.

9.9.1 Commentaries on Royal Customs

It should be noted that two commentaries on royal customs were written by Raja Ali Haji, the author of the *Tuhfat Al-Nafis*. They are:

(1) The *Mukadimah Fi Intizam,* which describes the three obligations (*wazifah*) which must be known and practiced by those in charge of government (Abu Hassan Sham, 1981); and

(2) The *Tsamaratu 'l-Muhimmati,* which consists of a preface and three chapters. The preface expounds the greatness of learning and the dangers of evil conduct. Chapter one describes the installation of a king and the appointment of major office holders such as ministers and the senior Muslim judge (*kadi*). The chapter also describes the processes involved in dismissing ministers and judges who do not perform their duties. Chapter two describes the administration of the state and the manner of choosing members of the courts of law. Chapter three states that the king and his officials must protect the souls, bodies and good names of their subjects. The chapter concludes with a discussion of various human defects, including pride, spitefulness, greed, stinginess, laziness, dishonesty, untrustworthiness, a lack of seriousness, and sloth (Cut Riowati Aziz, 1980).

REFERENCES

Abu Hassan Sham
1973. "Adakah hukum kanun Malaka mempengaruhi undang-undang Melayu yang lama," *DB*, 17 (4), pp. 146-159.
1973. "Unsur-unsur undang-undang Hindu di dalam teks Undang-undang adat Temenggung, khasnya hukum kanun Malaka," *DB*, 17 (7), pp. 310-321.
1981. "Mukadimah Di Intizam...", *Islamika*, Kuala Lumpur.

Buxbaum, David C.
1968. *Family Law and Customary Law in Asia*, The Hague.

Crawfurd, J.
1967. *History of the Indian Archipelago*, 3, London.

Cut Riowati Aziz
1980. *Tsamaratu 'l-Muhimmati*, Masters thesis, FSUI, Jakarta.

Drewes, G. W. J. & P. Voorhoeve
1958. "Adat Atjeh," *VKI*, 24.

Edwar Djamaris, et al.
1970. "Kitab undang-undang dalam kesusastraan Minangkabau," *Manusia Indonesia*, 4 (3&4), pp. 85-105.
1981. *Naskah Undang-undang dalam Sastra Indonesia Lama*, Jakarta.

Hasan Junus
1981. *Raja Ali Haji Budayawan Di Gerbang Abad XX*, Pekanbaru.

Hooker, M. B.
1968. "A Note on the Malayan legal digests," *JMBRAS*, 41 (1).
1970. *Readings in Malay Adat Laws*, Singapore.
1972. *Adat Laws in Modern Malaya*, Kuala Lumpur.
1984. *Islamic Law in Southeast Asia*, Singapore.

Kempe, J. E. & R. O. Winstedt
1948. "A Malay legal digest compiled for Abd al-Ghafur Muhaiyuddin Shah, Sultan of Pahang, 1592-1614," *JMBRAS*, 21 (1), pp. 1-67.
1952. "A Malay legal miscellany," *JMBRAS*, 26 (1), pp. 1-19.

Liaw Yock Fang
1965. "Undang-undang Luhak Tiga Laras," Masters thesis, FSUI, Jakarta.
1973. "Satu catatan tentang hukum kanun Malaka dan undang-undang Melayu lama," *DB*, 17, no. 9, pp. 420-424.
1976. *Undang-undang Melaka*, (Bibliotheca Indonesia 13), The Hague.
2003. *Undang-Undang Malaka dan Undang-Undang Laut*, Kuala Lumpur.

Maxwell, M. E.
1884. "The Law and customs of the Malays with reference to Tenure of land," *JSBRAS*, 13.
1890. "Law relating to slavery among the Malays," *JSBRAS*, 22.

Mohd Taib Osman & Hamdan Hassan
1978.   *Bingkisan untuk Pendita,* Kuala Lumpur.

Newbold, T. J.
1839.   *Political and Statistical Account of the British Settlements in the Straits of Malacca,* London.

Panuti Sudjiman
1983.   *Adat Raja-raja Melayu,* Jakarta.

Radja Labih
1922.   *Kitab Kesimpulan Adat dan Undang-undang,* Fort de Kock.

Raffles, T. S.
1818.   *Asiatic Researches,* Vol 12, London.
1879.   "The Maritime Code of the Malays," *JSBRAS,* 3.

Rigby, J.
1929.   "The Ninety-nine Laws of Perak," *Papers on Malay Subjects: Law, (Part 2),* Kuala Lumpur.

Ronkel, Ph. S. van
1919.   *Risalah Hoekoem Kanoen,* Leiden.
1929.   *Adat Radja-radja Melaju,* Leiden.

Shahari Talib, et al
1991.   *Tuhfat al-Nafis Naskhah Terengganu,* The House of Tengku Ismail.

Wilkinson, R. J.
1908.   "Law" Part 1, *Papers on Malay Subjects,* Kuala Lumpur.

Winstedt, R. O.
1923.   "A Brunei Code," *JMBRAS,* 1 (1), p. 251.
1928.   "Kedah Laws," *JMBRAS,* 6 (2), pp. 1-44.
1945.   "Old Malay legal digests and Malay customary law," *JRAS,* pts 1 & 2, pp. 17-29.
1948.   "A Malay Legal Digest compiled for Abd. Al-Ghafur Muhaiyuddin Shah, Sultan of Pahang 1592-1614 A.D with undated additions," *JMBRAS,* 2 (2).
1953.   "The date of the Malacca legal codes," *JRAS,* pts 1 & 2, pp. 31-33.
1953.   "An old Minangkabau legal digest from Perak," *JMBRAS,* 26 (1), pp. 1-13.

Winstedt, R. O. & P. E. de Josselin de Jong
1954.   "A digest of customary law from Sungai Ujong," *JMBRAS,* 27 (3), pp. 1-71.
1956.   "The maritime laws of Malacca," *JMBRAS,* 29 (3), pp. 22-59.
1958.   "A History of Classical Malay Literature," JMBRAS, 31 (3)

Zuber Usman
1962.   "Kitab-kitab hukum dan perundangan Melayu lama," *Pustaka Budaja,* 3 (9), pp. 30-34.

10 Poetic Forms: Pantun and Syair

10.1 *Pantun*

The pantun was originally a form of folk verse that was meant to be sung. Pantun are still meant to be sung. In his Account of a Voyage to Kelantan (*Pelayaran ke Kelantan*) Abdullah Munsyi noted various ways in which a pantun might be sung, including Lagu Dua, Lagu Ketara, Ketapang, Dendang Sayang, and so on. The pantun form first appears in Malay literature in the *Sejarah Melayu* and in some other chronicles from that time. It also occurs within the long narrative syair such as the *Syair Ken Tambuhan*.

There are various opinions about the word "pantun" itself. Some believe that it is based on the high Javanese *parik,* which is similar to the Malay *pari,* a proverb (*peribahasa*). In this sense it is close to the Indian sense of the seloka, a two-line verse form. Dr. R. Brandstetter, a Swiss comparative linguist, has suggested that the word originates from *tun,* which is found in a number of Indonesian languages; for example, in Pampanga, *tuntun* means "well organized"; in Tagalog, *tonton* suggests a skilful arrangement; in Old Javanese, *tuntun* means "a thread", *atuntun* means "well arranged", and *matuntun* is "to lead"; in Batak Toba, the word "pantun" means "polite, worthy of respect" (Djajadiningrat, 1933/34). R. O. Winstedt supports this opinion, noting that in many Indonesian languages, words which suggest "something set out in rows" gradually gain the new meaning of "well arranged words", in prose or in poetry (Winstedt, 1958: 158).

In Malay, the pantun is a quatrain, rhyming abab. In Sundanese, however, the pantun is a long narrative poem, recited with a musical accompaniment.

The pantun has been studied in considerable detail by many scholars. One of the points of discussion is whether there is any semantic connection between the first couplet and the second. Pijnappel, in a paper he read at the Sixth Orientalists' Congress held at Leiden in 1883, has argued that the two are always closely related (Pijnappel, 1883). He discussed a pantun that is to be found in the *Sejarah Melayu*:

> *Telur itik dari Sanggora*
> *Pandan terletak dilangkahi*
> *Darahnya titik di Singapura*
> *Badannya terlantar ke Langkawi.*

> A duck egg from Sanggora
> A pandan mat to be walked over
> His blood fell in Singapore
> His body came ashore in Langkawi.

According to Pijnappel, Sanggora is on the east coast of Malaya (near Siam) and can be considered to be at some distance from the speaker. But the woven rush mat is close. The whole poem suggests that the particular murder took place far from the grave of the victim. Twenty years later, in 1904, Ch. A. van Ophuijsen discussed this topic as part of his inaugural professorial lecture. He felt that it was a pointless task to search for the connection in every case. Usually a connection can be made but often these are forced and non-productive; they are probably far from the author's original intention in any case. He quoted two other pantun, suggesting that there was no reasonable connection between the two couplets (Ophuijsen, 1904: 13-14). The two pantuns are:

> *Jendral majlis mati di Bali*
> *Berkubur di tanah lapang*
> *Apa diharap kepada kami*
> *Emas tiada bangsa pun kurang.*

> The council's general died in Bali
> Buried in an open field
> What hope is there for us
> Who have neither gold nor status.

> *Satu, dua, tiga, enam*
> *Enam dan satu jadi tujuh*
> *Buah delima yang ditanam*
> *Buah berangan hanya tumbuh.*

> One, two, three, six
> Six and one are seven
> They planted a pomegranate
> But an arsenic tree grew in its stead.

Winstedt disagreed with van Ophuijsen, and tended to agree with Pijnappel that a connection could usually be found. He agreed with Pijnappel's explanation of the first pantun quoted above ("*Telur itik dari Sanggora*"), suggesting, however, that it contained a further metaphor. In Malay thought, the image of a duck egg being hatched by a hen suggests an unfortunate wanderer with no friends. A woven mat is often found in the homes of wealthy Malays and is not to be trodden on. The poem suggests a woman keen to be with us, of whom we should be suspicious. Winstedt also explains the pantun recorded by van Ophuijsen ("*Satu, dua, tiga, enam/ Enam dan satu jadi tujuh*") suggesting that it represents a Malay farmer counting his harvest. He has done well but he is surprised to see poisoned fruits growing whereas he planted pomegranates. Winstedt adds a similar pantun (Winstedt 1958: 163):

Satu tangan bilangan lima
Dua tangan bilangan sepuluh
Sahaya bertanam biji delima
Apa sebab peria tumbuh

One hand has five
Two hands have ten
I planted pomegranates
But why have edible gourds grown?

R. J. Wilkinson also accepts that the two couplets are connected through parallel patterns of sound. The first couplet foreshadows the meaning of the second couplet. To paraphrase Wilkinson's words, the first couplet must provide a poetic thought whose beauty is hidden, while the second couplet gives the same thought in all its manifest beauty (Wilkinson, 1907: 51-53).

H. Overbeck disagreed with R. J. Wilkinson. He believed that the first couplet carried no meaning. Overbeck argued that in creating a pantun, the author usually focused his attention on the second couplet and then tried to find corresponding rhymes to start the poem. There is absolutely no connection between the two parts. The first couplet commonly relies on clichés: "*Dari..., berlayar ke..., orang..., pulang ke..., Kalau tuan pergi ke..., carikan saya...*" (From ... sail to ... people ... return to ... If you go to ... find me ...). Overbeck may have been influenced by Abdullah Munsyi's opinion:

The pantun consists of four lines. The first two lines have no meaning. They simply serve as an accompaniment. The second pair of lines do have a meaning. (Overbeck, 1914: 17-18).

C. Hooykaas has discussed these various opinions and concluded: "Perhaps there is no connection between the first and second couplets of many pantun, but there is always a connection in the best ones".

Another problem that has often been discussed is the origin of the form. Ch. A. van Ophuijsen suggests that we can understand the pantun better if we are familiar with the Mandailing Batak symbolism of leaves and a particular type of folksong (Ophuijsen, 1904: 15-18). Mandailing young people use the symbolism of leaves to declare their affections. If a young man sends his sweetheart a posy comprising *sitarak, hadungdung, sitata, sitanggis, podom-podom* and *pahu,* he is saying: "Since we parted, I cannot sleep until I first weep." *Sitarak* rhymes with *marsarak,* to part. *Hadungdung* rhymes with *dung,* since. *Sitata* rhymes with *hita,* we. *Sitanggis* rhymes with *tangis,* weep. *Podom-podom* rhymes with *modom,* sleep; *pahu* is *au,* I.

Like the pantun, the Mandailing *ende-ende* verse consists of two parts. The first part records a scene or an event, while the second part carries the meaning of the poem. Consider this example:

Muda mandurung ko di pahu
Tampul si mardulang-dulang;
Muda malungun ho di au,
Tatap si rumondang bulan.

> If you go fishing in a pond
> Cut some tray leaves
> If you long for me
> Look at the light of the moon.

Like the *ende-ende*, the pantun may have developed from the language of leaves, although we cannot be certain that the Malays ever used this particular symbolism. However, flowers and fruits are still common in the pantun and to understand them fully we must understand what they refer to. Usually they refer to young maidens. A coconut destroyed by a civet cat, or a flower enjoyed by a bee, symbolizes a girl who has lost her virtue. The word "*selasih*" (basil) rhymes with "*kasih*" (love). The kiambang water lettuce has shallow roots; love will not last. The frangipani grows in graveyards and symbolizes eternal love. The delicate lime symbolizes a girl's sweet lips.

R. J. Wilkinson more or less agrees with van Ophuijsen. He recognizes that Malays commonly use symbolic language. But he asks whether the language of leaves has created rhyming equivalents or, rather, the use of rhymes has created the language of the leaves? There is no ready solution to this problem. Wilkinson prefers to see the origin of the pantun in the Malay enjoyment of allusion. The first couplet must inspire or foreshadow the sounds of the second. He provides the following pantun and its translation as an example of this (Wilkinson 1907: 49-501):

> *Dari mana punai melayang*
> *dari paya turun ke padi*
> *Dari mana kasih sayang*
> *dari mata turun ke hati.*

> The fate of a dove is to fly,
> It flies to its nest on the knoll;
> The gate of true love is the eye
> The prize of its quest is the soul.

R. A. Hoesein Djajadiningrat also supported van Ophuijsen's suggestion that the origins of the pantun an be found in the language of leaves. He offers a different proof. In Banten, West Java, young girls sometimes wear particular colours to indicate their affection for a certain young man. So *hejo* (green) means *nenjo*, to see; *hideung* (black) means *nineung*, longing; *beuream* (red) means *eureun*, I do not love you. Djajadiningrat admits that this practice is not an old one (Djajadiningrat, 1933/34).

The pantun is popular throughout the Archipelago. Besides Malay, it is also found in Minangkabau, Achehnese, Batak (the *ende-ende*), Sundanese (as *wawangsalan* or *sisindiran*) and Javanese (*parikan* or *wangsalan*). Scholars have been most particularly interested in *wawangsalan*, which is a form of riddle occuring in both prose and poetry, in speech and song. Like the pantun, *wangsalan* consist of four line verses; the first two lines have no particular meaning but establish a basic sound pattern that is picked up in the second couplet. Here is an example:

Jenang sela (apu)
Wader kalen sesonderan (sepat)
Apuranta
Jen wonten lepat kawula.

Limestone (chalk)
Wader fish (perch) in the river
Forgive me
If I have made any mistake.

Apu points to *apuranta, sepat* to *lepat* (Ikram, 1964: 263). There is no particular beauty hidden in the second couplet; the parallel rhymes are sufficient in themselves.

10.1.1 Beyond the Archipelago

Poetic forms similar to the pantun can be found far beyond the Archipelago and are indeed worldwide. Giacomo Prampolini has discussed various forms that are similar to the pantun, from such languages as Chinese, Japanese, Persian, Arabic, Spanish, German and so on (Prampolini, 1951). We will say a little more here about the Chinese and Spanish forms.

Overbeck in the work mentioned above has noted the similarities between Chinese poetry, especially the *Shi Ching* form, and the pantun. Winstedt has even suggested that the Chinese of Malaka may have contributed to shaping the pantun as we know it today. This is uncertain. There are certainly similarities between the *Shi Ching* and the pantun. Both are four-line verse forms and contain usually four words in each line. The first part of the *Shi Ching* usually presents a picture of a scene or an action that leads to the second couplet. It is worth noting that the *Shi Ching* was basically a form of folksong before Confucius formalized it. We might do better to turn our attention to the folksong itself.

Chinese folksongs commonly contain an indefinite number of lines, so there would seem to be no immediate connection with the pantun. But the overall structure is still the same. The first lines often present a picture of the world in all its variety: grass, the birds, mountains, rivers, boats, and so forth. Scholars suggest that these images serve no other function than to allow the speaker to pause politely before moving to the main topic he wishes to address. That is very similar to the pantun. Here is one example, freely translated:

There are many stars in the sky, the moon is hiding. There are many mountains, the ground is rocky. A lamp shines at home, I am far away. An apple comes from the city. Is there wine or not? Woman whom I love, do you love me? An eagle flies high above, his shadow crosses the ground. You sing so sweetly, my restless hearts beats rapidly.

W. A. Braasem has noticed some striking similarities between the pantun and the Spanish *copla*. The *copla* is also a humble folk verse form, sung to the accompaniment of a musical instrument. It too consists of four line verses, in which the first two lines present a picture that is elucidated in the next two lines. Here are two free translations of *copla*:

> I boarded a ship in Malaga,
> the ship sank.
> Whoever marries young,
> sells her soul to the devil.
> The moon rises over the ocean,
> And glides towards Valentia
> Marry you? Thank you very much,
> The thought has never crossed my mind.

Both *copla* are associated with proverbs. The girl who marries young has sold her soul to the devil. Boarding a ship is a metaphor for marriage. "*La luna de Valencia*" gestures towards a high cliff which ships usually avoid, except when the tide is very high and is a metaphor for a girl who steadfastly refuses to marry (Braasem, 1950: 34-38).

This concludes our discussion of the pantun. To summarize: the pantun is a form of folk poetry and has many similarities with other folk arts throughout the world. Each verse consists of two couplets that are often symbolically related to each other or employ related sound patterns. At other times, however, there is no apparent connection at all. The pantun may have developed from a playful use of language related to floral imagery.

10.2 *Syair*

Another form of traditional verse is the syair. Syairs consist of four-line verses, each line containing four words, that is eight to twelve syllables. Unlike the pantun verses that are self-contained, the verses in syair are part of a longer poem. Syair verses lack the element of mockery that is to be found in some pantun. The rhyme scheme is aaaa and an internal rhyme is common (A. Teeuw, 1966b: 431-432). Patterns of end rhyme are often, in fact, not very strict. *Nya* can be rhymed with *na, intan* with *hitam, pura* with *dua, -ih* with *i*. Further, if a syllable uses the same written form, that is sufficient as well. *U* is considered to rhyme with *o* and *au*, because in the Jawi script all are represented by the letter *wau* (و). Similarly, *i* rhymes with *e* and *ai*, because all three are represented by *ya* (ي)

When did the syair form first appear in Malay literature? This question led to a heated debate between A. Teeuw, Syed Naguib Al-Attas and Amin Sweeney. Originally scholars believed that the oldest recorded syair was that engraved on gravestone at Minye Tujuh (Acheh), dated 1380CE (Winstedt, 1958: 150-151). G. E. Marrison challenged this opinion, arguing that the poem was not a syair but an *upajati,* an Indian verse form (Marrison, 1951: 162-165).

Winstedt suggested that the first syair in Malay literature was the *Syair Ken Tambuhan,* written during the Malaka Sultanate. He referred to the use of Old Javanese words such as *lalangan* (garden), other Javanese words such as *ngambara* and *ngulurkan,* the diverse vocabulary overall, the use of Hindu myths, and the classical style of the work (Winstedt, 1958: 152). Teeuw disagreed, suggesting that the syair emerged as a distinct genre several generations after Hamzah Fansuri had composed his mystical verse in this form in the second half of the sixteenth century. Teeuw argued that the *Syair Ken Tambuhan* was written in the seventeenth or eighteenth century, and that the Javanese elements were common in literary texts of this time; they may not have been borrowings by the author but influences from Panji and wayang theatre texts (as we see in recent Kelantan wayang performances, for example). Many Malay authors, such as Raja Haji Ali, Abdullah, and the composer of the *Hikayat Hang Tuah,* use words drawn from many diverse sources.

Teeuw also insisted that the first extended poems using four-line verses and a monorhyme scheme were the work of Hamzah Fansuri, but noted that he called his verses *ruba'i*, although they were different from the Arabic/Persian form which consisted of single four-line verses. It was only later when his poems gained wide popularity that they came to be called syair. (For example, Valentijn records in 1726 that Hamzah Fansuri was famous for his "syair".) Later, other poets then took up the form and used it for non-religious subjects. In Javanese literature a new form arose, the *singir*. A historical poem written in Makasar in 1670, was entitled *Syair Perang Mengkasar*. Romantic subjects were also introduced, as in the case of the *Syair Ken Tambuhan*. By the seventeenth century, syair had been produced throughout the Archipelago: in Johor, Palembang, Riau, Banjarmasin, Batavia (Jakarta), and Ambon (A. Teeuw, 1966b: 442-446).

Before Teeuw, Voorhoeve also argued for the priority of Hamzah Fansuri in the history of the syair in Malay literature. In a lecture given to students of Malay in Paris in 1952, Voorhoeve offered these reasons to support his claim (they were almost the same reasons as Teeuw was later to give):

(a) No syair earlier than those of Hamzah Fansuri have yet been discovered;

(b) There are no syair from elsewhere in the Archipelago except for the Javanese *sangir*, and that is clearly influenced by the Malay syair;

(c) Ar-Raniri, Hamzah Fansuri's opponent, included several syair-like verses in the *Bustanus Salatin*, although he too still called them *ruba'i* (Voorhoeve, 1968: 277-278).

If Teeuw still hesitated to proclaim Hamzah Fansuri the author of the first Malay syair, Syed Naguib Al-Attas certainly did not. In two monographs (Syed Naguib Al-Attas, 1968, 1971), he attacked Teeuw for his reluctance to affirm Hamzah Fansuri as the creator of the first Malay syair and explained his role at some length, describing how Hamzah was influenced by the four-line syair form in Arabic literature. Al-Attas extensively quoted the work of the Iraqi poet, Ibnu-l Arabi, to prove his point (Syed Naguib Al-Attas, 1968: 58).

Was Hamzah Fansuri really influenced by the Arabic verse form, the syi'r? Amin Sweeney, who was then teaching at the National University of Malaysia, did not agree. He favoured the strong influence of the pantun form, such as was already to be found in the *Sejarah Melayu,* written after 1535. This conclusion was based on a study of various aspects of syair, including metre, rhyme, formal units and verse structures.

The metre of the syair is the same as that of the pantun; hence, not only do pantun often occur in syair, several lines of a syair may also be used in a pantun. (In his thesis, the Dutch scholar Doorenbos too showed that a number of lines in Hamzah Fansuri's poem may also found in pantuns.) Sweeney also pointed to the common use of *caesura* in both forms. Further, although the rhyme scheme is not that of the pantun, the poems contained in the *Sejarah Melayu,* which look like pantun, nevertheless use the aaaa rhyme pattern (see also R. Roolvink, 1966: 455-457). For example:

Cau Pandan anak Bubunya   (a)
Hendak menyerang ke Melaka   (a)
Ada cincin berisi bunga   (a)
Bunga berisi air mata   (a)

Cau Pandan and his minions
Wanted to attack Melaka
There was a ring filled with flowers
The flowers were filled with tears.

Hamzah may have felt that the common pantun pattern, abab, was too light for the serious topics with which he wished to deal.

On the other hand, Sweeney also argued, the aaaa pattern is seldom found in Arabic poetry. Again, each of Hamzah's verses consists of four lines; this is a further difference from Arabic verse that tends to favour two-line stanzas and not four-line verses at all. Finally, Hamzah's verses are linked together to form larger unities; this too is not a feature of Arabic verse (Sweeney, 1971: 58-66).

We may conclude, therefore, that although Hamzah Fansuri himself describes his poems in Arabic terms as ruba'i, they are not derived from this source but are much more strongly influenced by the original Malay form of the pantun (see also Hooykaas, 1947: 72).

We can group the contents of syair verse into five categories:

(1) Syair based on Panji narratives;
(2) Syair based on romantic narratives;
(3) Syair based on the use of figurative natural symbolism;
(4) Syair based on historical events;
(5) Syair based on religious themes.

10.3 Syair Based on Panji Narratives

In Chapter 3, we discussed the origin, spread and functions of Panji narratives at considerable length. Most Panji syair are based on prose originals: *Syair Panji Semirang* is a version of the *Hikayat Panji Semirang*, while the *Syair Angreni* is adapted from *Panji Angreni*. (Sometimes the contents remain the same while the title is changed.) The plots of syair are more straightforward than those of the prose originals. The poetic version may omit all of the subplots. The *Syair Ken Tambuhan* focuses on the love of Raden Menteri and Ken Tambuhan, and their marriage; the *Syair Undakan Agung Udaya* only tells of Panji's experiences in Daha and uses the single name Undakan Agung Udaya. Here are a few poetic Panji narratives.

10.3.1 *Syair Ken Tambuhan*

The *Syair Ken Tambuhan* is the most famous Panji syair and has been extensively studied by many scholars. Roorda van Eysinga translated it into Dutch in 1838. It was also published in 1866 by H.

C. Klinkert. A hundred years later, in 1966, a romanised version was published in Kuala Lumpur (Teeuw, 1966a). Here is a summary of the poem.

The poem begins by describing how the states conquered by the Ratu Kuripan competed with each other to send him tribute. Some rulers sent slaves and servants; others offered him their own daughters. The ruler of Tanjungpuri's daughter, Raden Puspa Kencana, "had a face like an angels," "she was sweet in nature," "her lips were red, her teeth like pomegranate seeds," "she was of medium height, slender, and when she smiled, she was even more attractive." The ruler named her Ken Tambuhan.

Ratu Kuripan's son was called Raden Inu Kertapati or Raden Menteri; he was handsome, intelligent and well mannered. One day Raden Inu went hunting. He shot a parrot with his blowpipe and the bird fell in the grounds of the residence where Ken Tambuhan was installed. Raden Inu climbed over the fence and came face to face with Ken Tambuhan:

> *serta terpandang hatinya berdebar*
> *lakunya tidak lagi tersabar*
> *arwah melayang berahi terkibar*
> *bagai penyakit tiada tertambar.*

> as soon as he saw her, his heart pounded
> he was so impatient
> his soul flew away, his desire increased
> he was like a sick man with no cure.

He coaxed and flattered Ken Tambuhan and eventually she agreed to be his wife:

> *Raden pun duduk bersukaan*
> *di dalam istana Ken Tambuhan*
> *bertambah kasih dengan kasihan*
> *pangku dan belai di atas ribaan.*

> Raden Inu stayed enjoying himself
> in Ken Tambuhan's palace
> their love grew
> she sat on his lap and he caressed her.

The queen was angry at Ken Tambuhan, believing that the girl was not worthy to be her son's wife. His father had already engaged him to the daughter of the ruler of Banjarkulon. The ruler of Kuripan had no such objection but this did not satisfy his wife who planned to have the girl killed.

The queen expressed a desire to eat fresh meat and sent Raden Inu into the forest to go hunting on her behalf. While he was away, an executioner took Ken Tambuhan into the forest and killed her. At her request, he placed her body on a raft and pushed the raft out into the river. Raden Inu found the raft and fainted. When he recovered, he committed suicide. News of these terrible events reached the king. In his anger, he had the executioner impaled. He drove the queen out of the palace and ordered her to look after the hunting dogs.

For forty days the king fasted, neither eating nor drinking, as he worshipped the supreme god, Batara Guru. The gods were moved by his plight and Batara Guru sent Batara Kala into the world to bring the two young people back to life. She brushed them both with the Gandapuri flower, formed from the milk of Dewi Sugarba's breasts, and they immediately revived. Raden Inu and Ken Tambuhan were formally married in a splendid ceremony. The king of Tanjungpuri heard the news. Ken Tambuhan was his long lost daughter (her name had originally been Puspa Kencana) and he was delighted at her marriage with Raden Inu. He quickly departed for Kuripan; the meeting with his daughter was extremely moving. Preparations were made to install Raden Inu as king of Kuripan, after which the king of Tanjungpuri returned home. So:

> *tetaplah kerajaan Raden Menteri*
> *Ken Tambuhan menjadi Suri*
> *suka dan ramal seisi negeri*
> *dengan punggawa sekalian menteri.*

> Raden Menteri's reign lasted
> Ken Tambuhan became his queen
> the people were happy and prosperous
> as were the chiefs and all the ministers.

The version of the *Syair Ken Tambuhan* edited by Teeuw is a short version, as are those of de Hollander (1856) and Roorda van Eysinga (1886). Teeuw also studied the longer texts: Kl 149, Cod. Or. 1997 and Cod. Or. 3375. These manuscripts tell how the pregnant Ken Tambuhan craved the exotic janggi fruit. Raden Inu was captured by the *garuda* who guarded the tree and held captive. After a very long time he was rescued by his son and Ken Tambuhan's brother (Teeuw, 1966a: xxvi).

We must admit that the *Syair Ken Tambuhan* is not very consistent in its description of Ken Tambuhan's origins. At first she is a prisoner of the king of Kuripan. Later, she is the daughter of the king of Tanjungpuri, whom the ruler of Kuripan has saved from a *garuda*. Even stranger, Tanjungpuri is also confused with Banjarkulon and Daha, Ken Tambuhan being described as the Princess of Daha (Teeuw, 1966a: xxx).

Syair Ken Tambuhan is a very popular syair and its language has been much praised by western scholars (Teeuw, 1966a: xxxv). Its contents also appear in a wayang story entitled *Hikayat Jaran Kinanti Asmaradana* and, in part, the *Hikayat Undakan Penurat* edited by Robson (Teeuw, 1966a: xxvii).

10.3.2 *Syair Angreni*

This syair has almost the same plot as *Syair Ken Tambuhan*. Raden Menteri, or Raden Inu Kartapati, secretly marries Ratna Angreni, the daughter of a minister. The King of Kuripan is angry, because he wanted his son to marry a princess of Kediri, Sekar Taji. He sends Raden Menteri out hunting and has Angreni executed during his son's absence. Raden Menteri is so sad that he decides to wander and to conquer the whole of Java. If he is killed, he will meet his beloved in heaven. There are many erotic descriptions of Raden Menteri's experiences with the various princesses he meets. The poem also tells the story of Carang Wespa, Panji's younger brother, and his love for Ratna Mindaka, Sekar Taji's younger sister. Panji's younger sister, Onengan, also falls in love with Gunung Sari.

According to Winstedt, Malays find the *Syair Angreni* difficult to undestand. Harun Mat Piah, who has studied the manuscript Raffles No. 65, held in London, does not agree. He thinks that the manuscript is easy to understand, although it does contain many Javanese words and expressions at a few points (Harun, 1980: 42).

10.3.3 *Syair Damar Wulan*

Syair Damar Wulan tells of a minister who becomes a stable hand, only to later marry a princess of Majapahit. Winstedt notes that the same story occurs in the *Sejarah Melayu* (Winstedt, 1958: 47). Although the syair was extremely widely circulated, it is now difficult to find copies of the manuscript. A text held in Jakarta (Bat. Gen. 190) has been transliterated by Jumsari Jusuf; it lacks a beginning and an end. Here is a summary of that work (Jumsari, 1971).

The poem begins by announcing that the work belongs to a man called Zakaria living in the area of Belandungan. Readers who borrow the book are asked to look after it carefully, and not spill oil or water on its pages. When they have finished, they should return it promptly. The story of Damar Wulan then commences.

Damar Wulan's father, Patih Majapahit, has retired from government service. When he grows up, Damar Wulan asks his uncle for employment. Because he is afraid that Damar Wulan will prove superior to his own sons, Layang Seta and Layang Kumitir, Patih Logender is unwilling to offer Damar Wulan any appropriate work and instead makes him a stablehand. Damar Wulan suffers greatly but Patih Logender's daughter, Anjasmara, feels sorry for him and soon the couple fall in love. Angry, Patih Logender throws them both into prison.

The ruler of Majapahit is the very beautiful Kencana Wungu. The king of Blambangan, Menak Jingga, proposes to Kencana Wungu, but she rejects him. Infuriated, Menak Jingga leads his army against Majapahit. Majapahit is no match for his troops and Menak Jingga rapidly advances against the kingdom. One night, the startled Putri Kencana Wungu dreams that only Damar Wulan can save Majapahit. She summons him but before he attends the court, Damar Wulan marries Anjasmara at her own request.

Putri Kencana Wungu is attracted to Damar Wulan, and offers herself and her kingdom to him if he can capture Menak Jingga. Damar Wulan sets off to fight Menak Jingga. Menak Jingga is very powerful and kills Damar Wulan. Menak Jingga's two wives revive him and help him steal Menak Jingga's magic weapon. With the help of the weapon, Damar Wulan challenges Menak Jingga and kills him in battle. Damar Wulan sets out for Majapahit, taking Menak Jingga's head with him.

Unfortunately he is attacked on the way by two of Patih Loginder's sons, Layang Seta and Layang Kumitir, and killed. The bandits take Menak Jingga's head. Damar Wulan's grandfather is an ascetic and he revives him, ordering Damar Wulan to continue his journey to Majapahit, bringing the treasure he has captured with him.

Patih Logender's sons announce Damar Wulan's death to the court. Princess Kencana Wungu is very sad. Damar Wulan appears, bringing his treasure and many of Menak Jingga's beautiful wives. He soon marries Princess Kencana Wungu and is appointed as the ruler of Majapahit. Anjasmara and the wives of Menak Jingga, who helped Damar Wulan kill Menak Jingga, become his secondary wives.

The spiteful Layang Seta and Layang Kumitir are not done with their evil plan and they turn Damar Wulan's half brothers against him. Fortunately the quarrel is soon resolved. Ashamed, Patih Logender and his sons leave Majapahit. Damar Wulan lives happily with his wives and as long as he rules Majapahit, the kingdom is peaceful and prosperous.

10.3.4 *Syair Undakan Agung Udaya* (Leiden Cod. Or. 1765)

This syair tells about a single incident. Ino Kertapati, prince of Jenggala, is an inveterate traveler. On his journeys, he marries two princesses, Raden Galuh Kusuma (of Singasari) and Candra Kusuma (of Bali). Then he changes his name to Undakan Agung Udaya Mesa Brangti and disguises himself as a puppet-master. In Daha, the princess falls in love with him and he kidnaps her. The rulers of Kediri, Gagelang, and Singasari attack Ino. The monk Sri Bupati appears and reconciles Ino and his enemies. The story ends at this point.

10.3.5 *Cerita Wayang Kinudang* (Leiden Cod. Or. 3367)

This syair was copied on the 30 November 1875 in Banjarmasin. The story is as follows.

The king of Kuripan goes to Sari Island to pray for a child. The king of Java also comes to the island. The queen of Kuripan becomes pregnant after eating the fruit of a palmyra palm and gives birth to two boys, Panji Mengarang and Panji Anom. The queen of Java delivers two daughters, Ratna Kumala dan Kembang Madani. When he grows up, his parents betroth Panji Mengarang to the elder sister, Ratna Kumala. On his way to Java, Panji Mengarang visits Mount Ledang where he marries Princess Domas Wayang. He then continues his journey. Discovering that she is pregnant, Domas Wayang goes to Kuripan, where she gives birth to a child whom she names Wayang Kinudang. After marrying the princess of Java, Panji Mengarang returns to Kuripan.

Forty great princes come to Java to compete for the hand of the princess Kembang Madani in an archery competition: whoever can shoot a ring fixed to a waringin tree will win the princess. No one is successful, except for Wayang Kinudang, who happens to be in Java searching for his father. Wayang Kinudang kills the forty princes but they are all revived. He marries the princess and they have a son, Raden Ulakan Jawa. When he grows up, Raden Ulakan Jawa visits Kuripan.

Domas Wayang has a dream in which she sees a deer with golden horns. Panji Mengarang sets out to find the deer. On the advice of the god Indra, Panji Mengarang undertakes ascetic practices on Mount Arga Sulasih. While he is absent, Domas Wayang gives birth to a son, Harimau Buwas (Wild Tiger). Ulakan Jawa marries Banyu Arum. Harimau Buwas sets out to find his father. On the way, he defeats Raden Asmana and marries his sister, Rumbayang Teja. Ulakan Jawa then changes his name to Citra Kusuma.He kills a king, Pudak Satagal, but then revives him at the request of the ruler's daughter, Sekar Kencana. Ulakan Jawa changes his name again and visits Karang Jajar. The poem ends with a description of the beautiful Princess Indra Kumala.

10.4 Romantic Syair

Romance is the most popular theme for syairs. Harun Mat Piah studied 150 syairs for his dissertation at the National University of Malaysia (1989) and found that 70 of them (47 per cent) dealt with romantic topics. This is not surprising, because the same themes occur in folk tales, oral narratives and prose chronicles. A kingdom is attacked by a *garuda*. The king (if he is still alive) leaves with his son and daughter. Then the love story begins. The prince or princess suffers because someone else, another king or princess, is jealous. Everything works out happily in the end. In some romantic syair, the heroine is a commoner, like the Chinese concubine in *Syair Sinyor Kosta*. Sometimes the poems are adapted from foreign languages; the *Syair Tajul Muluk* is derived from a Persian original. Here are a few of the more important romantic syairs.

10.4.1 *Syair Bidasari*

Syair Bidasari was extremely popular. There are at least ten manuscripts; they can be found in libraries in Jakarta, Leiden, and London. It has been translated into Dutch, English and French. In 1843, W. R. van Hoevell published an edition of this text (Hoevell, 1843); another appeared in 1886, edited by H. C. Klinkert (Klinkert, 1886: 270-419). According to Hoevell, the poem may have been composed in Palembang sometime after the coming of Islam and before the presence of Europeans in the Archipelago. According to the author (or the editor), the story was first composed in a prose form and then later turned to verse. Unfortunately the prose original has not survived, although it is possible that there is a version in Macassarese.

More recent versions have been published in Jakarta (Tuti Munawar, 1978) and in Kuala Lumpur (Jamilah, 1989). The Jakarta text is the same as that used by Klinkert; the Kuala Lumpur edition contains many incidents that are not in the Jakarta manuscript and there has clearly been a good deal of rewriting.

The copyist may well have been a *peranakan* Chinese. The Kuala Lumpur text states that copying manuscripts was the work of peranakans, while the Jakarta manuscript says:

> *Encik tuan-tuan yang punya surat*
> *Encik Cina (Klinkert: Husin) yang menyuratnya*
> *Barang siapa yang meminjamnya*
> *Pulangkan segera pada tuannya.*

> You sirs who own libraries
> A Chinese gentleman (Mr Husin?) copied this book
> Whoever borrows this book
> Should quickly return it to its owner.

The Leiden Cod. Or. 1942 names Mohd. Ching Said as the copyist of that particular manuscript. It is very likely that the Jakarta text came from a shop in Palembang that rented out books.

Here is a summary of the Jakarta (1978) edition.

There was once a king in Kembayat who was renowned for the just way in which he treated visiting merchants. One day a powerful *garuda* attacked the kingdom and destroyed its capital. The king and his wife fled the realm. On the way, the queen gave birth to an extremely beautiful princess. Sadly, the queen was forced to wrap the child in a golden blanket and leave her at the side of the river. A rich merchant from Indrapura, Lela Jauhari, found the child; he had no children of his own and he named her Siti Bidasari, because she was as beautiful as an angel (*bidadari*). To protect the child, he placed her soul in a fish and kept the fish in a golden bowl. As she grew, Bidasari became more and more beautiful:

Putih kuning wajah gemilang,
panjang nipis lehernya jenjang.

Her face was a pure pale golden colour,
her neck was long and slender.

The king of Indrapura was a just and generous ruler. After he died, his son, Raja Johan Syah, assumed the throne. Raja Johan Syah was married to the beautiful princess Lela Sari. On one occasion she asked him jokingly would he marry a more beautiful wife if he ever found one. The king, also jokingly, replied that if he ever found such a woman, he would appoint her to be the Princess's closest companion. Hurt by his response, the princess decided to find any woman who was more beautiful than herself and have her put to death. On the following day, she sent her maidservants to sell golden fans around the kingdom, as a way of finding out if she had any rivals.

Bidasari was keen to have one of the fans, despite her step-father's warnings, and bought one for two golden coins. When the Princess heard about Bidasari, she ordered that the girl be taken to the palace, where she was locked in a dark chamber. When Bidasari wept, she was punched and pummeled. After seven days, her body was sent back to her step-father. The merchant cared for Bidasari and she eventually recovered. Afraid for her safety, Lela Jauhari built her a house in the forest. She lived there alone, and he brought her food and drink every three days.

Raja Johan Syah and the Princess lived happily together. Then, one night, he dreamed that the moon had fallen into his lap, "illuminating his whole body". The dream was interpeted as meaning that he would soon take a new wife. The king was delighted, as he previously decided to marry any woman more beautiful than his present consort. The next day, he gathered his troops and went hunting. He toiled hard but could not capture anything. Suddenly he came across Bidasari's dwelling. Summoning up his courage, he went in and was overwhelmed by Bidasari's beauty. After a few days, he was able to speak to her and learn of her fate. With his encouragement, she her sanity returned and she was able to lead a normal life. The king decided to marry Bidasari. He established a new capital, complete with a new palace and grand markets, and moved the merchants and his subjects there. The wedding was held on a grand scale.

Meanwhile, the King of Kembayat had returned to his kingdom. He mourned the loss of his daughter and sent his son, Putra Bangsawan (the Noble Prince), to find her. While the prince was on board a ship, he met a young man called Senapati. Senapati was Bidasari's main servant and he was struck by their similarity in apearance, "they were like two halves of a betel nut, there was absolutely no difference between them." The two returned to Indrapura, where the merchant Lela

Jauhari (now called Mangkubumi Lela Mengindra) was keen to meet Putra Bangsawan. He took the young man to Raja Johan Syah, and Putra Bangsawan was finally able to meet his sister. The news quickly spread that Bidasari was the daughter of the King of Kembayat.

Senapati (now called Laksamana Menteri) was sent to take a letter to the King of Kembayat. The king and the queen came to Indrapura at once. The reunion was very emotional. The queen of Kembayat fainted, as she had finally been absolved of the sin of abandoning her own child. The King of Indraputra and his wife were crowned on an auspicious day.

The queen consort, Lela Sari, regretted her past actions. She was forgiven and given a new palace of her own. The king lived happily with his two wives. Putra Bangsawan married Putra Lela Sari's beautiful younger sister, Putri Lela Mengindra. The kingdom of Kembayat prospered, as did Indrapura:

> *Negerinya ramai tidak terperi,*
> *kabarnya masyhur segenap negeri.*
>
> The country was heavily populated,
> Her fame was known througout the land.

10.4.2 *Syair Yatim Nestapa* (The Poor Orphan)

This syair was first published in 1886 by H. C. Klinkert in *Drie Maleische Gedichten* (Three Malay Syairs, namely *Syair Ken Tambuhan, Syair Bidasari,* and *Syair Yatim Nestapa*). In 1968, it was transliterated into Romanised script by Mohd. Hashim Taib as part of his work for the B.A. (Hons) of the University of Malaya, and compared with an edition published in Singapore by Sulaiman Marie in 1934 (Mohd. Hashim Taib, 1968). Most recently, it has been studied by an Australian scholar towards his Master of Arts degree at Monash University (Julian Millie, 2004).

Here is a brief description of the story.

There was once a king, Sri Maharaja Indra Cita, who ruled over a vast empire. He had four wives and was most fond of the youngest one, always fulfilling her every wish. The second queen was jealous and decided to poison her young rival. Eventually Sri Maharaja appointed his son Ahmad Maulana (the son of the senior queen consort) as ruler and gave him the title of Raja Lela Mahkota. Raja Mahkota was instructed to treat his mothers and siblings equally.

The jealous queen obtained the poison and ordered one of her maids to add it to the youngest queen's food. Unfortunately, Sri Maharaja ate the food and died. The royal palace was in an uproar. Raja Mahkota ordered an immediate investigation. Because Sri Maharaja had died in the palace of the youngest queen, she was suspected of murdering him and the second queen supported this accusation. Raja Mahkota believed the lie; he had the youngest queen tortured in the marketplace and placed in prison. The second queen took possession of the youngest queen's two children.

After a long time, the youngest queen's son, Asmara Dewa, managed to escape and ran away, together with his younger sister, Intan Cahaya. A swallow showed them the way out of the forest. A snake first tried to swallow them but later gave Asmara Dewi a magic stone that had healing qualities. Eventually they reached the house of a fairy godmother.

Princess Indra Puspa of Indra Negara was bitten by a poisonous snake. Her physicians tried various medicines and potions, to no avail. The king Baginda Maharaja Indra Syah Johan sent heralds throughout the kingdom to announce that whoever cured the princess could marry her and would become the Crown Prince. Asmara Dewa heard the news and went straight to the palace. Thanks to the magic stone, he was able to cure Princess Indra Puspa; he was appointed Crown Prince and given the title Maharaja Muda Indra Negara. A magnificent wedding was held. Asmara Dewa's sister married a prince called Dewa Persada.

After some time, the Crown Prince successfully led his army against Raja Mahkota. He held Raja Mahkota captive for a while but eventually forgave him. The Crown Prince also freed the youngest queen and she was thus reunited with her two children. The Prince sentenced the wicked queen to death. Later the Crown Prince helped Dewa Persada kill a *garuda* that was attacking his kingdom of Belantapura. Dewa Persada was then crowned king. His brother, Dewa Syahadan, became king in another country. All these kings ruled justly and diligently.

10.4.3 *Syair Abdul Muluk*

The *Syair Abdul Muluk* is reasonably well known. It was first published in the journal *Tijdschrift van Nederlandsch Indie* in 1847, with a Dutch translation by Roorda van Eysinga. According to van Eysinga, the *Hikayat Abdul Muluk* (not the *Syair Abdul Muluk*) "was composed in the current form of Johor Malay by Seri Paduka Yam Tuan Muda Raja Ali Haji ibn Raja Ahmad." However, A. F. von de Wall has suggested that Raja Ali simply improved an existing text that had been written by his sister, Salihah. In 1934, Balai Pustaka published an edition based on three manuscripts, those of van Eysinga, Von de Wall and another published in Singapore that had been edited by Akbar Saidina and Haji Muhammad Yahya.

Here is a summary of the Roorda Van Eysinga text.

Sultan Abdul Hamid Syah ruled the land of Barbary; he was a wise and brave man. His brother, Abdul Majid, served under him. The queen's brother, Mansur, was the prime minister. After some time, the king was blessed with a handsome son, Abdul Muluk. After the death of another brother, Abdul Malik, the king offered his protection to his brother's wife. The wife gave birth to a very beautiful daughter, Siti Rahmat. After he finished his studies, Abdul Muluk married Siti Rahmat. Eventually the king fell gravely ill and was replaced by Abdul Muluk.

One day Abdul Muluk decided that he wanted to travel. He ordered his senior minister, Mansur, to prepare a boat. After sailing around the whole world, Sultan Abdul Muluk finally reached Ban. The Sultan of Ban had a daughter, Siti Rafiah, whom the astrologers predicted will be very devoted to her husband. Abdul Muluk was very attracted to Siti Rafiah; her father agreed to the match and, at an auspicious time, they were married in a lavish ceremony. Six months later, Abdul Muluk asked to be allowed to return to Barbary, taking Siti Rafiah with him. Siti Rahmat welcomed Siti Rafiah and treated the newcomer as if she were her own sister. Abdul Muluk was very happy with his two wives. He was as famed for his wisdom and courage as was his father before him.

The story then turns to the Sultan of Hindustan, who was bitter because his father's death in a prison in Barbary had not yet been avenged. He attacked Barbary without first sending a declaration of war; this was a serious breach of protocol. The war was ferocious. All of the ministers and generals of Barbary were killed, none of them survived. Abdul Muluk was also captured and imprisoned, as was Siti Rahmat.

Siti Rafiah escaped into the forest and, six months later, took refuge with a sheikh who treated her kindly. There she gave birth to an incomparably handsome son. Then she resumed her travels, leaving the boy with the holy man. She asks that her son be allowed to search for her when he is seven years old.

Dressed as a man and calling herself Dura, Siti Rafiah arrived in the land of Barbaham. She was surprised to discover that that the people were divided into two separate communities. One group, who supported Bahsan were "plentiful and happy, and their stores are well stocked". The other group, who supported Jamaluddin Mahkota, Bahsan's nephew, "are very unhappy, they are few in number and their shops are almost empty." Siti Rafiah helped Jamaluddin regain his throne and received Jamaluddin's sister, Rahat, as 'his' wife.

After some time, Siti Rafiah (still disguised as Dura) resumed 'his' travels to Hindustan. Pretending to be a merchant, 'he' became good friends with the ministers and leaders. Helped by the army of Berbaham, Siti Rafiah conquered Hindustan. The king was captured, imprisoned and eventually died. Siti Rafiah released Abdul Muluk and Siti Rahmat from prison and cared for them until they had fully recovered. When she revealed her identity to them, they were all delighted.

When Abdul Ghani turned seven, the holy man in the forest ordered him to find his parents, in accordance with Siti Rafiah's request. At one stage in his travels, he stayed at an inn where, coincidentally, a jeweler lost his merchandise. Abdul Ghani was accused of the theft as he had woken up during the night. Fortunately a wheat merchant paid his ransom and the boy went to live with him. One day, Abdul Ghani was involved in a fight with a young thug. He wounded his opponent and the youth's parents were angry. They brought him before the Sultan. Abdul Ghani described what had happened and the details of his life. The Sultan summoned the virtuous scholar and rewarded him with diamonds. He was also granted high religious and secular titles. The Sultan asked the sheikh to continue to teach Abdul Ghani various esoteric arts. Eventually Abdul Ghani became sultan of Ban. The land prospered because he ruled "in accordance with the teachings of the last prophet".

10.4.5 *Syair Seri Banian*

The *Syair Seri Banian* is also known as the *Syair Selindung Delima* and *Syair Indra Laksana*. There are many manuscripts. One, held in Jakarta (Bat. Gen. 34), was transcribed in Bukit Tinggi in 1850 and is full of Minangkabau words. This manuscript was lithographed in Singapore. Here is a summary of its contents.

The land of Badan Pirus was ruled by a powerful ruler, named Dewa Syah Peri. He had two children: a son, Bangsa Kara, and a daughter, Seri Banian. One day, the kingdom was attacked and destroyed by a *garuda*. The king vanished, but not before he had hidden his son inside a bamboo flute and his daughter in a box. A week later the chaos subsided and the children emerged from their hiding places. Unwilling to live in these miserable conditions, the pair decided to travel. They looked for a boat at the harbour but all the ships had been destroyed. Bangsa Kara began to build a boat. One day, Seri Banian went walking in a garden and ate a lime there. She felt unwell; her stomach hurt and she gave birth to a child, whom she placed in a box. Seri Banian ordered her brother to take the box with him when he set sail for his voyage, and breathed her last. Bangsa Kara was saddened by his sister's death and did as she had asked him.

Bangsa Kara sailed for seven days and seven nights. Large waves almost sank the boat but, thanks to the creator of the universe, it reached a kingdom whose ruler had just died. Carrying the box, Bangsa Kara went ashore and was chosen by a magic elephant to be the next king. He married the ruler's seven daughters. After a while, Bangsa Kara decided to go hunting. He left the box with the youngest princess, strictly instructing her not to look inside it. But the other princesses insisted that she open the box. When she did, out came a little girl, Selindung Delima. The six princesses thought that Selindung Delima was another of Bangsa Kara wives; they hit and insulted the girl. Only the youngest princess came to her aid.

The story now turns to Bangsa Kara. To his surprse, he did not find a single animal while he was out hunting and so he became very bored. He decided to go to Tanjung Pura. Selindung Delima presented herself before him and asked Bangsa Kara to take her to Bendu Island, so she could collect some cane and rocks. If he refused, she said that a fierce storm would come and he would never be able to return home. Bangsa Kara was taken aback by the girl's courage and intelligence. He had absolutely no idea that she was the child whom his sister had hidden in a box.

After he had lived in Tanjung Pura for three months and nine days, Bangsa Kara set out to return home. Suddenly a huge storm arose and the boat could not move. When the sails were furled, the sun shone. When they were opened, the storm returned. This happened several times. Only when Bangsa Kara made enquiries of a leading astrologer did he remember Selindung Delima's request. He visited Bendu Island and gathered cane and rocks with her. After he arrived home safely, Selindung Delima used the cane and rocks to bring Dewa Laksana and Seri Banian back to life. Bangsa Kara was delighted. He punished the six princesses and then quickly forgave them. After a while, Bangsa Kara and Seri Banian returned to their own land, Bandan Pirus. The *garuda* attacked the kingdom again but this time it was defeated by the brave Dewa Laksana who killed it. The kingdom of Bandan Pirus was rebuilt, complete with a palace, a capital, moats, marketplaces, and countless citizens. The king of Diwangsa asked for Selindung Delima's hand in marriage to his son, Dewa Udara. The proposal was accepted and the celebrations lasted forty days. Thus ends the *Syair Seri Banian*, "a deeply moving story, not without its moments of sadness."

10.4.6 *Syair Sinyor Kosta*

The romantic syair, the *Syair Sinyor Kosta,* is mentioned in many catalogues and has been much discussed by European scholars, who consider it to be the best and most popular of all travel verse narratives. The author has cleverly described the daily life, thoughts and customs of Malay merchants, using the colloquial language that was common in the ports at this time (Wieringa, 1998:150-151).

There are numerous copies of the manuscript and they can be divided into four groups.

(A) *Syair Sinyor Kosta*. This version is represented by Kl. 150, held in the library of Leiden University. The manuscript was transcribed in Tanjung Pinang about 1850 by a man called Incik Ibrahim. It is possible that this was Datuk Orang Kaya Ibrahim. The manuscript was lithographed several times, both in Singapore and Penang. In 1986, Mohd Yusof Nor published the text as part of his Honours studies. A photocopied version was published in 2004 by Teeuw et al.

(B) *Syair Sinyor Kista*. This version is represented by Kl 170, Leiden University library. The task of copying it was completed in Riau on 4 Dzukaidah 1261/4 November 1845 by a collleague of Haji Ibrahim. This is a short version of the text.

(C) *Syair Silambari*. This version is represented by Malay B 2609, India Office Library (Malay B 2609), London. It was copied by Ibrahim Ibn Kandu (Munsyi Ibrahim) in Penang, on 18 Syawal 1220/ 9 January 1806.

(D) *Syair Sinyor Kista*. This version is represented by Cod. Or. 1895, Leiden University library. It was copied in 1863 by Sultan Mahmud Badaruddin, who ruled from 1804-1822; he was exiled to Ternate by the Dutch in 1821.

The plot of the four versions is identical, apart from the endings. Here is a summary of the A text, based on Mohd. Yusof Nor and A. Teeuw et al.

The poem tells of a merchant named Sinyor Kosta (or Sinyor Gilang) who visits a particular port to trade. As he is walking around the town, he sees Siti Lela Mayang, the concubine of a Chinese merchant, Ceng Koa. Siti Lela Mayang, who comes from Pegu (Burma), is very beautiful: her nose is well shaped ("*hidung mancung bunga seria*"), her face is like a shadow puppet doll, pale yellow like a flower ("*bagai tulis wayang gambar/putih kuning bunga kembang*"). Sinyor Kosta falls in love with her. He sends a Balinese woman, Milam Perahu, to plead his case. Siti Lela Mayang refuses to meet him; she is a married woman, like a bird in a nest ("*bagai unggas dalam sarang*"). Sinyor Kosta does not give up hope. He bribes Milam to administer a love potion to Siti Lela Mayang. This is successful and Siti Lela Mayang agrees to run away with Sinyor Kosta.

Sinyor Kosta prepares to return home. He has just loaded his boat with goods when Ceng Koa invites him to attend a dance party. He is impressed by the merchant's good looks. Cunningly Sinyor Kosta encourages all the Chinese at the party, including Ceng Koa, to drink until they are completely inebriated. Then he takes Siti Lela Mayang aboard and sails away.

When Ceng Koa recovers from his drunkenness, he finds that Siti Lela Mayang has vanished, together with much of his wealth. Ceng Koa offers the sultan a large amount of money for his assistance and the next morning five boats set out after Sinyor Kosta. When they find him, a battle breaks out but Ceng Koa is defeated and suffers even further losses. Because of the war, he now has nothing at all. Sinyor Kosta returns to his own land and is received with great rejoicing by his parents.

The poem concludes with a colophon stating that the poem was written by Ibrahim in Riau, Tanjung Pinang. The colophon is not found in the Singapore edition (1887). Instead, we find the following pantun:

> *Buah bacang masak layu*
> *Makan oleh anak bandan*
> *Tujuh bintang sinyor rayu*
> *Sita tambar pulih badan*

> The horse-Mango ripens and wilts
> It is eaten by a child of Bandan
> Sinyor pleads to the seven stars
> Sita cures him and he recovers

This is the short version of the *Syair Sinyor Kosta*. Each of the texts, as we have noted, has a different ending. In A, Sinyor Kosta's parents proceed to scold him for stealing another man's wife and he is forced to agree with them. In B, Sinyor Kosta dies in battle and becomes a dragon. Siti Lela Mayang commits suicide and becomes a python (Teeuw et al., 2004: 42:62). In C, the Dutch help Ceng Koa to defeat Sinyor Kosta in a fierce battle. Siti Lela Mayang is taken back to Malaka; the Chinese community is delighted, and they sing and dance. In the longer version, D, Bandan, Sinyor Kosta's friend and assistant, marries Siti Lela Mayang's servant, a Persian girl. The wedding is celebrated with a grand feast.

10.4.7 *Syair Cinta Berahi* (Love Poem) (v.d. Wall Collection, 267)

This poem is also known as the *Syair Farahid*. It derives from a story in the *Hikayat Bayan Budiman* (number 9 in the Balai Pustaka edition). The plot is as follows.

Sultan Indra, the ruler of Branta Indra, had many wives. The most beautiful and the one he loved the most was Siti Lela Mengindra, the daughter of the Treasurer. Her beauty was widely praised. Mengindra Syahperi heard a parrot speak of Siti Lela Mengindra and wanted to see her face. Day by day he could dream of nothing else. After he met Siti Lela Mengindra, he was even more in love with her.

He stayed for a while with a fairy godmother, calling himself Muda Farahid. The magic arts he learned from her soon made him a good friend of the king. But when he flirted with Siti Lela Mengindra, the king became very angry. He offered to give him Siti Lela Mengindra if Muda Farahid could fulfill certain conditions, including catching a wild tiger and entering a mountain. Muda Farahid did all that he was asked but the Sultan refused to honour his side of the agreement and bribed an old woman to poison him. The old woman lied to Muda Farahid, saying that Siti Lela Mengindra had died. Overcome by grief, Muda Farahid committed suicide. When Lela Mengindra heard of his death, she too committed suicide. The whole country mourned her death. The Treasurer ordered that the old woman be killed. The king himself died of grief (Djadjuli, 1961).

10.4.8 *Syair Raja Mambang Jauhari* (Leiden Cod. Or. 1986)

This poem was composed by Panembahan Bupati of Palembang. It uses Palembang Malay but with many Javanese words. The plot is as follows.

The king of Langkara Indra died, leaving behind his daughter, Kusuma Indra, who was betrothed to Dewa Syahperi of Belantapura. Raja Mambang Jauhari heard of the princess's beauty and decided to kidnap her. Dewa Syahperi was defeated in the battle and was close to death. The god Batara Kala brought him back to life again and advised Dewa Syahperi to kidnap Raja Mambang Jauhari's sister, Puspa Indra. War broke out again between Raja Mambang Jauhari and Dewa Syahperi. Finally Batara Kala manifested himself and made peace between the two factions.

Dewa Syahperi then married Puspa Indra. Raja Mambang Jauhari returned to his kingdom. The manuscript ends abruptly.

10.4.9 *Syair Tajul Muluk* (v.d. Wall Collection 258, Jakarta Museum)

Djadjuli has made an extensive study of this syair (1961, 1971). He suggests that it was written in Penyengat, Riau, and completed on the fourteenth day of the month of Ramadhan, in the year of Arafat. It was republished in Singapore in a transcription made by Muhd. Idris in 1336 H /1917. The contents of the two manuscripts are the same.

Malik Sulaiman Syah was a great king. He was rich, just and generous. His wife was the daughter of Malik Zaharsyah and together they had one son, Tajul Muluk. One day when Tajul Muluk was out hunting, he met a man named Aziz, who told him about his sad life. Aziz was a rich merchant. He was engaged to Azizah but just before the wedding was about to take place, he was bewitched by another woman and as result forgot all about the event. Azizah forgave him his negligence and even helped him marry Dalilah. Dalilah was ashamed of her behaviour and sent Aziz back to Azizah. Unfortunately by the time he arrived, Azizah had already died. Aziz and Dalilah visited Azizah's grave and paid their respects to her.

After a while, Aziz was trapped by another woman and forced to marry her. He was only allowed to return home once the woman had given birth to a baby. Dalilah refused to accept him, as did the other woman. Aziz was forced to live with his parents, who gave him one of Azizah's handkerchiefs as a keepsake. To relieve his sorrow, Aziz had taken to wandering about, and this had led him to Tajul Muluk.

Tajul Muluk eagerly listened to Aziz's story, especially when he spoke of the beauty of Princess Saidatuddunia, the daughter of the king of Persia, who had made the handkerchief:

> *Rambutnya hitam beserta lebat*
> *manis laksana minum syurbat.*
> ......
> *Mukanya bujur, hidungnya mancung,*
> *laksana kalam baharu diruncing,*
> *jarinya halus, lentik diujung,*
> *bagai manikam sebuah, dijunjung.*
>
> *Lehernya jenjang seperti kendi,*
> *betisnya bagai bunting padi.*
> ......
>
> *Bulu mangsunya bagai dialas*
> *senyumnya patut dengan memalis*
> *dipandang jauh terlalu majlis*
> *laksana gambar baharu ditulis.*
>
> *Putih kuning cemerlang warna,*
> *cantik majlis bijaksana,*

lemah lembut usulnya kena,
memberi hati bimbang gulana.

Her hair was black and thick
as sweet as sherbert.
...
Her face was oval, her nose well-defined
like a newly sharpened quill,
her fingers were slender and curved at their tips
like pearls when raised in greeting.

Her neck was as slender as a gourd,
her thighs were like sheaves of rice.
...
Her eyebrows were black
her smile subtle
her gaze direct and noble
like a newly painted picture.

Her colour was light golden,
she was beautiful and wise,
soft and gentle in all she did,
she could stir the heart to melancholy.

Tajul Muluk wanted to marry Princess Saidatuddunia and sent an envoy to ask for her hand. She refused, saying that she did not want to be married.

Tajul Muluk set out for Persia, take one of his father's ministers and Aziz with him. When they arrived, he disguised himself as a merchant. Although he sent Princess Saidatuddunia several letters, she never replied to any of them. Finally he asked her why she did not want to marry and this was the story she told him.

Once, Princess Saidatuddunia had dreamed of a pair of doves. When the male was caught in a net, his mate helped him escape. But when she was caught, the male bird said nothing and refused to help her. After she died, he flew happily about, without a care in the world. That was why she did not want to marry: she believed that all men were untrustworthy.

When he heard the story, Tajul Muluk thought of a plan by which he could win his sweetheart. He ordered an artist to paint a picture of two doves. The male dove was trapped in a net. The female was standing by, just looking at him. Princess Saidatuddunia was surprised to see the picture. She realized that she had been tricked by her dream. At that moment, Tajul Muluk appeared in front of her and she immediately fell in love with him. They were together in her palace for many months until finally Malik Syaharman found out and, in his anger, had Tajul Muluk imprisoned.

His companions, Aziz and Wazir, returned home to tell the king, Malik Sulaiman, of Tajul Muluk's disappearance. His father led the army against Persia. The king of Persia was shocked. On the advice of his senior minister, the king married Tajul Muluk to Princess Saidatuddunia in a lavish ceremony, after which Malik Sulaiman Syah and his army left. Aziz was allowed to go back to his parents. Before long, Tajul Muluk became the crown prince and Saidatuddunia became his consort.

10.4.10 *Syair Sultan Yahya* (Leiden Cod. 1777)

This poem is also known as *Syair Saudagar Budiman* (The Poem of the Virtuous Merchant). There are two copies of this manuscript in the Jakarta Museum but they are very different from each other. The summary here is based on the manuscript held at Leiden, which was printed in Singapore. King Zamin of Iran renounced his throne and travelled around disguised as a merchant. He had a son, Jayaputra, and two daughters, Jauhar Manikam and Siti Bandahara.

Also disguising himself as a merchant, Jayaputra traveled to Zaman Turan, which was ruled by Sultan Yahya. One of Jauhar Manikam's suitors poisoned her father. Siti Bandahara married Sultan Hamzah. Jauhar Manikam too disguised herself as a merchant and, assuming the name of the Virtuous Merchant, set out to find Jayaputra. When she reached Zaman Turan, Sultan Yahya suspected that she was a woman and ordered her to catch fish, go hunting and leap over a ditch. Jauhar Manikam successfully did all these things. Finally she found her brother and revealed her true identity to him. Sultan Yahya was amazed and asked her to be his wife. Soon after this, Jayaputra ascended the throne in place of his father. Once he had a fight with Princess Belantapuri, Sultan Yahya's first wife, but they soon settled their differences and became good friends.

10.4.11 *Syair Putri Akal*

Syair Putri Akal (The Clever Princess) or *Syair Putri Handalan* (The Skilful Princess, Cod. Or. 1771) deals with a theme we also find in the *Hikayat Nakhoda Muda*: a clever young woman becomes pregnant to her own husband without his knowledge, and thereby wins back his love. Pijnappel claimed that this is a good quality work and deserved to be published. Here is a summary of an edition that was published in Singapore.

A wise and worthy king once had a very beautiful daughter, Putri Akal. When her fame reached Damascus, the ruler came and asked for her hand in marriage but he was rejected. The King of Damascus finally wins Putri Akal's heart after he makes her a golden doll that can dance. They are then married. There is drinking and great festivities. The couple is very much in love and cannot bear to be parted from each other for very long.

One day the King of Damascus takes the princess sailing. The yacht sails into the middle of the sea, swift as a bird in flight. When they reach that point, Putri Akal, for no obvious reason, receives a servant named Selamat (Cod. Or. 1771: Lamat). The King of Damascus decides to marry the Treasurer's daughter. Putri Akal is extremely upset. Devising a clever plan, she takes out the golden doll and gives it to the girl on the condition that they sleep in each other's beds. By the grace of God, the young woman accepts the offer. Each night, the Treasurer's daughter meets the wild Selamat. He knows that she is the Treasurer's daughter, the king's wife, but says nothing. Putri Akal sleeps in the simple bed; the king visits her each night but, somehow, does not recognize her. Before long, both women are pregnant. Putri Akal's son looks just like the king; the son of the Treasurer's daughter looks like Selamat. Their secrets are revealed. The King of Damascus is delighted by Putri Akal's intelligence and piety. He sends the Treasurer's daughter back to her father. The treacherous Selamat is impaled.

This concludes our discussion of romantic syair. We should note that, like the Panji syair, some romantic narrative poems are also adapted from prose chronicles: for example, the *Syair Indra Putra* comes from the *Hikayat Indra Putra*; and the *Syair Anggun Cik Tunggal* from the *Hikayat Anggun Cik Tunggal*. According to Hooykaas, the prose narratives offer simpler narratives, while the poems emphasise emotions at the expense of the plot and comprehensibility (Hooykaas, 1947: 73).

10.5. Figurative Syair

The Figurative syair describes imaginary romantic relationships. Not between people but between fish, birds, flowers and fruits. Hans Overbeck has called these "Malay animal and flower syairs" (1934), suggesting that they symbolize actual events in an implicit and mocking manner. The *Syair Ikan Terubuk* mocks a proposal made by the King of Malaka for the hand of a princess from Siak. The *Syair Burung Pungguk* mocks a young man who wanted to marry a woman of higher estate than himself. Other syair mock the affairs of traveling merchants and offer pertinent advice to their listeners. Our discussion below is particularly based on a number of poems found in the v.d. Wall manuscript 242 and follows Jumsari et al., 1978.

10.5.1 *Syair Ikan Terubuk* (The Herring)

We may begin by studying the *Syair Ikan Terubuk,* which is narrated in the v.d. Wall 242 manuscript. Herring lived in the Malaka Straits. One day, he fell in love with Princess Climbing Perch, who lived in a pool at the head of the river in Tanjung Padang. Each day, he dreamed of her beauty and sweet manners, her slender waist and ample bosom. The thought of her made him quite melancholy. So he assembled his ministers, guards and warriors to discuss the matter. Each of the fish was ready to sacrifice himself for his king, in his own unique manner. The Sea-perch advised him to be careful, because it was not easy to conquer another kingdom, one needed to have the right weapons. When the king asked who might betray him, Perch made no reply. Preparations were made to attack the pool where the princess lived and to bring her back by force, if need be.

Swamp Eel was fond of the princes. He warned a tilan fish of the forthcoming attack and Tilan immediately told the princess. She gathered all her subjects and said that, although she did not dislike the herring, the two countries were very different. Herring lived in the east, while they lived in the jungle; he lived in the sea, they lived upriver. The Perch said that they were ready to defend their kingdom. They suggested various ways in which they might avert the disaster. Finally the princess agreed to pray and ask the ancestors for their assistance. She prayed all night. A hurricane came, thunder crashed and lightning flashed, and the ancestors descended, bringing with them a lofty pulai trunk. The princess and her people hid in the layered foliage of the tree. When Herring arrived, he found that the pond was empty "as far as the eyes could see". He returned home, heart-broken.

Another manuscript, described by Hooykas, differs slightly from the v.d. Wall 242 held in Jakarta. When Herring and his army reach the pond, they are caught in a net by a fisherman.

Herring manages to escape but he realizes that it is not God's will that he should meet the princess. He also hears of the princess' taking refuge in a tree. Herring returns to his own kingdom and lives in misery for the rest of his days (Hooykaas, 1947: 73-75).

10.5.2 *Syair Burung Pungguk* (The Owl)

This poem tells of a love that fails because of the lovers' different social statuses. A young man pining for a girl of high estate is often said to be "like the owl longing for the moon". W. W. Skeat presented a somewhat different version in his book *Malay Magic* but the essence of the story is still the same (Overbeck, 1914: 190). There are not a lot of manuscripts of this text. Overbeck published one from Padang (dated 1310H) in the *JSBRAS,* vol. 67. Raja Iskandar bin Raja Muhammad Zahid studied several of the texts for his B. A. (Hons.) and found them to follow basically the same plot. Here is an outline of the story.

Owl fell in love with Princess Moon who was much higher in status than he was. She did not reject his love but neither did she encourage him. Owl could only gaze at the princess from afar.

The princess spent a lot of time in a very beautiful garden. One day, Owl visited the garden and, with the assistance of Bird-of-paradise, he was able to tell the princess how he felt. The princess fell in love with him. After this first meeting, the princess ordered Bird-of-paradise to tell Owl to come again. They sported to their hearts' content. When it was time for them to part, the princess gave him a cloth and he wore it with pride. A *garuda* recognized the cloth; he attacked Owl and killed him, leaving his body in a river. When the princess heard of the tragedy, she dared not say anything for fear of suffering the same fate. Owl's body turned into a mushroom that looked like a living creature. Ever since that time, the love-sick owl has longed for the moon. Each night he tries to fly to somewhere where he can be closer to her.

10.5.3 *Syair Kumbang dan Melati* (The Beetle and the Jasmine)

Two poems that tell of unrequited love are the *Syair Kumbang dan Melati* (The Beetle and the Jasmine) and the *Syair Nuri* (The Parroquet). The *Syair Kumbang dan Melati* tells of a Beetle who fell in love with a Jasmine flower. He sent an envoy to tell her of his love but she rejected him. Beetle was very disappointed but did not give up hope. He went and learned magic from Cricket. Thanks to his magic, Jasmine fell in love with him. She sent him a message and they spent some time together. When the king, who owned the garden where Jasmine lived, announced that he intended to kill Beetle, Beetle just laughed. Three manuscripts of this poem have been studied by Jumsari et al. (1978: 169-188). The poem was composed in Singapore but may be based on a story from Trengganu, Malaysia.

10.5.4 *Syair Nuri* (The Parroquet)

Syair Nuri (Bat. Gen. 8) tells of an impossible love between an Ariel and a Parroquet who is married to Worthy Parrakeet. They are forced to conceal their feelings. One day Parroquet can no longer restrain herself and she invites Ariel to visit her. When he comes, they can only look at each other because her husband is there. They console themselves by reciting pantun to each other (Jumsari et al., 1978: 223-233).

Overbeck has described a rather different *Syair Nuri*, in which Parroquet falls in love with a Frangipanni in another man's garden. The bird learns magic from Plover and is able to meet the flower. The two make love to their hearts' content. Then Parroquet leaves, never to return again. The flower remains forlorn in the garden (Overbeck, 1934: 119-122).

10.5.5 *Syair Bunga Air Mawar* (The Rose)

This poem too tells of an unfulfilled love. Bird-of-Paradise falls in love with Rose and sends Parroquet to tell her of his feelings. His declaration is rebuffed because Rose is ashamed to know that he is already married. Secretly, she really does love him. The bird is sad and goes to Java, where he dies (Jumsari et al., 1978: 89-99).

The manuscript claims to have been composed in 1275H by Pangeran Panembahan Bupati, brother of the Sultan of Palembang but Overbeck does not accept this. There are no doubt other manuscripts besides that held in Jakarta (Overbeck, 1934: 132).

10.5.6 *Syair Nyamuk dan Lalat* (The Mosquito and the Fly) (v.d. Wall Collection 239)

This poem describes the love of a Fly for a very beautiful Mosquito:

> *Badannya seperti gambar wayang*
> *Pipinya laksana pauh dilayang*
> ....
> *Alisnya laksana bentuk taji*
> *Anak rambutnya bagai disuji*
> ....
> *Dadanya bidang ramping pinggangnya*
> *Lilin dituang umpama lengan*
> ....
> *Bibirnya merah madu segara*
> *Giginya seperti karang mutiara*
> ....
> *Betisnya laksana batang padi*
> *Tumitnya seperti kilat permata*
> (Jumsari et al., 1972: 204-205)

> Her body was like a shadow-pupppet
> her cheeks like hanging mangoes
> ...
> Her eyebrows were curved like the spurs of a fighting cock
> her curls seem to have been embroidered
> ...

> Her breasts were full, her waist slender
> her wrists were like melting candles
> ...
> Her lips were red, like an ocean of honey
> her teeth were like rows of pearls
> ...
> Her thighs were like stalks of rice
> her heels were like jewels of lightning

The Fruit-fly was sent to propose to the Mosquito. The Mosquito rejected his proposal because the Fly was a low fellow, "of humble origins and unknown language". Besides, he was like the Basil plant, whom everyone scorned and avoided. The Fly fainted when he heard the news. Following the advice of the Fruit-fly, the Fly went to learn magic from a powerful Hornet. He applied what he had learned and the Mosquito fell in love with him. They met, kissed each other on the cheeks, and declared their undying affection for each other.

10.5.7 *Syair Kupu-kupu dengan Kembang dan Balang* (The Butterfly, the Flowers and the Balang Butterfly) (Bat. Gen. 255)

This poem tells of a very handsome butterfly. He visited many flowers in a garden, sucked their pollen, and left them to die. Finally he met a very beautiful Balang butterfly. "Her waist was slender, her breasts were full." Although he loved her very much, he did not dare approach her because her brother was so fierce and strong. So he pined for her day and night, and eventually wasted away. This is what happens to people who behave badly.

The poem was written by Muhammad Bakir bin Syafi bin Usman Al-Ghazali, who lived in Pecenongan.

10.5.8 *Syair Buah-buahan* (Fruits) (Bat. Gen. 254)

This poem consists of six tales. The first tells of Pomegranate who fell in love with the beautiful Grape. Unable to restrain his emotions any longer, Pomegranate sent Banana to plead his case with Grape. She accepted and they were married in a lavish celebration. The second story tells of Mango's love for Rambutan; the third of Sawo's love for Sweetsop; the fourth of Cempedak's love for Jackfruit. In each of the stories of Mango, Sawo and Cempedak, there are difficulties, but these difficulties are ovecome through the acquisition of magic, and eventually the couples are married.

The fifth story tells of the love of a Baba (Chinese-Malay) for his wife. The wife fell sick and the Baba spent all his money buying medicine. Finally he bought grapes and pomegranates at great expense. After eating the fruit, his wife died in peace. The Baba was very sad. He gave instructions that, when he died, he was to be buried near his wife; a jasmine bush was to be planted by her grave, a frangipani tree near his own. Having said this, he ate the remains of his wife's fruit and he too died. The trees were planted near their graves.

The sixth story tells of two beetles playing near the graves of the Baba and his wife. Mr Beetle decides to make posies and sell them at the market. In one of the posies he placed poems. The poems were sold to the princess, who fell in love with the beetle. The beetle had vanished, no one knew where to find him. To console herself, the princess made imitation posies (Jumsari et al., 1978: 34-86).

The poem was completed by Muhammad Bakir of Pecenongan on 22 November 1896. Muhammad Bakir apparently hired out copies of the text at ten cents for twenty-four hours. There is a list at the end of the text of 14 poems readers could hire. These readers were members of the Jakarta working class and the language used is full of Chinese words, for example:

Cempaka orangnya bopeng
Lakunya candal, *mulutnya* bengkeng
Kelakuannya seperti perempuan huakeng
Yang suka dengan main di pangkeng.

Frangipani is *bopeng* (pockmarked)
Her actions *candal* (sluttish), her mouth *bengkeng* (crude)
Her behaviour is like a *huakeng* woman
Who likes to play in the *pangkeng*

The *huakeng* was what we call "a good time girl" and the *pangkeng* is the bedroom.

This ends our discussion of figurative syair. If we accept that the animals and flowers represent human beings, then we will better understand the poems and their meanings.

10.6 Historical Syair

Historical syair are poems dealing with historical events. Wars are obviously one of the most important historical events and many syair therefore deal with conflicts. These include the *Syair Perang Mengkasar,* which deals with a war in Makasar, 1668-1669; the *Syair Kaliwungu* (Bat. Gen. 198), which deals with a war in Semarang, 1763; and the *Syair Perang Palembang* about the attack of the Dutch on Palembang, 1819-1821, which led to the fall of the Palembang Sultanate (this poem is also known as *Syair Perang Palembang,* Atja, 1967b).

Other major events were the rule of kings and Dutch residents. The *Syair Sultan Mahmud di Lingga,* for example tells the life of Sultan Mahmud Syah and his family, while the *Syair Residen De Brau* describes the role of De Brau in exiling the Minister of Palembang to Java.

Finally it needs to be noted that historical events could, on occasion, be such simple daily affairs as the marriage of the head of the Chinese community—the *Syair Perkawinan Kapitan Tik Sing* (Bat. Gen. 168)—or a fire—the *Syair Singapura dimakan Api* (v.d. Wall Collection 270). We will discuss a few of the most important historical syairs.

10.6.1 *Syair Perang Mengkasar* (The Makasar War)

This account of the conflict between the Makasarese and the Dutch was formerly known as the *Syair Sipelman.* C. Skinner, who wrote his Ph.D. thesis on this work at SOAS London, argued that the earlier title is inappropriate, as the Dutch admiral, Cornelis Speelman, is the not the main character in the work. He was not the only protagonist in the war by any means (Skinner, 1963: 45).

The author of the poem was Encik Amin. Skinner describes him as a mixed blood Makasarese Malay. Because he served as a scribe to the Sultan of Goa, he had a profound knowledge of life in the palace and the world of commerce, and of nearly all of the most important people involved in both. He was also well acquainted with mysticism and with Classical Malay Literature This knowledge may have helped him write in a pure Malay, without any use of Makasarese (unlike the history of Acheh, *Hikayat Aceh,* for example, which is filled with Achehnese words).

The poem was written between June 1669 and June 1670, making it one of the oldest syair known (Skinner, 1963: 43). This is Skinner's summary of the work.

After offering praises to God, the Prophet and the Sultan of Goa, the poet describes the origins of the war. Once, "Sipelman" (as he is called) encouraged the Buginese prince, Raja Palaka, to become King by leading his people against the Makasarese. Raja Palaka swore he would conquer the Makasarese fortress in a single day. The Dutch assembled their fleet and sailed to Makasar. The people of Makasar were determined to fight alongside their ruler. War broke out. The Makasarese leaders, the "Karaeng", were defeated and surrendered.

The story next tells of the Sultan of Ternate's offer to help the Dutch attack Makasar. The Sultan of Goa resolved to continue to oppose the Dutch, for which the author praises him highly. A separate war broke out. Sultan Tallok, the brother of the Sultan of Makasar, successfully defeated the Buginese and returned to Makasar. The Dutch played a major role in supporting Palaka. They shelled many parts of Makasar. The Makasarese mocked Sipelman's envoy and the Dutch continued to bombard the kingdom. Many Makasarese died but the Company was not successful in its attack. Eventually the Company signed a treaty with the Makasarese.

After a while some evil Makasarese Karaengs provoked the Dutch to attack Sanrabone. War broke out again. Makasar sent assistance to Sanrabone and the Dutch attack was defeated. The English fortress was burned to the ground. More fighting broke out and the Makasarese fort was razed to the ground. The Makasarese retreated to Goa. The poet finally mentions that the Makasar lost because they had been starved into submission. He gives his own name, Encik Amin.

10.6.2 *Syair Kompeni Welanda Berperang dengan Cina* (The Dutch Company Fights a Chinese Uprising)

Jan Rusconi made a detailed study of this poem and its historical context for his doctoral dissertation at the University of Utrecht (Rusconi, 1935). W. Kern has also provided some important notes on it (Kern, 1948).

The poem tells of a Chinese uprising against the Dutch in Jakarta, 1740, and of a related war in Madura. It is also prefaced by an account of a riot in Sailan (Sri Lanka). Kern says that the poem has several titles: *Cerita Welanda Berperang dengan Cina* (The Story of The Dutch War against the Chinese—with no mention of the Company; Van der Tuuk also records this title), and, in Banjarmasin, as *Syair Hemop*. Kern believes that this is the more correct title because Van Hemop, or Imhoff, is indeed the major character in the work. A copy of the manuscript in the Jakarta

Museum concludes with the words "the book of the famous Hemop is done" and "This concludes the Poem of Hemop ("*Syair Hemop tamatlah sudah*").

The author was a Banjarese mixed-blood who had lived for a long time in Jakarta. The manuscript uses many Javanese and Banjarese words. Kern also says that this is a good example of a Dutch-Malay syair. The Jakarta Museum manuscript describes Abdurrahman, a clerk from Jakarta, as being the author. Kern suggests that the text was written about twenty years after the uprising. The fact that he makes several small but important mistakes suggests that author was not present at the time of the event.

Here is a summary of the story based on that provided by Rusconi, together with some additional comments by Juynboll in his catalogue.

The Dutch asked permission to establish a post in Ceylon. Once they felt strong enough, they began to behave aggressively. The king of Kandi was angry and attacked the Dutch. A war ensued. The Dutch received reinforcements from Batavia five times but to no avail. Finally they sent Van Imhoff to negotiate with the king and a truce was declared, thus ending the war. Van Imhoff decided to rebuild the post, which had been destroyed in the war, and asked the Governor of Jakarta, Valckenier, to send him some unemployed Chinese. In his greed, the Governor deliberately misinterpreted the request. He summoned the Headman, telling him to round up all the Chinese and send them to Ceylon. By so doing, he extracted an enormous amount of money from the Chinese community.

Five years later, Van Imhoff returned to Jakarta. The king of Kandi farewelled him and gave him many expensive gifts.

The Chinese felt anxious and united under the leadership of Long (Si Panjang). They agreed to launch an attack. The Dutch were terrified by this threat. Governor Valckenier wanted to let them have the city; Van Imhoff disagreed and was prepared to resist any attack. Valckenier was furious that Van Imhoff had ignored him. He quietly stole Valckenier's authority and put the troops on stand-by at their various guard-posts. He also devised appropriate military strategies. The first Chinese atack was broken and many Chinese died. Long gathered his remaining troops and atacked Batavia from three different directions. Fierce fighting again followed. Many Chinese also died in this second attack. Finally the Chinese were defeated and they were forced to retreat into the jungle. The Dutch had won but they found that Jakarta was empty, as all the Chinese had fled.

Long and the Chinese reassembled and were able to convince the Susuhunan to attack the Dutch. They surrounded the Dutch trading post, killing many Dutchmen and forcing others to convert to Islam. Then the Chinese decided to send their army against Semarang.

In Jakarta, relations between Valckenier and Van Imhoff grew steadily worse. Both men accused each other of provoking the war. Van Imhoff also accused Valckenier of oppressing the Chinese by rounding up all the community and not just the indigent and unemployed. The accusation enraged Valckenier and he had Van Imhoff arrested and sent back to the Netherlands to be hung.

The cunning Van Imhoff had many allies. He succeded in having the charges overturned, claiming that he had performed a great service by saving Jakarta, whereas Valckenier would have surrendered it to the Chinese. He had also put down the insurrection in Ceylon. His clever oratory convinced many people. Van Imhoff was freed and generously compensated. He was made governor of Jakarta in place of Valckenier, who was subsequently arrested.

The Dutch could not withstand the Chinese attack and appealed for assistance. In this way, the attack was broken. The Susuhunan Kartasura lost his nerve and betrayed many local rulers who were sent into exile by the Dutch. Long angrily invaded Kartasura. The Susuhunan fled to Solo and, refusing to return, had a new palace built there. Van Imhoff was a just and wise ruler, and the people prospered. The Chinese asked his permission to return to Jakarta and Batavia once more returned to life. The Dutch attacked the Cakraningrat in Madura, defeating him after a lengthy and bitter struggle. The Cakraningrat fled to Banjarmasin and was arrested there.

According to Cod. 2095, held in Leiden, Van Imhoff eventually converted to Islam. He died soon afterwards and was replaced by Jakob Mossel, who proved to be a very unsatisfactory administrator. "The book was finished on the twentieth day of the month of Rabiul Akhir. It belongs to Major Parkur. The year was 1232 on the Muslim calendar."

10.6.3 *Syair Perang di Banjarmasin* (The Banjarmasin War)

There are two manuscripts of the syair that describes the Banjarmasin war of 1862, *Syair Peperangan di Banjarmasin*. The Jakarta manuscript was presented to F. N. Nieuwenhuysen; the Leiden manuscript (Cod, Or. 2094, Leiden) was given to C. C. Tromp, the Resident of Banjarmasin from 1870 to 1875. The Jakarta text consists of 69 chapters: 13 by Engku Raja al-Haj Daud, of Penyengat, Riau, 56 by Raden al-Habib Muhammad of Siak. Raden al-Habib Muhammad also wrote a version of this work in Johor-Malay when he was in Banjarmasin, during February 1871. The Leiden text was written by Engku Raja al-Haj Daud on the 16 June 1870 in Penyengat, according to Matheson. However, it consists of 23 chapters and a preface that summarises the whole poem (see Siti Hawa, 1987: 155-156). It should be noted that Van Ronkel includes an entry to the *Syair Perang di Banjarmasin* in the Supplement to his Catalogue (No. 191), claiming that it is identical to both the Jakarta and Leiden texts; the manuscript to which he refers has been edited by Arena Wati and deals with the multi-ethnic community of Pontianak, including the indigenous population as well as Chinese and Indian immigrants. This different text was composed by the Sultan of Matan on 27 Muharam 1313 Hijriah, that is 7 July 1895 (Arena Wati, 1989: 9). Here is a summary of the Jakarta manuscript.

The poem begins by praising the Dutch administration of the East Indies. When Major Verspijk was Resident, Banjarmasin was disturbed by a group of bandits led by Hidayatullah. Pangeran Syarif Hasyim was appointed to deal with them but was unsuccessful. Their activities grew worse and they even killed a Dutch regent. Pangeran Syarif Hasyim raided several of their hideouts and, because of this pressure, Hidayatullah and his followers surrendered. When he heard he was to be exiled to Jakarta, he escaped. Efforts were made on a large scale to find him. Pangeran Syarif Hasyim captured Hidayatullah's family and he reluctantly surrendered. The bandit was taken to Jakarta. Pangeran Syarif Hasyim was promoted to be ruler of Cangal Manunggal and awarded a medal.

The Dutch set out to arrest the remaining rebels. One of the leaders, Demang Wangkang, conditionally surrendered to the Resident but it took so long for his pardon to be granted that Demang Wangkang ordered his men to continue in their disobedience. He pillaged villages and eventually raided Banjarmasin. The Company sent military assistance and they bombarded the bandits. Unable to defend themselves, the rebels fled. Pangeran Syarif Hasyim was sent to various districts to explain the new arrangements. Rid of these rebels, Banjarmasin once more returned to peace (Atja, 1967a: 1-6).

Another poem dealing with Kalimantan is the *Syair Perang Wangkang* (Bat. Gen. 92). The poem tells how a number of merchants led by Haji Sulaiman were asked by the Dutch Company to fight the Wangkang who were ravaging the countryside. (The word "Wangkang" means "high sterned Chinese boats", according to Putri Minerva Mutiara who has edited this manuscript (1979: 11), but it may also refer to a location in southeastern Kalimantan.) The Wangkang begged for peace but the Dutch refused, knowing that further troops were on the way. The situation worsened and soon broke out into open warfare. The Company had the better of the fighting but the Wangkang continued to resist. The Malay merchants were reluctant to cooperate with the Company. The poem was composed by Haji Sulaiman, head of the Malay merchant community.

10.6.4 *Syair Raja Siak* (The King of Siak) (v.d. Wall Collection 273)

The poem *Syair Raja Siak* describes the development of Siak prior to its conquest by the Dutch in 1857. The syair was edited by Kosim H. R. (1978) and its contents are as follows.

The poem opens with a description of the extremely prosperous Port Bengkalis, which was continually visited by boats large and small. Unfortunately the state lacked a king. The ruler of Johor, who was a vassal of the Buginese, sent an envoy to Pagar Ruyung. His letter so infuriated the king of the Minangkabau region that the king gathered his army and they marched on Bengkalis. Next they attacked Johor. Quickly defeated, the King of Johor fled into the forest. The Minangkabau then marched on Siak and established a state there. The state quickly grew.

The king had two sons, who could never agree with each other. Their quarrels became so bad that the country descended into civil war and chaos. The king insisted that one of the two should leave the kingdom. The elder brother left. His younger brother became the crown prince and was to be the king after his father passed away.

After his formal appointment, the younger brother established a new kingdom called Indrapura. He went looking for his elder brother but couldn't find him. Shortly afterwards, the king became ill. Before he died, he ordered his sons to do their best to always live in peace and not to quarrel. The people mourned his passing. The younger son took his place on the throne and grieved his father's death.

After some time, the Dutch set out to attack Siak. The King put aside his grief and ordered his ministers to prepare fortresses, moats and weapons. The Dutch arrived and war broke out. For fifteen days neither side gained an advantage. After two months, the people of Siak attacked the Dutch ships. There was more fighting. Because the Siak weapons were inferior, they were forced to retreat and were eventually defeated. The war was over. The poem ends with a story of the king wanting to find a wife and sending his chief minister to negotiate on his behalf.

The *Syair Perang Siak* (KL. 154) was edited by Goudie, who also provided an English translation with relevant historical annotations (1989). There are some lines in the *Syair Perang Siak* which are not found in the *Syair Raja Siak*, for example,

51a	*Mendengar titah Paduka Ratu*
51b	*segala rakyat berhati mutu*
53c	*Negeri Buatan zaman sekarang*
53d	*ramainya bukan sebarang-barang.*

51a	When they heard the King's commands
51b	the people obeyed him
53c	Today the colony they established
53d	has a large and happy population.

"The colony they established" in line 53c may be Kuantan, which is another name for Indrapura as mentioned in the *Syair Raja Siak*. Goudie's edition includes Tenas Effendy's comments on two manuscripts held in Pelawan dan Siak respectively, as well as comments on the social functions of the syair (Goudie, 1989: 257-268).

10.6.5 *Syair Sultan Ahmad Tajuddin*

This poem describes events that took place during the reign of Sultan Tajuddin of Kedah, and is also called the *Syair Sultan Maulana* (The Poem of the Most Excellent Ruler) in his honour. There were few copies of this manuscript; the only one now surviving is ADD. 12394, held in the British Library. It has been edited twice in a very short period: firstly by Muhammad Yusoff Hasyim as *Syair Sultan Maulana, Suatu Penelitian Kritis tentang Hasil Pensejarahan Melayu Tradisional* (*Syair Sultan Maulana,* A Critical Study of a Traditional Malay Historical Text), Kuala Lumpur, 1980; and secondly, in 1985 by C. Skinner as *The Battle For Junk Ceylon,* with a translation and historical annotations. The two books are obviously similar, although Skinner's work is more detailed.

The poem was completed in 1810, soon after the Salang war. The name of the author is unknown, although Skinner suggests that he may have been the secretary of the Laksamana (Admiral) of Kedah, who had taken part in the war. A copy of the manuscript was given to J. McInnes, who served as a Malay translator in Penang from March 1812. McInnes is believed to have had a close relationship with the Kedah nobility, including the author of this poem. He passed the manuscript to John Crawford, who sold it to the British Museum (Skinner, 1985: 31). Here is a summary of the text (Muhammad Yusoff, 1980: xxiii - xxiv).

The manuscript opens with details of Kedah, a prosperous state, ruled by the just Baginda Sultan Maulana, together with his wise ministers and brave military officers.

It then describes how Patani rose up against Siam. Kedah was ordered to provide immediate assistance to Senggora. However, its troops could only reach Padang Terap, where they were stopped and unable to proceed. The Governor of Senggora was furious and the king was forced to send his Chief of Defence (Temenggung) and the army to Patani. When the Kedah troops arrived, the rebellion had been quelled. The king of Senggora was furious and had the Chief imprisoned. The king sent the Admiral to convey his apology. The apology was accepted and the Laksamana brought the Temenggung and the other senior officers home.

Later, Burma attacked many provinces and surrounded Pulau Salang. The king of Senggora ordered the coastal regions and the provinces to prepare their armies to fight Burma. The Admiral was ordered to take the Kedah troops and assist Pulau Salang. The fighting was fierce. The Burmese occupied Pulau Salang for six months before it could be taken back again. Datuk Maharaja, also known as Wazir (The Prime Minister), played an important part in the struggle. The poem ends with 25 stanzas that begin:

> *Sebab diperbuat sair ikatan*
> *supaya kerja nyata kelihatan*
> *tetap cara padang dan hutan*
> *tiada manis sajak sebutkan.*

> The reason for making these linked verses
> was to make clear what we have done
> enduring as the fields and forests
> that it is not for this poem to say.

The last verse concludes:

> *Patutlah kita sekalian umat*
> *membaca salawat pohonkan rahmat*
> *di atas fikir yang mencari hemat*
> *mematutkan sair hingga tamat.*

> It is right that all good Muslims
> should praise the Prophet and ask for blessing
> for the careful thought
> that has brought this poem to its end.

10.6.6 *Syair Siti Zubaidah Perang Melawan Cina* (Siti Zubaidah's War against China)

This syair contains very little historical material and might be better thought of as a romantic poem. Nevertheless, one of its editors believed that it did have some actual foundation and tried to locate it within a certain period of Chinese history (Abdul Mutalib, 1983: xlvi-xlvii). For this reason we will consider it in this part of our chapter.

There are not a lot of manuscripts of this poem. The oldest is held in the Library of SOAS (MS 37083) and bears the date 1256 H (1840). Its contents are as follows.

There was once a great king, Sultan Darman Syah, who ruled over a prosperous kingdom named Kembayat. The king had been married for many years but had no male heir. One day he told the queen that he intended to give alms to a holy man as a way of winning divine favour. In time, the queen gave birth to a very handsome son. They named him Zainal Abidin. At the age of six, he was sent to study the Koran and learn the arts of weaponry. He grew to be a splendid young man.

One day there was a disturbance in the kingdom. A merchant refused to honour his promise to sell goods to a visiting Chinese boat's captain and sold them to another merchant instead. They quarrelled and the captain was imprisoned for using coarse language. His boat was burned and his crew fled back to China. The ruler of China was angry and ordered his seven brave and wise sons to lead the army against Kembayat.

One night Zainal Abidin dreamed that he met an intelligent princess who was as beautiful as an angel. He immediately set sail to find the princess. When he reached Pulau Peringgi, he heard someone melodiously chanting the Koran and wanted to meet that person. Disguising himself as a royal water-carrier, he met Siti Zubaidah, the one who had been chanting the holy book. He was overwhelmed by her loveliness, "her black eyes, cute nose, curving eyebrows, long hair, slender waist and full breasts", and the wonderful way she looked around her. Siti Zubaidah was the daughter of the senior Muslim scholar, the former king of Iragan Kastan. Because of his devout nature, the king had handed over his kingdom to his son Muhammad Tahir and gone to live on Pulau Peringgi.

Zainal Abidin won the heart of Siti Zubaidah and they were married. On their way home to Kembayat, they visited Yaman and Zainal Abidin helped the King ward off an attack by the King of Menggala. As a reward, Zainal Abidin received Princess Sajarah as a second wife.

The King of Kembayat was delighted to welcome his son and the two women. The second wife treated Zubaidah with contempt and always spoke harshly to her, but she could not disturb the elder woman's patient demeanour. One day, the Chinese army attacked Kembayat and captured Zainal Abidin. He refused to marry the daughter of the emperor and was imprisoned in a poisoned well.

Zubaidah ran and hid in the forest, where she gave birth to a son. In order to continue her journey, she was forced to leave the child behind. Later she met Princess Rukiah, who had been driven out from her kingdom in Yunan. They became good friends and even studied weaponry together with a warrior who lived in seclusion on a hill. Then they disguised themselves as men and regained Rukiah's kingdom. Now it was Rukiah's turn to help Zubaidah. They disguised themselves as dancing girls and went to China, where, after various difficulties, they freed Zainal Abidin and his fellow prisoners, and took them to Yunan.

The story then tells how Muhammad Tahir invited his father, His Majesty the Senior Muslim Scholar, to Irakan Kastan. He knew that his sister, Zubaidah, had married and gone to Kembayat. One time, Muhammad Tahir went hunting and he met a "very handsome child, the colour of beaten gold", wearing an emerald ring, and bearing the name of The Senior Scholar Sultan of Irak. He realized that the boy was Zubaidah's son. Tahir cared for the child and gave him the new name, Raja Ahmad Syah Bangsawan Muda.

The king of Yunan's allies gathered and prepared to invade China. Muhammad Tahir and Ahmad Syah Bangsawan Muda also joined them. Zubaidah recognized her long lost son but did not immediately identify herself to him. Using the best of all strategies, the King of Yunan defeated the King of China, with the help of Zubaidah, his royal allies and their noble warriors. The Chinese princesses were forced to convert to Islam. Zainal Abidin married the Queen of China and then celebrated his nuptials with Princess Rukiah. Zubaidah revealed her identity and a joyful reunion followed.

The armies escorted Zainal Abidin back to Kembayat. The old king was very pleased to meet his son and the daughter-in-law whom he had treated so badly. The queen was ashamed of her actions. Following Zubaidah's appointment as Queen of Kembayat, the kings of the surrounding nations returned home.

> *Tamatlah syair Siti Zubaidah*
> *tiga bulan baru sudah*
> *Raja akhir habislah sudah*
> *tengah gelora hendak berpindah.*

> This completes the syair of Siti Zubaidah
> three months later
> the king passed away
> in the hustle and bustle of moving.

After this stanza, the author laments his own wretched fate, "no parents, my friends hate me, I cannot look them in the face." He leaves this advice for his readers:

> *Inilah pesan dagang yang lata*
> *kepada sekalian adik dan kakak*
> *membaca syair jangan dikata*
> *karena tulisan terlalu leta*
> ... ...
> *Pesan kedua ikhlas di hati*
> *kepada sekalian encik dan siti*
> *pikirkan kisah dengan seperti*
> *dari awal akhir ditamati.*

> *Encik dan tuan, lebai dan haji*
> *jika tuan berkehendak membeli*
> *syair dan kitab banyak sekali*
> *harganya murah tiada terperi.*

> This is the advice of this wretched pilgrim
> to all my brothers and sisters
> don't criticize this syair when reading it
> because of its poor writing
> ...
> My second piece of innocent advice
> to all you ladies and gentlemen
> think of this story as is proper
> from start to the very end.

> Gentlemen and squires, holy men of various degrees
> if you would like to buy
> a good many poems and books
> the price is cheap beyond compare.

10.7 Religious Syair

The most important syair are those that deal with religious topics. We have explained that Hamzah Fansuri was the first person to write poems of this type and his example was followed by other poets in Acheh such as Abdul Jamal, Hasan Fansuri and several other unnamed writers. Abdul Rauf himself wrote a poem entitled *Syair Makrifat*, A Poem of Mystical Knowledge (Van Ophuijsen, 78). The form first dealt with religious topics and only later slowly came to be used for topics that were not connected with religion.

There are various types of religious syair, depending on their contents. First are the Sufi poems written by Hamzah Fansuri and his contemporaries. Second are those which deal with Muslim doctrine, such as: *Syair Ibadat*, Religious Practice; *Syair Sifat Dua Puluh*, Twenty Attributes; *Syair Rukun Haji*, The Pilgrimage; *Syair Kiamat*, The Grave; *Syair Cerita di dalam Kubur*, Stories from Within the Grave, and so on. Third are poems describing the lives of the prophets, such as: *Syair Nabi Allah Ayub*, The Prophet Ayub (Job); *Syair Nabi Allah dengan Firaun*, The Prophet of God and Pharoah; *Syair Yusuf*, Yusuf (Joseph); *Syair Isa*, Isa (Jesus), and so on. The fourth category give advice and instruction to their readers and listeners, such as: *Syair Nasihat*, Advice; *Syair Nasihat Bapak Kepada Anaknya*, A Father's Advice to his Child; *Syair Nasihat Laki-laki dan Perempuan*, Advice for Men and Women, and so on. Poems such as *Syair Takbir Mimpi*, The Interpretation of Dreams, and *Syair Raksi*, Omens, may also possibly belong to this cateory. We shall now consider the works of Hamzah Fansuri and his contemporaries, as well as several other important syairs.

10.7.1 Hamzah Fansuri

Hamzah Fansuri was the first person to write syair but many of the works attributed to him by Doorenbos (1933: 16-89), such as *Syair Perahu*, The Boat; *Syair Bahr an-Nisa'*, The Sea of Women; *Syair Dagang*, The Merchant; *Syair Burung Pingai*, The Bird of Life, and a few others, are not by him at all (Drewes, 1986: 18). Thirty-two poems testify to his pre-eminence; these have been studied by Drewes and Brakel and translated into English. Their commentary has been of great assistance to me in writing this section.

Drewes suggests that the relatively small number of poems may be due to the burning of his works by Nuruddin ar-Raniri during the reign of Sultan Iskandar Thani. It may also have something to do with the high number of Arabic words and the difficulty of understanding the works in general (Drewes & Brakel, 1986: 35). This difficulty may be the reason Syamsuddin al-Sumatrani felt that it was necessary to write *syarah* (explanations) about some of the poems (1986: 194-224). The thirty-two poems can be divided into six different categories, depending on their contents.

The first group consists of 13 poems, I-XIII, of which twelve begin with the words, "*Aho segala kita yang*" (Oh, all of us who ...). The first poem commands the faithful to pray regularly and not to seek pleasure in secular learning. It also tells of the author's mystical experience:

> *Hamzah nin asalnya Fansuri*
> *mendapat wujud di tanah Syahrnawi*

> *Beroleh khilafat ilmu yang asli*
> *Daripada Abd. al-Qadir Jilani.*

> Hamzah who came from Fansuri
> attained his being in Syahrnawi
> He received his authority to convey the true knowledge
> from Abd. Al-Qadir Jilani.

Poem II orders mankind not to be negligent in the study of the Quran and to learn law (*syariat*), follow the path of the mystical brotherhoods (*tarikat*), and study esoteric wisdom (*hakikat*), in order to achieve divine union (*makrifat*). Poem III encourages mankind to obey the Tradition and the Scriptures, because they contain God's word. Poem IV introduces seven of God's important attributes: life, knowledge, will, almightiness, speech, hearing and seeing. Poem V orders mankind not to forget *ma'al-hayat* (the water of life), because all people will return to the *ma'al-hayat*, just as the wave returns to the sea. Poems VII and VIII again order mankind to seek *makrifat*, which contains *syariat*, *tarikat*, and *hakikat*. Poem IX encourages mankind to pray much, not to be greedy, and not to love the world. Poem X reminds mankind not to forget *rabbai-'alamin*, The Lord of all the Worlds, and to work to know one's own self. Poems XI and XIII advise mankind not to love the world, in order to: "*Hidup dalam dunia umpama dagang, datang musim kita kan pulang*" ("Live in this world like a voyager/ When the winds change, it is time to return home").

The second group of poems consists of seven works, XIV-XX, explaining God's perfection and eternal characteristics. God is the Creator and He sent the Prophet into the world with the Quran for the guidance of mankind. In Poem XVIII, Hamzah writes:

> *Cahayanya terlalu nyarak*
> *Dengan rupa kita yang banyak.*
> *Iya juga takir dan arak*
> *Jangan kau cari jauh hai anak.*

> His light is very bright
> It is in all our various forms
> He is the cup and the wine
> There is no need to search far for Him, oh child.

Drewes insists that these few lines contain the core of Hamzah Fansuri's teachings: "*Man' arafa nafsahu fa qad 'arafa Rabbahu*" (Whoever knows himself, knows his God) (Drewes & Brakel, 1986: 165).

The third group of poems consists of three works, XXI - XXIII. In Poem XXI, Hamzah recommends that Muslims pray more often and that they not desire the world that is no more than a passing parade. The poem concludes:

> *Hamzah Fansuri di dalam Makah*
> *Mencari Tuhan di bait al-Ka'bah*

> *Di Barus ke Kudus terlalu payah*
> *Akhirnya dapat di dalam rumah.*

> Hamzah Fansuri in Mecca
> Searched for God in the Holy Ka'bah
> From Barus to Jerusalem is a very difficult journey
> Finally I found Him in my own house.

Poem XXII encourages us to conquer our mind, feelings and desires, and learn to know ourselves. Whoever knows his ruler knows himself, because we and our king are like the waves and the ocean. Poem XXIII has the same theme: knowing yourself is the best way to find knowledge of God.

The fourth group consists of four poems on birds, XXIV-XXVII. In the first, Hamzah says that a person searching for God is like a bird without feathers (*tayr ul-'uryan*), and that we have no need of silver and gold. Through *syariat, tarikat, hakikat,* and *makrifat* we can attain our goal. In the fourth poem, XXVII, mankind is compared to a parrot that is created from God's pure light. The poem also states that the knowledge of God will give us eternal life.

The fifth group consists of three poems, XXVII-XXIX, on the sea. The relationship between mankind and God is like that of the waves and the sea. Strong winds create the waves; when the winds cease, the waves die away. In other words, the waves are not separate from the sea and mankind is not separate from the creator. We should recognize our true nature and make every effort to know ourselves.

The sixth group consists of two poems, XXXI dan XXXII. The first is also known as *Syair Ikan Tongkol* (The Tuna Fish) (Roolvink, 1964: 243) Hamzah compares the Sufi who knows his or her true origins to a fish that feels at home in the sea. The ignorant Sufi, who refuses to study with a Master, is like a stupid fish looking for water in a rock. In the second poem, the person searching for God in the wrong place is like the whale from the China Sea searching for water on Mount Sinai. Hamzah suggests that the searcher for knowledge should:

> *Satukan hangat dan dingin*
> *Tinggalkan juga loba dan ingin*
> *Hancurkan hendak seperti lilin*
> *Mangkanya dapat kerjamu licin.*

> Treat hot and cold as one and the same
> leave greed and desire
> have your wants melt like wax
> then your work will progress smoothly.

These are the 32 poems scholars consider authentic works of Hamzah Fansuri. As we have mentioned, there are another three that are often attributed to him, although there is considerable doubt about this: *Syair Perahu, Syair Dagang,* and *Syair Bahr an-Nisa'*.

10.7.2 Syair Perahu (The Boat) (Doorenbos, 1933: 16-21)

Hamzah Fansuri always included his name in the last stanza of each poem. This is the case in the works discussed above; it is not the case with copies of this poem. The versification is also not as smooth as the other works (Braginsky 1975: 407-408, note 2). However, the contents and the spirit of the writing are similar to the other poems, and we might just as well assume it is by Hamzah Fansuri until proven otherwise.

The poem compares human life to a boat sailing in a sea full of whales and sharks. Often we have to endure hurricanes and typhoons. The sailors therefore need to cling to LILA (*La ilaha illa 'llah*, There is no god but God), destroy all lusts (*nafsu*), and not bother about gathering gold and coins. Further, pilgrims are advised to know themselves in order to know the Creator, because "the servant and the Lord are not different". Finally the merchant is advised to study so as to be able to answer the questions of Mungkar and Nakir once one has died.

10.7.3 Syair Dagang (The Merchant) (Doorenbos, 1933: 21-33)

Although Teeuw (1952: 26) and Drewes (1986: 21) both doubt the authenticity of this poem, Syed Naguib does not. He suggests that the pen-names used, *Si Tukar* (The Exchanger) and *Si Tamthil* (The Exemplar), belong to Hamzah Fansuri (Syed Naguib, 1971: 8-9). I tend to agree with Teeuw and Drewes.

The poem tells of a merchant who has gone abroad to find his fortune. When he has much gold and silver, he has many friends. When he is sick or poor, his friends look at him with contempt. The merchant never has enough to eat or drink, but he always endures excessive suffering. He can only "write a poem to console himself". The idea behind the poem is in no way typical of Hamzah Fansuri, who warned travelers against a love of silver and gold, telling them to "leave greed and desire", because one should "Live in the world like a voyager/ When the winds change, it is time to return home". Drewes and Brakel claim that the pseudonym *Si Tama'ie* (Shallow) is indicative of "a gloomy Minangkabau" living away from home (Drewes dan Brakel, 1986: 21).

10.7.4 *Bahr An-Nisa'* (Sea of Women) (Doorenbos, 1933: 65-70)

Voorhoeve denies that this poem was written by Hamzah Fansuri (1968: 272). Syed Naguib, however, disagrees with Voorhoeve. He notes that many of the terms used—such as *bahr, al-bahryan, orang, insan, rajil* (plural, *rajul*), *pedang 'alat,* and *jauhar*—appear frequently in Hamzah's work and could not possibly be the work of anyone else (Syed Naguib, 1971: 1-23). He suggests that it was written during the reign of Syah Alam (Alauddin Ri'ayat Syah).

Drewes has studied four versions of this poem and found them to be very different from each other. None of them mentions Hamzah's name. He concludes that the four derive from an earlier text by an unknown author; the poem may be an adaptation of an Arabic poem (Drewes, 1986). Who is right?

Before we can answer this question, we need to survey the contents of the poem. The syair compares a man about to be married to a person sailing on *bahr an-nisa'* (a sea of women). His pleasure is perfect and the waters are as sweet as the waters of the "zam-zam" well in Mecca. But like the ocean, there are also high waves, corals as sharp as an axe, swift currents, fierce waves, and poisonous serpents. Many ships crack and sink. But if the boat is strong, if the teacher is wise and the navigator experienced, we can safely cross the ocean. In other words, this is a poem of pre-marital advice, encouraging the taking of advice from a wise teacher and marrying a woman whose faith is strong. If the woman is as perfect as the wives of the last prophet, both the man and his wife will be abundantly happy. But it is difficult to find a good woman unless one already has a wise teacher. The Achehnese version held in London quotes the Arabic proverb, *Man lam yajid ladhdhat fi 'l-nisa' fa-lam yajid ladhdhat fi 'l-akhira,* A man who finds no pleasure in women, will find no pleasure in the world to come.

The idea is very different from, and even contradicts, what we find in other poems by Hamzah. In his poetry, Hamzah always encourages his audience to renounce the world and its pleasures, because we will all pass away with only a "single covering of cloth" (Drewes and Brakel, 1986: 60-61). How could such a man encourage his readers to find pleasure in the world and, most particularly, in women?

The poem is certainly not the work of Hamzah Fansuri. According to Drewes and Brakel, the poem may have been composed by Leube Baba, whose name is to be found at the end of the version held in London (1986: 19). According to Ricklefs and Voorhoeve, Leube Baba lived at the time of Sultan Badruddin (1764-1765) (Drewes and Brakel, 1986: 19).

Doorenbos also included a number of other syairs in his dissertation, claiming that they had no titles. Drewes and Brakel disagree with this claim (1986: 21-24). The *Syair Jawi fasal fi bayan At-tawhid* (Doorenbos, 1933: 61-64) is the work of Hasan Fansuri, a pupil of Hamzah Fansuri; the *Al-naka'ith fi bayan al-awwalin* is the work of Abdul Jamal, the pupil of Hasan Fansuri. Syed Naguib disagrees with them, claiming that the name "Hasan Fansuri" is an incorrect transcription of Hamzah Fansuri (Syed Naguib, 1971: 31-32), and that Abdul Jamal is not a name but a Sufi concept referring to absolute beauty, i.e. Paradise or the souls in Paradise (Syed Naguib, 1971: 47-49). I am inclined to agree with Drewes, because the name Syekh al-Fakir Hasan Fansuri occurs several times in the *Syair Jawi fasal fi bayan at-tauhid,* and the author explains that he received the idea of writing his poem from Hamzah Fansuri. He also provides a summary of Hamzah's writings, including the mystical poems (Drewes and Brakel, 1986: 22). The name Abdul Jamal also occurs several times in the *al-Naka'ith fi bayan al-awwalin.* Hasan Fansuri is also mentioned twice by Abdul Jamal as the author of *Miftah al-asrar,* a commentary on Hamzah's *Asrar al-'Anfin.* I will not discuss these extra poems here because, as Syed Naguib has said, their contents are the same as the other works of Hamzah Fansuri (Syed Naguib, 1971: 31). And I have already described those ideas in considerable detail.

10.7.5 *Syair Kiamat* (Day of Judgement)

This poem tells about death, what happens in the grave, and the signs of the approach of Judgement Day. There are not many manuscripts of this work. The relationship of this syair to the *Syair Hari Kiamat* (KL 133C, KL. 152), held in Leiden, is difficult to establish from the description given in the catalogue. Muhammad Fanani (1978-1979) describes the contents of the *Syair Kiamat* (v.d. Wall. 228), held in Jakarta, as follows.

The poem first tells about what will happen on Judgement Day. Those who have done evil throughout their lives will be condemned to the flames of hell. Only those who have lived pious and virtuous lives will escape. Wealth will be of no assistance at the hour of death. Therefore we should obey our parents and worship God so that He will protect us from being punished.

Next the poem describes the signs of Judgement Day. The Prophet Isa (Jesus), the Messiah, will come into the world to fight the Anti-Christ, Yakjuj and Makjuj, Dabbatul Ard, and the King of Ethiopia. The work describes the punishments of hell and the pleasures of heaven. The descriptions are almost the same as those in the Arabic work by Nuruddin, *Akhbar al-akhirat fi ahwal al-kiyama,* discussed above in Chapter 7.

The author was Encik Hussin, a Buginese living in Keling (Kalang?). He finished the poem in 1281 H (1865), after moving from Trengganu to Singapore. In Singapore he became conscious of the sins he had committed; he desired to repent and undertake the pilgrimage to Mecca. The poem was written to remind Muslims to live wisely and not engage in sin or evil deeds.

10.7.6 *Syair Takbir Mimpi* (The Interpretation of Dreams)

The *Syair Takbir Mimpi* deals with the interpretation of dreams and resembles a Javanese almanac (*primbon*). Overbeck's English translation is based on an edition printed in Singapore in 1326 H (1908). The work has often been reprinted: an earlier manuscript from 1306 H describes Muhammad Taib as the printer and Ibrahim as the writer.

The poem explains the meaning of various dreams, in the following manner:
(1) if you dream of Allah, this is a sign you will become great;
(2) if you dream of the Prophet, this is a sign your wishes will come true;
(3) if you dream of an angel, this is a sign you will be blessed;
(4) if you dream of heaven, this is a sign you will be happy;
(5) if you dream that the sun and the moon fall into your lap, this is a sign you will be honoured;
(6) if you dream of an earthquake, this is a sign you will be imperfect;
(7) if you dream of a comet, this is a sign you will be prosperous;
(8) if you dream of thunder and lightning, this is a sign you will experience difficulties;
(9) if you dream of heavy rain, this is a sign your nation will be blessed;
(10) if you dream of taking a wife, this is a sign you will enjoy yourself;
(11) if you dream of suicide, this is a sign you will commit a crime;
(12) if you dream of being imprisoned, this is a sign you will have unlimited wealth;
(13) if you dream of being hit, this is a sign you will receive something which will make you happy;
(14) if you dream of going on a sea-voyage, this is a sign you will make a great profit;
(15) if you dream of sex, this is a sign you will do something wrong, don't play about;
(16) if you dream of becoming an animal, this is a sign you will be sick;
(17) if you dream of restraining a dog, this is a sign you will be fine, there is nothing to worry about;
(18) if you dream of a cat coming into your house, this is a sign you will receive a visit from a friend;

(19) if you dream of eating the flesh of a frisky mousedeer, this is a sign you will be granted a child;
(20) if you dream of being taken by a tiger, this is a sign something bad will happen to you. (Overbeck, 1929)

10.7.7 *Syair Raksi* (Omens)

The *Syair Raksi* is a book to help in predicting the future. It has been printed many times in Singapore. The text translated by Overbeck (1923) was composed by Haji Muhammad Amin. Overbeck describes its contents as follows.

The poem consists of six chapters. The first deals with marriage partners and whether they are suitable to each other or not. In order to decide this, give each letter in the first person's names a numerical value based on the Arabic alphabet. So, if the name is Hasan: *ha* = 6, *sin* = 60, *nun* = 50. Add the numbers together and then divide them by 9. In this case, the remainder is 1. Now do the same with the name of the woman. Add the two remainders together and divide by 9 one more time. If the final figure is 2, their prospects are excellent.

> *Kalau esa samanya dua,*
> *terlalu baik raksinya,*
> *kepada yang lain tiada kecewa,*
> *Umpama Adam dengan Hawa.*

> If one and two occur,
> the omens are very good,
> they will not be disappointed in each other,
> just like Adam and Eve.

The second chapter, *Syair Hari Bulan,* On Days of the Month, predicts auspicious and inauspicious days:

> *Inilah permulaan sehari bulan,*
> *tiap-tiap pekerjaan sangat handalan*
> *menghadap raja bertemu taulan*
> *berlayar berniaga sangat kebetulan.*

> On the first day of the month
> all tasks will turn out well
> meeting the king, being with a friend
> going on a trading expedition, everything will work for the best.

Chapter three advises readers to study diligently and avoid evil. Four tells of the misery of those who are in debt; five tells of the happiness of those who are free of debt and avoid evil. The sixth and last chapter describes the best times for meeting other people:

> *jika hendak bertemu orang*
> *bangsa yang baik atau kurang*
> *dipikirkan kelapangan orang*
> *jangan pergi waktu sebarang.*

> If you want to meet someone
> whether they be noble or not
> think of when they might be free
> don't just go any old time.

REFERENCES

Abdul Mutalib Abdul Ghani (ed.)
1958.   *Syair Siti Zubaidah Perang Cina*, Kuala Lumpur.

Akademi Pengajian Melayu
n.d.   *Syair Perang Mengkasar, Syair Marifat Islam, Syair Isma Yatim*, Kuala Lumpur.

Akbar Saidina & Haji Muhammad Yahya
1934.   *Syair Abdul Muluk*, Jakarta.

Al-Attas, Syed Naguib
1968.   *The Origin of the Malay Shair*, Kuala Lumpur.
1971.   *Concluding Postscript to the Origin of the Malay Sha'ir*, Kuala Lumpur.

Alisjahbana, Sutan Takdir
1954.   *Puisi Lama*, Djakarta.

Altmann, G.
1963.   "Phonic Structure of Malay Pantun," *Archiv Orientalni*, 31, pp. 274-286.

Altmann, G. & R. Stokovsky
1956.   "The climax in Malay Pantun," *Asian and African Studies* (Bratislaya), pp. 13-20.

Arena Wati
1989a.   *Syair Pangeran Syarif*, Kuala Lumpur.
1989b.   *Syair Pangeran Syarif Hasyim Al-Qudus*, Kuala Lumpur.
1989c.   *Syair Perang Cina di Monterado*, Kuala Lumpur.

Atja
1967a.   "Sjair Peperangan di Bandjarmasin," *Manusia Indonesia*, 1 (3), pp. 1-6.
1967b.   "Syair Perang Palembang," *Seri Sarjana Karya*, no. 1.

Braasem, W.A.
1950.   "Pantuns," *Orientatie*, XXVVIII, pp. 27-42.
1950.   *Pantuns, vertaald en ingeleid*, Djakarta.

Braasem, W. A. & R. Nieuwenhuys
1952.   *Volkspoezie uit Indonesia*, Groningen & Djakarta.

Braginsky, V. Y.
1975.   "Some remarks on the structure of the 'Syair Perahu' by Hamzah Fansuri," *BKI*, 131(4).

Chambert-Loir, H.
1982.   *Syair Kerajaan Bima*, Jakarta.

Dep P. dan K.
1981.   *Syair Carang Kelima*, Jakarta.

Dewan Bahasa dan Pustaka
1990.   *Kurik Kundi Merah Saga. Kumpulan Pantun Melayu*, Kuala Lumpur.

Djadjuli
1961.   "Transkripsi Sjair Tjinta Berahi," *Bahasa dan Budaya*, 9 pp. 91-133
1971   "Sedikit tentang Sjair Tadjul Muluk", *Bahasa dan Budaya*, 10, pp. 7-36.

Djajadiningrat, R. H.
1933/34. "Arti Pantun Melayu yang Gaib," *Pujangga Baru*.

Drewes, G. W. J.
1986 "Nur al-din al-Raniri Charge of Heresy against Hamzah and Shamsuddin from an International Point of View," in C.D. Grijns & S. O. Robson (eds.) *Cultural Contact and Textual Interpretation*. Dordrecht.

Drewes, G. W. J. & L. F. Brakel
1986. *The Poems of Hamzah Fansuri* (Bibliotheca Indonesica 26), Dordrecht.

Goudie, D. J.
1989. *Syair Perang Siak*, Kuala Lumpur.

Harun Mat Piah
1980. "Syair Angreni - sebuah syair panji yang tipikal," *Jurnal Budaya Melayu*, Vol. 2 (1), pp. 42-50.
1989. *Puisi Melayu Tradisional*, Kuala Lumpur.

Hoevell, W. R. van
1843. "Sjair Bidasari, een oorspronkelijk Maleisch gedicht," *VBG*, 19.
1856. *Sjair Ken Tamboehan*, Leiden.

Hooykaas, C.
1947. *Over Maleische Literatuur*, Leiden.

Ikram, A.
1964. "Pantun dan wangsalan," *Madjalah Ilmu-ilmu Sastra Indonesia*, 2 (2), pp. 263.

Jamilah Hj. Ahmad
1989. *Syair Bidasari*, Kuala Lumpur.

Jumsari Jusuf
1970. "Syair Sultan Mahmud Radja Muda," *Manusia Indonesia*, 4 (3 & 4).
1971. "Sjair Damar Wulan", *Manusia Indonesia*, 4 (1 & 2), pp. 172-238.
1972. "Sjair Singapura dimakan api" (W. 270), *Manusia Indonesia*, 6 (1 & 2), pp. 4-26.
1976. "Syair Burung Nuri," *Archipel*, 11, pp. 57-70.

Jumsari et al.
1978. *Antologi syair simbolik dalam sastra Indonesia lama*, Jakarta.

Kathirithamby-Wells J. & Muhammad Yusoff Hashim
1985. *The Syair Mukomuko: some historical aspects of a nineteenth century Sumatran chronicle*, Kuala Lumpur.

Kern, W.
1948. "Aantekeningen op de Sjair Hemop," *TBG*, 82.

Klinkert, H.C
1868. "Iets over de pantoens of Minnezangen der Maleijers," *BKI*, pp. 384-410.
1886. *Drie Maleische Gedichten*, Leiden.

Kosim, H. R.
1978. *Syair Perang Siak*, Jakarta.

Marrison, G. E.
1951. "A Malay poem in old Sumatran characters," *JMBRAS*, 24 (1), pp. 162-165.

Matheson, V.
1983. "Question arising from a nineteenth century Riau syair," *Review of Indonesian and Malaysian Affairs*, vol. 17, pp. 1-61.

Millie, J.
2004. *Syair Bidasari*, Leiden.

Mohd. Hashim Taib
1968. *Shair Yatim Nestapa*, Kuala Lumpur.

Mohd. Taib Osman
1968. "Pantun, Shair dan Sajak: dari segi pandangan diakronis dan sinkronis," *Penulis*, 2 (1).

Mohd. Yusof Md. Nor
1986. *Syair Sinyor Kosta*, Kuala Lumpur.

Muhammad Fanani
1978/79. *Naskah Syair Kiamat dalam Sastra Indonesia lama*, Jakarta.

Muhammad Hj. Salleh
1982. "Preliminary notes on the esthetics of the Malay pantun," *Jurnal Budaya Melayu*, 4 (1), pp. 70-78.

Muhammad Yusoff Hashim
1980. *Syair Sultan Maulana: suatu penelitian kritis tentang hasil pensejarahan Melayu tradisional*, Kuala Lumpur.

N. M. Rangkoto
1982. *Pantun Adat Minangkabau*, Jakarta.

Ophuijsen, Ch. A. van
1904. *Het Maleische volksdicht*, Leiden.

Overbeck, H.
1914. "Shaer Burong Punggok," *JSBRAS*, 76, pp. 193-218.
1922. "The Malay pantun," *JSBRAS*, 85, pp. 4-28.
1923. "Shaer Raksi," *JMBRAS*, 1 (2), pp. 282-307.
1929. "Shaer Ta'bir Mimpi," *JMBRAS*, 7 (2), pp. 338-375.
1932. "Shaer Dandan Setia," *JMBRAS*, 10 (1), pp. 141-158.
1934. "Malay animal and flower shaers," *JMBRAS*, 12 (2), pp. 108-148.

Phillips, N.
1981. *Sijobang: sung narrative poetry of West Sumatra*, Cambridge.

Pijnappel, J.
1883. "Over de Maleische pantoens" (On pantun Melayu), *BKI*, uitgegeven vanwege te Gelegenheid van het 6e Internationale Congress der Orientalisten te Leiden, pp. 161-175, 's-Gravenhage.

Prampolini, G.
1951. "De Pantoen en de verwante dichtvormen in de volkspoezie," *Indonesie*, 5 (3), pp. 234-243.

Putri Minerva Mutiara
1979. *Syair Perang Wangkang*, Jakarta.

Pyan B. Husayn
1974. "Struktur plot cerita pantun Sunda dan cerita penglipur lara," *DB*, 18 (4), pp. 163-169.

Raja Iskandar
1964. *Shair Burong Punggok*, Kuala Lumpur.

Roolvink, R.
1964. "Two New 'Old' Malay Manuscripts," *MIS*, pp. 242-255.
1966. "Five-line song in the Sejarah Melayu," *BKI*, 122, pp. 455-457.

Rusconi, J.
1935. *Sjair Kompeni Welanda berperang dengan Tjina*, Dissertation, Utrecht.

Siti Hawa Haji Salleh
1987. *Cendekia Kesusasteraan Melayu Tradisional*, Kuala Lumpur.

Skinner, C.
1963. "Sjair Perang Mengkasar," *VKI*, 40.
1973. "Shaer Kampong Gelam terbakar," *JMBRAS*, 45 (1), pp. 21-56.
1985. *The Battles for Junk Ceylon, The Syair Sultan Maulana, text, translation and notes* (Bibliotheca Indonesica 25), Dordrecht.

Sweeney, A.
1971. "Some Observations on the Malay Shair," *JMBRAS*, 44 (1), pp. 58-66.

Teeuw, A.
1952. *Taal en Versbow*, Amsterdam.
1966a. *Shair Ken Tambuhan*, Kuala Lumpur.
1966b. "The Malay sha'ir. Problems of origin and tradition," *BKI*, 122, pp. 429-446.

Teeuw, A. et al.
2004. *A Merry Senhor in the Malay World: Four Texts of the Syair Sinyon Kosta*, Leiden.

Thomas, P.
1979. "Syair and pantun prosody," *Indonesia*, 27, pp. 51-64.

Tuti Munawar
1978. *Syair Bidasari*, Jakarta.

Voorhoeve, P.
1968. "The Origin of the Malay Syair," *BKI*, 124 (2).
1970. "The author of the Sjair Raden Menteri,", *BKI*, 126, pp. 259-260.

Wieringa, E. P.
1998. *Catalogue of Malay and Minangkabau Manuscripts in the Library of Leiden University and other Collection in the Netherlands*, Vol. 1, Leiden.

Winstedt, R. O.
1943. "Nature in Malay literature and folk verse," *JRAS*, pts 1 & 2, pp. 27-33.
1958-9. *Kesusastraan Melayu: Rampai-rampai*, London.

Wilkinson, R. J.
1907. *Malay Literature I* (in Papers on Malay Subjects), Kuala Lumpur, pp. 51-53.

Woelders, M. O.
1975. "Het Sultanaat Palembang 1881-1825," *VKI*, 72.

Yustan Aziddin
1981. *Syair Carang Kulina*, Jakarta.

Yusuf Iskandar
1973. "Syair Perang Mengkasar sebagai sebuah karya sejarah," *DB*, 17 (1), pp. 20-32.

Zahir Ahmad
1991. *Syair Agung*, Kuala Lumpur.

Zainal Abidin Bakar
1983. *Kumpulan Pantun Melayu*, Kuala Lumpur.

Bibliography

Manuscript Catalogues

Abu Hassan Sham
1974 "Naskah-naskah Melayu di Museum Serawak," *DB*, 19 (7), pp. 336-342.

Achadiati Ikram
2004 *Katalog Naskah Palembang*, Tokyo.

Behrend, T. E.
1989 *Katalog Induk Naskah-naskah Indonesia Jilid I: Museum Sonobudoyo Yogyakarta*, Jakarta.
1998 *Katalog Induk Naskah-naskah Indonesia Jilid 4: Perpustakaan Nasional Republik Indonesia*, Jakarta.

Cabaton, A.
1912 *Catalogue Sommaire des Manuscrits Indiens, Indochinois et Malaya-Polynesians de la Bibliotheque Nationale*, Paris, pp. 217-268.

Chambert-Loir, H.
1980a "Catalogue des catalogues de manuscrits Malais," *Archipel*, 20, pp. 45-69.
1980b "Les manuscrits Malais de Bale, Lund, Singapour et Paris," *Archipel*, 20, pp. 87-98.

Chambert-Loir, H. & Oman Fathurahman
1999 *Khazanah Naskah: Panduan Koleksi Naskah-naskah Indonesia Sedunia*, Jakarta.

DBP
1999 *Ensiklopedia Sejarah dan Kebudayaan Melayu*, 5 Vols., Kuala Lumpur.

Gallop, A. T.
1994 *The Legacy of Malay Letters*, London.

Gallop A. T. & B. Arps
1991 *Golden Letters: Writing Traditions of Indonesia*, London.

Greentree, R. & E. W. B. Nicholson
1910 *Catalogue of Malay manuscripts and manuscripts relating to the Malay Language in the Bodleian Library*, Oxford.

Howard, J. H.
1966 *Malay Manuscripts: A bibliographical guide*, Kuala Lumpur.

Ibrahim bin Kassim
1973 "Katalog Manuskrip," *DB*, 17 (11), pp. 516-536.

Departement of Education and Cuture, Indonesia
1972   *Katalogus Naskah Melayu Museum Pusat,* Jakarta.

Iskandar, T.
1999   *Catalogue of Malay, Minangkabau and South Sumatran Manuscripts in the Netherlands,* Two Vols., Leiden. KITLV Press.

Juynboll, H. H.
1899   *Catalogus van de Maleische en Sundaneesche handschriften der Leidsche Universiteits-Bibliotheek,* Leiden.
1911   *Suplement op de catalogus van de Javaansche en Madoereesche handschriften,* Part 11, Leiden.

Kratz, E. U.
1989   *Katalog der Malaiischen Handschriften der Koniglichen Bibliothek in Berlin von C. Snouck Hurgronje,* Stuttgart.

Kumar A. & J. H. McGlynn
1996   *Illuminations: The Writing Traditions of Indonesia,* Jakarta.

Mohd. Taib Osman
1972   "Laporan: Naskah-naskah dan Alat-alat Budaya Melayu di beberapa pusat pengajian di Great Britain dan Jerman Barat," *Nusantara,* 1, pp. 60-82.

National Library of Malaysia
2002   *Warisan Manuskrip Melayu,* Kuala Lumpur.

Oman Fathurahman & Munawar Holil
2007   *Katalog Naskah Ali Hasjmy,* Acheh & Tokyo.

Overbeck, H.
1967   "Malay Manuscripts in the public libraries in Germany," *JMBRAS,* 4 (2), pp. 233-259.

Pearson J. D.
1989   *Oriental Manuscripts in Europe and North America: A Survey,* Switzerland.

Poerbatjaraka, R. M. Ng., P. Voorhoeve & C. Hooykaas
1950   *Indonesische handschriften,* Bandung.

Ricklefs, M. C. & P. Voorhoeve
1977   *Indonesian Manuscripts in Great Britain,* Oxford.

Ronkel, Ph. S. van
1896   "Account of six Malay Manuscripts of the Cambridge University Library," *BKI,* 46, pp. 1-53.
1900   "Over eene oude lijst van Maleische handschriften," *TBG,* 42 (4), pp. 309-322.
1908a   "Catalogus der Maleische handschriften van het Koninklijk Instituut", *BKI,* 60, pp. 181-248.
1908b   "Beschrijving der Maleische handschriften van de Bibliotheque Royalete Brussel," *BKI,* 60, pp. 501-520.
1909   "Catalogus der Maleische handschriften in het Museum van het Bataviasche Genootschap van Kunsten en Wetenschappen," *VKI,* 57.
1921   "Supplement Catalogus der Maleische en Minangkabausche handschriften in de Leidsche Universiteits Bibliotheek," Leiden.

Teeuw, A.
1967　　"Malay manuscripts in the Library of Congress," *BKI,* 123, pp. 516-520.

Tuuk, H. N. van der
1949　　"Kort verslag van Maleische handschriften in het East India House te London," *Tijdschrift voor Nederlandsch Indie,* 1, pp. 385-400.
1866　　"Short account of the Malay Manuscripts belonging to the Royal Asiatic Society," *JRAS,* 2, (new series), pp. 85-135.

Voorhoeve, P.
1952　　"Indonesische handschriften in de Universiteits Bibliotheek te Leiden," *BKI,* 108, pp. 209-219.
1963　　"List of Malay Manuscripts in the library of the Royal Asiatic Society," *JRAS,* pts. 1 and 2, pp. 58-82.
1973　　"Les Manuscrits Malais de la Bibliotheque Nationale de Paris," *Archipel,* 6, pp. 41-80.
1980　　"List of Malay Manuscripts which were formerly kept at the general secretariat in Batavia," *Archipel,* 20, pp. 71-77.

Winstedt, R. O.
1920　　"Malay Manuscripts in the libraries of London, Brussels and the Hague," *JSBRAS,* 82, pp. 153-161.

Wieringa, E. P.
1998　　*Catalogue of Malay and Minangkabau Manuscripts in the Library of Leiden University and other collections in the Netherlands,* Vol.1, Leiden.
2007　　*Catalogue of Malay and Minangkabau Manuscripts in the Library of Leiden University and other collections in the Netherlands,* Leiden.

General References

Bausani A.
1979　　*Notes on the structure of the Classical Malay Hikayat* (translated by Lode Brakel), Melbourne.

Bezemer, T. J.
1943　　*Vier eeuwen Maleische literatuur in vogelulucht,* Deventer.

Braginsky, V. I.
1992　　*The System of Classical Malay Literature,* Leiden.
1998　　*Yang Indah, Berfaedah dan Kamal. Sejarah Sastra Melayu dalam Abad 19,* Jakarta.
2004　　*The Heritage of Traditional Malay Literature,* Singapore.

Casparis J. G.
1975　　*Indonesian Palaeography:* A history of writing in Indonesia from the beginnings to c. A.D. 1500, Leiden.

Dankmeyer, J. W.
1945　　*Vergelijking in Maleische literatuur,* Dissertation, Utrecht.

DBP
1999　　*Ensiklopedia Sejarah dan Kebudayaan Melayu,* 5 vols., Kuala Lumpur.

Departement of National Education, Indonesia
2008　　*Kamus Besar Bahasa Indonesia.* Fourth Edition, Jakarta.

Encyclopaedia
1917-1940 *Encyclopaedia van Nederlandsch-Indie, I-VIII.*
1960 *Encyclopaedia of Islam,* new edition.

Emeis, M. G.
1973 *Bunga Rampai Melayu Kuno,* Kuala Lumpur, reprint.

Ghazali Dunia
1969 *Langgam Sastra Lama,* Kuala Lumpur.

Gonda, J.
1947 *Letterkunde van de Indische Archipel,* Amsterdam.

Grijns, C. P. & S. O. Robson
1986 *Cultural Contact and Textual Interpretation,* (*VKI,* 115), Dordrecht.

Harun Mat Piah et al.
2006 *Kesusasteraan Tradisional Melayu,* Kuala Lumpur.

Hellwig, C. M. S. & S. O. Robson (eds.)
1986 *A Man of Indonesian Letters: Essays in Honour of Professor A. Teeuw,* (*VKI,* 121), Dordrecht.

Hollander, J. J. de
1893 *Hondleiding bij de beoefening der Maleische tool en letterkunde,* Breda.

Hooykaas, C.
1947 *Over Maleise Literatuur,* Leiden.
1965 *Perintis Sastera,* (First Edition, Jakarta, 1953) Kuala Lumpur.

Iskandar, T.
1995 *Kesusastraan Klasik Melayu Sepanjang Abad,* Brunei, Universiti Brunei Darusalam.

Ismail Hussein
1973 "Pengajian akademik kesusasteraan Malaysia", *DB,* 17, vol. 11, pp. 486-493.
1974 *The Study of Traditional Malay Literature,* Kuala Lumpur.
1978a "Bibliografi Teks Cetakan Sastera Melayu Tradisi," Kertas Data, No. 2 (JPMUM).
1978b *Bibliografi Sastera Melayu Tradisi,* Kuala Lumpur.

Jan van der Putten & Mary Kilcline Cody
2007 *Lost Time and Untold Tales from the Malay World,* Singapore, NUS Press.

Maier, Henk
2004 *We are playing elatives. A survey of Malay writing,* Singapore, ISEAS.

Jamilah Haji Ahmad
1981 *Kumpulan Esei Sastera Melayu Lama,* Kuala Lumpur.

Mohamad Daud Mohamad
1987 *Tokoh-tokoh Sastera Melayu Klasik,* Kuala Lumpur.

Mohd. Taib Osman
1965 *Kesusasteraan Melayu Lama,* Kuala Lumpur.
1971 "Classical Malay Literature," *Asian Pacific Quarterly,* 3 (3), pp. 51-71.

Muljadi, S. W. Rudjiati

1968 "Sejarah Kesusastraan Indonesia Lama", *Bahasa & Kesusastraan I*, 4, pp. 3-9.

Niemann, G. K.
1907 *Bloemlezing uit Maleische geschriften*, 's-Gravenhage.

Penguin Companion to Literature
1969 *Vol. IV*, London.

Rogayah Hamid & Mariyam Salim
2006 *Kesultanan Melayu Kedah*, Kuala Lumpur, Dewan Bahasa dan Pustaka.

Roolvink, R.
1975 *Bahasa Jawi, de taal van Sumatra*, Leiden.

Siti Hawa Haji Salleh
1987 *Cendekia Kesusastraan Melayu Tradisional*, Kuala Lumpur.

Skinner, C.
1978 "Traditional Malay Literature: Pt. 1, Ahmad Rijaluddin and Munshi Abdullah," *BKI*, 134 (4), pp. 466-487.

Stutterheim, W. F.
1951 *Cultuur Geschiedenis van Indonesie*, I-III, Groningen & Djakarta.

Sweeney, Amin
1980 *Authors and Audiences in Traditional Malay Literature*, Berkeley.
1983 "The Literary Study of Malay-Indonesian Literature: Some Observations," *JMBRAS*, 56 (1), pp. 33-46.
1986 *A Full Hearing*, Berkeley.

Teeuw, A.
1961 *A Critical Survey of Studies on Malay and Bahasa Indonesia*, The Hague.
1984 *Sastra dan Ilmu Sastra*, Jakarta.

Teeuw, A., Dumas, R., Muhammad Haji Salleh, Tol, R., Van Ypere, M. J.
2004 *A Merry Senhor In The Malay World, For Texts of the Syair Sinyor Kosta*, KITLV Press, Leiden.

Universiti Malaya
1980 *Katalog Koleksi Melayu Perpustakaan Universiti Malaya*, Kuala Lumpur.

Wieringa, E. P.
1998 *Catalogue of Malay and Minangkabau Manuscripts, Leiden* University Library, Leiden.

Wilkinson, R. J.
1907 *Papers on Malay Subjects, Malay Literature I & III*, Kuala Lumpur.

Winstedt, R. O.
1907 *Papers on Malay Subjects, Malay Literature II*, Kuala Lumpur.
1958 "A History of Classical Malay Literature," *JMBRAS*, 31 (3). (Reprint O.U.P., 1969).
1958/9 *Kesusasteraan Melayu Rampai-rampai*, London.
1961 *The Malays, A Cultural History*, London. on *Malay Subjects, Malay Literature II*, Kuala Lumpur.

Index

Abbas, Abdullah ibn, 189
Abu Nawas, 11, 12, 24, 25, 26, 27
Aceh, 11, 224, 300, 301, 302, 305, 306, 310, 312, 319, 321, 322, 323, 326, 329, 330, 334, 337, 339, 346, 347, 355, 362, 367, 368, 370, 371, 372, 373, 374, 377, 402, 415, 421, 426, 447, 470, 478
adat istiadat, 425, 426
adat nan diadatkan, 426
adat nan sebenar adat, 426
adat nan teradat, 426
Adat Raja-raja Melayu, 438
Adatrechtbundel, 414
Adbhuta-Ramayana, 51
Adham, D., 396
afal, 307
Akhbar al-Akhira fi Ahwal al-Kiyama, 319, 483
Akhyayika, 264, 265
Al-Attas, Syed Naguib, 302, 303, 305, 447, 448, 481, 482
Al-Fatani, Daud Ibn Abdullah (Syaikh Daud), 337
Al-Ghazali, 335, 336, 338
Al-Hallaj, Mansur, 305, 318
Al-Kashani, Abd al-Razak, 316
Al-Muntahi, 303, 305, 318
Al-Muqaffa, Abdullah, 265
Al-Palimbani, Abd Al-Samad, 334, 335, 336
Al-Qusyasyi, Ahmad, 322
Al-Sumatrani, Syamsuddin, 301, 305, 306, 318, 478
Al-Suri, 238
Al-Tabari, 326
Al-Thalabi, 188, 212

Amin, Encik, 470
Amongsastra, Kyai Rangga, 9
animism, 92, 414
Anusyirwan, Raja Khosrau, 265
Arjuna Wiwaha, Kakawin, 80, 81, 90
Ar-Raniri, Nuruddin, 158, 301, 305, 306, 309, 336, 478
arthasastra, 50, 266
Asiatic Researches, 414, 419
Asmaradana, 451
Asrar Al-Insan Fi Ma'rifa Al Ruh Wa 'l-Rahman, 315
Azhari, Muhammad (Syaikh Nuruddin), 301

Babad Daha-Kediri, 114
Babad Tanah Jawi, 114
Baried, Siti Baroroh, 300
Barrett, E.C.G., 68
Being (*wujud*), 479
    Oneness, 186, 188, 230, 303, 304, 307, 308, 309, 316, 322, 330, 337
Berg, C.C., 116
Bhatti-Kavya, 51, 57
Blagden, C.O., 147
Brahman, 375, 376
Brakel, L. F., 142, 220, 221, 224, 225, 302, 303, 478, 479, 481, 482
Brandes, J., 9, 58, 90, 91, 267, 268, 279, 292
Brandon, James, R., 92, 93
Brandstetter, R., 442
Braasem, W.A., 446, 447
Broek, W. Palmer van den, 9
Bruyn, De, 438

Buddha, 8, 22, 51
Bulcke, C., 51
Bustanus Salatin, 158, 257, 294, 301, 305, 311, 312, 313, 334, 354, 448

Callenfels, Stein, 80
Cantri, 279
Caron, L.J.J., 425
Cense, A.A., 392
Cerita Maharaja Wana, 102
Cerita Si Umbut Muda, 42, 43
Cerita Sri Rama, 60
Chambert-Loir, Henri, 402, 404
Chaucer, 238, 276
China, 4, 31, 49, 92, 158, 184, 185, 186, 227, 251, 256, 269, 276, 292, 318, 353, 356, 357, 361, 368, 371, 386, 393, 397, 403, 406, 426, 475, 476, 480
Clowns (*punakawan*), 91, 94, 113
Coedes, G., 50
Collingwood, R.G., 355
Crawford, John, 404, 474

Daka'ik al-Huruf, 322, 324, 325
Dalang, 102, 115, 117, 119, 120, 138, 268
Daly, Peunoh, 323, 324
Dasarata Jataka, 51, 56
Daud al-Fatani, Muhammad b. Ismail, 339
Daudy, Ahmad, 310, 319, 321
De Pandji Roman, 113
Desai, Santosh, N., 73
Dharmawangsa, 76, 80
Dipodjojo, Asdi S., 11
Divine Attributes (*sifat*), 303, 307
Divine Essence (*zat*), 304, 306, 317, 319, 326, 327, 330
Djajadiningrat, Hoesein, 346, 442, 445
Djamaris, Edward, 204, 212, 294, 320, 334, 425, 433, 436, 437
Drewes, G.W.J., 171, 175, 302, 303, 305, 317, 335, 336, 337, 478, 479, 481, 482
Dulaurier, 419

Eysinga, Roorda van, 59, 152, 178, 179, 257, 329, 449, 451, 457

Fadi, Abdul, 306
Fakhruddin, Kemas, 334, 337
Fansuri, Hamzah, 301, 302, 303, 304, 305, 309, 310, 318, 319, 447, 448, 449, 478, 479, 480, 481, 482
  birthplace, 302
  teachings, 305, 309
Fath al-Mubin 'ala Al-Makhidin, 319
Feasts (*kenduri*), 13
Folk-romance (*cerita pelipur lara*), 27
Framed narratives, 264, 265
Furu' al-Masa'il wa Usul al-Masa'il, 338

Galland, A., 266, 276
Gibson-Hill, G.A., 352
Gonggrijp, J.R.P.F., 267, 268, 272
Goslings, B.M., 92, 114
Grierson, George A., 51
Gujarat, 184, 185, 348
Gunawarman, 49
Gush, Manomohan, 51, 192

Haji, Raja Ali, 383, 439, 457
Hall, E.G.E., 300, 347
Hamid, Syaikh Muhammad Jailani, 301
Hang Jebat, 245, 352, 405, 406, 407
Hazeu, G.A.J., 91, 92
Hidayat al-Saliki fi Suluk Maslak al-Muttakin, 335
Hidding, K.A.H., 114
Hikayat Abu Nawas, 24, 26
Hikayat Abu Syahmah, 224, 231
Hikayat Aceh, 346, 371, 438, 470
Hikayat Ahmad Muhammad, 143, 144, 171, 174
Hikayat Amir Hamzah, 174, 224, 245, 246, 247, 253
Hikayat Anggun Cik Tunggal, 33, 465
Hikayat Arjuna Mangunjaya, 94

INDEX

Hikayat Awang Sulung Merah Muda, 28, 29, 371
Hikayat Badi ul-Zaman, 253
Hikayat Bakhtiar, 27, 144, 264, 265, 291, 292, 294, 295, 297
Hikayat Banjar dan Kota Waringin, 392
Hikayat Bayan Budiman, 1, 170, 229, 264, 278, 279, 291, 294, 461
Hikayat Berma Syahdan, 143, 156
Hikayat Bulan Berbelah, 215, 217
Hikayat Cekel Waneng Pati, 114, 115, 119, 120, 124, 128, 133
Hikayat Dewa Asmara Jaya, 133, 134
Hikayat Galuh Digantung, 116
Hikayat Golam (*Hikayat Raja Azbakht*), 268, 295, 297
Hikayat Hang Tuah, 1, 102, 120, 245, 311, 344, 404, 405
Hikayat Indra Bangsawan, 102, 142, 143, 162
Hikayat Indraputra, 158, 159, 160
Hikayat Iskandar Zulkarnain, 238
Hikayat Isma Yatim, 143, 144, 178
Hikayat Jaya Langkara, 142, 143, 144, 166, 168
Hikayat Jumjumah, 297
Hikayat Kalilah dan Damina, 264, 265, 267, 268
Hikayat Koraisy Mengindra, 143, 161, 162
Hikayat Langlang Buana, 143, 152
Hikayat Maharaja Ali, 144, 147, 213, 297
Hikayat Maharaja Garebak Jagat, 94
Hikayat Mahasyodhak, 22
Hikayat Malim Deman, 31, 373
Hikayat Malim Dewa, 30
Hikayat Merong Mahawangsa, 346, 367, 371
Hikayat Mikraj, 215
Hikayat Misa Taman Jayeng Kusuma, 131
Hikayat Muhammad Hanafiah, 215, 220, 221, 224, 225, 228, 245, 365, 371
Hikayat Nabi Bercukur, 215, 219
Hikayat Nabi Wafat, 215, 220, 223
Hikayat Nakhoda Muda (*Hikayat Sitti Sara/ Hikayat Raja Ajnawi*), 144, 168, 170, 171, 297, 464
Hikayat Negeri Johor, 377, 379, 388
Hikayat Nur Muhammad, 212, 215, 217
Hikayat Pandawa, 81, 85, 86, 94, 402
Hikayat Pandawa Lebur, 81, 85
Hikayat Pandawa Lima, 81, 85, 86
Hikayat Panji Semirang, 127, 128, 449
Hikayat Parang Punting, 143, 150
Hikayat Patani, 399, 400, 402
Hikayat Pelanduk Jenaka, 5, 8, 9
Hikayat Puspa Wiraja, 143, 144, 147
Hikayat Raja Ambong, 38
Hikayat Raja Budiman, 28, 39
Hikayat Raja Donan, 28, 36
Hikayat Raja Handak (*Khandak, Hunduk*), 236
Hikayat Raja Jumjumah atau Tengkorak Kering, 212, 213
Hikayat Raja Muda, 32, 33
Hikayat Raja-raja Pasai, 346, 347, 348, 371, 377
   influence on the *Sejarah Melayu,* 347
Hikayat Saif Dzul-Yazan, 254
Hikayat Sama'un, 224, 233, 234
Hikayat Sang Boma, 81, 86, 87, 89
Hikayat Sang Kancil, 5, 7, 9, 10
Hikayat Seribu Masalah, 326, 327, 328
Hikayat Seribu Satu Malam (*Alf Laila Wa Laila*), 19, 144, 246, 265, 275, 276, 277, 295
Hikayat Si Miskin (*Hikayat Marakarma*), 142, 143
   Hindu motifs, 155
Hikayat Sri Rama, 58, 59, 60, 67, 70, 71, 72, 73, 74, 116, 142, 158, 280, 310, 311, 371
   origins, 69
   versions, 59, 60, 64, 68, 69
Hikayat Sultan Ibrahim Ibn Adham, 257
Hikayat Syah Kobat, 143, 160
Hikayat Syah Mardan, 143, 144, 175, 334
Hikayat Tamim al-Dari, 224, 229, 231
Hikayat Terong Pipit, 40, 42, 102
Hikayat Undakan Penurat, 135, 451
Hikayat wasiat Lukman Hakim, 333
Hill A. H., 348
Hill al-Zill, 318
Hindu, 4, 49, 50, 52, 56, 57, 73, 74, 77, 91, 142, 143, 155, 178, 184, 268, 353
   concepts, 353
   influence, 49, 150
   motifs, 143, 155, 162
   mythology, 108
Hooykaas, C., 4, 52, 57, 87, 238, 245, 247

Hollander, J.J.De, 175, 233, 329, 451, 449, 465, 466
Houtman, Frederick de, 306
Hujjatu'l-Siddik li daf i 'l-Zindik, 316
Hurgronje, Snouck C., 233, 323, 325, 337, 345
Hussin, Encik, 483

Idah al-Bab li Murid al-nikah bi 'l-sawab, 338
Ikram, Achadiati, 69, 94, 446
Index Islamicus, 186
Iskandar Muda, Sultan, 305, 306, 310, 355, 371, 373, 374

Jacobi, H., 50
Jawahir al-Ulum fi Kasif al-Ma'lum, 319, 339
Jinaka (atau *Jenaka*), 8, 11
Johns, A.H., 186, 300, 322, 325, 371
Jong, P.E. de Josselin de, 405, 419, 433
Juynboll, H.H., 57, 58, 69, 70, 94, 134, 157, 231, 233, 240, 305, 471

Kakawin Arjuna Wiwaha, 80, 81
Kakawin Ramayana, 51, 57, 69, 72
Kaeh, Abdul Rahman, 131
Kalidasa, 51
Kamban, 52
katha, 169, 264, 268
Kats, J., 73, 91
Kebayan, 29, 31, 32, 39, 40
Kelantan, 94, 101, 128, 295, 380, 405, 442, 448
Kingdoms, small, 49,
Ketemenggungan, Datuk, 426
Khairuddin, *haji*, 267, 268, 272, 384
Kifayat Muhtajin, 323, 339
Kisah Al-anbiya, 188, 189
Kisasul al- Anbiya, 188, 204, 205, 206, 212
Kitab Mir'at al-Muhaqqiqin, 306
Kitab Seribu Masa'il, 301
Klinkert, H.C., 8, 11, 152, 419, 450, 454, 456
Krom, N.J., 91

Lanang, Tun Sri, 354, 355

Lancaster, Sir James, 306
Lassen C., 50
Laufer, B., 92
Lebai Malang, 11, 12, 13, 14
Leur, J.C. van, 50
Leeuwen, P.J. van, 238, 239
Literature,
    historical, 345, 346, 347, 367, 371, 377, 387, 402, 403, 404
    mystical, 300
    theological, 300, 301, 339, 340
    transition, 142, 143, 155, 178
Loro Jonggrang, temple, 56

Mahabharata, 114
    in Javanese literature, 80
    in Malay literature, 81
Mahkota Alam, Sultan Iskandar Muda, 306, 372
Maier, Hendrik J., 371
Malat, 116, 136
Malikus-Saleh, al, 184
Marco Polo, 184
Marrison, G.E., 447
Mat Jenin, 19, 20, 267
Mat Piah, Harun, 133, 134, 452, 454
Maulana, Encik, 421
Maxwell, W.E., 4, 60, 64, 351, 352, 354, 367, 368, 387, 414, 421, 433, 434
Mees, C.A., 8, 396, 397
Misa Melayu, 374, 375, 438
Mpu Panuluh, 80
Mpu Sedah, 80, 81, 83
Mulawarman, King, 49
Munsyi, Abdullah, 267, 329, 350, 399, 400, 442, 444
Musang Berjanggut, 19, 20, 21
Mutalib, Abdul, 222, 475

Nasrullah, 265, 268
Negeri nan empat, 427
Netscher, E., 351, 404
Nieuwenhuijze, C.A.O. van, 306
nitisastra, 50, 266

North, Thomas, 265

Omar, Syaikh Abu Bakar ibn, 156
Omayya, Amir ibn, 248, 254
Ophuijsen, Ch. A. von, 155, 170, 267, 443, 444, 445, 478
Osman, Mohd. Taib, 2, 29
Overbeck, H., 74, 116, 384, 404, 405, 444, 446, 465, 466, 467, 483, 484

Pahang, 310, 312, 352, 353, 361, 362, 363, 364, 365, 366, 367, 378, 380, 381, 383, 386, 388, 389, 390, 391, 401, 415, 416, 434, 435, 437
Pak Belalang, 11, 12, 18, 19
Pak Kadok, 12, 13
Pak Pandir, 11, 12, 16, 17, 18
Pamoentjak nan Sati, Abas Datoek, 405
Pancatantra (*Hikayat Kalilah dan Dimnah*), 4, 265, 266, 267, 275, 279, 328
    difference from *tantri*, 279
    Malay version, 279
Panja Tanderan, 267
Panji Angreni, 135, 136, 138, 449
parik (*pari*), 445
Pearson, J.D., 186
Pelanduk dengan Anak Memerang, 5, 6, 10
Pigeaud, T.G.Th., 57, 80, 114
Pijnappel, 442, 443, 464
Pischel, R., 91, 92
Poerbatjaraka, R.M. Ng., 51, 57, 114, 116, 124, 128, 136, 138
Portuguese, 144, 185, 186, 224, 245, 301, 310, 346, 347, 351, 352, 356, 364, 365, 366, 367, 371, 373, 388, 407, 416
    and the fall of Malakan dynasti, 356
    conquer Malaka, 362
Prameswara (Megat Iskandar Syah), 185, 349
Panji stories,
    in Cambodia, 138, 139
    in Java, 113, 116, 136
    in Thai, 138
    social role, 115

Pseudo-Kallisthenes, 239

Purnawarman, King, 49

Quran, 13, 14, 20, 24, 27, 29, 34, 93, 172, 186, 187, 188, 217, 219, 226, 230, 232, 239, 241, 280, 289, 290, 292, 294, 297, 300, 305, 313, 316, 322, 325, 333, 349, 370, 373, 387, 403, 479

Raffles, Sir Stamford, 68, 69, 87, 229, 231, 232, 279, 329, 348, 351, 352, 354, 355, 356, 387, 390, 392, 414, 419, 452
Ramacaritamanas, 52
Rama Jataka, 56
Rama Keling, 58, 71, 72
Ramavatram, 52
Ramayana-Patani, 60
Ranir (Rander), 309, 310
Ras, J.J., 92, 114, 345
Rassers, W.H., 69, 70, 91, 113, 114, 129, 128
Rauf, Abdul, 321, 478
Rawana, 68, 74, 92, 93, 94, 114, 142
Ravana-Wadha (*Bhatti-Kawya*), 51, 57
Riddel, P.G., 325, 330
Robson, S.O., 135, 451
Ronkel, Ph. S. van, 152, 220, 224, 233, 234, 245, 246, 247, 254, 323, 327, 328, 329, 419, 438, 472
Roolvink, R., 187, 300, 313, 340, 345, 350, 351, 352, 354, 356, 404, 448, 480
Rosenthal, Franz, 186, 448, 449
ruba'i, 328
Rumi, Daud, 325

Sabai Nan Aluih, 42, 44, 45
Salasilah Kutai, 345, 396
Sarkar, H.B., 114
Sati, Tulis Sutan, 43, 44
Sejarah Raja-Raja Riau, 347, 381, 383, 388
Seltmann, F., 92
Semar, 12, 69, 85, 89, 91, 95, 96, 97, 99, 125, 127, 130, 131
Sen, Rai Saheb Dineschandra, 70
Serat Kancil, 9, 10
Serat Kanda Ning Ringgit Purwa, 57, 58, 72

Serat Rama, 57, 69, 72
Shellabear, W.G., 59, 60, 61, 62, 63, 64, 68, 69, 311, 351, 352, 405
Shifa al-Khulub, 319
Silsilah Melayu dan Bugis dan Segala Raja-rajanya, 347, 383, 384
Si Luncai, 11, 12, 14, 15, 16
Singkel, Abdur Rauf (Abd ar Rauf Ibn Ali al-Fansuri), 321, 478
Sirat al-Mustakim, 158, 308, 310, 324
Siyar al-Salikin ila 'Ibadat abb al-'Alamin, 335, 336
Stutterheim, W. F., 69, 70, 73, 114, 115
Sudjiman, Panuti H.M., 438, 439
Suhaili, Anwari, 265, 268
Sukasaptati, 4, 265, 278, 279
Sweeney, Amin, 92, 102, 348, 387, 447, 448, 449
Syah, Ali Ri'ayat, 301, 372
Syah, Sultanah 'Inayat Syah Zakiyatuddin, 301
Syah, Sultanah Tajul-'alam Safiatuddin, 301, 323, 374, 375, 376, 391, 415, 416,
Syah-Nama, 239, 246
Syah, Sultan Muhammad, 353, 359, 360, 367
Syah, Sultan Muzaffar, 353, 360, 366, 367, 370, 371, 374, 375, 376, 415, 416
Syair,
    Historical, 469
    Religious, 478
    Romantic, 454
Syair Abdul Muluk, 457
Syair Angreni, 449, 451, 452
Syair Bidasari, 454, 456
Syair Buah-buahan, 468
Syair Bunga Air Mawar, 467
Syair Burung Pungguk, 465, 466
Syair Cinta Berahi (*Syair Farahid*), 461
Syair Dagang, 478, 480, 481
Syair Damar Wulan, 452
Syair Ikan Terubuk, 465
Syair Ken Tambuhan, 125, 135, 442, 447, 448, 449, 451, 456
Syair Kiamat, 478, 482
Syair Kompeni Welanda Berperang dengan Cina, 470
Syair Kumbang dan Melati, 466

Syair Kupu-kupu dengan Kembang dan Balang, 468
Syair Nuri, 466, 467
Syair Nyamuk dan Lalat, 467
Syair Panji, 449
Syair Perahu, 478, 480, 481
Syair Perang Mengkasar, 448, 469
Syair Raksi, 478, 484
Syair Raja Siak, 473, 474
Syair Sinyor Kosta, 334, 454, 459, 460
Syair Seri Banian (*Syair Indra Laksana*), 458, 459
Syair Sultan Ahmad Tajuddin (*Syair Sultan Maulana*), 474
Syair Takbir Mimpi, 478, 483
Syair Undakan Agung Udaya, 449, 453
Syair Yatim Nestapa, 456
Syarab al-'Asyikin, 303, 304

Tajus Salatin, 294, 301, 328, 329, 334, 396
tantri, 275
   compared to *pancatantra*, 275
Tarjuman al-Mustafid, 325
Teeuw, A., 86, 135, 184, 348, 399, 400, 402, 404, 447, 448, 450, 451, 460, 461, 481
Thaib, Ahmad bin Muhammad, 128
Thani, Sultan Iskandar, 301, 306, 310, 316, 317, 478
Tibyan fi Ma'rifati 'l-Adyan, 317, 366
Tortoise, 4, 11, 270, 271, 274
Tuhfat al-Nafis, 347, 377, 381, 387, 388, 439
Tuhfat al-rahibin fi bayan haqikat Iman al-mukminin, 336
Tulisi, Das, 52
Tunggal, Anggun Cik, 29, 33, 34, 35, 465
Tuuk, H. N. van der, 8, 58, 81, 83, 94, 119, 144, 279, 470

Umdat al-Muhtajin ila Sulukl Maslak 'l-Mufridin, 323
Undang-undang Dua Belas, 425, 433
Undang-undang Kedah, 435, 436
Undang-undang Laut, 415, 419, 420, 425
Undang-undang Malaka, 414, 415, 416, 419, 420, 421, 425, 434, 435, 437, 438

Undang-undang Minangkabau, 425, 428, 433, 437
Undang-undang Nan Empat, 426, 427
Undang-undang Pahang, 416, 434, 435
Undang-undang Sembilan Puluh Sembilan, 437

Valentijn, F., 158, 178, 328, 329, 350, 351, 404, 405, 419, 448
von Capua, Johannes, 265
Voorhoeve, P., 302, 317, 325, 448, 481, 482
Vorm, Petrus van den, 350, 351
Vyasa, 75, 76, 78, 79

Wahab, Abdul, 295
Wall, A.F. von de, 19, 22, 212, 217, 218, 233, 236, 295, 435, 457, 465, 482
Wasiat Lukman al-Hakim, 301

Wayang Pandu, 94
Wayang Purwa, 57, 87, 90, 92
  origins, 90
Werndly G. H., 8, 131, 158, 160, 166, 175, 178, 219, 220, 267, 268, 295, 306, 329, 404
Wilkinson, R.J., 11, 68, 69, 238, 240, 312, 355, 367, 414, 437, 444, 445
Winstedt, R.O., 347, 348, 349, 352, 353, 355, 356, 368, 372, 375, 376, 378, 388, 389, 405, 415, 417, 420, 434, 435, 436, 437, 438

Yasadipura I, 57, 80
Ying-hi, 92

Zainal, Baharuddin bin, 295
Zieseniss, A., 59, 69, 73

Biographical Details

Liaw Yock Fang was born in Singapore on 14 September 1936. He received his BA in Indonesian Language and Literature from the University of Indonesia in 1963 and was awarded the MA degree in 1965. He then received the degrees of Doctorandus (MA) from Leiden University in 1971 and Doctor of Letters in 1976. His doctoral dissertation was a study of the *Undang-undang Melaka*.

Among his many publications are *Ikhtisar Kritik Sastra* (with H.B. Jassin, 1970), *The Complete Poems of Chairil Anwar* (with the assistance of H.B. Jassin, 1974), *Sejarah Kesusastraan Melayu Klasik* (1975), *Undang-undang Melaka* (1976), *Standard Malay Made Simple* (1988), *Speak Standard Indonesian* (with Munadi Patmadiwiria & Abdullah Hassan (1990), *Nahu Melayu Modern* (with Abdullah Hassan), *Easy Indonesian Vocabulary* (1995), *Indonesian Grammar Made Easy* (1996), *Malay Grammar Made Easy* (1999), *Essential Indonesian Reading, A Learner's Guide* I and II (with Leo Suryadinata (2005), *Undang-undang Melaka* (2003). He has published more than twenty articles with Dewan Bahasa dan Pustaka, Kuala Lumpur, and presented over twenty papers at conferences in Malaysia, Indonesia and Brunei Darussalam.

Razif Bahari is Adjunct Research Fellow at the School of English Communication and Performance Studies at Monash University, Melbourne, and was formerly Assistant Professor of Malay and Indonesian Literature at the National Institute of Education, Nanyang Technological University, Singapore (2006-2010). He was born in Singapore and educated at the National University of Singapore, Murdoch University, Perth, Western Australia, and the Australian National University. He is the author of *Pramoedya Postcolonially* (2007), a groundbreaking book that investigates, from a postcolonial theoretical perspective, the construction of the nation, history and gender in the novels of Indonesia's best-known novelist, Pramoedya Ananta Toer. His research articles have appeared in *Review of Indonesian and Malaysian Affairs, Contemporary Literary Criticism, Journal of the South Pacific Association for Commonwealth Literature and Language Studies, E-Utama Journal of Malay Education, Culture, Language and Literature,* and Cornell University's *Indonesia*. His most recent publication is an entry on "The Novel in Southeast Asia" in Blackwell's *Encyclopedia of the Novel* (2011). His previous translations from the Malay include the poems of Masuri S.N. in *Ode to Masuri S.N.* (Math Paper Press, 2012), the Introduction and a chapter on "The Art of Embroidery" in *The Crafts of Malaysia* (Editions Didier Millet, 1994), and from English to Malay, Richard Berengarten's "Volga" in *The International Literary Quarterly*. His poems, short stories, essays, reviews and translations have also been published in *The Straits Times, Berita Minggu, Singa: Journal of Literature and the Arts in Singapore* and elsewhere. He served as a member of the Arts Resource Panel (2010) and as External Assessor of Theatre and Drama (2006-

2010) in the Singapore National Arts Council, as editorial board member (2009-2010) of *Poestaka: Jurnal Ilmu-ilmu Budaya*, an international peer-reviewed journal published by the Faculty of Literature, Udayana University, Bali, Indonesia, and as editor (2008-2009) of *E-Utama: Journal of Malay Education, Culture, Language and Literature* published by the Malay Language and Culture Division, National Institute of Education, Singapore.

Harry Aveling holds an adjunct appointment as a Professor in Translation and Interpreting Studies at Monash University, Melbourne, and was Distinguished Visiting Professor in the Center of Southeast Asian Studies, Ohio University in 2011. He has taught courses in Classical and Modern Malay and Indonesian Literatures at Monash University; Universiti Sains Malaysia, Penang; Murdoch University, Perth, Western Australia; and La Trobe University, also in Melbourne; and in Translation Studies at Universitas Indonesia, Jakarta, Universitas Gadjah Mada, Yogyakarta, The Vietnam National University, Hanoi, and the University of Social Sciences and Humanities, Ho Chi Minh City. He holds degrees from the University of Sydney (MA Hons. in Indonesian and Malay Studies), the National University of Singapore (Doctor of Philosophy in Malay Studies) and the University of Technology, Sydney (Doctor of Creative Arts, DCA, in Literary Translation). He has written extensively on Indonesian and Malay literatures, including *A Thematic History of Indonesian Poetry* (Northern Illinois University, 1971), *Sastera Indonesia: Terlibat atau Tidak?* (Kanisius, Yogyakarta 1986), *Shahnon Ahmad: Islam, Power and Gender* (Universiti Kebangsaan Press, Bangi 2000) and *Rumah Sastra Indonesia* (IndonesiaTera, Magelang 2002). He has also translated widely from both literatures, including, from Malay, A. Samad Said *Salina* (Dewan Bahasa dan Pustaka, KL 1975), Ishak Haji Muhammad *Son of Mad Mat Lela* (Federal Books, Singapore 1983), Harun Mat Piah et al. *Traditional Malay Literature* (DBP, KL 2002), and A. Ghafar Ibrahim *Yang Yang, That's That* (Institut Terjemahan Negara Malaysia, KL 2010); and from Indonesian, *Secrets Need Words, Indonesian Poetry 1966-1998* (Ohio University Press, 2001) and Dorothea Rosa Herliany *Morphology of Desire* (Lontar Foundation, Jakarta 2013). Harry Aveling is a Fellow of the Stockholm Collegium of World Literary History. He was awarded the Anugerah Pengembangan Sastera by GAPENA (The Federation of Malaysian National Literary Associations) in 1991 for his "strong commitment to furthering the international understanding of Malay Literature".

Professor Riris K. Toha-Sarumpaet edited the Indonesian edition of *Sejarah Kesusatraan Melayu Klasik* on which this translation is based. She is Professor of Literature at the Faculty of Cultural Studies, University of Indonesia, where she teaches courses in drama, research methods and children's literature. She is actively engaged in poetry and theatre activities and has twice been the Chair of HISKI (Society for Scholars of Indonesian Literature). Among her many publications are *Isu yang Sama Emosi yang Sama: Inilah Cerita Kita*, in *Perempuan*, edited by Mochtar Lubis, *Pedoman Penelitian Sastra Anak* and *Batu Permata Milik Ayahanda: Dongeng Tradisional Indonesia*.

www.ingramcontent.com/pod-product-compliance
Lightning Source LLC
Chambersburg PA
CBHW080531300426
44111CB00017B/2676